THE ULTIMATE
DREAM DECODER

SURFACING DURING YOUR DREAMING SLEEP ✳ A COMPLETE GUIDE TO INTERPRETING THE SYMBOLIC MESSAGES THAT ARE LOCKED IN YOUR SUBCONSCIOUS,

THE ULTIMATE
DREAM DECODER

REVEALING THE SECRETS OF YOUR SUBCONSCIOUS MIND

M. JANE TAYLOR & CLARE GIBSON

Saraband

Published by Saraband (Scotland) Limited
The Arthouse, 752–756 Argyle Street,
Glasgow G3 8UJ, Scotland
hermes@saraband.net
www.saraband.net

ISBN: 1-887354-41-7

Printed in China

10 9 8 7 6 5 4 3 2 1

DREAM THEMES AUTHOR: M. Jane Taylor
ASSOCIATE EDITOR & PROJECT CONSULTANT: Clare Gibson
INTRODUCTION written by Clare Gibson
EDITOR: Sara Hunt
ART EDITOR: Deborah Hayes
GRAPHIC DESIGN: Phoebe Tak-Yin Wong

CONTENTS

Sleep hath its own world,
And a wide realm of wild reality,
And dreams in their development
have breath,
And tears, and tortures, and the touch of joy;
They have a weight upon our
waking thoughts,
They take a weight from off our waking toils,
They do divide our being.

LORD BYRON, *The Dream* (1816)

INTRODUCTION

Dreams have always intrigued and puzzled people. We know this
from the lore that we have inherited from ancient civilizations the
world over, from the tales of mysterious and powerful dreams that
were initially handed down from generation to generation by word
of mouth before eventually being recorded in more permanent
form by means of writing and drawings. The Aborigines of
Australia, for example, tell of the Dreamtime, or Dreaming, the
primeval period when their ancestors brought the landscape and
every creature—humankind included—that inhabits it into being,
and continue to celebrate this magical, mythical era in their artistic
traditions and sacred rites.

A Brief History of Dreams

The first dreams to have been set down in writing are thought to have been those contained in the *Epic of Gilgamesh*, a stirring piece of ancient Babylonian literature that is believed to date from around 1760 B.C. In column 31 of the section entitled "Ishtar and Izdubar," according to Leonidas Le Cenci Hamilton's translation of 1884, the king summons his seers and commands them to interpret a troubling dream that he has had, whereupon:

*The seers in silence stand, perplexed
    and think …
And they now prostrate fall before his
    throne,
"Forgive thy seers!" one cries, "O mighty
    One!
For we this dreadful dream do fear
    portends
Thy harm! A god some message to thee
    sends!
We know not what, but fear for thee."*

A strikingly similar story is told in the Old Testament Book of Daniel (2:2–3), which relates that King Nebuchadnezzar: "commanded to call the magicians, and the astrologers, and the sorcerers, and the Chaldeans, for to shew the king his dreams. So they came and stood before the king. And the king said unto them, I have dreamed a dream, and my spirit was troubled to know the dream." In the end it was Daniel, who, enlightened by a vision sent to him by God, interpreted Nebuchadnezzar's dream, first explaining: "The secret which the king hath demanded cannot the wise men, the astrologers, the magicians, the soothsayers, shew unto the king; But there is a God in heaven that revealeth secrets, and maketh known to the king Nebuchadnezzar what shall be in the latter days." (Daniel 2:27–28).

From these two pieces of evidence alone, we can conclude that nearly two millennia ago, dreams were taken extremely seriously as important portents, or messages, from a divine source, whose interpretation required equally divine inspiration or guidance.

Right: *The lion-vanquishing Mesopotamian hero Gilgamesh was said to be one-third human and two-thirds divine. Tales of his exploits are told in the* Epic of Gilgamesh, *which is believed to contain the oldest written references to dreams.*

Throughout the history of humankind, numerous tribes and civilizations have credited dreams with having an external cause. It was once almost universally believed that nightmares, for instance, were inflicted on defenseless sleepers by devils, demons, and other malevolent spirits, while enjoyable dreams were said to have their origins in benevolent supernatural beings. (This outlook is embodied in the concepts underlying the dreamcatcher—essentially a webbed hoop that resembles a spider's web or decorated tennis racket—that, in Native American tradition, is hung by a child's bed in order to trap, and thus fend off, bad dreams, while at the same time enabling happiness-infused dreams to enter the young sleeper's slumber.)

Other cultures have regarded dreamland as being a sort of parallel universe that only becomes accessible to us when we lose consciousness. The Inuit people of Hudson Bay, for example, hold that our souls temporarily leave our bodies while we are sleeping, and that we are witnessing their adventures as we dream. Likewise, some "New Age" theorists maintain that it is during sleep that the phenomena known as out-of-body experiences (O.B.E.s), astral projection, or astral travel, occur, when our disembodied spirits slip away from our cumbersome bodies (to which they remain harnessed by a silver cord, however) to travel freely through time and space.

Although few Westerners today are superstitious or unconventional enough to believe that dreams are literal omens or manifestations of real events, most of us would probably accept that they are not without personal meaning. Some researchers propose that dreams are a kind of side effect of the reexperiencing, sorting, and consequent forgetting or laying-down of memories that the brain undertakes during its "downtime," or sleep, a rational and compelling hypothesis that it would be difficult to reject out of hand.

Yet this does not explain why, as commonly happens, we may go to sleep mulling over a conundrum and awake in possession of a neat solution, one that came to us in a dream. Nor does it account for the delightful dreams that may hearten us in times of trouble, or for the recurring dreams that may plague our sleep, or for the absurd dream storylines, incongruous characters, and out-of-character behavior to which we may be party while we are sleeping. And if, as is sometimes claimed, dreams are merely muddled memories, why can they affect us so powerfully? "I've dreamt in my life dreams that have stayed with me ever after, and changed my ideas; they've gone through and through me, like wine through water, and altered the colour of my mind." Why do Emily Brontë's words, immortalized in her novel *Wuthering Heights* (1847), ring so true?

Left: The Old Testament tells us that King Nebuchadnezzar was tormented by his incomprehensible dreams. History tells us that King Nebuchadnezzar II ruled Babylonia from 604 B.C., captured Jerusalem twice, and that it was he who created the famous hanging gardens of Babylon, one of the Seven Wonders of the World.

The Interpretation of Dreams

Below: This dreamlike image arose from the visionary imagination of the English mystic William Blake (1757–1827). Unusually, in the Age of Reason, Blake trusted in the truth-discerning powers of the unconscious, writing in 1810, "Vision or Imagination is a Representation of what Eternally Exists, Really and Unchangeably."

The rejection of superstitious beliefs in favor of scientific ones, and the consequent search for a physiological or psychological prompt for our dreams, was initiated several centuries before the birth of Christ by such Greek philosophers as Heraclitus (*c.*544–483 B.C.), Plato (*c.*427–347 B.C.), and Aristotle (384–322 B.C.), along with Hippocrates (*c.*460–377 B.C.), the "father of medicine." And it was a Roman work, *Oneirocriticon (The Interpretation of Dreams)*, by Artemidorus (A.D. 138–180), that was probably the first dream "dictionary" of the symbol-based, self-help type with which we are familiar today. All of these thinkers proposed that our dreams originate within ourselves, and that while certain of their elements may be common to humankind, their meaning is largely personal, in that they arise from, and pertain to, the dreamer's individual circumstances.

Although many wise words about dreams were subsequently penned by poets, playwrights, novelists, and essayists—an example being William Hazlitt's astute observation "We are not hypocrites in our sleep" ("On Dreams," *The Plain Speaker*, 1826)—and the Romantic movement of the nineteenth century kindled a renewed, albeit somewhat vague, interest in the subject, it was not until the twentieth century that dreams again attracted serious, and sustained, general attention. That they then did so, and that research into dreams and their possible meanings has, a century later, developed into a significant field of scientific study, is largely due to Sigmund Freud (1865–1939), the Austrian "father of psychoanalysis" whose seminal work *Die Traumdeutung (The Interpretation of Dreams)* caused a sensation when it was first published in 1900. "In the following pages, I shall demonstrate that there is a psychological technique which makes it possible to interpret dreams, and that on the application of this technique, every

dream will reveal itself as a psychological structure, full of significance, and one which may be assigned to a specific place in the psychic activities of the waking state." The dry opening words of *The Interpretation of Dreams* may have seemed innocuous, but they introduced ideas so radical, and so shocking to the buttoned-up sensibilities of the pre-World War I era, that they earned their author widespread notoriety.

Freud proposed the theory that the human psyche comprises the superego, or conscience; the ego, or the conscious, "civilized" mind; and the id, or the nebulous realm of unconscious, "uncivilized" thoughts. While we are awake, the ego—despite being subject to modification by the superego—is essentially in control, perhaps its most important task being to suppress the "animal" urges, "antisocial" instincts, and sensory quest for self-gratification that emanate from the id. It does this in order to ensure that we behave

conventionally and, as a result, fit in with, and are accepted by, the society in which we live. When we are asleep, however, the ego loosens its stranglehold on the id, enabling these "animal" urges and "antisocial" instincts to float to the surface of our sleeping minds, albeit usually disguised in symbolic form, thereby preventing the conscious mind from instantly recognizing the nature of "the beast" and being shocked into wakefulness and the resumption of its repressive function.

Far left: The Greek philosopher Aristotle, the author of a work entitled On Divination Through Sleep, *was centuries, if not millennia, ahead of his time when he disagreed with the prevalent view of his contemporaries that dreams foretold the future. Aristotle instead dismissed so-called "prophetic" dreams as being "mere coincidences."*

Left: Just as Charles Darwin horrified God-fearing Creationists with his theory that humans and apes share a common ancestor, so Freud disgusted many by suggesting that we all possess an "animal" side, or id, and that it is this that comes to the fore and runs amok in our dreams.

Above: *Sigmund Freud, who, in* The Interpretation of Dreams, *stated, "The interpretation of dreams is the royal road to a knowledge of the unconscious activities of the mind."*

Below: *Freud's groundbreaking work launched dreams and their interpretation on a new, scientific course. Before then, it was sometimes thought that sweet dreams were the doing of good fairies or spirits.*

What really repelled the "respectable," strait-laced readers of *The Interpretation of Dreams* was Freud's proposition that the ego is constantly trying to quash the frequently amoral or even incestuous sexual drives and desires to which we have been longing to give free rein since infancy, and that it is these that are expressed, and that may find fulfillment, in our dreams. A very simplified summing-up of the Freudian view of dreams is therefore that they are wish-fulfillment fantasies that often focus on the gratification of the libido, but not overtly so, so that it is necessary to interpret the dream's manifest content, or symbolism, in order to reveal its latent content, or the truth. Freud believed that certain symbols were favored by the id in all of us: phallic symbols, for example: "It is quite unmistakable that all weapons and tools are used as symbols for the male organ: e.g. ploughshare, hammer, gun, revolver, dagger, sword, etc." (*ibid*). Yet while acknowledging our unconscious propensity to "dream up" the same types of symbols, Freud did not consider dreams to be concerned with anything more than personal wish fulfillment.

The Freudian View of Dreams as Wish Fulfillment

The ancient belief that dreams reveal the future is not indeed entirely devoid of truth. By representing a wish as fulfilled the dream certainly leads us into the future; but this future, which the dreamer accepts as his present, has been shaped in the likeness of the past by the indestructible wish.

—Sigmund Freud
The Interpretation of Dreams (1900)

Although twenty-first-century dream researchers and psychoanalysts respect and admire Freud for his groundbreaking work, most would not unreservedly endorse his theories. For while the Freudian viewpoint is certainly worthy of consideration, the modern consensus is that dreams should be examined from at least the Jungian angle as well. Their differences—first minor, but eventually unbridgeable—may eventually have driven these erstwhile colleagues to part ways, but today the joint legacies of Freud and the Swiss analytical psychologist Carl Jung (1875–1961) are regarded as the twin pillars on which a century's worth of dream-interpretation theories and practice have been constructed.

Given their brief collaboration, it is not, perhaps, surprising that many of Jung's ideas are comparable to those of Freud. He, too, surmised that the human psyche consists of three levels, for instance, but deviated from Freud by

identifying them as being the conscious mind, which regulates our waking thoughts; the personal unconscious, the realm of impulses that are unique to us as individuals; and the collective unconscious, effectively a repository of humankind's memories, experiences, and instincts, which we have inherited from our common ancestors and often take the form of archetypes, or universal symbols (see Chapter 5, Archetypal and Symbolic Figures, for a more detailed discussion of some of these). "I was never able to agree with Freud that the dream is a 'façade' behind which its meaning lies hidden—a meaning already known, but maliciously, so to speak, withheld from consciousness…" stated Jung in *Memories, Dreams, Reflections* (1962). Nor did he share Freud's conclusion that dreams were primarily concerned with wish fulfillment. Instead, Jung believed that dreams are therapeutic tools initiated by the self, or each human's psychic "core," with the purpose of trying to achieve individuation—"wholeness," or the perfect balance of the conscious and unconscious parts of our psyche.

It is usually only when we are asleep that the unconscious—personal and collective—is able to express itself without interference by the conscious mind,

and the dreams that flow from it, Jung averred, "give information about the secrets of the inner life and reveal to the dreamer hidden factors of his personality" ("Dream-Analysis," *Modern Man in Search of a Soul*, 1933). Jung believed that when the conscious mind reasserts itself and we leave dreamland and awaken, we should consequently consciously try to understand the dream messages generated by the unconscious mind, which "harbors no intention to deceive, but expresses something as best it can," often in the form of personal or archetypal symbols. In short, if you can comprehend the language of your unconscious, and are willing to heed what it is telling you, chances are that you will become a more balanced and happier individual.

Above: It was Carl Jung who "dreamed up" the theory of the collective unconscious, whose vocabulary, he proposed, includes archetypal symbols that resonate with us all.

Above, left: Freud believed that such long, narrow, pointed weapons as swords often symbolize the penis when wielded in dreams.

Left: Freudians may deem a dream of St. George and the dragon a sexual fantasy in which a man (perhaps the dreamer) makes a conquest of a "man-eating" woman. Jungians, on the other hand, may infer that by depicting the hero archetype (maybe the dreamer's masculine aspect) overcoming his or her personal "demon," the dream sets an example to follow.

The Jungian View of Dreams and the Unconscious

The view that dreams are merely imaginary fulfillments of suppressed wishes has long since been superseded. It is certainly true that there are dreams which embody suppressed wishes and fears, but what is there which the dream cannot on occasion embody? Dreams may give expression to ineluctable truths, to philosophical pronouncements, illusions, wild fantasies, memories, plans, anticipations, irrational experiences, even telepathic visions, and heaven knows what besides. One thing we ought never to forget: almost

the half of our lives is passed in a more or less unconscious state. The dream is specifically the utterance of the unconscious. We may call consciousness the daylight realm of the human psyche, and contrast it with the nocturnal realm of unconscious psychic activity which we apprehend as dreamlike fantasy. It is certain that consciousness consists not only of wishes and fears, but of vastly more than these, and it is highly probable that the unconscious psyche contains a wealth of contents and living forms equal to or even greater than does consciousness, which is characterized by concentration, limitation and exclusion.

—Carl Jung
"Dream-Analysis,"
Modern Man in Search of a Soul
(1933)

During the century or so since Freud and Jung first proposed their different theories and methods for decoding dreams, many other psychologists and psychiatrists have made notable contributions to this fascinating field of study, be it by advancing alternative proposals or by devising innovative interpretative techniques. And although none can unequivocally be said to be totally right or wrong, or to offer a "one-size-fits-all" explanation or key with which to unlock the hidden meaning of our dreams, many have nevertheless given us a better understanding of why we dream, and why we dream the dreams that we do.

Types of Dreams

Look through the body of research that is today available to anyone interested in dreams, and it soon becomes evident that dreams can be classified into a number of common types or categories, including the following:

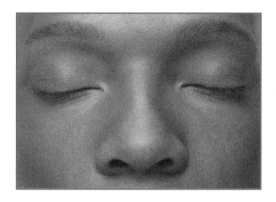

- literal, factual, and processing dreams
- physiological and punning dreams
- problem-solving and inspirational dreams
- cathartic and safety-valve dreams
- contrary, compensatory, or wish-fulfillment dreams
- recurring dreams
- nightmares
- precognitive and telepathic dreams

Left: Physical, as well as psychological, influences can flavor your dreams. If your head is exposed to the chilly air of a winter's night while you are sleeping, your dream may play itself out in arctic conditions, for instance.

Because you are likely to experience at least some of these types of dreams, you may find it useful to know a little about the form that they typically take and their possible causes. Note that dream types may also overlap, so that a nightmare in which you are struggling to breathe may also be a recurring dream, as well as a literal and physiological one, if, for example, your bedroom is constantly and grossly overheated.

Left: The unconscious mind may not conform to convention or reality when it conjures up a dreamscape. During the course of a twenty-first-century night, you may therefore find yourself dressed in medieval garb, on the outskirts of a walled European city, discussing, in Esperanto, your plans for a mountain-climbing expedition with some dainty lady companions. Small wonder that Surrealist artists were inspired by their dreams!

✳ ✳

LITERAL, FACTUAL, AND PROCESSING DREAMS

Literal and factual dreams reflect reality, or, as the Indian poet Rabindranath Tagore so elegantly put it, "In the drowsy dark cave of the mind / dreams build their nest with fragments / dropped from the day's caravan" (*Fireflies*, 1928). They can be concerned with the past, present, or future, although processing dreams, as literal and factual dreams are sometimes also called, are generally more concerned with the reexperiencing and digesting of memories. If you went to sleep at the end of a day spent shopping and dreamed of revisiting the same stores in which you had just spent real time, you experienced a literal, factual, or processing dream. If you dreamed that someone was knocking insistently on your bedroom door, and then awoke to find that this was indeed the case, you also had a literal, or factual, dream. And if you were mulling over the prospect of the many errands that you had to run the next day before losing consciousness and abandoning yourself to sleep, and then found yourself performing some of these chores in dreamland, your dream again falls into the literal or factual category.

Researchers generally do not consider such dreams to have hidden or especially significant meanings, but believe that they may highlight the dreamer's preoccupations, and may also be part of the process by which the brain recalls and reappraises its memories of the day before either jettisoning or preserving them.

PHYSIOLOGICAL AND PUNNING DREAMS

Physiological dreams are those that reflect the state of the dreamer's body. If, for example, you went to bed dehydrated, and then became increasingly parched as the night progressed, your actual thirst may have intruded into your dream, perhaps manifesting itself as a longing for a long, cool drink of refreshing water as you endured a hot and dry dreamland atmosphere. Or maybe your bedding obstructed your nose and mouth as you slept, prompting a physiological dream in which you were being suffocated by someone and were gasping desperately for breath.

Below: Knowing that you faced the ordeal of delivering an important presentation the next morning may have been weighing heavily on your mind when you turned out the light. And if your dream turned into a dress rehearsal for your "big moment," anxiety about your performance no doubt triggered your literal, or factual, dream.

✳ ✳

* *

Left: *If you were burning up with a fever as you drifted in and out of sleep in the real world, your high temperature may have triggered a physiological dream of being on the verge of succumbing to heatstroke as the sun blazed down upon you in an excruciatingly hot, arid, desert dreamscape.*

Researchers are divided about whether physiological dreams can reveal as yet undiagnosed internal problems. Some might say that a dream of an army of white-clothed ants battling against a horde of black aphids could depict, in symbolic form, the body's white blood cells struggling to vanquish the threat posed by a cancerous tumor that has started to develop within the dreamer's body. Others would dismiss this interpretation as being either fanciful (particularly if no tumor is subsequently diagnosed), coincidence (if it later is), or merely a reflection of the dreamer's health concerns or hypochondria, whether or not cancer subsequently rears its ugly head in the real world. There is currently no proof either way, so if you are troubled by a recurring dream that you believe may refer to your health, asking your doctor to check you over may at the very least put your mind at rest, thereby enabling you to enjoy a good night's sleep.

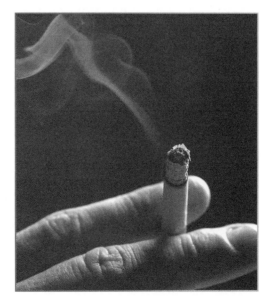

Left: *You may be consciously determined to beat your addiction in the waking world, but it's not always a case of mind over matter in the dream world, where, free of your conscious control, suppressed urges and desires can at last express themselves. So if you have recently quit smoking and dreamed of drawing lovingly and lingeringly on a cigarette, a very real craving for nicotine may have prompted your dreamland fantasy.*

* *

Above (left and right) and right: *If the significance of a dream's subject matter mystifies you, consider the possibility that it portrayed a pun. So if having a baby is out of the question in real life and you dreamed of cradling an infant, could the dream newborn have represented your "brainchild," or a pet project? If, while playing poker in dreamland, you observed your opponent draw an ace from his cuff, could your dreaming mind have been warning you that he has "an ace up his sleeve," or a "secret weapon" in the waking world? And, on the subject of weapons, could your unconscious have been trying to alert you to someone's real-life plan to "stab you in the back," or betray you, by homing in on a dagger in dreamland?*

Although punning dreams are not always, or exclusively, also physiological dreams, puns (plays on words) are often used in dreams as apt metaphors for how we are feeling. In such dreams, puns may be expressed in speech or writing, or they may be acted out. During a period in my life when I was so overwhelmed by working demands that there was no time at all for relaxation, I dreamed, for example, of keeling over every time that I stood up, while despairingly wailing "I've lost my balance!" for good measure. On waking, it was obvious to me that my dream referred to the loss of my usually healthy work–life balance in the waking world, which I was consciously trying to disregard in order to meet my deadlines. Similarly, if your waking hours are spent in a way that you find distasteful and you dreamed of vomiting uncontrollably, your unconscious may have been graphically portraying your real-life sense of being "sickened," or of being made to feel "sick to the stomach," by your waking circumstances.

Or if you dreamed of watching a dog slink into its kennel, a miserable expression on its face and its tail tucked abjectly between its legs as its owner berated it for having misbehaved, could the unconscious reference have been to the guilt that you feel for having cheated on your partner, and your sense of being "in the doghouse" now that he or she's discovered what you've been up to?

Punning dreams can—maybe incidentally, maybe not—also paint such ludicrous pictures that your conscious self can't help but smile at their memory, thereby lightening the negative mood that may have given rise to them. The Russian composer Igor Stravinsky (1882–1971) obviously felt aggrieved that unsympathetic music critics apparently "shut their ears" to his works, but cannot have taken them too seriously following his dream, reported in the English newspaper *The Evening Standard*, on October 29, 1969, that they "were small and rodent-like with padlocked ears, as if they had stepped out of a painting by Goya."

PROBLEM-SOLVING AND INSPIRATIONAL DREAMS

If no solution immediately springs to mind when we are faced with a dilemma, or are pondering an important decision or course of action, we may decide to "sleep on it." Having literally "slept on it," we may then wake up with a clear idea of how best to resolve our difficulties or of how best to proceed. Most researchers agree that problem-solving dreams, and sometimes also inspirational dreams, emanate from deep within our unconscious minds in response to a conundrum that the conscious mind has been unable to solve. Remember that although we distinguish our thought processes by labeling them as being "conscious" or "unconscious," "waking" or "dreaming," "reasoning" or "intuitive," all are generated by your brain, and all are therefore fundamentally "on your side." If you have been consciously preoccupied with a problem during your waking hours, it stands to reason that it has concerned you on an unconscious level, too, so that when you finally enter the realm of your unconscious in your dreams, you may find that the solution is waiting for you there, albeit maybe disguised as a symbol.

There are a number of famous examples of problem-solving dreams, and at least two have resulted in inventions that continue to play an important role in everyday life the world over. Ball-bearings, for instance, are said to have been invented by the Scottish engineer James Watt (1736–1819) as a result of his recurring dreams of being battered by a hailstorm of lead pellets, which eventually led him to realize that molten lead will form spheres if dropped from a significant height. And the idea for setting the lockstitch sewing-machine needle's hole in its tip, rather than its end, is said to

Left: In his problem-solving dream of men wielding spears with holes in their blades, Elias Howe unconsciously hit on the unconventional design solution that had eluded his conscious mind until then, namely, piercing the tip, instead of the end, of the needle that was destined for his new-fangled sewing machine.

Xanadu and Dreamland

In the note that he published, as a "psychological curiosity," with his poem in 1816, the English poet Samuel Taylor Coleridge (1772–1834) evocatively explained how "Kubla Khan" had its genesis in a dream, but revealed that it remained frustratingly incomplete.

In the summer of the year 1797, the Author [Coleridge], then in ill health, had retired to a lonely farm-house between Porlock and Linton…an anodyne had been prescribed, from the effects of which he fell asleep in his chair at the moment that he was reading the following sentence, or words of the same substance, in Purchas's Pilgrimage: "Here the Khan Kubla commanded a palace to be built, and stately garden thereunto. And thus ten miles of fertile ground were inclosed with a wall." The Author continued for about three hours in a profound sleep…during which time…he could not have composed less than from two to three hundred lines; if that indeed can be called composition in which all the images rose up before him as things, with a parallel production of the correspondent expressions, without any sensation or consciousness of effort. On awakening he appeared to himself to have a distinct recollection of the whole, and taking his pen, ink, and paper, instantly and eagerly wrote down the lines that are here preserved. At this moment he was unfortunately called out by a person on business from Porlock, and detained by him above an hour, and on his return to his room, found, to his no small surprise and mortification, that though he still retained some vague and dim recollection of the general purport of the vision, all the rest has passed away like the images on the surface of a stream into which a stone has been cast, but, alas! Without the after restoration of the latter!

—Samuel Taylor Coleridge
Written upon the publication of "Kubla Khan" (1816)

have come to U.S. inventor Elias Howe (1819–67) following a dream of tribesmen armed with spears that had pierced blades. Both of these inventions represented important breakthroughs to the men who had dreamed them up.

Problem-solving dreams can thus also be inspirational dreams, but inspirational dreams do not always arise in response to a waking-life problem. Whatever their cause, these types of dreams can have the most magical consequences for humankind. The haunting refrains that have permeated the dreams of distinguished musicians have sometimes lingered long enough to be captured on paper, a dream of Satan playing the violin, for example, in the case of the Italian composer and violinist Guiseppe Tartini (1692–1770) resulting in *The Devil's Trill* sonata of 1714.

CATHARTIC AND SAFETY-VALVE DREAMS

If you dreamed that you told some-one—perhaps a forbidding figure of absolute authority in your waking world—what you really think of them, beat them up, or otherwise asserted yourself aggressively or violently over them, you may have woken up feeling rather shocked by your dreamland actions. But if you also experienced a sense of release or relief, you probably had a cathartic or safety-valve dream. For if, during your waking hours, you have to accede to that person's will without question, you may have been feeling increasingly resentful of having to submit to the power that he or she wields over you, and may have been longing to reverse your respective positions so that you are the one who is in control and able to punish your erstwhile tormentor. By allowing you to do just that in the parallel world of dreamland, your dream may have enabled you

Left: A dream of lashing out at an infuriating colleague may have averted a real-life fight that may have had irreparable, career-damaging consequences in the waking world. Such dreams may be categorized as both wish-fulfillment and safety-valve dreams.

to let off steam, thus perhaps heading off a similar outburst or attack that may otherwise have occurred had your pent-up frustrations boiled over in real life, with, no doubt, disastrous consequences.

Left: If you are feeling increasingly frustrated by your sister-in-law's meddling ways during your waking hours, but are consciously biting your tongue because you daren't risk alienating your brother, letting off steam by telling her some home truths in dreamland may have been a cathartic experience.

CONTRARY, COMPENSATORY, OR WISH-FULFILLMENT DREAMS

Freudians would say that cathartic and safety-valve dreams are also wish-fulfillment dreams because they give the instincts of the id an outlet, thereby fulfilling "base" desires that the ego, regarding them as being socially unacceptable, generally successfully suppresses. They could equally be classed as contrary or compensatory dreams because they reverse, or are completely contrary to, one's real-life situation and thus compensate, albeit only in dreamland, for unsatisfactory waking conditions.

Indeed, contrary, compensatory, or wish-fulfillment dreams can give us a much-needed emotional high when our real-world circumstances are making us feel low and hopeless, which may be why we dream them up. If, for example, you are going through a period of relative poverty and spend your waking hours anxiously trying to devise ways of reducing your outgoings, you probably woke with a smile on your face after a dream in which you won a million dollars on the lottery and had a wonderful time splashing out on frivolous fripperies without even asking their price. Similarly, if you have secretly always longed to be an astronaut, but know that realizing your dream is out of the question in the real world, dreaming of zipping yourself into a spacesuit, taking your place on a space shuttle, and counting down the seconds to blast-off would be your unconscious mind's way of granting you your dream and boosting your morale.

Right and far right: If you are an impoverished, single student who is working flat out in the waking world to put yourself through school in the hope of passing your exams with flying colors, a dream of enjoying a luxurious vacation with your current crush, and of toasting your academic success with expensive champagne, may be classified as a contrary, a compensatory, and a wish-fulfillment dream.

✱✱✱

Left and far left: Maybe your most cherished wish is to be a blushing bride, whose radiance—and designer gown—arouses the admiration of all who set eyes on you, or perhaps you long to shop until you drop, money no object. In depicting you being, or doing, exactly that in dreamland, your unconscious may have done you a great service by giving you a memory to smile about, thereby lightening your mood in the waking world.

Wishful thinking may therefore be rewarded with wish fulfillment in dreamland, but, according to Jung, there may be another, less clear-cut, reason why we have compensatory dreams—particularly if they paint a negative dreamland picture—and that is to achieve, or maintain, a balanced psyche.

The psyche is a self-regulating system that maintains itself in equilibrium as the body does. Every process that goes too far immediately and inevitably calls forth a compensatory activity. Without such adjustments a normal metabolism would not exist, nor would the normal psyche.... The relationship between conscious and unconscious is compensatory. This fact...affords a rule for dream interpretation. It is always helpful, when we set out to interpret a dream, to ask: What conscious attitude does it compensate?"

—Jung, "Dream-Analysis," *ibid.*

According to this theory, if, for example, you are beset by crippling shyness in the waking world, your dreaming self may be transformed into a sparkling, superconfident, social butterfly. So if you find yourself puzzling over the possible meaning of a dream in which you behaved totally out of character, remember to take compensation into consideration.

✱✱✱

Right: Why would your normally placid pet have behaved completely out of character in dreamland, terrifying you so much by her spitting, scratching, and blood-curdling howls that you were relieved to awake from your nightmare? Could your dream have highlighted your suppressed fear that your best friend, usually an easy-going "pussy cat," will turn on you and hurt you in the real world?

Below: A recurring dream of having to sit an important exam for which one is completely unprepared is very common. Usually anxiety-induced, it may recur at times when we feel that we have to perform perfectly in the real world, yet feel unequal to the challenge, just as we did during our schooldays.

RECURRING DREAMS

Recurring dreams need not be identical in content, but the dream theme will usually be broadly consistent. If you often dream of competing in a race, of struggling to climb to the summit of a mountain, or of being humiliated by your classmates, for instance, the finer details of your dreamland experience may change, but the central issue remains the same, as, no doubt, does the emotional response that it elicits from your dreaming self.

Psychologists believe that recurring dreams—which may or may not be anxiety dreams or nightmares, but which generally provoke a profoundly negative reaction in us—are unconscious expressions of our deepest worries, fears, or memories that arouse such a powerful response in us that we push them to the back of our conscious minds because we find them so painful, uncomfortable, or embarrassing to confront. And because we have not consciously faced and worked them through, they continue to lurk in the depths of our unconscious, surfacing during our sleep in the form of recurring dreams. If you suffer from upsetting recurring dreams, putting a stop to them may therefore require some bravery on your part (see the following section on nightmares for further advice).

NIGHTMARES

Nightmares prove that many of our fears are "all in the mind," for if you think about it rationally, a dream is an intangible that can cause you no harm and is therefore nothing to be afraid of. But if that is the case, why do we sometimes wake up with a start, with a dry mouth, a racing heart, in a sweat, and on occasions even screaming?

The answer lies in whatever it is that we consciously fear, or that makes us feel exceptionally anxious, and that we therefore do our best to avoid or not to think about when we are awake. That consciously ignored fear remains dormant in our unconscious mind, however, and because we can exert little, if any, conscious control over dreamland, the province of the unconscious, it may come to the fore when activated by a certain trigger that we have encountered during the day. The trigger may be a stressful situation, an upsetting memory, or the arousal of a phobia: encountering a spider in the waking world may give rise to a nightmare about being entrapped by a monstrous spider if, for instance, you are an arachnophobic. But what if you are not at all bothered by spiders in the real world, yet your dreaming self was scared witless by a nocturnal encounter by a sinister black-widow spider? If you are determined to get to the bottom of a bad dream like this, it may help to ask yourself what the black widow could have represented, such as a predatory older woman who, if you are a younger man, you may have sensed has amorous designs on you, and who you fear may "eat you for breakfast" should you fall into her clutches.

If a spider, monster, ogre, or demon terrorized you while you were sleeping, remember that it was your unconscious, in other words, you, that conjured it up, and that, in the words of Jung, "The unconscious is not a demonic monster, but a thing of nature that is perfectly neutral as far as moral sense, esthetic taste and intellectual judgement go. It is dangerous only when our conscious attitude to it becomes hopelessly false. And this danger grows in the measure that we practice repressions. But as soon as the patient begins to assimilate the contents that were previously unconscious, the danger from the side of the unconscious diminishes." ("Dream-Analysis," *ibid.*)

Whatever it is that you decide that your menacing monster may have symbolized, most therapists would concur with Jung that the only really effective way of banishing it from your dreams for good is consciously to address it and to think about why you relate or respond to it in such an extreme manner. By making an effort to understand what it represents and why this has the power to frighten you so, you will, it is hoped, demystify the monster that terrorizes you in the darker depths of dreamland, gain control over your fear, and thus neutralize the threat that it poses to your psychic wellbeing. "Knowledge is power," it is said, and this is often especially true when you are able to pluck up the courage to confront your bogeymen or unresolved issues, whereupon you may

Below: Sometimes the fear underlying a nightmare requires no explanation. If you are a parent who dreamed that your child was snatched from you by a sinister someone in the street, for instance, your deepest real-life fear—one that you probably can't bear to think about while you're awake—was simply surfacing in your sleep. Unfortunately, not even the most skilled therapist can banish a parent's worries about the safety of his or her offspring.

see them for the pathetic things that they actually are, enabling you to overcome your fear and leave it behind you, in the past, as you move confidently on into the future. Be warned that this process is rarely quickly or easily accomplished, however, and if you regularly suffer from terrible nightmares, seeking the help of a trained therapist may be a wise strategy.

PRECOGNITIVE AND TELEPATHIC DREAMS

Now that scientific principles have been overwhelmingly applied to the study and analysis of dreams, the notion that we may receive psychic omens foretelling future events, or telepathic communications from others—be they hale and hearty, sick or dying, or even long dead—in our dreams is generally dismissed out of hand. And should an event that was apparently foreseen in a precognitive, prophetic, or clairvoyant dream actually come to pass in the real world, the explanation is usually put down either to coincidence or to an unconscious recognition of the inevitability of the event occurring. If you dreamed of crashing your automobile and later really did so, for example, the suggestion would be that you'd unconsciously picked up clues that your automobile's brakes were faulty and that there was consequently an accident "waiting to happen."

No one can yet claim to understand the workings of the human mind fully, however. And there have been many well-documented instances of individuals dreaming of disasters occurring on different continents that have later come to pass, as well as of people being visited by a loved one, or of hearing a message from a significant someone, in dreamland shortly before receiving news of their actual demise at around that very time. So if you strongly feel that you have had a precognitive or telepathic dream, you may well be right. If you think that this may indeed be the case, make sure that you record the details of your dream as fully as possible, along with the date (and if you can, also note down the time) on which you dreamed your portentous dream, so that you later have proof should the events of your dream really be played out in the waking world. Do not panic on waking from such an unsettling dream, however, because unless you already know that you have psychic abilities, a dreamland fantasy, or else unconscious knowledge, will still be the most likely explanation for it.

Right: Abraham Lincoln may have had a precognitive dream shortly before he was murdered in 1865. He recounted its details to his friend, Ward Hill Lamon: "Before me was a catafalque, on which rested a corpse wrapped in funeral vestments. 'Who is dead in the White House?' I demanded of one of the soldiers. 'The President,' was his answer; 'he was killed by an assassin!'"

Left: Before drifting off into dreamland, make sure that you have a pen and paper at the ready with which to record what happened to you there as soon as you awake.

Decoding Your Dreams

You may not think that you dream at all, but be assured that you do. If you awake with no memory of having dreamed, it may either be that the details of the night's dreams have been driven from your conscious mind by over-riding thoughts of what the new day will bring or that you woke at the "wrong" time during the sleep cycle.

Unless you suffer from insomnia or another type of sleep disturbance, you will usually spend the bulk of your night in "slow-wave" sleep, of which there are four distinct stages.

(Drifting off to sleep is the first stage, when your body and brain relax (sometimes triggering myoclonic jerks, or involuntary muscular spasms), your eyes roll, and you enter the hypnagogic state, during which you may see and hear random visions and voices. You do not dream during this stage, however.

(During the second stage, you sink ever deeper into unconsciousness, but still aren't truly asleep, nor are you dreaming.

(By the time that you enter the third stage, when you are at last fast asleep, you will have become utterly relaxed, but are still not dreaming.

(The fourth stage of sleep is known as orthodox, or nonrapid-eye-movement (N.R.E.M.), sleep, when your unconscious mind has come to the fore and your brain arranges for any damage to your body or breaches of your immune system to be repaired, also, it is thought, addressing the day's memories. Although you may be hit by night terrors, or unspecific feelings of dread, during this stage of sleep, these are not technically dreams.

It typically takes between ninety and one hundred minutes to pass through the four stages of slow-wave sleep, when your brainwaves are pulsing at their slowest rate and your vital functions have also slowed considerably, after which you move backward through the cycle, and then forward again.

Right and below, right: Writing down the details of your dream while they are still fresh in your memory will preserve them. This is a necessary precaution if you are serious about decoding your dreams, for, as the poet Samuel Taylor Coleridge (below) ruefully testified, dream-world visions are all too easily banished by real-world intrusions (see page 22).

You will probably have noted that dreams do not feature in any of the four stages of slow-wave sleep, so when exactly do you dream? The answer is after you have returned to the first stage, at which point you enter paradoxical, or rapid-eye-movement (R.E.M.), sleep, when your brainwaves and body functions quicken and your eyeballs flit around behind your closed eyelids. If you awake from a vivid dream now, you may not be able to move, for while the unconscious sends you off on dreamland adventures, it also takes the precaution of paralyzing you to prevent you from acting out the dramatic action of your dream in reality.

Your first taste of the R.E.M., or dreaming, phase of sleeps lasts for only around ten minutes before you reembark on the four stages of the slow-wave sleep cycle again, but each R.E.M. period—and they average four a night—gradually lengthens so that the ultimate, and longest, phase of dreams that you may experience can last for about forty-five minutes. And it is the dreams that occur during this final incidence, as you increasingly surface into consciousness, that you are most likely to remember.

You, like Samuel Taylor Coleridge, may already be all too ruefully aware of how quickly the details of your dreams elude your powers of recall once you have woken up and have started your early morning ritual. If you're serious about analyzing your dreams, this is why it's important to record them before your conscious thoughts of the day's "to-do" list, or that first shot of caffeine, crowd out, or otherwise banish, your ephemeral memories of events in dreamland. Capture your dreams as soon as you awake, before stirring from your bed, either by dictating them into a Dictaphone or by scribbling them into a notebook (depending on your preferred method, remember to keep your Dictaphone primed or a pen, paper, and perhaps also a flashlight, to hand by your bedside). Once you have recorded the crucial details, note the date because this may later help you to identify a waking-world trigger for, or real-time pattern to, your dreams. (You'll also find a space on each of the dream-subject pages that follows on which to jot down the gist of a relevant dream.) It may be, for instance, that studying your dream diary reveals that in December you invariably have disturbing dreams about family arguments, or that you consistently dreamed of inheriting a fortune at a time when money was particularly tight. It's particularly important that you log the atmosphere of your dream and how your dreaming self felt, for emotions prevail in dreamland, and will almost certainly provide you with the key to decoding your dreams.

Having acted as a human dreamcatcher while muzzily cocooned in your warm, cozy bed, you can then set the day under way and get on with the business of living life in the real world. Later on, when you have some free time, solitude, and emotional distance, you'll be able to pick up where you left off and consciously consider your dream in the cold light of day, your thoughts unclouded by emotive residual memories. Sometimes the message conveyed by your dream will be crystal clear. On other occasions, you may find the advice in this book enlightening as you grope your way toward settling on a likely interpretation. And if you are on the verge of giving up because you find a dream utterly baffling, you may find it helpful to use such Freudian tricks as free association, or writing down every little thing springs to mind when you think of a particular aspect of your dream, without giving it a second's thought; or Jungian techniques like direct association, or focusing intensely on a dream symbol and listing everything with which you associate it; or any other interpretive strategy, such as teasing out possibly significant considerations by

interviewing yourself (for instance, "Did the way that the gray cat in your dream looked or behaved remind you of anyone or anything?")

The Talmud (Berachot 55a) asserts that "A dream that is not interpreted is like a letter that has not been opened." Think about the life-changing messages that have been mailed to you in the real world: a declaration of love; news of an exam success or failure; of a birth; of an invitation to attend a job interview; of someone's proposed visit. It matters not who you believe the sender of your dreams to be—be it a divine agency, or your own, unconscious mind—but can you afford to remain ignorant of the potentially illuminating, if not life-altering, communiqués that are delivered to you in your sleep?

CLARE GIBSON

Above: We enter a rich parallel world when we fall asleep, and letting the strange, yet often sage, messages that emanate from dreamland go to waste would be a shame. After all, their source is you, and who else could possibly know you, your hopes and fears, your likes and dislikes, your sins and your virtues, any better?

In dreams and in love
there are no impossibilities.

János Arany, nineteenth-century Hungarian poet

CHAPTER 1

THE BODY

If you are consciously troubled by a niggling feeling that all is not
well with your health, and you had a worrying dream that appeared
to confirm your worst fears, your unconscious may merely have
been providing an outlet for the worries that your conscious mind
is trying to quash. (And if such dreams are recurring, consulting
your doctor may give you peace of mind.) It is more likely,
however, that your unconscious seized on and portrayed a
pun as a way of expressing your current state of mind.

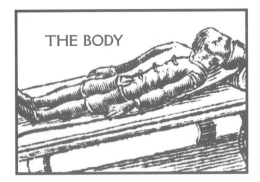

THE BODY

My Arms Dreams

----

* * * * * * * * * * * * * * * * * * *

Hugging Yourself

If you dreamed that you wrapped your arms around yourself, perhaps you are feeling vulnerable and in need of stronger emotional defenses in your waking life. Or were you keeping others at bay, or holding secrets close to your chest?

ARMS

In the world of dreams, a scenario that focuses on arms can mean a number of things. Depending on the circumstances of the dream, and on whether the arms were yours or someone else's, they can denote welcoming, comfort, and protection, strength, work, or a readiness to fight.

Symbolic and Verbal Associations
- Strength, work, productivity
- "Open arms," or welcoming
- "Linking arms," togetherness or solidarity
- Being someone's "right-hand man"
- Comfort, protection, and reassurance (when hugging is involved)
- Being "up in arms," fighting, or "arming" oneself for a forthcoming challenge
- Keeping your distance: holding someone at "arm's length"

Positive Interpretations: If you had a dream in which your mother, lover, or friend affectionately enveloped you in their arms, then this dream hug probably symbolized your real-life feelings of being loved and protected (or else your desire to have these feelings, perhaps after a recent loss or separation). A dream that someone welcomed you into their home with "open arms" can be similarly interpreted. Arms are often a symbol of strength, and therefore the appearance of arms in a dream can have a number of positive (or negative) associations related to this, such as linked arms representing support. Because of their association with strength and power, arms can also symbolize work and productivity. For instance, if you had a dream in which your boss told you that she considered you her "right-hand man," then this may symbolize your feelings of power and importance within your work position. Alternatively, could your unconscious have been telling you that it's time to take on more responsibilities on the job? Your reaction to the dream scenario should give you a clue as to the meaning of your dream.

Negative Interpretations: Because of their association with strength and activity, arms can be a symbol of violence, threats, and fighting. In English, the word "arms" itself can also be used to mean "weapons." If you had a dream in which someone was striking out at you, do you know the person? Could he or she be harboring some anger toward you that your unconscious is picking up on? A similar meaning could be applied to a dream in which you were "up in arms," or raising your own arms in attack—or in defense—against another person. Perhaps it is your own anger that is the issue? Or, more generally, could a dream in which you were taking up or wielding a weapon be your unconscious's way of alerting you to your need to "arm" yourself for a challenge, such as an upcoming exam? And if you were extending your arms against someone or something, perhaps you are trying to avoid a person or problem.

Related Dreams

pages 106, 199, 253, 264, 281 & 267

BACK & SHOULDERS

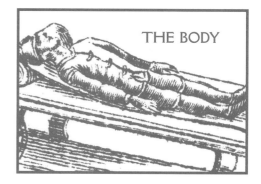

✽✽✽✽✽✽✽✽✽✽✽✽✽✽✽✽✽✽✽✽✽✽✽✽✽✽✽✽✽✽✽✽✽✽✽✽✽

Like the arms, the back and shoulders are often symbols of strength and vitality. In dreams, the back can signify power and determination, but can also be highlighted in the alternative context of weakness. Shoulders, meanwhile, often symbolize support, or responsibility for duties.

Symbolic and Verbal Associations
- Support; a "shoulder to lean on"; "shouldering" responsibilities
- "Putting your back into it," or hard work; "backing," or providing support
- "Spinelessness," or, alternatively, having "backbone"
- Things going on "behind your back"
- "Turning one's back" or "backing out" on someone or of something; abandonment
- "Backing down" or "backing off": retreating or withdrawing from confrontation
- "Getting someone's back up," or annoying them
- "Backbiting," or malicious gossip; being "stabbed in the back"

Positive Interpretations: If you had a dream in which you offered your friend your shoulder for support, could it be that he or she is in need of you for emotional or other support in waking life? Or if you had a dream in which you found yourself leaning on someone else's shoulder, consider whether it is you who is in need of "a shoulder to lean on." The back and shoulders can also appear as symbols of power, strength, and hard work. If you had a dream in which you were "shouldering" a heavy load, think about what this burden may represent in your waking life, and how it made you feel in your dream. Did you feel happy to make yourself helpful and useful? Or did you struggle with a burden that was "too much to bear"?

Negative Interpretations: A dream in which someone placed a heavy, or "back-breaking," load on your back or shoulders could indicate that someone is asking you to bear or "shoulder" too much weight or responsibility in waking life. Who was it who placed this load upon you? If it was your coworker, for instance, is he shirking his duties on the job, therefore leaving more work on your desk? If you had a dream in which you suffered from a backache, whereas you have no such complaint during waking hours, ask yourself why it was that your unconscious mind was directing your focus to your backbone. There are many possible interpretations for a dream such as this. Have you been feeling "spineless" in a particular area of your life? Or are you considering "backing down" over an important issue in your relationship? Otherwise, perhaps someone has been talking or doing something "behind your back"? In another scenario, if you dreamed that you were having a conversation with your mother and that she suddenly turned around and walked out of the room, could you be afraid that she disapproves of something that you are doing, and fear that she is about to "turn her back on you" in the waking world?

Related Dreams
pages 110, 200, 257 & 302

My Back & Shoulders Dreams

✽ ✽ ✽ ✽ ✽ ✽ ✽ ✽ ✽ ✽ ✽ ✽ ✽ ✽ ✽ ✽ ✽ ✽ ✽ ✽

A Shoulder Massage
A dream in which you were treated to a shoulder massage might well have been a form of wish fulfillment. Are you tense, overtired, or overburdened at the moment? Do you need a spa retreat or some relief from an emotionally draining problem?

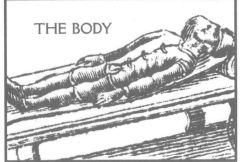

My Beauty & Ugliness Dreams

----

* * * * * * * * * * * * * * * * *

Mirror Images

A dream that featured the image of a beautiful stranger in a mirror, perhaps unusually dressed or from another era, was probably telling you something about yourself. If you realized that the stranger was you and you were looking intently at the mirror, are you anxious about a shameful secret, or perhaps worried about developing signs of aging?

BEAUTY & UGLINESS

* *

As much as we may try to counter such beliefs in the waking world, in the world of dreams, concepts of bodily beauty and ugliness are not always skin-deep: they are often representative of our hopes, fears, and feelings about the inner character of ourselves and others.

Symbolic and Verbal Associations

‹ Aspirations for the admiration and approval of others
‹ Fears about growing older; physical aging
‹ Our hopes and fears about the character of ourselves and others
‹ Revulsion, or being repulsed by someone; moral repulsion
‹ Harboring unhealthy or "ugly" emotions, or behaving in an obnoxious manner

Positive Interpretations: The image that we present to others, or the persona that we show to the world, is often represented in our dreams by a focus on the appearance of our physical self. If, in your dream, you looked into the mirror to see a vision of exquisite loveliness, it may be that this is how you want the world to see you. Do you wish for others to admire you for your beautiful appearance or moral character? Or did you have a dream in which someone else's physical beauty caused you to have feelings of yearning, attraction, or admiration? If this is the case, it may be that your dream self has encountered your anima (if you are a man) or animus (if you are a woman): a character who is the mirror image, or reverse, of your soul, and whose appearance in your dream may indicate the need for balance in your waking life. If you are a man, it may signal that it is time for you to get in touch with your emotional, intuitive, or empathetic side. Conversely, if you are a woman, the appearance of your animus may be your unconscious mind's way of prompting you to become more intellectually focused, practical, or confident.

Negative Interpretations: If you had a dream in which you looked into the mirror to find that your body had become twisted and ugly, could it be that you are harboring an "ugly" emotion, such as jealousy or envy, and that you are worried that others may "see" this in you and find you repulsive? Alternatively, if your dream self was horrified to see that you had become old and wrinkled, this may be your unconscious expression of your fears and/or regrets about the physical effects associated with aging. But if you were terrified, horrified, or revolted by someone else's ugliness in your dream, do you know who the person was? Your dreaming image of them may indicate that this person is—by means of their actions or their intentions—somehow plaguing you during waking hours, or that their attitude or their "energy" is repulsive to you in some way. The dream meanings associated with the relative beauty or ugliness of the specific body parts will be addressed in detail, one-by-one, in later sections of this book.

Related Dreams

pages 100, 119, 120, 125 & 265

BLOOD & GUTS

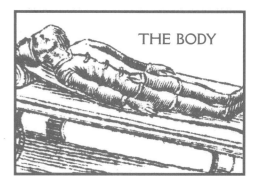

Because we don't usually see someone's blood unless they have been injured—and because, if a person loses enough blood, they are likely to die—the letting of blood in dreamland is often a powerful symbol of the life force ebbing from someone. Similar interpretations can be applied to a dream that focuses on intestines (either our own or someone else's)—though, depending on the context, there are a number of other explanations that should be considered.

Symbolic and Verbal Associations
- Mortality; the "life force"
- Menstruation; pregnancy
- Injury, or loss of vitality
- "Bleeding someone dry"
- Coming to terms with, "stomaching," or "digesting" new information
- Courage, or "having the guts" to do something

Positive Interpretations: If you are a woman of childbearing age and you had a dream that featured or spotlighted blood, then your unconscious may be honing in on your hopes or fears about pregnancy. Otherwise, it may just be that you are about to begin menstruating. However, if you had a dream in which you received a life-saving blood transfusion, you should think about who the person was who either administered the transfusion or donated the blood; perhaps he or she has the ability to revitalize or heal you in some way in the waking world.

Negative Interpretations: If you had a dream in which you were chopping up carrots for dinner and suddenly chopped into your finger by mistake, or if you dreamed that you were more seriously injured, perhaps that you were attacked and stabbed by someone, then your dream self's loss of blood may be representative of your feelings of having lost vitality in the real world. Could it be that you have been overworking yourself in order to finish the new addition on your house by the holidays? Or has someone else, perhaps an overly needy friend or relative, been wearing you down or "sapping your strength"? If you dreamed that your child knifed you in the belly, is he "bleeding you dry" in the waking world through his ceaseless demands for your time or money? Perhaps not so symbolic, a dream of intestinal pain could simply mean that you ate too much (or not enough) food for dinner and that you are suffering for it during your slumbering hours. Or is it that your unconscious is telling you that you are feeling "starved" of love or affection? If this is not the case, however, you might want to ask yourself whether you are finding it difficult to "stomach" or "digest" something in real life, such as your widowed mother having taken on a new boyfriend. Alternatively, could it be that you have been lacking the "guts" to do something in the real world, such as quitting the job that you hate?

Related Dreams
pages 50, 56, 87, 92, 239 & 254

My Blood & Guts Dreams

✱ ✱ ✱ ✱ ✱ ✱ ✱ ✱ ✱ ✱ ✱ ✱ ✱ ✱ ✱ ✱ ✱ ✱ ✱

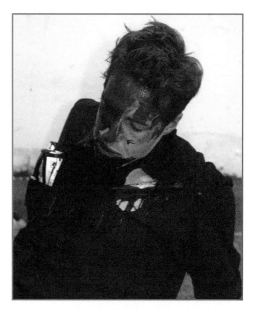

Your Bleeding Victim
Did you dream that you saw someone bleeding and losing consciousness and then realized that you had inflicted the wound yourself? If the victim was someone you know, you may be a drain on his or her emotional or practical resources in your waking life. If it was a stranger, the bloodletting probably signifies a pent-up frustration that you should deal with before lashing out in the real world.

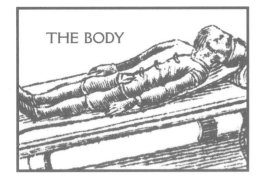

My Bodily Functions Dreams

----

* * * * * * * * * * * * * * * * * * *

Locked Out

If you were unable to get into the bathroom in your dream, what was the setting? Perhaps you were at your workplace, in which case you are probably burdened with a problematic situation whose inaccessibility is denying you a sense of relief. Alternatively, perhaps you literally needed to get up and visit the bathroom.

BODILY FUNCTIONS

* *

It's not a pleasant subject, in most people's opinion, but such bodily functions as urination and defecation do serve the important purpose of ridding our bodies of waste. And when we dream of ourselves performing these functions, the meaning is likely to be similar, though the dream probably has to do with the elimination of emotional matter, such as unpleasant memories.

Symbolic and Verbal Associations
- Elimination of emotional waste
- "Letting go" of unhealthy feelings or the past
- Emotional "blockage" or constipation; "anal retention"
- Cleanliness versus filth or foulness
- Being emotionally in, or out of, control

Positive Interpretations: A dream in which you found yourself urinating or defecating is likely to signify the need for an emotional purging of some sort, whether it is an unpleasant memory that you need to let go of or a past lesson that you have learned and can now put behind you, so that it may no longer trouble your mind. So, if you found your dream self frantically racing to get to the bathroom, and then finally emerging with relief, you may need to ask yourself if it is time to "flush out" your emotional system during waking hours. Have you felt that you have been emotionally burdened of late? Perhaps a recent visit to your hometown has caused your mind to be troubled by the memory of an argument that you had with your now deceased father? Or do you long to rid yourself of your jealous feelings toward your best friend, who has recently been promoted to an executive position within her company? Whatever the cause of the dream, it is likely that it was your unconscious mind's way of signaling to you that you would be happier if you were to dedicate yourself to performing some serious emotional purging.

Negative Interpretations: Did your dream self have difficulties due to constipation? Or perhaps your dreaming mind cast you in a scenario in which you suffered from diarrhea? An analysis of the dream situation should give you a clue as to whether you have been emotionally "blocked," constipated, or "anally retentive," or, alternatively, whether you have lately spun out of control in the emotional arena of your waking world. Or perhaps your dream self was desperately searching for a public restroom, only to look in vain, or to find one that was all locked up and to which you could not gain access. If this was the case, it may be that your waking self needs to find the key, or the catalyst, for a much-needed emotional release. In another scenario, if you had a dream in which you or your belongings were fouled by someone else's urine or feces, do you know who the person was? You may want to consider whether you have been taken advantage of or "dumped on" by this person.

Related Dreams
pages 70, 182, 257, 259, 271 & 302

BONES

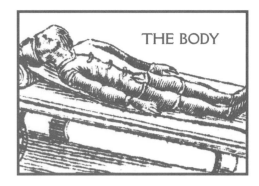

★★

As illustrated by the symbolism associated with such holidays as Halloween and the Mexican Day of the Dead, skeletons are a classic symbol of death and the world beyond. However, depending upon the context, there are several other associations that could explain the appearance of bones in a dream.

Symbolic and Verbal Associations
(Health and wellbeing
(The "bare bones" of an issue
("Skeletons in the closet"; shame
(Death; mortality; the afterlife
(A "skull and crossbones": a warning of danger

Positive Interpretations: If you dreamed that you were looking at an X-ray of your arm or leg, and that you saw that you had a fracture or a break in one of your bones, the symbolic meaning of the dream is not necessarily negative. If you know that you are in good health and have no particular fears about receiving an injury (if you haven't recently taken up hang-gliding, for instance), then it may be that your unconscious was prompting you to get down to the "bare bones" of an issue, such as a seemingly trivial dispute that has been troubling your marital relationship.

Negative Interpretations: On the other hand, if you are the star pitcher for your company's softball team and have a very important game coming up, then a dream in which you suffered from a broken arm is likely to have been a simple reflection of your worries with regard to your performance in the game. But—because X-rays and scans reveal hidden truths about ourselves—if you had a dream in which you were anxious that your best friend should not see an X-ray of your skull, could it be that you are worried that she will discover "the truth" about you, see you "as you really are," or else find out what you think of her? In another scenario, did you have a dream in which you opened a closet in your parents' basement and were shocked when a skeleton came falling out toward you? If so, it may be that you are unconsciously aware of some awkward family secrets that it would be healthier to "bring out into the open." However, because skeletons, skulls, and bones are such powerful symbols of mortality and death, having a dream involving any of these things—especially if you were frightened—could indicate your fear or anxiety regarding death (either your own death or that of a loved one). In a similar vein, a dream in which you were terrified by the sight of a skull and crossbones (a symbol of warning) could be your unconscious mind's way of telling you that there is danger ahead.

My Bones Dreams

★★★★★★★★★★★★★★★★★★★★★★

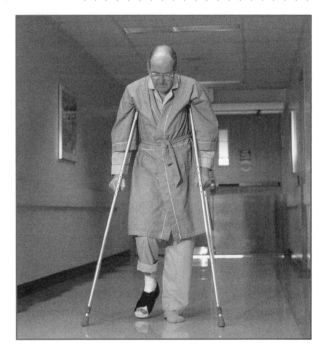

Broken Bones
If you dreamed that you were incapacitated by a broken leg, the significance probably lies in an emotional injury for which you need support. Alternatively, do you need to be forced to "put your feet up" and to relinquish some of the stressful burdens that may be getting on top of you?

Related Dreams
pages 35, 37, 92, 141, 207 & 273

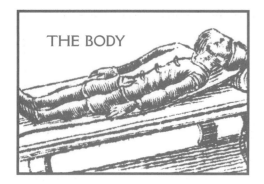

THE BODY

My Chills & Coldness Dreams

....
....
....
....
....
....
....
....

* * * * * * * * * * * * * * * * * *

A Refreshing Freeze

In your dream, did you step out into a winter wonderland of fresh, powdery snow on a bright, crisp new day? If so, perhaps you have been stifled by too much sticky heat or tension at home or work and need to clear the air or simply to step outside to "chill out."

CHILLS & COLDNESS

✱✱✱

When we talk about our passions, we often describe them in terms of temperature, whether they be "hot" or "cold." When we have a dream in which we find ourselves to be chilly or cold, it is therefore likely that our unconscious mind is directing our attention to our emotions, and the meaning can be positive or negative, depending on the context and our dream self's feelings.

Symbolic and Verbal Associations
- Being "cool," i.e., suave or calm and collected
- Mediating a dispute, or "cooling" tempers
- Relaxation: "chilling out"
- Emotional coldness; indifference
- An unwelcoming or "chilly" attitude or atmosphere; giving "the cold shoulder"
- Ruthlessness; doing something in "cold blood"
- Fear; something that makes the "blood run cold"

Positive Interpretations: While it seems that many of our associations with feeling chilled or cold are not positive ones, there are a few scenarios in which finding one's dream self feeling cool can bode happiness and mental wellbeing. If your dreaming self felt pleasantly cool, have you recently felt "cool" or suave because you finally worked up the courage to ask your big crush out on a date and he or she said yes? Or have you really buckled down to study for an upcoming exam, and now feel cool, calm, and collected about your ability to ace it? Alternatively, if you have recently been under a lot of stress during waking hours, could your dream have been your unconscious's way of fulfilling your need to relax or "chill out"? (The same explanation could be applied if you have been feeling very angry or "hot-tempered" in the real world.)

Negative Interpretations: If you dreamed that you were very cold, did you awake to find that you were, in fact, suffering from a chill? If this is the case, it may be that you were ill with a fever, or that you simply needed to put an extra blanket on your bed. But if this was not the case, then your unconscious mind may be reacting to your present mood or to the circumstances of your waking life. For instance, could it be that your relationship with your girlfriend has gone "cold," and that you need to find a way to "turn up the heat" or make things exciting again? Or could it be that someone in the real world has been giving you the "cold shoulder," behaving coldly toward you, or treating you with indifference? Or is it you who is giving off cold "vibes" toward someone else? If your dream involved feelings of apprehension or fear, has something or someone been making your "blood run cold" during waking hours? Or have you been feeling emotionally frozen or paralyzed? Alternatively, have you been contemplating committing an act in "cold blood"?

Related Dreams

pages 37, 92, 237, 239, 257 & 271

CONVALESCENCE

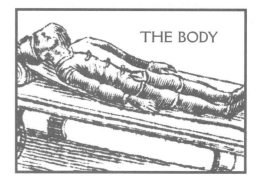

Apart from any meanings that might be associated with a dream of being sick, if you had a dream in which you were being nursed or cared for during an illness (or a recovery from an illness), then it is likely that the meaning of your dream has much to due with your emotional wants and needs.

Symbolic and Verbal Associations
- Being pampered, cherished, or otherwise taken care of
- Feelings of importance, or a lack thereof
- Taking the right "medicine" to heal an emotional wound
- Needing emotional care or attention
- Worries or fears with regard to health

Positive Interpretations: Did you have a dream in which you thoroughly enjoyed being fussed over and nursed lovingly and attentively back to health by someone? If so, it may be that you are in need of some emotional pampering or care in the waking world. Did you recognize the person who was nursing you? If so, you should consider whether this person may have the ability to care for or heal you emotionally in some way in the waking world. Alternatively, it may be that your self-esteem has been in decline and that you long to be made to feel important, in the way that a good nurse would make you feel the center of attention. Finally, if you felt an enormous sense of rest and relief in your dream, consider whether you have been overworking yourself and are now in need of a temporary release from your real-world duties and responsibilities.

Negative Interpretations: In the waking world, doctors and nurses have the duty of diagnosing and treating illnesses. When these figures appear in your dreams—especially in the context of them caring for you during a period of convalescence—then your unconscious mind may be reflecting your worries about some aspect of your health and signaling to you that it's time to be brave and to make that doctor's appointment that you've been putting off for so many months. Alternatively, your dream may indicate that you have been running yourself down and need to take better care of yourself so that you do not become ill. If you had a dream in which you were called upon to take some medicine, your dreaming self's reaction to the medicine should give you a clue as to the meaning. Did you gag or grimace in disgust at the awful taste of the stuff? If so, has someone been giving you "bad medicine," or terrible advice, in the waking world? Or did you swallow a sweet elixir that made your throat feel cool and soothed? If this was the case, then it is likely that your dream was reflecting your unconscious good feelings about some emotional care or "medicine" that you have been given in the real world or, alternatively, your desire to receive such a remedy or cure.

Related Dreams
pages 56, 113, 173, 179, 192 & 271

My Convalescence Dreams

....
....
....
....
....
....
....
....
....

* * * * * * * * * * * * * * * * * * * *

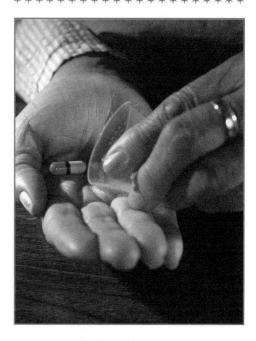

Self-medication

A dream that focused on medication rather than your being looked after by someone else might mean that your unconscious has recognized your need to attend to yourself and take charge of your physical or emotional health. Have you been neglecting yourself in either arena, or altogether? If so, take this dream as a reminder that you cannot get away with doing so forever.

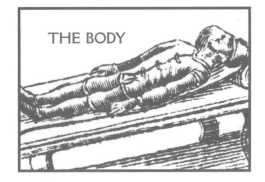

EARS & HEARING

A s hearing is one of the major senses that most people rely upon for taking in information, communicating, and navigating their way through the world, it is no wonder that there are so many symbolic associations and expressions relating to the organs with which we hear: the ears.

Symbolic and Verbal Associations

‹ Keeping an "ear to the ground," or staying alert or informed
‹ Focusing one's attention, or being "all ears"
‹ Not listening, or "closing one's ears," to the truth
‹ Ignoring, or "turning a deaf ear" to, what someone is saying
‹ "Wagging ears"; the circulation of gossip
‹ "Burning ears": sensing that someone is talking or gossiping behind one's back
‹ Being "up to one's ears," i.e., overburdened or fully occupied

Positive Interpretations: Hearing, or "listening out," is an important, primary way detecting things to come—both literally and figuratively—in the waking world. Did your dreaming mind cast you in a situation in which you were bent down, listening intently, with an "ear to the ground"? If so, then this could be an unconscious clue that you need to stay alert and informed about what is happening around you in the waking world—perhaps at work, where an upcoming company reorganization may lead to promotions and/or layoffs. Alternatively, a dream that focuses on your (or someone else's) ear may be a signal that you need to pay more attention to the things that people are telling you. In another scenario, if you had a dream in which someone's ears had grown to an extraordinary size, you may want to consider whether that person is "all ears" or ready to hear something that you have been wanting to tell them for some time.

Negative Interpretations: If you dreamed that you were deaf or hard of hearing, and if you do not suffer from hearing problems in the waking world, could it be that you have been "closing your ears" to some hard truth that you haven't wanted to hear in the waking world? In your dream, did you know the person who was trying to speak to you? Do they have some information that may be difficult—yet important—for you to "hear"? Alternatively, if you dreamed that someone else had gone deaf, has that person been "turning a deaf ear" to, or ignoring, something that you have been telling (or asking of) them in the waking world? Having a dream that places the focus on "wagging" or "burning" ears may be your unconscious mind's way of telling you that it is possible that someone you know has been gossiping or talking behind your back. Or is it you who has been doing the gossiping? The specific dream scenario involved, and your dreaming reaction to it, should give you a clue as to how to interpret your dream.

My Ears & Hearing Dreams

....
....
....
....
....
....
....
....
....
....

✱ ✱ ✱ ✱ ✱ ✱ ✱ ✱ ✱ ✱ ✱ ✱ ✱ ✱ ✱ ✱ ✱ ✱ ✱

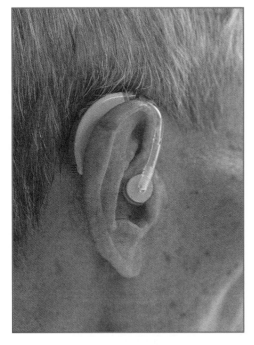

Hard of Hearing

Dreaming of wearing a hearing aid or losing your hearing suggests that you fear the aging process if this felt depressing to your dreaming self. However, if you were feeling upbeat, it could mean that you suddenly experienced better communication and an end to a period of isolation in the waking world.

Related Dreams

pages 106, 110, 114, 218, 266 & 278

EYES & EYESIGHT

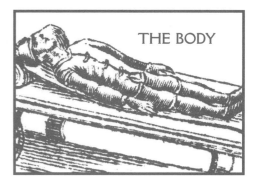

We often hear people say that the eyes are the "windows to the soul," which is, perhaps, an allusion to the eyes' crucial function in communicating and relaying emotions. The eyes, the organs of sight, have long been the subject of countless songs and stories, and when they feature in our dreams, the meaning can be as rich and multilayered as the ancient symbolism that surrounds these all-important organs.

Symbolic and Verbal Associations
- "Having an eye" or "having eyes" for (liking, being interested in, or having a flair for) someone or something
- Agreeing, or "seeing eye to eye"
- "Windows to the soul"
- The "third eye"; insight
- "Avoiding eye contact," or guilty behavior
- Looking at things in a skewed, or "cock-eyed," fashion
- "Turning a blind eye," or "closing one's eyes," to the truth
- Being near- or short-sighted; lacking imagination or insight
- The "green-eyed monster," jealousy

Positive Interpretations: If you had a dream that focused on someone's eye color, you may begin to understand its meaning by considering the color of the person's eyes and how it made you feel about him or her. For instance, did your dream emphasize the innocence of a "blue-eyed boy"? Were you overcome by a brown-eyed someone's warmth and affection? Or, conversely, was your dream subject a "green-eyed monster" of jealousy? Or perhaps you had a dream in which you found yourself gazing affectionately into the eyes of your wife. Can it be that your unconscious was reflecting your waking feeling that the two of you have been "seeing eye to eye" with one another, or was it expressing nostalgia for a time when you did?

Negative Interpretations: If you had a dream in which you were afflicted by a loss of vision or blindness, have you "closed your eyes" or "turned a blind eye" to some truth that you haven't wanted to "see" in the waking world? But if, in your dream, you found that putting on eyeglasses greatly improved your vision, then perhaps your unconscious was telling you that you need to examine or "focus on" some issue of importance in real life. Likewise, if your dreaming self was suffering from distorted vision or a squint, consider whether you have been looking at some issue in a skewed, or "cock-eyed," manner. Finally, if you had a dream in which you found yourself arguing with someone, and that someone told you to "Look me in the eye and tell me the truth," then have you been feeling guilty over a lie that you have recently told or a secret that you have been keeping?

Related Dreams

pages 192, 260, 265 & 278

My Eyes & Eyesight Dreams

20-20 Vision

If you looked upon the world with renewed clarity or donned glasses that gave you twenty-twenty vision in your dream, perhaps you have recently discovered something that was previously concealed from you. Alternatively, you may have gained more insight into an important issue, or let your imagination come to the fore.

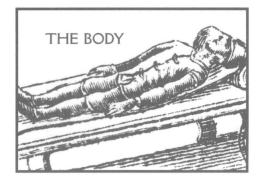

THE BODY

My Facial Hair Dreams

....
....
....
....
....
....
....
....

✶ ✶ ✶ ✶ ✶ ✶ ✶ ✶ ✶ ✶ ✶ ✶ ✶ ✶ ✶ ✶ ✶ ✶

A Dense Beard

If you dreamed that someone you know had grown a thick, luxuriant beard, perhaps you have realized that he is more mature, macho, or aggressive than you previously thought, depending on your opinion of him and on whether you looked with approval at the dream beard or found it somewhat overpowering.

Facial Hair

✶✶

Because of our traditional societal gender associations, the appearance of facial hair in a dream will usually have a specific meaning depending on the sex of the person whom our unconscious mind casts as having (or lacking) whiskers.

Symbolic and Verbal Associations
- Virility, vigor, courage, and strength (in men)
- Maturity (in men)
- "Unnatural" masculinity (in women); the "bearded lady" or circus "freak"
- Being dirty, "wild," or "uncivilized" (if a man's beard is unkempt)

Positive Interpretations: Many people seem to have strong feelings—either positive or negative—about facial hair, and your own feelings about beards and mustaches will direct your dreaming reaction to a person with whiskers (and will also give you a clue as to the meaning of the dream). For men, facial hair in its many forms (stubble, mustache, beard, goatee) has general connotations of masculine strength and vigor, and if this accords with your own personal feelings and you dreamed of a bearded or mustachioed man, then it is likely that you projected these feelings onto the dream character. If you are a woman, consider whether this is the sort of mate that you unconsciously desire, or whether your dream self has been visited by your animus (the reverse image of your soul, possibly indicating the need for more balance in your waking life). Likewise, if you are a man and you dreamed that you were pleased to find that you had grown a beard, then it may be worth asking yourself if you wish that others would view you as being a stronger, more mature character.

Negative Interpretations: As noted above, many people make negative associations with facial hair. Some people find stubble, beards, or mustaches a sign of degeneracy or poor grooming, while others feel that facial hair makes a man seem overbearing or too forceful. In addition, most people would agree that an out-of-control, unkempt beard makes a man seem "uncivilized." If your dream highlighted a whiskered man, then examining your own reactions to him will help you to understand the meaning of your dream. If you knew who he was, perhaps your unconscious mind was trying to highlight your feelings about him or his behavior in the waking world. In your dream, were you simply perplexed to see that your best friend had suddenly sprouted a beard on his chin? It is possible that your unconscious mind was alerting you to the fact that your friend may be hiding his "chinlessness," or lack of courage or honor, behind a showy display of machismo. On the other hand, if you are a woman who dreamed that you were horrified when you looked in the mirror and saw that your face was covered in whiskers, then this may reflect your anxiety and fears about seeming too masculine in the real world.

Related Dreams
pages 90, 100, 109, 120, 133 & 143

FEET & TOES

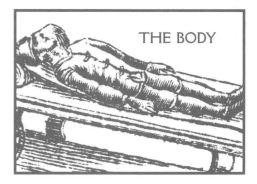

Unless you have an actual physical concern with regard to your feet, then dreams that focus on the feet or toes usually point to waking issues of progress, movement, or emotional support, or, alternatively, to a lack thereof.

Symbolic and Verbal Associations
- Progress or movement
- Putting "your best foot forward"
- "Grounding" (or calming and focusing) oneself
- Support, "standing on your own two feet"; being self-supporting
- Sore feet, or weariness
- Saying the wrong thing, or "putting your foot in your mouth"
- "Dragging your feet": reluctance

Positive Interpretations: Did you have a dream in which you luxuriated in the pleasure of walking barefoot through a lawn of cool grass? If so, and if your life has been particularly frenzied of late, then your dream could be an unconscious signal that you need to "ground" yourself better during waking hours. Bare feet put us in direct contact with the earth below us, and any dream in which you found yourself unshod could indicate your real-life feeling that you are finally "standing on your own two feet"—for instance, have you finally moved out of your parents' home, into your own apartment? A dream in which you had itchy feet could symbolize your waking desire to travel. Or a positive new beginning may be indicated if you "put your best foot forward" as you journeyed along a dream road or path.

Negative Interpretations: If you are a woman and you dreamed that you found yourself "barefoot and pregnant," then there are a few possible interpretations. If you really are pregnant, then are you worried about having enough money to support yourself and your child? Or do you feel that your partner is not giving you enough support (either financial or emotional)? In another dream scenario, if you found yourself frustrated by a foot pain or problem that caused you to limp or that otherwise hindered your progress as you raced to catch the bus to work, then could your unconscious mind have been telling you that something is interfering with your career progress? Similarly, a dream in which you found that you had no feet at all could indicate your waking sense that you are powerless to move forward in life. Finally, if you had a dream in which you were at a party where everyone was pointing and laughing at you because you had somehow succeeded in stuffing your toes or feet into your own mouth, are you feeling sorry or embarrassed about something that you have inadvertently said to someone during waking hours?

Related Dreams

pages 221, 224, 239, 289 & 368

My Feet & Toes Dreams

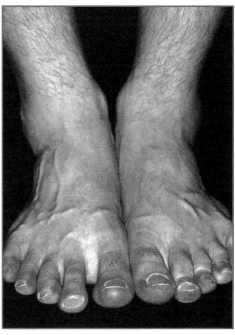

Healthy, Happy Feet
Observing with satisfaction your strong, clean, bare feet in dreamland is likely to reflect your confidence, wellbeing or sense of freedom in the real world, or perhaps the opposite, in which case such a dream may highlight the need to boost your morale or pay more attention to your health or emotional stability.

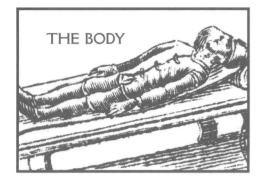

My Fingers & Hands Dreams

✴ ✴ ✴ ✴ ✴ ✴ ✴ ✴ ✴ ✴ ✴ ✴ ✴ ✴ ✴ ✴ ✴

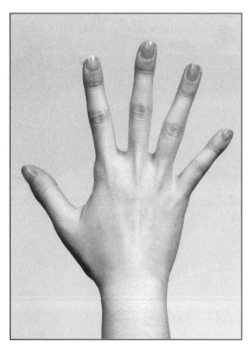

An Open Hand

Were you anxiously studying your spread fingers in your dream? This could mean that you are in danger of letting an opportunity slip through your fingers. Alternatively, perhaps you were reassured by a strong or firm-looking hand, indicating someone's comforting capability and decisiveness.

FINGERS & HANDS

I n dream symbolism, fingers and hands often refer to dexterity, but are otherwise closely associated with good will, working together, and also—particularly when in the form of a fist—with selfishness or fighting.

Symbolic and Verbal Associations
- "Lending a hand," or being "on hand" to help
- Being "in good hands"
- Asking for someone's "hand in marriage"
- Being someone's "right-hand man"
- A clenched fist: anger, or a willingness to fight
- "Out of hand": loss of control
- Being "tight-fisted," or stingy
- Getting into trouble; having your "fingers burned"

Positive Interpretations: Throughout many societies, the acts of shaking or holding hands carry a number of positive, "good will" meanings. If you had a dream in which you asked your girlfriend's father for "her hand," have you recently gotten engaged, or are you considering doing so? Or did you have a dream in which you found yourself contentedly holding the hand of your friend? If so, then could this reflect your feelings that your harmonious friendship is based on a healthy balance of give and take? If this is not the case, then do you wish that the two of you could "shake hands" and agree to make peace with regard to an old argument? Because our fingers and hands are the means by which we are able to do a number of "manual" tasks, the hands can also symbolize work and productivity. And if you had a dream in which your boss told you that she considered you her "right-hand man," then this may symbolize your feelings of power and importance within your workplace. Alternatively, could your unconscious have been telling you that it's time to take on more responsibilities on the job? Your reaction to the dream scenario should give you important clues as to the meaning. Finally, if you had a dream in which you developed a "green thumb" (or "green fingers"), might you be happier if you took up gardening or some other form of cultivation?

Negative Interpretations: Hands—specifically, fists—can also be used as weapons, or as the means of negative actions. For instance, a dream in which you noticed that your sister's hands were clenched tightly into fists may be reflecting the fact that the two of you have recently argued in the real world. Is it possible that she may be harboring some unresolved anger toward you? Or, alternatively, have you noticed that she has been acting in a "tight-fisted" or stingy manner? Could your dream of accidentally touching a hot stove be an unconscious warning that you're likely to get your "fingers burned" in a business venture that you recently entered into?

Related Dreams

pages 94, 110, 116, 253, 259 & 281

GENITALS

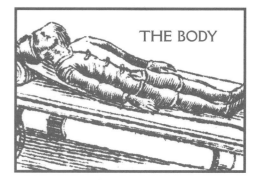

The most obvious and likely reference associated with the dream appearance of breasts and genitalia is sex. That said, sex is a large and complex subject—encompassing issues of intimacy, sexual orientation, and gender identity, virility, power, and so forth—and a dream that highlights genitals or breasts can have a number of other meanings, depending upon the specific context and your dreaming reaction.

Symbolic and Verbal Associations
- (Sex and sexuality
- (Virility; sexual potency
- (Gender identity
- (Mothering (when breastfeeding is highlighted)
- (Castration; emasculation
- (Impotence

Positive Interpretations: If you had a dream that homed in on genitalia, the most likely explanation is that it had to do with your real-life feelings about sex, intimacy, and/or—especially if you are a man—your anxiety about your sexual performance. The same can be said about the appearance of breasts in a dream, although—particularly if the dreamer is a woman, and if the dream involved breast-feeding—breasts can also symbolize one's hopes and fears with regard to childbearing and mothering. Of course, if your unconscious highlighted the genitals in a positive sexual way, it is most likely that you have experienced a wish-fulfillment dream. If you have a waking desire to undergo sex-change surgery, then wish fulfillment may also be the explanation of a dream in which you realized that you had developed the genitalia of the opposite sex. But if you have no such waking desire, then your unconscious mind may have been telling you that you need to balance your personality better by developing your masculine side (if you are a woman) or your feminine side (if you are a man), particularly with regard to your sex life (do you long to be more submissive or assertive in bed?).

Negative Interpretations: If you are a man who dreamed that your partner grew fangs and was about to bite off your penis, then you have experienced a classic male anxiety dream. The penis is a symbol of masculine power, and your dream may indicate that you are feeling impotent or emasculated because you perceive that your partner is the more dominant player in your relationship. (Dreams of impotence, which have to do with a loss of self-esteem, may also have a literal or real-life parallel.) On the other hand, if you are a woman who dreamed of castrating a man, then the meaning is the opposite: it is likely that you have waking feelings of resentment about this man's power over you, and that you long to render him impotent or less threatening or dominating in his behavior toward you.

My Genitals Dreams

----

* * * * * * * * * * * * * * * * * * * *

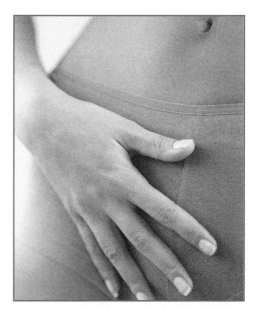

Genital Pain
If you experienced or feared pain in your genitals during a dream, a number of explanations are possible. Perhaps you unconsciously feel shame or regret over an illicit encounter or your waking desire for an adulterous affair. Or you may be repressing sexual anxieties relating to changes in your body, aging, or fear of dysfunction. Alternatively, this dream could reflect a more general blow to your self-esteem.

Related Dreams
pages 107, 112, 116, 237, 242 & 268

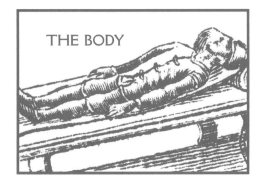

HAIR

In dreamland, as in the realm of the unconscious, hair is often a symbol of physical and intellectual power, as well as of male virility (or a lack thereof). And because hair is of crucial importance to our physical appearance, a dream that focuses on our hair may be a reference to how attractive we are feeling in real life.

Symbolic and Verbal Associations
- Physical strength; male sexual virility
- The intellect
- Physical attractiveness
- Physical and emotional wellbeing
- Wisdom and/or aging (when white or gray hair is depicted)
- "Knotty" problems or "entanglements"

Positive Interpretations: If you had a dream in which you grew a beautiful, thick head of hair, then this may reflect your waking feelings of physical attractiveness (or else your dissatisfaction with your physical appearance). Alternatively, a dream in which you asked your barber to shave off all of your hair may signify your desire to "lighten your load" (which may also apply if you dreamed of bleaching your hair), to be free of your worldly problems, or to lead a more simple or ascetic life. Hair color in a dream can have symbolic significance, depending on your associations with the color, though it may simply reflect your own personal likes and dislikes. But because silver, gray, or white hair is a universal symbol of the dignity and wisdom of old age, if you dreamed of a person with silver, gray, or white hair, consider whether your unconscious mind has called upon the archetypal wise man or woman (perhaps in the form of someone familiar to you, such as one of your grandparents) in order to give you some guidance or advice. If this character communicated with you in your dream, it is quite possible that his or her message has some relevance to the waking world.

Negative Interpretations: Like the biblical story of Samson and Delilah, if you had a dream in which your head was shaved against your will—particularly if you are a man—then did you know the person who was shearing you? Your unconscious may have been signaling to you that this person is draining your strength or potency in the real world. Similarly, a dream of balding may indicate a waking fear that your strength is failing—particularly with regard to sexual virility (if you are a man) or physical attractiveness (be you a man or a woman)—and may also be tied into anxiety about aging. Finally, if in your dream you became frustrated when you struggled in vain to run a comb through your tangled mass of hair, could this be an indicator that you are tussling with "knotty" troubles or "entangled" relations in your waking life?

My Hair Dreams

_____

_____

_____

_____

_____

_____

_____

_____

_____

Hair Extensions

Did you dream that you suddenly had a head of long hair, because you were either wearing a wig or had hair extensions? If so, you may unconsciously feel insecure and may wish that you felt more feminine (if you are a woman) or attractive. On the other hand, if your new hair was unmanageable, have you become embroiled in a complicated situation?

Related Dreams

pages 36, 100, 133, 134 & 258

HEADS & FACES

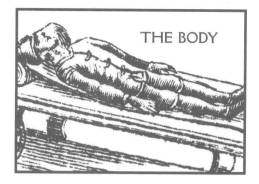

****

Because the head is the location of the brain, its symbolism involves thinking, the intellect, reasoning, and control (or the loss thereof). The head is also the location of the face, the part of us that we most often (and most prominently) present to the world. The face is a primary vehicle for determining how others will perceive us, and our dreams sometimes use the symbol of the face in order to direct our focus to our outer image or persona.

Symbolic and Verbal Associations
‹ The outer image or persona
‹ Thinking; reason; intelligence
‹ "Getting ahead"; progression
‹ "Losing face": humiliation
‹ Becoming "red-faced" or embarrassed
‹ Acting "big-headed" or "swollen-headed," i.e., self-importantly

Positive Interpretations: If you had a dream that focused on a head—no matter if it was your own head or someone else's—you should consider whether your dream was an unconscious reference to "getting ahead" (such as being promoted to the "head" of a board or committee), or else to reason or the intellect. When interpreting a dream in which, like the myth of Narcissus, you found yourself transfixed by the beauty of your own face, ask yourself if you wish that the world would recognize you for your good looks or for the attractiveness of your personality.

Negative Interpretations: If, in your dream, your boss delivered a painful blow to the side of your head, then is he or she putting too much pressure on you, and thereby giving you a "headache," in the real world? Or if you had a nightmare in which someone was about to cut off your head, who was that person? Is he or she aggravating or harassing you so much during waking hours that you feel that you are in danger of "losing your head" or acting rashly? Any dream in which your head swelled to a larger-than-life size could be an unconscious signal that you have become vain or "big-headed." If you were shocked to see that your dream face had frozen into a horrible grimace, could it be that you are worried that others may find you obnoxious or repulsive, perhaps because you have been consumed by an "ugly" emotion, such as jealousy or hatred? On the other hand, if you had a dream in which you were frightened by someone else's ugly face, this may be an unconscious warning that you will soon have to "face up" to something unpleasant. (Did you recognize the person in your dream? The unpleasantness to which your unconscious was referring may have something to do with that person.) Finally, if you dreamed that you looked into the mirror and saw that you had no face, do you feel that you have recently "lost face," or suffered a humiliation, in the real world?

My Heads & Faces Dreams

----

* * * * * * * * * * * * * * * * * * *

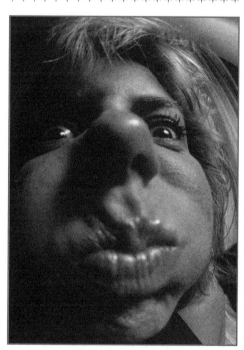

Distorted Faces
If your dream face was grotesquely distorted, you are likely to have some real-life anxieties relating to the gap between the "real you" and the image that you present to the world. Do you have a shameful or upsetting secret? Or perhaps you are feeling pressurized or controlled and are losing your sense of your true personality.

Related Dreams
pages 36, 125, 129, 182, 224 & 270

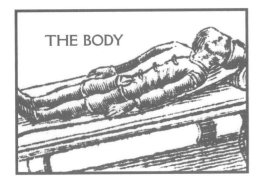

THE BODY

My Heart & Chest Dreams

_____

_____

_____

_____

_____

_____

_____

_____

✱✱✱✱✱✱✱✱✱✱✱✱✱✱✱✱✱✱✱✱✱

In Good Shape

Dreaming of someone you know working out to develop a brawnier chest could indicate that he or she is trying to summon up the courage to increase his or her assertiveness in the real world. If it was a stranger, however, a dream of this sort was probably wish fulfillment, when the fitness-conscious stranger may represent either you or a lover.

HEART & CHEST

✱✱✱✱✱✱✱✱✱✱✱✱✱✱✱✱✱✱✱✱✱✱✱✱✱✱✱✱✱✱✱✱✱✱✱✱✱✱✱

One of the most important internal organs, the heart takes love and romanticism as its primary symbolism. And because the heart is housed within the chest, the dream imagery associated with the heart and chest is fairly interchangeable.

Symbolic and Verbal Associations
- Love; matters of the heart
- Pride and courage
- Feelings of shock or excitement
- Fear and cowardice
- Having "a weak heart," or being emotionally vulnerable
- "Heartache"; disappointment in love
- Sickness; faltering vitality

Positive Interpretations: If, in your dream, the sight of someone you know caused your heart to "jump" or to beat faster in your chest, then your dreaming reaction to that person may indicate that you harbor waking feelings of romantic love for (or, depending on the scenario, fear of) him or her. The heart is a symbol not just of romantic love, but of love in general, and your dream should therefore be interpreted within the context of your waking relationship with the person of whom you dreamed. The heart is also associated with pride, and dreaming that your chest was "puffed out" with pride may be a reflection of your real-life sense of satisfaction with your son, for instance, who has recently earned straight As in school. If, on the other hand, your dream centered on someone else's chest in a similar fashion, then do you know who the person was? Is it possible that you have done something to make that person proud of you in the waking world?

Negative Interpretations: Because of the heart's vital function of pumping the blood around our bodies, a dream in which you felt your heart failing or faltering may possibly be your unconscious mind's way of telling you that your heart is not functioning as it should. If you have had a dream of this sort and it troubles you, then it is probably a good idea to have yourself checked out by a doctor. If you know that your heart is physically strong and healthy, however, then a dream of this sort is likely to have been a reference to the emotional realm. Is it true that you have been suffering from "heartache" since you broke up with your last boyfriend? Have you found that you have "a weak heart," i.e., that you tend to be emotionally injured, over and over again, in matters of love? Or is your emotional strength being sapped by an overly difficult partner? In addition to love and pride, the heart is a symbol of courage, as well as of its opposite: cowardice. Therefore, explanations involving courage and cowardice should not be ruled out when you are interpreting dreams that spotlight the chest or heart.

Related Dreams

pages 37, 242, 244, 257, 267 & 270

HEAT & FEVER

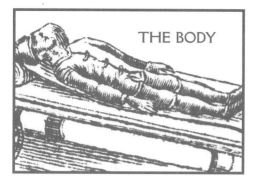

THE BODY

In our society, we often see words like "heat" and "fever" used as sexual references. However, these concepts are also symbolic of passion in the broader sense—zest for life, excitement, and obsession—and also of anxiety and mental troubles. In the realm of dreams, the possible interpretations are similar.

Symbolic and Verbal Associations
(Passion or excitement
(Sexual desire, or having the hots for someone
(Obsession
(Loss of control
(Anxiety, or having a troubled mind
("The hot seat"; a dangerous situation
(Anger and rage

Positive Interpretations: If you had a dream in which you suffered from an elevated body temperature, and you found yourself to be equally hot when you awoke, then your dreaming mind simply incorporated your actual body temperature into your dream. However, if this was not the case, then is it possible that you are in the grip of a "fever" (an excitement or an anxiety) over something (or someone) in the waking world? If so, this dream can have a positive or a negative interpretation, depending upon the context. If your dream fever came on with the appearance of a particular person, then do you find this person to be "hot," or sexy, or do you have the "hots" for him or her, in the waking world? Otherwise, if you dreamed that you were comfortably and pleasantly warm, cozy, or snug, what was the context of your dream? Was there another person (or other people) with you? You should consider whether you are developing "warm" feelings, or positive emotional ties, with regard to someone or some situation in your waking life.

Negative Interpretations: A dream in which you found yourself to be overheated could be a warning sign that you have gotten yourself into "the hot seat," or a dangerous or "hot" situation, in the waking world, and that you are likely to get yourself "burned" if you continue in the manner in which you have been behaving. Otherwise, could it be that you are "heated up," or full of rage, about someone or something during waking hours? Such a dream could also be an unconscious cue that you have developed an unhealthy obsession for someone or something, that you are experiencing anxiety about your obsession that you are in danger of losing control, and that you would benefit if you could somehow find a way to cool your passions. Alternatively, if you found yourself feeling hot and bothered when someone entered the room in your dream, do you know the person? Is she or he making things "hot," or uncomfortable, for you in the real world?

Related Dreams

pages 56, 253, 268, 371 & 384

My Heat & Fever Dreams

----

* * * * * * * * * * * * * * * * * * * *

Relaxing Warmth

Perhaps your dream took place in a sauna or steam room, and you felt suffused with a pleasant warmth. This sort of dream is often simple wish fulfillment. Are you working too hard and are you longing for a vacation, or are you desperate for winter to give way to spring in the waking world?

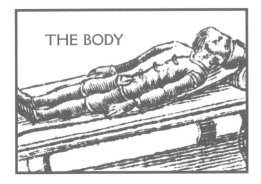

THE BODY

My Height Dreams

----

* * * * * * * * * * * * * * * * * * * *

Loss of Height

While height loss in dreamland often has negative interpretations, if you, or someone you know, was suddenly much shorter and felt happy about this, your dream may have reflected a desire to unburden yourself of responsibilities associated with your social status (or the other person's delight in his or her "downsizing").

HEIGHT

* *

Our height, or how tall we are, is an important marker of how others perceive us in our society. For better or worse, height functions as a mark of status, and there is an "acceptable" range of heights that we tend to expect people to fall into. Unfortunately, those who are "too tall" or "too short" are often discriminated against in a variety of ways. In our dreams, the unconscious mind may use height in order to comment on how we are feeling (or how others may feel) about our status, our functioning, or our power in the world.

Symbolic and Verbal Associations
- Power (when tallness is highlighted)
- Experiencing joy, or "walking ten feet tall"
- Avoiding, or "shrinking away" from, persons or situations
- Feeling insignificant or "looked down upon"
- Being overlooked; "disappearing" (or the desire to vanish)
- Feelings of being awkward or conspicuous

Positive Interpretations: Did you dream that you were overjoyed to find that you had grown into a giant, and that everyone around you was in awe of your phenomenal stature? If so, and your status in the real world has recently increased (have you been elected president of your neighborhood council?) then it is likely that your dream reflected your real-life feelings of pride by allowing your dream self to "walk ten feet tall." (If this is not so, then it is possible that you experienced a wish-fulfillment dream.) Of course, there are gender differences attached to our societal associations with height: for instance, being tall is a trait that is traditionally more desirable—and that provides a mark of status and power—that in men, more so than in women, for whom being "too tall" can even reduce status (though this has been steadily changing, along with our changing cultural ideals with regard to women's bodies). Your feelings about a dream that focuses on your height (and also your interpretation of the dream) will probably be linked to your gender or your own ideas and ideals regarding body image.

Negative Interpretations: If you had a dream in which you found yourself towering over everyone around you, as outlined above, except that in this dream you were mortified that people were heckling and ridiculing you, could it be that you are concerned about "sticking out," or appearing awkward or overconspicuous? By contrast, if your dream self was upset to find that you had shrunk to a miniature version of your normal self, have you been feeling insignificant, or "looked down upon," during your waking hours? Or do you wish that you could avoid, or "shrink away" from, your duties or from an uncomfortable situation? A dream in which you actually shrank to nothingness, or disappeared, may be similarly interpreted.

Related Dreams

pages 193, 224, 229, 247, 261 & 270

LEGS

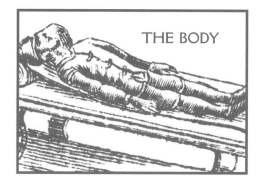

Like dreams of the feet, dreams that shine a spotlight on the legs are often an unconscious attempt to direct our attention to issues of progress or movement.

Symbolic and Verbal Associations
- Progression; the ability to move forward
- "Making a stand": resolution and determination
- Kneeling: a gesture of gratitude, respect, or humility
- Standing (or being unable to stand) "on one's own"
- "Standing up for" (or defending) oneself or others
- Having "shaky legs": being fearful or lacking confidence

Positive Interpretations: In your dream, did you find yourself effortlessly running along a track, at an easy pace, and breezing past those whom you were racing against? Do you know who your competitors were? If so, this sort of dream could be a reflection of your waking satisfaction with your level of success or advancement. In dreams, as in the real world, kneeling functions as an act of gratitude or humility. If you had a dream in which your brother was kneeling before you, has he recently admitted that you were right all along about an old disagreement (or do you wish that he would admit such a thing)? Or if you dreamed that your boyfriend went down on one knee before you, do you have hopes that the two of you will soon become engaged to be married? However, if you were the one who was kneeling, asking yourself who you were kneeling before and how this made you feel should help you to determine the meaning of your dream. (If it was your wife, and you have been hiding your gambling habit from her, for instance, then could your unconscious have been spurring you on to confess and to ask for her forgiveness?)

Negative Interpretations: Did you have a dream in which you were trying to run, but found that no matter how hard you tried, you could only advance very slowly (or else not at all)? If so, what was the goal that you were straining toward? Could something be interfering with your waking desire to achieve or reach whatever it was? Or were you struggling to keep up with someone else? If so, whom? Was there something in your dream—some obstacle—that impeded your progress? Or were you simply too tired or fatigued to run? Answering these questions will help you to interpret this sort of dream. Did you have a dream in which your legs were useless? If so, do you feel immobile or unable to propel yourself in the physical world? If you had a dream in which your legs shook (or had "turned to jelly") out of fear, then could your unconscious have been reflecting your waking fear, timidity, or inability to "stand up" for yourself (or for someone else)? In your dream, what caused you to be fearful?

Related Dreams

pages 45, 94, 257, 260 & 289

My Legs Dreams

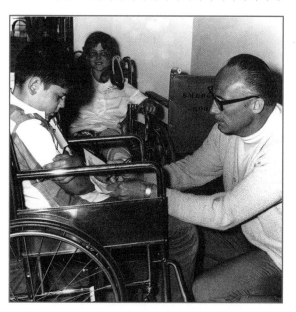

Sudden Disability

Dreaming of being wheelchair-bound may reflect your real-life loss of mobility or anxieties about this. However, such a dream could also be a result of your waking worries about achieving your career or family goals, irrespective of your physical health. If you felt a sense of relief at not being able to walk, you may be unable to cope with your commitments and may be longing to come to a standstill.

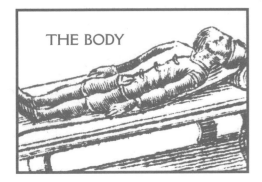

My Neck & Throat Dreams

----

* * * * * * * * * * * * * * * * * * *

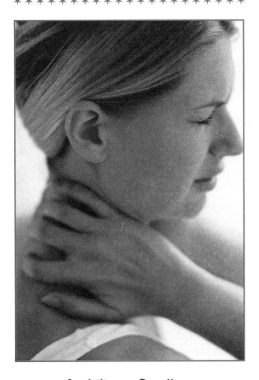

Inability to Swallow

Any dream situation that features the inability to swallow, or discomfort when swallowing, points to waking-life anxiety. This could be due to your general tension—should you think carefully about the underlying cause?—or to a specific problem that needs to be resolved.

NECK & THROAT

****

The neck houses the windpipe, as well as several large blood vessels that carry blood to and from the head, and if we are injured in the throat or the neck, or if anything chokes us or prevents us from breathing, then the situation is likely to become very serious, if not deadly. In the world of dreams, a spotlight on the throat or neck is often symbolic of the vital importance (and therefore potentially mortal danger) associated with this relatively vulnerable area of our body.

Symbolic and Verbal Associations

- "Sticking your neck out," or "risking your neck," for someone or something
- "A pain in the neck": annoyance
- Being "choked up" with sadness or grief
- Hostility: wanting to "wring" someone's neck
- Being "up to your neck" in work or problems
- "Necking" or intensive kissing

Positive Interpretations: The muscles of the neck are a location in which many people hold tension, which can lead to pain and rigidity. If you dreamed that you were delightedly or contentedly receiving a neck massage from someone, and that you were feeling more relaxed than you have ever felt in your life, then could it be that you have been overwhelmed by work or stress in the real world, and that you crave a release from your tensions? If you dreamed that someone was passionately kissing you or giving you love bites on your neck, then is your dream mirroring the real-life passion that you share with this person? Or do you wish that you could have the chance to kiss, or to "neck" with, him or her?

Negative Interpretations: Did you experience a nightmare in which a vampire crept up on you and sank his fangs into the side of your neck? If so, did you recognize the vampire? Is this person "sucking the life out of you" during daylight hours? Or did you dream that you were choking? If so, and you awoke to find no obstruction in your throat, then it is likely that your dreaming mind was playing out your waking feelings of unhappiness, or of being "choked up" with sadness or grief. But, if you had a dream in which someone had their fingers around your neck and was choking you, then the explanation is likely to be that someone in your waking world is exhibiting signs of hostility toward you. It is common to sleep uncomfortably on one's pillow and to awake with a "crick" in the neck, and, if you dreamed of having neck pain and subsequently woke with the same pain, this is the most likely explanation. If this was not the case, however, then your dream could signify that someone or something is being a "pain in the neck" in the real world. Or are you experiencing anxiety because you have been "sticking your neck out," or "risking your neck," for someone or something?

Related Dreams

pages 176, 179, 146, 219, 227 & 238

NOSE & SMELLING

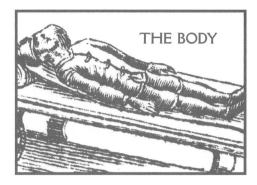

The nose is a sense organ that can detect things that are not readily visible: we can smell things that are nearby, in the next room, or sometimes far away—and we can even smell things that have already come into our surroundings and have then gone again. In the world of dreams, the symbolism associated with the nose is often associated with the detection of information.

Symbolic and Verbal Associations

- Being "nosy" or "nosing around": prying or searching
- Keeping one's "nose clean," or staying out of trouble
- Having "a nose" for the truth
- Something "smelling fishy" or not quite right
- Something "getting up your nose" or annoying you
- "Smelling a rat"; "sniffing out" trouble; "scenting danger"
- Irritating someone, or putting their "nose out of joint"
- "Turning up one's nose" or going about "with one's nose in the air": snobbery, a sense of superiority or disdain

Positive Interpretations: Though many people would now agree that it is wrong to judge people by the appearance of their body, the shape of their nose has been associated with a person's moral nature. These types of associations are still with us today in one sense or another, and can often be found in children's stories (think of the hackneyed character of the witch, with her twisted and mole-ridden nose). And if you dreamed of someone (perhaps yourself) having a straight, "Roman," or aquiline nose, is it possible that your unconscious mind is making a reference to that person's (or your own) leadership skills? Or did you have a dream in which you were walking through a garden enjoying the sweet fragrance of the flowers? If so, have you been feeling that "life is sweet"? Or could your unconscious have been telling you that you have been hurrying along through life, and that you should take some time to "stop and smell the roses"?

Negative Interpretations: If you had a dream in which your nose had been broken or twisted out of shape, then has someone in the real world been annoying or troubling you, putting your "nose out of joint"? Or if you had a dream in which your nose kept growing longer and longer, like Pinocchio's, have you been telling fibs or lies? Or could it be that you have been behaving in a "nosy" manner (perhaps you've been probing around to find out information about the family that has just moved into the house next door)? Did you have a dream in which you gagged at a terrible, obnoxious stench? If so, ask yourself if some corrupt, or "rotten," activity is going on "under your nose" in waking hours, or whether your unconscious is trying to tell you that it has "smelled a rat."

My Nose & Smelling Dreams

----

* * * * * * * * * * * * * * * * * * *

Pleasant Fragrances

Enjoying the aroma of flowers, favorite foods, or other pleasant smells in dreamland is likely to be a reflection of your real-life sense of well-being. Sometimes, though, a particular scent has a specific associations: does the smell of a rose make you think of a certain romantic encounter, or that of lilacs, springtime at your childhood home?

Related Dreams

pages 36, 60, 171, 179, 219 & 350

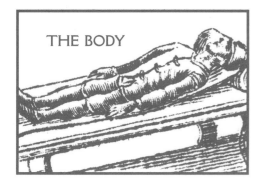

My Sickness Dreams

----

* * * * * * * * * * * * * * * * * * * *

Undergoing Surgery

If your dream featured you or a relative having surgery, have you been repressing fears about your, or his or her, health or state of mind? If, however, you were recovering from a major procedure, relief after an anxious time is the most likely explanation.

SICKNESS

* *

Unless you are really sick in the real world, or fear that you might be ill (in which case you should probably see a doctor in order to set your mind at ease), dream sickness rarely refers to physical health. Rather, sickness in a dream is usually a reference to our emotional wellbeing.

Symbolic and Verbal Associations
- Psychological or emotional wellbeing
- Emotional impairment
- Being in need of help or support
- A desire to be taken care of
- Being sickened or nauseated by something

Positive Interpretations: If you had a dream in which you were lying on your sickbed, or in which you felt terribly ill (when, in reality, you are quite physically healthy), then this could have been an unconscious warning that you are not taking care of your body or mind—either because you are overworking yourself, because you are not eating properly, or because you have been drinking too much alcohol or using other substances—and that, if you do not alter your habits, you could end up making yourself very ill (either physically or emotionally, or both). Or if you basked in the attention of someone who was taking care of you, it is possible that you experienced a wish-fulfillment dream, or else that you are in need of some emotional support in the waking world.

Negative Interpretations: Your unconscious may use different medical conditions to symbolize specific emotional problems. For instance, if you dreamed that you were ill and in the hospital, and that your doctor told you that you were suffering from cancer, then is something "eating away" at you during your waking life? Could it be your guilt about the fact that you maybe haven't spoken to your mother in a year? In another scenario, if you dreamed that you were vomiting uncontrollably, is something in the real world making you feel sickened or nauseated? Or else, do you wish that you could purge yourself of a "sickening" problem or situation? If you dreamed that you couldn't breathe, is something causing you to gasp or "fight for breath" in the real world? Do you feel "suffocated" by your overneedy partner? If you had a dream in which you were paralyzed, numb, or felt nothing at all, then ask yourself whether you have become emotionally "numb" or unfeeling in the waking world. If you had a dream in which you were walking with crutches, do you feel that you are emotionally "crippled"? Or are you reliant upon chemical "crutches," such as alcohol or drugs? Finally, if you dreamed that you had contracted a contagious disease, do you feel that you have become a "social outcast" in the real world?

Related Dreams

pages 41, 89, 113, 257 & 259

SKIN

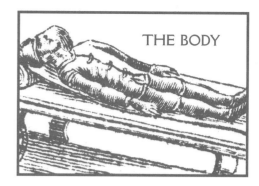

The skin is the outer covering of the body; it is our protection from the world, and it is the largest part of us that is visible to the world. It shoud be no surprise, then, that much of the symbolism surrounding skin has to do with things that "penetrate" us emotionally, or else with our feelings about how we are viewed by the world (and also with how we ourselves view others).

Symbolic and Verbal Associations
- Being "thin-skinned" or easily hurt
- "Itching" (or being eager) to do something
- Something that is "skin-deep"; superficiality
- Emotional "scars" or "blemishes"
- Someone or something that "gets under your skin"
- Fear and anxiety regarding aging
- Being irritated or "sore" (when a rash or sore is highlighted)
- A "skinflint" or miser

Positive Interpretations: If you had a dream in which you were young again, and in which your face was speckled with freckles from the hours and hours that you spent playing in the summer sun, then it could be that your unconscious mind was reflecting your real-life desire to be free or to romp outdoors like you did when you were young. Or if you dreamed that your scarred or blemished face was suddenly clear-skinned, have you recently tackled your emotional scars in waking life? There is an old superstition that having an itchy palm means that one is about to receive money, and if you dreamed that your palm was itching unbearably, are you anticipating receiving a windfall (or do you wish that you would come into some money)?

Negative Interpretations: Another interpretation of a dream in which your skin was itching, or in which you broke out in a rash or sores, is that someone or something is irritating you or making you feel "sore" in the waking world. Or if you dreamed that your friend's face had become covered in pimples (and if he or she does not suffer from acne in the real world), then could your unconscious mind have been telling you that your friend has been reverting to his or her adolescence, or acting immaturely? Did you have a dream in which you noticed a scar on your skin where there is no scar in the waking world? Scars are remnants of past wounds, and it is possible that your dream was an unconscious signal that you have been "scarred" by an emotional wound—perhaps a wound that you have gotten over long ago, but that still lingers in your memory. Finally, in your dream, were you aghast when you looked into the mirror and saw that your face had become exceedingly aged and wrinkled? If so, your dream was probably an unconscious expression of your anxiety and fears with regard to getting older.

My Skin Dreams

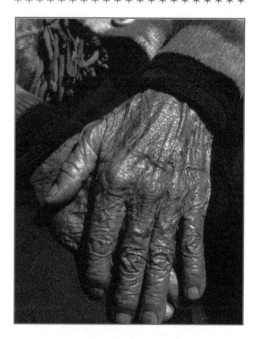

Wrinkled Skin

If your dream featured deeply lined skin, the most important question is whether it was yours or someone else's. Were you enjoying a nostalgic dream about your long-lost grandmother, whom you now miss, or were you horrified at the speed at which you were aging? Ask yourself, too, whether a body part was also significant in this dream scenario.

Related Dreams

pages 100, 111, 237, 274 & 341

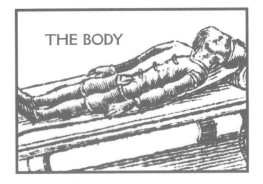

My Tattoos & Piercings Dreams

----

* * * * * * * * * * * * * * * *

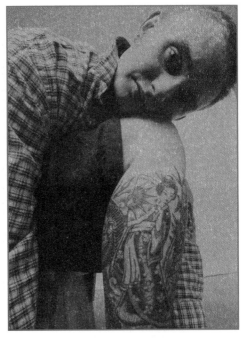

Elaborate Tattoos

If you dreamed that an elaborate design had been tattooed on your body, and you were keen to show it off, you may be ready to reveal something important about yourself to your loved ones. Have you been unable to explain your feelings, or have you been hiding your plans or decisions from others?

TATTOOS & PIERCINGS

* *

Tattoos and piercings are a means by which people make statements about themselves; they also reflect a person's self-image. Because tattoos and piercings are a form of decoration for the body, and because they draw attention to the person who has them, they can signal to the world that "I am happy and comfortable with my body." They can send an endless number of other messages, too, depending on the nature of the piercings and tattoos and where they are located. If you dreamed of having tattoos or piercings, then all of these specifics should be considered when you are trying to interpret your dream.

Symbolic and Verbal Associations
- Permanence (for tattoos)
- Happiness with, and confidence in, one's body
- Penetrating "beneath the skin"; emotional depth
- The desire to make a social statement
- Showing allegiance to a group or ideal; conformity
- Social rebellion; resistance to the status quo

Positive Interpretations: Any dream in which you were pleased that you had decorated your body with tattoos or piercings is likely to have reflected your conscious feelings of confidence and approval with regard to your physical appearance. Conversely, if your self-image is generally poor, then such a dream may have indicated that you would like to appear more attractive to others with regard to either your physical appearance or personality. If you dreamed that you were sitting in a chair in a tattoo parlor while the tattoo artist prodded her inky needles beneath your flesh, it is important to think about what it was that you were having tattooed onto your body and what this means to you. If it was the name of your girlfriend or boyfriend, could it be that you desire to form a lifelong partnership with her or him? Or if you dreamed that you had a flag branded onto your bicep, could this be a symbol of your real-life feelings of patriotism or allegiance to a club or group?

Negative Interpretations: If your dream tattoo was of a "darker" nature, such as a skull-and-crossbones (a symbol of danger, death, and destruction), then you should ask yourself if you have a habit of wreaking havoc or creating bedlam in the waking world. Or was your tattoo an identification number in a prison or institutional setting? If so, do you feel "branded" by some aspect of your life? Finally, because visible tattoos and certain piercings (facial ones, for instance) are still not quite acceptable in all social situations (in many places of work, for instance), then a dream in which you sported a controversial piercing or tattoo may have indicated your waking frustration with the status quo, and your desire to rebel against society in some symbolic or actual way.

Related Dreams

pages 57, 65, 73 & 84

TEETH

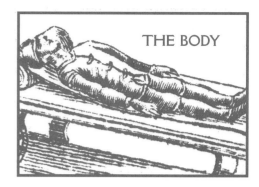

We don't often think much about our teeth unless there is something wrong with one of them, and when teeth feature prominently in a dream, it is rarely in a positive light. Dreams of teeth often have to do with anxiety about something, and may be tied into our feelings about a recent loss or life change.

Symbolic and Verbal Associations
- Youth, vigor, or "bite"
- Losing our baby teeth; leaving childhood behind
- Ruminating on something, or "chewing it over"
- "Wisdom" teeth
- Anxiety about change or loss

Positive Interpretations: One of the primary functions of teeth is chewing, and when we are thinking about, or ruminating on, some issue or problem, we sometimes say that we are "chewing it over." So if you had a dream in which you were chewing and chewing on the same morsel of food, this may have been an unconscious allusion to some problem that you have been faced with in your waking hours; your dream may be a signal that you should "chew over" the facts a lot more before coming to a decision about how to address the problem. Or if you dreamed that your wisdom teeth (the hindmost molars) were emerging, have you actually been feeling wiser or more mature and responsible in the real world?

Negative Interpretations: Many people have experienced an anxiety dream about their teeth crumbling or falling out. Having a dream toothache could simply be due to the fact that you were grinding your teeth as you slumbered and your unconscious mind incorporated this into your dream. Some people grind their teeth while they sleep when they are under excessive stress during waking hours, and if you awoke to find that your jaws were clenched and sore, you should probably see your dentist to discuss whether this could be the case for you. Dreams about tooth pain or loss could also signify that you are feeling anxious about a significant life change. Have you recently quit your job, or are you and your spouse discussing divorce? Or if you dreamed that your teeth fell out, have you recently lost a loved one? Are you about to move to another part of the country, leaving your friends and family behind? Or could it be that you are anxious about growing older and losing your vigor or your "bite"? Anxiety (whether about visiting the dentist or about a forthcoming event) is also the likely meaning if you had a dream in which a dentist shone a bright light in your face as he or she poked and prodded inside your mouth. The other major function of teeth is biting, and if you dreamed that someone you know threatened to bite (or actually bit) you, could it be that this person really harbors some anger or hostility toward you?

Related Dreams
pages 60, 84 & 233

My Teeth Dreams

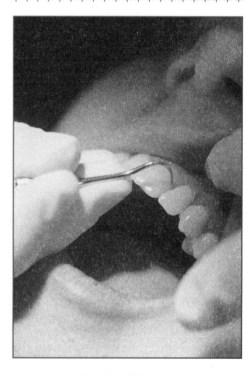

Perfect Teeth
In your dream, did you dread going to the dentist, but then find that her inspection revealed a perfect set of teeth? If so, and you experienced a sense of relief, you may be worrying too much about your abilities in a real-world situation.

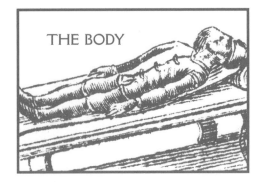

My Tongue & Mouth Dreams

✱ ✱ ✱ ✱ ✱ ✱ ✱ ✱ ✱ ✱ ✱ ✱ ✱ ✱ ✱ ✱

Prominent Lips

Did your dream feature glossy, unnaturally full lips, from which you could not divert your attention? This scenario indicates that a woman in your waking world is making you feel uncomfortable by making obvious sexual overtures to you. Think about whose lips they were, and how you reacted in your dream. If they were your lips, are you attracted to someone?

TONGUE & MOUTH

The tongue and mouth are among the most sensual areas of the body, and they perform a variety of functions, including talking, tasting, and kissing. Therefore, the interpretation of a dream in which the tongue or mouth was highlighted will depend greatly upon the context of the dream.

Symbolic and Verbal Associations
- Getting "a taste of" (or first-hand experience of) something; having "a taste of your own medicine"
- Scolding someone, or giving them "a tongue lashing"
- Being "tight-lipped," or not talking about something
- "Mouthing off" to someone
- "Losing your appetite" for something
- "Tongue wagging," or gossiping
- Having "loose lips," or not being able to keep a secret
- "Paying lip service" to someone or something

Positive Interpretations: If you had a dream in which you were devouring the most delicious food that you had ever tasted, could this have been a reflection of the fact that you have recently discovered how to relish life to the fullest? Or, did you dream that your mother was gazing at you with pleasure, a beaming smile on her face? Your dreaming mind may have been remembering a fond moment from your childhood, or else you may feel that you have recently made your mother happy with something that you have done. How we hold our mouth is a big indicator of how we are feeling (happy, sad, angry and so on), so if you had a dream that highlighted someone's mouth, consider what emotion or state of mind it seemed to be indicating. The lips, in particular, are also associated with female genitalia, and depending on the context of your dream, this symbolism should also be considered when you are attempting to interpret your slumbering visions.

Negative Interpretations: In your dream, did you bite into your favorite food, only to find that it was the most disgusting thing that you had ever tasted, or else that you couldn't taste anything at all? If so, have you recently "lost a taste" (or your "appetite") for something that you used to love? Did your dream home in on your boss's mouth as he scolded you for arriving late at work? If so, is he prone to giving you "tongue lashings" in the real world? Your dream could have reflected your growing frustration with his berating of you, or a fear that your position at work might not be secure. Or did you dream that your adolescent daughter refused to speak to you, or even to open her mouth? Is it possible that she is being secretive, or "tight-lipped," about something in waking life that you would like to know more about?

Related Dreams

pages 47, 59, 176 & 278

VOMITING

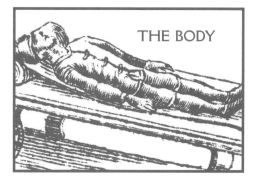

In the dream world, as in reality, vomiting is usually indicative of our need to purge ourselves of something that is making us sick, be it bad food or negative emotions. Similarly, a dream in which we experience nausea (which accompanies or precedes vomiting) may be an unconscious sign that we are having trouble "digesting" or "stomaching" something in the real world (see also the entry "Blood & Guts").

Symbolic and Verbal Associations
- Purging
- Being "nauseated" or emotionally "sickened" by something
- Difficulty "digesting" information, or an inability to "stomach" something
- Emotional upset
- An unhealthy approach to nutrition and weight loss

Positive Interpretations: While it may seem difficult to find a positive interpretation for a dream in which we find ourselves sick to the stomach, nauseated, or puking, there is at least one type of vomiting dream scenario that could be interpreted positively. If you had a dream in which you finally told your boss that you were quitting the job that you hate, promptly went into the restroom and vomited, making you immediately feel better (perhaps better and healthier than you have ever felt before), then your dream is likely to have been your unconscious mind's way of telling you that it really is time to quit that horrible job because it is making you ill—either physically ill or emotionally ill or both. This is just one example; if you have any dream in which you find yourself feeling remarkably better after vomiting, you should ask yourself what you were "purging" yourself of in your dream, what "sickening" problem or "ailment" this could represent in your waking world, and whether you should address it in actuality.

Negative Interpretations: As discussed in the entry "Sickness," dreams of being sick are usually unconscious references to something that is disturbing us psychologically or emotionally. That said, if you dreamed of being nauseated or of vomiting (and if you were not, in fact, experiencing an actual stomach ache because of something that you ate for dinner), then this is usually a clear sign that you are being emotionally upset by something during your waking hours. An examination of the details of your dream should help you to understand the problem. Was anyone with you in your dream? If so, was that person trying to help you? Or were they part of the cause of your illness? Can you tell what made you sick? The location or setting of the dream may also give you some clues. Finally, if you had a dream in which you ate a very large dinner and then forced yourself to throw up, consider whether you are suffering from a negative body image, and whether you have some unhealthy ideas regarding dieting and weight loss.

My Vomiting Dreams

----

* * * * * * * * * * * * * * * * * * * *

Eating While Nauseous

If you couldn't stop eating in your dream, but were feeling sick, you may be suffering from an eating disorder in waking life, or perhaps have simply overeaten. If neither of these apply, then your dream scene could have referred to an unhealthy emotional situation that you are "gorging on" rather than putting a stop to.

Related Dreams
pages 37, 56, 154, 172 & 182

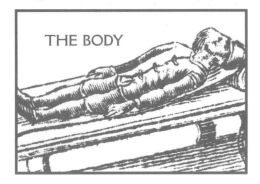

My Weight Dreams

✱ ✱ ✱ ✱ ✱ ✱ ✱ ✱ ✱ ✱ ✱ ✱ ✱ ✱ ✱ ✱ ✱ ✱

Positive Weight Gain

Despite concerns over weight and health, many people associate happiness and well-being with being heavier and not restraining the impulse to indulge in "forbidden" foods. If you have been dieting, then a dream featuring a well-fed, heavy, but happy person is probably simple wish fulfillment.

WEIGHT

★ ★

Now, more than ever before, our society is fixated on weight issues. At a time when most of the Western population is getting fatter and fatter, people are going to greater and greater lengths to be thin, with stomach-banding operations, liposuction, fad diets, and low-fat/low-calorie foods being the obsessions of the moment. When we dream of weight issues, it is sometimes a reflection of our real-life thoughts and feelings about our weight, but this is not always the case.

Symbolic and Verbal Associations
(Being "weighed down" by problems
(Someone who is "bloated up" with something
(Being "overloaded" by information, work, and so on
("Wasting away"
(Being "starved" of emotional, intellectual, sexual, or spiritual nourishment

Positive Interpretations: If, in the waking world, you have been worried about the fact that you have gained too much weight, and if you dreamed that you were standing on a set of scales in a public place and that many people were gathered around you, cheering for you because you had lost ten pounds, then this could be your unconscious mind's way of telling you that now is a good time to begin that weight-loss regimen you've been thinking about, or another challenging project you have been putting off, because you have lots of emotional support at this time. Similarly, if you are worried that you have become too thin in real life and dreamed that you had wasted away to "skin and bones" and were eating voraciously from a great pile of food before you, it is quite possible that your unconscious was telling you that you need to nourish your body better.

Negative Interpretations: If you are not preoccupied with your size, then a dream that focuses on your weight is probably a reference to something else. Did you dream that you had ballooned up to such a large size that you could not get out of bed? If so, have you been feeling "weighed down" by problems in the waking world? Or is it possible that your unconscious mind was trying to tell you that you have been overindulging—not necessarily in food—but perhaps in something else that is unhealthy for you in too large amounts? On the other hand, if your dreaming mind cast you as appearing much too thin, is it possible that your waking self has been feeling "starved" of some "nourishment" (whether it be emotional, intellectual, sexual, or spiritual)? And are you now metaphorically "wasting away"? If you dreamed that someone was withholding food from you, did you recognize the person? Could it be that he or she is withholding some vital nourishment from you in the real world? Or was this person simply trying to help you to curb your overactive, self-destructive appetite?

Related Dreams
pages 39, 172, 176 & 182

CHAPTER 2
CLOTHING & EMBELLISHMENTS

In dreams, as in real life, we use clothing and embellishments
either to project a certain image or to express our state of mind.
Such dreams may be particularly indicative of how successfully we
feel that we are fitting in with those around us, our self-perceived
status in relation to others, or how we hope or fear that
others regard us in the waking world.

My Coats Dreams

----

* * * * * * * * * * * * * * * * * *

Ocean-going

If you dreamed that your sea journey was an adventure, and that you were wrapped up warmly while sailing in calm waters, perhaps you're yearning for change. It could be that a real-life trip of some kind is imminent, or else that you're feeling frustrated with your present situation, but feel positive about taking the next step.

COATS

* *

Apart from adorning our bodies and making a statement to others about our image or "who we are," our clothing—and especially a coat—serves the important function of protecting us from the environment. We wear coats to shield us from the rain, the wind, and the cold, and, in the world of dreams, the function of a coat is likely to be that of emotional or psychic protection.

Symbolic and Verbal Associations
- Protection from the environment
- Camouflage or concealment
- An "icy" situation
- Dealing with a "dirty" or "messy" situation (when a work coat is highlighted)
- Travel; escape

Positive Interpretations: Because we usually don our coats when we are going to go outside, dreaming of wearing a coat can be symbolic of travel. If you had a dream in which you went to the closet, put on your coat, and eagerly headed for the front door, where was it that you were leaving from? Do you know where you were going? Your dream could have been an unconscious indication that you need either a temporary or a permanent escape from some place where you are currently unhappy. Perhaps it's time for that long-overdue vacation you've been meaning to take? It's also possible that your dream signaled the need for an escape of a more emotional nature. For instance, if, in your dream, you were leaving your parents' home, could it be that you are in desperate need of some emotional distance from them?

Negative Interpretations: Did you have a dream in which you were sitting down to dinner in your home with your husband, and are you perplexed because in your dream you were wearing your winter coat? If you had a dream of this sort, in which you were wearing a coat indoors or in warm weather, the dream could have been your unconscious mind's way of expressing that you are involved in an emotionally cold or "icy" relationship or situation in the real world. Have things between you and your husband become "cool" of late? Or did you have a dream in which you were wearing coveralls or a laborer's jacket at the office? If so, you should ask yourself if you are trying to protect yourself from a "dirty" or "messy" situation. (Perhaps there are some behind-the-scenes office politics going on that you'd rather not be a part of?) Finally, if you had a dream in which you were prowling around at night in a large, dark trench coat, or in which you were donning a camouflage jacket, is there something that you are trying to conceal from others around you in the waking world? Or are you in fear of a potential attack from someone? Otherwise, could it be that you have undertaken some task or duty that will require anonymity and stealth? The details of the dream should give you some clues as to its meaning.

Related Dreams

pages 40, 125, 224, 229, 260 & 375

COSMETICS

My Cosmetics Dreams

✱ ✱ ✱ ✱ ✱ ✱ ✱ ✱ ✱ ✱ ✱ ✱ ✱ ✱ ✱ ✱ ✱

Because we usually associate the wearing of makeup or cosmetics with femininity, the meaning of a dream in which you were applying cosmetics to yourself is likely to be influenced by your gender. However, whether you are a man or a woman, it is possible that a dream in which you were applying makeup to your face has to do with either confidence in your appearance, the desire to appear attractive, or else a wish to "cover up" or conceal something about yourself.

Symbolic and Verbal Associations
- Self-esteem
- Confidence (or, alternatively, a lack of it)
- The desire to appear attractive
- Concealing "blemishes" or "flaws"
- Putting on a different "face": transformation

Positive Interpretations: Did you have a dream in which you were seated in front of a mirror, busily applying makeup to your face, and did you gaze at the finished "product" with approval and happiness? If you are a woman, this sort of dream could indicate your conscious feelings of confidence and self-approval with regard to either your physical appearance or the "face" that you present to the world. However, if your waking self-image is generally poor, your dream could signal your wish to present a more attractive image to others. And because of the symbolic association between lips and female genitalia, if you had a dream in which you were carefully applying lipstick to your mouth, this could be an indication of your desire to attract a lover. (In your dream, were you preparing for a date? If so, with whom?) If you are a man who is perplexed to have had a dream of applying or wearing cosmetics, it is possible that your unconscious mind is telling you that you would benefit from embracing your feminine side. Perhaps you could better solve a problem or improve a relationship in your waking life if you adopted a more "feminine" approach to it—by being more compassionate, for instance?

Negative Interpretations: Did you have a stressful dream in which you were trying to cover up blemishes on your face with foundation or concealer? Regardless of your gender, such a dream is likely to be indicative of your desire to conceal or hide some character "flaw" that you perceive that you have. In your dream, was it pimples that you were trying to cover up? If so, are you concerned with hiding your "adolescent" attitude from others? Or did your dream self have dark circles under the eyes? In the real world, are you trying to hide your mental or emotional fatigue from those around you? Makeup is also used for theatrical purposes. If you had a dream in which you used makeup to put on a totally different "face," are you trying to play up to an "audience" in the real world?

Related Dreams

pages 36, 49, 95, 125, 273 & 276

Lip Gloss

If you are a man and you dreamed that a woman was flirting with you while applying her lipstick, this may have been simple wish fulfillment. If you had this dream as a woman, were you trying to attract someone's attention? You may be harboring feelings of attraction.

CLOTHING

DISGUISES & COSTUMES

My Disguises & Costumes Dreams

----

* * * * * * * * * * * * * * * * * *

Dressing Up

A positive dream about putting on a costume could mean that your playful side is coming out in your sleep. You may be uninhibited while you're sleeping, but is this a side of yourself that you're ready to express in your waking life? If you were dressing up to go to a dream party, it may mean that you want to be more of an extrovert in your social life.

D isguises and costumes (including masks) both conceal our identity and give us a "new" identity: with them, we can "become" whomever we want. Masks are one of the oldest (and most effective) theatre props, as their power to create a sense of drama is as effective today as it was when they were used by the ancient Greeks.

Symbolic and Verbal Associations
- Identity: who we are
- The persona or face that we present to the world (with regard to a mask)
- Someone who is "false-faced"
- "Putting on an act" for someone: pretense
- Parties, events, and holidays
- Flirtation; mystery
- Concealment
- Darkness and/or death (when hoods and capes are depicted)

Positive Interpretations: Did you have a dream in which you were thrilled and excited to attend a fancy masquerade ball? If so, what sort of costume were you wearing? If it was a princess gown and tiara, is this the sort of elegant and royal image that you wish to present in the real world? Or if you were dressed as a Civil War general, for instance, would you like others to view you as being more of a powerful leadership figure? If you are a man who found yourself dressed as a woman, or a woman who was dressed as a man, consider whether your dream choice of costume was an unconscious attempt to highlight your underlying feminine or masculine side. Because they present an air of mystery, masks, veils, and fans (which partially cover the face) also denote flirtatious behavior. So if you had a dream in which you were hiding your face behind a fan in order to tease or attract someone at a party, did you recognize the person? Could it be that you are sexually attracted to him or her in the waking world?

Negative Interpretations: Because disguises, masks, and costumes hide our true identity, they can be symbolic of falsity and pretense. Did you dream that you were frustrated because you were trying to have a discussion with your best friend, but she refused to take off the mask that she was wearing? If so, do you feel that she has been wearing a "false face" around you, or attempting to deceive you in some way, in the real world? In your dream, did you attempt to "unmask" her? Or did you have a dream in which you were the one wearing the mask? If so, is there some aspect of your personality that you are trying to conceal from those around you? Dreams that involve characters in hoods or hooded capes may have connotations of grief, misery, or death, so if these types of costumes featured in a dream that you had, can you draw any connection with your waking reality?

Related Dreams

pages 49, 125, 127, 143, 276 & 286

DRESSES & SKIRTS

✦✦✦✦✦✦✦✦✦✦✦✦✦✦✦✦✦✦✦✦✦✦✦✦✦✦✦✦✦✦✦✦✦

The meaning of dream skirts and dresses is likely to vary greatly depending upon whether you are a man or a woman, and also depending on your feelings with regard to these items of clothing. For instance, while some women find it liberating when they put on a skirt, others view such items of clothing as symbols of patriarchy and the suppression of women.

Symbolic and Verbal Associations
- ☾ Femininity; feminine sex appeal
- ☾ "Dressing up"; formality
- ☾ Freedom or, alternatively, restriction
- ☾ Vulnerability; weakness

Positive Interpretations: If you are a woman, the meaning of a dream in which you wore a dress or a skirt will depend upon the specific type of dress or skirt that you wore, as well as on your dreaming reaction to your appearance. If you dreamed that you were wearing a beautiful formal gown, and if you felt yourself to be very pretty and elegant in your dream, then this could be a reflection of your real-life feelings of happiness and confidence in your "femininity." (Otherwise, your dream could reflect your desire to feel this way.) A dream in which you were frolicking in a long, flowing skirt could indicate your feelings of freedom and joy, or else your need to "let loose" in the waking world. Or if your dress was exceptionally desirable or expensive, could it be that you long to live a life of luxury? If you are a man who found your dream self happily sporting a dress or a skirt, might you be happier in the real world if you allowed others to see more of the "feminine" side of your personality? Dresses and skirts are traditionally associated with female sex appeal, so this should also be considered when you are interpreting a dream that highlights one of these articles of clothing.

Negative Interpretations: If you are a woman who would never, ever wear a dress or a skirt in the real world because you find such articles of clothing to be symbols of female suppression by the "patriarchy," and if you were appalled and extremely uncomfortable to find your dream self wearing a dress to your company picnic, then have you been feeling bullied or kept down by your male colleagues at work? If you are a man who had a similar dream, is it possible that you have been feeling emasculated in the waking world? Finally, if you are a woman who dreamed of wearing a skirt or dress in a totally inappropriate situation—for instance, if your dream self was extremely frustrated because you were trying to ride a bicycle and your long skirt kept getting in the way of the pedals and kept getting caught up in the chain—then have you been feeling frustrated at being restricted in the real world, perhaps because of your gender?

My Dresses & Skirts Dreams

✦✦✦✦✦✦✦✦✦✦✦✦✦✦✦✦✦✦✦✦✦

Evening Dresses

If you are a woman and you dreamed of wearing a glamorous outfit, are you yearning to feel attractive and to be noticed? Perhaps you have been overwhelmed by your domestic duties and would benefit from a romantic evening out—or maybe you are worried that your husband's eye is roving.

Related Dreams
pages 65, 125, 172, 218, 265 & 268

My Eyewear Dreams

✴ ✴ ✴ ✴ ✴ ✴ ✴ ✴ ✴ ✴ ✴ ✴ ✴ ✴ ✴ ✴ ✴ ✴ ✴

Clear-sightedness

If you dreamed that your child was wearing glasses, are you concerned about his or her progress or performance at school? Or perhaps your dream was a return to your own childhood, which may suggest a desire either to relearn something or a regret that you didn't study as hard as you should have done during your schooldays.

EYEWEAR

Though wearing eyeglasses was once considered "uncool" ("Men seldom make passes/At girls who wear glasses," as poet Dorothy Parker famously wrote) or, at best, they were perceived as giving one the appearance of being "bookish," eyewear has now become a very hip and trendy fashion statement. The result is that dreams that focus our attention on eyeglasses, sunglasses, or contact lenses can vary greatly in their meaning, depending on the type of eyewear depicted and on the specific dream situation.

Symbolic and Verbal Associations
- ‹ Intelligence; bookishness
- ‹ Seeing the world through "rose-colored glasses"
- ‹ Someone who is shortsighted
- ‹ Feeling boring or "nerdy" (because of wearing eyeglasses)
- ‹ Appearing "cool" or "suave" (when wearing sunglasses); stardom
- ‹ Hiding one's emotions (by covering the eyes with dark glasses)

Positive Interpretations: Did you dream that you put on a pair of sunglasses and that you then began to see the world in hues of happy pink? If so, your dream may have been indicating that you have been viewing the world "through rose-colored glasses"—something that we say that people do during times of extreme happiness, such as when they have fallen in love. Did you have a dream in which you wore a pair of spectacles to a cocktail party, and everyone at the party was impressed and amazed by your clever and sharp witticisms? This type of dream is an example of an unconscious play on the old stereotype that people who wear glasses are somehow more intelligent than those who don't. If you experienced this sort of dream scenario, have you been feeling especially bright or learned in your waking life? Or do you wish that others would view you as such? Or did you dream that you were wearing a pair of special-effect contact lenses—perhaps the kind that make your eyes look like a cat's (with vertically elongated pupils)? If so, do you, in real life, feel that you are especially alert to things that might go undetected by others (so that you feel as if you can "see in the dark")?

Negative Interpretations: If you had a dream in which you were frustrated to find that you could not see clearly, so that you had to put on a pair of spectacles in order to gain some perspective on what was going on around you, then could this be an unconscious cue that you are being shortsighted with regard to some issue or problem in your waking life? Or did you dream that you were having breakfast with your husband and that you refused his request that you take off the dark sunglasses that you were wearing? If so, have you been attempting to hide your true feelings from him in the real world?

Related Dreams
pages 43, 49, 197, 288, 330 & 384

FOOTWEAR

CLOTHING

* *

Because feet are a primary means of mobility, dream feet—and the shoes and socks that adorn them—often symbolize some sort of advancement in the real world. When we have a dream that focuses on footwear, it is important to consider the type and quality of the footwear that our unconscious mind conjured up, and your reaction, when determining the meaning of the dream.

Symbolic and Verbal Associations
- Mobility and advancement
- Travel and exploration
- Inhibition and restrictions, or, alternatively, freedom from restrictions
- "Walking in someone else's shoes"
- Someone "walking all over" another person
- "Socking it to" (or impressing) someone
- Hitting or "socking" someone

Positive Interpretations: Did you have a dream in which you excitedly laced up your hiking boots and then eagerly set off to explore new pastures? If so, your dream may have been your unconscious mind's attempt to encourage you to be more adventurous in your life—either literally, by finding more opportunities for travel, or figuratively, by allowing yourself to "explore" other ways of being (or opportunities) in life. (For instance, have you always wished that you could take a trip to France, but have never done so because of your inhibitions or because of your lack of knowledge of the French language? Your dream could be an unconscious prompt that it's time to venture forth on such a journey.) Or if you had a dream in which you were wearing platform shoes or high heels, have you been feeling "heads above" everyone else in the waking world?

Negative Interpretations: In your dream, were you depressed to see that your shoes were shabby, dirty, and coming unglued at the seams? If so, have you been feeling "worn out" and downtrodden in real life? (The same interpretation may apply if you had a dream in which your socks were full of holes.) Or if you had a dream in which you were wearing a pair of shoes that pinched or rubbed your feet, so that you hobbled along in horrible pain, are you feeling inhibited or restricted in the waking world? (A similar message may apply if you had a dream in which you limped along on concrete pavement because you had lost your shoes.) Alternatively, if your dream foot pain was caused because you were wearing someone else's shoes, whose shoes were they? Could it be that your unconscious mind is telling you that if you were to "walk in this person's shoes" for a while, you would find that he or she has a much harder time progressing than you do—and that you should be more compassionate toward him or her?

Related Dreams
pages 45, 125, 239, 247, 273 & 306

My Footwear Dreams

----

* * * * * * * * * * * * * * * * * * * *

Party Shoes

Wearing shoes suited to a particular occasion, or inappropriate to your situation, could be an indication of whether you were comfortable in your dream scenario. If your high-heeled evening shoes were giving you blisters and your dream took place at work, does one of your real-life colleagues eye you with disapproval, or perhaps flirt with you against your wishes?

CLOTHING

My Formal Dress Dreams

★ ★ ★ ★ ★ ★ ★ ★ ★ ★ ★ ★ ★ ★ ★ ★ ★

Formally Dressed Children

Dreaming of your child or younger sibling wearing formal clothing might be your unconscious mind's way of pointing out that he or she is growing up. If the clothing looked unnatural, is he or she shouldering adult responsibilities or doing too much, too soon? If the child was you, do you feel that you can't cope with or control a waking-life situation?

FORMAL DRESS

★★★★★★★★★★★★★★★★★★★★★★★★★★★★★★★★★★★★★★

People normally dress in formal clothing in order to attend "grand" occasions or celebrations, such as weddings or even birthday celebrations, although formal clothing is also worn on more somber occasions, such as funerals. In the world of dreams, the donning of formal dress can symbolize some "marked" occasion in life—whether or not we have acknowledged this occasion in the waking world—or else our feelings with regard to our lifestyle, our image, or our social status.

Symbolic and Verbal Associations
- Celebration
- Wealth; luxury
- Leisure
- High self-esteem
- A ceremony of some sort; a "grand" occasion

Positive Interpretations: If you had a dream in which you found yourself dressed in a beautiful silk evening gown (if you are a woman) or in a dashing tuxedo (if you are a man), then it is possible that your unconscious mind depicted you in this formal wear in order to express your waking desire to mark or celebrate some "grand" occasion in your life. Have you recently gotten engaged, or are you about to graduate from college? Or else could it be that your dream was merely a reflection of your real-life self-esteem? Of course, it could also be that you have been desiring a "night out," or that you wish that you had more wealth, excitement, or leisure time in your life. In your dream, did you relish the admiration of everyone around you, and, in the waking world, do you wish to present a more "elegant" image of yourself to others? An assessment of your waking situation and of your specific reactions to your dream will give you clues as to its meaning.

Negative Interpretations: Did you have a dream in which you suffered and sweated because you were "suffocating" in the many layers of formal attire that you found yourself wearing? If so, are you feeling restricted or weighed down by your "formal" duties or by the need to "keep up appearances" in real life? Or have you become overly "stiff" or humorless during your waking hours? If your dream self was tortured by the uncontrollable itchiness of your chiffon dress, could this be indicative of some irritant that is hassling you in the real world? If you found your dream self desperately and ineffectively trying to loosen the tie or scarf that you wore around your neck, is there something that is "choking" you in your daily life? Or if your dream self tore off your uncomfortable clothing, have you been feeling "buttoned up" in the real world, and do you long to "let loose" and to relax?

Related Dreams

pages 90, 102, 114, 125, 224 & 247

GLOVES

There are many, many types of gloves: boxing gloves, formal "ladies'" gloves, gardening gloves, winter gloves, driving gloves, and so on. So if you had a dream in which gloves were featured, the meaning will depend upon more than the context: it will also depend on the type of gloves that your dreaming mind conjured up.

Symbolic and Verbal Associations
‹ Not revealing "your hand"
‹ Treating someone gently, with "kid gloves"
‹ "Taking the gloves off"
‹ "Fighting dirty"
‹ Not wishing to leave fingerprints
‹ An "ace up the sleeve"
‹ Not wishing to "dirty your hands"

Positive Interpretations: The origin of shaking hands was to show the person whom we were greeting that we did not hold a weapon in our hand—and therefore that we meant them no harm and that we were hailing them in friendship. So if you had a dream in which you pulled off your right-hand glove in order to shake hands with someone, your dream probably reveals your waking feelings of friendship and goodwill toward that person. In addition, people often wear gloves when they are dressed for travel or for a formal occasion, so these meanings should also be considered when you are trying to determine the meaning of a dream in which you found yourself wearing gloves. Or did you have a dream in which you were putting on "kid gloves" in order to "deal" with someone? If so, who was this person? Is it possible that you consider this person to be vulnerable, so that you feel the need to treat him or her extra gently?

Negative Interpretations: If, in your dream, you squared off against your brother while wearing a pair of boxing gloves, do you feel the need to have it out with him over some issue in the real world? Since boxing gloves somewhat cushion the blow of a punch, your feelings of anger toward your brother may be even more severe if, in your dream, you took off your gloves and continued to "fight dirty" with him. Alternatively, if you had a dream of putting on gloves, are you hiding something from someone, so that you're worried about "revealing your hand"? Or, in your dream, did you pull on a pair of gloves so that you wouldn't leave any fingerprints behind? If so, are you engaged in some undercover, clandestine activity during waking hours? Otherwise, did you pull on a pair of dream gloves in order to undertake some messy or undesirable task? If so, might this be a metaphor for a task or responsibility that you have to take on in the real world—and are you hesitant to "dirty your hands" in the process?

My Gloves Dreams

★ ★ ★ ★ ★ ★ ★ ★ ★ ★ ★ ★ ★ ★ ★ ★ ★ ★ ★ ★

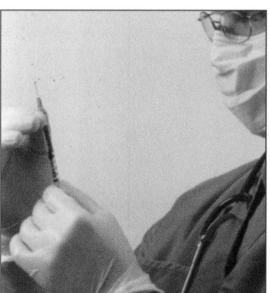

Surgical Gloves
Donning a pair of protective gloves in a dream scene indicates the need to avoid direct contact with someone or something. Are you trying to keep your distance from someone in your waking world? If your dream involved someone else approaching you wearing surgical gloves, this could reflect either a literal fear of medical or dental treatment or someone's real-life coldness toward you.

Related Dreams
pages 40, 46, 70, 256, 266 & 281

CLOTHING

My Hats Dreams

----

* * * * * * * * * * * * * * * * * * *

Getting Ahead

Dreaming of wearing a hat while you're on vacation could suggest a laid-back approach to your waking life. Perhaps you were lazing on the beach, with the hat shielding you from the sun, feeling at peace with the world. If others in your dream were also wearing hats, this could point to your feeling of fitting in.

HATS

* *

Throughout history, different types of hats have meant many things to many people—and, like other types of clothing, the meaning of a dream hat will vary greatly depending on the type of hat and the scenario of the dream.

Symbolic and Verbal Associations
- Putting on your "thinking cap"; a "feather in your cap"
- A laid-back attitude (when a casual hat is highlighted)
- Festivities
- Being "crowned" in glory
- "Tipping your hat" to someone
- Covering the head for religious purposes
- Work; manual labor (depending on the type of hat)
- Protection from a "rainstorm" or from "bad weather"

Positive Interpretations: In Western society today, few people wear hats for formal or religious purposes on a day-to-day basis, yet one can walk down any busy street and see many people wearing baseball caps, scarves, or casual hats. Therefore, if you donned one of these casual types of hats in a dream, this could denote a laid-back or casual attitude in your waking life. Or if, in your dream, you wore a festive hat, then have you been feeling happy, celebratory, or playful in your daily life? (Or do you need to incorporate more festivity into your waking hours?) If you had a dream in which everyone was wearing the same kind of hat, this may be a metaphor for team spirit or for collective values. Alternatively, if you dreamed of yourself or of someone else wearing a skullcap, a traditional and still contemporary sign of religious observation (in the Jewish and the Roman Catholic religions, for instance), then you should consider whether your unconscious mind was making an allusion to piety and religion. Since hats are worn on the head, they can also be a symbol of authority, intellect, and higher consciousness. So did your dream depict you putting on your "thinking cap"?

Negative Interpretations: In certain historical periods, hats were worn by men and women out of social compulsion. Therefore, dreams of old-style hats can be metaphors for antiquated values. Did you have a dream in which you felt frightened or intimidated by a man who was wearing an old-fashioned-style hat? If so, did you know who the man was? Whether or not you knew him, how did the dream make you feel? If you can identify the era—and the values—that he represented, this should give you a clue as to the meaning of your dream. Or did you have a dream in which someone came along and knocked a tall hat off your head? If so, is it possible that this person was accusing you of behaving (or of having ideas) "above your station"?

Related Dreams

pages 49, 121, 149, 247, 261 & 270

JEWELRY

* *

Jewelry—whether it is made of gold, silver, gemstones, or imitations thereof—is representative of the precious things in life. It is also a traditional symbol of wealth, and therefore shows the value of the wearer. Because of its personal nature, when someone gives us a gift of jewelry (whether in dreamland or in the waking world), it is likely to symbolize this person's love of, and appreciation for, us.

Symbolic and Verbal Associations
- Love and romance
- Precious things; wealth (both literal and metaphorical)
- Excitement; "sparkling" or "glittering" feelings
- Loyalty and friendship
- Partnership, wholeness, and eternity (when rings or bangles are represented)
- Having "a heart of gold"
- Someone who is "a diamond" (perhaps "in the rough")
- A "weak link"

My Jewelry Dreams

----

* *

Positive Interpretations: If you had a dream in which someone gave you a piece of precious jewelry, then your dream was likely to have been either an unconscious reflection of your waking desires to be loved and appreciated by the dream jewelry-giver, or else a metaphor for your happiness and satisfaction with how this person actually treats you in the real world. Because of their circular shape, rings (and also bangles) represent partnership, wholeness, and eternity. So if, in your dream, your boyfriend gave you a diamond ring, are you hoping that he will actually make you a proposal of marriage? Or did you have a dream in which a medal or brooch was pinned on your chest? If so, what was the medal, and for what were you being honored? Although some gemstones have specific meanings attached to them (diamonds mean love, for instance), if you dreamed of a particular stone, you should ask yourself what this stone means to you. (Is it your birthstone? Or does the color remind you of your mother's eyes?)

Negative Interpretations: Did you have a dream in which you were panicked and grief-stricken to realize that you had lost your favorite necklace because the clasp had come undone? If it was a string of pearls that your partner had given you, is it possible that there is "a weak link" in your relationship? Or if you had a dream in which you took the gold and diamond necklace that your husband gave you to be appraised, and you were shocked to find out that it was a fake, your dream may be indicative of your feelings about the "worth" or the "genuineness" of your marriage. Is it possible that your husband has been "stringing you along"?

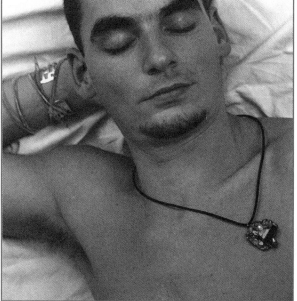

Precious Metal

Did someone who doesn't know that you are attracted to them in real life give you the necklace in your dream? If so, this may be wish-fulfillment. If you are single, the necklace may signify a desire for intimacy. But what if you're in a relationship? If the necklace wasn't associated with your partner, it could mean that you have eyes for someone else.

Related Dreams
pages 94, 102, 198, 233, 245 & 267

CLOTHING

My Nightwear Dreams

✶ ✶ ✶ ✶ ✶ ✶ ✶ ✶ ✶ ✶ ✶ ✶ ✶ ✶ ✶ ✶ ✶

Sweet Dreams

Dreaming that you are young again in the house in which you grew up, and that you are wearing your favorite old pajamas and cuddling your childhood bear, could be a sign that you are seeking comfort in your past. Maybe you are trying to revive feelings of being looked after as a child in an unconscious attempt to suppress worries about your adult responsibilities.

NIGHTWEAR

✶✶✶✶✶✶✶✶✶✶✶✶✶✶✶✶✶✶✶✶✶✶✶✶✶✶✶✶✶✶✶✶✶✶✶✶

In dreams, the appearance of nightwear can have various meanings, depending on the type of nightwear depicted and the situation in which it is worn.

Symbolic and Verbal Associations
- Comfort
- A casual attitude or mood
- Rest and relaxation
- Sex and eroticism (when certain types of lingerie are represented)
- Sexual guilt
- Anxiety
- Humiliation

Positive Interpretations: Did you have a dream in which you were comfortably lounging around your home, during daylight hours, while wearing your favorite nightgown or pajamas? If so, your dreaming mind may have been highlighting your need for more rest and relaxation. (Have you been depriving yourself of sleep because you've been working long hours at the office while trying to keep up with your social life?) Or did you have a dream in which you enjoyed parading your body before someone while you were dressed in sexy lingerie? If so, who was the person for who you were "showing off"? Is it possible that you have real-life feelings of sexual attraction for this person? In your dream, did your baiting behavior work? If so, you probably experienced a wish-fulfillment dream.

Negative Interpretations: Did you have a dream in which you were trying to impress someone with your sexiest lingerie, but in which you were embarrassed when you looked down and realized that your outfit was stained or dirty? This sort of dream may indicate that you have feelings of sexual guilt—either in general, because of your inhibitions, or because of something specific that you have done (do you feel that you have betrayed your lover, for instance?) Or was your dream self humiliated when you realized that you had accidentally gone to work while wearing your pajamas? If so, it is possible that your dream was an unconscious indication that you are feeling anxiety for one reason or another—perhaps connected with your perception of there being a blurred line between your work and home lives. (Do you feel like your coworkers know too much about your private affairs?) Another explanation for this type of dream is that you feel you have taken on a "too-casual," nonchalant attitude toward your career, and if this is the case, your unconscious mind may have placed you in this embarrassing dream predicament in order to encourage you to adopt a more professional attitude during working hours.

Related Dreams
pages 112, 155, 218, 224 & 268

PURSES & WALLETS

* *

CLOTHING

Purses and handbags are symbols of female identity, but they (along with brief-cases, for men and for women) also hold the everyday and emergency objects that are the keys to keeping us in communication with the world.

Symbolic and Verbal Associations
- Money
- Personal identity; anxiety about loss of identity
- Female sex organs or the womb (when handbags or purses are depicted)
- Communication (because purses hold cell phones, address books, identification cards, etc.); alternatively: isolation

Positive Interpretations: Not only are they symbols of femininity, but handbags and purses are also symbolic of female sex organs and the womb. So if you had a dream that focused a spotlight on a new, gorgeous handbag that your dream self purchased, you should consider whether your dream was a metaphor for your real-life feelings with regard to your sex appeal. Was your dream a reflection of your waking feelings of satisfaction with your sexuality? Or could it be that you desire to appear more sexually attractive to others? In addition, purses and handbags (and also briefcases) are the means by which we carry those highly personal items that identify us as individuals (identification cards and photos, for instance). So if you had a dream in which you were searching through a purse or handbag that belonged to another person, could it be that, in the real world, you would like to find out more about this person?

Negative Interpretations: If you are a woman who had a dream that someone snatched or ran off with your purse, who was it? If it was a man, do you feel sexually threatened by him in the waking world? Or if you dreamed that you lost your wallet or purse, did your nightmare simply reflect your general anxiety with regard to losing your possessions—perhaps because you view yourself as absentminded or irresponsible? If this is the case, your unconscious mind may have been telling you to be more careful with your things. However—because purses, handbags, and brief-cases are the vehicles that carry our symbols of individuality and identity, and also those things that help us to maintain communication with our friends and family (cell phones, address books, etc.)—a dream in which you lost your purse or brief-case could reflect your real-life feelings of anxiety about some sort of loss of iden-tity (have you recently lost or retired from your job, for instance?) or about our ability to stay connected to others. Finally, if you are a woman who dreamed that you snapped your purse closed in order to keep your partner from taking money out of it, could it be that you are feeling angry with him and that you are, therefore, with-holding sex from him in the real world?

My Purses & Wallets Dreams

----

* * * * * * * * * * * * * * * * * * *

Money Talks

Having a dream in which your purse or bill-fold was stuffed with cash may mean that you are experiencing feelings of self-confidence. Or have you been worrying about your finances, and was your dream sheer wishful thinking? If you dreamed that you lost a bulging wal-let, this could suggest that a general feeling of anxiety is pervading your waking life.

Related Dreams
pages 233, 268, 278 & 302

CLOTHING

My Shabby Clothing Dreams

✱ ✱ ✱ ✱ ✱ ✱ ✱ ✱ ✱ ✱ ✱ ✱ ✱ ✱ ✱ ✱ ✱

Patched Up

If you normally dress snappily and dreamed that you were wearing your oldest jeans and a faded T-shirt, but felt comfortable in yourself, it could simply mean that you crave more relaxation time. Or were you at a social event where you were dressed down and everyone else looked smart? If so, this dream may point to a sense of social insecurity or a feeling of isolation.

SHABBY CLOTHING

✶✶✶✶✶✶✶✶✶✶✶✶✶✶✶✶✶✶✶✶✶✶✶✶✶✶✶✶✶✶✶✶✶✶✶✶✶✶

For better or for worse, the way that we dress says tells others something about "who we are," and when people meet us for the first time, a large part of the impression that we make upon them will most likely come from the clothing that we are wearing—not only the type or style, but also (and very importantly) the quality and the condition of our garments.

Symbolic and Verbal Associations
‹ A relaxed attitude
‹ Leisure activities
‹ Self-consciousness; shame
‹ Something in your life that needs "patching up"
‹ Sadness; depression

Positive Interpretations: If you are a meticulous dresser during waking hours (perhaps you have a career that requires you to look prim, proper, and tidy whenever you leave the house), and if you had a dream in which you were "bumming around" in an old raggedy sweat suit or something of a similar nature, then your dream may have been your unconscious mind's way of giving you a break from your real-life obligation to "keep up appearances." This may especially be the case if, in your dream, you felt particularly relaxed or relieved of stress. Or, similarly, did you have a dream in which you had donned your old fishing hat and jacket and your most comfortable pair of old, "knock-around" boots, and that you were gleefully heading out of your house with your fishing pole slung over your shoulder? This is another example of a type of wish-fulfillment dream—one that indicates that you would probably be much happier if you could find a way to introduce more rest, relaxation, and fun into the routine of your daily life.

Negative Interpretations: In the real world, do you pride yourself on being well-dressed, and did you have a dream in which you were dressed in clothing that was old, shabby, or of poor quality? If so, then the key to the meaning of your dream will depend, in large part, on how the dream made you feel. If your dream made you feel sad or depressed, then it is quite likely that your unconscious was trying to alert you to the fact that this is how you've been feeling during your waking hours. (And it is worthy of noting that, in dreams, dark or drab shades generally represent depression or gloominess, while bright colors denote cheerfulness, white conveys innocence, and black conveys mourning—though these are just generalizations and should not be taken as rules.) In your dream, were people jeering or laughing at you because of your bedraggled appearance? If this is the case, then have you been feeling self-conscious or ashamed of the "image" that you have been presenting to the world during your waking hours?

Related Dreams
pages 125, 224, 235, 237, 273 & 271

Shirts & Neckties

****

CLOTHING

Most of the symbolism and metaphors having to do with shirts, collars, and neckties comes from a time when these items of clothing were almost exclusively worn by men. Regardless of the origin of our shirt and necktie associations, however, it is quite reasonable to apply similar interpretive criteria whenever these garments crop up in the dreams of either men or women.

Symbolic and Verbal Associations
- The penis (symbolized by a necktie, according to some)
- Restriction (when a tight collar or necktie is depicted)
- Rolling up your shirtsleeves; hard work
- Losing or giving someone "the shirt off your back"
- Clinging to someone's shirttails

Positive Interpretations: Did you have a dream in which you were engaged in the task of vigorously rolling up your shirtsleeves? If so, is there a big task ahead of you in the waking world that has been on your mind of late? In the corporate world, where the acceptable range of clothing diversity is fairly small—particularly for men—the necktie has become a means of expressing one's individuality. Therefore, if you dreamed of someone (maybe yourself) who was wearing a necktie that caught your attention, what did it look like, and how did it make you feel?

Negative Interpretations: Did you have a panicked dream in which you were rushing out of your house in the morning, only to realize that your shirt was dirty or needed ironing—or, even worse, that you had no shirt on at all? If so, this type of stress dream could simply be due to the fact that your unconscious mind remembered that you had a big meeting the next morning and that all of your business shirts were, in fact, either wrinkled or soiled. However, if this was not the case, your slumbering mind may have been trying to tell you something with this tense scenario. For instance, if you found your dream self bare-breasted, are you, perhaps, in danger of going bankrupt—or of "losing the shirt off your back"—in the real world? Or did you awake from a dream in which you felt as though you were being choked to death by an exceedingly tight collar or necktie? If so, are you feeling restricted or constrained during waking hours (perhaps, in particular, in relation to your place of work since these items are generally worn in a professional setting)? On the other hand, if you dreamed about a necktie, you should consider the fact that many people have associated this item of clothing with the penis—both because of its phallic shape, and because neckties were traditionally worn by men solely (and have therefore been considered as a symbol of "male power"). So if you are a man who dreamed that you were being strangled or suffocated by your own necktie, is it possible that your machismo has spun out of control, so much so that it has become self-defeating?

Related Dreams
pages 34, 54, 219, 237 & 247

My Shirts & Neckties Dreams

****

Tied in Knots
Did you awake from a dream in which your necktie was choking you? If so, it could be that you're feeling trapped or somehow suffocated during your waking hours, particularly at your place of work. Is it time for things to change in that section of your life? Perhaps there's a dispute that needs to be resolved, or maybe it's time for you to consider breaking free before moving on to pastures new.

CLOTHING

My Shorts & Pants Dreams

----

* * * * * * * * * * * * * * * * * * *

The Long and the Short of It

If you were wearing shorts in your dream, perhaps you're feeling nostalgic about the days of your youth, a time when things were simpler. If you were wearing shorts as part of a sports outfit, perhaps while playing a game of soccer, could it be that you're craving more fun, or else the opportunity to collaborate more as part of a team, be it at home or at work?

SHORTS & PANTS

* *

From talk about who "wears the pants in a relationship," to being caught "with your pants down," the garments that cover our nether parts have been the subject of countless sayings, jokes, and anecdotes. By their very nature, because part of their function is to cover the genital area, these items of clothing have numerous sexual associations.

Symbolic and Verbal Associations
- Sexuality
- Sexual potency
- Youth, or a youthful (or casual) attitude (when a dream has us in shorts)
- The person who "wears the pants," or who is "in control," in a relationship; also, male dominance or potency (or the undermining thereof)
- Being caught "with your pants down"; sexual shame
- Someone who is a "smarty pants" (e.g., a "know it all")
- Embarrassment (when a dream has to do with soiling—or losing—one's pants)

Positive Interpretations: If you had a dream in which your girlfriend or your wife paraded or danced across your path of vision—especially if your attention was drawn to the pair of pants that she wore—then this is, perhaps, an easy metaphor to interpret. Could it be that your unconscious mind was musing on your partner's role as being the one who "wears the pants" (i.e., the one who is "in control" or who is dominant) in your relationship? If this is the case, how did your dreaming self react to this scenario? Or if you had a dream in which you were enjoying a warm day on the beach while you wore your favorite, most comfortable pair of shorts, is it that you are in need of some rest and relaxation from your demanding work schedule?

Negative Interpretations: Did you have a dream in which you stood up to give a presentation before a large group of people, only to realize with shock and embarrassment that you weren't wearing any pants? This is a classic anxiety dream, which possibly has to do with fears about some sort of exposure. The simplest explanation for this type of dream is that you are nervous about some task that you must undertake in the waking world. In a similar vein, if you had a dream in which you were horrified and humiliated because someone—perhaps your girlfriend or wife caught you "with your pants down," you should ask yourself whether you feel at risk of being discovered for something that you are doing unbeknownst to her—for instance, have you been having (or considering having) an affair? Alternatively, if you had a dream in which you were panic-stricken and ashamed to discover that your exposed, pants-less self was the focal point of a jeering crowd, could it be that the true nature of your sexuality is in danger of being "exposed"? Otherwise, could such a dream have to do with your concerns or fears about your own virility or sexual potency?

Related Dreams

pages 47, 79, 224, 235 & 237

SWIMWEAR

* *

Bathing suits come in many shapes and forms—from polka-dotted bikinis to floral one-pieces to slick wet suits (such as surfers wear). Because of our societal obsession with weight and body image, many people—especially women—have a lot of anxiety about baring so much of themselves in order to sport swimwear, and the approach of summertime has a lot of people in dread (and engaging in desperate acts of eleventh-hour dieting and gym-going). Therefore, the meaning of a dream in which someone finds themselves wearing a bathing suit will depend greatly upon (among other things) the body image of the dreamer.

Symbolic and Verbal Associations
- ◖ Relaxation; vacation
- ◖ A "bathing beauty"
- ◖ Summertime
- ◖ Self-confidence
- ◖ Feelings of sexual attractiveness

Positive Interpretations: Did you dream that you were running down a beach in a bathing suit, and that you were laughing as the waves licked at your heels? If so, this could have been a wish-fulfillment dream—perhaps signaling that it's high time you took a vacation. Bathing suits, beaches, and swimming all have strong associations with summertime, leisure time, and vacationing. Therefore, if you had any dream that dressed you in a swimsuit, you should consider whether it might have been an unconscious expression of nostalgia, particularly for your childhood (since summertime is a time of freedom for most children). Or, if, in your dream, your bikini-clad self was parading around in front of someone whom you were trying to attract, do you know who the person was? This sort of dream probably denotes your actual feelings of self-confidence and satisfaction with your appearance, and it may be also be a hint that you are sexually attracted to your would-be dream lover in real life. If you had any dream that focused your attention on your swimsuit, you should also consider the color and the pattern (if any) of the suit, what that color or pattern means to you, and how it made you feel in your dream.

Negative Interpretations: Did you have a dream in which you were swimming in the ocean, and in which you were suddenly horrified because a big wave swept your swimsuit away, leaving you exposed for all of the people on the beach to see? If so, are you concerned that something personal about you is about to be exposed to the world—perhaps something that relates to your sexuality? Or did you dream that you were aghast at the mirror image of yourself because your fat was spilling out of the bikini that fitted you so well last summer? If so, it is likely that your dream was a metaphor for your actual dissatisfaction with your current "image."

My Swimwear Dreams

----

* *

Making a Splash
Dreaming about swimwear often suggests a desire to get away from the routine of daily life. Is it time to start planning that long-deserved trip abroad? Or if the unattractive appearance of your dream self didn't match how you really look, are you concerned about baring all? Have you been harboring negative feelings about your body image?

Related Dreams
pages 78, 81, 237, 291, 383 & 384

CLOTHING

My Umbrellas Dreams

✱ ✱ ✱ ✱ ✱ ✱ ✱ ✱ ✱ ✱ ✱ ✱ ✱ ✱ ✱ ✱ ✱

Rainy Days

If you dreamed that you were young again, and were not only dressed up snugly on a rainy day, but were equipped with an umbrella, this may suggest a feeling of wellbeing and security. If the umbrella was shielding you from the elements, were you unconsciously taking refuge in the past by returning to a time when you felt cocooned and protected?

UMBRELLAS

✱✱

Because they shield us from the rain, umbrellas are symbols of protection—and, in the world of dreams, this often means emotional protection.

Symbolic and Verbal Associations
- "Taking cover"; physical and emotional protection
- A "stormy" environment
- An emotional "rainstorm"
- Keeping "dry," or staying out of whatever drama might be going on around you

Positive Interpretations: Did you dream that you were walking along with your friend when it suddenly started to pour with rain, and that your friend opened up a large umbrella and pulled you in under it with her so that you would not get wet? If so, could this friend be a source of help or protection for you from some onslaught of troubles in the waking world? Or, in your dream, were you the one that shared your umbrella with someone else? If so, who was that person? Is it possible that you feel that you are in a position to offer help or protection to that person in the real world? Did you have a dream in which you were standing in the middle of a large crowd of people when it started to rain, and did you calmly pull out your umbrella to keep yourself dry, while everyone else around you got soaked? Since rain shares water's symbolic association with the emotions, your dream could indicate that you have been keeping yourself aloof or "dry" in the midst of a "rainstorm" of drama that has been taking place all around you.

Negative Interpretations: If you had any dream that placed you in a rainy situation that required the use of an umbrella, you should ask yourself whether you are being besieged by a storm of emotions (either your own or someone else's) during waking hours. In your dream, how well did your umbrella shield you from the rain? The answer could be a clue to how well you are protecting yourself from the emotional battering that you have been undergoing in the real world. Were you frustrated to find that your dream umbrella leaked, so that a steady trickle of water fell upon your head and face? If so, perhaps your unconscious mind was trying to tell you that you need to find a new means of defense from whatever is besieging you in real life. The same may be true if, in your dream, your umbrella was broken or blown away by a big gust of wind. Did your dream self dump the broken umbrella in the trash and march on without it (perhaps to find that the rain wasn't so bad, after all)? Or, finally, did you have a dream in which you found yourself caught out in the rain without any protection at all? Did you search desperately in your bag for your umbrella, only to realize that you had left it at home? If so, your unconscious may be warning you that you need to "think ahead" in order to protect yourself because there are "rainy days" ahead.

Related Dreams

pages 223, 366, 372, 380, 387 & 389

UNDERWEAR

✶✶

Because underwear (which includes bras, panties, briefs, and boxer shorts) is just what it is called—what we wear underneath our clothing—it is both highly personal and, particularly in the world of dreams, representative of a part of ourselves that very few other people ever see.

Symbolic and Verbal Associations
(That which is "beneath the surface" or "seldom seen"
(One's private life
(Sex and sexuality
(Femininity, and also male virility and sexual potency
(Fear of being "exposed" or caught with one's "pants down"; sexual guilt

Positive Interpretations: If you are a woman, did you dream that you were by yourself, lounging around your home in a lacy and frilly bra-and-panty set, and that you were basking in the luxury of how your garments made you feel? If so, do you feel that your true self is exceptionally feminine and/or sexually attractive, even though this might not be a side of yourself that you allow many others to see? It is also possible that you experienced a wish-fulfillment dream (and perhaps your unconscious mind was trying to prompt you to go out and splurge on that bra-and-panty set that you've been eyeing at the shopping mall). Did you have a dream in which you were pleasantly amazed to see that your bra (and breast) size had grown several cups larger? This is another example of a possible wish-fulfillment dream, signaling that your real-life body image could possibly do with some boosting. Or if you are a man who dreamed that you were gazing with approval at the image of your brief-clad body in a full-length mirror, have you been feeling especially sexy and attractive (or do you wish that you could be more like this) in real life?

Negative Interpretations: Did you have a dream in which you undressed at your doctor's office, only to be hit by a wave of humiliation as you saw that your bra and/or underwear was dirty, stained, or torn? If you suffered from this type of nightmare, you may want to consider whether you are harboring sexual guilt—either over some aspect of your sexuality, or with regard to something that you have done (or have thought of doing)—about which you fear some sort of public exposure. (For instance, do you feel that you are too promiscuous? Or have you been thinking about cheating on your girlfriend?) In another scenario, did you dream that you stood up to deliver a speech, and that everyone started to snicker and laugh at you because you were wearing only your underwear? This is a classic kind of anxiety dream (and of a similar nature to dreams of being "caught with your pants down") that is probably indicative of some real-life anxiety that you are experiencing, possibly with regard to your sexual identity or habits.

My Underwear Dreams

✶✶✶✶✶✶✶✶✶✶✶✶✶✶✶✶✶✶✶✶✶✶

What Lies Beneath
Dreaming about underwear often signifies a focus on your real self, the one underneath all of the layers of clothing that others don't normally see. If you were wearing sensual lingerie in your dream, your unconscious may have been expressing your sexually playful side. Would you normally wear leopard-print underwear? If not, it could be that you secretly long to be more sexually confident.

Related Dreams
pages 47, 78, 79, 224, 235 & 237

CLOTHING

My Uniforms Dreams

----

* * * * * * * * * * * * * * * * * * *

Banged Up

Did you dream that you were in jail, wearing striped prison uniform? If so, this may suggest guilty feelings about something you've done returning to haunt you in your dream. Were you uncomfortable in the uniform, and were other prisoners around you also wearing it? This may point to a feeling of losing your sense of self, or of being one of many.

UNIFORMS

****

In the world of dreams, as in the real world, military and police uniforms are symbols of authority and the rule of state, while work uniforms represent certain types of manual labor. All uniforms, however, to one extent or another, are emblems of depersonalization, self-discipline, and the work ethic.

Symbolic and Verbal Associations
- Authority; official business
- The rule of state; law and order; the social code
- Depersonalization; a team mentality
- Self-discipline; the work ethic
- Manual labor
- Male power and virility

Positive Interpretations: Did you dream that you were lost in a crowded, unfamiliar city, and that you didn't know which way to turn until a friendly, uniformed officer came to your rescue? If so, do you feel that you are in need of help or guidance from some "higher" authority in the real world? If you had a dream in which you yourself were dressed in a uniform of official business, and that you were pleased to find that everyone treated you with respect and admiration, could this be an unconscious indication that you would get along better in your current life if you would present yourself as being more "official," authoritarian, or more of a "team player"? Because police and military positions were, at one time, only open to men, these types of uniforms have retained their traditional association with male power and virility. Hence, for many people, uniforms are a strong sexual turn-on (even to the point of being a fetish for some)—and, depending on your personal feelings with regard to uniforms, and depending on the specific scenario of your dream, the possibility of this type of meaning should not be overlooked.

Negative Interpretations: Did you have a nightmare in which you found that you had been enlisted into the army, and that you were lined up, your head shaved, along with several other uniformed soldiers, and that you were filled with homesickness and a dread of what lay ahead? If so, then your unconscious mind may have been reflecting your real-life disenchantment with authority, the law, or with whatever social code you have been forced to live under. Or, in your dream, did you feel uncomfortable and out of place because you were the only one out on a baseball diamond who was not in uniform? If so, your unconscious may have been depicting your waking feeling that you have "fallen out of line" with the team mentality of those around you. Finally, did you dream of being detained or arrested by a team of uniformed police? If so, are you feeling guilty about some social offense that you feel that you have committed in the waking world?

Related Dreams

pages 121, 227, 228, 234, 247 & 290

CHAPTER 3
THE LIFE CYCLE

Dreams of being younger or older than you actually are may have been triggered by all manner of latent emotions, such as feelings of nostalgia or worries about aging and a desire to turn back your body clock. Dreams like these may alternatively symbolically portray your conscious or unconscious state of mind, and especially your desires and dreads. That said, sometimes they merely echo your conscious preoccupations with aspects of your real-world situation.

THE LIFE CYCLE

My Adolescence Dreams

_____

_____

_____

_____

_____

_____

_____

_____

* * * * * * * * * * * * * * * * * * *

Hanging Out

If you dreamed of your youth, of a time when you were footloose and fancy-free and spent many exciting hours skateboarding with friends, this could suggest a desire to have more fun in your adult years. Or maybe your life needs an injection of some fast-paced action.

ADOLESCENCE

* *

Adolescence is a very special time of transition in life as it is the segue from childhood to adulthood. In dreams, the appearance of teenagers often has to do with youthful attitudes and behavior, as well as with those issues that people generally must face during adolescence.

Symbolic and Verbal Associations
- Youthful attitudes and behavior
- Rebellion
- Enthusiasm and ambition
- Stubbornness; willfulness
- A carefree attitude

Positive Interpretations: If you had a dream that focused on a teenager, particularly if this teenager was unknown to you and if you found yourself reacting to him or her with admiration, then this may have been your unconscious mind's way of urging you to adopt a more youthful outlook on life. If you are a man who dreamed of an adolescent boy, what about him did you admire? Was it his carefree abandon? His rebellious idealism? His energy and vitality? Or if you are a woman who dreamed of a teenaged girl, what struck you about her? Was it her enthusiasm for life? Her sense of wonder at the world? Her positive outlook? Whatever the quality, it may be that this aspect of your own self has become atrophied or faded over the years—and if you worked to redevelop it, then you may find that you would be much happier, with a restored joy of living. On the other hand, if you are a woman who dreamed of a teenaged boy, or if you are a man who dreamed of a teenaged girl, then you should consider whether you may have been visited by your animus (if you are a woman) or your anima (if you are a man)—a character whose appearance in your dream may indicate the need for your waking self to develop a better internal gender balance.

Negative Interpretations: If you dreamed of being a teenager again, could it be that you are in mourning over the loss (or the perceived loss) of your youthful looks, vitality, and/or outlook on life? Or could it be that you regret that you did not "make the most" of your youthful potential at a time when (you now realize, with hindsight) "the world was at your feet"? If you had a dream in which you were upset by a teenager's rudeness, willfulness, or bad behavior, then this may have been your unconscious mind's attempt to push you to recognize such behavior in your waking self. For instance, have you been rebelling against the advice of an authority figure (such as a professor or a boss) because you do not want to recognize that you are wrong about some issue? Or if you had a dream in which a teenager hurt your feelings by ridiculing you, what was it that he or she said that most wounded you? Was it your stodgy unwillingness to open your mind to new ideas? If so, then could he or she have been right?

Related Dreams

pages 95, 105, 115, 119, 120 & 235

ADOPTION

✶✶

THE LIFE CYCLE

The act of adopting (or even fostering) a child involves taking a young person into your home, with the assumption that you will love and care for them as you would for your own flesh and blood. Dreams that have adoption as a theme will often be related to a waking desire to lavish love and affection on someone; in short, a desire to give of oneself and, in turn, to receive love back.

Symbolic and Verbal Associations
‹ Showering someone with love and attention
‹ The urge to care for someone
‹ Familial happiness and satisfaction
‹ The desire for unconditional love
‹ Feeling disconnected from one's family
‹ Mentorship

Positive Interpretations: Did you dream that you adopted a baby or a child, and that you welcomed him or her into your home with love and delight? If so, and if you have actually been thinking about adopting or fostering a child, then it is likely that you experienced a wish-fulfillment dream (and that your unconscious mind was giving positive reinforcement to your waking desire to bring a child into your family). But if you are in no way considering such an action in the waking world, then it is likely that your unconscious was casting a spotlight on your real desire to lavish love and affection on someone. In reality, has an object of affection been lacking from your life? You should consider the possibility that you would do well to find an outlet (not necessarily a child, but perhaps a partner, a pet, or a friend) through which to release your pent-up desire selflessly to care for and love someone. In another scenario, did you dream of fostering or adopting someone whom you actually know in the waking world? If so, it may be that you would like to demonstrate your love or affection for that person, or that you would enjoy acting as a mentor for him or her.

Negative Interpretations: Did you dream that when looking through your mother's things, you were dazed and upset when you accidentally came across a certificate that documented your parents' adoption of you? If so, and you have no such suspicions in the real world, then could your dream have been an unconscious reflection of your real-life feelings of disconnection from (or of not "fitting in" with) your family? Or could it be that you feel that your parents have been hiding something from you—perhaps something very important that pertains directly to you ? If, in your dream, you angrily confronted your parents about your discovery, and if they reacted by "coming clean" and apologizing, then your unconscious may be telling you that a similar waking confrontation may have some positive consequences.

My Adoption Dreams

✶ ✶

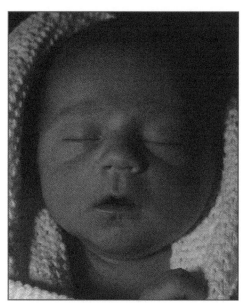

Baby Love
Did you dream that you had adopted an infant? If so, and it was a comforting dream, perhaps you crave the intimacy and unconditional love that is represented by a child. If you do not have children, could you be unconsciously yearning for a baby? But if the dream baby was swaddled in your feelings of stress and uncertainty, the message may have been that you are not yet ready for parenthood.

Related Dreams
pages 87, 101, 105, 252, 266 & 267

THE LIFE CYCLE

My Anniversaries & Holidays Dreams

✱ ✱ ✱ ✱ ✱ ✱ ✱ ✱ ✱ ✱ ✱ ✱ ✱ ✱ ✱ ✱ ✱

Celebrate Good Times

Have you had a positive dream about celebrating your anniversary with your real-life partner? If so, this could have been an unconscious reflection of your strong feelings for him or her. Are you easily able to express these feelings in your waking life? If not, maybe that's why these emotions are flooding into your dreams. Would it hurt to be more open about your love for your partner?

ANNIVERSARIES & HOLIDAYS

Anniversaries are usually celebratory occasions (often having to do with marriages or relationships), though anniversaries can also be of a more somber kind (the death of a loved one, a national tragedy etc.). But, in general, anniversaries usually mark the milestones of our lives—those events upon which we hitch our identity.

Symbolic and Verbal Associations
‹ A milestone
‹ Celebration; festivities
‹ Achievement
‹ Pride
‹ Excitement
‹ A demonstration of love (with regard to a wedding anniversary)

Positive Interpretations: If you had a dream about a special date or occasion, whether it was an anniversary or a seasonal holiday, this may have been an unconscious reflection of the fact that your waking self is looking forward to this annual celebration. Did your dream concern the anniversary of an attainment that you are particularly proud of? Or, could your dream have been a metaphorical self-"pat on the back" for having stayed with the same partner or employer for so long? Have others, in the real world, been indifferent to your "staying power," and do you wish that they would take notice and congratulate you for it? Alternatively, did you dream of celebrating a holiday that you especially enjoy? Celebratory holidays like Thanksgiving, Christmas, New Year's Eve, and Independence Day can mean many different things to different people, and it is important to think about your personal associations with a particular holiday (including your experience of this day) when it occurs in your dreams. For instance, if you dreamed of celebrating Christmas, and if Christmas is one of the few times when your entire family comes together and when the mood is happy and festive, then could your unconscious mind have been providing you with a wish-fulfillment dream (perhaps a sign that you could use some "family time" in the real world)?

Negative Interpretations: If you had a dream that highlighted a somber anniversary (be it the death of a friend or family member, or any other tragedy or sad occasion), then your unconscious may have been mirroring your actual dread of this approaching date. Or could it be that something in your waking life has triggered your memories of this unhappy event? On the other hand, if you dreamed of a holiday celebration "gone bad" (perhaps you had a dream of a family feud during Thanksgiving dinner), then are you afraid that a family problem or issue is about to erupt into a terrible argument or battle in the real world?

Related Dreams
pages 88, 102, 178,
253, 261 & 286

Birth

✳✳

When the unconscious mind summons the theme of birth into our dreams, the meaning often has less to do with a real-life baby than with a metaphorical one. Dreams of this nature may be a reference to the "inner child," or the "baby" within, or even to a part of yourself that longs to be reborn.

Symbolic and Verbal Associations
- The "inner child"
- Rebirth or a reawakening of some part of oneself; new potential
- Hopes and fears with regard to an actual pregnancy
- Laboring to give birth to an idea; a "brainchild"

Positive Interpretations: If you are a pregnant woman who dreamed of giving birth to your baby, then it is likely that your dream was a reflection of your hopes and fears with regard to your impending due date. (A similar interpretation will apply if you are a prospective father who dreamed of your partner giving birth.) If the dream labor and birthing were easy, then your unconscious was probably attempting to set your mind at ease with this wish-fulfillment dream. However, if you are a woman who dreamed of giving birth and if you are not actually pregnant in the real world, then it is possible that your dream was pointing to your desire to have a child. On the other hand, whether you are a man or a woman, a dream of giving birth may also be a reference to a "brainchild"—an idea, plan, or project that you have been thinking about during waking hours. Did the labor go smoothly? And were you ecstatic because you had given birth to a healthy newborn? If so, your unconscious mind was probably trying to reassure you that your plans will pan out well. Did your dream self give birth to twins? If so, your dream may have been a reference to "twin" ideas or aspects of yourself, such as your writing and musical talents.

Negative Interpretations: Did you dream of undergoing a difficult and painful labor? If so, and if you are actually pregnant, then your dream was probably mirroring your anxieties—perhaps in an effort to force you to face up to your fears, thereby strengthening you and preparing you for the upcoming day or night when you actually will go into labor. In your dream, were you surprised to see that you'd given birth to an animal, or even to a monster? Again, this sort of dream is likely to be a reference to your real-life worries. Or a dream of a difficult labor may be a reference to an idea or a "brainchild." Was the umbilical cord wrapped around your brainchild's neck? If so, then your unconscious may have been indicating that your idea is in danger of being "strangled at birth." Or if you labored in vain, unable to give birth to your baby, it is possible that your unconscious was trying to tell you that your waking plans or ideas will be difficult—if not impossible—to carry out at this time. The same interpretation may apply if, in your dream, you were aggrieved to have given birth to an unhealthy or a stillborn child.

Related Dreams
pages 91, 105, 109, 113, 145 & 240

My Birth Dreams

✳✳✳✳✳✳✳✳✳✳✳✳✳✳✳✳✳✳✳✳✳✳

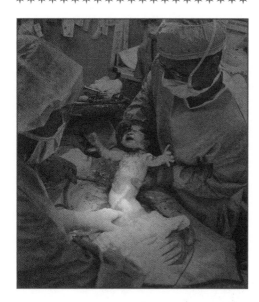

Labor Day

Are you a pregnant woman who dreamed about your baby being born? If so, this could have been a straightforward anxiety dream reflecting your hopes and fears surrounding not only the birth, but also your new life ahead, with a baby to care for. Was the birth easy or difficult? Was it something that you felt prepared for or not? Your dream experience may tell you more about how you really feel about bringing a child into the world.

THE LIFE CYCLE

My Birthday Dreams

✶ ✶ ✶ ✶ ✶ ✶ ✶ ✶ ✶ ✶ ✶ ✶ ✶ ✶ ✶

Make a Wish

Did you dream that it was your child's birthday and that you were celebrating together, yet felt inexplicably sad? If you really do have a child, this could mean that you sense how quickly time is passing and are concerned that you're missing out on your son or daughter's childhood. Do you wish that you could spend more time together during your waking hours?

BIRTHDAYS

In our youth, most of us look forward to our birthdays. As we grow older, however, many people begin to look with dread upon the occasion of adding another year to their age. In the same vein, some people love their birthday because it makes them the center of attention, while other people try to avoid celebrating their birthday for the same reason. When you are attempting to interpret a dream that threw a spotlight on your birthday, then, it is important to consider, among other things, your real-life feelings about this annual event.

Symbolic and Verbal Associations
- Being put in the spotlight: being the center of attention
- Excitement and anticipation
- Aging: the transition from one life stage to the next
- Knowledge, as in "another year older, another year wiser"
- Giving and receiving (gifts)

Positive Interpretations: Did you have a dream in which you looked at the calendar that hung on your wall and noticed, with glee, that the day of your birthday was circled in red and that it was just a few days away? And do you actually look forward to this annual celebration of your birth with excitement and anticipation? If so, is this because you love being the center of attention, if just for a day? If your birthday isn't for another six months, however, and you had a dream such as this, then could it be that you long to be made to feel special by those around you during your waking hours? Do you feel that others don't give you due acknowledgement for your special qualities, talents, or achievements?

Negative Interpretations: If you dreamed that your birthday was fast approaching or that the day itself had actually come, and if your dreaming reaction to this was the opposite of happiness, then did your dream express the way that you generally feel about celebrating your birthday in the real world? Does it make you feel uncomfortable when people make a fuss over your birthday because it puts you in the limelight—which your rather introverted and withdrawn nature cringes from? If so, is it possible that you have recently experienced discomfort in the real world because you feel that those around you have been giving you more credit for a waking achievement than you feel that you are deserving of? Or if your birthday is truly around the corner, then could your dream have been an unconscious manifestation of your anxiety about growing older? After a certain age, many people begin to dread the "big birthdays"—such as turning thirty, fifty, or seventy. So, if you are about to turn forty, and you dreamed that your loved ones surprised you with a birthday cake that had so many candles that it set the house on fire, then it is likely that your nightmare was an unconscious expression of your anxiety about reaching this milestone.

Related Dreams

pages 86, 87, 184, 245, 261 & 286

CHILDHOOD

✶✶

A dream youngster is often a symbol of the "inner child"—the aspect of oneself that is carefree, playful, and innocent. Childhood is also a time when we learn many of the lessons that we will keep with us and reference later in life, so that a dream in which you revisited some scenario from your childhood may have been an unconscious reminder of an important lesson that may have some relevance to your current situation.

Symbolic and Verbal Associations
◖ The "inner child"
◖ Fun; play
◖ Having a simple perspective on life
◖ Innocence and wonder
◖ Lessons learned

Positive Interpretations: Did a dream take you back to a pleasant memory from your childhood? Perhaps you were sitting contentedly on your father's lap while he read to you from your favorite book? There are two likely explanations for a dream of this sort. The first explanation is that your dream was an unconscious manifestation of your nostalgia for a simpler time, when life was filled with fun and you had no responsibilities and few worries. (The second explanation will be discussed below, in Negative Interpretations.) If your dream called up a child who you did not know, then your unconscious mind may have been summoning the archetype of the "inner child"—either as a representation of the part of you that never grew up, or as a reference to a part of you that you have lost (but that you would do well to regain).

Negative Interpretations: The other explanation for a nostalgic childhood dream is that, by reminding you of how happy and secure you felt as a small child, your unconscious mind was attempting to comfort you and to compensate for your adult unhappiness. If you are facing a difficult problem or situation in the real world, then it is also possible that your dream called upon the image of your father because he was someone who always gave you good advice; your unconscious mind may have been hinting that you would do well to remember the lessons that he taught you, or it may have been prompting you to seek out someone who would be likely to give you wise counsel in your present life. Alternatively, did you dream of a child who upset you with his or her bad or immature behavior? If so, could this have been a dream reference to your own childish bad conduct in the waking world? For instance, did you dream that you were watching a group of children playing, and that you were appalled when a bigger boy went up to a smaller girl and pushed her down into the dirt? If so, have you been playing the bully with someone less powerful than you—perhaps a junior colleague whom you've been dumping your workload onto?

Related Dreams
pages 99, 105, 109, 115, 282 & 287

THE LIFE CYCLE

My Childhood Dreams

✶ ✶ ✶ ✶ ✶ ✶ ✶ ✶ ✶ ✶ ✶ ✶ ✶ ✶ ✶ ✶ ✶ ✶ ✶ ✶

Playtime

If you dreamed that you were a small child again, playing with your soft toys, this could have been a case of nostalgia for those halcyon days when you could let your imagination run riot and your life was filled with fun. Consider slotting more creative and relaxation time into your daily routine.

THE LIFE CYCLE

My Coming of Age Dreams

✶ ✶ ✶ ✶ ✶ ✶ ✶ ✶ ✶ ✶ ✶ ✶ ✶ ✶ ✶ ✶ ✶

A Rite of Passage

Dreaming about graduation, one of life's significant milestones, could signify that you're anticipating entering a new phase. Have your circumstances recently changed, or are they on the verge of doing so? Or perhaps you unconsciously crave greater recognition of, and praise for, your achievements, be it in the workplace or at a more personal level.

COMING OF AGE

✶ ✶

In our culture today, there seems to be no consensus on when we enter adulthood. This is no wonder, when we are given adult freedoms in such small increments; for instance, we can get a driver's license at age sixteen, join the military at age eighteen, purchase alcohol at age twenty-one, and rent a car at age twenty-five! Each of these milestones will have varying degrees of personal significance for different people, however, and each of them (as well as many more, such as going to college, getting married, and achieving financial independence) are moments in which we step farther into the world of adults.

Symbolic and Verbal Associations
❨ Freedom
❨ Taking on adult responsibilities and making adult decisions
❨ Having to "stand on your own two feet"
❨ "Flying the nest," or leaving one's parents' home
❨ The "empty nest"

Positive Interpretations: Did you have a dream in which you relived some moment from your past that you felt represented the end of your childhood and that ushered you into your adult life? Perhaps it was the first time that you stood up to your father, or the day you moved into your first apartment? If so, and if you awoke from this dream with a thrilling rush of adrenaline, then it is likely that your unconscious mind summoned up this memory in order to remind you that it is once again time to take the initiative and to "stand on your own two feet" in the world. If you've been feeling somehow "smothered" or "kept down" in the real world—perhaps by an over-dominant partner or parent—then your unconscious may have been trying to remind you how positive and good it felt to "break loose" on your own.

Negative Interpretations: Did you dream that you stood weeping as your son read from the Torah at his bar mitzvah (the ceremony in which Jewish boys, at age thirteen, are initiated into adulthood)? And, in reality, did your son have his bar mitzvah years ago? If so, is he about to take another big life step, such as going away to college, joining the army, or getting married? If so, then your dream was probably a reflection of your sadness and fears with regard to "losing" your son; perhaps you feel as though your home will be an "empty nest" once he is "gone" from you. Or, did you dream that your daughter (who, in reality, is now happily married, with children of her own) was once again in her first term at college and rebelling against your authority by staying out at all hours and using illegal drugs or alcohol? If so, then could it be that you feel as though your daughter no longer consults you or wants to be "mothered" by you in the waking world? Or, as when she was in college, is she once again engaging in some activity that you feel is dangerous or destructive?

Related Dreams

pages 97, 194, 195, 258 & 296

CONCEPTION

✶✶✶

Conception has been a high-profile media topic for some time now, as many people who oppose the right to abortion maintain that life begins at the moment that we are conceived, while their opponents often argue that life truly begins at a later stage of fetal development, or even at birth. Everyone must agree, however, that conception is at least the dawn of the creation of a new potential life, and dreams that involve conception may be literal (especially if becoming pregnant has been on your mind) or they may be metaphors for creation of another type.

Symbolic and Verbal Associations
- Sexual union; the merging of male and female
- New beginnings; fresh potential
- Creation and creativity; the "fertilization" of a concept
- Apprehension about or fear of becoming pregnant

Positive Interpretations: If you are a woman, did you awake from a sexual dream in which you were certain that you had just conceived a baby? And were you overjoyed by that knowledge? If so, and if you are hoping to become pregnant in the real world, then you have probably experienced a wish-fulfillment dream (although it is also possible that your unconscious mind has detected that you are, in fact, pregnant, and that it sent you this dream in an attempt to bring this fact to your conscious attention). If you are a man who dreamed that your partner had conceived, which made your dream self very happy, then, likewise, your unconscious mind was probably giving expression to your fervent wish to have a child. However, there is another line of interpretation for dreams of this type. If you dreamed that you (or your partner) had conceived, and if nothing is farther from your mind, then your dream conception may have been a reference to the fertilization of a creative concept. Have you recently hit upon a good idea in the waking world?

Negative Interpretations: If you are a woman who had a dream in which you were apprehensive or uneasy because you thought that you had conceived a baby, then have you been debating whether to try to become pregnant in the waking world? If so, then your dream may have been a reflection of your real-life uncertainty as to whether having a child would be a good idea at this time. (Perhaps you feel you are not ready to expand your family, but have been feeling pressured to do so by your partner or your relatives.) If you were horror-struck by your dream conception, then it is likely that your dream was expressing your waking fears that you have accidentally conceived (or could accidentally conceive) a child—and your unconscious may have been attempting to jolt you into taking more sound precautions against pregnancy. Similar interpretations will apply if you are a man who reacted ambivalently or negatively to a dream that your partner had conceived.

Related Dreams
pages 87, 101 & 105

My Conception Dreams

✶ ✶ ✶ ✶ ✶ ✶ ✶ ✶ ✶ ✶ ✶ ✶ ✶ ✶ ✶ ✶ ✶ ✶ ✶

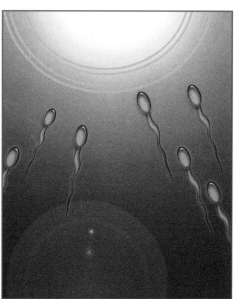

Fertile Thoughts

If you are a man who dreamed that you were a sperm, racing toward an egg, your dream may have pointed to a feeling of anxiety about your virility. Are you in a relationship in which your partner is trying to conceive? If so, your worries may be surfacing in your sleep. If, in your dream, you reached your goal and fertilized the egg, are you feeling macho and self-confident, either sexually or more generally?

My Death Dreams

✱ ✱ ✱ ✱ ✱ ✱ ✱ ✱ ✱ ✱ ✱ ✱ ✱ ✱ ✱ ✱ ✱ ✱

A New Phase

Dreaming about death, or about visiting a loved one's grave in a cemetery, doesn't necessarily signify something ominous or negative. Death doesn't only represent an ending, it also symbolizes a beginning, and may point to a period of profound change. Did you dream about the death of someone you know with whom you haven't been in touch for some time? If so, this could be your guilty conscience telling you to make contact.

DEATH

✱✱

Although everyone knows that they and their loved ones must one day die, not many people like to think about this fact, and, for most people, dreams that involve death are among the most disturbing. When our unconscious mind forces us to experience dreams about death, however, there are many possible interpretations, and not all of them have to do with the actual ending of someone's life.

Symbolic and Verbal Associations
- Loss
- Endings (and beginnings); the end of a relationship
- Life changes
- Loneliness

Positive Interpretations: Did you awake in tears from a dream in which you watched as your grandmother died? If so, and if your grandmother's health is failing in the real world, then your dream probably reflected your sadness at the thought of losing her, and it may also have been your unconscious's way of preparing you for her inevitable demise. If, in your dream, you felt greatly relieved at your grandmother's passing, then it may be that you have already come to terms with her approaching death, which you know will release her from her suffering. But if you dreamed of the death of a loved one who is quite well in the real world, then it could be that this person represented some part of yourself or your life that either is passing away or that you would like to be done with. Unless your own death is near (if you suffer from a fatal disease, for instance), then a dream that highlights your own death is highly unlikely to portend your actual demise. There are three possible explanations for a dream such as this: first, that you are concerned about your health (in which case, a visit to the doctor may be in order); second, that you seek an "escape" from the world; or, third, that your dream death signaled a life change that you are about to make (which is a sort of metaphorical death, but also a new beginning).

Negative Interpretations: A dream involving the death of a loved one may also reflect our own feelings of guilt about having neglected our responsibilities to that person or about our failure to tell them how much they mean to us. This type of interpretation may apply if, for instance, you dreamed that your sister had died, and if you were deeply saddened—not just by her passing, but also because you had not gotten a last chance to tell her that you love her. Another interpretation is that you feel as though your sister has been drifting away from you, and you feel that your relationship with her is in danger of ending altogether (in which case, your unconscious may have been trying to prompt you to mend the rift between your sister and yourself). Alternatively, if you felt happy or liberated by your sister's dream death, this may reflect your unconscious desire to end your relationship with her, perhaps because you feel it has become unhealthy for you.

Related Dreams

pages 96, 100, 223, 252, 254 & 272

DIVORCE

✶✶

The unhappy flip side of marital happiness, divorce tends to be a messy and cheerless thing to go through—for both divorcee and divorcer alike. Likewise, dreams that involve a separation or divorce from one's spouse tend to be equally cheerless. However, like most dream symbols, a dream divorce does not always stand for a real-life divorce, and dreams that have to do with divorce are not always negative.

Symbolic and Verbal Associations
- Anxiety about one's marital health
- Longing to escape a marriage
- A desire to separate from something to which you are "wedded"
- Independence
- Reinvigoration; freedom from inertia

Positive Interpretations: If you had a dream in which you were shocked and grieved because your wife told you that she wanted to divorce you, it is possible that your unconscious mind sent you this dream in order to remind you how lucky you are to have such a wonderful wife—and also to warn you not to take her for granted. However, there is another line of interpretation for divorce-related dreams, which may have nothing at all to do with your actual marriage. It could be that, in your dream, your wife or husband stood for something else to which you are "wedded," such as a job or an ideal, but which has started to make you unhappy. If so, your unconscious mind may have been trying to tell you that it's time to quit your job or to open your mind to other ideals or points of view, thereby reinvigorating your life or your mindset and freeing you from the inertia that has set in.

Negative Interpretations: Did you have a nightmare in which your husband told you that he was moving out and that he wanted a divorce? If so, it could be that you are concerned about the health of your marriage—a concern that may be well-founded, but which also could be a figment of your imagination (and only you will know which is true). If, in your dream, your husband told you that he had been cheating on you with another woman, then this may reflect your insecurity about your husband's love for you, whether or not this insecurity is grounded in reality. It could also be that you have unconsciously detected signs that your husband might really be cheating on you, in which case your dream may have been an unconscious attempt to prepare you for this worst-case scenario. But if your dream self was relieved to hear your husband tell you that your marriage was over, or if, in your dream, it was you who told your wife that you wanted to separate or divorce, then you should consider whether you may have a desire (although it may be unconscious) to escape from your marriage, perhaps because it has become stagnant or because you and your spouse have grown apart emotionally.

Related Dreams
pages 102, 107, 116, 218, 252 & 258

My Divorce Dreams

✶✶✶✶✶✶✶✶✶✶✶✶✶✶✶✶✶✶✶✶✶✶

A Parting of the Ways

Did you dream that you and your husband rowed and that he told you that he wanted a divorce? Such a dream could be a manifestation of your anxiety about the health of your marriage. How did you feel in the dream? If you were filled with a sense of relief, could it be that you secretly desire a divorce or separation, but don't want to be the one who first suggests it? Perhaps it's time to be more forthcoming about what you really want.

THE LIFE CYCLE

My Engagement Dreams

★ ★ ★ ★ ★ ★ ★ ★ ★ ★ ★ ★ ★ ★ ★ ★ ★

Diamonds are Forever

Did you have a dream in which your boyfriend proposed to you and presented you with an engagement ring? If so, this may point to your desire for a greater level of commitment from others, whether in your romantic relationship, a friendship, or at work. Or perhaps it is conventionality that you desire. Alternatively, do you feel that your life has taken too many dramatic turns, so that you're longing for more stability?

ENGAGEMENT

✴ ✴

To engage, in the strictest literal sense, means "to seize" or "to occupy." And, in a way, that is what we do when we get engaged to be married: we choose to make a commitment to stay with someone, ideally not to part until death separates us (as the traditional marriage vows state). Whether or not a dream of getting engaged is a reference to a real-life engagement to be married, it is almost certainly a reference to making a commitment of some sort.

Symbolic and Verbal Associations
‹ Love and romance; devotion to someone or something
‹ Commitment
‹ The union of two opposing ideas or characteristics
‹ A contract or business venture
‹ The balance or unification of masculinity and femininity

Positive Interpretations: If you are a woman, did you have a dream in which your boyfriend got down on one knee, declared his endless love for you, and slipped a large diamond ring onto your finger? If so, and if you fervently wish that your boyfriend would propose to you, then your dream was almost certainly mirroring your desire to become engaged. The same interpretation is likely to apply if you are a man who dreamed of proposing marriage to your girlfriend, whom you love dearly. However, if you are already happily married, or if marriage is the farthest thing from your mind, and if you dreamed that someone pleaded with you to marry them, then you should think about who this person is and what you associate them with in the real world. Their proposal most likely symbolized a commitment that you may have been (or are about to be) asked to make. For example, if, in your dream, it was your best friend who asked you to marry her, then could her proposal have symbolized her real-life desire for the two of you to quit your jobs and go into business together? If so, then your dreaming reaction to her proposal may give you a clue as to how you really feel about her business idea.

Negative Interpretations: Did you have a dream in which your boyfriend asked you to marry him, and did your dream self react with ambivalence or indecision? If so, and if you feel that he may be about to "pop the question" in the waking world, then your dream may indicate that you are unsure about whether you would want to commit to spending the rest of your life with him. Or if, in your dream, you reacted with extreme negativity, perhaps by throwing the engagement ring back into your boyfriend's face and telling him that you had no wish ever to marry him, then this may also be an indication of how you really feel about your boyfriend. But if it seems unlikely to you that your dream was referencing a real-life proposal, then an examination of the details and the situation of the dream may give you clues as to its meaning. Who was it who made you the proposal, and what in your waking world might the proposal represent?

Related Dreams

pages 73, 102, 116,

242 & 267

FIRST DATE/KISS

* *

THE LIFE CYCLE

Nostalgic dreams, in general, are often unconscious attempts to bring us comfort—particularly during times when we are unhappy or dissatisfied in our waking life. This is also true for dreams that take us back to the first time that we went out on a date or kissed someone, memories that are often (though not always) happy ones.

Symbolic and Verbal Associations
- Nostalgia
- Comfort
- Romance
- Unhappiness with one's present relationship
- Hope for future happiness in love
- Coming to terms with unhappy memories: resolution

Positive Interpretations: Did you have a dream that took you back to that first time that you went out on a date with your husband, when the two of you drove in his convertible to see a drive-in movie? And did your dream depict that electric moment when you leaned toward each other, over the bucket of popcorn that sat between you, and let your lips join together in your first kiss? If so, and if your life with your husband now is less than electric—perhaps things have become routine, and your sex life is barely existent—then your unconscious mind may have sent you this dream in order to bring you comfort in your sadness, and also perhaps to remind you of a time when you were happy with your (then future) husband, and why you fell in love with him in the first place, so that you might take heart and decide to do something to try to rekindle the romance between you. Another possible interpretation for a dream of this sort—especially if it seems unlikely that it pertains to your current love life—is that it was your unconscious mind's attempt to spur you into adding more romance back into your life—not necessarily with a partner, but perhaps in your work, play, or creative pursuits.

Negative Interpretations: Not all of our first-date and first-kiss memories will be positive ones—especially if things went terribly bad, if our partner is now deceased, or if we are no longer together with him or her for some other reason. Sometimes the unconscious will send us unhappy nostalgic dreams in order to force us to face up to painful memories, so that we can move beyond them and get on with our lives. So if your wife has been dead for three years, and if you recently dreamed about the first night that the two of you got together as a couple, a memory that you have been desperately trying to push out of your conscious thought because it hurts you too much to think about it, then it is likely that your unconscious mind gave you this dream in order to help you to embrace your pain and to move past it (and maybe you should consider whether it's time to start dating again).

My First Date/Kiss Dreams

----

* * * * * * * * * * * * * * * * * * * *

Young Love

Dreaming about your first kiss, that electric moment when your lips first touched someone else's, could be a sign of dissatisfaction with your current situation. Could it be that returning to a memory that represents sexual and emotional awakening and excitement is a way of unconsciously comforting yourself for the lack of these elements in your life at present?

Related Dreams

pages 90, 112, 267, 268 & 272

My Funerals Dreams

✳ ✳ ✳ ✳ ✳ ✳ ✳ ✳ ✳ ✳ ✳ ✳ ✳ ✳ ✳ ✳ ✳ ✳

Passing Away

Having a dream about a ritual associated with death could indicate a need to lay something to rest. This may not necessarily mean saying goodbye to a person who has died, and could instead suggest letting something else go: perhaps a job, a fixed idea, a relationship, or something that you have been banking on. Through the symbolism of the funeral ritual, you may unconsciously be working through these issues and preparing to move on.

FUNERALS

The rituals associated with death—funerals, burials, and cremations—are carried out in different ways by different peoples, and these rites have changed over time. However, the basic tenets behind these customs have not changed, the primary purpose being to allow people a chance to say their goodbyes to their loved one, and to dispense with the body in some ritualistic and respectful way. And in the world of dreams, funerals and the like oftentimes have to do with the recognition of something that is passing from our lives.

Symbolic and Verbal Associations
- Something that you wish to "bury" or "lay to rest"
- Mourning over the loss of something
- Praise for one's positive attributes; eulogizing
- The need for validation and praise
- Having to "undertake" a disagreeable task
- Feeling as though you are "boxed in"
- Transformation or rebirth (with regard to cremation)

Positive Interpretations: If you had a dream that involved a funeral, it is likely that your unconscious was not pointing to a literal death in the real world. Unless you have been troubled with worries about your (or someone else's) health or safety, it could well be that your dream funeral was a representation of something in your current life that you would like to (or which you are about to) "bury" or "lay to rest." This could even be a relationship that you would like to end—particularly if the funeral was not your own. And if your dream focused in on an undertaker—or especially if you were cast in that role yourself—you may want to ask yourself whether your dream could have been an unconscious reference to an unpleasant task that you must soon "undertake" in the waking world.

Negative Interpretations: Did you dream that you stood by, unseen by others, watching your own funeral take place? If so, was your dream self curious about what your friends and family would say about you? Because eulogies tend to focus on the positive qualities of the dear departed (there is an old superstition that it is bad luck to "speak ill of the dead"), your dream may signal that you are in need of an ego boost: perhaps you have been feeling overly criticized by your loved ones, who you wish would give you more praise in the real world. And especially if your dream self felt satisfied or validated at watching others grieve over your death, it is likely that you have been feeling hurt or ignored by those whose approval and appreciation you seek. Or did you have a dream in which you were aghast to find yourself lying in a coffin? If so, have you been feeling isolated or "boxed in" during your waking hours?

Related Dreams

pages 92, 149, 207, 212, 254 & 272

LOSS OF VIRGINITY

✦✦✦✦✦✦✦✦✦✦✦✦✦✦✦✦✦✦✦✦✦✦✦✦✦✦✦✦✦✦✦✦✦✦✦✦✦✦

The loss of virginity is a milestone in most people's lives, having to do with growing up and assuming an adult identity. A dream of losing your virginity can have a number of different meanings, depending on whether you are someone who has yet to have had sex for the first time or whether you lost your virginity long ago (and also depending on the current state of your love life).

Symbolic and Verbal Associations
- Sexual curiosity
- Maturation; entrance into adulthood
- Losing one's "innocence"; disillusionment
- Anticipation of, or anxiety about, losing one's virginity in real life
- The need to rejuvenate, or reintroduce excitement to, one's sex life

Positive Interpretations: The onset of puberty causes many hormonal changes to our bodies, and it is normal for adolescents to have erotic dreams. So if you are a young person who has never had sex and you dreamed of losing your virginity, this was probably a combination of your natural physiological changes, together with a healthy waking curiosity regarding what it would be like to have sex with someone. In this case, your dreaming mind was probably reflecting your conscious anticipation and worries about losing your virginity—and also giving you the opportunity to experience, in the safety of the dream world, how you would feel. But if you lost your virginity many years ago and you recently had a dream that carried you back to the excitement and the exhilaration of the first time that you had sex, then it is quite possible that your unconscious mind was mirroring the real-life sexual "renaissance" that you have been going through. For instance, have you recently begun dating someone who thrills you more than anyone has in a long time, so that when you make love with this person, you feel as excited and expectant as if you were once again making love for the first time ever?

Negative Interpretations: If you are far from being a virgin and you dreamed of the time that you first made love with someone, and if your waking sex life has become dull, routine, or nonexistent, your unconscious may have sent you this dream as a wish-fulfillment—and perhaps also to remind you of how good and healthy it felt to have exciting, passionate sex, so that you might seek out ways to reinvigorate this aspect of your life. Or if you awoke disappointed or saddened by a dream of losing your virginity, then could your unconscious mind have been pointing to your recent disillusionment or "loss of innocence" in the real world? Perhaps you have found out that someone whom you cared for or trusted deeply has turned out to be a back-stabbing liar or cheater. (Thinking about the details of your dream may give you a clue. Where did your dream take place, and who was it that you lost your virginity to?)

Related Dreams

pages 47, 90, 95, 242, 268 & 274

THE LIFE CYCLE

My Loss of Virginity Dreams

✦✦✦✦✦✦✦✦✦✦✦✦✦✦✦✦✦✦✦✦✦✦

Like a Virgin

The meaning of a dream about losing your virginity depends entirely on how the experience was in the dream. Were you scared and insecure about experiencing this milestone, one that represents a transfer into the adult world, or were you relieved and happy? Also, to whom did you surrender your virginity? Could your dream have been an unconscious expression of your desire to be seduced by that person in real life?

THE LIFE CYCLE

MISCARRIAGES

* *

My Miscarriages Dreams

----

* * * * * * * * * * * * * * * * * *

Loss and Disappointment

If you are a pregnant woman who longs for your baby's safe arrival, but dreamed of miscarrying, your nightmare was probably simply a reflection of your hopes, anxieties, and fears. Otherwise, could your dream miscarriage have represented the actual, imminent, or threatened termination, abortion, or failure to reach fruition of a cherished plan in the waking world?

If you dreamed that you had a miscarriage, an abortion, or a stillbirth, you probably awoke feeling saddened and disturbed (at the very least). All of these things have to do with an expulsion of something (or someone) from ourselves, which will also be reflected in the various dream-world meanings.

Symbolic and Verbal Associations
- Anxiety (possibly—but not necessarily—about pregnancy)
- A concept or idea that is doomed to failure
- The desire to abort (or rid oneself of) something
- Feelings of guilt
- A "miscarriage" of duty or justice

Positive Interpretations: A dream of having a miscarriage, an abortion, or a stillbirth (particularly if you are actually pregnant) probably left you feeling deeply upset when you awoke. However, if you are really pregnant, while it is always a possibility that your nightmare was a message from your unconscious mind that your unborn child is not developing properly, the far more likely scenario is that your unconscious was reflecting your normal feelings of anxiety with regard to your pregnancy. Alternatively, could your dream abortion or miscarriage have been an unconscious clue that you are not ready to make some great personal sacrifice, such as becoming a mother (and therefore assuming complete responsibility for another human being) would require?

Negative Interpretations: Particularly if you are a man, or if you are a woman who is not pregnant, the vast majority of dream miscarriages, abortions, or stillbirths will refer to an idea or concept that you have "conceived," which your unconscious mind may be telling you is doomed to fail. How did your dream self react? Was the termination of your dream pregnancy against your will? If so, was someone else responsible? And could you identify that person? It is possible that your unconscious mind cast him or her in the role of your abortionist in order to signal that he or she is set on thwarting some plan of yours in the real world. (Perhaps it was your neighbor, who has been secretly hacking away at your rose bushes because he is jealous that they might grower higher than his own.) However, if your dream self wanted the abortion, or was glad for your miscarriage, then it is possible that (for whatever reason) your unconscious mind was warning you against the current plan or idea that has been developing in your mind. Or could your dream of having an abortion have been a metaphor for something that you feel guilty about in the waking world? (If so, your unconscious may have been prompting you to "kill off" or to "get rid of" the evidence of whatever has been causing you distress.)

Related Dreams

pages 87, 92, 105, 254, 271 & 273

NAMING CEREMONIES

****

Naming ceremonies and Christian baptisms, which involve name-giving, are both initiations and formal presentations of either a child or an adult to the community. In the language of dreams, baptisms and naming ceremonies often have to do with "transformation" or "cleansing," since the person who undergoes one of these ritual initiations is usually considered to have been in some way "reborn."

Symbolic and Verbal Associations
- The formal presentation of a concept or idea
- Community acceptance
- The washing-away or cleansing of "original sin" (the Christian baptism)
- Being "reborn"; transformation
- Taking on, or turning to, advisors or guides (godparents)

Positive Interpretations: Did you dream that you stood holding a small baby, with your family and friends gathered all around you, as the child went through its formal naming ceremony? If so, and if it is not likely that your dream had to do with a real-life child, then could your dream baby have represented an idea or concept that you have been thinking about, which you are about ready to present (or have recently presented) to those around you? Perhaps you have been seriously thinking about forming your own business, in which case your unconscious may be saying that now is the right time to move forward and "go public" with your plan. (If so, how did your dream self feel as you stood holding the child? Were you proud? Excited? Nervous?) In your dream, were there any godparents standing by? If so, who were they? Your unconscious may have been saying that these people will be able to offer you help and support with your new project.

Negative Interpretations: In Christianity, baptisms and christenings (whether they are of babies, children, or adults) have to do with the washing-away of the "original sin" that was brought on humankind by Adam and Eve when they ate of the forbidden fruit in the Garden of Eden. Baptism also represents a symbolic death (being submerged in water) and also a renewal (re-emerging from the waters of rebirth). So if you are a Christian and you dreamed of someone (perhaps it was you) undergoing baptism, your dream may have been mirroring your waking desire for that person (perhaps yourself) to undergo a life-changing transformation. For instance, if it was you who was being baptized in your dream, have you been feeling depressed or unhealthy in your waking life? Could your unconscious mind have been urging you to make the necessary changes to turn your life around in a positive direction, to be "reborn" as a new, more healthy, person?

Related Dreams
pages 87, 105, 149, 212, 261 & 270

My Naming Ceremonies Dreams

....
....
....
....
....
....
....
....
....

* *

A Life-changing Experience
Did you dream that you were holding a baby as it underwent a formal naming ceremony? Dreaming about these kinds of rituals can symbolize the idea of transformation or of something being reborn. Are you currently in the process of coming up with a new idea or plan that you wish to impart to others? If so, "going public" may also be represented by the naming of the baby in your dream.

THE LIFE CYCLE

My Old Age Dreams

✱ ✱ ✱ ✱ ✱ ✱ ✱ ✱ ✱ ✱ ✱ ✱ ✱ ✱ ✱ ✱ ✱ ✱

A Wisdom Quest

Are you a young person who dreamed of growing old? This could point to a feeling of anxiety about aging, but if the dream was positive, it could suggest that you are seeking a sense of wisdom and serenity in your waking life. Perhaps, in the dream, you were at peace with yourself and the world. If so, is this a state of mind that you find difficult to attain while coping with the stresses of modern life?

OLD AGE

✱✱✱✱✱✱✱✱✱✱✱✱✱✱✱✱✱✱✱✱✱✱✱✱✱✱✱✱✱✱✱✱✱✱✱✱✱✱✱

When our unconscious mind places an older person at the forefront of our dreams, it may do so in order to highlight those positive qualities that we associate with old age: experience, wisdom, and kindness. But, like most dream symbols, old age also has a flip or dark side, having to do with cruelty and the selfish use of power.

Symbolic and Verbal Associations
‹ Wisdom and guidance
‹ The archetype of the priest or the priestess
‹ The archetypal witch or the black magician
‹ Anxiety with regard to growing older
‹ Mortality: decline and death

Positive Interpretations: If your dream cast a spotlight on an older man or woman, did you know who he or she was? If it was one of your grandparents, for instance, then his or her appearance in your dream may have filled you with a feeling of happy nostalgia, perhaps reminding you of how simple and good life could be when you were a child. And because we tend to associate growing older with achieving a certain amount of wisdom, you may want to consider whether the older person whom you dreamed of could have represented an archetype—perhaps the priestess (the wise old woman) or the priest (the wise old man)—thereby indicating that you are in need of some guidance in the waking world. (In your dream, what did the older person say to you?) Or if your dream image was one of yourself, well-aged and contented, perhaps sitting on your front porch and bouncing your young grandchild on your knee, then have you been feeling stressed and frazzled in your waking hours? Do you wish that you could retire from your job and enjoy the rest of your days in peace? Your unconscious may have sent you this dream in order to give you a taste of the release that you seek.

Negative Interpretations: Did you dream of an older person who, by their wickedness, filled you with dread? The negative aspects of the priestess and the priest are the archetypes of the witch and the black magician. Though equally knowledgeable and powerful, these characters use their knowledge and power destructively, to advance their own dark agendas. Did you recognize the evil elder in your dream? Your unconscious may have been warning you that you should scrutinize the motives of this person, who may be intending to do you ill. Or could the witch's or the black magician's appearance in your dream have been a signal that your own dark side has begun to gain power over you? Alternatively, if you had a dream in which you were horrified to discover that you had rapidly advanced in years, so that you had become, all of a sudden, an old man or woman, then it is likely that your unconscious was expressing your fears or regrets about the inevitability of growing older and—ultimately—your own mortality.

Related Dreams
pages 92, III, 133, 134 & 197

PARENTHOOD

✦✦✦✦✦✦✦✦✦✦✦✦✦✦✦✦✦✦✦✦✦✦✦✦✦✦✦✦✦✦✦✦✦✦✦✦✦✦

THE LIFE CYCLE

T‌he parent–child relationship is one of the strongest and most fundamentally important relationships that exist, and, therefore, the concept of parenting lends a generous load of fodder to the symbolic world of dreams.

Symbolic and Verbal Associations
- ‌ Care-giving (both physical and emotional)
- ‌ Providing guidance to (and exerting authority over) someone
- ‌ The "child within"
- ‌ Your hopes or fears with regard to a symbolic "child" (a plan or idea, perhaps)
- ‌ Frustration with demands that others make upon us; lack of personal time

Positive Interpretations: Did you dream that you were the proud parent of a healthy, happy son or daughter? If you do not have any children in the real world—and if, in fact, having children is the farthest thing from your mind—then it is likely that your dream was a reference to a symbolic "child"—perhaps a plan or idea of yours that has begun to grow and prosper in the real world. If the child was excessively demanding of your attention, then your unconscious may have been indicating that your "brain-child" will require a lot of nurturing from you in order for it to thrive. Alternatively, did you find your dream self "parenting" someone whom you know in the real world—maybe a friend or a coworker? If so, then you may want to ask yourself whether you have been feeling protective of, or responsible for, this person, or if this person somehow needs your help or guidance. (And your dream self's reaction is likely to be an indication of the health of your relationship with him or her in the waking world.)

Negative Interpretations: If you had a dream in which you were the parent of a child who screamed constantly, so that your peace of mind was wrecked to bits, then your unconscious mind may have been indicating that you have been neglecting or failing to care for your new idea or project properly (perhaps you have taken on more responsibility than you are currently capable of handling). Or if you had a nightmare in which you lost, injured, or otherwise allowed some harm to come to your dream child, then do you fear that your self-perceived flaws or inadequacies will cause a similar fate to befall the budding blossom of your imagination (or your hard work) in the real world? However, if your dream child corresponded with someone from your waking world (perhaps your actual child), then it is likely that your dream was mirroring your current mental state. Have you been feeling overburdened (and guilt-ridden) by the demands of others (perhaps your real-life children), so that you find that you are unable to cope with everyday life?

Related Dreams
pages 105, 109, 113, 121, 259 & 267

My Parenthood Dreams

✦✦✦✦✦✦✦✦✦✦✦✦✦✦✦✦✦✦✦✦✦✦

Bringing up Baby
Did you dream that you were a parent, and that you and your partner were playing with your child? Dreaming about such an idyllic domestic setting may indicate that you desire this situation in your waking life. Or perhaps you would like to feel more connected to, and intimate with, younger family members or friends. Alternatively, do you long to feel more needed and appreciated by others?

My Wedding Dreams

----

* * * * * * * * * * * * * * * * * * *

A Special Day

Are you a woman who dreamed that it was your wedding day, and that you were standing before a congregation facing the love of your life? Was the groom a man who you secretly desire, perhaps a friend who has no idea that you feel this way about him? If so, it is likely that your dream represents your suppressed yearnings. Or perhaps the groom was faceless and your wedding dream represents a more general longing to be in a relationship and to share your life with someone special.

WEDDINGS

* *

For many people, their wedding day is a day on which their life changes significantly, and (presumably) forever, because it is the day when they formally bind themselves to another. In dreams, weddings often have to do with unions and partnerships, but also with sacrifice.

Symbolic and Verbal Associations
- Romance, love, and desire
- Union (perhaps of your masculine and feminine aspects); a working partnership
- Being "tied" to someone, theoretically for life
- Self-sacrifice
- "Losing" someone to marriage, as in "giving away" the bride

Positive Interpretations: Did you dream that you stood before a congregation of your family and friends as you gazed into the eyes of someone and pledged to love him or her for the rest of your days? If you are actually engaged, then your dream was probably reflecting your hopes and wishes. However, if you have no immediate plans to marry in the real world, there are a number of possible interpretations for a dream such as this. It could be that you have romantic feelings for your dream bride or groom. Or it could be that your unconscious was telling you that you would do well to form some sort of partnership with this person (perhaps a joint business venture). Alternatively, especially if you did not recognize the person who you were marrying, or if you dreamed of watching someone else get married, your dream may have been signaling the need to unite two different (but complementary) aspects of your character—perhaps your masculine and feminine (or intellectual and intuitive) aspects.

Negative Interpretations: Did you have a dream in which you realized, with terror, that marrying your betrothed was the last thing in the world that you wanted to do, and did you seek to escape while, at the same time, you felt compelled to continue down the aisle toward the altar (which, in symbolic terms, denotes sacrifice)? If you are engaged to be married in the real world, then your nightmare may have been highlighting your misgivings in order to make you face and evaluate them on a conscious level before your wedding day arrives—and, ultimately, either to come to terms with them or to call off the wedding. Or if you had a dream in which you watched unhappily as someone you know got married, could it be that you are afraid of "losing" that person to another, or else that you feel jealous of the bridegroom or the bride? Finally, if you dreamed of going through a wedding ceremony with your current spouse, and if you feel that the love or the intimacy in your marriage has waned, then your unconscious may have been prompting you to take steps to bring romance back into your relationship (perhaps by planning a special dinner or a second honeymoon).

Related Dreams

pages 70, 94, 116, 149 & 242

CHAPTER 4
RELATIONSHIPS

Because we see or communicate with them regularly, and perhaps even daily, or they remain present in our thoughts even if physically absent, it is hardly surprising that our dreams are typically populated by the people with whom we interact in the real world. And when they materialize in dreamland, they may either represent themselves and the type of relationship that we actually have—or else hope or fear having—with them, or they may symbolize a certain characteristic within ourselves.

My Acquaintances Dreams

★ ★ ★ ★ ★ ★ ★ ★ ★ ★ ★ ★ ★ ★ ★ ★ ★ ★ ★

Close Encounters

Did you dream that you were rubbing shoulders with someone whom you barely know? Perhaps it was someone who is on the periphery of your life, whom you see regularly, but have never actually spoken to. If so, your dream may have been a simple expression of your desire to know this person better. Is there a special someone whom you've had your eye on, yet are too shy to approach?

ACQUAINTANCES

When the dreaming mind focuses in on someone whom we are only acquainted with, whom we don't know very well at all, it usually chooses to do so for a reason—though the reason might not have anything to do with this person directly.

Symbolic and Verbal Associations
- The desire to know someone better
- A budding friendship
- Romantic attraction
- An aspect (or a desired aspect) of one's own personality
- A warning of danger (depending on the circumstances of the dream)

Positive Interpretations: Were you surprised by a dream that cast a spotlight on someone whom you hardly know? If so, then your unconscious mind may have had a significant reason for sending you this dream. For instance, if you dreamed that you were sharing an intimate dinner with this person, and that the two of you were telling each other personal things—things that you only share with your closest friends—then it is possible that your dream was an unconscious indication that you would like to get to know this person better, and perhaps to become their friend in the real world. It is also possible that you have romantic feelings for this person (and only you will know whether or not this is true). But if neither of these explanations seems likely, you may want to ask yourself what this person represents to you. What aspects or qualities do you associate with him or her? Your unconscious may have been urging you to develop these qualities within your own personality better.

Negative Interpretations: Did you have a nightmare in which someone whom you are only vaguely acquainted with played a sinister role? For instance, did you dream that the man who lives a few doors up the street was prowling around outside your house with a knife in his hand? If so, there are a few possible explanations as to why your dreaming mind might conjure up such a scenario. One explanation is that your unconscious has picked up on something about this person that it is trying to relay to your conscious mind. Perhaps you have unconsciously decided that your neighbor has predatory qualities and that he is up to no good. Another explanation is that your unconscious has detected that you may be in danger of some sort of attack (though not necessarily physical) from outside your immediate sphere, and it cast your innocent neighbor in this menacing role in order to alert you and to put you on your guard. Alternatively, it is also quite possible that your unconscious was pointing to some dark or disturbing aspect of your own personality (or your recent behavior). Whether or not any of these explanations seem likely, thinking about the details of your dream may give you more information as to the message that your unconscious was trying to relay.

Related Dreams
pages 110, 130, 188, 278 & 286

CHILDREN

Because the parent–child relationship is usually very strong, and because most parents are deeply in tune with what is happening with their children, the meaning of a dream that involves one's own child is often very clear-cut and easy to deduce.

Symbolic and Verbal Associations
* Maternal or paternal feelings
* Ideological progeny: a "brainchild"
* A masculine or feminine archetype
* Childlike attitudes or behavior

Positive Interpretations: If you are a parent who had a dream that involved your child, then the meaning of your dream is probably a straightforward one. For instance, if you dreamed that you were filled with pride and love as you watched your daughter perform the lead role in a school play, then it is likely that your dream was an expression of the pride and love that you feel for your daughter in the real world. On the other hand, if you had a dream such as this, but, in reality, you do not have any children, then it is possible that you experienced a wish-fulfillment dream. It is also possible that your dream child represented a "brainchild"—an idea, plan, or project that you have given (or are about to give) life to. However, if none of these explanations seems likely, then you should ask yourself whether your dream child could have represented one of the many masculine or feminine archetypes—especially the princess (the unspoiled heroine), the prince (who represents the idealistic and questing nature of youth), the amazon (who represents the intellect and practicality), the warrior (the archetypical hero), or the trickster (an attention-seeker who uses jests and tricks to sabotage the status quo—often for good reason).

Negative Interpretations: Again, because a dream that involves one's own child can usually be taken at face value, if you are a parent who dreamed that your daughter was in danger or that she had been injured, then you are probably worried about her safety in the real world. (Has she recently taken up a sport or hobby that involves physical risk, such as skateboarding?) Or did you have a dream in which your son railed against you for not understanding where he is "coming from" or for not taking his opinions seriously? If so, it is likely that your unconscious mind was trying to alert you to the fact that, in reality, you haven't been listening to, or giving enough attention to, your son, and that you would do well to prioritize spending some "quality" time with him. However, especially if you do not have children of your own, you should consider whether your dream child may have represented one of the dark or more sinister archetypes, including the siren (or selfish seductress), the wastrel (the irresponsible philanderer), the huntress (who hunts down and uses others for her own purposes), or the villain (who uses cunning or violence for evil ends).

My Children Dreams

✳ ✳ ✳ ✳ ✳ ✳ ✳ ✳ ✳ ✳ ✳ ✳ ✳ ✳ ✳ ✳ ✳ ✳ ✳

Child's Play
Are you a parent who dreamed of your children? If the dream was positive, and you were watching them play while basking in feelings of love, this suggests that you are feeling comfortable with, and, indeed, are reveling in, your parental role. Are you currently at a point where you feel practically and emotionally able to support your children, so that you are simply enjoying them?

Related Dreams
pages 87, 89, 101, 126, 127 & 131

My Enemies Dreams

....

....

....

....

....

....

....

....

....

✴ ✴ ✴ ✴ ✴ ✴ ✴ ✴ ✴ ✴ ✴ ✴ ✴ ✴ ✴ ✴ ✴

Friend or Foe?

Did you dream that you rowed with your enemy and said all of the things that you really think of him, but have never had the nerve—or chance—to say? Although this could be a straightforward wish-fulfillment dream, echoing your real-life desire to tell a certain someone your true feelings, it may otherwise point to a more internalized conflict. Perhaps your enemy represented an aspect of yourself that unconsciously troubles you.

ENEMIES

✶ ✶

If you awoke from a dream that centered on your arch enemy or rival, this was probably an unpleasant experience (to say the least)—unless, of course, your dreaming mind transformed your worst foe into a trusting friend, in which case you are probably more perplexed than upset. But what do dreams of this nature mean?

Symbolic and Verbal Associations
- Conflict or hostility; a challenge
- A warning of an attack (not necessarily physical); the need to stay "on your toes"
- Atonement, or a desire to make peace with someone
- An internal conflict; "the enemy within"

Positive Interpretations: Were you surprised by a dream in which you quarreled and then made up with your worst enemy? Did your dream end with the two of you having drinks together and laughing over your old feud? If so, your dream may be an unconscious indication that the two of you may be able to "bury the hatchet," or come to a settlement over whatever it is that has divided you in the real world. Or if, in your dream, you were making a sincere apology to your enemy, and were pleading with him or her to forgive you for something that you have done, could it be that you are feeling guilty over the way that you have treated this person in the waking world? Your unconscious may have been telling you that you should take responsibility and make amends for your role in the conflict that you have had with this person.

Negative Interpretations: If you dreamed that you had a heated argument or fight with your most hated enemy, the most likely explanation is that your unconscious was merely mirroring your waking-life dislike of that person, his or her antipathy toward you, or your mutual abhorrence of each other. And if, in your dream, it was you who instigated and dominated the conflict, then your dream may have served as a safety valve, providing you with an outlet for the pent-up anger and aggression that you feel toward this person. Alternatively, if you had a dream that you were under some sort of attack (be it physical or psychological.) by your enemy, your unconscious mind may have been warning you that this person has been plotting against you, and that you are in danger of a similar attack in the real world. Finally, if your dreaming mind conjured up an enemy whom you did not recognize, then you may want to consider whether you are in conflict with some aspect of yourself, or "the enemy within". What did your dream enemy look like? And can you remember what it was that you were arguing or fighting over? (For instance, if you are a somewhat conservative man and you dreamed that you argued with a teenager over politics, then the teenager may have represented a more youthful and adventurous part of yourself that longs to be expressed in the waking world.)

Related Dreams

pages 190, 221, 253,
262, 264 & 281

EX-LOVERS & EX-SPOUSES

Though a few people manage to cultivate good, healthy friendships with their exes, most people tend not to have very positive feelings toward their ex-lovers and ex-spouses. And if you had a dream in which you were visited by an ex, you were probably left wondering why your unconscious mind chose to put you through such grief.

Symbolic and Verbal Associations
- Jealousy
- Guilt
- Anger; rage; hostility
- Insecurity
- Deceit

Positive Interpretations: Were you perplexed by a dream that took you back to a scene from a less-than-happy old relationship, and are you in a positive, loving relationship now? Perhaps you dreamed of your ex-husband coming home in the middle of the night, when you knew that he had been cheating on you with another woman. Your unconscious mind's reason for forcing you to relive such a scenario may have been simply to remind you of how lucky and happy you are to have your current husband or boyfriend. Alternatively, did you dream of happy times with an ex? If so, there are a few possible explanations. It is possible that your unconscious mind was reminding you of the inherent goodness that lies inside your ex-partner, perhaps so that you might find the courage to "bury the hatchet" and become friends with (or, at least, let go of your anger for) this person. Of course, it is also possible that your dream is an indication that you still have romantic feelings for your ex, and only you will know if this is the case.

Negative Interpretations: Did your ex-wife make an appearance in your dream, and did she "push your buttons" in the same way that she did before you were divorced? If so, and if she is still a part of your life in some way (perhaps you have to see each other because you share custody of a child), then your dream was probably just a reflection of your real-life feelings for your ex-wife. It is also possible that you are worried about a threat that you perceive that she may be posing to you. (For instance, has she been threatening to seek full custody of your child, or do you feel that she has been "poisoning" your child's mind against you?) Or did you have a dream in which you knocked your cocky ex-husband on the head with his favorite golf club? If so, you probably experienced a safety-valve dream—i.e., your unconscious mind was allowing you to act out the rage that you feel toward your ex in the safety of dreamland. However, it is also possible that your dream was a warning that your feelings of anger are overtaking you and that you are in danger of losing control and actually committing some violent act toward your ex.

Related Dreams

pages 102, 116, 218, 252, 253 & 264

My Exes Dreams

----

* * * * * * * * * * * * * * * * * *

The "Ex" Factor

If you dreamed that you stepped back in time into an old relationship, perhaps your dream involved a particular memory of an old flame. If the dream was positive, this could suggest a yearning for your ex, for the comfort of that relationship. But if the dream left you in a cold sweat, it could highlight feelings of guilt and anger concerning your ex that you haven't yet confronted.

My Extended Family Dreams

✦ ✦ ✦ ✦ ✦ ✦ ✦ ✦ ✦ ✦ ✦ ✦ ✦ ✦ ✦ ✦ ✦ ✦

Relative Values

Have you been dreaming about a relative with whom you find it difficult to get on? Perhaps you have an overbearing mother-in-law who has been interfering with your dreams recently. Was she reminding your spouse of everything that you're doing wrong? If so, and you defended yourself, maybe it's time that you stood up to her in the real world.

EXTENDED FAMILY

✦✦

Because dreams that involve an extended-family member will often reflect your feelings toward, or your relationship with, the person whom you dreamed of, the meaning of these dreams is (in most cases) quite direct.

Symbolic and Verbal Associations

c One's feelings toward a family member
c An aspect of one's own character
c A masculine or feminine archetype
c Insecurity and/or rivalry

Positive Interpretations: If you were perplexed by a dream that involved a member of your extended family—perhaps a distant cousin or an in-law—and if you are having trouble making sense of the message that your unconscious mind was trying to send you, then it may be that your dream actually had nothing at all to do with the person whom you dreamed of. It is possible that your unconscious called up an image of this person in order to point to an aspect of your own character or personality (or else to the character or personality of someone else). For example, if you had a strong reaction of empathy and admiration when you dreamed that your second-cousin-once-removed was volunteering in a soup kitchen to help to feed homeless people, this may be a signal that you yourself would be more fulfilled if you sought out ways in which you could work to help people in need. However, if you are still finding it difficult to determine the meaning of your dream, you may want to consider whether the extended-family member whom you dreamed of could have represented a masculine or feminine archetype. For instance, did you have a dream in which your great-aunt (who lives a long distance from you and whom you hardly know) came to you, took you in her arms, and gave you advice and instilled you with hope for the future? If so, could your great-aunt have been a personification of the feminine archetype of the priestess, the spiritual and intuitive wise woman?

Negative Interpretations: The darker archetypes may also appear in your dreams in the form of extended-family members—a dream niece as the siren, for instance, or a dream father-in-law as the ogre—though a negative dream about a parent-in-law or a step-parent (or even a stepbrother or -sister) is also likely to have been a simple reflection of your real-life feelings of insecurity and/or rivalry with regard to this person. Because having a new authority figure in your life (even a benign one) is bound to threaten your individuality to a certain extent, these sorts of feelings and dreams are normal and natural. Therefore, if you dreamed that your step-mother locked you in the basement and told you to stay away from her son, have you been feeling bullied and overpowered by her in the waking world?

Related Dreams

pages 121, 134, 127, 228, 264 & 278

FATHERS

✶✶✶

For many people, their father is one of the most dominant, significant influences in their lives. (And even if you grew up without a father, his absence was likely to have exerted a considerable force and influence on your psyche.) When interpreting a dream that centered on your father, you should take into consideration what sort of relationship you have (or had) with him (if any at all)—particularly when you were a child—as well as how this makes you feel.

Symbolic and Verbal Associations
(Love and caring
(Dependence on someone
(Authority and discipline
(Respect
(Benevolence
(The ogre (or the negative, power-hungry father)

Positive Interpretations: If you had a dream in which your gentle and loving father put his arm around you and told you how proud of you he was, then your dream was probably underlining the important, positive role that your father has played in your life (though your dream may also indicate that you have been feeling somewhat insecure lately and that you could use some loving reassurance). Or were you surprised by a dream in which your father, who, in real life, was always overly aggressive and hurtful, acted in a way that was compassionate and loving? In this case, your unconscious mind may have invoked the archetype of the ideal male parent, possibly because you are in need of this type of father figure in your current life, or possibly to tell you that it's time for you to fulfill this role for your own self (or even for someone else in your life).

Negative Interpretations: Did you dream that your father gave you a stern lecture about your spending habits? If so, and if you have memories of him chiding you for wasting your money when you were a teenager, then your dream was probably pointing to your own judgment against yourself because you feel that you are not living up to the standards that your father set for you. However, if your father was always gentle and loving, and if you had a dream in which he behaved aggressively or cruelly toward you, then your unconscious may have conjured up the archetype of the power-hungry ogre—perhaps to alert you to someone who is behaving like an "ogre" in your current life. (For instance, could the dream ogre have represented your over-controlling boss, who has been bullying and demeaning you at work?) Finally, if you have recurring negative dreams about your father, this may be an indication that you need to become more independent of him (or of his memory), and that it's time for you to live your life according to your own rules and values.

My Fathers Dreams

✶ ✶

Daddy Dearest
If you dreamed that you were young and riding on your father's shoulders, were you happy in the dream, and did you feel loved and secure? If so, this could point to a need to feel cared for and protected in your waking life. Perhaps you longed for a closer bond with your father during your formative years, but he wasn't around much, so that you're now putting things right in dreamland.

Related Dreams
pages 89, 121, 132, 133, 199 & 227

My Friends Dreams

....
....
....
....
....
....
....
....
....

★ ★ ★ ★ ★ ★ ★ ★ ★ ★ ★ ★ ★ ★ ★ ★ ★ ★

Lean on Me

Did you dream that you were hanging out with a group of your closest friends? Dreaming about people who know you well—and the other way round—and feeling comfortable and confident in their company, may reflect the important role that they play in your life. In your waking world, have you been finding it difficult to make time for your friends? Perhaps your unconscious self is telling you to pick up the phone.

FRIENDS

O ur closest friends are a source of companionship and emotional support, and we depend on them for many things. Most people will have a number of similarities with their friends, in term of personality and interests, as well as differences, and a dream that involves a friend may highlight an aspect of that friend's character or personality or of our relationship with him or her (sometimes in order to tell us something about ourselves, as the unconscious will often project aspects of ourselves onto those who are closest to us).

Symbolic and Verbal Associations

‹ Camaraderie
‹ Trust
‹ A reunion
‹ Emotional dependence
‹ An aspect of your own character

Positive Interpretations: Did you have a dream in which you and your closest friend participated in an activity that the two of you always do together? Perhaps you dreamed that you and your friend were chatting and listening to music as you shared a pot of tea at her house—something that you do at least two times a week. If so, then your unconscious was probably mirroring your real-life relationship with your best friend, and the important role that she plays in your life. The same interpretation will apply if you and your best friend no longer live close to each other, and face-to-face interactions have become infrequent—although, in this case, your dream was probably a signal that you miss your friend and that it may be time for a visit.

Negative Interpretations: Did you dream that you looked on with terror and dismay as your best friend, who has a bit of a hot temper, started a fist fight with a group of people at a bar, so that he was handcuffed and arrested by the police? When the unconscious highlights or exaggerates a characteristic or the behavior of one of your friends, it may do so for one of two reasons. On the one hand, your dream may have been a sign that, although you make light of, and are often amused by, your friend's temper, his tendency to "blow up" is making you feel uneasy or afraid. On the other hand, however, your dream may have been a warning that it is you, and not your friend, who is in danger of letting your temper lead you into real trouble. Alternatively, in your dream, did your friend turn his violent temper against you? If so, you probably awoke feeling extremely troubled, and perhaps angry with your friend. This type of dream may indicate that there is some underlying trouble in your relationship with your friend—perhaps something that neither of you is consciously aware of—and examining the details of the dream and your friend's behavior (both in the dream world and in real life) will provide clues.

Related Dreams
pages 104, 218, 253, 261, 278 & 286

GRANDPARENTS

Because grandparents are often a source of unconditional love and affection, and because they also often serve as a go-between or a buffer between their children and their grandchildren, many people hold their grandparents in extremely high esteem—and it is likely that you awoke feeling pleasant and reassured if a grandparent put in an appearance in one of your dreams.

Symbolic and Verbal Associations
‹ Wisdom and experience
‹ Unconditional love and encouragement
‹ Fairness and impartiality
‹ Nostalgia for happy times
‹ The past; traditional values

Positive Interpretations: Did you have a dream in which one of your grandparents—who, perhaps, has been dead for many years—came to you and comforted you with regard to some problem that you have been dealing with in the real world? Perhaps it was your grandmother, who, in your dream, held you on her knee and stroked your hair like she did when you were a child. The unconscious mind may invoke this sort of dream, particularly in troubled times, to remind us of how happy and secure we once felt (and, presumably, to remind us that it is possible to feel this way again). A dream such as this may also indicate that, as you navigate life's problems, you are in need of the sort of sage-like guidance and wisdom that your grandparents provided you with. However, if your real-life relationship with your grandparents was not loving or positive in this way, you may want to consider whether your dream grandparent could have been a metaphor for the archetype of the priestess (or wise old woman) or the priest (or wise old man).

Negative Interpretations: Did you have a dream in which you were bewildered or confused by something that your grandfather did or said? When a dream ancestor gives you advice—even if the meaning of the message is unclear—this is usually an unconscious signal that you should look to the past for the answer to some problem or trouble that you are currently facing. This could either be a lesson learned from an actual event that happened in your family (perhaps something that has been passed down in family lore), or, otherwise, a genetic or family trait that you have inherited, which you may be able to scrutinize more objectively in someone else (i.e., your dream grandfather). Finally, if you had a dream about a grandparent and none of the above interpretations seems satisfactory, especially if you were disturbed by your dream grandparent's words or actions, then it may be that your unconscious mind used the image of your grandparent to conjure up the dark archetype of the witch or the black magician (the darker, more sinister aspects of the priestess and the priest respectively)—perhaps to highlight some dark aspect of your own personality or recent behavior.

Related Dreams
pages 101, 133, 134, 222, 267 & 263

My Grandparents Dreams

----

* * * * * * * * * * * * * * * * * *

Innocence and Experience
Have you been dreaming about your grandparents? We often respect these relations as sources of both fun and wisdom, so if you have, chances are that your dreams were positive ones. Perhaps you dreamed of a grandparent who has passed away, who returned to you in your sleep to impart some advice. This suggests that you are seeking guidance from someone whom you trust and look up to about an issue that is troubling you in your waking life.

My Lovers Dreams

★ ★ ★ ★ ★ ★ ★ ★ ★ ★ ★ ★ ★ ★ ★ ★

Heated Passion

If you dreamed that you were making love with someone whom you consciously desire, was this person your partner or someone whom you are lusting after who doesn't know how you feel? If it wasn't your partner, and your real-life relationship has become sexless, it may be that you crave an injection of passion into your love life. Perhaps you have been with your partner for so long that your sex life has become strangled by routine and your frustration is playing itself out in your sleep.

LOVERS

★★

A fixation on love and sex—or on seeking or wooing a lover—is a major preoccupation in the lives of many, many people. The desire for love and sex is basic to human nature, and it is not surprising that dreams of these themes are quite common.

Symbolic and Verbal Associations
- Love and affection
- Romance
- Sexual desire
- Partnership
- Commitment

Positive Interpretations: Did you have a dream in which you felt the vibrant euphoria of sharing a passionate moment with your current lover, whom you are desperately in love with? If so, your dream may have been simply reaffirming your waking feelings of love for him or her. Or if things have begun to settle into a routine with your lover, so that the feelings of romance and desire are no longer as strong as they used to be, then your dream may have been a reminder from your unconscious of how you used to feel toward your lover (and may continue to feel, although you may not be as conscious of your feelings as you were before). If this is the case, then your unconscious may have been prompting you to make a conscious effort to rekindle the romance between yourself and your lover. Alternatively, if you experienced this sort of romantic dream and if you have no lover in the real world, then your dream was probably reflecting your desire to be in a relationship. (And did you know your dream lover? What qualities did he or she possess that attracted you?)

Negative Interpretations: Were you upset by a dream in which you and your lover were engaged in a vicious argument? If so, can you remember what you were arguing about? Your unconscious mind may have been highlighting a problem that has, thus far, gone under the radar of your conscious mind. Alternatively, were you taken aback or unsettled by a dream in which you were in love with someone whom you regard as playing a relatively minor role in your life (such as a coworker, or the cashier at your supermarket)? (Perhaps, even, you are actually attracted to this person in real life, but you have been fighting your feelings because you feel that they are not appropriate.) If so, you were probably extremely troubled by your dream—especially if either you or the person you dreamed of are in another relationship. However, as difficult as it may be to admit, your unconscious mind probably sent you this dream in order to provide an outlet for the romantic feelings that you have suppressed in the waking world. And it is also possible that your dream was encouraging you to express your feelings for this person in the real world.

Related Dreams

pages 95, 97, 116, 242, 260 & 268

MOTHERS

Perhaps no bond is stronger than the mother–child relationship when it is in its ideal form (i.e., gentle, loving, and nurturing). For a significant part of your life, you were probably emotionally and physically dependant on your mother (or—if she was absent from your life—on an alternative mother figure). And how you react to a dream that involved your mother will be tied into your feelings for her in the real world.

Symbolic and Verbal Associations
(Selflessness
(Tenderness and affection
(Nurturing
(The desire to "mother" (or to be "mothered" by) someone
(The archetype of the "terrible mother"

Positive Interpretations: Did you dream that your mother (who was always affectionate, tender, and loving toward you in the real world) held you in her arms, kissed you, and told you how much she loved you? If so, your dream was most likely mirroring your mother's importance in your life. It is also possible that your dream was an indication that you are currently in need of some "mothering" (perhaps because you have been feeling sad, lonely, or insecure). On the other hand, did you dream that your emotionally withdrawn, perhaps even spiteful or vindictive, mother had become full of love and compassion? If so, you probably awoke feeling a bit confused. The most likely explanation for this sort of dream is that your unconscious mind may have conjured up the archetype of the ideal mother (such as the Virgin Mary of Christianity), who represents selfless nurturing and unconditional love—perhaps indicating that you are in need of a "mothering" influence in your life (even if it is your own self who must mother you), or perhaps indicating that you are being called to "mother" someone else.

Negative Interpretations: Did you have a dream in which your overly critical mother was in prime form, berating you because of her disapproval of your hairstyle or clothing? If so, then your dream may have been an unconscious form of self-admonishment, signifying that you are feeling badly about yourself because you feel that you are not living up to the standards that your mother instilled in you. However, if you dreamed such a dream and, in reality, your mother has never had an unkind word to say to you, then it may be that your dream self was visited by the archetype of the "terrible mother," the mother's dark side, who is cruel, dominating, critical, and undermining. If so, you should ask yourself whether someone in your current life has had a damaging effect on you by being overly controlling or selfish. Finally, if you have recurring negative dreams about your mother, you may want to consider whether you are too focused on her values and expectations of you; it may be time to set off on your own course in life.

My Mothers Dreams

★ ★ ★ ★ ★ ★ ★ ★ ★ ★ ★ ★ ★ ★ ★ ★ ★ ★ ★

The Maternal Bond?
Did you have a dream in which you were trying to talk to your mother, yet she was giving you the cold shoulder and ignoring everything that you said? In this case, you may be feeling a need to be mothered that is not being met. Could it be that you want to reach out to your mother, but fear that she won't be there for you? Or perhaps you are seeking someone else's approval in your waking life, and your disinterested dream mother represented the person who is being withholding.

Related Dreams
pages 85, 89, 101, 134, 252 & 267

My Rivals Dreams

✶ ✶ ✶ ✶ ✶ ✶ ✶ ✶ ✶ ✶ ✶ ✶ ✶ ✶ ✶ ✶

Healthy Competition

Did you dream that you were competing against an old rival in a game of soccer? When we dream of rivals, we are, in fact, often focusing on an aspect of ourselves because we tend to have things in common with those against whom we compete. Maybe you have recently been suppressing your active, physical side during your waking hours, and your dream rival symbolized this aspect of your character fighting to overcome your conscious control.

RIVALS

✶✶✶✶✶✶✶✶✶✶✶✶✶✶✶✶✶✶✶✶✶✶✶✶✶✶✶✶✶✶✶✶✶✶✶✶✶✶✶

Whether we like it or not, our rivals are usually people whom we are similar to—at least in some way, otherwise we would not be competing with them in the first place. And, because of this, our dreaming mind may conjure up the image of a rival in order to point out some quality—be it positive or negative—about ourselves.

Symbolic and Verbal Associations
- Competition
- Jealousy
- Ambition and success
- Similarity to, or comparison with, another person
- The "rat race"

Positive Interpretations: Did you have a dream in which you were competing in a race against a colleague whom you consider to be a rival (perhaps the two of you are on a similar career path, and you find that you are always competing for raises and promotions)? When we dream of competing against those whom we naturally compete with in the real world, such as colleagues or school mates, this almost always represents our competition in the waking world to win a prize—whether it is recognition or admiration, money, status, or power—that we have set our sights upon. If you experienced a dream such as the one above, for instance, it is likely that you feel somehow threatened by the person whom you were racing against—and the outcome of the race may signify your feelings about how you are faring against this person. Were you flying ahead of her as you approached the finish line? Were the two of you running neck and neck? Or did she leave you struggling in her wake?

Negative Interpretations: If you dreamed of competing against a rival, and if he or she was winning the competition, then your unconscious may have been signaling to you that your rival is better equipped than you to achieve whatever goal you are competing for. So if you dreamed that you were racing your coworker, who dashed past you toward the finish line, then your dream may have been a warning that you are in danger of "falling behind" in your struggle to gain an important promotion that the two of you are up for. (However, your dream may also have been simply reflecting your fears with regard to the "worst-case scenario" that could happen, thereby preparing you emotionally for such a setback in the real world.) Finally, it is also possible that your unconscious was using the image of your rival to point out some quality about yourself. So if you dreamed that your old arch rival from high school was cheating on an exam that you had spent weeks preparing for, then you may want to ask yourself if you have been somehow "cheating" to get ahead in your current life.

Related Dreams
pages 190, 192, 198, 221, 265 & 281

SIBLINGS

Because our brothers and sisters are usually around the same age as us, our relationships with them are probably less encumbered by the quest for independence that so often causes difficulties in our interactions with our mother and father. However, this is not to say that our relationships with our siblings are simpler or less troubled: in fact, the conflicts that arise out of sibling rivalry tend to surface frequently in most people's conscious—and unconscious—minds.

My Siblings Dreams

---

* * * * * * * * * * * * * * * * * * *

Symbolic and Verbal Associations
(Sibling rivalry
(Platonic love
(Jealousy
(Bullying
(One's own self

Positive Interpretations: If you had a dream that mirrored the real-world, positive, and loving relationship that you have with your brother or sister, then your dream can almost certainly be taken at face value. However, if you are an only child and you dreamed of having a brother or sister, or if you dreamed that your real-life brother or sister behaved completely out of character, then it is quite likely that your dream had absolutely nothing to do with your family. Instead, your unconscious mind may have called up the image of a sibling in order to place the spotlight on some characteristic or aspect of your own self. For instance, if your normally angry and rude sister behaved courteously and lovingly in your dream, then your unconscious may have used the image of your sister in order to "set an example" for you to follow in your daily life. In another scenario, if your dream cast someone unrelated to you in the role of your sibling, this usually means that you have brotherly or sisterly feelings for him or her—along with all of the undercurrents of rivalry and platonic love that come with a sibling relationship.

Negative Interpretations: If you had a dream in which your brother or sister behaved in a way that angered or disturbed you—especially if their dream behavior was typical of the way that he or she behaves (or the way that he or she used to behave) in the real world—then your dream was likely to have been a reflection of your unresolved childhood issues with regard to that sibling. So if your brother teased and bullied you in your dream in the same way that he did when you were children (and in the same way that he may continue to do today), then your unconscious may have been prompting you to take action and confront your brother about his behavior. However, as discussed above under "Positive Interpretations," it is also possible that your dream sibling's bad behavior was really a reflection of your own self—and thinking about your sibling's real-life behavior, as well as your own, should help you decide if this is the case.

Family Ties
Are you an only child who dreamed that you had a number of siblings? This could be an example of a wish-fulfillment dream. Perhaps you dreamed that you and your brothers and sisters were hanging out together, laughing, and looking out for one another. Yearning for this kind of sibling relationship, one that is often characterized by feelings of intimacy and comfort, suggests that these positive emotions are currently missing from your life.

Related Dreams
pages 89, 105, 108, 114, 263 & 265

My Spouses Dreams

....
....
....
....
....
....
....
....
....

* * * * * * * * * * * * * * * * * *

Married Life

The meaning of a dream about your spouse largely depends on your real-life situation. If you are in a relationship or marriage that makes you happy and you dreamed that you and your spouse were sharing a loving, intimate moment, your unconscious may simply have confirmed how you consciously feel. But if you are having difficulties in your relationship, your positive dream may have pointed to your desire for a greater level of mutual respect and passion in your marriage.

SPOUSES

* *

Marriage has many abstract, yet powerful, associations, including love, commitment, and partnership. And in the world of dreams, when the unconscious calls up the image of a wife or a husband (whether or not they represent an actual person in the real world), it is to these primary associations that we should first look when we are trying to make sense of our dream.

Symbolic and Verbal Associations
‹ Love and commitment
‹ Contentment and security
‹ Anxiety about the stability of one's domestic life
‹ Partnership
‹ A masculine or feminine archetype

Positive Interpretations: If you had a dream in which you found yourself sharing a happy, loving moment with your husband or wife, the meaning of your dream will depend, in part, on your current life situation. So if your real-world partnership with your spouse is as loving and warm as it was in your dream, then your dream was surely reflecting and affirming this reality. However, if your marriage has been plagued by difficulties or quarreling, then it is likely that your unconscious sent you the dream in order to remind you of the love that you feel for your partner, and perhaps to encourage you to not give up hope of regaining a functional, caring relationship with him or her. On the other hand, what if you experienced such a dream but, in reality, you are unmarried? If it is your deepest desire to find someone to share your life with, then you may have experienced a wish-fulfillment dream. But if you have no plan or desire to become wedded, then you may want to consider whether your dream spouse could have been a female or male archetype—possibly even your anima or animus, the alter ego of your soul.

Negative Interpretations: Did you have a nightmare in which your worst fears regarding your husband or wife were played out upon the stage of your mind? Perhaps you woke up feeling like your heart was in your throat because you'd dreamed that you caught your wife of twenty years engaged in a sex act with another man. If so, your dream was probably just an expression of your insecurity or worries about your wife's faithfulness and dedication to you—although the dream may also have been an indication that you have unconsciously (or even consciously) perceived that your wife may, in fact, be cheating on you, in which case your unconscious mind may have been trying to prepare you to confront and deal with this reality. Lastly, if you dreamed of arguing or fighting with your spouse, then your unconscious may have been pointing to some issue or problem in your relationship—and if you can remember what it was that you were quarreling over, then this may give you a clue to the real-life issue.

Related Dreams

pages 93, 102, 112, 119, 120 & 267

CHAPTER 5

ARCHETYPAL & SYMBOLIC FIGURES

According to Jung, the archetypes are symbolic representations
of human emotions, traits, and behavioral patterns whose form
has been hardwired into our brains by millennia of inherited
experience. When they appear in dreams, they generally reflect a
similar presence in your waking life, as well as your gut reaction to
it, or else suggest a need for the incorporation of the characteristics
that they represent into your waking existence. The unconscious
may similarly recruit other symbolic figures to appear on the dream
stage in wish-fulfillment and warning dreams.

My Amazon/Huntress Dreams

----

* * * * * * * * * * * * * * * * * *

Endurance Test

Are you a woman who dreamed that you were out in the wild, on a long journey, and that you were climbing confidently and rapidly toward your destination? Adventure dreams in which you are in a position of power and control suggest that this is a situation in which you would like to find yourself in your waking life. Could it be that you're currently feeling undermined, manipulated, or bullied at home or work?

AMAZON/HUNTRESS

* *

The amazon represents the feminine principle in its intellectual and practical form. She can be symbolized by a successful professional woman—a fierce competitor who may be much more focused on her career than she is on her romantic and/or family life. The amazon's dark side is the huntress, who ruthlessly stalks her prey—be it someone or something that she desires—only to spit it out and discard it after she has had her way.

Symbolic and Verbal Associations
- Intellect
- Practicality
- Power
- Competition
- Stealth
- Female sexual aggression

Positive Interpretations: If you are female, did you dream that an armor-clad and sword-wielding warrior woman came to your defense at a company meeting in which you were being ignored or otherwise maltreated by your male coworkers? If so, did you relish your feelings of vindication and triumph as your heroine unleashed chaos, ruin, and defeat upon your enemies? Perhaps, even, you found yourself transformed into an amazonlike warrior, whose power and stealth struck fear into the very souls of those who oppose you? If so, then your dream may have served a dual function: both to fulfill your desire for success, authority, and/or revenge, and to hearten you in your real-world struggle to advance your career. Your dream need not have been so dramatic, however: the amazon may appear in a variety of forms and guises—even in animal form—and any time that your dream highlights a powerful, self-assured female, then you should consider whether the amazon has paid you a nocturnal visit. If you are a man who dreamed of the amazon, she may have represented an actual woman in your waking life, or else your need or desire for a strong female companion or influence.

Negative Interpretations: Did you have a dream that highlighted the amazon-gone-bad? Perhaps, in your dream, you were being chased by a sinister female predator who chilled you to the very soul with her evil war cry. If so, was your assailant someone who was recognizable from your waking life? It may be that your unconscious conjured the image of the huntress to alert you to someone who is attempting to hurt or even destroy you for her own dark ends. And, especially if you are a woman, you may want to consider whether you yourself have been acting the part of the huntress. The huntress is also associated with sexual aggression, and she may appear in your dreams as an overly forceful female suitor, especially if you are male.

Related Dreams

pages 121, 124, 140,

221, 244 & 281

ANIMA

★ ★

For men, the anima is a personal female archetype: she is the "soul image"—not a mirror image, but the reverse of one's self, which is one of the reasons why the anima (and the animus, for women) is manifested as a member of the opposite sex. For example, if you are a shy, inwardly drawn man, your anima might take the form of a gregarious, outgoing woman.

Symbolic and Verbal Associations
- ❨ A mirror image of one's self
- ❨ A man's feminine qualities
- ❨ Positive or negative aspects of one's character
- ❨ Emotional, intuitive, or empathetic impulses
- ❨ Internal gender balance

Positive Interpretations: If you are a man who dreamed of a woman who was very different from yourself, you may have had a glimpse of your anima. And if this is the case, the details of your dream and your reaction to your anima will help you to interpret the reason why your unconscious sent her your way. For instance, perhaps you are a conventional, somewhat conservative, man who dreamed that a youthful, carefree woman approached you at a party and asked you to dance with her—something that you would never dream of doing in the real world—then how did your dream self react? If, in your dream, you threw off your old inhibitions and allowed yourself the freedom and enjoyment of dancing with your anima, then the message from your unconscious is fairly clear, and it is that you might find that you are happier and have more fun in your life if you would loosen up some of your self-controls and allow yourself to act in a less inhibited way more often. In general, any time that you dream of your anima, your unconscious mind may be trying to tell you that you need to counterbalance your overriding male tendencies or behavior. For many men, the appearance of the soul image may signal that they have been ignoring their emotional, intuitive, or empathetic impulses, for instance. Following the example of your anima will usually help you to develop into a more balanced, happier person, and it is likely that it will also fortify and improve your relationships with women.

Negative Interpretations: A man's anima is the outline of his feminine side; as such, his anima was originally based on the example set by his mother (or by a motherlike figure in his life), although it eventually expands to encompass the characteristics of all of the women whom he has come to know in his life. And depending upon the nature of these female influences, the anima may be either positive or negative in character. When the anima is negative, she will often share qualities with one or more of the principal negative female archetypes: the terrible mother, the siren, the huntress, and the witch. (Please see the individual entries for these archetypes.)

Related Dreams
pages 113, 118, 127, 130, 134 & 140

My Anima Dreams

★ ★

Opposites Attract

Are you a man who dreamed of a woman who was the nurturing, maternal type? If so, it may be that you glimpsed your anima, and that you are unconsciously attempting to access and develop your feminine side. Are you someone who finds it difficult to express this caring side of yourself? Perhaps you're involved with someone who has been complaining that you don't look after them as much as they would like.

My Animus Dreams

✱ ✱ ✱ ✱ ✱ ✱ ✱ ✱ ✱ ✱ ✱ ✱ ✱ ✱ ✱ ✱ ✱

Mirror Image

If you are a woman who dreamed about a man who was very different to you, could it be that he was your animus? Did he fit the male stereotype of being rational, mathematically inclined, and decisive? If so, have you recently felt that you lack these qualities? Perhaps someone has been putting you down, making you feel as though you aren't intelligent or hard-headed enough, and maybe the dreamtime appearance of your animus signifies your concern about this.

ANIMUS

The animus is a woman's "soul image": a male archetype that represents the reverse image of her self, which is one of the reasons why the animus (and the anima, for men) is manifested as a member of the opposite sex. For example, if you are a spontaneous, somewhat reckless, woman, your animus might take the form of a cautious and reserved man.

Symbolic and Verbal Associations
- A mirror image of one's self
- A woman's masculine qualities
- Positive or negative aspects of one's character
- The intellect, practicality, and confidence
- Internal gender balance

Positive Interpretations: If you are a woman who dreamed of a man who behaved quite differently from yourself, then you may have been visited by your animus. And if so, the details of your dream and your reaction to your animus will help you to determine why your unconscious summoned his presence. Perhaps, for instance, you are a reserved and withdrawn woman who dreamed that a confident, outgoing man offered to show you around the big gambling casinos in Las Vegas. How did your dream self react? Did you take him up on his offer, and were you surprised to find yourself in fantastic spirits as you learned how to place bets at the blackjack tables? If so, then the message from your unconscious is fairly straightforward: if you would allow yourself to be less inhibited and more outgoing (perhaps if you would sometimes take more of "a gamble" on life), then you might find yourself to be happier and having more fun. In fact, whenever you dream of your animus, your unconscious mind may be trying to tell you that you need to counterbalance your overriding female tendencies or behavior. For many women, the appearance of the soul image may signal that they would benefit from striving to become more confident, pragmatic, or intellectually focused. Following the example of your animus will usually help you to develop into a more balanced, happier person, and it is also likely to strengthen and enrich your relationships with men.

Negative Interpretations: Because the animus is the blueprint of a woman's masculine side, it was originally modeled on the example set by her father (or by someone who acted as a father figure in her life), although it eventually expands to encompass the characteristics of all of the men whom she has come to know in her life. And, depending upon the nature of these male influences, beginning with the father, the animus may be either positive or negative in character. When the animus is negative, it will often share qualities with one or more of the principal negative male archetypes: the ogre, the wastrel, the villain, and the black magician. (Please see the individual entries for these archetypes for a detailed description of their characteristics.)

Related Dreams

pages 109, 126, 130, 132, 133 & 140

AUTHORITY FIGURES

Typical authority figures include police officers and judges, teachers and professors, doctors, heads of state, spiritual authorities (such as priests and rabbis), parental figures (traditionally the father), and even referees and umpires. When they appear in our dreams, it is usually for one of three reasons: to rebuke us for some transgression (whether it is of thought, word, or deed); to act as our advisor or guide; or to warn us that we may be abusing our own authority.

Symbolic and Verbal Associations
‹ The law; reprimands and punishment
‹ Spiritual, intellectual, and social lessons
‹ The example of one's "elders and betters" as advisors and guides
‹ The voice of one's conscience

Positive Interpretations: Did you dream that you sat in an austere university lecture hall, listening in rapture as a professor talked about the evolution of humans? And did you awake feeling surprised because, in reality, you've never gone to college and you've had very little waking curiosity about science or evolution? Your unconscious might have summoned the authority figure of the professor in order to provide your mind with some much-needed intellectual stimulation—and also to encourage you to seek out more knowledge-expanding experiences in your waking life. Or did you dream that a doctor had hooked you up to a heart monitor and was taking your blood pressure? If so, have you been placing yourself under too much stress and strain lately, so that your health may be in jeopardy? And if your dream doctor advised you to get more rest and to exercise more, then you should probably consider doing just what your "internal physician" has recommended. Or did someone important, such as the queen of England, come to a dream tea party that you hosted? And were you delighted when Her Majesty praised you for your elegant décor and for the high quality of the tea and cakes that you served? If so, your unconscious mind may have been compensating for your perception that you are unappreciated by others in your waking life.

Negative Interpretations: If you are a Roman Catholic, did you have a dream in which you went to confession and the priest reprimanded you for not having visited your mother in a very long time? If you have you been feeling guilty about your lack of attention to your mother, then your unconscious probably summoned the dream priest to advise you that visiting her would bring you peace of mind. Finally, did you find your dream self in a position of authority? Perhaps you were dressed in the robes of a judge, and you were presiding over a case against your best friend? If so, what was he or she accused of doing? And do you feel that your judgment was fair? If not, your dream may have been a warning that you have been unfairly condemning your friend in the waking world.

Related Dreams
pages 109, 123, 124, 128, 150 & 199

My Authority Figures Dreams

Judgment Day
Did you dream that you were on trial in court, and that the judge was giving his verdict? If so, perhaps you called this authority figure into your dream to represent your own conscience. Are you feeling guilty about something that you've done that you're scared to own up to? Or is it that you are unconsciously seeking an authoritative pronouncement or decision on an issue that has been troubling you?

My Beggars Dreams

----

* * * * * * * * * * * * * * * * * * *

On the Streets

Did you dream that you were a homeless person, with hardly any belongings, living on the streets? If so, perhaps you are currently experiencing some financial worries and this dream spelled out your fears for the future. Or could it be that you are feeling isolated and spiritually "homeless," or lost and unstable, in your waking situation, and that by begging, your dream self was reaching out for a bit of comfort and security?

BEGGARS

* *

When we have a dream that casts our mind's spotlight on the image of a beggar or a homeless person, just as when we encounter these characters in reality, we may be deeply impacted with feelings of guilt, sadness, or even a fear of becoming destitute ourselves.

Symbolic and Verbal Associations
‹ Monetary losses; poverty; bankruptcy
‹ Loneliness
‹ A part of one's personality that is starved
‹ A dearth of affection or emotional support

Positive Interpretations: Dreaming of a beggar or a homeless person can be an unconscious indication that you are in danger of suffering a significant monetary loss. However, this type of meaning generally only applies if you are, in fact, either living beyond your means or if you have been concerned about your financial situation. But what if you feel that you are in good financial standing, but you dreamed that you were sleeping on a sidewalk heat grate, with only a cardboard box and an old, holey blanket to protect you from the wind and the rain? The details of your dream will help you to interpret its meaning. For instance, if you were searching desperately for a pen and paper, is it time that you sat down to write that novel that you've been thinking about for so long? By portraying your dream self as destitute, your unconscious may have been trying to tell you that your creative side has been starved. Or did you dream that someone approached you on the street and begged you to give them some change? If the beggar was your wife, could it be that you have placed her in a state of emotional impoverishment by denying her your love and support? A dream in which you watched with excitement and envy as a caravan of traveling circus folk made their way through your town may indicate that your own life has become too stagnant and monotonous, and that you would welcome a chance of a more carefree, adventurous existence.

Negative Interpretations: Did you dream that you were destitute and living a dirty and piteous life on the streets? And are you, in reality, worried about the state of your financial affairs? If so, your dream may have been an unconscious warning that unless you make some changes in your life, then you may find yourself "out in the cold" in the waking world. But if this interpretation seems unlikely, your dream may have been an unconscious reference to poverty of another sort. Have you been feeling "starved" in another aspect of your life? Perhaps you feel that you are suffering from a lack of friends, perhaps by your own choice or doing (whether this is conscious or unconscious), in which case your dream may have been an attempt to tell you that you might be headed for "lonely street" if you do not make more of an attempt to reach out to others.

Related Dreams

pages 179, 185, 211,
236, 269 & 273

CELEBRITIES

✦✦

ARCHETYPAL & SYMBOLIC FIGURES

Most people, at least at some point in their lives, have wished that they could be more like the celebrities that grace the television and movie screens and the pages of the popular fashion magazines. Dreams that involve the appearance of a famous person often serve to fulfill our unconscious wishes and desires—especially if we are somehow singled out by the dream celebrity.

Symbolic and Verbal Associations
- Beauty and glamour
- Hypermasculinity or -femininity
- High fashion
- Wealth
- Fame
- Power

Positive Interpretations: Did you have a dream in which you had some personal contact with a famous person, perhaps someone whom you admire greatly? For example, in your dream, did Brad Pitt approach you in a bar and ask you for a cigarette? Or were you dumbfounded when you realized that Halle Berry was seated beside you on an airplane? Whatever the dream scenario—and no matter whether you wish that you were as good-looking, rich, famous, or powerful as the person whom you dreamed of, or whether you simply find this person attractive—if a celebrity paid you a nocturnal visit, then it is very likely that you experienced a wish-fulfillment dream. And in addition to giving you the temporary pleasure of being so close to the face of fame and fortune, your dream may have also served a deeper function: the celebrity whom you dreamed of may have been cast in the role of your anima (if you are a man) or animus (if you are a woman). For example, he or she may have represented some personal characteristic that you would do well to develop within yourself. So if you dreamed about the famous late comic actor Charlie Chaplin, your unconscious might have been hinting that you should try to cultivate the mischievous, fun, and entertaining qualities that were prominent in so many of the characters that Chaplin played.

Negative Interpretations: Having a dream in which you gained the attention of a famous person—and particularly if you have this sort of dream on a frequent basis—can be an indicator that you feel that you are undervalued by those around you, and that you are, perhaps, suffering from a low sense of self-esteem. In your dream, did your contact with a celebrity significantly raise your social standing among your peer group or friends? If so, then your dream may have been an unconscious attempt to boost your self-esteem (albeit temporarily), but also to prompt you to take the necessary steps to improve your self-confidence in the waking world.

My Celebrities Dreams

✦ ✦ ✦ ✦ ✦ ✦ ✦ ✦ ✦ ✦ ✦ ✦ ✦ ✦ ✦ ✦ ✦ ✦ ✦

The Fame Game
Did you dream that you were at an awards ceremony, surrounded by glamour and glitz? Were you a celebrity yourself, dressed up to the nines and strutting your stuff, or were you an overawed onlooker? If you were a vital part of the stellar scene and felt exhilarated, maybe the message from your unconscious was to try to nurture your inner exhibitionist and to engage in ego-boosting social activities.

Related Dreams
pages 119, 120, 125, 242, 243 & 247

My Leaders Dreams

★ ✱ ★ ✱ ★ ✱ ★ ✱ ★ ✱ ★ ✱ ★ ✱ ★

Power Trip

Perhaps the iconic image of an all-powerful leader like China's Chairman Mao keeps making random appearances in your dreams. This could point toward an ongoing issue that you have with an authority figure, such as a parent or boss, in your waking world. Do you feel as though this person is ordering you around or controlling you to such an extent that you can never entirely escape his or her dominating and demanding presence?

LEADERS

★✱★✱★✱★✱★✱★✱★✱★✱★✱★✱★✱★✱★✱★✱★✱★✱★✱★✱★

In a perfect world, our leaders would be those who have in mind the best interests of the people, and they would care for us and guide us much as a good mother or father would their children. In the world that we live in, however, this is sometimes, but not always, the reality, and dreams that involve a leader can be symbolic of the father or mother archetype in either their positive or their negative aspects.

Symbolic and Verbal Associations
‹ Direction and control
‹ Wise and just rule
‹ Royalty and ceremony
‹ The symbolic "father" or "mother" of a nation
‹ Tyranny and dictatorship; abuse of power

Positive Interpretations: Did you wake up from a dream in which the head of the United Nations called you into her office for a special meeting because she wanted to ask your advice about the state of affairs of the world? If so, your dream may have been an unconscious validation of your waking feelings of intelligence and competence (although it could have been compensating for your feelings of inadequacy, as discussed below under Negative Interpretations). If you dreamed of a leader or monarch, it is also possible that this person represented someone who has power over you in your waking life, such as your boss—and if you think that this may be the case, the person's behavior in your dream will probably either reinforce or compensate for the way that he or she treats you in the real world. For instance, did you have a dream in which your usually cold and unsympathetic supervisor was transformed into your state governor, and did he take you aside and tell you what a good job you've been doing and ask you if there was anything that you would like to see changed? Alternatively, were you moved by a dream in which you listened to the famous civil-rights leader the Rev. Dr. Martin Luther King Jr. give a speech about love and fairness? Sometimes when we dream of a leader, this can be a signal that we should try to develop this person's qualities within our own self.

Negative Interpretations: Did you have a dream in which the country had been taken over by a power-consumed madman who was threatening to spread his tyrannical and cruel control over the entire planet? Your dream autocrat may have represented someone in your waking life who is behaving in this despotic way, or he may have been a messenger bearing a warning from your unconscious that you yourself have been acting the part of the tyrant. Finally, dreams of being singled out by someone famous, including an eminent leader, may be an unconscious attempt to both compensate for and boost a low sense of self-esteem.

Related Dreams

pages 109, 113, 121,
123, 199 & 247

PERSONA

* *

The word "persona" comes from the Latin word for an actor's mask. Each and every one of us has a persona: it is the face that we present to the world. In fact, people usually have more than one version of the persona, each carefully tailored to suit its intended audience, be it one's family, friends, colleagues, or strangers. Most people's personas have one thing in common, however: they are almost always meant to portray their "wearer" in the most positive light possible.

Symbolic and Verbal Associations
- The personality that one presents to the world
- Image; character
- Disguises and masks
- "False face"
- An aspect of oneself that is concealed

Positive Interpretations: When we dream of altering our appearance, this is likely to be an unconscious reference to our persona, the personality that we present to others. Did you have a dream in which you put on a disguise? For instance, perhaps you dreamed of putting on a mask that made you look much older than you really are, which caused others in your dream to treat you with much greater respect and deference. If so, and especially if you awoke with good, positive feelings, then your unconscious may have sent you the dream in order to advise you that you should take on a new persona in order to help you achieve your goals. For instance, using the dream example above, it may be that you have been thinking of running for some political office, such as on the city council, but you are much younger than any council member who has ever been elected. Your dream of donning a mask that made you seem older may be an indication that you should take steps in the waking world to make yourself seem more adult—perhaps by dressing more maturely, or by behaving in a more self-assured manner.

Negative Interpretations: Did you dream that you were standing in front of the bathroom mirror at your office, desperately trying to scrub off the clown face paint that you wore? If so, do you feel that you have been "playing the clown" for your coworkers—when, in reality, this is against your true nature? Your dream was probably a warning that your clownish image is in conflict with your true, inner self, and that you would be happier and more comfortable if you would cast off this "false face," at least to some degree, and show your coworkers that you also have a very serious, matter-of-fact side to your character (which may be a necessary step in order for you to receive that promotion that you really want, which would give you many more responsibilities than your current position holds).

Related Dreams
pages 65, 66, 131, 143, 202 & 276

My Persona Dreams

----

* * * * * * * * * * * * * * * * * * * *

Behind the Mask

Dreaming about wearing a mask tends to relate to issues of personal identity. It could be an unconscious expression of your desire to conceal something about yourself from others. Alternatively, putting on a mask could mean that you are feeling emotionally vulnerable and wish to prevent yourself from exposing your true feelings in case you end up being wounded.

My Prince/Wastrel Dreams

✱ ✱ ✱ ✱ ✱ ✱ ✱ ✱ ✱ ✱ ✱ ✱ ✱ ✱ ✱ ✱ ✱ ✱

Young at Heart

If you dreamed about the prince figure, the archetype of the youthful seeker, your dream may have been an unconscious attempt to recapture your youth. The dream prince may have been a stranger to you, or else someone whom you know, but it is nevertheless likely that he represented something that you admire and desire. Perhaps you're feeling weighed down by your adult responsibilities and want to regain the idealistic and questioning nature that you had when you were younger.

PRINCE/WASTREL

✶✶✶✶✶✶✶✶✶✶✶✶✶✶✶✶✶✶✶✶✶✶✶✶✶✶✶✶✶✶✶✶✶✶✶✶✶✶

A younger version of his forebear, the positive father archetype, the prince represents the hopeful, idealistic, and questing nature of youth. He is the young hero of countless fairy tales. However, like all archetypes, the prince has a dark side: the wastrel, whose selfishness and irresponsibility lead him down the road of debauchery and idleness.

Symbolic and Verbal Associations
- Hopeful idealism
- A questing nature
- Irresponsibility
- A philanderer
- Lack of intellectual or moral purpose
- A desire for immediate sensory gratification

Positive Interpretations: A dream that involves the prince may be a signal from your unconscious that you would do well to try to "loosen up," and to recapture some of the freedom and idealism that you may have experienced in your youth. The prince often makes an appearance in dreams in the form of a young man. This can be someone you know or it can be a youth who is a stranger to you, and it may take some thinking about the dream and its context in order to determine that it was, indeed, the prince who paid you a nocturnal visit. For instance, did you have a dream in which you watched with admiration as a youngster trained with his master in a martial art? The prince also represents the hopeful and questing nature of the young-at-heart, and he is ever in search of bettering himself through the attainment of knowledge and experience. Your dream might not have been a cue from your unconscious that you yourself should take up a martial art (though, depending on your interests, this may be the case), but it is likely that your dream was an unconscious attempt to encourage you to seek out new avenues for personal growth.

Negative Interpretations: If you experienced a dream that focused on the negative attitude or actions of a young man, then it is very likely that you have encountered the archetype of the wastrel, the prince's dark side. The wastrel is the embodiment of youth-gone-bad: lazy, irresponsible, selfish, and lacking in intellectual or moral purpose. His appearance in your dream may be a message from your unconscious that you have been letting your obligations and duties to others slide for too long, and that it's time for you to grow up and take some responsibility for your actions. For example, did you dream that a young man persuaded you to hire him as a helper around your house, and then proceeded to sleep "on the clock," leave a mess wherever he went, and eat up all of your food without asking? If so, could it be that you have been playing the part of the wastrel in some aspect of your waking life? Or was the wastrel your immature brother or partner?

Related Dreams
pages 109, 120, 123, 130, 242 & 244

PRINCESS/SIREN

✶✶

The fairy-tale princess is forever a symbol of youthful hopes and wishes. She is the innocent, romantic girl with the bright future, for she is sure to meet and fall in love with her handsome prince—unless, of course, she gives way to her dark side: the siren, whose selfishness and sexual voracity leave a trail of destruction wherever she goes.

Symbolic and Verbal Associations
- Happiness
- Innocent romanticism
- Hopes and wishes
- A positive destiny
- Selfishness
- A seductress; voracious sexuality

Positive Interpretations: If you dreamed of the archetypical princess, this may have been a prompt from your unconscious that you have become too cynical or stuck in your adult ways, and that it is time that you released yourself from the old ties that have bound you and find ways to retrieve some of the freedom, joy, and optimism that you probably had ample amounts of in your younger days. In dreams, the princess will often appear as a whimsical young girl; she may come in the form of someone whom you are familiar with, or she may be a stranger to you. Thinking about the details and the context of your dream, and your reaction to the dream situation, will help you to determine whether the princess has paid your sleeping self a visit. For example, did you dream that you were walking down a wooded path when a young girl came out of the forest, took your hand in her own, and entreated you to join her on a journey to find butterflies? The archetypical princess represents the care-free happiness of youth—and though your dream might not have been an unconscious prompt for you to run barefoot through the forest (or perhaps it was), it might have been a sign that you should seek out ways to experience more of the fun and the beauty of the world around you.

Negative Interpretations: Did you have a dream that highlighted the negative aspects of a girl or a young woman? If so, it is quite possible that you have encountered the archetypical siren, the princess's dark side. A selfish and ill-meaning predator, the siren uses her powers of seduction to weave her spell of doom over anyone who stands in her way. Her appearance in your dreams may be a sign from your unconscious that you are in danger of allowing your own selfishness to thwart your relations with those around you. For instance, did you dream that a young woman charmed you into doing her some great favor, only to turn around and ridicule or harm you behind your back? If so, could it be that you have been acting in the role of the siren in some aspect of your waking life?

My Princess/Siren Dreams

✶✶✶✶✶✶✶✶✶✶✶✶✶✶✶✶✶✶✶✶✶

A Fairy-tale Princess
The princess often appears in dreams as a young, fancy-free girl, who is beautiful, kind, and innocent. Did you dream of such a character? If so, were you charmed by her artlessly winning ways? If you enjoyed encountering the princess in dreamland, it could be that you want to view the waking world through her eyes. Maybe you yearn for more fun and romance in your life and regret that you have become cynical over the years.

Related Dreams

pages 113, 119, 123, 130, 242 & 245

ARCHETYPAL & SYMBOLIC FIGURES

My Professionals Dreams

----

* * * * * * * * * * * * * * * * *

Working Life

Did you dream that you were watching a lawyer eloquently present his case in court? If so, is this a profession that you're interested in, and were you longing to be in the lawyer's position? If you answered "Yes" to both questions, your dream was probably an indication that you're feeling dissatisfied in your current job and want to make a career change. Was your unconscious nudging you to consider studying law during your waking hours?

PROFESSIONALS

****

If you had a dream that focused in on someone at work, in their professional role, then it is likely that their particular occupation or job bears some relevance to your current waking situation—and your reaction to and/or feelings about this person and their profession may give you some insight into the specific message that your unconscious was trying to send you.

Symbolic and Verbal Associations
- Work; manual labor
- Discipline
- Expertise in some particular area
- Duty
- Skill and dexterity
- Experience; knowledge

Positive Interpretations: Did you dream of watching someone at work in a profession that you greatly admire? Perhaps you had a dream that you were watching with wonder and admiration as a sculptor chiseled out a marble bust? If so, then your dream sculptor may have been a messenger from your unconscious that you would be happier if you could find ways to express your own creativity. Some occupations have general, across-the-board associations. For instance, if you dreamed of an accountant or a bookkeeper, this may have been your unconscious's way of saying that you would benefit from taking a more objective or analytical approach to some problem or situation that you are facing in your waking life.

Negative Interpretations: Did you have a dream in which feelings of sickness and fear arose in your stomach as you watched a group of soldiers marching past your house? If so, can you remember why you felt this way? If you were afraid that you would be drafted into their army, or if it was because you associate the military with having too little personal freedom and too much discipline, then the interpretation of your dream is fairly clear: could it be that your unconscious was warning you that your life and/or your ideals have become too regimented and stiff? Any time that you dream of an occupation that is particularly abhorrent to you, you should think about the specific reasons why you feel this way. So what if you simply cannot stand lawyers because you feel that they are generally insincere, fraudulent, and deceitful, and you dreamed that you had decided to study for a degree in law? In this case, could it be that you have been slipping into a pattern of being dishonest or insincere with those around you? There are some occupations that carry negative connotations for almost everyone. And if you had a dream that featured a pimp or a drug-dealer, for instance, the message that they brought should be fairly straightforward.

Related Dreams
pages 82, 121, 191, 195 & 200

SHADOW

* *

The shadow is an archetypical character that is individual to each person. Usually appearing in the form of someone who is the same gender as you are, the shadow is the representation of all of those qualities that you find particularly loathsome in others—such as, for example, violent aggression, cowardice, bigotry, or unfaithfulness. And though you may despise these qualities, they exist, to some degree, within the character of each and every person, including yourself. Because your unconscious mind probably does such an excellent job of repressing your shadow, its one and only outlet may be the dream world.

Symbolic and Verbal Associations
- The polar opposite of the persona
- Any quality that you despise in others
- Repulsion
- Cowardice
- Hatefulness
- Bigotry
- Brutality

Positive Interpretations: If you dreamed of your shadow, it will do you well to remember that although your conscious mind is prejudiced against the qualities that your shadow demonstrated, they are not always bad in and of themselves. In fact, if you would take the cue from your unconscious and allow these qualities more of a presence in your waking personality (either by consciously acknowledging them or by embracing them, even), then you might find that your creativity and your joy of life would be greatly enhanced. For example, did you dream of someone—perhaps someone who looked somewhat like yourself—who embodied the very trait that you hate the most: physical aggression? If so, perhaps you would benefit from finding a physical outlet for your own pent-up frustrations, such as kickboxing or karate.

Negative Interpretations: Sometimes the traits that we most abhor in others are those traits that we ourselves have to struggle most fiercely to contain. By fixating our loathing on others who possess these qualities, we can pretend that the qualities do not exist within our own psyche. And sometimes, when you dream of your shadow, the symbol of everything that you loathe within yourself, it can be a sign from your unconscious that these very qualities that you hate are threatening to bubble over in your conscious, waking life. So if you are a young woman whose pet peeve is people who gossip, and if you dreamed of a young woman of about your age who stunned and upset you with the haphazard way in which she slandered her friends and enemies with equal fervor, you may want to consider whether you yourself are the one who has been telling tales behind the backs of your friends and cohorts.

My Shadow Dreams

----

* * * * * * * * * * * * * * * * * * * *

The Other Side

Did a shadowy, faceless figure lurk menacingly in your dream? And did it finally confront you in a rude and aggressive fashion, thereby displaying qualities that you consciously abhor? If so, you may have encountered your shadow, particularly if you spend your waking hours trying to repress your mean temper, in which case its only outlet may be through your shadow while you are sleeping.

Related Dreams
pages 137, 139, 253, 256, 264 & 273

ARCHETYPAL & SYMBOLIC FIGURES

My Strangers Dreams

✳ ✳ ✳ ✳ ✳ ✳ ✳ ✳ ✳ ✳ ✳ ✳ ✳ ✳ ✳ ✳ ✳ ✳

Unfamiliar Territory

Did you dream that you picked up a hitch-hiker in your automobile? If so, did you feel drawn to the stranger in your dream? How you responded to him or her may be the key to how you feel about yourself or your life. If your dreaming self admired the hitchhiker's fearlessness and free spirit, maybe it's time to take a chance or two, or to be less cautious and more adventurous, in the waking world.

STRANGERS

✳✳

When our dreaming mind focuses in on a stranger, it usually has an agenda. Dream strangers often represent some aspect of our character, or of a real-world relationship, that we either have not consciously acknowledged or that we have neglected. This is why they seem unfamiliar or "strange." When interpreting the meaning of a dream stranger, it is very important to consider how the stranger looked or behaved, and how our dream self reacted to him or her.

Symbolic and Verbal Associations
‹ Someone or something that is unfamiliar or alien
‹ A newcomer
‹ A mystery
‹ An unacknowledged aspect of one's own character
‹ A threat

Positive Interpretations: Dream strangers often appear as the "embodiment" of our anima (if we are a man) or our animus (if we are a woman)—an archetype that is the reverse image (and the opposite gender) of ourselves. If you are a man, did you dream that an unknown woman knocked on your door and begged you to take her in and help her because she had just been beaten up and robbed? If so, your unconscious may have sent your anima in order to alert you that someone in your life has been hurt (though not necessarily physically) and to call on you to access your nurturing, caring, feminine qualities in order to help this person. Or if you are a woman, did you have a dream in which a strange man rode up to you on his motorcycle and invited you to climb on for a sightseeing ride through the countryside? If so, your animus may have been a messenger, sent from your unconscious to urge you to embrace the outgoing, masculine side of your personality that longs for adventure and excitement.

Negative Interpretations: Did you have a dream in which you and your husband found yourselves locked in a prison cell that was guarded by a jailor whom you did not recognize? The stranger who was your dream jailor may have represented some aspect of your marriage—a problem that the two of you have ignored or not acknowledged—that is somehow "locking up" your relationship and preventing it from growing or moving forward. If you can remember what "crime" you were being imprisoned for, this may be a clue as to the nature of the problem. (And if, in your dream, you and your husband worked together to defeat the jailor, then your unconscious may have been encouraging you to work together with your husband to overcome the issue or problem in the real world.) Finally, if you dreamed of a stranger who behaved in a way that caused you to feel contempt for him or her, you may want to consider whether this person was actually your shadow, a character who represents the qualities that you particularly despise in others (but that probably exist, to one degree or another, within your own psyche).

Related Dreams

pages 104, 119, 120, 121, 129 & 228

TRICKSTERS & CLOWNS

A wild, rebellious maverick, the trickster (or clown) rejoices in overturning the status quo and causing chaos wherever he roams. This archetype, neither completely positive nor completely negative, is represented in mythology by the Greco-Roman gods Hermes and Mercury and by the Norse Loki. He is analogous to the king's fool: a seemingly capricious prankster who is actually the bearer of much wisdom—and, as such, his appearance in our dreams should be a matter of immense interest to us.

Symbolic and Verbal Associations
- Pranks
- Shapeshifting
- Rebellion; wildness
- Mockery
- Anarchical behavior
- Sabotage

Positive Interpretations: Did a red-nosed clown cavort across the stage of your dream, just as you were making a speech before a large audience about the importance of upholding traditional morality? And did this clown steal the attention of the crowd as he berated and mocked the "moral" issues about which you spoke? If so, your dream trickster was most likely a representation of the inner aspect of yourself that believes that you have become too conservative and narrow in your views—sent in by your unconscious on a daring mission to sabotage your dream speech in order to shake you up and (presumably) out of your boring conventionalism. And—though he may have annoyed, angered, or even embarrassed your dream self—if you heed the trickster's message, you may find yourself transformed into a happier, more open and carefree person.

Negative Interpretations: Did you awake in a sweat, having had a nightmare in which a black-clad anarchist was chanting "Down with corporate education" as he poured gasoline all over your neighborhood's elementary school and lit a fire? If so, your dream anarchist was almost surely a form of the trickster, who is ever challenging those traditions and values that are held in society's highest esteem. But what purpose could your unconscious have had in sending this criminal maverick to upset your nocturnal slumber? It may be that someone in your waking life—perhaps even yourself—has "gone over the deep end" in his or her battle against the forces of the status quo. And if you think that it might be you, you should ask yourself if you have been allowing the ends to justify your means. Perhaps it's time that you reevaluated your methods before some serious, irrevocable damage is done to yourself or others.

My Tricksters & Clowns Dreams

Fool's Gold

In dreams, the trickster often represents the "wise fool," a figure who is trying to tell you something serious, even though he or she seems to be merely clowning around. If the trickster was playing the fool in a formal situation in your dream, embarrassing you, but causing those around you to roar with laughter, perhaps the message from your unconscious was to stop being so earnest and to see the funny side once in a while.

Related Dreams
pages 66, 84, 203, 224, 235 & 264

My Warrior/Villain Dreams

★ ★ ★ ★ ★ ★ ★ ★ ★ ★ ★ ★ ★ ★ ★ ★ ★

Playing the Hero

If you dreamed that you were looking on as a warrior surveyed his territory and barked commands at others, this could be a sign that you need to assume a similar role in your waking life. Is there a situation at home or work that needs to be resolved, but that you're reluctant to face head on? If so, your unconscious may have been prompting you to be assertive, to state your opinion or make your demands, to be ready to go into battle if necessary, and to relish watching the sparks fly!

WARRIOR/VILLAIN

★★★★★★★★★★★★★★★★★★★★★★★★★★★★★★★★★★★★★

The archetypical hero of myths and legends, the warrior is the mature man whose strength, valor, and conviction have led him to victory after victory on the battlefield. In the language of dreams, he represents positive action. The warrior's arch enemy is his dark side: his own nemesis, the villain.

Symbolic and Verbal Associations

‹ The hero
‹ Courage and valor
‹ Conviction
‹ Physical strength
‹ Harmful intent
‹ Criminality

Positive Interpretations: When the warrior makes an appearance in your dreams, this is often a signal from your unconscious that you need to play the part of the warrior in your own life and take necessary, positive, and decisive action in order to achieve a desired goal. For instance, did you have a dream in which you looked on as a knight in armor, his sword raised high over his head, turned his horse and rode off across a field of battle? If so, do you know what he was fighting for (or against)? Perhaps he bore a special symbol on his shield. Think about the details of your dream, and try to draw parallels with your waking reality. Is there some issue, problem, or hurdle that you have been deliberating whether to "take on"? If you can pinpoint the thing that your dream was referring to, then this should help to clarify the action that your unconscious mind was prompting you to take. Beyond all else, the purpose of your dream warrior was to fortify your soul with the courage and determination to meet all of life's obstacles head on.

Negative Interpretations: Like all of the archetypes, the warrior has a flip side. When he allows himself to succumb to his own selfish desires, with a disregard for all that is right and good, then the warrior is transformed into his dark alter ego, the villain. And whenever the villain plays some part in the drama of your dreams, the message from your unconscious is almost always clear: "This is the way not to behave!" For example, did you dream that you were on the train, making your way to work, when a masked gunman burst into the train car and demanded that everyone hand over their money and jewelry? If so, could it be that you been somehow acting as the "bad guy," either in thought or in deed? (And if, in your dream, you played the role of the warrior and fought back against the gunman, then you are probably already well on your way to defeating the "villain within.")

Related Dreams

pages 106, 109, 121,
124, 140 & 244

WISE MAN/WARLOCK

* *

ARCHETYPAL & SYMBOLIC FIGURES

The ever-popular symbol of goodness, wisdom, and magic, the wizard is also the high priest, who represents masculine spirituality. A solitary spiritual guide, guru, or mentor, the wizard has been famously personified as the Merlin of Arthurian legend and as Tolkien's Gandalf. His counterpart is the black magician—a conjurer who is on a par with the wizard, but a figure who chooses to use his powers in the service of darkness.

Symbolic and Verbal Associations
- Masculine spirituality
- Wisdom
- Magic
- A guide
- Lust for power
- The forces of darkness

Positive Interpretations: Did you have a dream that involved the archetype of the wizard or the high priest? For instance, did you dream that an older gentleman in white robes told you that he had some important information about your future? If so, do you remember what else he said to you? And did you recognize the man? Or with whom in the real world do you associate this character? If you can identify your dream wizard with someone in your waking world, then your unconscious mind may have been trying to tell you that this person has your best interests at heart, and that he is willing and able to act as your guide and mentor (or it may be that this person has already been acting in this role, and that your dream was an unconscious prompt for you to heed his advice and guidance.) Taking the example dream above, if the wizard told you that you should "follow your heart and not your mind," could he have meant that you should reconsider pursuing that art degree that you have been yearning to sign on for—meaning that you would have to quit your job, which pays well, but which makes you very unhappy?

Negative Interpretations: Do you think that you may have dreamed of the wizard's polar opposite, the black magician? For example, did you have a dream in which a dark-clad, hooded figure pointed his staff in your direction, causing you to cower in fear as lightning bolts flew from the end of the staff toward your head? If so, did you recognize the black magician? Or with whom do you associate this character? Trying to answer these questions, as well as considering the details of your dream, will help you to understand why your unconscious sent you such a nightmare. It could be that you have unconsciously detected that someone in your life, most likely someone who has some amount of power over you, has been plotting to use this power to your detriment.

Related Dreams
pages 44, 100, 111, 121, 142 & 143

My Wise Man/Warlock Dreams

----

* * * * * * * * * * * * * * * * * * *

The High Priest
Did an older, bearded man in flowing robes come to you in a dream to impart words of wisdom and guidance? The wise old man can appear in dreams when we are seeking advice, but haven't yet mustered the courage to share our problems and fears. What did he tell you? Perhaps you need to consider whether the guidance that he offered is relevant to your waking reality.

WISE WOMAN/WITCH

My Wise Woman/Witch Dreams

★ ★ ★ ★ ★ ★ ★ ★ ★ ★ ★ ★ ★ ★ ★ ★ ★ ★

Consulting the Oracle

If the wise woman of folklore appeared in your dream, did you recognize her, or was she a stranger? If she resembled someone in your everyday life, perhaps her appearance in your dream was your unconscious mind's way of urging you to seek her out after you've woken. It could be that you have somehow sensed that she has the power to help or guide you.

The most advanced of the feminine archetypes, the dual character of the priestess/evil sorceress is also called by the names wise woman and witch. She is, by nature, both good and evil, positive and negative; in fact, like all of the archetypes, her light aspect cannot exist without her dark side.

Symbolic and Verbal Associations
- Feminine spirituality
- Wisdom
- Magic
- Guidance
- Selfish use of power; manipulation
- Chaos and destruction

Positive Interpretations: Did your dreaming mind conjure up the archetype of the high priestess, the wise woman of folklore who uses her knowledge and power for the collective good? For example, perchance you dreamed that you went on a quest to find knowledge or an answer to some question, and that, after much searching, you found yourself prostrate before an oracle: an older, white-haired woman with a gentle, yet confident, demeanor. If so, do you remember what she said to you? And did you recognize her? Or with whom in the real world do you associate the character of the high priestess? If you can identify your dream wise woman with someone in your waking world, then your unconscious mind may have been trying to tell you that this woman may be willing and able to act as your guide and mentor. It is also possible that this person has already been acting in this role, and that your unconscious was sending you the message that you would do well to heed her advice and guidance.

Negative Interpretations: Is it possible that you may have dreamed of the evil sorceress, who shares all of the high priestess's knowledge, but who uses her powers for her own selfish ends? For instance, did you have a nightmare in which a dark-robed witch had cast her spell on you? Perhaps, in your dream, this evil woman had confined you within a magical circle and she was planning to boil you alive in her great pot of supernatural stew? If so, did you recognize your dream witch? Or with whom do you associate this character? Whenever you dream of the evil sorceress or witch, you will probably want to pay close attention: it could be that you have unconsciously detected that someone in your life, most likely someone who has some amount of power over you, has been plotting to use this power to harm you. Finally, you may also want to consider whether you yourself have been acting the part of the evil sorceress, perhaps by behaving in a selfish, manipulating way that has only served to alienate you from others in your waking life.

Related Dreams

pages 48, 100, 111,
121, 142 & 143

CHAPTER 6

SPIRITUALITY &
THE SUPERNATURAL

Dreams that revolve around issues of spirituality and religion will usually be colored by your own beliefs and experiences in these areas. They can, however, point toward a need or desire to "rise above" one's day-to-day problems or else to be guided by a "higher" authority. And depending on whether they are negative or positive in tone, dreams that incorporate magical or supernatural beings or events may signify that you do not feel in control in your waking world or that you long for the impossible to become a reality.

My Angels Dreams

★ ★ ★ ★ ★ ★ ★ ★ ★ ★ ★ ★ ★ ★ ★ ★ ★ ★ ★

A Guardian Angel?

Dreaming of angels is often a sign of an unconscious desire for an element of spirituality in your daily life. Are you currently experiencing a spiritual awakening, contemplating your faith, or searching for life's deeper meaning? Or has someone—maybe a close friend or your sibling—taken on the role of your "guardian angel" by helping you to make some positive, life-changing decisions?

ANGELS

★ ★

Regardless of their religious association, angels (and also saints, bodhisattvas, and avatars) are perfect beings, the embodiments of goodness and purity. They are not gods themselves, but they do have access to heavenly wisdom, and they are traditionally viewed as being messengers or intermediaries between humans and the divine. Angels are typically represented with wings, which are symbols of transcendence, and haloes, signifying their holiness and divine illumination. And when they appear in the world of dreams, there is generally some spiritual or divine meaning, or perhaps a test of faith, at hand.

Symbolic and Verbal Associations
‹ Perfection
‹ Spiritual purity and goodness
‹ Transcendence
‹ Holiness; divine illumination
‹ Otherworldliness

Positive Interpretations: In general, when our dreams are graced by the presence of an angel, a saint, or a similar being, the meaning probably has to do with goodness and the quest for spiritual betterment—qualities to which we should try to aspire. As you slept, did you feel that you were being blessed and protected by your guardian angel? If so, this may have been an unconscious affirmation that you have made a correct choice or decision, or that you have been behaving in such a way that is righteous and good. However, sometimes the message that a dream angel brings can be relatively straightforward. If you are familiar with Christian teachings and you dreamed of St. Michael, the angel who cast the rebel Lucifer out of heaven, could it be that your unconscious mind was telling you that there is some negative person whom you would do well to eject from your waking sphere? (For instance, perhaps the new boarder in your house has been plaguing you and your family with his loud music and parties, his bad attitude, and his general disregard for the rules that you have set.) Finally, dreaming of an angel or a similar being may be a sign that you are opening up to a higher level of spiritual consciousness. If you are unsure as to the meaning of the angel's appearance, try meditating on your dream; this may help you to gain new spiritual awareness and insight.

Negative Interpretations: If you were visited by a dream angel, he or she may have brought you a message from higher up (whether you believe the message to have come from the divine, from your unconscious, or from both together). Did the angel warn you that you have made some transgression of thought or deed? If so, you will probably want to consider whether you should take a more ethical position with regard to some issue that you are struggling with in your waking world.

Related Dreams
pages 144, 148, 150, 212, 267 & 339

DEVILS

✶✶

In Christian lore, devils and demons were originally fallen angels. Cast into hell for their rebellion against God, they now owe their allegiance to the devil (also known as Satan, Lucifer, Beelzebub, and Old Nick). These demons retained their supernatural powers, however, which they now use to tempt and torment humankind. If you dreamed of the devil or his wicked cohorts, this does not signify that you are hurtling toward damnation. Everyone who has ever lived must navigate the convoluted course between good and evil, and sometimes our own personal demons can be viewed as messengers: unconscious warnings that we are in danger of straying from the trail of righteousness.

My Devils Dreams

....
....
....
....
....
....
....
....
....
....

✶ ✶

Symbolic and Verbal Associations

- ☾ Evil; malevolence
- ☾ Immorality
- ☾ Hell; darkness
- ☾ Temptation
- ☾ Unhappiness; misery

Positive Interpretations: Were you perplexed by a dream that featured a devil or demon because you feel that you are an ethical, decent person who strives for goodness in everything that you do? Perhaps, in your dream, a demon had latched onto your back and, no matter how hard you fought, you were unable to shake him off. If so, your dream may not refer to your current life at all. Instead, the dream demon may have been summoned by your unconscious to remind you of a past wrong that you committed that has never been corrected. (For instance, did you borrow money from your brother many years ago—so long ago that you both seem to have forgotten that you never paid him back? Now that you have consciously acknowledged the debt to your brother, the demon that you dreamed of may continue to harass you until you have settled the matter.)

Negative Interpretations: Did you awake from a fantastical nightmare in which the devil and his cohorts were dancing around your bed in celebration of their conquest of your eternal soul? If so, is there something in your waking life that you are feeling unsettled or guilty about? Perhaps you have been considering whether to take an action that you feel is not quite right, but that would bring you some immediate benefit at the expense of others. Your dream devil may have been a warning from your unconscious that you are in great danger of falling into the spell of an evil temptation that, in the end, will lead you to your own unhappiness. It is also possible that a dream that involves devils or demons is an alert to an external threat rather than a reference to a demon that skulks inside of you. Could it be that you have unconsciously detected negativity from someone in the real world? If you think that this is the case, you will probably want to pay close attention to the message of your dream, and to be on your guard when you are dealing with this person.

Personal Demons

Devils can symbolize evil or temptation when they appear in dreams. They don't always signify that you are straying from the path of goodness by behaving badly, however. Instead, they may reflect your struggle to make a decision or choice between something dull, but worthy, that you know you should opt for and something that may be deeply tempting, but morally questionable.

Related Dreams

pages 141, 145, 257, 260, 311 & 338

My Fairies, Elves & Imps Dreams

✶ ✶ ✶ ✶ ✶ ✶ ✶ ✶ ✶ ✶ ✶ ✶ ✶ ✶ ✶ ✶ ✶ ✶

Fairy Stories

Fairies, elves, and imps often flutter or hop into our dreams. Whether they take the form of a fairy godmother waving her wand and granting your wish or elusive creatures flitting around at the bottom of the garden, fairies are typically linked to magical possibilities and fantasy. Are you about to embark on a creative journey in the waking world?

FAIRIES, ELVES & IMPS

✶ ✶

In most cultures throughout the world and over many centuries, there has been a belief in a class of beings that are of another realm, who inhabit the wild areas of nature and the sea. Called fairies, elves, imps, sprites, dwarfs, or many other names, these magical beings sometimes excel over humans in terms of their power and knowledge—and, if they so choose, they can be a terrible force to reckon with, or they can be the source of very good fortune. In the language of dreams, fairies and the like represent the realm of fantasy and the forces of fate.

Symbolic and Verbal Associations

‹ Fantasy and creativity
‹ Mischief
‹ Magic and transformation
‹ The forces of nature
‹ Fate

Positive Interpretations: In your dream, did your fairy godmother appear and announce herself to you, perhaps offering to grant you your deepest, most secret desire? Then, with a wave of her wand and sprinkling of her fairy dust, did she transform you and your home into an image of beauty and elegance? No matter what the specifics were, if you had a dream in which some good fortune came to you via the realm of fairy, then it is very likely that you experienced a wish-fulfillment dream. Because they may uncover our deepest fantasies, these types of wish-fulfillment dreams may also help us consciously to solidify what it is that we really want out of life—perhaps helping us to make the choices that will lead us closer to our desires. If you dreamed of fairies, who symbolize fantasy and the creative forces of nature, it is also possible that your unconscious was attempting to spur you into better developing and utilizing your creative, artistic talents.

Negative Interpretations: As discussed above, not all fairies are friendly and helpful all of the time. In fact, some fairies of legend are notorious for wreaking misery and woe upon humankind, and many fairy tales have to do with the mischief that these creatures like to get up to. So if you dreamed that a gang of snickering, impish sprites had invaded your home and was injecting chaos and upset into the daily lives of everyone in your family, then could it be that you unconsciously suspect that, in the absence of any plausible, mundane explanation for a recent string of mishaps and misfortunes, supernatural forces beyond your control are at play? Or did you have a dream in which you caught a leprechaun, who promised that if you would set him free, he would lead you to a pot of gold? And, in your dream, did the leprechaun somehow trick or outsmart you, so that you ended up with no gold (and perhaps the worse for wear)? (However, though leprechauns are notorious for their mischief, they may also be a sign that a hoard of real hidden treasure is within your reach.)

Related Dreams

pages 131, 136, 137, 143, 146 & 259

GHOSTS

✶✶✶

If the popular movies are any measure, Western culture is obsessed by the idea of ghosts. Perhaps the allure has to do with our curiosity about the unknown, and our anxiety about what happens to us when we die. If you dreamed that you received an ethereal visitor, you may have been left quite shaken, and trying to determine the unconscious reason for your dream may help you to feel more at peace with your experience.

Symbolic and Verbal Associations
- A loved one who has died
- Nostalgia for the past
- Guilt over wrongdoings
- Fear of the unknown
- Shadows and darkness
- Incubi and succubi

Positive Interpretations: Did you dream that your beloved grandfather, many years dead, walked into the room with you and began talking to you as if nothing was out of the ordinary? And did you feel no fear—and were you, in fact, comforted by your dream? If so, it is likely that your grandfather has lately been on your mind. Maybe his birthday is coming up, or perhaps the anniversary of his death; or maybe you saw someone on the street who resembled him in some way. Whatever the explanation, you will probably be reassured by knowing that your dream is a sure sign that your grandfather remains very close to your heart. And if, in your dream, your grandfather gave you any advice, then he may have been acting in the role of the archetypal wise man, and you will probably want to pay close attention to what he told you.

Negative Interpretations: In your dream, did you cower under the covers in an attempt to conceal yourself from whatever shadowy phantom had found its way to your bedside? If so, did you recognize the specter? Or did the spirit say or do anything that has some association with someone in your present or past waking world? You may want to consider whether your visitor represented a source of guilt that you are feeling—either a person whom you feel that you have wronged or a "ghost" from your past that continues to haunt your conscience. Or, while sleeping, did you feel as though a great, unmovable force was crushing your chest so that you could not move and you could barely even breathe? In times past, when sexual pleasure was taboo, people who had erotic dreams were said to have been attacked by a sexually voracious incubus (a male demon) or succubus (a female demon). Today, the words "incubus" and "succubus" are still used to describe the nocturnal sensation of a weight pressing down on one's chest, together with a feeling of dread and an inability to move, a phenomenon that dream experts think may be due to temporary breathing difficulties combined with sleep paralysis (which we all experience while sleeping, but which we rarely become aware of).

Related Dreams
pages 92, 111, 133, 134, 254 & 260

My Ghosts Dreams

✶ ✶ ✶ ✶ ✶ ✶ ✶ ✶ ✶ ✶ ✶ ✶ ✶ ✶ ✶ ✶ ✶ ✶ ✶

Ghostly Apparitions

A figure from the past, a family member who has passed away, or simply a shadowy specter—ghosts are far from uncommon in dreamland. Such ethereal visitors can imbue dreams with a variety of meanings, not all of them scary. It may be, for instance, that your dream ghost's manifestation merely reflected your conscious curiosity about what happens to us when we die.

My Gods & Goddesses Dreams

✴ ✴ ✴ ✴ ✴ ✴ ✴ ✴ ✴ ✴ ✴ ✴ ✴ ✴ ✴

Divine Inspiration

Gods and goddesses symbolize the vast range of human emotions, so the appearance of one in your dream may have signaled that you are harboring powerful feelings regarding a real-life situation. Were you entranced by the beautiful Venus? Or did you tremble in fear before the mighty Zeus? Either way, thinking about your dream deity may help you to clarify how you're feeling at present.

GODS & GODDESSES

✶✶✶✶✶✶✶✶✶✶✶✶✶✶✶✶✶✶✶✶✶✶✶✶✶✶✶✶✶✶✶✶✶✶✶✶✶

As divine archetypes, gods and goddesses are eternal symbols of the spectrum of human emotions and experiences. As such, their symbolism is timeless, transcending the partitions of culture and geography. Throughout the ages, gods and goddesses have been said to use their powers to manipulate and control the lives of mortal humans—sometimes for a greater good, and sometimes for their own self-serving reasons. So if you dreamed of a god or a goddess, you will want to take into account any associations that you have with that particular deity when you are attempting to interpret your dream.

Symbolic and Verbal Associations
- Divinity
- The male and female archetypes
- Raw energy; human emotion
- Creation
- Law and order

Positive Interpretations: Throughout history, the characteristics of many gods and goddesses have been shared from culture to culture, and many deities have nearly identical counterparts that are called by a different name. For instance, the Canaanite Ba'al, the Greek Zeus, the Roman Jupiter, the Celtic Taranis, the Vedic Indra, the Hindu Vishnu, the Germanic Donar, and the Norse Thor all share the predilection of hurling thunderbolts to demonstrate their divine discontent. They are all archetypes—symbolizing emotions and experiences that are so universal as to render their base meanings ageless and unchanging. Are you a man who dreamed that you were being courted and seduced by a stunningly beautiful goddess of love? If so, you may have encountered Venus or one of her many counterparts. In fact, even if you do not recognize or know the name of the specific god or goddess that you dreamed of, you will probably recognize the emotions that he or she represents. And if you think that you may have dreamed of a deity, but you are unsure, if necessary consult the male and female archetypes described in Chapter 5 of this book to see if you can recognize your dream god's or goddess's role and, ultimately, understand his or her message to you.

Negative Interpretations: As discussed above, the gods and goddesses of the world represent the full range of human emotions, including those emotions that we tend to think of as being negative, such as aggression, jealousy, anger, and vengeance. So if you dreamed that you were trembling in fright before a divine, wrathful warlord, do you find your hostile male supervisor so intimidating that your fear is affecting your ability to do your job? Or if you dreamed of the Greek goddess Hera, who was ever consumed by jealousy over her husband, Zeus, could it be that you yourself have fallen into the lap of that green-eyed brute?

Related Dreams
pages 118, 126, 127, 131, 132 & 150

HEAVEN & HELL

More than anything else, dreams of being in heaven or hell usually refer to your current feelings or state of mind, in that you have probably been finding your life particularly heavenly or hellish of late. You may be relieved to know that such dreams are not predictive of where your soul is destined to spend the afterlife—if you believe in this form of life after death.

Symbolic and Verbal Associations
- States of mind
- Hopes and fears for the future
- Paradise
- Damnation
- Something very good, or "heavenly"
- Something that is outstanding (i.e., "one hell of a racehorse")

Positive Interpretations: Did you have a dream in which you were relaxing in the luxury of heaven, however you imagine heaven to be? Your dream version of paradise may have looked a lot like your favorite vacation destination. Maybe you found yourself upon a bright, tropical island with warm, glittering beaches filled with colorful parrots and coconut trees. If you did have a dream such as this, and if you have been feeling as though you are "in heaven" in the real world, then your dream was most likely mirroring your current state of mind, and affirming what you already know: that life is good. However, if you find yourself perplexed by such a dream because your life, as of late, has been anything but good, then what could have been the meaning of your dream vacation in paradise? It is possible that your unconscious sent you this sort of dream as a wish fulfillment, to make up for the current lack of bliss in your life, and also to hearten you to remember that life can, indeed, be good.

Negative Interpretations: Did you have a dream in which you found that you had died and gone to hell, where the devil and his army of demons were planning to do nasty, tortuous things to you? If so, there are two likely explanations for your nightmare, and only you will know which of the two is more probable. The first is that you are feeling guilty about some wrongdoing that you have committed (or that you have been tempted to commit) in the real world. And if you think that this explanation is valid—particularly if you are wracked with guilt over whatever you may have done—and if you have recurring dreams of this sort, then "righting" your "wrong" may be the only way for you to find peace in dreamland. The other possible explanation for dreams of this type is that, for whatever reason, your current waking life feels like a living hell, and in sending you the nightmare, your unconscious mind was simply mirroring your waking reality (and, perhaps, attempting to prompt you to do something about it).

My Heaven & Hell Dreams

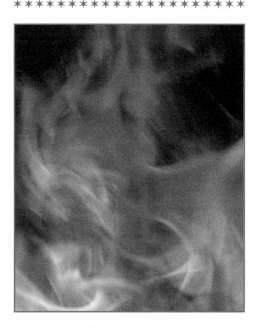

Paradise Lost
Dreaming of heaven or hell has less to do with the direction in which your soul may be heading when you shuffle off this mortal coil than with your current state of mind. So if you dreamed of burning fires and torture, are you going through a hellish time? Conversely, dreaming of heaven may signify that you've found peace and happiness in the waking world, at least for now.

Related Dreams

pages 92, 136, 137, 150, 260 & 261

My Magic, Rituals & Spells Dreams

....

....

....

....

....

....

....

....

* * * * * * * * * * * * * * * * *

The Magic Touch

Did you dream that you were the beneficiary of a spell that bestowed magical powers upon you or a possession, like Aladdin's lamp? If so, who performed the ritual? Understanding the meaning of your dream often hinges on the identity of the person who was working the magic. And if it was you, was your dream concerned with wish-fulfillment?

MAGIC, RITUALS & SPELLS

* *

In folklore, magical spells and rituals have often been cited as the cause of human good luck, as well as misfortune. However, unlike the type of magic worked by gods, demons, or fairies, rituals and spells are usually said to be the works of some member of the human community. And when magic rituals and spells feature prominently in your dream, an all-important clue as to the meaning of your dream will have to do with the identity of the magician.

Symbolic and Verbal Associations

‹ Wizards and witches
‹ The occult; hidden mysteries
‹ Being "bewitched" or "charmed" by, or "enchanted" with, someone or something
‹ Control; power
‹ Curses and blessings
‹ Psychic attacks and defenses

Positive Interpretations: Did you have a dream in which you were imbued with wonderful powers of magic? Perhaps, in your dream, you found yourself casting a magical circle, pentagram, or hexagram (all symbols of protection) on the earth, while chanting some ancient spell, which you knew was causing your lottery-ticket number to become the jackpot winner? If so, and if you wish that you could magically make yourself rich in the real world, then you probably experienced a simple wish-fulfillment dream—although it is also possible that your dream was mirroring your real-life feelings of vitality and euphoria. Dreams of magical rituals and spells can also be references to our hopes for the future. For example, if you are an expectant mother, did you dream that a magical guardian held your newborn baby in her arms and blessed her? (If so, and if you recognize the guardian, your unconscious may have been telling you that this person may be willing and able to act as your child's protector in the real world.) Or are you a man who dreamed that your girlfriend was brewing a large cauldron full of a magical elixir that was meant to cause you to fall in love with her? If so, your unconscious mind may have been pointing out that you have been "bewitched" or "enchanted" by your girlfriend (in which case, it may be interesting to note that cauldrons symbolize the womb).

Negative Interpretations: Did you have a dream in which your neighbor, with whom you often quarrel, pointed his magic wand at you, over the fence that separates your properties, and turned your prized herb garden into a rotting swampland of weeds? If so, could it be that you have unconsciously detected that your neighbor is planning to do you ill? (And it may or may not be relevant for you to know that, in the language of dreams, wands are considered to be both phallic symbols and conductors of powerful magical energies.)

Related Dreams
pages 133, 134, 144, 149 & 229

MAGICAL SHAPESHIFTING

In the realm of dreams, transformations happen all of the time. For instance, your mother-in-law may suddenly shapeshift into the family dog, or your family dog may turn into a unicorn! Often, when these fantastical dream transformations happen, we do not even think that anything is out of the ordinary or odd—that is, not until later, after we have awakened and when we are trying to recall our nocturnal adventures. However, when you dream that magic has been used to turn one being or thing into another before your dreaming eyes, then the being or thing that has been transformed (or destroyed) and the being or thing that has been created anew are likely to be significantly associated in your unconscious mind; and the recognition of this association may enlighten you to an important truth about yourself or your current reality.

My Magical Shapeshifting Dreams

Symbolic and Verbal Associations

(Destruction and creation
(Personas; the different masks or faces that a person wears
(Shapeshifting
(Rites of passage
(Someone's "real" personality or inner character

Positive Interpretations: Did you dream that you had turned into a winged Pegasus, and that you were joyously soaring up and over the mountains, valleys, and rivers of your fantasy dreamland? If so, have you been feeling blissfully free, light, or adventurous during your waking hours? Or do you wish that you could be so? In another scenario, if you dreamed that you had been transformed into a wizened and powerful wizard or priestess, could it be that you feel as though you have gone through a rite of passage and that you are now, finally, a wise elder who can serve as a guide to others? Or did you have a dream in which, as in the story of King Midas, everything that you touched turned into gold? This may have been a wish-fulfillment dream, but it may also have been an unconscious reflection of your current financial fortunes (and perhaps now is a good time to gamble on that big business venture that you've been pondering over for so long!)

Negative Interpretations: Did you have a dream in which you looked on with terror as your new landlord shapeshifted into a long-fanged, hairy werewolf? If so, then your dream may have carried an important message. It may be that you have unconsciously detected that your landlord, for all his seeming friendliness, is really a ferocious, hungry animal who will prey on you at any given chance. Or were you upset or frightened by a dream in which some everyday object was transformed into something more ominous? For instance, did you have a terrible nightmare in which your daughter's automobile was transformed into a hearse? If so, are you worried that your daughter's automobile is unsafe, or that she has been driving in a dangerous or reckless manner?

Amazing Transformations

Were you magically transformed into a different person, or else an animal or object, in your dream? Shifting shape in dreamland can reveal much about your current real-life situation. If you dreamed of being transformed into a mermaid, for example, have you recently seduced someone in waking life, or do you yearn to? See also page 146, on mythical creatures, when interpreting this dream.

Related Dreams

pages 87, 131, 133, 134, 145 & 146

My Miracles Dreams

✴ ✴ ✴ ✴ ✴ ✴ ✴ ✴ ✴ ✴ ✴ ✴ ✴ ✴ ✴

Make a Wish

Did you have a fantastic dream in which your every wish came true? Or did your nightmare of having a life-threatening illness come to an end when your dreaming self experienced a miracle cure? As well as being concerned with wish-fulfillment, such dreams can signify that you long to be rewarded for your suffering or sacrifices in the waking world.

MIRACLES

✴ ✴

Miracles are what many people call those (usually positive) occurrences that seem to have no other explanation except for divine intervention. In fact, except for their association with religion or spirituality, the idea of miracles is very much akin to that of magic.

Symbolic and Verbal Associations
(The supernatural
(The will of the supreme being or deity
(A reward for piety or goodness
(Religious faith, piety, or devotion
(Something wonderful

Positive Interpretations: Did you have a dream in which something marvelous and wonderful happened to you or to someone else? For instance, if you have a loved one who is gravely ill, perhaps in a coma, did you dream that he or she underwent a miraculous recovery? Or did you dream that your old, beloved, pet dog, who has gone almost entirely blind and deaf, was suddenly able to see and hear as well as when she was a puppy? If so, then you have almost certainly experienced a wish-fulfillment dream. (However, if you are religious, then you may feel that your dream came from whatever god or goddess, or gods or goddesses, you believe in, and that it was a sign that your loved one or dog will surely undergo the miraculous transformation of which you dreamed.) Alternatively, did you dream that, by a miracle, the world had been transformed into a planet of peace and love? If, lately, you have been feeling depressed or downhearted because of the dire state of the world's affairs, then your dream may have been sent by your unconscious in order to boost your morale and to give you hope for the future.

Negative Interpretations: The idea of a "negative miracle" may seem strange, but it may help to think of an event that might be called a miracle as being like a "reward" for some people while, at the very same time, it may be a "punishment" for others. A good example is found in the Old Testament of the Bible: when Moses raised his staff to part the Red Sea, this was a positive miracle for the Israelites, but it was surely a negative miracle for the Egyptians from whom they were fleeing, who were swallowed up and drowned by the returning waters. (The same can be said of the biblical story of the plagues on Egypt.) So if you are an avid competitive bowler, did you dream that, just before you were to bowl in a championship game, your fiercest opponent prayed for, and received, a divine miracle that caused your thumb to swell up so large that it would not fit into the hole of your bowling ball? If so, could it be that, deep down, for one reason or another, you feel that you are undeserving of the championship, and that, if justice were served, God would intervene and carry your opponent to victory?

Related Dreams
pages 136, 138, 140, 142, 143 & 150

MONSTERS

As a child, you may have been afraid of the monster that you thought lived in your closet or under your bed, and you may have had nightmares about the fiend's emergence from its lair. Your childhood fear of monsters probably had to do with the fairy tales that your parents may have read to you. But sometimes even adults have nightmares about monstrous beasts. Most dream analysts agree that, in the language of dreams, monsters represent our deep-rooted fears, "ugly" emotions, "monstrous" urges, or painful experiences, problems, or phobias.

Symbolic and Verbal Associations
- Fears and worries
- The unknown
- Danger; a predatory beast
- Evil; dark forces
- Someone or something that is of an exceedingly large, "monstrous" size
- Ugliness; a misshapen form
- Bestial urges

Positive Interpretations: Not all apparent "monsters" are bad, as many, especially modern, fairy tales will attest to. And not all of the emotions that our unconscious might represent as monsters are really unnatural or evil—sometimes, their materialization in dreamland is a sign that they are struggling for self-expression, and the best thing that you may be able to do is to try to come to terms with them. For example, perhaps you are someone who, because of your own internalized bigotry, has been fighting against your attraction to members of your own sex; because of your deep-rooted fears, your feelings of same-sex desire may manifest themselves in your dreams in the form of some monstrous beast. If you can bring yourself to face and accept the "beast" within, you may find that it is not really a monster at all.

Negative Interpretations: Did you have a nightmare in which you were running as fast as you could from a hideous, misshapen ogre that you knew was planning to devour you alive? If so, can you identify your dream ogre with anyone in your waking world? Perhaps there is someone, particularly an older man who might have power over you (such as a boss), whose cruelty and maltreatment of you has turned your daily life into a misery? (And, especially if you are a woman, could your dream ogre have represented a lustful, predatory man whom you feel threatened by?) In another scenario, you may have dreamed that you were being stalked by a blood-sucking vampire. Again, in interpreting your dream, it is important to consider whether you can identify your dream monster with someone in the real world—in this case, someone who might be threatening to "sap your life force" or "bleed you dry." Identifying your dream monster may not only set your mind at ease, it is also likely to bring the nightmares to a halt.

Related Dreams
pages 129, 137, 139, 143, 146 & 221

My Monsters Dreams

Wild Thing

The ravening monster that you dreamed about may have represented either an external threat or a fear or negative feeling that lurks within you yourself. If you dreamed that you were confronted by a hideous beast, could the beast have symbolized a menacing situation you're facing in your professional life, or else an ugly emotion that you are suppressing?

My Mythical Creatures Dreams

✦ ✦ ✦ ✦ ✦ ✦ ✦ ✦ ✦ ✦ ✦ ✦ ✦ ✦ ✦ ✦ ✦

Fables and Fantasies

Mythical creatures can signal fantasy and a desire for adventure when they appear in dreamland. Do you long for some excitement in your everyday life? A change of direction or a new career, perhaps? If you dreamed of a unicorn, could you be subconsciously preparing to turn over a new leaf, or might its pallic symbolism be significant?

MYTHICAL CREATURES

✶ ✶

If you dreamed of a fantastical creature, your unconscious may have borrowed its image from the chronicles of mythology and folklore, which are filled with tales of such beasts. Some of them are combinations of two or more real-world creatures, and some of them are strictly from the realm of fancy. If you are familiar with the myth from which your dream creature emerged, or if you can identify it with something in your waking world, or what it means to you personally, then this will help you to determine the message that it brought.

Symbolic and Verbal Associations
❲ Fantasy and adventure
❲ Unconscious instincts
❲ The predators or protectors of humans
❲ A hybrid being (such as the half-man, half-bull Minotaur of Greek myth)
❲ The forces of the natural elements (earth, air, fire, and water)

Positive Interpretations: Did you dream of a creature that inhabited the sky or the air, such as a winged Pegasus or dragon? Mythical creatures that are said to inhabit the air are symbols of freedom and spiritual or intellectual transcendence—and if you dreamed of one of them, then your unconscious may have been prompting you to "soar above" the humdrum problems that are afflicting your daily life by tapping into your spiritual or intellectual potential. Or did you dream of the unicorn, whose all-white coat is associated with purity and goodness? (If so, you may also be interested to know that the unicorn's horn can be a phallic symbol, which lends another layer of meaning to the legend that the unicorn can only be tamed by a virgin.) And if you view the dragon in terms of Chinese mythology, as a protector and a bringer of good fortune, happiness, and children, then you were probably quite thrilled if you dreamed of this beast. Alternatively, did you dream of watching a phoenix consume itself in fire and then rise from its ashes, renewed? If so, your unconscious may have been hinting that your own life is due for a renewal.

Negative Interpretations: In Western lore, the dragon's symbolism is quite different from the meanings that it carries in Chinese mythology. And if you have been influenced by the Western idea of the dragon, which associates this creature with hostility and aggression, then its appearance in your dream may have alarmed you. The inference of such a dream may be that a hostile authority figure is threatening to overwhelm you—unless you can gather the courage to defend yourself. Or perhaps you dreamed that you were being beckoned to by a siren? According to legend, these lovely sea nymphs sang songs that would lure sailors toward the jagged rocks on which they sat, causing them to wreck their ships and to drown. Could your dream have been a warning to be wary of a seductive woman in your life?

Related Dreams

pages 143, 145, 368, 371, 363 & 387

PARALLEL WORLDS

As strange as most dreams are, some dreams are stranger still, especially when we awake with the conviction that we have spent our slumbering hours not resting peacefully in bed, but traveling through a world that was very similar to, but also quite different from, our waking one. Examples of these "parallel-world" dreams include dreams of alien abductions, out-of-body experiences, and lucid dreams.

My Parallel Worlds Dreams

★ ★ ★ ★ ★ ★ ★ ★ ★ ★ ★ ★ ★ ★ ★ ★ ★ ★ ★

Symbolic and Verbal Associations

- Escape
- Emotional trauma or upheaval
- Wish fulfillment
- Fear of the unknown, or of death
- Feelings of "alienation"

Positive Interpretations: Did you have a dream in which your consciousness or spirit had left its body, allowing you to soar freely through space and time? Some people believe that these types of exhilarating experiences are actually out-of-body experiences (also known as astral travel or projection). Many people report having had these sorts of experiences during times of physical or emotional trauma or illness. Whether you believe that you had an out-of-body experience or that it was only a dreaming fantasy, it was likely to have been an indication that, for whatever reason, you are now in need of an escape (however temporary) from your current reality. In a similar vein are lucid dreams. You have probably, at some time or another while you were sleeping, suddenly become consciously aware of the fact that you were dreaming. Most people wake up when this occurs, but it is possible to train yourself to remain sleeping and dreaming, thereby giving you the ability to, at least partially, control your dreams. The ability to have lucid dreams is a powerful tool, which opens up many possibilities—not only for facing your dream "monsters," but also for enjoying wish-fulfillment dreams.

Negative Interpretations: Did you dream that you were visited, or even abducted, by aliens or "spacemen"? When we have a dream that puts our sleeping selves into contact with extraterrestrials, this is often an indication that we feel that we are under threat or attack from "alien" forces. Though it probably won't be easy, if you can bring yourself to begin a dialogue with these "alien" influences—either in the dream world, in reality, or in both—then you may be able to come to understand them, thereby helping to alleviate your fears of the unknown. Another possible explanation of dreams involving aliens is that you feel that you have become "alienated" from those who were once close to you, such as your friends or your family. Again, in this instance, you may be able to assuage much of your anxiety by cultivating better communication with those whom you feel alienated from.

Alienation?

Did you dream of an alien landscape peopled with otherwordly creatures that, on closer inspection, turned out to be fake? If your dream fear then subsided, perhaps your unconscious was urging you to face up to a situation in which you have felt alienated unnecessarily.

Related Dreams

pages 130, 141, 165, 222, 229 & 292

SPIRITUALITY & THE SUPERNATURAL

My Prophets & Saints Dreams

----

* * * * * * * * * * * * * * * * *

Guiding Light

Dreaming of a prophet or messenger from a higher plane may suggest that you're experiencing some kind of spiritual crisis for which you crave a resolution. Are you feeling lost and in need of direction in waking life? If so, heeding any message that was conveyed to you in your dream may offer a clue as to how best to achieve closure and move on.

PROPHETS & SAINTS

Prophets and saints may be most likely to appear in our dreams at moments of deep spiritual crisis. Because they are traditionally considered to be divine messengers, or intermediaries between the supreme being and humans, their function and symbolism is similar to that of angels—the main difference being that those who believe in prophets and saints believe that these divinely blessed figures were once mortal, flesh-and-blood human beings (unlike their angelic counterparts).

Symbolic and Verbal Associations
- Divine guidance
- A messenger
- Universal truth
- Higher spiritual awareness
- Someone who is a "false prophet"

Positive Interpretations: Did you dream of a prophet or a saint who has a spiritual significance for you? For instance, are you a Buddhist who dreamed of Gautama Siddhartha, a Muslim who received a vision of Muhammad, a Christian to whom Christ or St. Peter appeared, or a Jew who dreamed of the Messiah or the prophet Elijah? If so—no matter what your specific spiritual beliefs are or which saint or prophet your sleeping mind conjured up—the fact that your unconscious mind summoned a symbol of such great significance to you indicates that you may be in the midst of a profound spiritual crisis or crossroads in your life—and you were probably deeply affected by your dream. Have you been feeling particularly anxious about some important decision that you are being called upon to make, perhaps a decision that is so big that it is likely to change the course of your life? If so, it is advisable that you listen closely to the message that your prophet or saint brought to you because, as a conduit of divine wisdom, this spiritual guide is likely to represent your best interests. And even if you are not religious, or if you dreamed of a spiritual figure of a religion that is not your own, do not simply dismiss your dream messenger as being a "false prophet" as your unconscious probably understands that all religions share some part of the universal truth.

Negative Interpretations: If you dreamed of a prophet or a saint, did he or she bear a message of warning regarding something that you feel sorry for or embarrassed about (i.e., some transgression that you have committed, or some "faulty" aspect of your personality)? Again, as above, you will want to consider the point that your spiritual guide bore; his or her dream manifestation may be an unconscious prompt that you are ready to make a change in your life, and to ask for, and receive, absolution for your "sins." Or, finally, could your dream saint or prophet's appearance have been an unconscious attempt to balance out the fact that your waking life is largely lacking in spirituality?

Related Dreams

pages 133, 134, 136, 149, 150 & 212

RELIGIOUS CEREMONIES

If you dreamed of an elaborate religious ceremony, you may have been comforted, unsettled, or puzzled—depending upon your religious background and feelings, which must be taken into account when you are attempting to interpret your dream, as well as the setting and any religious paraphernalia that was involved. And although the primary significance of such a dream will often accord with your own particular religious education and beliefs, it is also true that some interpretations are fairly universal, even for atheist dreamers.

Symbolic and Verbal Associations

‹ A request for divine assistance or intervention
‹ A religious congregation or community
‹ Joy; an uplifting experience
‹ Enlightenment
‹ Healing; renewal
‹ Mystical transformation
‹ A stagnant ritual or tradition, lacking in spiritual vitality

Positive Interpretations: If you had a dream in which you were chanting, singing, or reading some sacred scriptures, or if you dreamed that you heard any of these things, then this may have been a signal from your unconscious mind of your desire to receive a divine answer to some question (which may be of a spiritual nature). Or did you have a dream that you were watching or participating in some religious ceremony or rite with which you are very familiar? For instance, if you were raised as Roman Catholic and you dreamed of lining up to receive the Holy Communion, how did this make you feel? If you felt comforted, blessed, or uplifted, then, depending on your current religious practices, your dream may have been a reflection of your sense of security and joy because you feel that you are living in accord with the moral code that you believe in, or else of your desire to reconnect with your religious background. And it may be interesting to note that dream chalices, which enclose the water of life (as well as, for some Christians, the blood of Christ), may reflect how you see yourself and your potential in the world. (So was your dream chalice made of gold and jewel-encrusted? Or was it a humble pewter cup?)

Negative Interpretations: Did a dream in which you were witnessing a religious ceremony kindle your feelings of anger, rejection, or rebellion? If so, then your unconscious mind may have been pushing you to break away from convention and assert your individuality (which is possibly being stifled by a rigid belief system or moral code). Or if you dreamed that you were praying fervently, perhaps tearfully, it may be that you are in search of some divine or spiritual advice, assistance, or intervention to help you with a troubling problem or dilemma.

Related Dreams
pages 99, 102, 121, 142, 148 & 212

My Religious Ceremonies Dreams

Act of Worship

Dreaming of praying or watching someone offering prayers and gifts can point to a desire for effective assistance with a problem that you are facing in everyday life. If a real-world situation is proving difficult to handle, do you wish that you could receive divine inspiration or enlightenment? And did your dream provide it, be it obviously or obliquely?

My Supreme Being Dreams

....
....
....
....
....
....
....
....
....

* * * * * * * * * * * * * * * * * * *

Meeting His Maker

In your dream, did you watch as someone knelt reverently before his supreme being? And did you feel comforted by the sight of him receiving spiritual or emotional support as a result of his supplications? This dream could mean that you sense that there is someone or something that may be able to relieve your own waking-life troubles.

THE SUPREME BEING

* *

"God," "Goddess," "the Creator," "the Alpha," "the Everything": whatever you call the supreme being—if you believe in a supreme being, that is, and even if you do not—a dream involving this omnipotent "all" is likely to have had a significant effect upon your psyche. In fact, when interpreting your dream, your own personal understanding or envisaging of the supreme being is not as significant as your recognition (either conscious or unconscious) of its transcendent, all-powerful, divine authority.

Symbolic and Verbal Associations
‹ Universal, absolute wisdom
‹ Omnipotence; the universal forces
‹ Creation (and destruction)
‹ The eternal life force
‹ Perfect enlightenment

Positive Interpretations: Did you have a dream in which the supreme being—however you envision him, her, or it—appeared before you? If so, how did your dream self react? If you felt blissful, blessed, or joyously uplifted, then your dream may have been a sign that you are on a spiritual quest for divine illumination (or else that your life has been lacking a spiritual element, which you need). (But if you felt fear or guilt, then you will probably want to consult below, under Negative Interpretations.) In your dream, did you ask anything of the supreme being? Or did the supreme being share with you any divine wisdom? An additional layer of interpretation may be that your dream was a reflection of your feelings of joyfulness and of being at peace and in harmony with the eternal forces of the universe.

Negative Interpretations: If you dreamed of the supreme being during times of trouble (perhaps your life seems doomed or chaotic and out of your control, or perhaps you have been feeling powerless and insignificant), then your unconscious may be seeking guidance or wisdom from the uppermost spiritual plane. However, particularly if you felt fear or guilt in the presence of the supreme being, it is also possible that your dream was a message that you have fallen into some moral corruption, and that you should make a close examination of the nature of your motives and actions. And if the supreme being appeared in the guise or form of someone you know, then another interpretation is that you have developed an excessive amount of reverence for someone in your life—someone who may have power over you, such as a teacher or a boss—so much so that your "worship" of this person has become detrimental to your own interests (and, depending on the details of your dream, your unconscious may also have been hinting that your feelings toward this person are somewhat misplaced or inappropriate, in that this person may be unworthy of such loyal veneration).

Related Dreams
pages 109, 113, 121, 140, 141 & 148

CHAPTER 7
THE HOME

The dreaming mind sometimes summons a house into our sleep to
represent the self. A dream home may therefore house your hopes,
fears, memories, and secrets, and may also reflect how you are
feeling about yourself, be it in isolation or in relation to the other
people in your waking life.

THE HOME

My Attic Dreams

✷ ✷ ✷ ✷ ✷ ✷ ✷ ✷ ✷ ✷ ✷ ✷ ✷ ✷ ✷ ✷ ✷ ✷

A Past Reminder

Did you dream of rummaging through dusty boxes full of long-forgotten items—old photograph albums, perhaps—that had been stored in the attic? If you did, it may be that you are seeking a connection with your past. Could it be time to call a friend or relative whom you haven't seen for a while?

ATTICS

✶✶✶✶✶✶✶✶✶✶✶✶✶✶✶✶✶✶✶✶✶✶✶✶✶✶✶✶✶✶✶✶✶✶

In the symbolism of dreams, attics can represent either higher consciousness (because of their lofty location at the top of the house) or memories (having to do with their traditional function as a storage repository). When interpreting the meaning of your dream attic, it will also be important to consider your personal associations with this often cluttered and seldom-visited room (i.e., fear, nostalgia, repulsion, etc.).

Symbolic and Verbal Associations
- Higher consciousness
- Ideals and aspirations
- Spirituality
- Nostalgia; cherished items from the past
- Family history (as documented in journals and photo albums)

Positive Interpretations: Did you have a dream in which you had gone back to the house where you grew up, which your parents sold long ago, but which, in your dream, was remarkably restored to how you remember it from when you were a child? And did you find yourself wanting, more than anything, to explore the attic? In your dream, perhaps you sifted and sorted through old family photo albums, clothing, and other family "junk." If so, your dream self may have found much delight in going through these old family things. A dream of this sort is an indication that, for whatever reason, your unconscious mind felt the need to remind you of your past. Could it be that you have been feeling nostalgic, and that you desire to get back in touch with your family and roots? Or is there some old family business that is undone, such as the settling of your deceased aunt's estate? Alternatively, might you need reminding of a family lesson, perhaps something that you learned as a child, which could help you with a current problem that you are facing? Of course, because the other meaning of a dream attic has to do with ideals, aspirations, and higher consciousness, a dream that involves an attic may signal that it's time for you to evaluate the things in life that are really important to you (and if, in your dream attic, you rediscovered some long-forgotten "treasure," then consider whether you have let slip some aspiration or ideal that you once held dear).

Negative Interpretations: If you dreamed of rummaging through the old family attic, did it bring up painful or difficult memories for you—memories that you have spent many years trying to forget? Your dream may have been a signal that these memories are still with you, no matter how hard you try to push them out of your conscious mind, and that you will need to deal with them, one way or another, before you will be able to move on. And if, in your dream, you were boxing things up to give to charity, then you may well be on your way to doing so. A similar interpretation may apply if you were cleaning or sweeping up your dream attic.

Related Dreams

pages 49, 111, 153, 164, 165 & 213

BASEMENTS

My Basement Dreams

In the world of dreams, basements and cellars, which are usually underground and at the very bottom of a house, are symbols of things that lie "below" the surface: the unconscious, basic urges, and instincts, and also things that we may want to conceal from others, such as sources of guilt or shame. And it is perhaps significant to note the classic horror-movie portrayal of the basement, where there is likely to be a body stashed away or a foul fiend lurking—or even a gateway to the underworld!

Symbolic and Verbal Associations

‹ The unconscious
‹ Basic instincts and urges
‹ Things concealed
‹ Guilt or shame
‹ Valuables or treats, stored away for future use

Positive Interpretations: Did you dream that you entered a house—perhaps a house that is familiar to you, that you may have once lived in—and marched straight down to the basement, pushing aside your fears, in order to confront some issue that has remained buried in (but not gone from) your unconscious? If so, your dream confrontation may have been a step toward your peace of mind with regard to the troubling issue. But in addition to being hiding places for things that we do not wish anyone to see (for more on this, see below, under "Negative Interpretations"), basements and cellars are also where people store valuables, goodies, and treats (such as wine) that they may only bring out on special occasions. In your dream, did you go down to the basement in order to bring back up some quality or character trait that, for whatever reason, you have concealed or suppressed during your waking hours? Another function of basements and cellars is as places of safety and protection, particularly in geographical areas that are subject to hurricanes and cyclones—so when trying to make sense of your dream, you should also consider whether this type of interpretation may apply.

Negative Interpretations: Did you have a dream in which you were descending the basement stairs with dread and trepidation? If so, do you know what you were afraid that you might encounter down there? If it was a monster or a "boogeyman," might this creature represent something that you feel uneasiness about—perhaps a source of guilt or shame that you (or someone close to you, such as a parent or a sibling) have attempted to bury deep below the level of consciousness? In your dream, did you turn and flee from the boogeyman, or did you bravely face him? (And if you did face him, you may have found out that he is not such a monster after all.) Finally, because they are symbolic of the unconscious, and because of their underground location (which may remind us of a grave, or of the underworld), dream basements and cellars may also reference our anxieties or fears of the unknown or of death.

Out of Sight

Basements are often places where we keep things out of sight. Dreaming of being in a basement may consequently mean that you are concerned with issues that lie beneath the surface in your day-to-day life. Are these feelings that you are repressing? Or is something that you've been keeping secret starting to weigh heavily upon your conscience?

Related Dreams

pages 145, 160,

165 & 385

THE HOME

My Bathroom Dreams

✳ ✳ ✳ ✳ ✳ ✳ ✳ ✳ ✳ ✳ ✳ ✳ ✳ ✳ ✳ ✳ ✳ ✳ ✳

Cleaning and Cleansing

Dreaming of washing may mean that you want to cleanse yourself of some unwanted issue or concern. Or did you dream that you were soaking in a bathtub, relaxing after a tough day? A dream like this may signify that you need to slow things down a little, or to take a few days off work, in order to make more time for yourself.

BATHROOMS

✳✳

In dream-house symbolism, bathrooms are sometimes associated with an upper story, which represents a level of consciousness that is one step higher than our normal, everyday concerns. In reality, bathrooms are places where we wash our bodies and rid ourselves of unwanted waste—and in the language of dreams, it is easy to apply these functions to the emotional realm.

Symbolic and Verbal Associations
- Cleansing
- Renewal
- A need to relieve or purge oneself of something (or someone)
- Self-examination and -critique
- Cosmetic transformation; covering one's "blemishes"

Positive Interpretations: If you have a large family, the bathroom may be the only place in the house where you can manage to get any time and space to yourself! Did you dream of luxuriating in a hot bubble bath, perhaps with soft music playing and only a few candles for light? If so, your unconscious was probably taking the opportunity to give you a bit of the rest, renewal, and rejuvenation that you are so desperately craving during your waking hours. The bathroom is also the place where many people primp or "make themselves up" in preparation for special occasions, by shaving, doing their hair, and applying cosmetics, perfumes, etc. If you dreamed of doing this, do you know what you were preparing for? And regarding your self-examination, did you like what you saw in the mirror? (Or, conversely, was there something about your face that you were trying to "cover up"? For more on this, read below under "Negative Interpretations.")

Negative Interpretations: If you had a dream in which you were taking a shower or a bath, is there something that you are anxious to cleanse yourself of? Some trouble that you'd like to send down the drain? Or, in your dream, were you frantically trying to "wash your hands of" something? Or, as in the song, is there someone that you wish that you could "wash out of your hair"? Dreaming of any of these activities implies a need to cleanse your conscience of some problem or issue, and, similarly, a dream of using the toilet is likely to have been a reference to your need to rid or purge yourself of some unwanted thoughts, feelings, or memories. We also tend to look at ourselves critically when we are standing in front of the bathroom mirror, and dreams of looking into a mirror are likely to be very telling about our self-image. If you dreamed that you were applying makeup or cosmetic "cover up" to your face, what were you trying to conceal? Or did you look into the mirror and see that you had been transformed into someone else entirely? If so, what did your new face look like, and how did this make you feel?

Related Dreams

pages 44, 48, 56, 57, 125 & 387

BEDROOMS

✦✦

Like bathrooms, bedrooms are usually associated with an upper story in terms of dream-house symbolism, meaning that they have to do with a level of consciousness that is a step higher than our day-to-day, "ground-level" thoughts and concerns. Specifically, dream bedrooms have to do with such widely varied associations as safety and refuge, rest and dreams, and eroticism and sex. Therefore, when attempting to interpret the meaning of your dream bedroom, you will want to consider as many details of your dream as you can remember.

Symbolic and Verbal Associations
(A personal refuge
(Safety and security
(Sex and eroticism
(Rest and sleep
(Sickness and recuperation

Positive Interpretations: Did you dream of your ideal bedroom, a place that was your personal refuge, where you felt safe and sound enough to let yourself fall into a peaceful, deep sleep? Or was your dream bedroom the ideal setting for a romantic, erotic, sexual encounter? Your answers to these questions are likely to indicate your current needs and yearnings—whether for rest, convalescence, and recuperation, or for erotic stimulation and sexual fulfillment. And if your dream bedroom was complete with a big, fourposter bed, you may be interested to know that this indicates a desire for old-fashioned-style romance (however you envision this to be)! Most people spend periods of illness and recuperation mostly in bed. So if you dreamed that you were lying ill in your "sickbed," or were convalescing in your dream bedroom, there are a number of possible interpretations. For example, could your dream have been an unconscious warning that you need to take better care of yourself? Or do you desire a temporary release from your real-world, daily duties and responsibilities? (For more on this, see "Sickness," page 56.)

Negative Interpretations: Did you dream that your bedroom, which should be a place of safety and comfort, was instead a scary, menacing place? In your dream, did you cower in the corner or beneath the covers of your dream bed? Did you fear that there was a ghost, monster, boogeyman, or an intruder hiding in your closet or underneath your bed, who was just waiting for the opportunity to spring upon you? If so, are you feeling unsafe in your daily life—not necessarily physically, but perhaps emotionally insecure? Or could your dream monster, ghost, or boogeyman have represented some deep-rooted fear or problem, an "ugly" emotion, or a "monstrous" urge that you are harboring, or else some painful past experience or phobia? Or is it possible that your dream was more literal, and that your unconscious has detected that someone in your waking world is planning to do you ill?

Related Dreams

My Bedroom Dreams

✦✦✦✦✦✦✦✦✦✦✦✦✦✦✦✦✦✦✦✦✦✦

Sleep or Seduction?

Your dream bedroom may have provided lots of clues as to how you are truly feeling. The type of room that you saw in your dream—be it a private, comfortable space or a romantic boudoir—may have hinted at what you are yearning for. Is it rest and relaxation? Is it more involvement in personal interests and hobbies? Or does your sex life need spicing up?

My Dining Room Dreams

✱ ✱ ✱ ✱ ✱ ✱ ✱ ✱ ✱ ✱ ✱ ✱ ✱ ✱ ✱ ✱ ✱ ✱

Food for Thought

Did you dream of preparing for a meal with your family and friends in a cozy dining room? A dream like this may indicate that you are concerned with issues of emotional sustenance. Are you hungry for attention or love? Or did your dream reinforce the satisfaction that you derive from the warmth of your real-life relationships?

DINING ROOMS

✱✱

In dream homes, as well as real ones, the dining room is usually located on the ground floor, the floor that symbolizes the conscious mind. The dining room is a place where we wine and dine our guests, and its appearance in your dreams (whether elegant, cluttered, or shabby and dirty) will offer clues about how you regard your social and entertaining skills.

Symbolic and Verbal Associations
‹ Comfort and hominess
‹ Elegance; formality
‹ The gathering-together of family
‹ Emotional sustenance
‹ Family drama and arguments

Positive Interpretations: Was your dream dining room a warm, inviting, vibrant place where you hosted wonderful and exciting soirées? If so, do you regard yourself as a charming, gracious host or hostess? Are your "people skills" honed to sharpness? The appearance and condition of your dream dining room is not only an indication of the level of skill and ease with which you entertain those whom you invite into your home, but it will also be a sign of how you interact and socialize with people in general. So if you were pleased with the welcoming, positive energy of your dream dining room, are your own social skills easy and welcoming? Because the dining room is a place where we eat, its appearance in your dream may also have to do with emotional sustenance. So in your dream dining room, were you enjoying a delectable meal? Or were you happily serving food to someone else (and if so, whom)? And what sort of furnishings did your dream dining room have? For instance, were they Victorian, Colonial, modern, or contemporary? The answer to this question may reflect your communication style. In addition to being a place where we entertain guests, the dining room is also a place where families will gather to eat together. And if you have positive associations with family mealtimes, then your dream dining room may symbolize comfort, security, and love.

Negative Interpretations: Was your dream dining room grandiose, cold, and formal? If so, is it possible that you are rigid, formal, or cold in your interactions with others, so much so that people may find you to be rather intimidating? Or if your dream dining room was exceedingly cluttered and untidy, are you confused and disconcerted when interacting with others? If your dining room was dirty, dusty, or shabby, with decaying, old furniture, are you simply awkward or "rusty" in your social dealings? Or do you associate the dining room with family arguments during mealtimes? For many families, dinnertime is one of the few times when they come together, and the dining-room table is one of the most popular stages for family dramas to be acted out. If this line of interpretation rings true, have you been preoccupied with family conflicts?

Related Dreams

pages 161, 162, 178,

278 & 286

FAÇADES

In the language of dreams, the façade, or outward appearance, of a house, is related to your persona, or how you present yourself to other people. It has to do with your feelings of self-respect, how you view yourself, as well as how you relate to others and (particularly if there were walls, gates, or fences surrounding your dream home) how emotionally "open" or "closed off" you are to those around you.

Symbolic and Verbal Associations
- The persona: one's outward image or appearance
- Interpersonal relations
- Stability (or lack thereof)
- Pride, or, conversely, depression and apathy
- Fences or barriers, put up to ward off others

Positive Interpretations: What did your dream house look like? Was it a mansion, a farmhouse, a row house, a trailer, or a condominium in a high-rise building? Whatever form your dream home took, it was likely to be a metaphor for both how you view yourself and how you relate to others. If you dreamed that you lived in your literal "dream home"—perhaps a grand, palatial mansion, or in an inviting, shorefront cottage—then you may have experienced a wish-fulfillment dream. And because mansions, cottages, farmhouses, and the like are usually set apart from other properties, your dream ownership of them may suggest that you are an independent, self-sufficient person, unlike residents of town homes, apartments, or condominiums, who inevitably have a much greater level of interaction with their neighbors. What was the condition of your dream home's façade? If it was in good shape, being structurally sound and with a fresh coat of paint, then you probably give off an air of stability, confidence, and self-pride. And if your dream home appeared open and inviting, then this may signify that you are open, honest, and easy in your relations with others.

Negative Interpretations: If, in your dream, you found yourself living in a home that was run-down or dilapidated, with the wood siding rotting away and most of the paint long gone, then this may be a sign that you have begun to "let yourself go." Have you been feeling sad or depressed, so that you are emotionally withdrawn and you no longer care what others think of you? (And, in your dream, did you begin to clean up and renovate your home? If so, this may have been an unconscious prompt to begin taking better care of yourself.) Finally, was the entrance to your dream house blocked by a wall, gate, fence, or other barrier (such as tall hedges)? Physical barriers to your dream home may be a sign that you have put up emotional barriers and that you are shut down to others who may want to get close to you. Conversely, these dream barriers may suggest a need for you to protect yourself better from the demands of others—and your dreaming reaction may help you to determine which interpretation is closer to the truth.

Related Dreams
pages 104, 125, 159, 166, 211 & 213

My Façades Dreams

On the Surface
Dreaming of the outside of a house may relate to how you are feeling about the way in which you present yourself to others in the waking world. So was your dream of a neglected exterior telling you that you're looking tired and dated and that it's time for a new look? Or was it suggesting that you'd welcome a radical change of image?

My Foundations & Walls Dreams

✶ ✶ ✶ ✶ ✶ ✶ ✶ ✶ ✶ ✶ ✶ ✶ ✶ ✶ ✶

Shaky Foundations?

Dream walls can reflect the state of the support structures that sustain our everyday lives. So if you dreamed that the walls of the bedroom that you share with your long-term lover were moldy or crumbling, does their appearance tell you anything about your real-life relationship? Is some patching-up or rebuilding required to avert the complete collapse of your love life?

FOUNDATIONS & WALLS

✶✶✶✶✶✶✶✶✶✶✶✶✶✶✶✶✶✶✶✶✶✶✶✶✶✶✶✶✶✶✶✶

Foundations and walls are both structural features: they determine the organization of a house, and they help to make it stable and sturdy—and they serve the very same functions for your dream house. In terms of dream symbolism, the meanings of foundations and walls are likely to be quite straightforward.

Symbolic and Verbal Associations
- Structure
- "Solid foundations": stability (or lack thereof)
- Security and protection
- Confinement
- "Putting up walls" against others: emotional isolation

Positive Interpretations: Was your dream home built upon a solid foundation, able to withstand wild windstorms and torrents of rain and flooding? If so, then your unconscious mind was probably indicating that you have based your life upon a good, solid foundation of beliefs and/or relationships, and that, accordingly, you are able to withstand the occasional "bad weather" that life inevitably sends your way.

And, likewise, did the solidity of your dream house's walls make you feel safe, secure, and protected from any hostile forces that might be lurking outside? (And if you can remember what color your dream walls were, this should also be taken into account when you are attempting to interpret your dream.)

Negative Interpretations: Did you dream that your house sat upon a weak, rickety foundation, so that it trembled and shook when you merely walked across the floorboards? Or did you dream that your house was built on a soft, slippery hillside, and that you could feel the whole house beginning to sink or slide in the mud? In your dream, did the fierce wind blow right through your house's decrepit walls, so that you were left cold and unprotected from the elements? If you dreamed of any of these scenarios, then you may want to ask yourself whether the values and relationships that you have based your life upon are weak or faulty, so that your world as you know it is in danger of giving way and collapsing around you. The walls of a house can offer protection, but they can also feel very isolating. In your dream, did the strong, sturdy walls of your home make you feel confined or claustrophobic? If so, have you reacted to past hurts or disappointments by building or putting up walls around you, which were meant to protect you and to shut others out, but which, instead, have ended up isolating you and shutting you in? If you think that this may be the case, then it is important to remember that it was you who put the walls up, and, therefore, you also have the power either to build them higher and stronger or else to tear them down.

Related Dreams

pages 153, 157, 160, 164, 204 & 211

GARDENS & YARDS

* *

If your dream house had a garden, its appearance may say much about your personality, your personal growth, and your growth potential. Gardens are also private places of relaxation and meditation and, in the language of dreams, they may have to do with issues of privacy.

Symbolic and Verbal Associations
- Personal growth
- Cultivating "seeds" of potential
- Self-nurturing
- Self-neglect
- Quiet contemplation or meditation and relaxation

Positive Interpretations: Was your dream garden a colorful, living wonderland, full of a variety of lush, healthy plants? And, in your dream, did you notice that many different types of animals, such as birds, squirrels, rabbits, and perhaps even fish in a pond, were thriving within your garden? If so, this may indicate that your real-life endeavors, as well as your personality, are flourishing and blossoming. In your dream garden, were you lying blissfully in a hammock or lawn chair, taking in the warm sun rays and feeling the gentle wind on your skin? If so, your dream may have been mirroring the joyous peace and spiritual harmony that you have been experiencing in the waking world. But if, given your current life, this seems highly unlikely, then your dream was probably a wish fulfillment, and a sign that you are in need of some peace, quiet, and solitude during your waking hours.

Negative Interpretations: Conversely, was your dream garden a dead, barren, or dark, swampy, and overgrown place? Perhaps it reeked of foul-smelling rot, and when attempting to pass through, you became helplessly and frustratingly tangled in thorny weeds and vines? If so, then your unconscious may have been signaling that you have been neglecting your personal growth and that you have given up your self-control. Is it time for you to take back command over your life, to clear away the "weeds," let in the sunshine, and begin nurturing your talents and potential? Alternatively, was your dream garden an overly prim, pruned, and sterile place, with sparse, waxy plants and lots of close-cropped grass that stuck into and hurt your feet? And had the rose blossoms all been clipped from their hedges, leaving only the stems and the thorns? If so, then your unconscious may have been warning that you have gone overboard with your excessively rigid life organization, and that, as a result, your personality growth has been stunted and prevented from "flowering" and reaching its fullest potential. In another scenario, were you upset when a trespasser entered your dream garden? If so, your unconscious may have become aware that someone has been threatening your emotional privacy by attempting to become too close to you.

Related Dreams
pages 125, 157, 163, 283, 350 & 379

My Gardens & Yards Dreams

----

* * * * * * * * * * * * * * * * * * *

A Growing Concern
Plants take root, grow, and develop in gardens, but only if the conditions are right. Dreaming of a well-tended and blooming garden may suggest that you are feeling content with your personal growth. Maybe a recent decision to take up a hobby, learn a new skill, or otherwise nurture your potential is proving rewarding in the real world.

THE HOME

My Hallways & Stairs Dreams

✶✶✶✶✶✶✶✶✶✶✶✶✶✶✶✶✶✶✶

Stepping Up

Dreaming of staircases or hallways may be linked to a period of real-life change. Were you walking toward a flight of stairs that led to an unknown dream destination? If so, are you pondering lots of options regarding the future, or do you have no idea where you are headed in life?

HALLWAYS & STAIRS

✶✶

Hallways, corridors, and stairs are usually not destinations in and of themselves, but instead they are places that we go through in order to arrive at other places. Therefore, in the symbolism of dreams, halls and stairs are associated with periods of transition. And since stairs lead us either up or down, they can be symbolic of either an ascent to the realms of higher consciousness or a descent into the workings of the unconscious mind.

Symbolic and Verbal Associations
‹ Transition
‹ Exploration
‹ Choices to be made
‹ Ascent to higher consciousness; rising aspirations
‹ Descent into the depths of the unconscious

Positive Interpretations: If you dreamed that you were walking down the hallway of your dream home, do you know where you were going or what you were looking for? And what was the mood of your dream? It may be that you are now in a period of transition in your life, and that you have some important choices to make about what direction you will go in and where you would like to end up. For instance, are you finally about to graduate from school, or have you been thinking more and more seriously about quitting your job and changing careers? Or, in your dream, were you climbing a flight of stairs? If so, this may have been a sign of your waking endeavors (or your desire) to tap into a higher level of consciousness, perhaps by engaging in mediation or yoga, or by focusing on and thinking more about your sense of spirituality. But if, in your dream, you were standing at the foot of a staircase that you felt unable to ascend, even though you wanted to, has something in your life been impeding your ability to explore the loftier realms? And if you found yourself roaming through your dream house, through the many corridors, and up and down the stairs, then your unconscious was probably giving expression to your need for adventure and exploration in your life and/or of yourself and your internal workings.

Negative Interpretations: Did you dream that you were walking though the halls of a house and that you felt uneasy, lost, or upset? If so, have you been feeling "lost" in your life, so that you do not know where you want to go? It may be time for you to devote some serious time and energy to thinking about your life goals and how you might go about achieving them. If you found yourself descending a flight of dream stairs, this may indicate that you are at a point in your life where you need to explore the depths of your unconscious mind (perhaps by engaging in some creative or artistic activity). And, depending on the mood of your dream, it is also possible that your descent symbolized lowered aspirations, or intellectual or emotional decline.

Related Dreams
pages 152, 153, 225, 234, 277 & 303

KITCHENS

In modern homes, kitchens are almost always located on the ground floor, which, in symbolic terms, represents the conscious mind. And whether or not you grew up in a traditional family, you are probably very familiar with the associations having to do with kitchens, which include images of aproned mothers and grandmothers merrily cooking or baking cookies, hot chocolate on a cold, winter day, and a warm, glowing stove to sit next to. Therefore, in dream symbolism, the kitchen is a place of emotional warmth and welcoming.

Symbolic and Verbal Associations
- Warmth (or coldness)
- A welcoming atmosphere
- Emotional nourishment
- "Food for thought": psychological and intellectual stimulation
- The transformation of "raw" ingredients into a new creation
- Heat or danger

Positive Interpretations: If you dreamed of a kitchen, was your dream kitchen welcoming and warm, perhaps with a pot of good-smelling soup simmering on the stove and all of the closets fully stocked up with a variety of nutritious foods? Kitchens are the places where we cook, or transform raw ingredients into complex, nourishing meals; therefore, in the language of dreams, kitchens are also symbolic of psychological and emotional nourishment. So if your dream kitchen was full of good foods to eat, this may have been an unconscious reflection of your healthy and complete emotional "diet," or of your ample psychological satisfaction.

Negative Interpretations: Was your dream kitchen bare and cold, with only a few uncomfortable chairs to sit on? And, in your dream, were you exceedingly hungry, and did you frantically search the cabinets and refrigerator for food, but there was not a scrap to be found? If so, have you been "starving" for love and affection in the waking world? Or was your dream kitchen overflowing with rotten, putrid food and garbage? In this case, could it be that a formerly nourishing and loving relationship has gone bad or "foul"? Alternatively, did you find that your dream kitchen was incredibly hot—so hot that you found yourself wanting to leave right away? If so, your dream may have been a reference to something that is making your waking life "hot" or unpleasant, in which case, your unconscious may have been guiding you to follow the advice of the old phrase, "If you can't stand the heat, get out of the kitchen." There is another old phrase having to do with kitchens, "Out of the frying pan, into the fire"—in other words, a situation that has gone from bad to worse—and if you dreamed that you were scalded or burned at the stove, this may have been an unconscious warning of a situation that is full of potential danger (of getting "burned") in the real world.

Related Dreams
pages 113, 170, 171, 179, 181 & 371

My Kitchen Dreams

Creature Comforts

Kitchens are often the heart of the home. And if you dreamed of luxuriating in a warm kitchen whose surfaces were piled high with food, and of appreciatively sniffing the delicious aromas wafting from the oven, it is likely that you are either relishing a period of emotional and intellectual nourishment in the waking world or that you long to do so.

My Living Room Dreams

----

* * * * * * * * * * * * * * * * *

Leisure Time

If your dream was set in a living room, your unconscious may have been signaling that you could do with relaxing with your friends or family during your waking hours. People come together in living rooms to socialize or simply to hang out, so are you craving more interaction with your friends, or should you be spending more downtime with your nearest and dearest?

LIVING ROOMS

* *

Being associated with the ground floor of the dream house, living rooms are symbolic of the conscious mind. In practical terms, they are places where we receive and entertain guests, and—like dream dining rooms—the condition and décor of your dream living room can tell you much about how you interact and socialize with others. In times past, before many people's bedrooms were equipped with stereos, telephones, computers, or televisions, the "living" room was the place where people would spend the bulk of their nonsleeping time at home—and even today, this room may also double as a "family" room, a place where family members spend time together, perhaps playing games, watching television, talking, or simply relaxing in companionable silence.

Symbolic and Verbal Associations
- A room in which to welcome guests
- Conversation and socializing
- Entertainment; games
- Relaxation
- "Family time"

Positive Interpretations: If you had a dream in which you found yourself within the living room of a house, what did the room look like? Was it a warm and homey place that made you feel comfortable and cozy? If so, you are likely to be warm, inviting, and sociable in your interactions with others. Further, when you invite people into your home, you are probably a cheerful and gracious host or hostess. Some people refer to their living room as the "family room," though a family room may be separate from the living room in some houses. Either way, because living rooms and family rooms are also places where family members may gather together for various purposes (to watch television or a movie, to play a game, or to socialize), these rooms are also representative of "family time." Therefore, could your cozy dream living room or family room have been a sign that your familiar relations are strong, loving, and healthy? When interpreting your dream, you may also want to take into account what style and color of furniture and appliances your family room had, and to consider what this particular kind of décor means to you.

Negative Interpretations: Are "warm" and "cozy" two of the last adjectives that you would use to describe your dream living room? If so, what was it like? If it was messy, dirty, or decorated with stained, shabby furniture, you may want to consider whether you need to clean up, or update, your social skills, which may be confused or awkward. Alternatively, if your dream living room was overly formal and austere, do you tend to be cold or aloof in your social interactions? Or is it possible that your dream was a reference to the "chilly" state of your familial relations?

Related Dreams

pages 104, 125, 156, 157, 285 & 292

OUTBUILDINGS

If the dream home represents the self or the soul, its outbuildings (including garages, sheds, greenhouses, and barns) can represent, among other things, various moods, stages, or states of being.

Symbolic and Verbal Associations
- Inactivity; idleness (symbolized by a garage)
- Lack of direction
- Security and stability; accomplishments
- Criticism, or the need to be compassionate (symbolized by a greenhouse)
- The personal qualities or "tools" that one has to work with (a shed)
- Instincts, or natural urges (a barn)

Positive Interpretations: Did you have a dream in which you were parking your automobile in a garage? The primary function of a garage is to protect your vehicle, the means of your locomotion, from the elements, and a dream of driving your vehicle into a dream garage is symbolic of a period of stability, which you may have earned for yourself through your own efforts. If you dreamed of opening a garage door as if to retrieve your vehicle in order to go somewhere, this may signify that you have made a decision with regard to an important life issue. For instance, perhaps you have decided upon the route or "road" by which you will travel in order to reach some personal goal. A dream of going into a shed may be a sign that, in order to deal with a current life problem or situation, you will need to access and utilize some personal characteristic that you generally keep latent, or stored away. In the world of dreams, barns can symbolize those basic or "animal" instincts or urges that we may try to keep reigned in or shut away from the rest of our psyche. So if you dreamed of entering a barn, ask yourself whether you have a current need or curiosity to explore these natural instincts and urges.

Negative Interpretations: If you dreamed of closing a garage door, this may be a sign you are feeling stuck, or unable to move forward in your current life. And if you dreamed that you were inside a garage, it may be that you are currently in a period of idleness or stagnation, and you feel that you lack direction in achieving your life goals. In your dream, were you frustrated because the door of your shed had a large lock clamped onto it, for which you did not have the key? If so, it may be that you have not yet found a way to tap into the full potential of your personal resources (in which case, your dream may have been an unconscious sign that you are beginning to seek a way to do so). Or did you dream that you were inside a greenhouse? Like the old saying, "People who live in glasshouses shouldn't throw stones," your dream may have signified that, in light of your own flaws, you should be less critical of, or more compassionate toward, others.

Related Dreams

pages 159, 226, 232, 283, 296 & 297

My Outbuildings Dreams

Personal Maintenance

When we dream of houses, it's often an indication that we are thinking about ourselves, about who we are, how we are feeling, and how we relate to others. Dreaming about outbuildings suggests that we are preoccupied with matters that are a little more on the periphery of our lives, such as the "tools" or transport that we use to maintain our appearance or lifestyles.

My Roofs & Chimneys Dreams

✱ ✱ ✱ ✱ ✱ ✱ ✱ ✱ ✱ ✱ ✱ ✱ ✱ ✱ ✱ ✱

Smoke Signals

The hearth is traditionally the heart of the home, which is why dreaming of smoke wafting gently from a chimney may have signified that you are feeling content and at one with your loved ones. Chimneys can also be a symbol of passion or sexual heat, so, alternatively, was your dream reflecting the recent stoking-up, or hotting-up, of your love life?

ROOFS & CHIMNEYS

Your dream home represents your entire self, and, as on a real house, your dream house's roof is that which protects you from spiritual wind, rain, and snowstorms. Chimneys have two symbolic meanings in the language of dreams: emotional warmth, as represented by the hearth, and passion and sexual "heat."

Symbolic and Verbal Associations
- Emotional and spiritual protection
- Structural soundness (or lack thereof)
- The hearth; a warm place of gathering
- A message
- Emotional warmth
- Sexual energy; passion

Positive Interpretations: Dream chimneys and fireplaces often represent the hearth, a warm place of gathering for family. And if you dreamed specifically of a smoking chimney, its smoke signal was probably a message or indication that an environment of emotional warmth reigns within you. However, another layer of interpretation to take into account is that, in symbolic terms, the chimney can be seen as a phallus or a vagina, and the fireplace as a scrotum or a womb—symbolizing sexual "heat," passion, and the creative forces of the universe. Was your dream house topped with a sound and solid roof? Perhaps, in your dream, you and your loved ones were gathered around a warm, crackling fire, feeling safe and protected even though you could hear a terrible storm raging overhead. If so, this was probably an unconscious sign that you are feeling well-protected from the emotional and spiritual storms that blow through life from time to time.

Negative Interpretations: If your dream house had a rotten, dilapidated roof, this may be an unconscious warning that your life is in danger of structural collapse, and that, at any moment, the "ceiling" may fall in atop your head. Is it time to put a new roof on your spiritual or emotional home? A dream that you were being annoyed by a constant drip, drip, dripping of water is likely to have been a sign that some irritation has been wracking your nerves during waking hours (unless, of course, your sleeping mind incorporated into your dream the actual sound of water dripping, in which case you may want to call in a plumber or a roofer!) Or did you have a nightmare in which you were lying in bed when a great, windy tempest suddenly kicked up, which filled you with terror when it actually sucked the roof right off your home? A dream of this sort is probably a sign that you are feeling vulnerable to, or inadequately protected from, either the perils of the world at large, or some specific spiritual or emotional storm that you have sensed is approaching (or that you may already be in the middle of).

Related Dreams

pages 158, 211, 371, 380 & 389

SECRET ROOMS

THE HOME

I n the strange world of dreams, a dream of searching or exploring your dream home is often symbolic of a spiritual or emotional quest—a quest to find or know your "inner" self. And stumbling across a secret room in your dream home may be akin to finding a quality or talent that you never knew you possessed.

Symbolic and Verbal Associations
- Curiosity
- The unknown
- A hidden or latent quality or talent
- Inspiration
- A new life direction

Positive Interpretations: Did you have a dream in which you were wandering through your dream home, opening doors and looking into the various rooms, when you unexpectedly came upon a door that you had never noticed before, which opened into a room that you never knew existed within your house? If so, what did your "secret" room look like? Was it the sort of room that you have always wished for? Perhaps a warm, bright, fragrant place full of plush, comfortable sofas and many soft pillows to relax on? In your dream, there may even have been some serene, pleasing music playing. If so, could it be that your secret room was a symbol of an inner peace, stillness, and tranquility that you never knew you possessed? Or, in another scenario, did you open the door to find a room full of easels, paints, and blank canvases? And did you enter and, without hesitation, begin painting? If so, this sort of dream may be an unconscious indication of your latent creative side—and your unconscious may have been prompting you to cast off your inhibitions and to express yourself freely and imaginatively.

Negative Interpretations: Alternatively, in your dream, was your secret room a not-so-inviting place? Was it, in fact, a place that filled you with anxiety, fear, or apprehension? Did you spring open the door to discover a terribly dirty and messy room that was packed high and full of old junk and garbage that you thought you'd given away or thrown out years ago? If so, your dream room may have represented pent-up feelings or emotional wounds that, though buried deeply in your unconscious, remain with you and affect you nevertheless. Or was your secret room set up like a torture chamber, a dark place containing shackles and implements of pain and suffering? If so, you may want to ask yourself whether you have been unconsciously tormenting yourself in some way—perhaps by prodding at your own sore spots or by continuously reopening your old wounds. Or did you find that your secret room was a place where, once inside, you could not find the door again, nor any other means of escape? If so, your secret room might represent an addiction or an unhealthy pattern or cycle of behavior that, once you allow yourself to enter into it, you may find difficult to break free from.

My Secret Room Dreams

Hidden Treasures
Stumbling across a secret room in your dream may have been an indication that you are going through a period of illuminating introspection or that you are on the verge of discovering something new about yourself, if you haven't already done so. The dream room's appearance and function may tell you more about the nature of your hidden resources.

Related Dreams
pages 152, 153, 160, 166, 228 & 232

THE HOME

My Windows & Doors Dreams

----

* * * * * * * * * * * * * * * * * *

A Different Viewpoint

Are you ready for a change in your waking life? A new outlook, perhaps? Dreaming of looking through a strange window may suggest that you are itching to alter your perspective, that you are yearning for a change of scenery, or else that you are longing to let some light and fresh air into your real-world existence.

WINDOWS & DOORS

* *

In dream homes, doors are transitional points that represent many things, including choices, new opportunities, adventure, escape, and outside influences. And since our dream house is symbolic of the self, its windows are akin to the "eyes" of our soul, or how we view life and others glimpse our true selves.

Symbolic and Verbal Associations
- Transition; new beginnings; choices; opportunities
- A point of entry for outside influences
- Escape
- The "eyes" of the soul; viewpoint
- Openness; letting in "light" or "fresh air"

Positive Interpretations: In your dream house, did you open a door? What lay behind it? As transitional points, dream doors can represent opportunities, possibilities, and new beginnings—and also the excitement or worry that accompanies these transitions. Specifically, a front door is usually the entry point for new people or influences in our lives, while a back door may be the favored entry and exit for those whom we are more familiar and comfortable with. (And if your dreaming mind focused in on a doormat, have you been allowing others to "walk all over you"?) If, in your dream, you stepped across a threshold, this may signal that you are open to change. On the other hand, if your dream self opened a door to let someone in, this may be a sign of your willingness to engage with this person. A dream of being overwhelmed by many doors may indicate that you are trying to decide between a number of choices in your waking life. If you dreamed of looking through a window into the home of someone you know, it may be that you wish to know or understand this person better. But if you dreamed that you were inside a house, looking out of a window, what did you see? Whatever it was—and, perhaps more importantly, how it made you feel—may reflect how you view your life and the world, or else the way you wish that the world could be.

Negative Interpretations: In your dream, were you frantically searching for a door through which to escape? If so, are you feeling trapped by some situation in the real world? A doorway can also be symbol of the mouth, so a dream of this sort may indicate your inability to express yourself. If, however, your dream self was confronted with a locked door, what was your reaction? If you were angry, then it may have represented some opportunity in the waking world that you feel is closed to you. But if you were curious, then it is likely to have represented something that you have been longing for. If you dreamed of looking into a window, longingly observing a happy, domestic scene, it is likely that you are currently feeling a lack of comfort, love, and security. Or if, in your dream, you looked out of a window to see an ugly, barren landscape, this may denote how you feel about the world at present, or else your fears for the future.

Related Dreams

pages 43, 60, 157, 160, 165 & 232

CHAPTER 8
SUSTENANCE

Unless you are deliberately denying yourself certain foods or drinks because you are on a diet, for example, when dreaming about them may give expression to your preoccupation with, and craving for, such "forbidden fruits," such dreams should rarely be taken literally. Instead, dreams that revolve around sustenance, or a lack thereof, often refer to our emotional needs, and to how satisfactorily they are being met and nourished.

SUSTENANCE

My Alcohol Dreams

✱ ✱ ✱ ✱ ✱ ✱ ✱ ✱ ✱ ✱ ✱ ✱ ✱ ✱ ✱

Cheers!

Dreaming of enjoying a drink with friends may signal that you're in need of spending some quality time with people who expect nothing more of you than your company and conversation. Have you been too busy working, or coping with family commitments, to socialize? Perhaps it's time to pick up the phone and arrange a fun-filled evening.

ALCOHOL

✱✱✱

Like coffee and tea, alcohol is something that we often consume when we want to enjoy ourselves and be sociable. As such, in dreams, alcoholic beverages can be a symbol of friendship and good cheer. We also drink alcohol in order to celebrate happy occasions, and in recognition of our pleasure in living. When we dream of consuming alcohol in gross quantities, however, this can signal overindulgence and loss of control.

Symbolic and Verbal Associations
‹ Enjoyment
‹ Conversation; friends
‹ Celebration
‹ Spiritual sustenance
‹ Intoxication; loss of control; overexuberance

Positive Interpretations: If you dreamed that you were filled with a sense of happiness and wellbeing as you shared a bottle of wine and good conversation with someone, this may be a sign that you would benefit from relaxing amidst some stimulating dialogue with friends. Or did you dream that you were at your favorite bar, having a beer, and trading stories and jokes with your best friends? And has your waking social life been lacking? Your dream may have been wish fulfillment, as well as a sign that it might be time to reprioritize your life in order to make room for more socializing and fun. If, in your dream, you uncorked a bottle of wine or champagne, is there some achievement or occasion in your life that calls for a celebration? (Or, alternatively, is there something that you are hoping that you will soon be able to celebrate?) For some Christians, wine is also a sacred symbol of the blood of Christ, so if this meaning has resonance with you, then you may want to consider if it applies to your dream of drinking wine.

Negative Interpretations: If you were disturbed by a dream in which you were terribly drunk, perhaps swaying and careening as you tried to make your way home from a party, then there are a number of possible interpretations. First of all, you may want to ask yourself whether the amount of alcohol that you consume has increased to an unhealthy level. But if you drink only rarely or in moderation, a second possible explanation is that your dream may have been an unconscious cue that you are in danger of losing emotional control in your waking life. Or, thirdly, have you been feeling "drunk" on power or success? If so, your unconscious may have been warning you that it's time to "sober up" a bit because your swaggering exuberance is starting to annoy those around you. Any of these interpretations may also be applied if you had a dream that a friend was intoxicated. But if, in your dream, your drunken friend accused you of mistreating him in some way, you may want to consider whether your unconscious sent you this dream in order to alert you to what you already know, on some level, is the truth.

Related Dreams

pages 90, 149, 170, 176, 174 & 286

BREAD

SUSTENANCE

For many, many centuries, bread has been a staple food among Western peoples, which is why the primary symbolism of bread has to do with life and survival. For many Christians, bread is also a symbol of spiritual sustenance (and it is bread that, in the Roman Catholic sacrament of Holy Communion for the Eucharist, becomes transformed into the body of Christ).

Symbolic and Verbal Associations
- Life and survival
- Spiritual sustenance
- "Breaking bread" with friends or family
- Something that is your "bread and butter"; financial support
- "Bread" or "dough" as slang words denoting money

Positive Interpretations: If you have been influenced by the Christian symbolism regarding bread, could your dream of eating bread have been a reference to spiritual sustenance? Likewise, for Jews, unleavened bread is what fed the Israelites as they were fleeing from the Egyptians who had enslaved them—which is another possible interpretation to consider if you are familiar with the Jewish tradition. Or did you dream of "breaking bread" with your friend, who may have a real-life problem for which she needs your help or advice? Or perhaps you dreamed of "casting your bread upon the waters"—in other words, selflessly helping someone whom you know will be unable to return the favor. If you dreamed of baking buns, could this unconscious reference to having "a bun in the oven" have referred to your suspicion that you might be pregnant, or else to your desire to have a child? Finally, could the "bread" or the "dough" in your dream have actually been a reference to money? For example, if you had a dream in which your kitchen was overflowing with loaves of bread, could this have been an unconscious reflection of your current plum financial state?

Negative Interpretations: Did you have a dream in which, while hiking or traveling, you were dismayed to find that you had lost the only thing left to eat: a hunk of bread? If so, then it is possible that your lack of dream bread was a reference to either spiritual or monetary poverty or loss—and thinking about the details of your dream, as well as your current life situation, should help you to decide which (if either) of these interpretations applies. Did you have a dream in which your husband ate a sandwich in front of you, and, though you were hungry, refused to give you even a bite? If so, has he been controlling (and withholding) the "bread and butter" that the two of you must live on? Or if, in your dream, you were eating a sandwich during your lunch break at work, are you working in a "bread-and-butter" job—one that pays you well, but that you have no interest in otherwise?

Related Dreams

pages 149, 161, 179, 233 & 358

My Bread Dreams

----

* * * * * * * * * * * * * * * * * * *

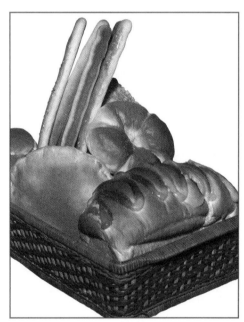

Kneads Must

Bread is a simple and satisfying staple food, of course, but in dreams it can be a symbol of spiritual sustenance, or, alternatively, of money. So if you dreamed of trying to steal loaves from a bakery, are you struggling financially? If so, maybe your dream was an unconscious expression of your desire to solve your money problems.

SUSTENANCE

My Coffee & Tea Dreams

✦ ✦ ✦ ✦ ✦ ✦ ✦ ✦ ✦ ✦ ✦ ✦ ✦ ✦ ✦

Break Time

Having a cup of tea or coffee is often something that we do when we're taking a break from work. Dreaming of enjoying a leisurely cup of coffee with your colleagues may therefore suggest that you're craving some time away from the treadmill in order to recharge your batteries, and perhaps to get to know your workmates better, too.

COFFEE & TEA

✶✶✶✶✶✶✶✶✶✶✶✶✶✶✶✶✶✶✶✶✶✶✶✶✶✶✶✶✶✶✶✶✶✶✶✶✶✶

Perhaps because they are hot beverages, and so must be consumed slowly, coffee and tea are symbolic of relaxation, socializing, and thought and reflection. And since many people consume tea or coffee habitually, at specific times of the day, they can also represent ritual and routine. Many people drink caffeinated coffee or tea for stimulatory purposes, and so these beverages may also symbolize mental acuity or alertness.

Symbolic and Verbal Associations
- Taking a break: relaxation
- Conversation; time with friends; a "tea party"
- Mental stimulation
- Morning, afternoon, or evening; ritual and routine
- Thought; reflection

Positive Interpretations: In your dream, were you filled with a sense of satisfaction and comfort as you sat down to a pot of your favorite tea with a good friend? If so, have you been feeling harried or frazzled in the real world? Your dream may have been a sign that you would benefit from enjoying some relaxing "down time" with friends. Or did you dream that you were at your local corner café, enjoying a steaming cup of coffee and some good conversation with a few of your best buddies? If so, and if your waking social life has been diminished of late, then your dream may have been wish fulfillment, as well as a sign that you might fare better if you would allow yourself more time to relax and unwind among friends. The caffeine content of coffee (and, to a lesser extent, tea) makes this drink a favorite mental stimulant for many. Did you dream that you had sat down at your desk, a hot cup of coffee in hand, in order to do some serious writing or studying? If so, have you been feeling overwhelmed by your worldly duties, and are you yearning for some quiet time and the space in which to think?

Negative Interpretations: Did you have a dream that you were brutally aroused from a very peaceful sleep when the high-volume beeping of your alarm clock sounded in your ears? And, in your dream, were you fumbling, half-blind from sleepiness, toward the kitchen so that you could brew yourself a much-needed cup of coffee? Of course, if you had any dream in which you were thirsting for a cup of coffee, it is possible that your unconscious mind was portraying your body's actual addictive need for caffeine (in which case, you may want to consider trying to wean yourself off it a bit)—though if this doesn't seem to be the case, then you may want to ask yourself whether you have been getting enough sleep lately. Do you dread the morning hour when your clock awakes you, and are you totally reliant on the caffeine jolt that you get from coffee because it seems to be the only thing that enables you to function at the most basic level?

Related Dreams
pages 168, 173, 185 & 188

COOKING

As well as providing nutritional sustenance, cooking is a means that we use to express our love of, and affection and appreciation for, others—in other words, it is also a source of emotional sustenance; and, in the language of dreams, the act of cooking is likely to be a reference to this latter meaning. But because it has to do with the transformation of raw ingredients into a palatable meal, dream cooking can also be a symbol of plans, rumination, and industriousness. And cooking is also a symbol of sexual passion for many reasons, including the rich, sensory experience of eating, the idea of certain foods as being aphrodisiacs, and, of course, the heat that is involved in the cooking process!

Symbolic and Verbal Associations
- Giving love, comfort, and support to others
- A plan that you are "cooking up"; rumination
- Happenings and excitement (as meant by the expression, "What's cooking?")
- Work; industriousness
- Sexual passion

Positive Interpretations: If you dreamed that you were cooking a large meal for your family, this was probably an unconscious confirmation that your family members rely on you for love, support, and comfort in the waking world. If you had a dream in which you were mixing raw ingredients and dishes together in a creative or experimental way, is there some plan or scheme that you are "cooking up" in the real world? Or were you surprised by a dream in which someone was cooking a meal for you because this person would be unlikely to treat you with such special consideration in the real world? If so, there are a few possible explanations. It could be that you are craving attention from this person, or else that your unconscious has detected that this person is appreciative of you (though he or she may be unlikely to express this to you). And if you dreamed of cooking a meal together with a possible love interest, the unconscious meaning is most definitely to do with passion and sex—in which case, the various nuances of your dream (such as what you were cooking and how your dream made you feel) will help you to interpret its meaning further.

Negative Interpretations: Did you have a frustrating dream in which you were cooking an important meal for guests—but, in your dream, did everything possible seem to be going wrong? Did you burn the rice and overcook the tuna while you were trying to whip up the dessert custard, which you just couldn't get to achieve the right texture, for all of your sweat, tears, and cursing? If so, have you been feeling as though your real-world plans and aspirations have gone all wrong? (Like in your dream, it could be that you have been trying to do too many things too quickly, and that you need to slow down, take a step back, and restrategize.)

My Cooking Dreams

Home Cooking

Is there anything more heart-warming than a home-cooked meal? Making dinner for someone is a way of showing just how much he or she means to you. So if you dreamed of cooking a warming soup, who was your dinner guest? And is he or she someone whom you want to impress, seduce, or simply love and look after in the real world?

Related Dreams
pages 113, 156, 161, 178, 179 & 182

My Dieting Dreams

----

* * * * * * * * * * * * * * * * * *

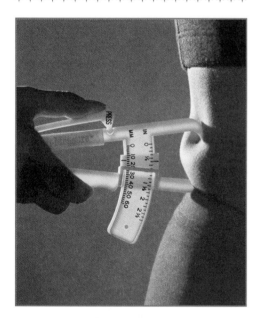

Slim Pickings

Dreaming of dieting could be a straightforward sign that you are concerned about your body image and weight. Have you been overindulging recently? Or perhaps your vacation is looming, and you're worried that you may not fit into the expensive bikini that you've splashed out on. Otherwise, could your dream have referred to some other form of self-denial relating to your current circumstances?

DIETING

* *

Dieting is currently one of the largest societal obsessions in the Western world. Every week, it seems, there are news stories about a new wonder diet that doctors have discovered, which usually involves some variation of high-protein, low-carbohydrate, or low-fat eating. If you are concerned that you might be overweight and you dreamed about dieting, then you can probably take your dream at face value, as a reflection of your real-world preoccupation with your health, your body image, or both. However, if it seems unlikely that your dream had to do with your actual food intake, then it may have had a more symbolic meaning, possibly having to do with issues of self-denial, control, or problems that might be "weighing you down."

Symbolic and Verbal Associations
- Control
- Self-denial
- A person's self-image
- Societal pressure; "ideal" body type
- Feeling "weighted down" by problems; carrying a "heavy load"

Positive Interpretations: In your dream, were you over the moon because you found that you were finally able to observe your ideal diet, which involves a modest daily intake of healthy foods, without feeling overly hungry or longing to "cheat" by eating candy or snacks? If so, and if you have been preoccupied with dieting during your waking hours, then your dream may have been a literal reflection of your dietary concerns. But if you were perplexed by such a dream because you are not in the least concerned with dieting in the real world, then there are a few possible interpretations that you may want to consider. First of all, could it be that you have been imposing too much control over your life, so that you are in a state of emotional self-denial? Alternatively, it is possible that your dream may have signaled that you would benefit from having more self-control. The details and mood of your dream, as well as—most importantly—how it made you feel, should help you to know which interpretation might be closer to the truth.

Negative Interpretations: Did you have a dream in which you had gone on a radical diet in a desperate attempt to shed the many pounds that you had put on? If so, and if you have not recently experienced any significant real-life weight gain, then could it be that you have been feeling "weighted down" by problems that you wish that you could shed in the waking world? (For more interpretations along this line, see this chapter's "Overeating" entry.) If, however, you dreamed that you had eaten so little that you were starving or wasting away, have you been feeling deprived of emotional, sexual, spiritual, or intellectual "nourishment" in the waking world? (And if so, is this a self-imposed "diet" or one that has been thrust upon you?)

Related Dreams

pages 62, 176, 179, 182, 184 & 273

DRUGS

Drugs include manufactured medicines, herbs, and also recreational drugs, cigarettes, alcohol, caffeine, and hallucinogens, but all act to produce some physiological or psychological change. There are many possible kinds of interpretations for dreams of taking drugs—depending on the type of drug that we dream of, its effect on us, and the mood and circumstances of the dream.

Symbolic and Verbal Associations
- A "quick fix"
- Escape
- Shielding or suppressing one's emotions
- Exploring expanded consciousness
- The need for emotional or spiritual healing
- Purification
- Rebellion against society's standards

Positive Interpretations: If you had a pleasant or positive dream of using a hallucinogenic drug, such as marijuana or L.S.D., it may be that you are currently experiencing a greater awareness, a broader insight, or an expanded or elevated sense of consciousness in your life. This sort of dream may also signal a need for you to look inward, inside yourself, for guidance and answers to your life questions. A dream of using an illegal drug may also be a sign that you are feeling at odds with, or rebellious of, society's rules and standards. And if you dreamed of taking any type of medicine or herb, it may be that your unconscious was prescribing a remedy for some sort of health problem that it has detected. Of course, the meaning of such a dream may also be more metaphorical: for instance, if you dreamed of gathering sage, this may be an indication that you are in need of one of this herb's primary ascribed uses: spiritual purification.

Negative Interpretations: If you dreamed that you were in possession of, or that you were taking, drugs, this may be an indication that you are in need of a "quick fix" for some problem that you are having in the waking world. In your dream, do you know why you were taking the drugs? The answer to this question may help you to interpret the meaning of your dream. For instance, if you dreamed that you took a pill to make you taller, have you been feeling "dwarfed," or small and insignificant, during your waking hours? Conversely, if you took something to make you invisible, who, or what, are you trying to escape or hide from? Or did you dream that you were taking a common street drug, such as speed or cocaine? If so, this may be an indication that you wish that you could shut down or dampen your painful emotions, or that you desire to escape from, or to deny, your worldly responsibilities. On the other hand, because these drugs are both "uppers," your dream may have been a sign that you are feeling driven or compelled quickly to complete some task or duty.

Related Dreams
pages 84, 143, 168, 170, 176 & 258

My Drugs Dreams

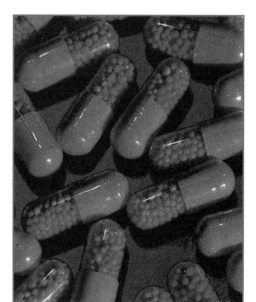

Magic Medicine
A dream of taking drugs—legal or illegal—may indicate that you're looking for a way to block out or escape certain difficulties that are blighting your life in the waking world. If you'd like nothing more than to banish your problems with a magic pill or painkiller, you may find that talking to friends or family provides the solutions or support that you're after instead.

SUSTENANCE

My Eating Out Dreams

....
....
....
....
....
....
....
....
....

✦ ★ ✦ ★ ✦ ★ ✦ ★ ✦ ★ ✦ ★ ✦ ★ ✦ ★ ✦

On the Menu

Dreaming of going out on a dinner date may hint that your mind is turning to affairs of the heart. Has it been too long since you and your lover treated yourselves to some fabulous food, fine wine, and frivolous conversation? Or has someone with whom you'd love to share an intimate table for two recently entered your waking world?

EATING OUT

✦✦✦✦✦✦✦✦✦✦✦✦✦✦✦✦✦✦✦✦✦✦✦✦✦✦✦✦✦✦✦✦✦✦✦✦✦

The explanation for a dream of eating out will depend upon, among other things, where you were eating (be it an upscale restaurant, a diner, or a fast-food-chain outlet), who you were with, and the mood and details of your dream.

Symbolic and Verbal Associations
- Joyousness and socialization; emotional sustenance
- Relaxation
- Celebration
- Loneliness and depression
- Choices and decisions
- Seeking emotional support outside of one's normal network

Positive Interpretations: Did you dream that you were having a festive meal at a restaurant, with all of your best friends gathered together? If so, the unconscious implication may be that you have healthy, solid relationships with these people, and that you provide each other with emotional sustenance (though your dream may also have been wish fulfillment, indicating that you wish that this were the case). If wine was served in your dream, the unconscious reference may have been to relaxing and unwinding together. But if a bottle of champagne was uncorked, this may have been a reference to something in your waking world that is a cause for celebration. Or if you generally cook every meal for your family and dreamed that you were enjoying a gourmet dinner at a five-star restaurant, then this may be a sign that you wish that you could have a break from your cooking duties once in a while, and be treated to a nice meal out. However, because a restaurant is a place where we seek nourishment, a dream of eating in one may suggest that you are seeking emotional nourishment or support outside of your normal support system.

Negative Interpretations: If you dreamed that you were at a restaurant, but that you were having difficulty selecting a dish from the menu, then this may indicate that you are puzzling over a waking problem or that you are in a dilemma over some choice or decision that you must make during your waking hours. And if an impatient waiter caused you to feel nervous or rushed to make a decision, have you been feeling similarly rushed to take action in the waking world? If you dreamed of eating alone in a restaurant full of people, it may be that you have been feeling sad, depressed, rejected, or socially isolated in the real world. Finally, if you dreamed that the waiter or busboy cleared away your plate before you had finished eating, do you feel that your inferiors, or those who are meant to serve you, have been rebelling against your authority undermining your efforts in the real world?

Related Dreams

pages 156, 168, 176, 178 & 286

EGGS

Because of their function as vessels of new life, eggs are ancient symbols of feminine fertility—a symbolism that transcends the realm of the physical and extends into the realm of the spiritual or the metaphysical.

Symbolic and Verbal Associations
(Birth; creation
(Spiritual growth and renewal
(Easter (for Christians)
(The gestation of an idea
(Putting "all of your eggs in one basket," or taking a big risk
(Having "egg on your face": shame or embarrassment

Positive Interpretations: Did you dream that you were you cracking eggs for an omelet, when you suddenly decided to leave one particular egg intact? In your dream, did you find yourself sitting on the egg to keep it warm, much as a hen would do? If so, is there some plan or idea that you have been incubating in the real world, with the hope of "hatching" it successfully? Of course, if you are a woman who is hoping to have a baby, such a dream may be taken more literally, as an unconscious reflection of your desire to conceive a child. Or did you have a dream in which you participated in an Easter-egg hunt? In Easter-egg hunts, which have become a Christian tradition, children sometimes receive special prizes for the eggs that they find. So if you had a dream such as this, have you been seeking some reward or goal? If so, in your dream, were you hunting successfully, so that your little basket became piled high with the brightly colored eggs? Or were you searching in frustration in vain, while others around you seemed to snatch up the eggs that were almost within your own reach? The relative success or failure of your dream egg hunt is likely to mirror your feelings, hopes, or fears regarding your real-life quest.

Negative Interpretations: In your dream, were you gathering eggs from a henhouse, and were you transferring them from their nests into one large basket? If so, your dream may have signaled that you have been "putting all of your eggs into one basket," or taking a large, all-or-nothing gamble on some real-world venture. In your dream, did you successfully deliver the basket of eggs to their destination, or did you trip and drop it on the ground, causing most of your eggs to crack? The answer to this question may provide a clue as to your unconscious estimate (as well as your hopes and fears) of the likely success or failure of your worldly venture. Or did you have a dream in which you had dinner at a fancy restaurant, after which you excused yourself to go to the restroom, there to see, with horror, that you had egg all over your face? If so, have you recently done something that has caused you public shame or embarrassment, or has made you feel a laughing stock?

Related Dreams
pages 85, 87, 105, 320, 333 & 339

My Eggs Dreams

....
....
....
....
....
....
....
....
....
....

✳ ✳ ✳ ✳ ✳ ✳ ✳ ✳ ✳ ✳ ✳ ✳ ✳ ✳ ✳ ✳ ✳ ✳ ✳

A Good Egg

If you came across some eggs in an abandoned nest in dreamland, did you cover and cherish them until your efforts were rewarded by the emergence of two healthy hatchlings? If so, could your dream eggs have symbolized the plans that you're incubating? Eggs can symbolize the gestation of ideas, but may also represent "nest eggs," so was the reference to your finances or savings?

SUSTENANCE

My Forbidden Foods Dreams

✴ ✴ ✴ ✴ ✴ ✴ ✴ ✴ ✴ ✴ ✴ ✴ ✴ ✴ ✴ ✴

Tempting Tastes

Dreaming of foods that you're not supposed to eat—be it for religious or spiritual reasons, or maybe to safeguard your health—may signify that you're feeling curious or guilty about straying from the path of righteousness, or else that you're feeling rebellious. The circumstances of your dream and how your dreaming self felt should help you to ascertain what your "forbidden fruits" represented.

FORBIDDEN FOODS

✴✴

Many religions and cultural traditions have rules or decrees against eating certain foods. For instance, practicing Jews and Muslims are forbidden from eating pork, Hindus may not eat beef, and Catholics may not eat meat on Good Friday. Likewise, it is also frowned upon in most of the Western world to eat horse or dog meat. And when we dream of eating a food that is a taboo for us, the message from our unconscious is likely to do with spiritual or metaphorical "contamination."

Symbolic and Verbal Associations
‹ Religious taboos
‹ Traditions and rules
‹ Being spiritually "contaminated" or "dirty"
‹ A transgression of thought or deed
‹ Temptation

Positive Interpretations: Did you have a dream in which you took delight in eating some food that, because of your religious or cultural traditions, is forbidden to you? For instance, if you are Jewish, did you dream that you sat down at the dinner table and gorged yourself on a large bowl of spiced shrimp (which is a taboo, under Jewish law)? Was this dream feast the best, most delectable meal that you had ever tasted? If so, you may want to ask yourself whether the statutes of your religion have been acting to confine you, or somehow to hold you back in your life aspirations. Do you have a deep, perhaps unconscious, desire to explore the world beyond the bounds of your upbringing? And because your dream involved eating, it may be that there is something that is new or foreign to you that you have become attracted to or infatuated with, so that you have a longing to consume or to take it within you. Or have you already strayed from the territory of your religion or culture? If so, your dream may have been an unconscious affirmation of your happiness at having chosen your own path in life, regardless of your learned mores or traditions.

Negative Interpretations: Did you dream that you accidentally ate—or were forced to eat—some food that is forbidden to you by your religion or your cultural traditions? For example, are you a Muslim who had a dream in which you believed that you were eating a barbecued-beef sandwich, only to realize, with horror, that what you had just eaten was, in fact, pork? And, in your dream, were you then flooded with a sense of nausea and guilt? If so, it is very probable that your nightmare was an unconscious reference to the guilt and impurity that you feel because you believe that you have committed some transgression that has left you spiritually "contaminated" or "dirty." In your dream, did someone force or tempt you to eat the forbidden food? And, if so, did you know the person? It may be that you feel that he or she is a bad influence on you in the waking world.

Related Dreams

pages 56, 156, 168, 172, 180 & 260

FRUITS

Fruits are symbolic of both feminine fertility (because of their often rounded shape, suggesting the womb or breasts, and because of the seeds that they contain) and immortality. And, in line with Freudian theory, certain long, rigid fruits and vegetables (including bananas and cucumbers) are considered to be phallic symbols (and nuts are often associated with testicles). The bottom line for all of these associations is sexuality, which is a very likely reference for a dream that involves fruit. Another line of interpretation for dreams of eating fruit has to do with reaping "the fruits" of your efforts.

Symbolic and Verbal Associations

- The "fruits of your labor"; a plan that has come to "fruition"
- Sweet rewards: the "sweet taste" of success
- Feminine fertility
- Immortality
- Phallic symbols

Positive Interpretations: When attempting to interpret any dream that had to do with fruit, it is important to consider the dream fruit's shape, texture, ripeness, and freshness. Did you have a dream in which you were enjoying a ripe, succulent pear? If so, could this fruit have represented a "sweet" victory or success that you have recently had in the real world? Or could your dream of eating a peach have represented your current "peachy" outlook or circumstances? Or is your delightful new teacher "a peach" of a person? In fact, the English language is filled with life metaphors having to do with fruit. Do you feel that your life is like "a bowl of cherries"? Is your daughter "the apple of your eye"? Or was your dream of a full bowl of fruit an unconscious indication that your life is overflowing with blessings? Of course, you should also consider whether your dream fruit might have had to do with your sex life. For instance, did your dream of round apples or oranges represent breasts? Or did your dream of a ripe banana symbolize a sexually mature and virile man?

Negative Interpretations: Did you have a dream that involved underripe, overripe, mealy, or rotten fruit? Could your dream of biting into an unripe plum have been a sign that your new girlfriend is too young for a serious relationship? Or has your husband been acting as if his life is nothing but "sour grapes"? Or, if you are a school teacher, was your dream of a "bad apple" actually a reference to the new kid in your class who you are afraid may "spoil the barrel," or negatively influence the other students with his unruly and defiant behavior? And if you have been influenced by Judeo–Christian beliefs, could your dream of eating an apple have been a symbol of the "forbidden fruit" that the serpent tempted Eve into tasting? (And, if so, what, in your waking life, could the apple have represented? Perhaps, if you are married, an affair that you have been tempted to engage in?)

My Fruits Dreams

★ ★ ★ ★ ★ ★ ★ ★ ★ ★ ★ ★ ★ ★ ★ ★ ★

Apple of Your Eye

In dreams, fruit often symbolizes delicious rewards. So did your dream of dozens of crisp, juicy apples represent the sweet success that you've recently tasted? Alternatively, does the phrase "An apple a day keeps the doctor away" strike a chord with you? If so, was your dreaming self setting your waking self a good example to follow?

Related Dreams

pages 184, 283, 350, 352, 358 & 186

SUSTENANCE

My Holiday Dinners Dreams

★ ★ ★ ★ ★ ★ ★ ★ ★ ★ ★ ★ ★ ★ ★ ★

Desperate Housewife?

Celebrating the holidays with family can be fun, but also stressful, particularly if you're responsible for providing the meal. If you're the designated cook this year in the real world, and you dreamed of overcooking the turkey in the dream world, it may be that you're worried about failing to meet your accomplished sister-in-law's impossibly high standards. (If so, relax—it's being together that counts.)

HOLIDAY DINNERS

★ ★

Whether religious or secular, many of the major holidays tend to center around a meal—and, as such, if you dreamed of a holiday, it is quite likely that you dreamed of sitting down to a large dinner with family and friends. Dreams that involve holiday dinners may be more of a reference to the specific holiday that you dreamed of than to the food that you were eating (though, if your dream did focus in on certain foods, you may want to consult other parts of this chapter for their symbolic associations). Moreover, the same holidays will hold varying significances for different people, so it is very important that, when trying to determine the meaning of your dream, you think about what the holiday that you dreamed of means to you.

Symbolic and Verbal Associations
- Celebration; happiness and festivity
- Rare indulgence (as in eating special foods or seasonal dishes)
- Excitement
- Gathering together with family and friends
- The turning of the seasons

Positive Interpretations: Did you have a pleasant, happy dream that involved gathering together for a holiday dinner? For instance, if you have always had a particular love for Thanksgiving (perhaps because it is the one day of the year when both sides of your family come together in celebration), did you dream of sitting down to Thanksgiving dinner with all of your family members? If so, then you may have experienced a wish-fulfillment dream, an unconscious signal that you have been missing the comfort and security that being together with your loving family brings you. (And perhaps it's time to plan a trip to visit some of your more distant relations.) Or, if you are Jewish, did you dream that you were eating the ritualistic Passover meal? During the Passover dinner, each dish is consumed in a particular order, with prayers, and interspersed with glasses of wine. If you dreamed of such a dinner, how did it make you feel? If you felt deeply reverent and spiritual, then your dream of consuming the sacred Passover meal was likely to have been a sign that you find happiness, contentment, and solace in your religion. However, if you have strayed from the tenets of Judaism, the consumption of your dream meal may have been an unconscious signal that you wish to reimbibe the Jewish beliefs and traditions.

Negative Interpretations: Did you have an unpleasant dream about a holiday meal? For instance, did you dream that you were traveling to your grandparents' house for Christmas dinner, but your flight was delayed and you missed the festivities altogether? In dreams, the act of eating together with others can be a symbol of emotional nourishment—so have you been feeling, for whatever reason, that you are unable to "connect" with your family anymore?

Related Dreams
pages 86, 108, 149, 156, 168 & 174

HUNGER

SUSTENANCE

Unless we are craving a "midnight snack" in our sleep, dreams of being hungry usually have to do with some sort of nonfood-related deprivation in the waking world. Among other things, these types of dreams can signal a real-life lack of love, physical affection, sex, or even intellectual stimulation.

Symbolic and Verbal Associations
- Emotional deprivation
- Being "starved" of love, physical affection, etc
- Longing to replace something that is missing from one's life
- A lack of "food for thought," or intellectual stimulation
- Comfort eating
- Being "hungry" for success etc

Positive Interpretations: Although hunger is painful, it is a good and necessary sensation because it lets us know when our bodies need food—and it also motivates us to take steps to feed ourselves (something that was very important earlier on in our evolutionary history—though perhaps a bit less important today in the Western world, where, for most people, food is not generally in short supply). Likewise, emotional, spiritual, or metaphorical "hunger" lets us know that we are lacking something that we desperately want or need. So if you had a dream in which you were thoroughly searching your place of work for something to eat, you may want to ask yourself if you are anxious or "hungry" to succeed in your career. Is there a promotion that you are vying to gain? Or have you been thinking of asking your boss for a raise? Your dream self's failure or success (and relative difficulty) in finding something to eat may be a clue as to your hopes and fears regarding your real-life goal, or else may represent your unconscious estimate of your actual chance of success.

Negative Interpretations: Did you have a dream in which you found yourself so famished that you were wandering the streets at night, frantically looking for a place to buy some food? And were you perplexed by your dream because when you awoke you found that you were not really hungry at all? If so, you should ask yourself if there is something that is currently lacking from your life, so that you are "hungry" for it in your waking and dreaming worlds. For example, could it be that you are lacking intellectual stimulation? Perhaps it's time to sign up for that course that you've been interested in taking at the local college. Or might you be missing a romantic or sexual relationship? If so, was your dream an unconscious plea for you to go to that singles group that you've heard so much about? Alternatively, did you have a dream in which someone was withholding food from you? Who was this person, and what could the food that they withheld have represented? For instance, if it was your wife has she become withdrawn from you, so that she has been denying you emotional sustenance in the waking world?

Related Dreams

pages 62, 161, 172, 185 & 266

My Hunger Dreams

★ ★ ★ ★ ★ ★ ★ ★ ★ ★ ★ ★ ★ ★ ★ ★

Midnight Snack

Were you rifling through the refrigerator, frantically looking for something tasty to munch on, in your dream? Dreaming about being hungry can indicate that there's something lacking in your life. What sort of "nourishment" might you be "starved of" in the waking world? Companionship? Or stimulation? Or had you gone to bed on an empty stomach, so that your dream merely reflected reality?

My Meat Dreams

✱ ✱ ✱ ✱ ✱ ✱ ✱ ✱ ✱ ✱ ✱ ✱ ✱ ✱ ✱ ✱ ✱ ✱ ✱

Meaty Matters

If you dreamed that you were preparing meat for a home-cooked dinner, this may hint that you are preoccupied with "meaty," or substantial, issues. Are you chewing over a major life decision? If you were trying to trim off fat from the meat, could the message have been that you need to cut back on your spending and live a "leaner" life?

MEAT

✶✶

In the English language, "meat" is a metaphor for very many different things. It can be used to mean information that is "meaty" or rich, it can mean the center or core of an issue, and it also has a plethora of somewhat crude sexual meanings. And in the language of dreams, the act of eating meat may take on any combination of these symbolic denotations.

Symbolic and Verbal Associations
- "Meaty" or substantial news or information; the "meat" or core of a matter
- Being "in a stew," or having "a beef" with someone
- "Sins of the flesh"; lust
- Being in a "meat market" (a "pickup spot")
- Someone who is "fresh meat" (an often offensive term for a new or young object of sexual desire)
- "Animal," or base, instincts or desires

Positive Interpretations: Did you have a dream in which you were busily consuming a large plateful of steak or roast beef? If so, is there some "meaty" or substantial news that you have recently been presented with in the real world? Or have you been "chewing over" some issue or information during your waking hours? Or is it that you feel that you have finally come to "the meat," or the core, of some matter of importance to you?

Negative Interpretations: If you dreamed that you were obsessively stirring a pot of boiling beef stew, you may want to ask yourself whether you are upset, or "in a stew," over some trouble in the waking world. Could it be, for instance, that you have "a beef" with your friend's tendency to ask you for lots of last-minute favors, while she herself is never willing to help you out in return? Or did you dream that you had a terrible desire for the taste of meat, which caused you a good deal of guilt because you knew that you were staying in a vegetarian household? If so, could it be that you have been lusting after the "sins of the flesh" to satisfy your carnal cravings, even though you know that the object of your lust is somehow forbidden to you? In a similar vein, if you dreamed that you were voraciously tearing through a platter of raw meat, it may be that your "animal," or base, instincts or desires are longing for expression in the waking world. Alternatively, did you have a nightmare in which you and your friends were hanging out at your favorite bar, when you realized that everyone around you had been transformed into walking, talking sides of beef? If so, could your unconscious have been trying to force you to see what you have thus far been in denial of: that your favorite hangout is really just a "meat market," or a "pickup spot" for singles? Or were you frightened by a dream in which your new girlfriend suddenly turned into a rack of lamb? If so, maybe you unconsciously view her as nothing more than "fresh meat," someone in whom you are interested only for your own sexual gratification.

Related Dreams
pages 176, 319, 320, 331, 334 & 336

MILK

For humans, as well as for other mammals, milk is the first form of nourishment that we subsist on in the world. Because of this reason, and because it is typically provided by our mothers, milk has many strong, positive symbolic associations with comfort, warmth, and security.

Symbolic and Verbal Associations
- "Mother's milk"; warmth, comfort, and security
- "The milk of human kindness"
- "Milking" something or someone (exploiting a person or a situation)
- Someone who hasn't yet lost their "milk teeth": a young or immature person
- A "milksop" (a person who is timid or weak)
- Semen; a sexual relationship

Positive Interpretations: Did you dream about a chilly, winter evening, when you were sipping from a warm mug of milk? And did your dream remind you of how, when you were a child, your mother would often heat up some milk for you to drink before bedtime? If so, have you been finding your waking life to be particularly cold, lonely, or hectic? By sending you your dream, your unconscious may have been trying to provide you with some warm comfort and security, in order to compensate for your waking woes. It is also possible that your dream was a reference to your need or desire to be mothered or pampered by someone. On the other hand, if you are a woman who dreamed of breastfeeding a baby, or of giving a cup of milk to a child, then are you either pregnant or hoping soon to have a child in real life? Another possible interpretation for a dream that highlighted milk is that your unconscious was making a reference to semen, and therefore to your desire to have a sexual relationship with a man.

Negative Interpretations: Were you disturbed by a dream in which you found that you had turned into a large, lowing dairy cow, and that someone was busily milking you? If so, did you know the person? Is it possible that your unconscious was attempting to tell you that he or she has been "milking" you (i.e., somehow exploiting or taking advantage of you) in the real world? Or, in your dream, were you shocked and disgusted when you took a big sip from a glass of milk that had gone sour? If so, has some previous source of security or comfort in your waking life also gone bad? For example, have things recently "soured" between you and your boyfriend? Alternatively, if you are a woman, did you have a dream in which a hungry baby was crying for food, but when you went to breastfeed the baby, were you frustrated and dismayed because you had no milk to give? If so, your dream may have been an unconscious indication that you feel inadequate in terms of your ability to "mother," or give comfort to, others in the waking world.

Related Dreams
pages 87, 101, 113, 170, 185 & 319

My Milk Dreams

_____

_____

_____

_____

_____

_____

_____

_____

The White Stuff
Milk often symbolizes comfort and security because it's the first nourishment that we receive as babies. If you dreamed of pouring milk, it may be that you are thinking about parenthood. But if you dreamed that you gratefully sipped a glass of milk that someone had given you, could you yourself do with some mothering in waking life?

SUSTENANCE

My Overeating Dreams

----

* * * * * * * * * * * * * * * * * *

Weighty Issues

In your dream, had your healthy pet suddenly become obese, or did you see a squirrel that had gorged itself to supersized proportions? If so, it is most likely that your dream reflected your guilt or anxiety about your own tendency to overeat. But if this isn't the case, could the animal have represented an obsession you are developing?

OVEREATING

* *

In the waking world, overeating is the act of taking in too much food, which can result in nausea, lethargy, weight problems, and general ill-health. In the world of dreams, overeating is probably to do with the overconsumption of, or overindulgence in, things other than food—such as information, work, hobbies, and even other persons—which, like overeating, can also result in poor physical and emotional health. And, like dreams of being hungry, dreams of overeating can signal a lack of something in the dreamer's waking life.

Symbolic and Verbal Associations
- "Weighty problems" that you wish that you could shed
- Overindulgence
- Obsession
- "Taking in" too much information, etc; overload
- Comfort eating (as a response to emotional distress)

Positive Interpretations: Did you dream that you were at a large feast, with all of your favorite foods at hand, and that you took great delight in stuffing yourself full of everything in sight? If so, and if you have been feeling a lack of something vital in your life (such as love, support, friendship, fun, etc), then your unconscious may have sent you your dream as a form of wish fulfillment—a happy session of "comfort eating" temporarily to "feed" your desires, if only in the dream world. If this is the case, you may want to consider ways, other than eating, in which you can begin to fulfill your needs in the waking world.

Negative Interpretations: Did you dream that you were quickly gorging yourself on a large plateful of food, and though you felt disgust and revulsion at your behavior, you could not make yourself stop eating? If you have a habit of bingeing on food in the waking world, then your dream may have been simply mirroring your waking worries about your tendency to overeat. However, if you were perplexed by your dream of overeating because you do not have these sorts of tendencies in the real world, then there are a few possible explanations. First of all, you might want to consider whether you have been feeling overloaded by something (work, problems, etc), or whether you have felt compelled to "take in" too much of something (such as information or emotional pain) in the waking world, so that you are metaphorically "weighted down" by whatever it is that you are consuming in large amounts. On the other hand, it is also possible that your dream was a reference to some waking obsession that you have been overindulging in: your work, a hobby, a game or sport, or even a person whom you may be (or wish to be) in a relationship with. Whatever it is, your dream may be an indication that the amount of time that you are spending on your obsession has reached an unhealthy level, and that your hearty appetite has become self-destructive.

Related Dreams

pages 62, 156, 161, 172, 179 & 268

SPICY FOODS

★★★★★★★★★★★★★★★★★★★★★★★★★★★★★★★★★★★★★★★

Just as spices make food more interesting to the palate, in symbolic terms, the word "spice" is used to mean variety, excitement, and fun—which is a likely line of interpretation if you had a dream of eating spicy food.

Symbolic and Verbal Associations
- A desire to "spice up," or add interest and variety to, your life
- A need to "pep yourself up" (become happier or more lively)
- Someone with a "peppery" (or stingingly candid) tongue
- Someone who is "vinegary" or acerbic
- Being capable, or "worth one's salt"
- Taking something or someone "with a grain of salt"; skepticism
- Sexual passion

Positive Interpretations: Did you have a dream in which you clandestinely crept into the kitchen while your wife was cooking, and did you secretly pour some extra spices into the dream dish that she was making? If so, have you been wishing that you could "spice up" your marriage in the waking world? (And because "spice" is often used as a sexual metaphor, your dream may have indicated your desire to bring more sexual passion into your marriage bed.) Or if you dreamed that you were grinding pepper over your son's plate of food, have you noticed that he has been sad or lethargic in the real world, and do you wish that he would "pep up," or be happier and livelier? Or did you have a dream in which your boss congratulated you for your good work and presented you with a bag of salt? If so, your unconscious may have picked up on the fact that your boss is happy with the job that you've been doing, and that he or she feels that you are definitely "worth your salt" as an employee.

Negative Interpretations: In your dream, were you aghast when you noticed that your effusive neighbor's wagging tongue looked just like a jalapeno pepper? If so, your unconscious was probably mirroring your waking feeling that your outspokenly critical neighbor has quite a "peppery tongue." Or did you dream that this same neighbor was dumping vinegar all over the food that she was about to eat? If so, could this have been an unconscious allusion to her "vinegary" (or harsh) outlook on life? Alternatively, did you have a dream in which the woman whom you are dating presented you with a plate of food, but when you took a bite of it, did you begin to choke and gasp at its overwhelming spiciness? If so, do you feel that your new girlfriend, though exciting, is just a bit too "spicy" for your taste? Or, finally, did you dream that you sat down to eat with your father-in-law, who is opinionated and prone to giving you unsolicited advice and guidance, and asked him to pass the salt? If so, might your unconscious mind have been advising you to take his assertions skeptically, or "with a grain of salt"?

Related Dreams

pages 51, 174,
178 & 185

My Spicy Foods Dreams

★★★★★★★★★★★★★★★★★★★★

Hot Stuff

Dreaming of serving up a hot and spicy dish may signify that you are longing for more excitement and variety in your life. Is it high time that you "spiced up" your dull daily existence by enrolling in a salsa class? Or was the reference to sexual "heat," and to that "hot," exotic-looking stranger whom you are thinking of asking out on a date?

CHAPTER 8: SUSTENANCE ❬ 183

My Sweet Foods Dreams

----

* * * * * * * * * * * * * * * * * * *

Chocolate Heaven

In your dream, were you enjoying the experience of choosing your favorite from a box of luxury Belgian chocolates and anticipating the pleasure your choice would bring? If so, and your waking circumstances are not pleasant at the moment, this may have been a wish-fulfillment dream. Or was your unconscious simply reflecting the wealth of "sweet" options that are currently within your grasp?

SWEET FOODS

B ecause of our early evolutionary history, when sugar was often hard to come by, humans have a highly developed taste (and desire) for sugar—which is, no doubt, why "sweet" is one of the most common and clichéd metaphors for "nice," "good," or "amiable" in the English language. Consequently, when we dream of foods that taste sweet, the meaning is often quite straightforward.

Symbolic and Verbal Associations
- Having a "sweet" life; satisfaction with one's circumstances
- Someone who is as "sweet" as pie (or sugar, candy, etc): a person who is charming or amiable: a "sweetheart"
- Something that is as "easy as pie"
- Getting one's "piece of the pie (or cake)"; monetary success
- Childish fun and excitement
- "Sweet talk" (flattery)
- Having a "sweet tooth" (a liking or craving for candy)

Positive Interpretations: Did you have a pleasant dream that you were inside a large, fully-stocked candy store, and that you had free rein to try anything and everything that caught your eye? If so, and if you are fairly happy with your current life, then your unconscious may have been mirroring your happy waking sense that "life is sweet." Otherwise, if you have been less than happy of late, then your dream of being in a candy store may have represented your desire to incorporate more excitement and childish fun into your life. Or if you had a dream in which your favorite aunt gave you a piece of chocolate pie, this was likely to have been an affirmation of your feeling that your aunt is as "sweet as pie" to you. Alternatively, if you have an important exam coming up and you dreamed of sitting down to take the exam while eating a piece of pie, your dream may have been an unconscious indication of your confidence in your performance in the exam because you feel that it will be as "easy as pie" for you.

Negative Interpretations: Did you have a dream that your boyfriend was trying to talk to you about something, but that whenever he opened his mouth, pieces of candy fell from his mouth into your lap? If so, this may have been an unconscious indication that your boyfriend has been trying to "sweet talk" you (i.e., he has been flattering you in an attempt to persuade you of something) in the real world. Or, in your dream, did someone give you a cup of coffee that was so sickly sweet that it made you gag and cough when you took a sip of it? If so, who was the person who gave you the coffee? Your unconscious may have been indicating that this person is too excessively "sweet" for your taste (perhaps because you feel that so much apparent "sweetness" has to be forced or phony).

Related Dreams

pages 62, 170, 172, 176, 177 & 182

THIRST

In symbolic terms, water is associated with the emotions. Therefore, if you dreamed of being thirsty, this may have signaled a lack of some basic emotional "sustenance" (unless, of course, you actually became parched during the night—a common occurrence for many people—in which case, your unconscious mind may have incorporated this real sensation into your dream).

Symbolic and Verbal Associations

- Emotions
- Feeling emotionally "parched"
- "Thirsting" for love or affection
- A desire to "drink in" love from someone
- Spiritual "dehydration"

Positive Interpretations: In your dream, did you find yourself wandering through a desert—the hot sun beating down on your body—and all that you could think about was a cool drink of water? And, seemingly miraculously, did you stumble across a lush, green island flowing with cold, freshwater springs, from which you drank long and deeply until your thirst was quenched? It is likely that such a dream was an unconscious indication that you have been feeling emotionally "parched" in the waking world, and, specifically, your dream may have signaled that you have recently found (or that you soon hope to find) an emotional "watering hole" (i.e., someone or something that will fill your emotional void and act to "revive" you emotionally). When attempting to interpret the unconscious meaning of any dream of having your thirst quenched, it will be important to consider where you found the much-needed water, or who gave it to you. For instance, if you were seeking a glass of water and you found it in a church, could it be that you have been suffering from a lack of spiritual sustenance? Or if you were joyfully relieved of your thirst when you found a water fountain in a nursery for children, do you desire to experience the love of a child of your own? And if you were thirsting and someone gave you a drink of water, did you know the person? Your dream may have been an unconscious cue that you would gain emotional sustenance by deepening your relationship with him or her.

Negative Interpretations: Did you dream that you were overcome with thirst and that, though you searched everywhere for a drink of water, not a drop could be found? If so (and if you do not believe that you experienced your dream of thirst because you had, in fact, become thirsty during the night), then your dream may have been an unconscious allusion to your emotional needs. In the real world, have you been single for so long that you feel emotionally "dehydrated"? Are you "thirsting" for affection, and yearning to "drink in" love from someone?

My Thirst Dreams

Water Baby

Few things feel better than quenching one's thirst with a long, satisfying drink of water. If you had a dream of this nature and don't think that you were actually dehydrated as you lay in bed, could you be thirsting for something intangible in waking life? Are you feeling emotionally or spiritually "parched,"? Do you know what it is that you crave?

Related Dreams

pages 51, 60, 168, 170, 181 & 387

SUSTENANCE

My Vegetables Dreams

✱ ✱ ✱ ✱ ✱ ✱ ✱ ✱ ✱ ✱ ✱ ✱ ✱ ✱ ✱ ✱ ✱

Fast-growing Fungi

Did you dream of a specific vegetable? If mushrooms grew and multiplied in your dream, for instance, perhaps some aspect of your waking world is undergoing a period of expansion. Could the reference have been to your rapidly expanding business or family? Or, if your dream turned into a nightmare, was your unconscious alluding to your "mushrooming" problems?

VEGETABLES

❋✱❋✱❋✱❋✱❋✱❋✱❋✱❋✱❋✱❋✱❋✱❋✱❋✱❋✱❋✱❋✱❋✱❋✱❋✱

Because vegetables provide important vitamins and nourishment, their appearance in our dreams often has to do with basic emotional sustenance, whether or not we "know what is good for us." And some long, rigid vegetables (such as carrots) may be dream phallic symbols.

Symbolic and Verbal Associations
- Basic emotional sustenance
- A person who is dull or lazy
- "Vegetation": an idle existence
- Someone who is clinically comatose
- Being forced to "eat your vegetables"; punishment ("for your own good")
- Phallic symbols

Positive Interpretations: Did you have a dream that highlighted a particular vegetable? If so, considering the symbolic associations of that vegetable (your personal associations, as well as more general ones) will help you in deciphering the meaning of your dream. For example, if you are having trouble getting your employees to make good use of their work time, could your dream of a carrot have been an indication of the carrot, or reward for good behavior, that you should wave under their noses to encourage them to increase productivity? If you dreamed of watching mushrooms grow and multiply, has your business been "mushrooming," or growing at a rapid pace? Or did you dream of a few persons who are "like two peas in a pod"? Finally, anytime that you have a dream that focuses in on a long, rigid vegetable, such as a carrot or a leek, consider whether your unconscious mind has called up a phallic symbol (perhaps as a reference to your sexuality or to intimacy issues).

Negative Interpretations: If you had a dream in which your lethargic, television-watching brother turned into a giant potato on the couch that he sat on, then the meaning of your dream is probably fairly obvious. Similarly, if you dreamed that you looked into the mirror and saw that you had broccoli sprouting all over your face, you may want to consider whether this was an unconscious reference to your tendency toward idle "vegetation." However, you may have been a bit perplexed if your dreaming mind cast you back in time to your childhood, to a dinnertime scene in which your parents were forcing you to sit at the table until you had eaten all of your vegetables. This sort of dream—of being forced to undergo something akin to punishment, "for your own good"—may be an unconscious indication that you have been failing to carry out some (perhaps unappetizing) action or task that it would serve you well to complete. (For instance, has it been weeks since you've been to the gym for a workout? Or has your diet degenerated into a feast of snacks and fast food?) But if your dreaming mind highlighted a hot potato, was the reference to a waking problem?

Related Dreams

pages 159, 171, 177, 283, 358 & 368

CHAPTER 9
SCHOOL & WORK

If you spend a large proportion of your waking hours at school or work and found yourself in the same environment in dreamland, the setting per se is not likely to have had much symbolic significance, reflecting as it did merely your daily reality. If you are no longer a student, however, with what do you associate your schooldays? Is there a lesson that you consciously need to relearn, perhaps? And if you do not have a job, would you be happier "working at" something in the real world, or are you feeling "slave-driven" or "bossed around"?

My Colleagues & Friends Dreams

✱ ✱ ✱ ✱ ✱ ✱ ✱ ✱ ✱ ✱ ✱ ✱ ✱ ✱ ✱ ✱ ✱

Diving for Gold

Did you dream that you and your coworker were on a diving vacation? Perhaps, in your dream, you were swimming together in the sea, feeling relaxed and sharing a laugh. Such a dream could point to your desire to enjoy an easier working relationship with your colleague in the real world if he is someone whom you find it difficult to relate to.

COLLEAGUES & FRIENDS

Our social circle of friends and/or colleagues can be a source of fun, emotional support, comfort, and security. However—particularly during childhood and adolescence—our friends can also cause us to feel anxiety and the pangs of peer pressure (i.e., they may exert a "bad influence," leading us to do things that, otherwise, we would not do). And when we dream of interacting with our peers, any of these types of situations and influences may assume importance.

Symbolic and Verbal Associations
- Nostalgia for happy times
- Camaraderie
- Comfort; feelings of "belonging"
- Peer pressure
- Rebellion

Positive Interpretations: Did you have a dream in which you were at the office, enjoying a coffee break and pleasant conversation with your coworkers? If so, you probably basked in the good feelings of comfort and belonging that your dream gave you. If your relationship with your coworkers is good, then it is possible that your dreaming mind was simply reiterating this fact. But if your relations with the people whom you work with are currently strained or poor, then your dream may have been either wish fulfillment (signaling your deep desire that you might develop better social interactions with your colleagues) or—particularly if your work has been especially harrowing of late—a reminder of some of the personal reasons why you have remained in your job, despite the current hardships. Alternatively, did you dream about a time, long ago, when there was nothing else in the world that you would rather be doing than hanging out with your best buddies after school? This sort of dream may indicate a longing or nostalgia for a period of your life when you were free and unburdened by adult responsibilities, or when it seemed that more opportunities were open to you.

Negative Interpretations: Did your dream of spending time with your old school friends make you squirm with discomfort, perchance because your dreaming mind replayed a typical scene that recalled the way in which you and your friends used to bully and tease each other so relentlessly? If so, is some present life situation, such as your interactions with your current coworkers, reminding you (perhaps unconsciously) of how you and your old school chums used to behave? If this is the case, your dream may have signified that you are suffering from social anxiety regarding how you measure up to your peers and colleagues and how you feel that they perceive you. In particular, if your dream cast a spotlight on a scene in which you were feeling peer-pressured to do something that you knew was wrong, is there a waking parallel?

Related Dreams

pages 104, 106, 110, 114, 190 & 247

DEADLINES

I f your waking life is filled full of plans and deadlines, then the pressure that you are under may also plague you in your dreams—thereby disturbing your sleep time (which may be the one and only time that you have to relax) and also, perhaps, signaling that you may be close to breaking point.

Symbolic and Verbal Associations
- Feeling hurried or rushed in one's life
- A sense that "time is running out"
- Unresolved issues; things left undone
- Motivation; action
- A feeling of being "under pressure"; a need to relax
- A desire for excitement or intellectual stimulation

Positive Interpretations: Were you thrilled or galvanized by a dream in which you had one hour to produce a research report on some topic of interest to you? For instance, have you always had a lay interest in astronomy, and did you dream that you were charged with compiling a report for N.A.S.A. on the most recently discovered stars in our galaxy? If so, it may be that you are craving intellectual stimulation, and that you would benefit by enrolling in school or by making more time in your life for reading and study. Or if you have been working on a long-term project (such as writing your memoirs or compiling a family history) and you dreamed that a deadline for completion was drawing near, this might have been an unconscious attempt to spur you into action so that you might finally finish your project.

Negative Interpretations: Did you have a dream in which you realized, with panic, that you had to produce a ten-page paper by the following day, which you had not even begun to research? If so, are you under an exceptional amount of stress in the waking world, so that you feel that you are beginning to lose control over your life and your work? It may be that you are so much "on the go" and are filled with so much anxiety during your waking hours that you are unable to give yourself permission to relax even in the dream world. In addition, it is possible that your dream may have been your unconscious's way of trying to tell you that there is something in the real world that has slipped from your conscious mind—perhaps a work deadline or an upcoming meeting that you must prepare for. And if you had a dream in which you were working yourself ragged, but with the overall feeling that you were accomplishing nothing at all, could it be that you have taken on so many tasks and responsibilities during your waking hours that you are not really doing justice to any of them? If so, you may benefit from delegating or letting loose of some of your responsibilities, which would both allow you to do a better job on the duties that you retain and give you a greater peace of mind.

My Deadlines Dreams

....
....
....
....
....
....
....
....
....
....

* * * * * * * * * * * * * * * * * * * *

A Ticking Clock

Deadline dreams are often the unconscious mind's way of reminding you that time is running out. If your dreaming self was under pressure to meet a deadline, what was the nature of the assignment that you had to complete? Did it have any relevance to a real-world task that you've been putting off? If so, it may be time to deal with it.

Related Dreams
pages 192, 193, 196, 231, 240 & 260

My Enemies & Rivals Dreams

....
....
....
....
....
....
....
....
....

* * * * * * * * * * * * * * * * * *

Lashing Out

Dreaming about coming to blows with a workplace rival could reflect your actual frustration with a coworker. It may be that you feel unable to express your views, so that your only outlet is getting physical in dreamland. Perhaps your unconscious was telling you that it's time to say what you think before you lose control and replicate your violent dream in the real world.

ENEMIES & RIVALS

* *

Because schools and workplaces are places where there may be severe competition between classmates or coworkers, almost everyone is bound to have had school- or workplace enemies and rivals at one time or another. (And sometimes our best friends can also be our top rivals, and they may occasionally even become our enemies.) The appearance of our enemies or rivals in our dreams may signify that we are feeling shamed, conflicted, competitive, or angry in the real world—perhaps indicating that there is some past problem, issue, or hurt that we have never fully dealt with.

Symbolic and Verbal Associations
‹ Humiliation
‹ Conflict
‹ Anger and grudges
‹ Rivalry: competition
‹ Emotional wounds

Positive Interpretations: If you had a dream that highlighted the contemptuous relationship that you currently have with one or more of your coworkers, your unconscious may have been simply reflecting your conscious preoccupation with the strained workplace issues that you face in the waking world every day. And if, in your dream, you lashed out at your rival(s) with your words or your fists, your dream probably served as a safety valve, allowing you to vent your frustrations in a way that will cause no real harm to anyone nor have any repercussions in the waking world. If you feel that you are the underdog in your relations with your enemies or rivals, a dream like this may also serve to bolster your confidence in dealing with real-life conflict. But if you dreamed that you offered kindness or forgiveness to an enemy from your past or your present, there are a few possible explanations. A dream like this may be an unconscious attempt to help you to heal and to move on from past hurts, and it may also serve as an encouragement for you to forgive and make peace with your current enemies.

Negative Interpretations: Did you have an unpleasant dream that played out a scene portraying competition or hostility between you and a real-life enemy or rival? And, in your dream, did you feel that your rival was getting the better of you? If so, this may be a cue that you are feeling insecure and inadequate in the game of power-positioning that is played out on a daily basis by you and your rival. A dream such as this may also be indicative of a general anxiety with regard to how well you relate to others and how others perceive you. But if your dreaming mind carried you back to a period of school or to a job in which you were made miserable because your peers picked on or bullied you, it may be that you haven't resolved your feelings about that life experience and that you have consequently been unable to move on with your life.

Related Dreams
pages 106, 114, 188,
253, 264 & 281

EQUIPMENT & TOOLS

Equipment, machines, and tools—including (and, perhaps, most importantly in today's world) computers—help us to do work faster and more efficiently. In the language of dreams, equipment and tools may be a veiled reference to emotional tools and abilities; i.e., our ability to cope and to navigate in the waking world.

Symbolic and Verbal Associations
- Skills
- Practicality or creative expression
- Energy or health, including emotional
- Capabilities: mental or physical performance
- One's personal, or "life," tools

Positive Interpretations: Did you have a dream in which you were working with a computer, a tool, or a piece of machinery? In the language of dreams, computers can be equated with the brain and with thought processes, and machines with the body or with physical energy. So if, in your dream, you were sitting quietly and contentedly at your desk as you concentrated on your computer screen, this may be a sign that your thought faculties (your ability to think and to focus) are in good working order. Similarly, if you dreamed that you were driving a forklift trick to move extremely large, heavy objects, this may have been a statement about your physical fitness and high energy levels. Both of these types of dreams reflect positively on your skills, capabilities, and practical ability to accomplish your work. On a deeper level, a dream of this sort may also indicate that you are well-equipped with the "life" tools that you need in order to succeed and prosper in the real world.

Negative Interpretations: If you dreamed that the machinery or equipment that you were using had jammed or failed, this may have been an unconscious reflection of your feeling or fear that you are not armed with the proper tools for success, or else that you lack the knowledge to use them properly. For instance, did you dream that the computer that you were using began to go haywire, so that you had no control over which programs you could open or close? Or, in your dream, did your computer screen go completely blank, filling you with great dread because you suspected that your hard drive might have been fried? If so, have the stresses of your job left you feeling mentally "fried" in the waking world? Or if you had a dream in which the work truck that you were driving broke down, have you been feeling physically run-down or "broken," so that you are in need of some major "repairs" or even a complete "engine overhaul"? Alternatively, if you work on an assembly line in a factory, could your dream that the line jammed up so badly that the whole floor was shut down have been an indication of your sense that the disarray of the company that you work for may soon reach a point of crisis?

Related Dreams
pages 204, 226, 253, 259, 278 & 296

My Equipment & Tools Dreams

----

* * * * * * * * * * * * * * * *

Keys to Success
If you've been dreaming about working at your computer and actually spend much of your time doing just that, it may be that your dream was underlining your uneven work–life balance. Or was your unconscious urging you to express or record your ideas in writing, or else to work through your thoughts on paper? Your dreaming self's mood should tell you more.

My Examinations Dreams

✴ ✴ ✴ ✴ ✴ ✴ ✴ ✴ ✴ ✴ ✴ ✴ ✴ ✴ ✴ ✴ ✴ ✴

Testing Time

Dreaming about taking an exam is often perceived as an expression of anxiety and a fear of failure. But perhaps, in your dream, you felt prepared, and, upon glancing at the paper, realized that you knew exactly how to respond. A dream like this suggests that your self-esteem and confidence are currently high, whether or not an exam is really looming.

EXAMINATIONS

I f you dreamed of preparing for, or of taking, an examination, the most important factor in determining the meaning of your dream is probably how it made you feel (i.e., nervous, anxious, pleased, proud, etc). These sorts of dreams often have to do with our feelings of self-esteem and self-worth, and are likely to reflect our feelings with regard to our relative success or failure in the "testing" situations that life often brings.

Symbolic and Verbal Associations
- Performance anxiety
- Fear of failure
- Hopes for success
- Trying or "testing" situations
- Feelings of self-esteem and self-worth

Positive Interpretations: Did you dream that you were sitting in a large lecture hall, a sharpened pencil in hand, and that you felt confident and eager as your professor passed out an examination paper and instructed you to begin? And as you answered the questions one by one, did you find that you knew the material so well that you were sure that you would receive 100 percent? A dream of aceing an exam is likely to have been an unconscious statement regarding your positive self-esteem and confidence in your brains and abilities. And if you do have an exam or test looming in the real world, your dream may serve as a confidence-boost—an unconscious effort to reassure you with regard to your performance ability and to cheer you on to success. It is important to note that the real-world exam or test that your dream was alluding to need not be a test or exam in the traditional sense, but could be a "testing" or trying situation that you must deal with during your waking hours.

Negative Interpretations: Did you have a dream in which you were sitting in a classroom, sweating and panicking as your teacher passed out an exam paper because you had forgotten to study and were completely unprepared? If so, there are a few possible explanations for this sort of nightmare. First of all, if you had a dream such as this and you have a real examination coming up soon, then your dream may have been a reflection of your anxiety and fears with regard to how you will fare. And, as discussed above, under "Positive Interpretations," it is important to remember that your dream may have been drawing a parallel not with an actual exam, but with a difficult or "testing" situation in the real world. But if there is no examination or other sort of trial looming in your near future, then you may want to consider whether you are suffering from low self-esteem, or whether you feel that you do not measure up to your peers or are unable to do things as well as most other people (i.e., general performance anxiety). A similar interpretation may apply if you dreamed that your teacher handed you back an exam paper marked with an "F." (For more on this, see the next page.)

Related Dreams

pages 191, 193, 195, 196, 199 & 240

FAILURE

✴ ✴

Though dreams of failing are not likely to be predictive of the actual outcome of a real-life test that you must undergo, or of a feat that you must accomplish, they may indicate how you feel about your relative chances of success. This type of dream may also be an unconscious reflection of your general feelings of worth or inadequacy, or else of your hopes and fears for the future.

Symbolic and Verbal Associations
- Feelings regarding one's relative worth or inadequacy
- Shame
- Preoccupation with, or worries with regard to, waking problems
- Measuring oneself against others
- Competition and rivalry

Positive Interpretations: Did a dream that cast a spotlight on a past failure give you a new, positive perspective on the incident? For example, did you dream about that second-grade spelling bee that has haunted you for years—the one you lost at the very last minute, when you misspelled a word that you knew well because you were nervous and you answered too quickly? But, in your dream, instead of breaking down into tears, running from the stage, and locking yourself in the restroom for an hour, as you did in real life, did you calmly acknowledge your loss, shake hands with the winner, and happily accept your trophy for second place? If so, then your dream may be a sign that you have finally gotten past your pain and that—even more importantly—you have discovered a valuable real-world lesson about dealing with loss. On the other hand, if you dreamed of failing an exam or some other challenge that you must soon face in the waking world, then you can rest assured that your dream was not necessarily predictive of how you will fare in reality: instead, your dream may have been an unconscious attempt to explore how you would feel and what you would do if you did fail, thereby helping you to prepare for the possible worst.

Negative Interpretations: In your dream, did you revisit the horrors of some past failure, which caused all of the terrible feelings and heartache that you felt at the time of the incident to return in full? If so, and especially if this is a recurring dream, it may be that you have not resolved your painful feelings from this incident and, as a result, have been unable to learn from your experience and move on. Also, whether your dream highlighted an actual (past) or a hypothetical failure, you may want to consider whether your dream might have been an indication that you are suffering from feelings of low self-esteem or worth. Alternatively, if you dreamed that you received an "F" for a real-world exam or that you somehow failed a trial that you must soon undergo, then your dream may be a sign that you are not yet as primed as you should be (in which case, your unconscious may have been attempting to push you into action).

My Failure Dreams

★ ✴ ★ ✴ ★ ✴ ★ ✴ ★ ✴ ★ ✴ ★ ✴ ★ ✴ ★

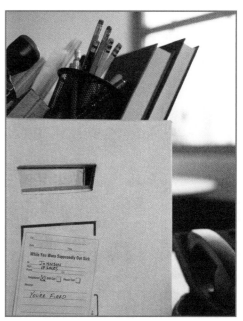

A Cleared Desk

Did you dream that you arrived at work to discover that your possessions had been bundled into a box ready for you to take home, and that you were then overcome by the terrible realization that you'd been fired? If so, you may, consciously or unconsciously, feel that your performance has been judged and found to be wanting, even if only by you yourself.

Related Dreams
pages 191, 192, 226, 231, 233 & 240

My First Day Dreams

✱ ✱ ✱ ✱ ✱ ✱ ✱ ✱ ✱ ✱ ✱ ✱ ✱ ✱ ✱ ✱ ✱

School Days

In your dream, did you return to your first day at school? Perhaps you relived feelings of uncertainty and confusion that you experienced in reality. If so, and you woke up in a sweat, are you about to undergo a major change in your life, maybe at work? Your dream could have been a manifestation of your fear of taking on this new challenge.

FIRST DAY

✱✱✱✱✱✱✱✱✱✱✱✱✱✱✱✱✱✱✱✱✱✱✱✱✱✱✱✱✱✱✱✱✱✱✱

The first day of kindergarten, school, college, or a new job is usually some combination of exciting and terrifying—and if your dreaming mind carried you back in time to a first day of school or work, it may be that you are in the midst of another big life change that is causing you to feel as insecure and uncertain as you did on that day that you dreamed of.

Symbolic and Verbal Associations
- Loneliness
- Uncertainty; confusion
- Insecurity and anxiety
- Excitement
- Life changes

Positive Interpretations: Did you dream that you were a small child, once again heading into the classroom for your first day at school? If so, have you recently started working in a new job, moved to a new city, or had some other major life change? Your dreaming mind may have conjured up your past experience of the first day of school in order to mirror your reaction to, and your feelings regarding, your current life change. So, in your dream, how did you feel? If your dream self felt excited, happy, or anxious to get started with your lessons, then this bodes well for how you are feeling about your new job, home, or other life change. An exciting dream about the first day of school may also indicate that you are feeling bored or dull in your current life, and that you long for the opportunity to stimulate your intellect through learning, to be trained in a new skill, or to develop a natural talent.

Negative Interpretations: Did your dreaming mind cause you to relive a past first-day-of-school trauma in which you felt highly insecure, apprehensive, lonely, or fearful? In your dream, did you weep and run from the classroom, back into the arms of your mother as she attempted to depart the school? If so, and if you have recently undergone a major life change (such as a change of employment or residence, as discussed above), then your dream have been an indication that you are feeling uneasy in your new situation. It may be that you are unsure of how to behave in your new environment, that you are worried and uncertain about what others expect of you, or that you are simply feeling lonely because you miss your old friends or colleagues and because you haven't yet formed any real friendships in your new situation. Having this type of dream may also be a sign that a childhood insecurity about being judged or derided by your peers, or even shunned by others, has been reawakened in the real world. For instance, have you recently been feeling as if you are the brunt of the jokes around your office? Or have your former friends at work treated you coldly ever since you took a public stand against a company policy that you felt was wrong?

Related Dreams

pages 130, 200, 224, 231, 235 & 266

GRADUATION & PROMOTION

Graduations and promotions are milestones in our lives, when we are recognized for our achievements and when we officially move upward, from one level to the next one. As such, they are occasions of pride and celebration. Having a dream that highlights a graduation or a promotion may be an unconscious reflection of the fact that you have completed one phase of life and that you are moving on to the next one, though it may also indicate that you wish to be publicly recognized for your efforts and accomplishments.

Symbolic and Verbal Associations
(Recognition for hard work and accomplishments
(The end of a life stage
(New beginnings
(Pride and joy
(Success and opportunities

Positive Interpretations: Did you dream that you were dressed in the cap and gown of a graduate, and that you felt a great swell of pride and emotion as your name was called out and you rose, amidst clapping and cheering, to receive your diploma? Or did you have a dream in which your boss publicly congratulated you for your good work, shook your hand, and welcomed you as the newest junior executive of your firm? If you had any dream of this sort, might your unconscious mind have called up the image of a graduation or a promotion in order to mirror a culmination or a new beginning in your waking world? For instance, have you recently made some important accomplishment, received a promotion at work, or moved on from one stage of life to the next (e.g., have you recently closed the deal on your first home, or were you recently married)?

Negative Interpretations: If you had a happy dream of receiving a promotion or of graduating from an educational program, and if, in your waking life, you are feeling disgruntled, discontented, or unrecognized for your efforts and accomplishments, then you may have experienced a wish-fulfillment dream (in which case, your unconscious mind was giving you a taste of the attention, recognition, and public acclaim that you so desperately crave in the real world). However, if your dream depicted you being recognized for some accomplishment that you have not yet completed, but that you plan to complete in the future, then your unconscious may have been attempting to urge you to do so. For example: if, in your dream, you were receiving your PhD diploma, this may have been an unconscious prompt for you finally to finish writing that dissertation that you've been dragging out for so long. Finally—particularly if you can draw no immediate parallel with a major life event or change in the real world—it is also possible that your dream signified a desire on your part to take some positive action, such as enrolling in college classes or launching a new project at work.

My Graduation & Promotion Dreams

----

* * * * * * * * * * * * * * * * * * * *

Onward and Upward
If you dreamed of your graduation, of accepting your diploma dressed in a cap and gown, this could represent the ending of a phase in your life. Perhaps you feel as though you have learned as much in your current job as you can, and your unconscious mind was telling you that it's time to seek a new venture.

Related Dreams
pages 90, 192, 198, 245, 250 & 270

My Interview Dreams

✳ ✳ ✳ ✳ ✳ ✳ ✳ ✳ ✳ ✳ ✳ ✳ ✳ ✳ ✳ ✳ ✳ ✳

A Missed Opportunity

Interviews tend to be highly stressful occasions, when we feel vulnerable and exposed to others' judgment, so small wonder that they often feature in anxiety dreams. In your dream, did you feel unprepared, unsure of yourself, or inappropriately dressed? Were you unable to answer any of the questions? If so, it is likely that you feel inadequate in the face of a stressful real-world situation.

INTERVIEWS

✳ ✳

Whether they go well or poorly, interviews tend to be highly stressful situations, and a dream of sitting for an interview is likely to be stressful as well. You may ask why your dreaming mind would choose to put you through such an ordeal. Though the answer will depend on the specific details of your dream, any dream of sitting for an interview or of otherwise being put on the spot is liable to be reflective of your self-image and your feelings and anxiety about how others perceive you.

Symbolic and Verbal Associations
- Self-image; persona
- Nervousness with regard to new people and situations
- Anxiety about how one is perceived
- Opportunities
- Challenges or tests
- Fear of failure

Positive Interpretations: Did you have a dream that depicted you sailing through an interview smoothly and confidently? And do you have an interview coming up in the near future? If so, your dream may have been an unconscious attempt to prepare you for the interview and to reassure you about your ability to perform well and to make a good impression on the interviewer. In general, any dream of performing well when put on the spot may also be an indication of your general feelings of confidence and security regarding your social and intellectual abilities. However, because we generally go to interviews in order to better ourselves in some way (for example, to attend a new school or to seek a better job prospect), having a dream such as this may also be a sign that you desire to pursue new and better opportunities in your life.

Negative Interpretations: In your dream of sitting for an interview, did you fumble nervously through your briefcase, drop your pen and papers into a pile of disarray, and stumble and stutter for the correct words to say as you felt the sweat collect on your forehead and begin to soak through the armpits of your suit jacket? Or did you dream that you were in the audience of a comedy-club show, when the comedian suddenly singled you out to come up and be his "assistant"? And, in your dream, did you begin to shake with fear and dread as the spotlight shone on you and the crowd began to clap and call for you to ascend to the stage? Dreams like this usually highlight some waking worry or angst, either regarding a specific situation that you must face or a general anxiety about how you are perceived by those whom you may regard as your superiors. (Most people feel this sort of social anxiety from time to time, but if you have recurring dreams of this sort, you may want to consider whether you have a more serious issue with your self-respect.)

Related Dreams

pages 121, 192, 193, 222, 240 & 257

LESSONS & LEARNING

✶✶

SCHOOL & WORK

When you are attempting to interpret the meaning of a dream that placed a focus on a past event or lesson that you learned, it will be helpful for you to try to draw a parallel with your current life as it is highly probable that this past event or lesson has, once again, become relevant to your waking world.

Symbolic and Verbal Associations
- ❬ A hunger for knowledge and intellectual stimulation
- ❬ Revisiting or relearning lessons from the past
- ❬ New methods of problem-solving
- ❬ Personal potential; abilities
- ❬ A need to expand or broaden one's mindset

Positive Interpretations: Did you have a dream in which the major focus was on a particular lesson that you were learning? If so, in attempting to interpret your dream, it will help to consider the dream lesson in the context of your past, present, and future. For example, did you dream that you were listening with excitement to a lecture about the American Revolution—a subject that you have long been interested in, but have never pursued to your fullest desire? If so, and particularly if you have been feeling frustrated by a lack of intellectual stimulation in your life, your unconscious mind may have been encouraging you to pursue your historical interest (perhaps by enrolling in a class or by reading more history books in your leisure time). Any dream of learning or studying a subject of interest to you may be an unconscious reference to your unrealized personal aptitude, talents, or abilities (thereby prompting you to nourish them). It may also be that knowledge of the particular subject that you were studying in your dream may be of help to you in solving a current real-life problem. Alternatively, if you had a dream of learning about a subject that is unfamiliar to you, such as a foreign language, this might have been an unconscious sign that you would benefit from expanding or broadening your mindset, or from attempting to view or understand the world from other people's points of view.

Negative Interpretations: Did you dream of relearning a lesson that was taught to you long ago, but that you have long since forgotten or put out of your conscious mind? For example, if you dreamed of learning the fundamentals of English spelling and grammar, have you become sloppy in your written communication, so that your letters and e-mails are full of badly worded sentences and spelling errors? If so, could your unconscious mind have been reminding you of your English lessons in order to encourage you to review those important rules of the language so that you might make a better impression on your business colleagues with whom you communicate in writing (which will, in effect, better your career prospects)?

My Lessons & Learning Dreams

✶✶✶✶✶✶✶✶✶✶✶✶✶✶✶✶✶✶✶✶✶✶

Back to School
Were you back in class in your dream, being taught a particularly inspiring lesson? If so, are you feeling stimulated at work? If not, your dream could have been a nostalgic return to a time when you were being pushed to your intellectual limits, which you're now missing as an adult. Maybe it's time to enroll on that course that you've been thinking about!

Related Dreams

pages 199, 200, 206, 210, 278 & 288

CHAPTER 9: SCHOOL & WORK ❬ 197

My Prizes & Raises Dreams

....
....
....
....
....
....
....
....

✱ ✱ ✱ ✱ ✱ ✱ ✱ ✱ ✱ ✱ ✱ ✱ ✱ ✱ ✱ ✱ ✱ ✱

Well Done!

If you dreamed that you were a student again, and that you were thrilled to receive a prize for your hard work, has your self-esteem recently received a boost? Or could your dream have reflected your longing to have your conscientiousness rewarded in the real world? Do you feel that you deserve a raise or bonus at work, for example?

PRIZES & RAISES

✱✱

When we have dreams that depict us receiving symbolic or monetary school or workplace payments or rewards—namely, wages, bonuses, or prizes—the reference may be fairly straightforward, having to do with our sense of personal value, pride, and accomplishment.

Symbolic and Verbal Associations
- Being valued (or undervalued) for one's worth or services
- Public recognition for one's accomplishments
- Pride
- Self-esteem
- Financial security (or a lack thereof)

Positive Interpretations: Did you have a workplace dream in which a significant focus was placed on your wages, or in which you received a bonus or a raise? If your dream self was pleased with your earnings or your reward, and if you are similarly pleased with the financial benefits of your job in the waking world, then your dream can probably be taken at face value, as an unconscious affirmation of your pleasure and contentment regarding your monetary earnings. A dream such as this is a sign that you have a great sense of security and comfort in your job, and that you feel adequately recognized and acknowledged for your work and your accomplishments, and is a likely indication that you have a good overall sense of self-esteem and that you feel that you are competent and worthy. In fact, any time that you have a dream of being paid, your unconscious may be reinforcing your waking knowledge that you and your family rely on your earnings in order to live, thereby underlining the importance that you place on your job and your wages. Similarly, a dream of winning a prize in school is likely to be a reflection of your sense of self-esteem and self-worth, and may parallel an event in your current waking life (such as receiving a bonus or a raise). And if you dreamed of receiving a billion-dollar paycheck, your dreaming mind was probably simply fulfilling your waking desire for wealth or for public recognition as a person of worth and importance.

Negative Interpretations: Did you dream of being paid for your work, and are you consciously concerned about your precarious financial situation in the waking world? If so, then your dream may have been mirroring your waking preoccupation with your finances, and also reinforcing the importance of your job in making ends meet. But if you are not struggling financially in the real world, did you have a dream in which you were outraged because you were underpaid for your work? Or did you have a dream in which a coworker received a raise or a bonus that you felt you deserved, or in which a classmate was given the prize that you knew should have rightfully been yours? If you dreamed of any of these types of scenarios, the unconscious message may be that you are feeling undervalued or somehow cheated in the waking world.

Related Dreams

pages 114, 192, 195, 199, 245 & 249

TEACHERS & BOSSES

Like all of the adults whom we encounter in our early lives, our teachers have the power to make a strong impression on us—one that can be very good or very bad, or something in between, depending on how they used, or abused, their power over us. The "stamp of authority" that they place on us may leave a deep impression on our unconscious mind, to emerge later in our dreams.

Symbolic and Verbal Associations

‹ Worries with regard to one's personal worth, or how one measures up (as judged by an authority figure)
‹ Nostalgia for happier times
‹ Unresolved pain or anger
‹ Vulnerability and humiliation
‹ Misuse of authority; an ogrelike figure
‹ Respect and obedience
‹ Resentment and rebellion

Positive Interpretations: In your dream, was your mind agreeably cast back to your old classroom, where you found yourself once again standing before, and conversing pleasantly with, your most favorite teacher of all time? If so, it may be that your unconscious was giving expression to your feelings of nostalgia for that time in your life. Another possible explanation for a dream such as this is that your memories of that early, loved teacher have been triggered by someone in your current life—perhaps your boss at work, who has earned your respect and your obedience because of her kindness and patience. Or if you are in a position of power with regard to others, a third explanation is that your dream was an unconscious reminder for you always to treat your subordinates with dignity and with compassion.

Negative Interpretations: Did you have a dream in which you found yourself face to face with a former teacher whom you feared and hated, and did this dream teacher berate and humiliate you in the same nasty way that he or she did when you were a child? A dream like this may signal current real-life insecurity, perhaps sparked by a hostile or overbearing boss, or by a similar set of circumstances in your current life. It is also possible that you have never really come to terms with the pain and suffering that you experienced because of this cruel teacher, and perhaps you are still very angry at this person—in which case, your dream was probably a signal that this is a good time for you to reassess this painful experience, and to think about it from an adult perspective so that you may be released from the hurting and begin to move past it. But if none of these interpretations ring true, is it possible that you yourself have been acting the part of the cruel monster in your dealings with others, possibly the people who work under you?

Related Dreams

pages 121, 124, 128, 200, 247 & 255

My Teachers & Bosses Dreams

✶ ✶ ✶ ✶ ✶ ✶ ✶ ✶ ✶ ✶ ✶ ✶ ✶ ✶ ✶ ✶ ✶

Mentoring Memories

Teachers often make strong impressions on our younger selves. And having a dream about a sports teacher, someone whom you perhaps respected, and who taught you certain skills, may suggest that you are seeking such a figure in your adult life. Alternatively, has someone who is already part of your waking world— possibly your boss—triggered this memory of being mentored?

My Workplaces & Schools Dreams

★ ★ ★ ★ ★ ★ ★ ★ ★ ★ ★ ★ ★ ★ ★ ★ ★

Nine to Five

Have you been dreaming about the mind-numbingly monotonous aspects of your real-life job? And if such dreams have been blighting your sleep, are they reinforcing your waking feelings of frustration at work? If you really are feeling unmotivated and under-valued in your workplace, these dreams may be prompts from your unconscious to look for more stimulating and rewarding employment.

WORKPLACES & SCHOOLS

Workplaces and schools are buildings that, either for better or for worse, hold many strong emotions for most people. (You are probably well aware of this if, as an adult, you have ever gone back to visit your old elementary school.) In reality, schools and workplaces have many similarities: they are both centers of physical and intellectual industry, as well as anxiety, ambition, competition, and a myriad of social interactions—which is why they are fairly interchangeable as dream metaphors.

Symbolic and Verbal Associations
❅ Physical and intellectual industry
❅ Nostalgia, or (alternatively) unresolved pain or trauma
❅ Anxiety about one's performance, and about being judged by one's superiors
❅ Social anxiety
❅ A sense of restriction, due to a preoccupation with work or study
❅ Feeling constrained by social, emotional, or moral rules and regulations

Positive Interpretations: In your dream, did you find yourself to be a young child once again, and were you standing outside your old elementary school, delighted to see that the playground was populated with your old friends, many of whom you haven't seen since that time? This sort of dream can be a simple reflection of nostalgia for a time in life when things were simpler, when you had fewer responsibilities, and when the world seemed alive with possibilities. It is also possible that your current life feels this way once again, which has sparked your unconscious into drawing a dream parallel with that earlier time; this may be particularly true if you have recently retired, switched jobs to one that is less demanding, moved out of the city to a more peaceful place, or otherwise simplified your life in any way.

Negative Interpretations: Dreaming that you are at work may signal a preoccupation with your job during waking hours, particularly if you are finding it stressful. A workplace dream may also be an unconscious attempt to draw your conscious attention to an issue or problem, such as a coworker's passive–aggressive hostility toward you. Or if you dreamed of working at an assembly line, drilling holes into a never-ending convoy of nondescript products, do you find your current life to be boring, monotonous, or mindless? Alternatively, if you had a dream in which you found yourself back at the high school that you hated (perhaps because your classmates picked on you or because you struggled with emotional or family problems that made your school life a torture), has a similar situation in your waking life sparked your memories of your angst-ridden teenage years? For example, do your coworkers pick on, or tease, you, or are your personal problems interfering with your work, so that you feel as though you are falling farther and farther into an abyss? (If this is the case, then coming to terms with your past trauma may help you in dealing with your current situation.)

Related Dreams

pages 84, 89, 199, 204, 210 & 247

CHAPTER 10

BUILDINGS & THE URBAN ENVIRONMENT

A building's real-life purpose usually holds the key to the meaning
of a dream in which it was prominent. When musing on a dream
in which a type of building or urban environment seemed
important, you may consequently find employing some direct
association helpful. If you dreamed of being in hospital, a place
where sick and injured people are cared for, are your waking
circumstances making you yearn for some form of mental
or physical nursing or healing, for example?

My Cinemas & Theaters Dreams

----

* * * * * * * * * * * * * * * * * *

Picture This

Did you dream that you were sitting expectantly in an empty movie theater, when you suddenly realized that the movie had already finished and you had missed it? This dream could mean that you are not living your life fully in the present: are you being held back by regret about something you wish you'd done when you had the chance? Do you feel life is passing you by?

CINEMAS & THEATERS

* *

Cinemas and theaters are places where we go to escape from reality, if only for a little while. They are centers of fantasy and drama, and, if we allow them to, they can transport us to other worlds and realities. When we dream of watching or participating in a dramatic performance, we should pay close attention to the plot and the mood, as they are likely to contain a message from our unconscious.

Symbolic and Verbal Associations
- Escape from worries
- Entertainment; drama
- Mental and emotional stimulation
- Illusion and transience
- Information or warnings

Positive Interpretations: If you had a dream in which you were acting in a play or movie, and if you have always wished for stardom, then you may have experienced a simple wish-fulfillment dream. But if the focus of your dream was more on the drama than on your pleasure in acting a role, or if you dreamed that you watched as a drama unfolded on the stage of your mind, then you will want to consider whether there may have been an unconscious message contained therein. For instance, if you dreamed that you were playing the role of a knight who was on a quest to find a princess to take as a bride, are you seeking a love interest (perhaps with the intent to marry) in the real world? Or if you took delight in watching a comedy that made you laugh until you felt that you would split in two, might you benefit from trying to have more fun during your waking hours? If you watched a romantic play, do you desire more romance in your own life? Or was it a drama or a fantasy that you saw, perhaps signaling a simple, unconscious desire temporarily to escape from the drama of your own waking life?

Negative Interpretations: The unconscious mind may use the ruse of a dream movie or play to give expression to your deepest fears or worries. For example, if you are terrified of the possibility of nuclear war, did your dreaming self watch a movie about a nuclear holocaust? Or if you are the parent of a teenage child who has recently begun driving, did you watch a play about an automobile accident in which a teenager was seriously injured or killed? Dreams like these need not be predictive, but instead they may be simply providing an outlet for our worst fears, also giving us the chance to consider how it would feel and what we would do if they actually came to pass. That said, a cinematic or theatrical dream may, indeed, contain information or a warning regarding something that you have unconsciously realized or suspected. So if you were extremely upset by a dream in which you watched a play about a cheating husband, do you suspect that your own husband may be having an affair?

Related Dreams

pages 66, 123, 125,
214, 276 & 292

CIRCUSES

Circuses are wild and chaotic places, with a multitude of wonders and oddities that are meant to entertain, amaze, and even frighten us. And just as the circus contains many worlds within worlds, there are many possible meanings for a dream of the circus—which is why it is very important to consider your specific dream scenario, what you were doing, what you saw and heard, and how you reacted.

Symbolic and Verbal Associations
- ‹ Illusion
- ‹ Spectacle
- ‹ Chaos
- ‹ Wonders and oddities
- ‹ Magic and mystery

Positive Interpretations: Did you dream that the circus crowd sent up a great cheer as you rolled and soared on the flying trapeze, several stories up beneath the dome of the big tent? If so, your dream trapeze act may have symbolized your rising aspirations, and also the attention and approval of others (which you may either be receiving or seeking) in your waking world. Or did you dream that a spotlight shone on you in the center ring as you cracked a lash over the head of three roaring, yet obedient, lions? If so, have you become a master at successfully controlling your waking environment? Could the lions have represented some powerful persons or forces that you have "tamed," or gotten to do your bidding, in the real world? Or if you were amazed and excited by some dream circus spectacle or wonder, might this have been an unconscious expression of your desire for magic, mystery, and adventure in your life?

Negative Interpretations: If you dreamed that you were lost and terrified in the chaos of the circus, has your waking life become "like a circus" (perhaps because there are always too many people in your home, or because all order seems to have been lost)? Or if you dreamed that you were a sideshow "freak," on display for others to taunt and laugh at, have you been feeling as though people see you as strange or freakish in the real world? Or, in your dream, were you a circus puppet, and was someone pulling the strings to make you dance? If so, do you know who the puppeteer was? Could this person be manipulating you during your waking hours? If you dreamed that you were juggling in a circus act, are you juggling a multitude of real-world duties and responsibilities? (And did you let any of the balls drop, or did you manage to keep them all in the air?) If you dreamed of walking a tightrope, are you having to tread "a fine line" in the waking world? Finally, if you, or someone you know, was dressed as a clown, could this have been a metaphor for an attempt to conceal sadness with a painted, happy face? Or is someone (maybe you) acting in a way that is clumsy, irritating, rude, or foolish in the waking world? Or was your dream clown actually the archetypal trickster?

Related Dreams
pages 66, 131, 202, 214, 235 & 314

My Circuses Dreams

Acting the Clown

Who was acting the clown in your circus dream? If it was you, could the message from your unconscious have been that you are currently behaving like a buffoon in other people's eyes, or else that that huge, fake smile that you've plastered on your face in an attempt to conceal the emotional pain that you are experiencing is actually fooling no one?

BUILDINGS & THE URBAN ENVIRONMENT

CONSTRUCTION SITES

My Construction Sites Dreams

----

* * * * * * * * * * * * * * * * * *

Building Blocks

A dream of a construction site may occur when, in the waking world, you are about to set an ambitious real-world project in motion or feel that you are on the verge of making a fresh start in life. Such dreams may also allude to "unfinished business," and to the work—perhaps including "building bridges"—required to achieve completion or closure.

I n attempting to interpret a dream about a construction site, it is very important to consider things like the mood of the dream and how it made you feel, as well as the dream's details. What time of day was it? What was being constructed? Was there active work being done, or was the site desolate? Or was the site in the demolition phase?

Symbolic and Verbal Associations
- Productivity
- Industry
- Potential
- Destruction
- Loneliness; solitude
- Danger; a hazardous zone

Positive Interpretations: Did you have a dream in which you and a team of others were constructing a new building? If so, what sort of building was it? If it was a school, for instance, this may signify the societal importance that you place on education. Or if you were thrilled to be working on the eightieth story of a half-constructed skyscraper, this may signify your rising aspirations in life, and your efforts to achieve them. And if you delighted in constructing something new, are you feeling happily productive in your waking life? Could the unfinished building represent the slow, but steady, realization of your personal potential?

Negative Interpretations: In your dream, did you find yourself alone on a desolate construction site, and did you pull your jacket around you more tightly to fend off the chilling wind that rattled at the construction tarps? A dream such as this may symbolize feelings of loneliness or isolation in your waking life, and perhaps you also feel that you are in a place in life in which things are at a standstill, and in which what you have been trying to build up around you is left unfinished. Alternatively, did you have a frightening dream in which you were in the midst of a large, commercial construction site, and were you confused and worried as large steel beams swung just over your head and you dashed and darted to avoid falling débris? If so, this may indicate that you are feeling aimless, lost, or confused in the midst of the industry of others. A dream like this may also be an unconscious warning of some danger that lies "overhead" (signaling a need for you to "look up" to see what might be coming at you)—and if you lacked a hardhat or any protective equipment, do you feel similarly unprotected in the real world? Finally, did you dream of the very beginning phase of a construction project: the demolition of another structure? If so, this may have been a metaphor for the destruction of some "structure" in your waking world, such as a relationship or an ideal—and thinking about what the old building might have been used for and how its destruction made you feel will offer clues to the meaning of your dream.

Related Dreams
pages 72, 128, 191, 211, 234 & 277

COURTHOUSES & JAILS

As both symbolic and functional emblems of the law, dream jails and court-houses may signify guilt at having transgressed against a social or moral code, or else a sense of being "on trial," or even imprisoned, in the waking world.

Symbolic and Verbal Associations
- Justice
- Authority
- Guilt
- Social and moral codes
- A feeling of being "on trial"
- Feeling imprisoned or trapped

Positive Interpretations: Did you have a dream in which you successfully argued a case before a court? For example, if you have been fed up in the real world with the way in which your paper boy always tosses your morning newspaper into the bushes, and if you convinced a dream judge and jury of his crime and his due punishment (hopefully, a sentence that was not too harsh), you probably awoke feeling exhilarated and vindicated. If so, you have probably experienced a wish-fulfillment dream. A similar interpretation is likely to apply if you dreamed of watching as someone who has transgressed against you—perhaps someone who has physically harmed you or a member of your family—was carted off to prison. Although these types of wish-fulfillment dreams may make us feel good at the time, they are a probable indication that we are harboring some inner anger or hostility that, in the end, will only serve to harm ourselves. You may be able to relieve yourself of your negative feelings in the real world if you either take some positive action to right the situation and to deliver justice, such as making a phone call to your paperboy's boss, or if you seek to come to terms with your anger and to forgive the person who has wronged or hurt you.

Negative Interpretations: Dreams of being on trial or of being thrown in jail may indicate that you are feeling as if you are "on trial" during your waking hours, or else that you are feeling guilty about having broken some moral or social rule. In your dream, were you filled with sickness or dread as police officers prodded you, handcuffed, through a pack of angry spectators toward the front doors of a courthouse? If so, what was your crime? Are you worried that the professors of your university program will soon judge you to be a deficient student and will seek to cast you out of the school? Or have you been repressing the guilty and shameful memory of the time that you stole twenty dollars from your grandmother's purse, even though you believe that she never realized your crime? Alternatively, if you dreamed of being locked up in a prison, are you feeling "imprisoned" by something in the real world, such as your mother's passionate mission to be informed of, and to control, your every move?

My Courthouses & Jails Dreams

....
....
....
....
....
....
....
....
....

* * * * * * * * * * * * * * * * * * * *

Judge and Jury

Did you find yourself transformed into a lawyer, passionately arguing your case in front of a judge and jury in a suspenseful dream scene? If the dream judge was your real-life boss, and the jury members were your coworkers, can you link your argument with a workplace issue that you feel strongly about? Was your unconscious encouraging you to make a similar stand at work?

Related Dreams

pages 82, 121, 227, 228, 260 & 273

My Galleries & Museums Dreams

✹ ★ ✹ ★ ✹ ★ ✹ ★ ✹ ★ ✹ ★ ✹ ★ ✹ ★ ✹

Exhibit "A"

If an object is taken out of its usual context before being professionally framed, lit, and displayed in an art gallery or museum, the implication is that it merits attention. So if your unconscious set your sleeping self in front of a dream-world exhibit, how does it relate to your waking reality, and why might it deserve your scrutiny?

GALLERIES & MUSEUMS

The act of visiting a gallery or a museum is a boon of having some amount of leisure time—and, in many ways, these places are the crown of a civilized society, offering citizens culture, knowledge, and the pleasure that beauty, education, and learning bring. Dream galleries and museums, therefore, are related to the functions of the thinking mind, to aesthetic appreciation, to the higher consciousness, and to an elevated spirituality.

Symbolic and Verbal Associations
- Knowledge (history, art, science)
- The past
- Art; beauty
- Inspiration and creativity
- Culture; the "collective consciousness" of a society
- An alternative perspective; other worlds and realities; transcendence

Positive Interpretations: Museums offer knowledge by giving the visitor an opportunity to study historical or scientific objects from (and information about) the past. If you dreamed of visiting a museum, this may denote your waking desire to seek out new knowledge and intellectual stimulation. Or if you dreamed that you were passing an enjoyable day by viewing art in a museum or gallery, your dream may have been an unconscious expression of your waking desire to seek out more beauty and deeper meanings in your waking world. And if, in particular, you were admiring a colorful acrylic painting that reminded you of paintings that you yourself used to make, might your dream have been an unconscious attempt to inspire you to return to your own creative endeavors?

Negative Interpretations: Did you have a dream in which you were strangely obsessed by a museum piece, perhaps a dress that reminded you of something that your great-grandmother used to wear? If so, your dream may have been pointing to something in the past that may have a bearing on a present situation or difficulty in your life—in this case, it might be a problem or a troublesome trait that you have "inherited" from your family. In another scenario, did you dream that you felt highly uncomfortable and out of place when you entered a private art gallery, a feeling that was compounded because the docents peered at you in disapproving silence? If so, do you feel uncultured or somehow "out of place" within the real-world social circle in which you are currently moving? (Your dream may have signified that you feel that others are critical and not accepting of you, or else that you have a poor attitude toward yourself, so that you act in a way that denigrates yourself before others.) Or if you dreamed that a painting of you was on display in an historical museum, might the message have been that your thoughts and ideals are antiquated or out of date, and should you reevaluate them?

Related Dreams

pages 197, 212, 279, 288 & 292

GRAVEYARDS

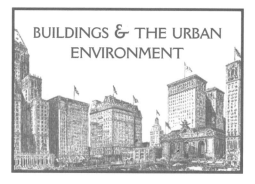

Like many types of dreams, dreams that involve gravestones and graveyards do not usually refer to the obvious. Although they may have connotations of mortality and death, they are much more likely to point to the past, to things "buried" in the unconscious mind, or to a metaphorical or symbolic death.

Symbolic and Verbal Associations
- The past
- Nostalgia
- Something that is "buried" in the unconscious
- The death of a relationship, a phase of life, etc
- Symbolic death and rebirth

Positive Interpretations: Did you dream that you went to visit your grandfather's grave? If so, your unconscious mind may have been recalling your memories of your grandfather in order to remind you of a characteristic of his, or of some advice that he gave you, that may be relevant to your current waking situation. For instance, if you always turned to your grandfather for advice and comfort when you experienced difficulties in your relationship with your father, are you now in need of your deceased grandfather's love and wisdom? By invoking his memory, your unconscious may have been trying to help you to find the part of your grandfather that remains within you and that can help you still. It is also possible that your dream was a result of your feelings of nostalgia for the happy days of your childhood, when you could pay your grandfather a visit whenever you liked. But if you dreamed that you stood by, watching someone dig a grave, do you desire to die a symbolic death, and thereby to be reborn as a "new" person? The same meaning may apply if you yourself were digging the grave, although the implication may also be that there is something, perhaps a negative emotion or a difficult experience, that you wish to "bury" and be done with.

Negative Interpretations: Were you confounded by dream in which you were mourning at the grave of someone who, in the real world, is still very much alive? If so, your dream may have been warning you that your relationship with this person may be fatally "ill" and headed for the grave—and that, unless you take some action to keep your relationship alive, you may soon be mourning this person's actual passing from your life. Or did you have a dream in which you were terrified to find yourself in a cemetery at night? If so, are there some "ghosts" from your past, perhaps the memories of things that you have struggled to keep buried in your unconscious, that you fear may rise up "out of the grave" in order to haunt you in the waking world? You may be able to allay your fears and to halt these sorts of dreams by braving a face-off with whatever it is that you have been attempting to keep covered up.

Related Dreams
pages 92, 96, 139, 149, 212 & 254

My Graveyards Dreams

Dead and Buried
Did you dream that you stood in front of a gravestone and read its inscription with satisfaction? If so, who—or what—were you pleased to see was "dead and buried," or no longer part of your life? If you are trying to quit smoking and the grave was that of a certain "Nick O'Teen," for instance, you probably experienced a wish-fulfillment dream.

HOSPITALS

✦ ✦

In reality, hospitals are places for people who are in need of healing from sickness or injury. And, likewise, when we dream of being hospitalized, this may point to a need for physical or emotional healing, or simply to a desire for someone to pamper and take care of us for a little while.

My Hospitals Dreams

✦ ✦ ✦ ✦ ✦ ✦ ✦ ✦ ✦ ✦ ✦ ✦ ✦ ✦ ✦ ✦ ✦

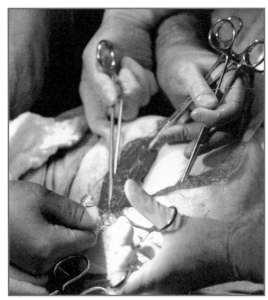

Operation Fix-it

If you dreamed of having open-heart surgery, do you fear that you have developed heart disease? If so, your unconscious may merely have been reflecting your worries. Alternatively, could your dream have portrayed your "broken heart" in the process of being fixed? If so, did you know the dream surgeon, and could he or she have the power to heal your "heartache" in real life?

Symbolic and Verbal Associations

‹ Illness or injury
‹ Physical or emotional rehabilitation
‹ Rest and recuperation
‹ A desire to be pampered and taken care of
‹ Relief from duties and responsibilities

Positive Interpretations: In your dream, did you find yourself a patient in a hospital, and did you enjoy being pampered and cared for by a group of kind and gentle nurses? If so, might you be in need of some emotional attention and care in the real world? Your dream hospital stay may have been an unconscious indication that you desire to be cherished, indulged, and coddled, to have your every need met for you, to be made to feel important, and to be relieved of your real-world duties and responsibilities (if just for a little while). A dream such as this may also indicate that you are feeling physically and/or mentally overworked and overtired, and that you are in desperate need of some serious rest and recuperation. So is it time for you to take that vacation that you've been putting off for so long?

Negative Interpretations: Did you have a dream in which you were very scared when you woke up, in a hospital bed, hooked up to a heart monitor and to various other tubes and machines that you couldn't even identify? If so, have you been worried about your health in the waking world, and have you been burying your fears because you are frightened that they might be confirmed by a doctor's examination of you? Most likely, your unconscious mind dreamed up your hospitalization in order to force you to confront your fears since you probably will not be able to alleviate them completely until you do—and since avoiding the doctor will certainly not make any potential illness go away. At the very least, seeking medical attention will ease your mind. It is also possible that your dream illness was a reference not to your physical health, but instead to some emotional or spiritual sickness. So, for instance, if you dreamed that you were taken to the hospital after suffering a heart attack, and if you believe your real heart to be healthy and functioning well, then are you feeling "lovesick" in the real world, or has someone recently "broken your heart"? Or if you suffered from dream concussion, do you fear that your faculties are slipping, so that you have begun to feel "cracked" in the head? If you dreamed of visiting someone else in a hospital, you will probably find the same logic useful in interpreting your dream.

Related Dreams

pages 56, 74, 121,
128, 257 & 294

HOTELS

* *

If you dreamed of checking into a hotel, you may have felt excited or depressed, depending on the quality of the accommodation and your dream reason for traveling. On a higher symbolic level, a dream of staying in a hotel may indicate a transitional phase or a spiritual journey.

Symbolic and Verbal Associations

‹ Vacations; relaxation
‹ Luxury or (alternatively) shabbiness and filth
‹ A transitional stage in life; a journey
‹ Impersonality; anonymity; transience
‹ Loss, or lack of, identity

Positive Interpretations: In your dream, were you thrilled to be checking into a five-star hotel? And was your delight even more pronounced when the porter led you to your room, a lavish penthouse suite with a view of the city and another of the ocean? If so, and if you are scheduled to take a real-life vacation soon, then your dream may have been a simple reflection of your excitement at the thought of the luxurious temporary dwelling that you may get to inhabit (perhaps also with a bit of wish-fulfillment thrown in!) However, if you are not planning a waking vacation or journey, then your dream may have had a more metaphorical meaning. Is it possible that your unconscious may have been hinting that you have entered a transitional stage in your life—a journey of the spirit, so to speak? As a provisional home, your dream hotel (which, like any dream home, is a symbol of yourself) may have echoed how you are feeling about your spiritual quest; and, in this case, have you recently obtained "the perfect" job, or has a risky business venture begun to pay off in a big way? Or because hotels are also impersonal places where you can remain fairly anonymous if you so choose, might your dream have signified that you are yearning to get away from everyone and everything for a while?

Negative Interpretations: Did you have a dream in which you were depressed to find yourself checking into an old, run-down hotel or motel? And did your dream get even worse when you saw your room—a stinking hole, with filthy, torn furniture, with cockroaches crawling on the walls, and with only a bare fluorescent light for illumination? If you are soon to take a vacation in the waking world, your dream may have been reflecting your anxiety and your worst fears about where you may end up staying. But if you have no vacation planned, then your dream may have been an unconscious signal that you have recently entered into a depressing transitional stage in your life (i.e., that you have embarked on a spiritual journey into "unknown territory") and you are feeling pessimistic. And because of the impersonality of hotels (and the consequent anonymity that they offer), do you fear a loss of identity?

Related Dreams

pages 155, 160, 166, 296, 301 & 302

My Hotels Dreams

----

* * * * * * * * * * * * * * * * * * * *

Hotel Paradiso

If you spend your days struggling to keep on top of the household chores and dreamed that "home" had suddenly become a deluxe hotel, complete with luxurious linen, maids, and room service, it is more than likely that you enjoyed a wish-fulfillment dream. Can you follow your dream cue and take a real-life vacation, or at least a rejuvenating break from your homemaking responsibilities?

BUILDINGS & THE URBAN ENVIRONMENT

My Libraries Dreams

----

* * * * * * * * * * * * * * * * * *

By the Book

In both the real and the dream worlds, libraries signify repositories of learning, and books, nuggets of knowledge. So if you dreamed of perusing a library's bookshelves, are you looking for answers to a real-life conundrum? If so, and you selected a book in your dream, its title or subject may provide the key to a possible solution to your problem.

LIBRARIES

* *

Because they symbolize accumulated learning, dream libraries often suggest a pursuit of knowledge—either knowledge for knowledge's sake, or the knowledge required to solve a real-life problem.

Symbolic and Verbal Associations
- The pursuit of knowledge
- Ideas
- Problem-solving
- The past; history
- Peace and quiet
- Solitude

Positive Interpretations: Did you find yourself in a dream library, and were you scanning the rows of shelves looking for a specific book? If so, can you remember the title or the subject matter of the book that you were looking for? Because real-world libraries are storehouses for the accumulation of human knowledge and ideas (in the form of books, newspapers, magazines, audio and video devices, and other electronic sources), your dream library may have referred to a pursuit of knowledge on your part. If so, your search may either be for general knowledge and intellectual stimulation or for a specific solution to a waking problem—the type of book that you were searching for in your dream will help you to decide which. So if you pulled a divinity-studies volume from the shelf, are you in search of answers to religious or spiritual questions? If it was a philosophy book that you took down, do you seek a greater understanding of philosophical or existential issues? If you sought a history book, is it possible that the solution to a current problem lies in the past? Or if you sought a book about automobile repair and maintenance, could your unconscious have been prompting you to find the source of that strange sound that has been coming from your vehicle's engine? Also, because libraries are relatively silent places, might your dream have pointed to your desire for some peace and quiet?

Negative Interpretations: In your dream library, did you find yourself searching for a book on an unhappy or a difficult subject? Your unconscious may have used your dream book search as a means to send you a message or advice about things that may be happening in your current life. So if you found yourself taking down a book on relationships, could it be that your unconscious has detected an issue or difficulty in your relationship with your partner that needs to be addressed? Or if you sought a book about substance abuse, might this have been an unconscious warning that your alcohol consumption has reached an unhealthy level?

Related Dreams

pages 121, 191, 197, 200, 206 & 288

RUINS

Though we tend to associate the idea of ruins with the remains of ancient civilizations, there are actually plenty of modern-day ruins to be seen in the cities and towns of now. And if you dreamed of viewing or walking through some ruins—whether they were ancient or contemporary—you will want to ask yourself if the ruined state of your dream environment was a reflection of your feelings about your current life.

Symbolic and Verbal Associations
- Desertion
- Desolation
- Loneliness
- Abandonment; feeling forsaken
- Feeling as if one's life is "in ruins"

Positive Interpretations: In your dream, were you hiking among some ruins with a camera strapped around your neck, and were you busily taking photos and writing down notes about what you saw? A dream such as this denotes some "archeological" interest on your part with regard to a structure (such as an ideal or a belief or a relationship) that may have once stood firmly in your life, but has now fallen into ruins. For instance, if the ruins that you were investigating were of your grandparents' house, could your dream have represented the antiquated or obsolete ideals and traditions that your grandparents held dear and that they taught to you as a child, but that are now antiquated or obsolete and of no value to you in your current life except as subjects of historical or archeological interest? Or if you walked through the dream ruins of the church or synagogue that you used to attend with your family, might your dream have indicated that you no longer embrace or find refuge in the religious beliefs and strictures that you were brought up with? Alternatively, did you find your dream self investigating a ruined site while you were thinking and planning how you would begin to rebuild the structure? If so, do you remember what the ruined structure was, or how or why it came to be destroyed? And were you planning to rebuild it exactly as before, or did you plan to make modifications or improvements?

Negative Interpretations: In your dream, did you find yourself alone, walking among the desolate remains of a ruined and abandoned city? If so, did your dream mirror how you are feeling during your waking hours—perhaps isolated, lonely, and forsaken? Do you feel estranged from your family and friends, and does your entire life seem to be "in ruins"? In interpreting your dream, you will want to consider what was ruined (i.e., the town that you grew up in, your first school, the city that you live in now, etc) and how it made you feel. Whatever was in ruins in your dream may have been a metaphor for the downfall or destruction of some "structure" in your waking world, such as a relationship or an ideal.

My Ruins Dreams

Rack and Ruin

One possible explanation for a dream of returning to the street on which you grew up, only to find that it had gone to rack and ruin is that, at some level, you feel that you cannot revisit your past. Have you neglected your relationships with your family members or childhood friends to the extent that they have crumbled away to dust?

Related Dreams
pages 157, 158, 204, 216, 234 & 369

My Sacred Places Dreams

✱ ✱ ✱ ✱ ✱ ✱ ✱ ✱ ✱ ✱ ✱ ✱ ✱ ✱ ✱ ✱ ✱

Spiritual Sanctuary

Maybe you dreamed of vacationing in the Far East, of ducking into a temple to escape a swarm of beggars, and of being suffused with a sense of serenity as you gazed at the Buddha figure within. If so, and you are feeling harried by others' demands when you are awake, perhaps making time for some quiet contemplation would similarly calm and fortify you.

SACRED PLACES

✶✶✶✶✶✶✶✶✶✶✶✶✶✶✶✶✶✶✶✶✶✶✶✶✶✶✶✶✶✶✶✶✶✶

Whether or not you are religious in your waking life, a dream of being in a religious building or a sacred place is likely to have symbolized your spiritual or idealistic needs, tendencies, or potential. Furthermore, dreams of this sort are likely to send an uplifting message from your unconscious.

Symbolic and Verbal Associations

- ☾ Spiritual guidance or fulfillment
- ☾ Idealism
- ☾ Peace; a sanctuary from worldly problems
- ☾ Wellbeing; happiness
- ☾ Reflection, meditation, or contemplation
- ☾ The need to treat your body as "the temple of the soul"

Positive Interpretations: Did you dream that you were rushing through the city streets, feeling hurried, stressed, or lost, when you suddenly saw and entered a church, sank down into a pew, and were overcome with a feeling of calm and blissful peace? If so, has the real world become so stressful and full of obligations (maybe to your work, your family, and your friends) that you find that you never have a moment to reflect, meditate, or contemplate your life? Your unconscious mind may have been urging you to seek a temporary refuge from your life problems and responsibilities to others, even if this simply means a retreat into the safe haven of your own inner consciousness. Is it time that you gave some thought to your own goals and needs, and to what is really important to you in life? Doing so may help you to find or plan a way to achieve your goals, thereby allowing you greater inner peace. In addition, have you been so busy taking care of your worldly duties and satisfying the needs of others that you have neglected your own spiritual needs? Your dream may have been an unconscious prompt for you to seek out, or return to, that which nurtures your spirit.

Negative Interpretations: Depending on your waking circumstances and on the details of your dream, there are a number of other interpretations for a dream of entering, or of being inside, a sacred building. If you have recently been doing something to harm your health, or if you have been otherwise disregarding your body, your unconscious may have been sending you a portent of the happiness and wellbeing that you would feel if you would begin to treat your body "as the temple of your soul"—thereby taking better care of your physical, emotional, and spiritual health. Alternatively, could it be that you are feeling guilty for having disregarded the humanitarian or altruistic ideals that you once passionately believed in and strove to live your life by? Or do you wish for spiritual guidance in solving a waking problem? In light of some current issue or ethical dilemma, do you long for the support and comfort of a system of unalterable and unquestionable moral rules?

Related Dreams

pages 96, 99, 102,
121, 148 & 149

SKYSCRAPERS & TOWERS

As tall, soaring structures, dream towers and skyscrapers may represent the dreamer's "towering" spiritual or intellectual aspirations. But because they are also isolating structures, which raise and hold a person above, and away from, the rest of the world, the possibility of this type of meaning should also be considered—as should the Freudian interpretation of skyscrapers as phallic symbols. The context of your dream and your dreaming reaction should help you to decide which type of meaning is closest to the truth.

Symbolic and Verbal Associations
- Feeling "removed" from the rest of the world
- Isolation; imprisonment
- Spiritual or intellectual aspirations
- Putting oneself in an "ivory tower": arrogance or intellectual aloofness
- Someone who is "a tower of strength"
- A phallic symbol; machismo; aggression
- Corporate or personal wealth and prestige

Positive Interpretations: In your dream, were you standing at the top of a tower or skyscraper, gazing down at the people who were scrambling to get to their various destinations far, far below? If so, how did your dream make you feel? Were you relieved and glad to be away from everyone else and the never-ending demands that they seem to make of you? A dream tower may also represent someone who is "a tower of strength," or a person whom others rely on for protection or support. Of course, because of their elongated and upright or erect shape, towering structures are interpreted by Freudian dream theorists as phallic symbols—and hence are also associated with macho tendencies, including a drive for power, wealth, and prestige. So if you dreamed that you were living in a lavish penthouse apartment, is it possible that this was a reference to your rising social or professional ambitions?

Negative Interpretations: Did you dream that you gazed out from the top floor of a tower, and did you feel sad or lonely because you felt that you were being held prisoner, against your will? If so, have you been feeling isolated from others in your waking world, perhaps because of your own arrogance, intellectual aloofness, or stubborn unwillingness to come out of your "ivory tower" and to mingle at the level of those around you? Or was your dream a reflection of the loneliness that you feel because of your exceptional intellect or your rarified beliefs, which prevent you from interacting normally with "the common man on the street"? Finally, considering the Freudian interpretation of towers as phallic symbols, might your dream tower have been a reference to the thrusting, ruthless aggression that you have used to climb high above others (in social or professional terms), so that all may see and envy your power and your position?

My Skyscrapers & Towers Dreams

----

* * * * * * * * * * * * * * * * * * * *

Aiming High

If you dreamed of surveying a glittering cityscape from a glitzy penthouse apartment, it is likely that your lavish, lofty vantage point represented the height of your personal aspirations. But if you felt dwarfed, or hemmed in, by a concrete jungle of skyscrapers in dreamland, are certain people's towering ambitions making you feel small, or restricting your room for maneuver, in the waking world?

Related Dreams

pages 152, 160, 164, 204, 228 & 277

BUILDINGS & THE URBAN ENVIRONMENT

My Sporting Venues Dreams

....
....
....
....
....
....
....
....
....

* * * * * * * * * * * * * * * * * * *

Slip-sliding Away

Did you dream that you and your friends were ice-skating? If so, the details of the dream scene may tell you a lot about your relationships with one another, and possibly also how successfully each of you is coping with a slippery, or tricky, waking situation. So, in your dream, who propped up whom; who sped along smoothly; and who lost control and fell?

SPORTING VENUES

Like movie theaters and playhouses, sporting venues are places where acts of triumph and tragedy are played out for the viewing pleasure of others. In symbolic terms, dreaming of viewing a sports event can be interpreted as either wishfulfillment (i.e., seeking the thrill of the match in order to divert our attention from our own problems) or else as a channel for a specific message or warning from the unconscious.

Symbolic and Verbal Associations
- Competition
- Bets and wagers
- Excitement: stimulation
- Triumph
- Tragedy

Positive Interpretations: Did you dream of entering a horsetrack, placing a bet on your favorite equine athlete, and excitedly taking your seat in the stands as the horses were led out to the track? And, in your dream, were you overjoyed as your horse quickly assumed his position at the head of the pack, never once fell back, and almost seemed to fly across the finish line to victory? If so, could this have been a sign of your own inevitable success in the real world? Was your intuition telling you that a recent real-world bet or gamble is about to pay off in a large way? (Alternatively, if you dreamed that your horse achieved victory after running a more difficult course—perhaps he came from behind to win the race in the last few seconds—then your unconscious may have been predicting that your own success or victory will come only after a difficult struggle.) Of course, it is also possible that you simply experienced a wish-fulfillment dream (a possibility that may be even more likely if you frequent the track during your waking hours). A dream of being excited and entertained by a sporting event may also be an unconscious stress outlet—a means of allowing you to escape your own real-world worries, if just for a little while.

Negative Interpretations: Did you dream of sitting in a football stadium, banner and beer in hand, as you readied yourself to watch your favorite team square off against its arch-rival in the most important match of the season? And, in your dream, were your hopes and spirits dashed as you watched your team being absolutely trounced? If so, have you recently experienced—or do you fear—a similar loss for yourself in the real world? For instance, has a new business venture suffered setback after setback, so that it looks as though it is sure to fail altogether? And if, in your dream, a fight broke out between the two teams, was this a reflection of the real-world battle that you have been fighting in order to try to save your business? If so, have you found yourself resorting to aggressive or "illegal" tactics in order to keep your company alive? Or was the game rained off? If so, this may signify that your own affairs are at a standstill.

Related Dreams

pages 82, 114, 190, 202, 282 & 289

STORES & MALLS

As places where we go to obtain our basic needs for living, as well as those things that we desire, but do not really "need," stores and shopping malls are symbolic of fundamental emotional sustenance and, also, of the desire to "better" oneself or to project a more attractive image to the world.

Symbolic and Verbal Associations
- Basic requirements
- Objects of desire
- Money; purchasing power
- "Retail therapy"
- Emotional sustenance

Positive Interpretations: In your dream, did you spend an enjoyable day at the mall, going from store to store, trying on clothes, and buying lots of wonderful things at bargain prices? If so, your unconscious was probably providing you with a little "retail therapy" in order to allow you to have a good time while temporarily escaping your worries, duties, and troubles. And if, in your dream, you purchased lots of "unnecessaries" (such as cosmetics, hair-care products, or fancy clothing or shoes), might this have mirrored your waking desire to project a better, or more attractive, image to the world? Or if you found yourself shopping in stores that sold clothing that was far outside the bounds of your usual style, might this have signaled an unconscious desire to change your "look" (and perhaps your attitude or outlook on life, as well)? If so, were your new dream clothes funkier than your usual wardrobe? Or were they sportier, or more conservative? Alternatively, did you have a dream in which you were pushing a cart down the aisles of a supermarket, scanning the shelves, and selecting grocery items as you scratched them off a list that you held? A dream such as this may indicate that you are successfully taking care of your fundamental needs by providing yourself with the emotional sustenance that you require—although if a much-needed shopping trip is due, then your dream may have simply been your unconscious's way of reminding you of your "to-do list."

Negative Interpretations: Did you have a stressful shopping dream in which you were unable to decide between two items, such as a red shirt and a blue one, and you only had enough money to purchase one? If so, have you been suffering from an agony of indecision over some issue during your waking hours? Or if, in your dream, you could not decide between purchasing a book or a dress, are you facing a real-world dilemma between focusing your energy on advancing your intellect or trying to appear more attractive? And if you were frustrated by a dream in which you couldn't find any clothing that you liked, or nothing that you tried on fitted, are you feeling similarly out of sorts, or like a "misfit," in the waking world?

Related Dreams
pages 75, 161, 169, 236 & 249

My Stores & Malls Dreams

Shopaholic Heaven
If you're a shopaholic of modest means and your unconscious transported your sleeping self to a purchaser's paradise—an Aladdin's cave of luxury and designer goods—and, what's more, equipped you with a credit card with no limit, you must have relished your wish-fulfillment dream. Don't assume that it was literally a sign of things to come, however!

STRONGHOLDS

✱✱✱✱✱✱✱✱✱✱✱✱✱✱✱✱✱✱✱✱✱✱✱✱✱✱✱✱✱✱✱✱✱✱✱

A dream of barricading oneself in a castle, fortress, or any stronghold may point toward emotional vulnerability and a desire to protect or defend oneself against outside attacks. In terms of Freudian dream interpretation, strongholds are associated with the desire to make a sexual conquest, or else to fend off one.

My Strongholds Dreams

....
....
....
....
....
....
....
....
....

✱✱✱✱✱✱✱✱✱✱✱✱✱✱✱✱✱✱✱✱✱

Symbolic and Verbal Associations
- Protection or defense from aggressors
- Emotional barricades
- Emotional self-reliance
- Isolation
- A sexual "conquest"

Positive Interpretations: Did you have a dream that highlighted your self-imposed isolation from others? For instance, did you dream of happily barricading yourself within a fortress or stronghold? If so, do you derive a great sense of security and contentment from being emotionally self-reliant? Alternatively, do you feel that you rely on others to satisfy your emotional needs? If so, your dream may have been an unconscious prompt for you to seek ways to meet your own emotional requirements.

Negative Interpretations: Did you have a dream in which you hurried into a medieval castle, raised the drawbridge behind you, lowered the portcullis, and then took up a position of defense with your bow and arrows? If so, you may be wondering why your unconscious mind would cast your dreaming self in such a scenario. Is it possible that, in the waking world, you have been feeling like you are on the defense against aggressive outside forces? This could be a rival or a group of rivals at school or at work, or anyone who may be seeking to attack you (not necessarily physically) in the waking world. Or have you been feeling so emotionally vulnerable that you are throwing up a virtually impenetrable emotional barricade in order to prevent anyone from breaching your persona (or façade) and therefore coming too close to "the real you"? And if, in your dream, your stronghold came under attack, could you identify your besiegers? Were they, indeed, your rivals or your enemies? Or were they your friends and your loved ones, from whom you have withdrawn emotionally in the waking world? (And did your defenses hold firm, or did they crumble under the attack? The answer to this question is likely to give you a clue as to how well your real-life defenses are holding up.) Finally, if you are a man, it may be relevant to know that Freudian dream interpreters equate a dream of storming a castle with a man's desire to make a sexual conquest of a woman who has resisted his advances. And if you are a woman who dreamed of pouring boiling oil over a man as he stormed the ramparts, might your dream have mirrored your real-life desire to defend yourself against someone's aggressive and persistent sexual advances?

Keep Out!

Did you dream that you were desperately trying to gain access to a fortress in order to speak to your friend, who had barricaded himself inside, and with whom you have fallen out in real life? In a dream like this, the castle walls may have symbolized the impenetrable barrier that your friend has built up around himself to avoid communicating with you.

Related Dreams
pages 106, 118, 132, 158, 213 & 228

CHAPTER 11
ANXIETY DREAMS

Anxiety dreams are among the most commonly remembered,
probably because, in a sort of vicious cycle, they feed the very fears
of which they are an expression, fears that the conscious mind
often tries its utmost to suppress. Some dream experts believe that
consciously and rationally identifying, facing, and dealing with
the often irrational worries and insecurities that give rise to
such recurring nightmares will banish them from your sleep.

ANXIETY DREAMS

My Betrayals Dreams

....
....
....
....
....
....
....
....
....

* * * * * * * * * * * * * * * * * * *

Being Cold-shouldered

Dreaming that your real-life partner gave you the cold shoulder and instead paid court to another woman almost certainly reflects your own insecurities regarding your ability to keep his attention and prevent him from straying. That said, you may have unconsciously detected signs that he really is losing interest in you or is attracted to someone else.

BETRAYALS

* *

Betrayals have been the fodder of drama and tragedy through the ages. The idea of betrayal is made much more sinister by the fact that, in order to betray someone, the betrayer must first have that person's trust—so, by definition, we may only be betrayed by a friend or loved one. There is no doubt, therefore, that in the world of dreams, betrayals are among the most highly stressful of subject matters.

Symbolic and Verbal Associations
(Suspicion
(Loss of trust
(Someone who is "two-faced"
(A turncoat
(Being "stabbed in the back"

Positive Interpretations: Did you have a dream in which you betrayed one of your dearest friends, albeit for good reason? For example, if, in the real world, your best friend has been hiding her drug problem from her family, whom she has been also stealing money from in order to support her habit, did you dream that you "blew the whistle" on her with her family, in order that she might receive professional help for her addiction? If so, your unconscious mind may have been trying to tell you that—although it may cause your friend to become very angry with you—betraying your friend's trust, in this instance, may be the best thing that you can do for her.

Negative Interpretations: Did you awake feeling very angry or embittered because you had a dream in which your best friend "stabbed you in the back," or betrayed your trust, perhaps by telling your most intimate secret to someone else? For instance, in your dream, were you infuriated and deeply hurt when you found out that your best friend, to whom you tell almost everything, had gone behind your back and told someone who is your rival or your enemy a secret of yours that you would never have told anyone else in the world (and, even worse, a secret that is likely to cause you public shame and ridicule if it ever became known)? If so, what could have been the meaning of your dream? If you have no cause to believe that your friend has actually exposed the secret that was featured in your dream, is it possible that your unconscious mind has detected that your friend's loyalty to you may be wavering? Or was your dream a simple reflection of the growing distance that you have felt between yourself and your friend, which you may have internalized as your friend's rejection or emotional betrayal of you? Or, alternatively, are you feeling guilt over some betrayal that you have committed against your friend—a situation that was inverted by your dreaming mind, perhaps to make you feel somehow righteous or blameless for your own disloyalty?

Related Dreams
pages 93, 235, 252, 253, 260 & 264

BREATHING DIFFICULTIES

✦✦✦✦✦✦✦✦✦✦✦✦✦✦✦✦✦✦✦✦✦✦✦✦✦✦✦✦✦✦✦✦✦

In many traditions and spiritual practices, breath is the tangible expression of the life force or the spirit (and, in fact, the Latin word *spiritus* means "breath"). Indeed, breathing is perhaps the most obvious sign that one is alive. It is no wonder, then, that, in dreams, as in reality, the inability to breathe properly is a high cause for panic and anxiety.

Symbolic and Verbal Associations
- Feeling restricted or "suffocated"
- Being harried, and therefore unable to "catch one's breath"
- Life; spirit
- Speech; one's voice
- Being "breathless" with anticipation
- Guilt; something that is "weighing on one's chest"

Positive Interpretations: Did you have a dream in which you were "breathless" with anticipation over something—perhaps an upcoming party, the results of an exam that you took, or word from a school that you have applied to? If so, your dream was probably simply mirroring your mounting real-world excitement over whatever it is that you are waiting for. Alternatively, if you generally suffer from health- or stress-related breathing difficulties, did you have a dream in which you were overjoyed to find yourself breathing easily, deeply, and evenly? If so, your unconscious may have been either allowing you a brief period of free and easy breathing or it may have been attempting to guide you toward becoming more calm and peaceful during your waking hours.

Negative Interpretations: Did you awake gasping for air, albeit with a flood of relief, after having had a dream in which you felt that you were suffocating? If so, and if you can think of no real-world reason why you might have had such a dream (such as a sinus infection or a respiratory problem, or a sheet or blanket that was covering your sleeping head), then your dream may have been an unconscious reflection of how you are feeling during your waking hours. So are you feeling stifled or suffocated because your boyfriend will not allow you out of his sight? Or are you feeling guilty about something that is "weighing on your chest"? Alternatively, while you were sleeping, did you feel as though a great, heavy force was crushing your chest so that you could not breathe or move? In past times, when sexual pleasure was considered taboo, people who had erotic dreams were said to have been attacked by a sexually voracious incubus (a male demon) or succubus (a female demon). The words "incubus" and "succubus" are still used to describe the nocturnal sensation of a weight pressing down on one's chest, together with breathing difficulties, an inability to move, and a feeling of dread—a phenomenon that dream experts think may have to do with natural sleep paralysis (which we all experience, but rarely become aware of).

My Breathing Difficulties Dreams

✦✦✦✦✦✦✦✦✦✦✦✦✦✦✦✦✦✦✦✦

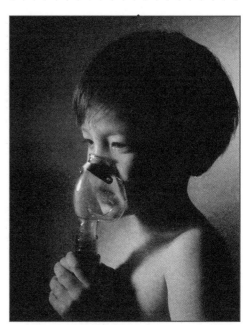

Gasping for Air

If you remember gasping for air in your sleep, could your breathlessness have had a simple explanation, such as a blocked nose or mouth? Otherwise, do you feel somehow suffocated by your present circumstances in the waking world, and could your dream consequently have portrayed you panting for a "breath of fresh air" or the "oxygen" of freedom?

Related Dreams

pages 50, 55, 220, 221, 223 & 227

My Buried Alive Dreams

_____
_____
_____
_____
_____
_____
_____
_____
_____

* * * * * * * * * * * * * * * * * * * *

That Sinking Feeling

When we are feeling anxious, but can't consciously pinpoint why, the unconscious mind may reflect our anxiety in dreamland by depicting us in the grip of a real-life phobia, such as claustrophobia. This is one possible explanation of a dream of being buried alive; another is feeling crushed, or suffocated, by an overwhelmingly oppressive situation in the waking world.

BURIED ALIVE

The fear of being buried alive is what led some people, in earlier times, to decapitate their deceased loved ones before putting them in the grave. In the language of dreams, being buried alive may symbolize a feeling of being overwhelmed or overtaken by problems or worries.

Symbolic and Verbal Associations
- Feeling hemmed in or claustrophobic
- Worldly demands, obligations, and worries
- A "black hole" that one cannot climb out of
- A "living death"
- Hostility or anger

Positive Interpretations: In your dream, were you walking through a lush forest, and did you come across a riverbank, where you lay down and gave in to the pleasurable sensation of your body sinking into the soft, warm mud? And, in your dream, were you overcome by a great sense of peace and comfort as the wet soil began to cover your body completely? If you had a dream of this sort, do you feel as if your waking life has become too frantic or frenetic, and do you wish that you could "ground" (i.e., calm or steady) yourself, or let go of your waking troubles, if just for a while? And if you had a dream in which you willingly went to your grave, do you wish that you could undergo a symbolic death and therefore be "reborn" as a "new" person?

Negative Interpretations: Did you have a terrible nightmare in which you found yourself trapped inside a dark, deep, earthen hole, with soil being thrown over your head so that you were being slowly, but surely, buried alive? And no matter how hard you tried to claw your way out, did your dream self seem to sink deeper and deeper into your grave? If you did have such a dream, you were probably deeply disturbed and mystified as to why your unconscious mind would subject you to this nightmare experience. The most likely interpretation for this sort of dream is that the demands, obligations, and worries of your waking life have become so overwhelming to you that you feel as if you were at the bottom of a "black hole" that you are unable to climb your way out of. If this is the case, and if you feel as if your life has become like a "living death," then you may want to consider seeking the help of a professional counselor. In a slightly different scenario, did you have a dream in which someone was deliberately burying you alive? If so, who? If it was the star player on your rival bowling team (for instance), then your unconscious mind may have been trying to force you to recognize the deep hostility that this person has for you, and his or her wish to see your goals and ambitions "dead and buried."

Related Dreams

pages 96, 207, 219, 368, 369 & 385

CHASES

ANXIETY DREAMS

Perhaps one of the most common and universal anxiety dreams is that of being chased. When interpreting a dream of this sort, it is important to try to identify who (or what) you were fleeing from, and to try to draw a connection with a person or a thing (perhaps even something within yourself) in the waking world.

Symbolic and Verbal Associations
(Escape from danger
(Fear of one's inner urges or traits
(Suppressed feelings; guilt
(Hostility
(Unsolved problems

Positive Interpretations: If you had a dream in which you were being chased by someone whom you did not recognize, it is possible that your pursuer was actually your shadow: a quality or an aspect of yourself that you are anxious to escape or to hide from. (This may be particularly true if your dream pursuer's appearance was repulsive to you and if he or she was of the same sex.) If so, what was it about him or her that frightened you so much? Was it his or her sadness, greed, or lust? Whatever your shadow represents, your unconscious may have been telling you that it is time for you to acknowledge and come to terms with this aspect of yourself.

Negative Interpretations: Did you awake with your heart pounding and your body soaked with sweat after having had a dream in which you were being hunted or chased by someone or something? If so, can you remember who or what you were running from? Was it a person whom you know in the real world? Or was it an unknown pursuer? A ghoul or monster? Or a vicious wild animal? Your dream is a likely indicator that you are feeling threatened by someone or something in the real world, and the answer to the previous questions will tell you who or what you feel threatened by—be it an actual person, a situation, or something that lies within yourself. For instance, if you dreamed that you were being chased by your mother-in-law, do you know why you might feel threatened by her? Has your unconscious assessed that your mother-in-law (or perhaps your wife's entire family, which your mother-in-law represents) disapproves of you and seeks to undermine your marriage? Or, in your dream, did your boyfriend transform himself into a werewolf and chase you for hours on end? And did you somehow know that he was planning to tear you into shreds and then eat you? A dream such as this may signify that you are feeling overwhelmed or dominated by your overbearing boyfriend, perhaps even more so because he has been pressuring you to make a commitment to marriage. However, unless you know that they represent someone whom you know in the real world, nonhuman dream pursuers usually symbolize an internal fear or need (an "animal" instinct) rather than an external threat.

My Chases Dreams

✶ ✶ ✶ ✶ ✶ ✶ ✶ ✶ ✶ ✶ ✶ ✶ ✶ ✶ ✶ ✶ ✶ ✶

The Intruder
Dreaming of being chased by a terrifying pursuer and of making it to safety, only to cower in horror while helplessly watching the monstrous predator smash down our defenses, is a classic "boogeyman" nightmare. Can you identify the horrific quality that your dream pursuer represented? If so, you may find that consciously facing it head-on neutralizes its power to petrify.

Related Dreams
pages 106, 114, 129, 190, 257 & 289

CHAPTER 11: ANXIETY DREAMS (221

My Communication Gaps Dreams

✶ ✶ ✶ ✶ ✶ ✶ ✶ ✶ ✶ ✶ ✶ ✶ ✶ ✶ ✶ ✶ ✶ ✶ ✶

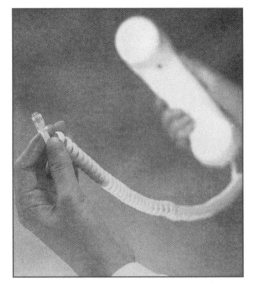

A Severed Connection

Because they enable us to bridge enormous distances and speak to people who are many miles away, telephones symbolize direct communication when they feature in dreams. Dreaming of deliberately terminating a conversation with someone by unplugging the telephone from the phone line suggests that you similarly long to sever your connection with him or her in the waking world, be it permanently or temporarily.

COMMUNICATION GAPS

As in the biblical story of the Tower of Babel, when communication breaks down, so does the functionality of a society. A dream of having difficulty in communicating may signal a real-world misunderstanding, an inability to voice your feelings or opinions, or a sense of emotional isolation.

Symbolic and Verbal Associations

- Confusion
- Getting your "wires crossed" with someone: a misunderstanding
- Emotional isolation
- Being unable to "speak your mind" or express yourself
- Freedom from responsibility

Positive Interpretations: Did you have a dream in which you felt happy or relieved to be free of the burden of communicating with others? For instance, did you dream that you were recovering from having your tonsils out and that you were under strict orders not to speak for several days? Or, in your dream, were you isolated in a wilderness cabin with no electricity and no access to a telephone or a computer? And did you enjoy the peace and tranquility that you felt because you were left alone with your own thoughts? If so, there are a few possible explanations. Your dream may have signaled that you are feeling overwhelmed by your real-world responsibilities, and that you long for a temporary release from the burden of communicating with others. Another explanation is that you feel misunderstood, or that everything that you say is misconstrued, so that you wish to shut off your willingness to communicate as an "I'll show them" tactic.

Negative Interpretations: Did you have a nightmare in which you were in some sort of danger—perhaps a hairy ghoul had you in its clutches—but when you opened your mouth to cry out for help, no sound would emerge? If so, do you feel unable, for whatever reason, to ask for help in the real world? Or, in your dream, did you seem to speak a different language from everyone else, so that no one could understand what you said? If so, do you feel similarly misunderstood by others in the waking world? Or did you have a dream in which you were invisible, so that, for all your efforts to communicate, no one could hear or see you? If so, do you feel that others ignore you or treat you as if you were invisible? Alternatively, did you have a dream in which you were trying to call someone, but, although you knew that the person was at home, he or she would not pick up the telephone? If it was your mother, do you feel that she doesn't listen to what you say in the waking world? Or if you dreamed that someone had gagged or taped your mouth shut, who was it? Have they, or something that they represent, taken away your real-world freedom of speech? Finally, any dream in which you were unable to communicate may point to a problem with expressing yourself in the real world.

Related Dreams

pages 60, 196, 227,

239, 259 & 278

DROWNING

In symbolic terms, dreams of drowning may indicate overwhelming trouble or problems, or a conflict with one's environment (including other people), so that there may be a feeling of "swimming against the tide," being out of one's "emotional depth," or struggling to keep one's "head above the water."

Symbolic and Verbal Associations

‹ Being "over one's head" in trouble, etc
‹ Conflict, as in "swimming against the tide," or struggling "against the current" (of opinion, etc)
‹ A desire to "go with the flow"
‹ Being out of one's "emotional depth"
‹ "Treading water"; trying to keep one's "head above the water"
‹ Being in need of help, or a "lifeline"

Positive Interpretations: Did you have a dream in which you were miraculously saved from drowning when someone threw you a rope and pulled you up into their boat? If so, did you recognize the person who tossed you the "lifeline"? Your unconscious may have been hinting that he or she has the ability to throw you an "emotional lifeline" in the real world, thereby saving you from your own inner turmoil, which is threatening to swallow you up. Alternatively, in your dream, did you find yourself becoming exhausted and giving in to the idea of drowning—only to discover that the moment you stopped fighting the water, you began to drift gently and peacefully downstream? If so, your dream may have signaled an unconscious desire to stop fighting some real-world battle and instead just to let yourself "go with the flow."

Negative Interpretations: Did you have a nightmare in which you were fighting for your life as you struggled against a mighty current of water? If so, have you been battling the "current" of popular opinion, or "swimming against the tide" in the waking world? Or, in your dream, were you swimming in the ocean when you drifted too far away from the shore, so that you were out of your depth? If so, are you out of your "emotional depth" in the real world (perhaps because you have gotten romantically entangled with someone who is already married, or because your girlfriend is sending you contrary signals regarding her feelings for you)? And if, in your dream, you found yourself desperately thrashing and flailing about, trying to keep your head above the rough and tossing waters, are you inundated with problems in the real world, so much so that you feel that you are beginning to lose all emotional control? (In other words, are you so distressed by your current waking situation that you fear that you may be headed for a nervous breakdown?)

Related Dreams

pages 219, 257, 291, 372, 383 & 387

My Drowning Dreams

----

* ★ * ★ * ★ * ★ * ★ * ★ * ★ * ★ * ★ *

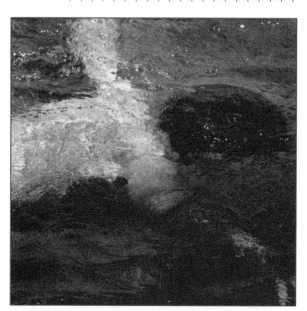

In Deep Water

Dreams of drowning are all about loss of control, or feeling "out of one's depth," during one's waking hours. When trying to interpret your dream, bear in mind water's symbolic association with emotions and try to remember what happened. Did someone deliberately hold you under water, for example? If so, is he or she immersing you in deep and dangerous emotions in real life?

My Embarrassment Dreams

....
....
....
....
....
....
....
....
....

* * * * * * * * * * * * * * * * * * * *

Oh No!

Does recalling your cringe-making dream make you squirm with embarrassment? If so, how did you humiliate yourself in dreamland? If you put your foot in it by saying something crass to a witty, sophisticated someone whom you admire in the real world, your dream may have reflected your feelings of anxiety about your ability to inspire that person's respect.

EMBARRASSMENT

★

Embarrassment is the base of many different types of anxiety dreams. Generally speaking, dreams of being embarrassed may signify insecurity, and a fear of appearing foolish in public or in front of someone whom the dreamer wishes to impress.

Symbolic and Verbal Associations
- Insecurity
- Exposure (of private thoughts, feelings, etc)
- A fear of looking silly or foolish
- Public shame
- Inappropriate behavior, or fear of acting inappropriately

Positive Interpretations: In your dream, did you commit some act or error, or find yourself in a situation, that caused you public embarrassment? For instance, did you stand up to deliver a speech with food stuck between your front teeth? If so, when your folly became known to you, did your dream self feel embarrassed, yet deal with the situation gracefully? For instance, in your dream, did you laugh along with everyone else and make a joke about the food in your teeth, and then move on smoothly to the more serious topic of your speech? If so, your dream may have been an unconscious affirmation that you are able to take the jokes and punches that life throws your way, and that you are a fairly confident person who is usually able to hold your own in tricky situations.

Negative Interpretations: Did you have a dream in which you did something that caused everyone around you to laugh at you, so that you turned hot- and red-faced with utter embarrassment? For instance, did you dream that you were walking through the cafeteria at your work, with your lunch tray in your hand, when you slipped and fell, scattering your tray and food everywhere? And, in your dream, did your coworkers roar with laughter, while not one single person bothered coming over to help you as you attempted to pick yourself up and clean up the mess? This sort of dream is likely to indicate that you feel insecure (particularly in the presence of your coworkers), and that you fear doing things that will make you appear silly or foolish in public. If so, asking yourself why you are feeling insecure will help you to move toward laying your fears to rest. Or if you had a dream in which you were embarrassed in front of someone in particular, who was the person? Do you feel a fervent desire to impress this person in the waking world, and if so, why? (For instance, perhaps you harbor unacknowledged romantic feelings for him or her.) Finally, if your dream had to do with an embarrassing public exposure of your private thoughts or feelings, were they something that you feel shame about in the real world? If so, why? Your dream may have been an unconscious signal that it is time for you to come to terms with whatever it is that you so desperately wish to keep covered up.

Related Dreams

pages 131, 194, 235, 237, 260 & 273

FALLING

While dreams of falling are quite common, we may have these types of dreams for a number of different reasons. Sometimes there is a purely physiological trigger for a dream of falling. These dreams may also reflect a conscious fear or phobia of heights, which may or may not have been rekindled by something in the waking world. Other times, dreams of falling may point to anxiety with regard to failure.

My Falling Dreams

✳ ✳ ✳ ✳ ✳ ✳ ✳ ✳ ✳ ✳ ✳ ✳ ✳ ✳ ✳ ✳ ✳ ✳ ✳

Symbolic and Verbal Associations
- Insecurity
- Fear of losing control, or of "letting yourself down"
- Fear of failure, or of "falling down"
- "Falling from" grace, fame, power, etc
- "Falling for" someone; "falling" in love
- A conscious phobia of heights

Positive Interpretations: If you have a great fear of heights in the real world and you had a nightmare in which you were dangling over a deep chasm as you clutched onto the side of a cliff, your dream may have been simply reflecting your waking phobia (particularly if you recently watched a movie about mountain-climbing or if you are planning to go hiking in the hills). Another common dream of falling occurs as people are just going to sleep: as you were "falling" asleep, did you dream that you were walking along a road and that you suddenly slipped into an empty hole? If so, you probably experienced a type of muscular spasm known as a myoclonic jerk (which sometimes occurs during the hypnagogic state, before we are fully asleep), and your unconscious reacted by incorporating it into your dream. Finally, is it possible that your dream was triggered by your real-life experience of "falling for," or "falling" in love with, someone?

Negative Interpretations: Perhaps the most disturbing of falling dreams are those that our unconscious mind uses to alert us to our insecurity or fear of losing control, failing, or "falling down" in some aspect of our lives. In these cases, the details of your dream can help you to determine the specific meaning. For example, if you dreamed that you were in danger of plummeting from the top of a skyscraper, the skyscraper was probably a metaphor for your high expectations of yourself (or the high expectations that others have for you). Perhaps you are afraid of "letting yourself down," or of your career "coming to a fall." If none of these interpretations seem likely, then you may want to ask yourself whether there is something in the real world that you are clinging to as if it meant life or death, perhaps because you are afraid of letting it go. In your dream, what happened next? Did you lose your grip and actually fall? If so, and if your dream self hit the ground, you may have been surprised to find that there was no real damage done to you—thereby indicating that the real-world "fall" that you are afraid of may not be as bad as you have anticipated.

Plummeting Hopes

Unless you discovered that you were able to fly, and could therefore swoop up, up, and away before crashing to the ground, a dream of falling was probably terrifying. Such nightmarish scenarios generally relate to a fear of failing or losing control, or else of having one's hopes dashed. Do any of these interpretations ring true in relation to your own situation?

Related Dreams
pages 164, 166, 213, 284, 294 & 363

My Faulty Equipment Dreams

----

* * * * * * * * * * * * * * * * * * *

An Antiquated Airplane

If you dreamed that you had to attend a far-flung business meeting as a matter of urgency, but that when you drove to an airfield to commandeer a Learjet, only a World War I-vintage biplane stood at the ready, your dream self must have been incandescent with frustration. Could the antiquated airplane have symbolized your outdated methods, which are slowing you down at work?

FAULTY EQUIPMENT

* *

In today's world, as we rely increasingly on computers and other machines to help us to do our work and to function at home and in society, equipment breakdowns are a particularly irritating and commonplace source of frustration—which makes this topic a first-rate candidate for use by our unconscious when it wishes to send us an anxiety dream.

Symbolic and Verbal Associations

- ◖ Problems and setbacks
- ◖ A faulty or malfunctioning aspect of oneself
- ◖ Losing one's energy or "drive"
- ◖ Running out of "fuel"
- ◖ Explosive anger: "blowing a fuse"

Positive Interpretations: Have you recently failed an important exam in the real world, and did you have a dream in which you found out that your failure was a mistake on the part of the computer that graded the exam, which you really aced? If so, you have probably experienced a wish-fulfillment dream, in which your unconscious blamed your exam failure on the common, real-world problem of computer malfunction. Wish fulfillment is also the most likely reason for a dream of a beneficial machine failure: for instance, did you have a dream in which you were using an ATM (automated-teller machine) to withdraw cash from your bank account, when the machine suddenly went haywire and began spitting out hundreds of dollars at you? This is the sort of equipment failure that almost everyone fantasizes about, along with such scenarios as city hall losing its parking-ticket records or your credit-card company losing its electronic record of your debt.

Negative Interpretations: In your dream, were you horrified when your work computer froze up just minutes before your deadline to turn in an important report to your boss? If so, your dream may have been an unconscious warning that your computer is cluttered up with so many unnecessary programs and applications (and possibly viruses) that it is teetering very close to a real-world crash—unless you "clean it up" or run an antivirus program very soon. It is also possible that your dream computer was a metaphor for some aspect of yourself—in this case (because dream computers generally denote the mind), probably your thoughts or intellect. Have you been infected by a destructive or poisonous idea? Or is your brain simply so "full" at the moment that it feels as if you are near overload? In a similar vein, could your dream of your automobile breaking down have been a signal that you are running out of energy or "drive," or that you are in danger of running out of "fuel"? And if you dreamed that a piece of electrical equipment blew a fuse, have your own anger and frustration gotten so out of hand that you are in danger of similarly "blowing a fuse" in the waking world?

Related Dreams

pages 161, 191, 204, 259, 295 & 296

FORCIBLE RESTRAINT

T hough they may excite some people, dreams of being forcibly restrained or held down are likely to be quite scary for most. Whatever the specific dream scenario or meaning, most of these sorts of dreams are a likely indicator that we are feeling powerless or unable to escape from a person or situation in the waking world.

Symbolic and Verbal Associations

- Powerlessness
- Feeling "chained down," perhaps to a person or a thing
- Someone who is one's "ball and chain"
- Being stuck "between a rock and a hard place"
- Being "all tied up"; the inability to act freely or to "move forward"
- Sexual "games" or domination

Positive Interpretations: Were you having what was seemingly a normal and banal dream when, suddenly, you found that you were unable to move or being forcibly restrained? If so, there may have been a physiological cause for your dream. Particularly during R.E.M. sleep, during which most dreams occur, the brain shuts down the body's nerve impulses, especially to the limbs (but not the eyeballs), to prevent us from literally acting out our dreams. And, while dreaming, if then you happened to regain a measure of awareness, you may have become conscious of your inability to move freely and have incorporated it into your dream.

Negative Interpretations: Did you dream that someone had tied or chained you up so that, although you struggled fiercely with all your power, you could not escape or even barely move? If so, do you remember who (or what) it was who was restraining you? Dreams like this may denote being held back by a powerful force that is beyond your control, or they may denote your feelings of powerlessness regarding a seemingly unsolvable problem in your waking life. Is someone or something "chaining you down"? Is your clingy and overly needy boyfriend making you feel as though you are wearing a "ball and chain"? Or do you feel as though you are stuck "between a rock and a hard place"? In another example, if you dreamed that you were tied to a chair in the home of your elderly parents, while they sat by as if nothing was out of the ordinary, are your responsibilities for your parents' care and wellbeing making you feel as if you are "all tied up," or unable to act freely in your own life? Or did you have a dream of a sexual nature, in which someone had tied you up in order to have their way with you? If so, your dream self's feelings and reactions will be important in making an interpretation. However, it is vital to note that dreams of being sexually restrained or forced may highlight feelings of being violated or victimized in the real world (though not necessarily sexually), often by someone who is in a position of power or has a dominating personality.

Related Dreams

pages 205, 220, 228, 230, 232 & 239

My Forcible Restraint Dreams

----

* * * * * * * * * * * * * * * * * * *

Tied Hands

Never disregard an obvious pun when analyzing your dreams. A workplace dream in which your hands were immobilized by a pair of handcuffs may have expressed your feeling that your "hands are tied," for example, or, in other words, that you cannot act as freely as you would wish at work due to the constraints that have been imposed on you by others.

ANXIETY DREAMS

My Imprisonment Dreams

----

* * * * * * * * * * * * * * * *

Behind Bars

A dream of being imprisoned may have amplified a conscious sense of having lost your liberty in the real world, and the circumstances of your dream may tell you more. If your dream jailer was your possessive partner, for instance, was the message from your unconscious that he or she is depriving you of your freedom of action in the waking world?

IMPRISONMENT

* *

Dreams of being confined or imprisoned are often a reflection of our real-life frustration at not being able to do as we please or to reach for our ambitions or our potential. In interpreting dreams of this sort, it is helpful to take a look at who (or what) was imprisoning you.

Symbolic and Verbal Associations

- Feeling confined or restrained
- The inability to reach one's fullest potential
- Someone who is "boxing you in"
- Being "locked into" (or trapped within) a situation, such as a relationship
- Self-imposed emotional constraint

Positive Interpretations: Did you have a dream that depicted you breaking out and escaping from a jail or a prison? If you did, in your dream, as you ran farther and farther toward liberation, did you feel a great sense of joy and thankfulness welling up in your heart? If so, you may have been perplexed by your dream (unless, of course, you are an inmate in a real-world prison, in which case your dream was probably a form of wish-fulfillment). By casting you in this sort of dream scenario, your unconscious was probably prompting you to set yourself free from whatever it is that is keeping or holding you back in the waking world; for more on this, see below, "Negative Interpretations."

Negative Interpretations: Did you dream that you were locked in a dark, dreary cell, with only a small window for sunlight to come through, and your only furnishing being a tiny, old prison cot? If so, you probably felt extremely lonely and/or frustrated, which may be how you are feeling during your waking hours (which is probably why you dreamed such a thing in the first place!) In general, dreams of being locked up or restrained usually signify that you are feeling frustrated because someone or something is preventing you from acting freely or from realizing your aspirations or your fullest potential in the waking world. In your dream, did you see your captor? If so, who was it? Is this person "boxing you in" in the real world? Are you being forced to live according to someone else's rules or plan? Or are you feeling "locked into" or trapped within a waking situation, relationship, or responsibility from which you feel you cannot escape? It is also possible that your imprisonment is self-imposed. Have you been constraining or hiding your emotions in order to protect yourself from emotional hurt or to prevent others from getting too close to you? Did the bars of your dream prison stand for your own inhibitions? Whatever the case, your unconscious was probably highlighting your feelings of confinement in order to urge you to break free from whatever it is that is holding you back—be it your own emotional inhibitions or else a deadening or draining job, a bad or stifling relationship, or a hefty commitment that is taking its toll on you. Is it time that you face down your fears and take a long-awaited taste of freedom?

Related Dreams

pages 166, 205, 220, 227, 230 & 259

INVISIBILITY

Depending on the context and the mood, a dream of being invisible can either be very liberating (in that real-world invisibility could allow one to escape from problems and responsibilities), empowering (because one could presumably come and go and do as one pleased), or disempowering (probably a reflection of your real-life feeling that you are "invisible" to, or overlooked by, others).

Symbolic and Verbal Associations
- Powerlessness
- Feeling "overlooked"
- A desire to escape from one's troubles
- Avoidance; "shrinking away" from persons or situations
- An inability to allow others to see you "as you really are"
- Someone who is emotionally "transparent"

Positive Interpretations: In your dream, were you excited and thrilled to discover that you had become invisible, so that you could simply walk away from or ignore your problems and responsibilities with no one bothering or hassling you about them? If so, do you wish that you could escape from your duties and problems in the real world? Do you long for the peace and solitude that being invisible would bring you? Or, in your dream, did you revel in the power that your invisibility brought you? For instance, did you find that you were able to come and go and do as you pleased, perhaps playing "tricks" on your enemies and performing beneficent acts for yourself and your friends? If so, your dream may have been a form of wish-fulfillment (particularly if you are a person with a somewhat high profile, thereby signifying that you wish to taste the freedom and power of anonymity).

Negative Interpretations: Were you depressed and saddened by a dream in which, for all of your efforts to communicate, no one could see or hear you because you had become completely invisible? If so, do you feel powerless in the waking world because people seem to ignore or overlook you on a regular basis? Or is your waking "invisibility" self-imposed because you are unwilling, or feel unable, to allow others to see you as you truly are? If so, your unconscious may have been urging you to assert your unique personality more often so that others may get to know the "real you." Or, on the contrary, did you have a dream in which you had become translucent, so that others could see all of the way inside of you and know everything that you were thinking and feeling? If so, are you feeling emotionally "transparent" (sometimes referred to as "emotionally incontinent") in the real world? In other words, do you reveal too much about what you think and feel when it is inappropriate to do so (such as at work or among people whom you do not know very well)? Could your unconscious have been encouraging you to "cover up" your innermost thoughts and emotions?

My Invisibility Dreams

----

* * * * * * * * * * * * * * * * * * * *

Blending In
Chameleons are renowned for their ability to adjust the hue of their skin to blend in with their surroundings, thereby camouflaging themselves. If you had an anxiety-inducing dream in which you were one of these creatures, but had difficulty changing color in a dangerous jungle, do you currently feel exposed and vulnerable, rather than invisible and safe, in an edgy waking situation?

Related Dreams

pages 143, 237, 258, 259 & 266

My Kidnapping Dreams

....
....
....
....
....
....
....
....
....

★ ★ ★ ★ ★ ★ ★ ★ ★ ★ ★ ★ ★ ★ ★ ★ ★ ★

Controlling Behavior

Did you kidnap your boss in dreamland? Dreams like this suggest that we long to have total control over someone, either for the power kick or to force a concession from that individual. So did your dream reflect your desire to turn the tables on your controlling boss, or do you wish that you could force him to promise you a raise?

KIDNAPPINGS

★ ★

Dreaming that you have been kidnapped may signify feelings of being trapped or emotionally restricted. However, dreaming that you have kidnapped someone else may mean that you are trying to contain or inhibit some aspect or aspects of that person (perhaps within yourself), or else that you are trying to force your will or your opinions upon them.

Symbolic and Verbal Associations
‹ Feeling trapped or controlled; emotional restriction
‹ The desire to inhibit or contain aspects of oneself
‹ A diversion from your goals
‹ Holding onto something that it would be better to let go
‹ Forcing one's views or opinions on someone else

Positive Interpretations: If you dreamed of a kidnapping, were you the victim, the kidnapper, or merely a witness? If you had a dream in which you had kidnapped someone else, did you know the person? Who was it? And what qualities or characteristics do you associate with this person? Especially if your victim was the same gender as you, your unconscious may have cast this person in the role of your shadow—the polar opposite of the persona that your ego has constructed, which embodies all that you find irritating and loathsome in others (and in yourself). Your dream of kidnapping this person may have been symbolic of your desire to suppress his or her qualities within yourself. And if you think that this may be the case, then your dream was probably an unconscious cry for you to acknowledge and face up to your shadow, and perhaps consciously to embrace that part of yourself that you have thought of so negatively. However, if this explanation seems unlikely, you may want to ask yourself whether you have been trying to force your views or your will on someone. If so, do you desire to control this person because you have developed an unhealthy romantic infatuation with him or her, or because he or she embodies something that you desire? It is also possible that your victim represented something in your life that you are holding onto, when you would perhaps be happier if you could let it go.

Negative Interpretations: Did you have a dream in which you had been kidnapped? If so, there are a number of possible explanations. Do you feel trapped or controlled by your dream captor in the real world? For instance, was your dream self kidnapped by your ex-husband, who continues to bully and control you even though you are no longer married? Or was your dream kidnapper someone who distracts or diverts your attention from your waking goals and ambitions? Another possible interpretation is that your kidnapper represented some force or situation that you feel is victimizing you in the real world. This may be your own beliefs or views on life, which may be so rigid that they are restricting your personal growth.

Related Dreams

pages 129, 227, 228,
253, 257 & 259

Lateness

For many people, the prospect of being late is enough to send them into a mad panic. The same is likely to be true of a dream of being late, which may have been an unconscious reference to either missed opportunities, impeded progress, overload and fatigue, or stress and worries.

Symbolic and Verbal Associations

- Missed opportunities in life: having missed "the bus," "the boat," or "the train"
- Being left behind
- Hindered progress
- Fatigue
- Worries

Positive Interpretations: Did you have a dream in which you were running late for work in the morning? But, in your dream, instead of rushing and fretting (as you usually do), did you slow down and calmly make your way to a coffee shop, where you sat down, ordered breakfast, and passed an enjoyable and relaxing morning eating, sipping coffee, and reading the newspaper? And do you find that you are living your waking life in a constant state of movement and distress, perhaps because you have taken on more obligations and activities than you can comfortably fit into your schedule? A dream like this may have been an unconscious plea for you to stop living your life in a hurry and to slow down and relax.

Negative Interpretations: Did your dream self run as fast as you could, while obsessively checking your watch out of dread that you might miss your train, only to arrive at the platform just as it was pulling away? If so—unless you are consciously worried about the logistics of a journey that you are soon to make in the waking world—then your dream may have been an unconscious expression of your anger and frustration at having missed an important real-world opportunity. In your dream, was someone responsible for your hold-up? And do you blame this person for impeding your progress in life? These types of dreams may also be a signal that you have been running yourself ragged, either physically or mentally, so that you are literally "out of steam"; this may be especially true if your dream depicted you almost making the train, except that you were unable to summon the small extra burst of energy that would have enabled you to catch it. In analyzing your dream of lateness, it will be helpful for you to identify what the missed "bus," "boat," or "train" (or anything else that your dream self missed) could have represented in your waking world. Was it a job that you wish you hadn't turned down, or the attractive woman whom you failed to ask out because you were too shy? And, since buses, trains, and boats are forms of mass public transportation, do you feel that others around you are forging onward while you are left behind?

My Lateness Dreams

....
....
....
....
....
....
....
....
....

* * * * * * * * * * * * * * * * * * * *

Falling Behind

If you dreamed that you were running late for a crucial date, that your legs were pumping as rapidly as pistons as you hurried along, but that the hands of your watch were whizzing around even faster, it is likely that you are worried about missing an important opportunity in waking life. Is it because you fear that time is no longer on your side?

Related Dreams

pages 194, 196, 259, 298, 300 & 304

ANXIETY DREAMS

My Locked In or Out Dreams

....
....
....
....
....
....
....
....
....

* * * * * * * * * * * * * * * * * * * *

No Entry!

How did you respond to a dream of being locked out? Were you curious? Frustrated? Furious? And do you know what lay beyond the door that was barred to you? The answers to these questions should tell you whether your interest has been piqued by a tantalizing secret or whether you feel that you are being denied access to an opportunity or hidden knowledge.

LOCKED IN OR OUT

* *

In the language of dreams, locks and keys symbolize secrets, problems or conundrums, and solutions, and any of these meanings may be implicated by a dream of being locked in or out of someplace. Dream locked doors may also be associated with secrets, as well as closed opportunities or things that are being withheld.

Symbolic and Verbal Associations
- Secrets
- Problems and solutions
- "Closed" opportunities
- Shame
- Mystery and curiosity
- Vaginal and phallic symbols (in Freudian theory)

Positive Interpretations: In your dream, did you come across a locked door, and were you filled with an overwhelming sense of curiosity to know what was in the room or the building that you were locked out of? In dreams, locks often symbolize problems or puzzles, and keys symbolize answers or solutions. A locked door may symbolize a secret or a mystery. In your dream, did you find the key to unlock the door? The dream key that you were searching for may have represented the "key" to a real-life problem or puzzle that has been preoccupying your conscious mind. Or were you only able to peer through the keyhole or the crack under the door? What did you see on the other side? Can you relate your discovery to a waking problem or situation? If you found a key, but it was not a match for the lock, your unconscious may have been telling you that you will have to continue searching before you will be able to "unlock," or release, the solution to your problem. Finally, it is probably worth noting that Freudian dream-interpreters associate locks with the vagina and keys with the phallus. So if you had a dream that placed a focus on a lock and key, you may want to consider whether your dream may have had an erotic or sexual meaning.

Negative Interpretations: Did you have a dream in which you were highly frustrated because you were either locked in or out of someplace? If so, your dream may have signified your waking frustration that an opportunity seems to be closed off to you, or that something is being withheld from you. Did the locked door lead to a room? (If so, what type of room? Consulting the chapter "The Home" may give you more clues as to the meaning of your dream.) Or were you locked out of a closet (which, in the language of dreams, may denote the self and secret or latent qualities)? Is there some hidden "skeleton" that is haunting your unconscious? Alternatively, in your dream, did you find yourself locked inside a room from which you were hysterically trying to escape? If so, do you feel trapped, or "locked in," by some situation, person, or relationship in the waking world?

Related Dreams

pages 165, 166, 205, 227, 228 & 259

LOSING SOMETHING

In interpreting a dream of having lost something, it is important to consider what was lost, as well as any meanings associated with this item. Dreams of this sort may have nothing at all to do with the dream thing that was lost, but instead with some aspect of the dreamer's self or waking situation.

Symbolic and Verbal Associations
- A warning from the unconscious
- Information; the solution to a problem
- Distraction
- Something that is missing from one's life
- The search for fulfillment

Positive Interpretations: Did you have a vivid dream in which you had lost something precious to you, such as your favorite necklace, which was passed down to you from your great-great-grandmother, so that when you awoke you had to get up to reassure yourself that your necklace was still in your jewelry box where you had left it? If so, then your unconscious mind may have noticed that the clasp on your necklace has become loose and sent you your dream in order to urge you to have it repaired before you really do lose the necklace in real life. And if you have lost something in the waking world and had a dream in which you found it, it is possible that you experienced a wish-fulfillment dream, but you may wish to check the location in which you found the item in your dream because you may be unconsciously aware of its whereabouts, even though this information has slipped your waking mind.

Negative Interpretations: Did you dream that you were frantically searching for something trivial, or else for something that, upon waking, you couldn't remember what it was? Dreams of losing things may be a sign that you are under so much stress and strain in the real world that you are starting to "lose" your waking focus and concentration and, therefore, your ability to manage and stay on top of the details and minutiae of your life. However, if this explanation seems unlikely, then your unconscious may have orchestrated your dream loss as a metaphor for something that is missing or lacking from your life, or for something that has been eluding you. Can you make an association between the lost dream item and something that you may be searching for in your waking world (such as happiness, love, or anything else that may be missing from your waking reality)? For instance, if you dreamed that you were searching for a key, could this have been a symbol of a solution to a waking problem? Or perhaps it was the key to self-knowledge or spiritual enlightenment? And if, in your dream, you found the key that you were looking for, your unconscious may have been telling you that whatever it is that you are seeking will soon be within your reach.

My Losing Something Dreams

Lost and Found
Sometimes the unconscious can act as an early-warning system by subjecting us to a stressful dream of losing a possession (a watch, for example, should its strap really be deficient in some way). Dreams of losing something may otherwise point to a more abstract potential waking-world "loss," such as of one's sense of perspective or humor, or even of others' respect.

Related Dreams
pages 97, 98, 254, 263 & 290

My Being Lost Dreams

....
....
....
....
....
....
....
....

* * * * * * * * * * * * * * * * * * *

Where Am I?

A dream of being lost usually points to such issues as a loss of identity, not knowing one's "place in the world," losing one's sense of "direction," or finding oneself in "unknown territory." Dreams like this usually occur following major real-life changes like starting at a new school or workplace or moving to a new town, which we don't yet know our way around.

LOST

* *

If we think of life as a long, zigzagging road, as it often seems to be, then it is easy to see how a dream of being lost may pertain to one's loss of direction in the waking world. This may have to do with the dreamer's goals and ambitions, important decisions, or with personal identity or beliefs.

Symbolic and Verbal Associations
- A loss of direction in life
- A lack of goals
- Confusion
- The need to get "back on track"
- A murky sense of personal identity

Positive Interpretations: Did you have a dream that depicted you wandering through the wilderness, hopelessly lost and afraid? And, in your dream, were you relieved and joyful when you found a map that would put you back "on the right track" to known territory? A dream like this may have been an unconscious attempt to hearten you with the knowledge that, although you have recently "lost your way" in life, you will soon find your proper direction once again. A similar interpretation may apply if, in your dream, you observed or followed someone who seemed to know the right way to go. Did you know the person? Your unconscious may have been trying to tell you that he or she is a good example to follow, or else that he or she has good advice to give you.

Negative Interpretations: In your dream, were you terribly frightened to find yourself lost in a foreign city? If so, your unconscious may have been reflecting your loss of direction or focus in the waking world. Have you lost sight of your goals, or strayed from the path that you must take in order to reach them? Or have you given up on your ambitions altogether? For example, are you confused about the next step that you should take on your career path? Or are you unsure of how you want to proceed in your current relationship (be it moving forward, toward marriage, or giving yourself more distance in order to decide how you really feel)? It is also possible that your dream was highlighting your loss of identity or self-knowledge—perhaps because you have recently undergone some major life changes, which have "thrown you for a loop" and changed your "path" in the world, so that you no longer know "who" you are or how you want to live. If this is the case, then thinking about what brought on the changes, or in what ways you have changed (which, therefore, may aid you in discovering the specific nature of your dilemma), will help you to decide "the best way forward." You may find that you have developed completely new goals and ambitions, of a nature that you would have never previously dreamed of.

Related Dreams

pages 259, 277, 289, 296, 303 & 306

MOCKING & TEASING

Whether or not they mirror reality, dreams of being teased or mocked are a likely indicator of feelings of insecurity in social situations—and, particularly if these dreams are recurring, they may point to deeply held pain, anger, and views of the self as a victim.

Symbolic and Verbal Associations
- Insecurity; social awkwardness
- Hostility
- Bullying
- Unresolved pain and anger
- Feelings of victimization

Positive Interpretations: In your dream, did your unconscious mind carry you back to a painful incident in your childhood, when all of the neighborhood kids banded together to tease you relentlessly? But, in your dream, did something happen that never happened in the real world: did you face up to the gang of bullies, so that they cowered away in shame? If so, what would cause your unconscious to turn your childhood memory into a story of vindication? It may be that, in the real world, you have finally come to a place in your life where you feel confident and self-assured, and your dream may have been your sleeping mind's way of helping you to come to terms with your old pain, anger, and feelings of victimization by depicting your younger self behaving in a way in which your current, confident self would behave. But if you do not feel that you have yet achieved a great level of self-confidence, then your dream may have been your unconscious's attempt to encourage you to become more self-assured.

Negative Interpretations: Did you dream that you had become the target of a barrage of jokes and teasing at your place of work, so that you felt waves of anger flowing through you and your face was burning with embarrassment? If so, and if you feel that you truly are the "black sheep" of the office, then your dream may have been simply mirroring your perception of reality. But if you are rarely the real-life focal point of your coworkers' mirth, then your dream may signify that you have a general sense of insecurity and social awkwardness (in this example, probably related to your performance at work or your social skills in relation to your coworkers). If you think that this may be the case, ask yourself why you feel insecure or awkward, and what you can do to get over these sorts of feelings. However, if you feel that you are a fairly confident person, then your dream may have been a message from your unconscious mind, which may have detected that certain of your coworkers harbor hostility toward you. (Is it possible that they are jealous of the promotion that you recently received?) Finally, whether or not your dream depicted you as the teaser or the "teasee," you may want to ask yourself if you yourself have become a bully of others in your waking world.

Related Dreams

pages 131, 218, 224, 255, 264 & 273

My Mocking & Teasing Dreams

....
....
....
....
....
....
....
....
....

* * * * * * * * * * * * * * * * * * *

Catty Comments

A dream in which you overheard your coworkers swapping mocking stories about your supposed faults may have been an unconscious expression of your niggling worries that others regard certain of your quirks and traits as character flaws. If your dream colleagues were giggling about you in an affectionate way, however, the message may have been not to fret too much about it because your imperfections are endearing.

My Money Problems Dreams

_____

_____

_____

_____

_____

_____

_____

****

The Good Life

Perhaps you dreamed that automobiles, supermarkets, and central heating were no longer part of your life, and that you had become reduced to a meager existence? If so, and you found your poverty did not trouble you, could you be ready to downshift and leave your stressful job? Or are you in danger of becoming "impoverished" in some way?

MONEY PROBLEMS

N o matter how much or how little of it we have, worries about money tend to occupy a large part of most people's conscious thinking. Dreams that focus on money problems may be a reflection of our conscious money worries, but they may also have to do with a perceived decline of nonmaterial wealth.

Symbolic and Verbal Associations
- Owing "a debt of honor"
- Loss (of a nonfinancial type)
- Money that is "burning a hole in your pocket"
- Emotional destitution
- Moral "bankruptcy"

Positive Interpretations: Did you have a dream in which all of your waking financial worries and problems were instantly solved? For example, did you dream that you won the lottery and became a billionaire overnight? If so, and if you do tend to spend a lot of time fretting about money problems, then your dream was probably a simple form of wish fulfillment. However, it is also possible that your dream riches were a metaphor for something of a nonmonetary nature, and doing some free association may help you to determine if this is the case. Are you blessed with a "wealth" of friends and loved ones? Could your dream of gold have signified a "heart of gold"? Or was your dream treasure a symbol of your own personal "treasure" of wisdom, experience, or compassion?

Negative Interpretations: Did you awake feeling very depressed because you had a dream in which you had hit financial "rock bottom"? In your dream, were you about to lose everything of value that you own in order to pay off the great debt that you had incurred? If you have a real-life financial debt that is weighing on your mind, then your dream may have been simply reflecting your waking preoccupation with your troubles. However, if this is not the case, then your dream may have been a reference to a "debt of honor," or a favor that you feel obligated to repay to someone. To whom do you feel indebted in the waking world? Is it to your brother because he took time off from his job to help you when you were ill? Or is it to your best friend, who has babysat your children on numerous occasions without asking for anything in return? Your dream may have signified that you are feeling guilty—a feeling that you may be able to alleviate if you would "make good" on your "debt." Another interpretation of a dream of going bankrupt is that your unconscious was making a reference to some nonfinancial resource that you are running short of. This could be your looks, your talents, your ethics—anything of value that you feel you would be the worse off for losing. Whatever your dream loss represents, your unconscious may have been sending you a warning and a call to take action, to avert a real-life "crash" of some kind.

Related Dreams

pages 75, 122, 193, 205, 215 & 233

NAKEDNESS IN PUBLIC

I n both practical and symbolic terms, the clothing that we wear acts as a costume or disguise that we use to hide our "true selves" from others. When we dream of being naked in public, the meaning of the dream will depend, in large part, on our dreaming emotional reaction—be it of shame, rebellion, or joyous liberation!

Symbolic and Verbal Associations

- Fear of behaving inappropriately
- Feelings of inadequacy
- Humiliation or shame
- Fear of "emotional exposure"; emotional vulnerability
- Allowing others to see us as we "truly are"
- Liberation
- Anxiety with regard to public scrutiny

Positive Interpretations: Did you have a dream in which you were at a party that was being thrown by one of your coworkers when you suddenly realized that you weren't wearing any clothes? And instead of feeling embarrassed or ashamed, did your dream self revel in the scandal and disapproval that you elicited in the room? If so, your unconscious may have been encouraging you to "cast off" the waking restrictions, inhibitions, and pretenses with which you have "clothed yourself" (not your literal clothing!) and to allow others around you to see and know you as you really are. And if, in your dream, you were the only one who seemed to notice that you were naked, then your unconscious may have been trying to assure you that it is safe for you to allow others to see your "true," exposed self because no one will even "bat an eyelid" at your self-exposure.

Negative Interpretations: In your dream, were you deeply ashamed or humiliated to realize that you were completely naked in the middle of a crowded shopping mall? If so, there are a number of possible interpretations of your dream. If, in your dream, you stood cowering and trying in vain to cover your naked body as the people around you pointed and jeered, then your dream may signify that you feel "exposed" and vulnerable under the scrutiny of others. It may be that you worry that you are an object of ridicule and mockery, either because you suspect that you may be behaving inappropriately or because you are worried that the "true you" is somehow flawed or blemished. For instance, do you feel inadequate at family functions, perhaps because many of your relatives have more formal education than you? Or do you feel rejected or derided by your coworkers? The most important question to ask yourself is: what is it about yourself that you most fear exposing to others? Are you afraid that, if you were to lower your defenses and behave naturally, you would be rejected by those around you?

My Nakedness in Public Dreams

Baring All

We wear clothes for the sake of "modesty" and "decency," and also to project an image, which could be businesslike, glamorous, rebellious, and so on. So if you had an anxiety dream in which you found yourself stripped naked amid a crowd of disapproving or laughing, fully-clothed people, do you fear that a glimpse of the "real you" would elicit a similar response?

Related Dreams

pages 66, 125, 224, 235, 258 & 273

ANXIETY DREAMS

My Obstructions Dreams

....

....

....

....

....

....

....

....

....

* * * * * * * * * * * * * * * * * * * *

Keep Out!

When they crop up in dreams, obstructions signify bars to our progress. If you dreamed of being stopped in your tracks by a formidable fence, can you equate it with a real-life problem? And did your dreaming self scale it or turn around and trudge away? Your answer will tell you more about your attitude, which may be "can do" or defeatist.

OBSTRUCTIONS

****

Sometimes our unconscious mind can be exceedingly cruel and torturous, especially when it forces our dream selves to expend precious physical and mental energy engaging in acts of futility for what can seem like hours on end! However, you can rest assured that, when you do have this sort of anxiety dream, your unconscious has a good reason in mind.

Symbolic and Verbal Associations
- A "dead end"
- An emotional "impasse"
- Feeling emotionally "penned in"
- Being stuck "in a jam"
- Carrying "a weight" on one's shoulders
- Hitting a "stumbling block"

Positive Interpretations: Did you have a dream in which you were walking along a trail that was so disused and overgrown that you had to struggle and fight your way through the dense foliage that blocked your way? And, in your dream, was your way blocked by a large boulder or a fallen tree, or was there a giant, muddy sinkhole in the middle of the path? And did your dream self persist onward, clearing the foliage, scaling over and past the boulder or tree, and sidestepping the sinkhole? If you dreamed of overcoming the obstacles that blocked your way in dreamland, it is a likely sign that you will have (or are having) similar success in the real world. Or if your dream depicted you giving up and turning back with a feeling of great relief because you knew that you were going back to the comfort and warmth of your home, then your unconscious may have been trying to tell you that your domestic happiness is more important to you than the achievement of your current life goals.

Negative Interpretations: Did you awake in the morning feeling utterly stressed out and exhausted because you felt like you had spent the entire night stuck in a dreamland traffic jam? If so, do you feel "stuck" in your efforts to "move forward" in the waking world (perhaps because you feel that everyone else is trying to go the same way that you are)? Or have you been telling lies that have led you into a "jam," or a troubling situation, in the real world? Alternatively, did you have a dream in which you were running a race, and did your unconscious portray you stumbling at the first hurdle that you came to, so that your competitors left you far behind? No matter what the specific scenario was, your unconscious may have been using your dream to draw a parallel with your efforts to "get ahead" in the waking world, and with how quickly and smoothly you may be advancing toward your goals. So if you dreamed of bicycling down a bumpy road, have you hit a "rough patch" in the real world?

Related Dreams

pages 53, 145, 290, 369, 374 & 385

PARALYSIS

****

In the English language, we talk about things like "paralyzing fear" and "emotional paralysis." These types of symbolic paralyses are likely to be the trigger or the root cause for dreams in which we find ourselves being held down by some invisible force, so that we may be unable to move or to flee from someone or something that means to do us harm (which is, perhaps, the most frightening type of scenario for this type of dream).

Symbolic and Verbal Associations
- Inability to escape danger
- Feeling "rooted" against one's will
- Emotional paralysis
- Feelings of powerlessness
- Hopelessness

Positive Interpretations: While sleeping, for no apparent reason, did you suddenly feel as if you were paralyzed or being held down by a heavy, unmovable force that restricted even your breathing? If so, there may have been a simple physiological cause. As we sleep (particularly during the dreaming stages of sleep), our brain shuts down the body's nerve impulses, rendering us effectively paralyzed, in order to prevent us from acting out our dreams and thereby causing harm to ourselves or others. It may be that you happened to regain a measure of your awareness while you were in this state, causing you to become conscious of your sleep paralysis (a normal phenomenon that happens to many people from time to time, though experts are unsure of the exact cause).

Negative Interpretations: Did you have a dream in which someone or something was coming after you with the intent of causing you harm, but, for all of your efforts, you found that you could not move even an inch from the spot where you stood? If so, you may be wondering why your unconscious mind would choose to sabotage your dream escape and put you through such stress and anxiety. There are actually a number of possible explanations for a dream like this. Could it be that you are suffering from "emotional paralysis" in the face of some distressing waking dilemma, such as the decision whether or not to put your elderly mother into a nursing home or to try to care for her yourself at home? It is also possible that your dream signified your waking feelings of powerlessness and/or hopelessness. If so, what do you feel powerless or hopeless about? Does some person or some waking-life situation make you feel as though you have no control whatsoever? Do you fear that you may be in some sort of danger (not necessarily physical danger), from which you feel unable to escape? (It will help in determining the meaning of your dream if you can identify who or what was chasing after you.)

My Paralysis Dreams

----

* * * * * * * * * * * * * * * * * * *

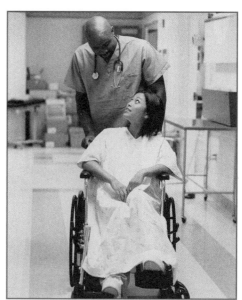

Comfortably Numb
Dreams of being unable to move are usually anxiety-inducing, particularly if our dreaming selves have been paralyzed by fear. There are instances when paralysis dreams can be soothing, however, such as if you enjoyed being waited on hand and foot as a result. Dreams like this suggest that you'd like to relinquish your waking-world responsibilities and instead be taken care of for a while.

Related Dreams

pages 145, 193, 208, 221, 257 & 259

ANXIETY DREAMS

My Unprepared ness Dreams

----

* * * * * * * * * * * * * * * * * *

Running Scared

If you really are due to sit an exam or perform at an important business meeting in the near future, a dream of not having studied or prepared for your "test" may have reflected either reality (in which case your dream may have been a warning and spur to action) or a more irrational fear of falling flat on your face and failing.

UNPREPAREDNESS

* *

Everyone has had them: dreams in which you walk into class and the teacher is passing out an exam that you knew nothing about. Even worse—your dream self may not even have gone to class all term! Many people have these sorts of dreams even years after they last set foot in a classroom; the universality and sheer terror aroused by this sort of scenario makes it excellent fodder when our unconscious wishes to send us an anxiety nightmare.

Symbolic and Verbal Associations
- Fear of failure
- Feelings of inadequacy
- An inability to "get it together"
- Self-criticism; low self-esteem
- Anxiety regarding a real-life testing situation

Positive Interpretations: If you have been preparing and studying very hard for an upcoming real-world exam, were you perplexed by a dream that depicted you walking into the exam room completely unprepared? If so, your dream may have simply been giving expression to your worst fears and worries regarding your performance in the exam, as well as preparing you for (though not necessarily predicting) your possible failure. Or did you have a dream in which you completely blew off preparing for your weekly team meeting at work (an event that you happen to loathe in the real world)? And, in your dream meeting, did you sit back and text-message your friends while your coworkers blandly hashed through the boring business at hand? If so, your unconscious may have been allowing you to have a brief reprieve and a bit of fun by sending you a wish-fulfillment dream, though you may also want to consider whether your dream was an unconscious call for you to reevaluate your career or job choice.

Negative Interpretations: If you dreamed that you were surprised by a test or an exam that you had not studied for at all, this may have been a metaphor for some testing or trying situation that you must face in the real world. Have you taken on, or been assigned, a real-world challenge that you feel unable to meet? Your dream may also point to a general lack of confidence or self-esteem. Do you feel as if you do not measure up to others around you? Of course, if you are a student and you do have a real-world exam coming up, which you have not been studying for as diligently as you know you should, then your dream may have been an unconscious effort to spur you into studying harder. Alternatively, did you stand up to give a dream speech before a group of people, only to realize, with dread, that you had no idea what you wanted to say? And when you opened your mouth to speak, were you even more upset because all that you could do was stammer and stutter? If so, your unconscious may have been highlighting your waking feelings of uncertainty, as well as your fear of scrutiny and criticism.

Related Dreams

pages 192, 193, 226, 231, 233 & 305

CHAPTER 12

WISH-FULFILLMENT DREAMS

Wish-fulfillment dreams are generally little treats, compensations,
or morale-boosts from you to yourself, especially if your waking
existence is currently grim or you are feeling unloved or
unappreciated. They may even make you feel so wonderful that
they inspire you to work toward recreating the circumstances of
your dream in the waking world, in which case your unconscious
may have given you a much-needed incentive literally to make
your dream come true!

WISH-FULFILLMENT DREAMS

My Dream Lovers Dreams

✳ ✳ ✳ ✳ ✳ ✳ ✳ ✳ ✳ ✳ ✳ ✳ ✳ ✳ ✳ ✳ ✳ ✳

Forbidden Love

Did you dream of a night of unbridled passion with someone whom you know, but who is "out of bounds" because you are happily married, or else because your dream lover is unavailable? If so, your unconscious was probably acting out your repressed desire for him or her in the safety of dreamland.

DREAM LOVERS

✶✶✶✶✶✶✶✶✶✶✶✶✶✶✶✶✶✶✶✶✶✶✶✶✶✶✶✶✶✶✶✶✶✶

In the language of the unconscious, dream lovers may signify a number of different things. In trying to interpret such a dream, the first step is to try to determine who, or what, your dream lover could have represented in the waking world.

Symbolic and Verbal Associations
- Euphoria
- Romance
- Suppressed attraction to someone; repressed sexual desire
- A need for affection, love, or comfort

Positive Interpretations: In your dream, were you filled with a warm and euphoric rush of feelings because you were in love? If so, who was your dream lover? If it was your real-life partner, whom you are very much in love with, then your dream was likely underlining and reaffirming your feelings for him or her. But if the romance between you and your partner has waned, then your unconscious may have been trying to remind you of the reasons why you fell in love with him or her in the first place—and of the love that you continue to feel for your partner, though it may be suppressed to an unconscious level. And if you think this latter interpretation may be true, then your dream was probably a call to action, from your unconscious, for you to take steps toward rekindling the spark in your relationship.

Negative Interpretations: Were you unsettled or disturbed by a dream in which your lover was someone whom you regard as a mere friend or acquaintance in the waking world? For instance, did your unconscious play out a scene in which you were basking in the loving embrace of your neighbor or a coworker? By sending you this dream, your unconscious may have been trying to alert you to your attraction to this person, though you may consider your feelings inappropriate for one reason or another—which can make this type of dream extremely disturbing, especially if you are already in a committed relationship. So if you think that this interpretation may apply, then your unconscious mind was probably allowing your desires to be expressed in the venue of dreamland, where no actual harm or pain will be caused to anyone. However, if you are in a relationship and yet you continually have sexual dreams about others, then it may be advisable to try to determine the reason or the problem (sexual frustration, for instance) and to work toward resolving it in the waking world. Alternatively, if your dream caused you to view someone in a new, romantic light, then consider whether it is time for you to acknowledge and express your feelings for him or her in the waking world. And, finally, if you dreamed that you were in love with someone, but that your feelings were unreciprocated, are you uncertain of how this person feels about you in the waking world, and are you afraid of being rejected by him or her?

Related Dreams
pages 95, 112, 116,
259, 267 & 268

FAME

✳✳

Almost everyone experiences the desire to be famous at some point in life. We may wish for fame—and also dream of being famous—at times in our life when we are craving more recognition and respect from those around us.

Symbolic and Verbal Associations
- Recognition, admiration, and respect for one's efforts or abilities
- Power
- Success
- Desired personal qualities or characteristics
- The fruits of diligence and hard work

Positive Interpretations: Did you dream that you were famous for some talent or skill that you nurture and take pride in during your waking hours? For example, if you play the cello in a local orchestra, did you have a dream in which you were hailed and celebrated as the very best cello player in the entire world? If so, your dream may have reflected your real-life desire for more recognition of your musical talent, but it may also have been an unconscious call for you to continue your quest to fulfill your highest aspirations for your musical career. And if you dreamed of a real-life famous person, what qualities does this person symbolize to you? He or she may have been acting as your anima (if you are a man) or your animus (if you are a woman), highlighting a personal quality or characteristic that you admire in others and would like to possess yourself, or a quality or characteristic that is relevant to a current life situation you are faced with. (So, for instance, if you dreamed of Mother Teresa, do you wish that you could have more compassion for others, or does a current situation in your waking life call for you to practice self-sacrifice?)

Negative Interpretations: Did you have a dream in which hundreds of thousands of people cheered and called out for you as you were paraded through the streets in a grand limousine? If your dream self savored the adulation that was heaped upon you, this may signal that you feel unrecognized or undervalued by others, and that you crave recognition and admiration from those around you, either for what you consider to be your outstanding personal qualities or for some talent or expertise that you feel you possess. So can you remember what your dream self was famous for? A similar interpretation may apply if you had a dream in which you were greeted or singled out by a famous person whom you admire—in which case, your unconscious was likely attempting to give your self-confidence a boost, if only a temporary, dreamland one. (Yet the effects of your dream may be more long-lasting if you heed the message from your unconscious and take the necessary steps to raise your self-esteem in the real world.)

Related Dreams
pages 123, 119, 120, 245, 247 & 250

My Fame Dreams
....
....
....
....
....
....
....
....
....

✳✳✳✳✳✳✳✳✳✳✳✳✳✳✳✳✳✳✳✳✳✳✳

Feeling Special
In your dream, did you have the trappings of a successful celebrity, such as a dressing room and an entourage to take care of your every whim? This dream may have been your unconscious mind's way of telling you to pamper yourself or to ask a loved one to pay more attention to your emotional needs.

My Heroism Dreams

★ ★ ★ ★ ★ ★ ★ ★ ★ ★ ★ ★ ★ ★ ★ ★ ★

Rescue!

If you dreamed of being saved by a hero in the rescue services, are you under intense waking-life pressure that you feel you cannot alleviate or escape? Such dreams may indicate that you need to ask others for help or else to find ways of relaxing in order to cope with your oppressive real-world situation.

HEROISM

★★★

Whenever our unconscious portrays us taking some sort of positive action, it is usually a good idea to heed the dream example and to strive to behave in such a way in the waking world. This applies to dreams in which we find ourselves committing heroic deeds of bravery and/or rescue: the unconscious may be signaling that it is time for an act of bravery (though perhaps in the service of emotional, not physical, heroism) in our waking life.

Symbolic and Verbal Associations
- A "knight in shining armor"
- "Riding to the rescue"
- An emotional "savior"
- Inspiration to do "good deeds"
- Guidance and encouragement

Positive Interpretations: Did you have a dream in which you, a "knight in shining armor," were riding to the rescue of an innocent victim who had been taken captive by a villain? Dreams of this sort may be meant to inspire or encourage you to behave in a similarly brave or gallant way in the face of some real-life problem or challenge, even though the nature of the problem or challenge may not be clear to you at this time. Did you know the person whom you rescued? And do you regard yourself as this person's actual or potential "savior" in the real world? Or, in your dream, did someone else ride to your rescue? If so, who was it? Do you regard him or her as your savior in the real world? (It is also possible that your unconscious summoned a heroic archetype in order to inspire you to cultivate these qualities of bravery and courage in your own waking life.) What did your dream savior rescue you from? Answering these questions may help you to identify what element of your life needs rescuing, what is threatening it, and how best to try to save it.

Negative Interpretations: If you had a dream that a hero rescued someone from a villain (and, in your dream, you may have played the part of either the hero or the victim), do you know who the villain was, or who (or what) he or she may represent in your waking world? Is it possible that your unconscious has determined that this person is "up to no good"? Or was your dream a signal that you yourself have been acting the part of the villain during your waking hours? And if you dreamed that a strong and brave hero or heroine rescued you from the clutches of evil, do you wish that a courageous savior would liberate you from a difficult real-world situation? For instance, have you been feeling increasingly uneasy because of your boss's threatening sexual advances, and do you wish that someone (perhaps the company manager) would recognize that you are in jeopardy and would take steps to extricate you from your boss's menacing reach?

Related Dreams

PRAISE & ADMIRATION

* *

Most people take pleasure in being praised and admired, even if they have difficulty accepting such praise outwardly or expressing their enjoyment. When we are openly praised or admired, this is a sign that others recognize us for our talents, our achievements, or for our inherently good qualities. Dreams of being praised may either be literal or compensatory, depending on our real-life situation.

Symbolic and Verbal Associations
- A need for recognition or respect
- Success; glory; real-world achievements
- Goals and ambitions
- Personal pride

Positive Interpretations: If you had a dream in which you were lavished with praise and admiration, have you indeed recently been praised or received public recognition for something? For example, if you dreamed that everyone in your office suddenly stood up to toast and applaud a speech that your boss gave in praise of your hard work and your positive contribution to the company, do you feel as though your coworkers have been forthcoming in their verbal acknowledgment of, and gratitude for, all of your professional efforts, talents, and abilities? If so, then your dream was probably a reflection of your waking pleasure at receiving such professional recognition and appreciation. Alternatively, did you have a dream in which a worker at your grocery store—a person to whom you never say more than "hi," "thanks," and "bye"—approached you and told you how much he or she admires and appreciates you? If the person who admired and praised you in your dream is only an acquaintance in the real world, then your unconscious may have been alerting you to the admiration and respect that this person has for you, which you may have intuitively, but not consciously, recognized. Alternatively, could it be that you crave recognition from this person, perhaps signaling that you yourself admire him or her and that you would like to get to know him or her better?

Negative Interpretations: A dream of being praised and admired (whether such praise is public or private) may be your unconscious's way of trying to compensate for a lack of such recognition in the real world. So if you had such a dream, what were you being praised and celebrated for? Whatever it was—for instance, your creative talents, your beauty, or your charm—it is likely that you feel that this aspect of yourself merits appreciation and recognition, which you have not been receiving in sufficient quantities. Or do you wish that a loved one would be more demonstrative of his or her appreciation of you? For example, did the praise and admiration that your husband heaped on you in your dream make up for his lack of the same during waking hours?

My Praise & Admiration Dreams

----

* * * * * * * * * * * * * * * * * * *

Turning Heads
A dream in which you literally turned heads as you walked confidently along the street is likely to have meant one of two things. Perhaps you are filled with a new sense of confidence because you have recently achieved an ambition. Or, on the other hand, you may be feeling insecure and in need of appreciation or a makeover to boost your self-esteem.

Related Dreams
pages 36, 89, 198, 243, 247 & 266

WISH-FULLFILLMENT DREAMS

My Revenge Dreams

★ ★ ★ ★ ★ ★ ★ ★ ★ ★ ★ ★ ★ ★ ★ ★ ★ ★

Getting Even

Did you dream of turning the tables on someone who has been threatening or bullying you in the real world? If so, perhaps your unconscious was demonstrating that you can conquer your fear and feelings of powerlessness by visualizing a situation in which you, rather than your enemy, are in control, and can perhaps find a way to confront or challenge him or her in waking life.

REVENGE

★★★★★★★★★★★★★★★★★★★★★★★★★★★★★★★★★★★★

Dreams of exacting revenge on those whom we feel have harmed us may bring the temporary pleasure of "getting even," and such dreams may also have a safety-valve effect, allowing us to vent our negativity in the safe space of dreamland. However, if dreams of this type recur, this may signal an unhealthy fixation on past wounds.

Symbolic and Verbal Associations
- A grudge; emotional wounds
- "Rubbing it in"
- "Getting even"
- "Revenge is sweet"

Positive Interpretations: In your dream, did you finally take revenge on someone from your past who abused their power over you? For instance, did your dream self travel back to the fourth grade, when your cruel and imperious teacher made your life a misery by singling you out for ridicule day after day? And in your dream, did you lead your class in a mutiny, causing the malicious teacher to cower under her desk? If so, your unconscious was probably compensating for the disempowerment and emotional pain felt by your fourth-grade self by affirming that your adult self would not put up with such treatment. Or did you have a dream in which you were able to "hit back" at someone in your waking life whom you feel has the upper hand and uses it against you? For example, if your father uses money to control your actions, did you dream that you did something to cause him public embarrassment, such as showing up at his birthday party in your underwear? A dream like this may be serving a few functions. For one, it may be an unconscious warning that your father's dictatorial attitude is pushing you to your limits, thereby signaling that you had better find a reasonable way to free yourself from his control. Your dream may also have been serving as a safety valve, allowing you to "blow off some steam" in dreamland so that you won't have as great a need to do so in the real world.

Negative Interpretations: Were you disturbed by a dream in which you took revenge on someone in an exaggerated or extremely violent manner? Did you dream that you went back to your old place of work, from which you were fired, and that you pulled out a shotgun and opened fire on your former colleagues? If so, you probably awoke feeling enormously upset—and rightfully so—but it is important to note that your dream was not necessarily a reflection of your conscious wishes. Instead, your unconscious may have been using the dream to alert you to your feelings of pain and anger, which you may have repressed so well in the waking world that you are not even conscious of them. If, upon reflection, you think that this may be the case, the healthiest course of action is to face up to your feelings, however painful this may be—perhaps with the help of a professional counselor.

Related Dreams

pages 106, 114, 132, 190, 253 & 281

STATUS

✶✶

Dreams of having an increased status—i.e., being the boss—in either the professional or domestic (or in any) realm of life may mirror a general desire to rise in status in the waking world. Such dreams may also be an unconscious comment on our attitudes and actions within our waking roles.

Symbolic and Verbal Associations
- Power and control
- The person "at the top" or "at the helm"
- Being "in charge" or "in control"
- Someone who is "bossy" or overly pushy
- A tyrant or "ogre"

Positive Interpretations: In your dream, did you find that you had been named as the C.E.O. of the corporation that you work for? If so, how did your dream self feel about being "at the helm"? Did you feel confident? Pleased? Energized? Were you a just leader who sought the best for your company and the people who worked for you? Your dream may be a reflection of your professional goals and ambitions, indicating that you feel that your professional abilities and work habits may potentially lead you to the top of the corporate ladder. Or if you have recently received a real-life increase in your status at work (for instance, if you were promoted to the level of junior executive), then your dream may have been both underlining your new elevation in status and encouraging you to continue following your ambitions.

Negative Interpretations: A dream of being the boss or of being in control or having power over others may also have been a simple form of wish fulfillment—an unconscious signal that you feel unrecognized or undervalued for your work and your abilities. In your dream, how did you behave and feel? Did you have a dream in which you found yourself acting the part of an "ogre" in your role as boss or leader? For example, in your dream, did you assume the position of head of your company and immediately fire all of the people with whom you have ever been in competition, even though they may always have done their jobs very well (which is, perhaps, why they made you feel competitive)? Or, in your dream, did you rewrite the company rules so that no one except yourself could take off any personal time for things like doctor's appointments or special family events? If so, ask yourself whether you've been acting like a tyrant during your waking hours—whether at work, within your family, or in any arena of your life. And if you wish that you had greater status or power so that you could either make yourself feel more important by taking advantage of others, or could take revenge on those you feel have wronged you, then you should consider whether you suffer from low self-esteem or whether you have difficulty controlling and managing your anger.

My Status Dreams

✶✶✶✶✶✶✶✶✶✶✶✶✶✶✶✶✶✶✶✶✶✶

Wearing the Suit

If you have been pushed too hard at work, and have not received the recognition that you feel that you have earned for your efforts, a dream of wearing the boss's suit, and of enjoying the trappings of his or her office, may be your unconscious mind's way of making up for the unsatisfactory way in which you've been treated by your boss.

Related Dreams

pages 114, 188, 190, 198, 243 & 249

WISH-FULLFILLMENT DREAMS

My Vacations Dreams

```
............................................................
............................................................
............................................................
............................................................
............................................................
............................................................
............................................................
............................................................
............................................................
```

★ ★ ★ ★ ★ ★ ★ ★ ★ ★ ★ ★ ★ ★ ★ ★ ★

Paradise

Did you dream of basking in an idyllic vacation paradise, where you relaxed on a palm-fringed beach, your waking worries reduced to a distant memory? If you have recently booked a vacation, your unconscious may simply have been anticipating the well-earned rest that you are so looking forward to. If not, and you are feeling exhausted, it's almost certainly time to plan a restful vacation.

VACATIONS

✦ ★ ✦ ★ ✦ ★ ✦ ★ ✦ ★ ✦ ★ ✦ ★ ✦ ★ ✦ ★ ✦ ★ ✦ ★ ✦ ★ ✦ ★ ✦ ★ ✦ ★ ✦

When the unconscious sends our dream selves on vacation, it usually does so in order to urge us to take some time off from our dull or demanding daily routines in order to revitalize our bodies, our minds, and our spirits. This generally applies whether the dream vacation was relaxing or more adventurous.

Symbolic and Verbal Associations
- Rest and relaxation
- Needing a break
- The desire to "get away from it all"
- Adventure
- Peace and tranquility
- Feeling "out of place" in one's environment

Positive Interpretations: In your dream, did you find yourself lazily sunning yourself as you lay back and relaxed, sipping an iced cocktail on a sparkling beach in the Caribbean? If so, have you been feeling worn out, overworked, or stressed out in your waking life? Your dream may have been an unconscious attempt to provide you with a bit of dreamtime relaxation and rejuvenation, as well as to urge you to go ahead and book that vacation that you've been meaning to take for so long now. At the very least, your unconscious was probably trying to encourage you to expose yourself to fresh or "foreign" ideas and influences. Alternatively, did you take a dream vacation of a more exciting type? For instance, in your dream, were you backpacking through the Amazon or traveling on a safari through Africa? Perhaps you were with a team of climbers, making an ascent toward the top of Mount Everest? If you had an exciting dream adventure such as this, and if you are feeling bored with the tedium or monotony of your daily waking life, then your dream may have been your unconscious's attempt to encourage you to reenergize and reinvigorate yourself by adopting a more adventurous lifestyle—not necessarily by climbing Mount Everest, but perhaps by joining a rock-climbing club, learning to snowboard, or engaging in some other exciting activity that you are interested in.

Negative Interpretations: Did you awake feeling bewildered or even frightened because you had had a dream in which you found yourself in a foreign environment? For example, in your dream, did you feel utterly lost and confused—and possibly even threatened—because you could not speak the language or read the writing of the land that you were in, nor could you find anyone who could speak your language? If so, your dream may have been reflecting your feeling of being "out of place" in your current waking environment. In the course of your dream journeys, did you encounter any problems or obstacles? For more possible interpretations of this sort, see Chapter 15, Travel.

Related Dreams

pages 41, 192, 228,

376 & 384

WEALTH

✶✶✶✶✶✶✶✶✶✶✶✶✶✶✶✶✶✶✶✶✶✶✶✶✶✶✶✶✶✶✶✶✶✶✶✶✶✶

WISH-FULFILLMENT DREAMS

A dream of being wealthy may be a form of simple wish fulfillment, thereby "making up" for a lack of wealth in the real world. However, dream riches may also be a reference to nonmonetary wealth (i.e., the things in life that "can't be bought").

Symbolic and Verbal Associations
- ❨ Getting your "just deserts"
- ❨ Security and comfort
- ❨ Social status; feelings of self-worth
- ❨ Things that are of intrinsic, or emotional, value
- ❨ Being "rich" in love, friends, and so on

Positive Interpretations: Did you have a dream in which you "struck gold"? For example, in your dream, did you discover that you owned some land that was worth a fortune, perhaps because it contained a vast quantity of underground oil reserves? If so, and if you have indeed recently come into some money in the real world, then your dream was probably an unconscious reflection of the pleasure you have gained from your new real-world wealth. Or if this is not the case, do you feel that you deserve a pay raise at work? (If so, it may be time to ask for one!) However, if your finances (for better or for worse) are the farthest thing from your mind, then it is possible that your dream fortune was a metaphor for wealth of a nonmonetary type. Thinking about the details of your dream in relation to your waking-life situation may help you to decide if this may be the case and, if so, what your dream wealth referred to. For instance, did your dream gold represent a "heart of gold"? And if so, whose? Are you blessed with a "wealth" of love in your life? Do you have a "treasure" of knowledge, faith, or inner strength?

Negative Interpretations: In your dream, were you exulting because you had suddenly landed a fortune—so much money that you knew that you would never need to work or worry about your finances ever again? Dreams of "striking it rich"— especially if you have them often—may point to a preoccupation with monetary problems or issues; dreams like this may serve as a form of wish fulfillment, an unconscious attempt to make up for a lack of financial security (and/or its accompanying social status) in the waking world. Alternatively, did you have a dream in which you were obsessed with the fear of financial ruin? If so, what was threatening your financial security? It is possible that your unconscious was making a reference to some nonmonetary resource that you are in jeopardy of losing. For instance, this could be anything that you fear running short of, such as your ambition, your will, your ethics, or your youthful perspective. No matter what your dream loss represented, your unconscious may have sent you your dream in order to urge you to take the necessary steps to secure your resources.

My Wealth Dreams

✶✶✶✶✶✶✶✶✶✶✶✶✶✶✶✶✶✶✶✶✶

Winning the Jackpot
A sudden windfall is so widely seen as the cure for all kinds of problems that a dream in which you won the lottery may have signified your desire for a dramatic change of real-life circumstances in almost any domain. When your unconscious gives you a wish-fulfillment dream like this, it may help to relieve some of your real-life pressures.

Related Dreams
pages 179, 193, 198, 215, 236 & 247

WISH-FULLFILLMENT DREAMS

My Winning Dreams

_____

_____

_____

_____

_____

_____

_____

_____

* * * * * * * * * * * * * * * * * * *

Taking the Trophy

If you dreamed of holding aloft a coveted trophy, and of making an emotional acceptance speech, do you sense that a real-life reward is within your grasp? Are you feeling confident that you can obtain an outstanding result in a forthcoming test or audition? Such a dream may help you to overcome your nerves if you are indeed preparing for an important exam, interview, or presentation.

WINNING

* *

Dreams of playing a game or a sport may reflect how well we feel we are doing in some area of our life—particularly in a competitive arena, such as in our career. And apart from wish fulfillment, dreams of winning may reflect our confidence, or lack of it, in our ability to achieve our goals and ambitions.

Symbolic and Verbal Associations
 ‹ Goals and ambitions
 ‹ Competition; success
 ‹ Having "an ace up your sleeve"
 ‹ "Playing dirty"; cheating

Positive Interpretations: Did you have a dream in which you were racing against rivals, whom you left behind as you sailed toward the finish line amidst wild cheering? If so, and if you are employed, your dream most likely refers to your working life (which is often called "the rat race"), and your dream of winning may be an indication that you feel that your career is in tip-top shape. Of course, if you have no job, or if your job is not going well, then you may have experienced a simple wish-fulfillment dream, or your dream race may have been a reference to some other aspect of your life—in which case, the details of the dream may provide clues as to its meaning. Did you recognize your rivals? Or did you have any teammates in your dream? If so, who were they? Do you know what sort of prize or trophy you stood to win? Or did you dream that you ran down a soccer field, successfully keeping the ball from your competitors' reach, and that you strategically passed the ball to your teammate, who scored the game-winning goal just before the clock ran out of time? Unless you are actually a soccer player, your dreaming mind may have been reliving, and congratulating you for, some real-life triumph, such as a successful business maneuver that you were recently part of.

Negative Interpretations: Did your dream depict you winning at a game or a sport, but only after a very hard struggle? For instance, did you dream of winning a marathon, but only after a grueling, hours-long run in which you encountered a plethora of obstacles and setbacks? If so, the message from your unconscious may have been that while achieving your goal is possible, it won't be done without struggle and hardship. It may be helpful to think about the obstacles and problems that your dream self encountered, and to consider what they may represent in the real world. Alternatively, did you have a dream in which you resorted to cheating to win? Dreams of cheating and deception are often literal reflections of a dishonest action that we have taken in the waking world. So have you been "playing dirty" in order to get ahead at work? Do you always feel the need to have "an ace up your sleeve"? If so, your unconscious may have been emphasizing the need for you to be true to yourself and others.

Related Dreams

pages 114, 124, 190,

195, 198 & 247

CHAPTER 13

THE EMOTIONAL ROLLERCOASTER

Many of us suppress our emotions in the waking world—especially extreme ones—for fear of somehow alienating those around us, or else of appearing dangerously vulnerable, or even of disgusting ourselves. This means that the only way in which we can "safely" express our true feelings is in dreamland. Dreams that are flooded by a positive emotion may furthermore often be categorized as wish-fulfillment dreams, while those that are blighted by a negative emotion may be classed as safety-valve dreams.

THE EMOTIONAL ROLLERCOASTER

My Abandonment Dreams

----

* * * * * * * * * * * * * * * * * * *

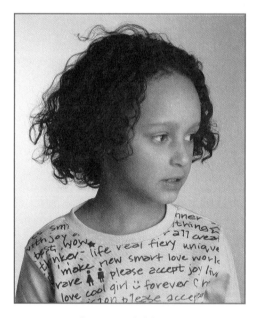

Lost and Alone

In your dream, did you revert to your childhood fear of becoming separated from your parents, and did you feel small, lost, and alone? Such dreams may not signify that you are feeling excessively insecure, vulnerable, or needy, but may instead be an emotional response to a distressing recent event, such as a bereavement or a hurtful argument that you've had with your friend or partner.

ABANDONMENT

* *

Though one teaches a child to fear being abandoned by his or her parents, it is usually one of the very first anxieties that we ever encounter in life and seems to be ingrained in our psyche. As adults, this fear may manifest itself in dreams of being abandoned or rejected by our partners or our friends.

Symbolic and Verbal Associations
‹ Childhood fear of being deserted
‹ Emotional (and physical) dependence and sustenance
‹ Fear of rejection; relationship insecurities
‹ Feelings of liberation
‹ Acting or behaving "with abandon"

Positive Interpretations: In your dream, did you initially feel shocked, and then ecstatically liberated, when your best friend told you that she never wanted to see you again? If you have a troubled real-life relationship with your friend, or if your relationship with her is a source of anxiety for you, then your dream may have been an unconscious message that severing your ties with her may not be a negative thing at all—and, in fact, such a "break up" would likely bring you some welcome freedom and peace of mind. However, if you do not feel that cutting all ties with your friend would be in your best interests, then your unconscious may have used your dream in order to prompt you to take a (perhaps temporary) step back from the friendship to give yourself some "head space" in which to evaluate the relationship's effect upon you and to think of ways in which you may wish to change your relationship so that it can better meet your needs.

Negative Interpretations: Did a dream of being abandoned by a loved one trigger your old childhood fear of being deserted by your parents? A dream like this may point to feelings of insecurity about the relationship in question, or to your doubts about the strength of the love and regard that the partner, family member, or friend (or even the group of people) who abandoned you in your dream has for you in the waking world. Although these sorts of feelings and dreams are completely normal, it may indeed be that your unconscious mind has detected a cooling in this person's feelings for you. And if this is the case, then your dream may have been a warning from your unconscious that you had better do something to strengthen this relationship, if possible, before it is lost to you. Alternatively, did your dreaming mind force you to relive a real-life abandonment? For instance, did you have a vivid dream about the day that your partner walked out on you? If so, then it is likely that you still harbor unresolved abandonment issues, and your unconscious may have been trying to compel you to confront this past rejection so that you can work through your feelings of loss, put this incident behind you, and begin to move on with your life in a positive manner.

Related Dreams
pages 89, 107, 218, 234, 254 & 266

ANGER

THE EMOTIONAL ROLLERCOASTER

✦✦✦

Dreams of being extremely angry or of fighting or arguing with someone are a likely sign that our waking efforts to suppress our anger are merely relegating it to the deeper levels of consciousness—especially if these dreams are recurring. And, as with any negative emotion that is released in the dream world, it is important to try to determine the source or trigger of your anger.

Symbolic and Verbal Associations
- ◖ Suppressed negativity
- ◖ Pent-up rage
- ◖ Loss of emotional control
- ◖ Violence
- ◖ Uncomfortable or disturbing memories

Positive Interpretations: In your dream, did you finally have the unbridled pleasure of telling your cantankerous and pushy next-door neighbor exactly what you think of her? If so, you probably awoke feeling vindicated and empowered, and then also probably somewhat relieved to know that you did not vocalize your true feelings so bluntly to your neighbor in the waking world—which was likely to be the exact mission of your unconscious! Although many people or things may anger us in our waking lives, we rarely have the freedom to let off some angry emotional steam by exploding with rage, for fear of the consequences. Therefore, any dream in which you reacted with wrath and fury to someone or something may have had a safety-valve purpose, allowing you to vent your rage and frustration in the safe environment of the dream world, where no one will be hurt (either physically or emotionally) and where there are no real or lasting repercussions.

Negative Interpretations: Another interpretation for a dream in which you exploded with rage at someone or something is that your unconscious mind was sending you a warning that you are coming dangerously close to "the edge" and that your pent-up anger is becoming so overwhelming that you are likely to lose control in the waking world. If you feel that this interpretation may be true, then you will probably want to try to remember who, or what, caused you to become so angry in your dream, and to think about ways of beginning to defuse your anger in the real world (such as some sort of peaceful confrontation with whomever or whatever is aggravating you). If you can remember anything that you said (or, more likely, shouted) in your dream, then this may provide more valuable clues about the source or the nature of your agitation. But if you have recurring angry dreams regarding some person or incident from your past, then the unresolved negativity that you are harboring is likely to keep plaguing you in your dreams until you make a conscious effort to face up to your anger so that you may then let it go and move on with your life.

Related Dreams

pages 106, 107, 218, 222, 259 & 264

My Anger Dreams

....
....
....
....
....
....
....
....
....

✦✦✦✦✦✦✦✦✦✦✦✦✦✦✦✦✦✦✦✦

Road Rage

Did you dream that you let your anger and frustration burst out of control while you were negotiating heavy traffic, resulting in reckless driving that caused an accident? If so, your unconscious was probably warning you that you are under too much pressure in waking life, and that you should do something to alleviate it before your rage is released in a similarly catastrophic explosion.

My Bereavement Dreams

----

* * * * * * * * * * * * * * * * *

Dream Desolation

If you dreamed that you were grief-stricken by the loss of the king or queen of your heart, yet your loved one is actually alive and well, have you recently betrayed your partner's trust, or do you suspect that he or she has been unfaithful? Your unconscious may have been flagging up a real-life threat to, or even the possible demise of, your relationship.

BEREAVEMENT

Dreams of being bereaved are quite common among people who have recently suffered the loss of a loved one, but you may have been disturbed by a dream in which you mourned the loss of someone who is still alive. However, in the language of dreams, death (like so many things) does not always mean the obvious.

Symbolic and Verbal Associations
- Catharsis; emotional release
- Preparation for the worst
- Guilt and sadness
- "Putting an end" to something
- The death of a relationship

Positive Interpretations: Did you wake up in tears because you had a dream about a loved one who has recently died? Though upsetting, such dreams are often an unconscious attempt to help us to work through pain and grief and eventually to accept loss. And because they allow us to express and release our sadness more openly and dramatically than we may feel able to in the real world, these dreams also tend to serve a cathartic purpose. You may also have been comforted by a dream about a departed loved one, particularly if your dream self got a chance to speak with the person who has died, or if you felt somehow reassured that he or she has moved on to a better place. If you dreamed of the death of someone who is gravely sick in the real world, then this may have been your unconscious's way of trying to prepare you for the worst by giving you a chance to experience how you would feel and react in the event of this person's death. Dreams like these may also be the unconscious's way of encouraging us to express our love and our gratitude to our loved ones before it is too late.

Negative Interpretations: Were you deeply upset by a dream in which your deceased brother accused you of never having shown him enough love? Dreams involving feelings of guilt after a bereavement are a natural part of the grieving process and are, ultimately, useful in helping you to accept your loss, however painful. Beareavement counseling or self-help research may help you to come to terms with these distressing feelings. Or were you confused by a dream in which you were mourning the death of someone who is actually in good health? Your unconscious may have chosen this person to represent something in your life that you would like to put an end to (such as recklessness or sloth), or else something that you feel you have already lost (such as your independence). Finally, it is also possible that your dream was an expression of your fear that your relationship with this person is in jeopardy, particularly if you have recently quarreled. If you think this may be the case, then your dream may have been pointing to the need for resolution and closure—either by settling the conflict between you or by coming to terms with it in your own mind.

Related Dreams
pages 56, 92, 139, 252, 260 & 272

CRUELTY

✶✶✶✶✶✶✶✶✶✶✶✶✶✶✶✶✶✶✶✶✶✶✶✶✶✶✶✶✶✶✶✶✶✶✶✶✶✶

Dreams that depict us behaving cruelly toward others may highlight our own feelings of hostility or our controlling tendencies, which may be underlined by feelings of powerlessness, self-loathing, and frustration.

Symbolic and Verbal Associations
- Hostility
- Controlling tendencies; abuse of power
- Self-loathing
- Frustration
- Feelings of powerlessness

Positive Interpretations: Unless your unconscious mind was replaying an incident that happened in the past (in which case it was probably urging you to confront and come to terms with the memory), having a dream in which you treated someone with cruelty may have been an unconscious attempt to defuse your mounting hostility toward this person in the real world. Did you dream that you were arguing with your sister and that your anger and hostility mounted to such a level that you lashed out at her with some extremely cruel words—things you would feel very ashamed and remorseful about if you had actually said them to her in the real world? If so, and if your sister is driving you crazy during your waking hours with her constant neediness, then your dream may have served as a safety valve, allowing you to vent your frustration with your sister in the safe space of the dream world. When interpreting a dream in which you acted cruelly, it is also important to consider whether the target of your unkindness could have represented an aspect of yourself, which may be even more likely if your dream victim was a stranger. For instance, in your dream, if the intolerable whining and complaining of someone of the same sex caused you to give this person a cruel tongue lashing, could your dream self have been trying to quell your own tendency to whine and complain?

Negative Interpretations: Any dream in which you behaved cruelly and sadistically toward someone may also imply a desire for control and power; perhaps, because you feel disempowered in most aspects of your waking life, you may be abusing what power you do have. Could a dream in which you behaved like a brutal ogre, wreaking physical or emotional abuse on someone else, have denoted your waking feelings of frustration and self-loathing? Or could your unconscious mind have been pointing to your real-life tendency to treat others, especially your subordinates or those whom you perceive as being weaker than you, with rash, unfeeling viciousness and cruelty? This sort of dream may also be a sign that you are struggling for self-control, particularly if you felt disconnected from or unmoved by (i.e., neither sorry for, nor relieved by) your malicious behavior.

Related Dreams
pages 106, 121, 165, 256, 259 & 273

My Cruelty Dreams

✶✶✶✶✶✶✶✶✶✶✶✶✶✶✶✶✶✶✶✶✶

Bound and Gagged

Were you shocked to awaken from a dream in which you overpowered an acquaintance, tied him up, and then bound and gagged him? If so, perhaps your dream victim has been spreading malicious gossip about you in the waking world, thereby arousing your anger, in which case your dreaming cruelty may have facilitated a harmless, cathartic release of your pent-up feelings of fury.

THE EMOTIONAL ROLLERCOASTER

My Disgust Dreams

....
....
....
....
....
....
....
....
....

✳ ✳ ✳ ✳ ✳ ✳ ✳ ✳ ✳ ✳ ✳ ✳ ✳ ✳ ✳ ✳ ✳

Nauseated

In your dream, did your friend appear disgusted with you? If so, and you had no idea why, are you harboring a sense of shame about something that you have done in waking life? If you have behaved badly, for instance, maybe you should express your remorse, but if your conscience is clear, could your friend be somehow undermining you in the real world?

DISGUST

✳✳✳✳✳✳✳✳✳✳✳✳✳✳✳✳✳✳✳✳✳✳✳✳✳✳✳✳✳✳✳✳✳✳✳✳✳✳

There are a few possible explanations for a dream that focused on someone whom you find disgusting or repulsive in some way. For one, your unconscious may have summoned your shadow, the "dark" or hidden part of your psyche that is battling for expression. Such dreams may also be your unconscious's way of alerting you to, or reinforcing, your feelings for someone in your waking life.

Symbolic and Verbal Associations
- Repulsion; loathing
- The "shadow"; one's "dark side"
- Unpleasant feelings or personal characteristics
- Someone whom one finds obnoxious or distasteful

Positive Interpretations: Did you dream about someone who was the same sex as you who behaved in a way that you found obnoxious, distasteful, or repulsive? If so, and especially if this person was a stranger, then you may have encountered your shadow, an archetypal character who is the polar opposite of the ego or persona that you show to the world, but which is a part of your psyche all the same. A good sign that you have met your shadow is that he or she will exude some character or quality that you find particularly disgusting in others, such as cowardice, cynicism, arrogance, or aggressive or violent tendencies. Since your conscious mind works very hard to suppress your shadow during your waking hours, its only outlet may be in your dreams. But it is important to remember that your shadow is not necessarily evil or bad, and that its appearance in your dreams is a likely sign that it is time to acknowledge and embrace whatever quality or qualities your shadow represents. By doing this, you may find that you become happier and more balanced.

Negative Interpretations: There is also a more straightforward line of interpretation for these types of dreams. If you had a dream in which you felt an overwhelming sense of disgust at someone whom you recognized from your waking life, then your unconscious may have been highlighting or reinforcing your feelings of repulsion for this person—even though these feelings may have not yet seeped into your conscious awareness (in which case your unconscious was probably attempting to alert you to the negative emotions that this individual arouses in you). A similar interpretation may apply if you dreamed that you rejected someone's romantic or friendly advances toward you. But what if the object of your dream disgust was not human at all, but was instead some sort of monstrous creature? The creature may symbolize something that you find repulsive, which may continue to lurk in your dreams unless you find a way of dealing or dispensing with it in the waking world. The first step is to try to figure out what, or whom, the monstrous object of your dream disgust represents in the real world.

Related Dreams

pages 129, 182, 224, 253, 262 & 273

FEAR

THE EMOTIONAL ROLLERCOASTER

✦✦

If you had a nightmare that left you paralyzed with fear, you probably awoke feeling very relieved to realize that it was just a dream, and you may have spent most of the next day trying to push it out of your memory. However, these types of dreams are underlined by our waking fears—which are very real, though perhaps repressed—which are likely to appear in our dreams again and again until we confront and resolve them.

Symbolic and Verbal Associations
- Unconscious fears; phobias
- Something (or someone) that one finds "monstrous"
- Repressed personal qualities or characteristics
- External threats
- A call to action; the "fight or flight" response

Positive Interpretations: If you have a waking phobia of spiders, did you wake up in a panic after dreaming that hundreds of giant, hairy arachnids were crawling all over you? Or, if you suffer from a fear of heights, did you have a nightmare in which you found yourself dangling precariously over the edge of a very high cliff? If so, your dream was probably just mirroring your waking phobias, especially if something in the real world has recently triggered your fear. And, as scary as your dream may have been to you, your unconscious mind probably selected the nightmare scenario as a "call to action," in order to urge you to confront and conquer your fear. If you have a recurring scary dream, you may find it helpful to tell yourself that when you next have the dream, you will not run from whatever it is that frightens you, be it spiders or boogeymen, but will instead stand and face whatever it is. If you do, you may be surprised to find that the dream consequences are not as bad as you imagined them to be, which will help to allay your fear and hopefully put an end to the dreams.

Negative Interpretations: The unconscious will sometimes portray our fears in monstrous form. Did you have a dream in which you were being pursued by a hideous, fanged monster that had run you down and was about to overtake you? If so, the monster was most likely a symbol of something that you fear in the waking world that you feel is threatening to consume you. Doing some free association may help you to figure out whom or what your dream monster represented. Was it your predatory lover? An ogrelike teacher? Your own "green-eyed" beast of jealousy? Could your dream vampire have represented your energy-sapping friend? (Or had you just watched a vampire movie on late-night television?) Once you have identified the source of your fright, you will be better able to arm yourself in order to do battle with whatever it is that is troubling you.

My Fear Dreams

✦ ✦ ✦ ✦ ✦ ✦ ✦ ✦ ✦ ✦ ✦ ✦ ✦ ✦ ✦ ✦ ✦ ✦ ✦

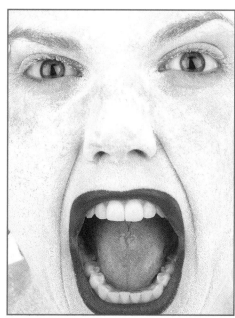

Nightmare Scenario
If you awoke trembling from a nightmare in which you were screaming with fear, yet there was no obvious cause for your terror, your dream may have been an indication that you need to deal with a situation that is making you feel uneasy or fearful in waking life. Have you been repressing your dread that a past wrongdoing will be exposed, for example?

Related Dreams
pages 38, 145, 153, 196, 273 & 294

My Freedom Dreams

* * * * * * * * * * * * * * * * * * *

Flying High

If you experienced an exhilarating dream in which you soared like a bird through clear, blue skies, you probably had a wish-fulfillment dream. A dream like this may have been triggered by a period of stress or a looming exam or deadline that has been constraining you, or perhaps by the emotional demands of caring for a sick relative or young children.

FREEDOM

✱✱✱✱✱✱✱✱✱✱✱✱✱✱✱✱✱✱✱✱✱✱✱✱✱✱✱✱✱✱✱✱✱

Sometimes our dreams may fill us with an exhilarating sense of freedom or liberation. And when we awake from this sort of dream, we may feel somewhat let down or disappointed to realize that we must now deal with the more mundane reality of the world. Dreams of flying may be the most literal or obvious form of freedom dreams, but almost any dream scenario may fall into this category, depending on our own subjective feelings and experiences.

Symbolic and Verbal Associations
- Exhilaration
- Escape; release
- Casting off your shackles
- "Being yourself"
- "Flying high," or "floating free"

Positive Interpretations: In your dream, were you soaring over beautiful mountains and valleys, or running carefree through a meadow of wildflowers? Or did your dream self rise up and walk out of your tedious office job for the last time? Dreams in which we finally break away from the chains and shackles that bind us—physically or emotionally—are likely to fill us with an overwhelming feeling of euphoria. Wish-fulfillment, escapist fantasy dreams of this sort are special treats from our unconscious minds, sent to us in order to make up or compensate for the tedium or drudgery of our day-to-day lives. These dreams may provide us with the little extra boost that we need in order to cope with daily life—and if we heed their message, they may even encourage us to release ourselves from whatever (or whoever) is holding us back or sapping our vitality in the waking world.

Negative Interpretations: If you felt extremely sad or depressed after waking from a dream in which you experienced ultimate freedom, do you feel that the dreariness and the confines of your current life have chained you down so firmly that there is no way of ever escaping to happiness? For instance, are you in a relationship that is making you feel trapped or claustrophobic? Are the demands of others, or of your workload, stealing your time, your energy, or your individuality? Do you long for a more exciting, stimulating relationship, job, or life? Do you desire the freedom to "be yourself"? If so, your unconscious mind was probably using your dream in order to urge you to seek appropriate help to take the necessary steps to release yourself from whatever situation is confining you. Though your dream may have provided you with a temporary release from your troubles, you may continue to experience your waking sadness until you make a conscious effort to cast off your shackles—whether they were put on you by yourself or by others—and to live your life in whatever manner you find personally fulfilling.

Related Dreams
pages 248, 261, 279, 289, 339 & 374

FRUSTRATION

✦✦✦✦✦✦✦✦✦✦✦✦✦✦✦✦✦✦✦✦✦✦✦✦✦✦✦✦✦✦✦✦✦✦✦✦✦✦

O ur waking frustrations may play themselves out in a variety of dream scenarios: dreams of going unprepared into a test, being confined or paralyzed, running late, or dealing with machinery malfunctions are all common. Everyone experiences such irritations in the waking world, but their repeated appearance in our dreams may signal a need for us to find ways in which to cope with our frustration better.

My Frustration Dreams

✦✦✦✦✦✦✦✦✦✦✦✦✦✦✦✦✦✦✦✦✦✦

Symbolic and Verbal Associations

- ☾ Anxiety; stress
- ☾ Fear of failure; self-perceived inadequacies; self-criticism and -judgment
- ☾ Difficulties, hindrances, and obstructions

Positive Interpretations: Did you have a dream in which you were struggling with a frustrating situation, and must you soon face a similar situation during your waking hours? For instance, if you are planning to take the test to get your driver's license, did you dream that you were under the pressure of the clock to successfully parallel park the car you were driving? If so, your unconscious was probably trying to give you an opportunity to rehearse and prepare for your upcoming test. If you had a dream in which you were frustrated by some sort of machinery malfunction, ask yourself what your dream machine may have represented in the real world, because your unconscious may have been trying to warn you that something is beginning to go wrong. For example, if you dreamed that your lawnmower died, are you, yourself, in danger of running out of "fuel"? But if your dream depicted you dealing calmly and collectedly with whatever frustrating problem you encountered, your unconscious was probably encouraging you similarly to "keep your cool" when you become aggravated in the waking world.

Negative Interpretations: Dream frustrations are likely to be references to things that are causing us frustration during our waking hours; though because symbolism is so rife in the dream world, it may take a bit of thought in order to figure out what real-world frustration was being highlighted. So if you had a dream in which you were struggling in vain to free yourself from a straightjacket, might this have been an unconscious reference to your frustration about something (or someone) that is restricting your freedom in the waking world? Or if you dreamed of running as fast as you could to catch a bus, only to see it pull away just before you reached the stop, might this have denoted your frustration at having missed an important real-world opportunity? Finally, if you dreamed that you were evaluated or questioned by a team of judges, whose sharp criticisms were causing you to feel more and more nervous and frustrated (and to perform more and more poorly), ask yourself who these merciless judges could have represented in the real world. Might your pitiless evaluators have represented the self-critical and –judging aspects of yourself, which are undermining your confidence and frustrating your waking endeavors?

Snap!

Did your boss lose patience with your poor performance in your dream, and do you worry that you have been underperforming during your working hours? Are you out of your depth, or do you have domestic problems? Your dream may have been a prompt to talk to your boss about whatever it is that is on your mind.

Related Dreams

pages 189, 193, 226, 228, 240 & 257

THE EMOTIONAL ROLLERCOASTER

My Guilt Dreams

✶ ✶ ✶ ✶ ✶ ✶ ✶ ✶ ✶ ✶ ✶ ✶ ✶ ✶ ✶ ✶ ✶ ✶

Busted!

Not all guilt dreams involve dark or shameful sins and taboos. Did you dream that you were caught red-handed while perpetrating a harmless prank or taking the last chocolate from the box, and did you find your predicament funny? If so, and if your conscience is sometimes overactive, your unconscious may have sent you your dream to encourage you to lighten up a little.

GUILT

✶ ✶

Depending upon your background, guilt may play either a small or a large part in how your unconscious encourages you to behave in the waking world. If you dreamed that you gave in to a temptation that you consider to be taboo, then you may have felt very guilty upon waking and reflecting upon what your dream self had done. However, it is important to note that dreams such as this are merely fulfilling our deepest desires and urges, which the conscious mind may be trying to suppress.

Symbolic and Verbal Associations
‹ Temptation; suppressed needs and desires
‹ "Immoral" acts; sexual frustration and curiosity
‹ Being troubled by one's conscience

Positive Interpretations: If, in your dream, you gave in to a temptation that your conscious mind considers immoral, then you probably felt guilty when you awoke. But instead of trying to repress the desire to which your dream self succumbed, you should acknowledge and to try to come to terms with it. In giving your suppressed desire free rein in the dream world, your unconscious may have been trying to point out that the desire may not be immoral, after all. For instance, if your dream portrayed you engaging in a same-sex erotic encounter, and if this made you feel guilty upon waking, consider why you feel this way. Same-sex relationships in dreamland may denote healthy sexual curiosity or refer to an intense emotional relationship.

Negative Interpretations: Sexual infidelities and the transgression of sexual taboos are probably the most common types of guilt-inducing dreams. Did you have a dream in which you were seduced by an attractive and charismatic stranger, and are you happy in a settled and committed relationship in the waking world? If so, you most surely woke up with a sense of guilt. However, in recognizing that your unconscious most likely sent you your dream in order to reflect and fulfill powerful needs and urges that your waking mind has tried to suppress, you may find that your best course of action is to face and acknowledge the problem, which may be sexual frustration or feelings of emotional isolation, and to work to resolve it in your waking life. Alternatively, did you dream that you cheated or "sinned" against someone you love? For example, did you dream that you sabotaged your sister's wedding plans? If so, your conscience may be troubling you about some aspect of your waking feelings or behavior toward your sister, whether or not you are consciously aware of it. For instance, are you jealous of your sister's relationship with her fiancé? The same interpretation may hold true if you dreamed of being punished for some crime, and—whatever your dream crime was a reference to—you may find that your conscience won't allow you any peace of mind (including in your dreams) until you right whatever wrong you feel you have committed.

Related Dreams

pages 107, 129, 176, 254, 268 & 273

HAPPINESS

Dreams in which we feel profoundly contented, happy, or joyful are rarer than those in which we are filled with negative emotion, perhaps due to the difficulties we often experience in life and our consequent anxieties about things like our relationships, our livelihoods, and our health. However, the unconscious mind sometimes attempts to bring us a bit of happiness in dreamland, perhaps to comfort and encourage us and to compensate for our waking troubles.

My Happiness Dreams

----

* * * * * * * * * * * * * * * * * * * *

Symbolic and Verbal Associations

- Security, comfort, and contentment
- Wish fulfillment
- Compensation for waking doubts and anxieties
- A sense of wellbeing
- The attainment of one's "heart's desire"

Positive Interpretations: If you dreamed that you were deeply contented or happy, without a worry or a care in your mind, and if this more or less sums up how you feel in your waking life, then your dream was probably merely reflecting your real-life situation and feelings, and you should consider yourself to be a very lucky person! Alternatively, it is also possible that, in sending you your dream, your unconscious mind was attempting to present you with the key to your own real-life happiness. What details can you remember from your dream? Can you recall what made your dream self feel so happy? Was it another person? Being in a certain place? Something you were doing? Once you have identified the source of your dream happiness, then you can consider whether your unconscious was fulfilling a wish that is out of your reach or that is unrealistic in your waking life, or whether the realization of your "heart's desire" may be obtainable if you choose to reach out for it.

Negative Interpretations: No matter how happy we are with our waking lives, most of us are at least somewhat beleaguered by nagging doubts or worries about such things as our relationships, our family life, our careers, our health, politics, the environment, and so on. Has something in the real world been causing you to fret or worry, or are you currently having an unhappy or difficult time in your waking life, and did you nevertheless dream that you were in a blissful state of contentment and wellbeing? For example, are you currently undergoing the stress of getting divorced, which is putting a strain on all the other aspects of your life, and did you dream that you were in a loving relationship and that all of the elements of your life were in complete health, balance, and harmony? If so, then it is possible that your dream was an unconscious attempt to comfort you in compensation for your real-life troubles—and perhaps also to hearten you to carry on in your quest for happiness by giving you a glimpse of what the future could hold for you.

Sheer Bliss

Did you dream that you were imbued with a sense of innocent, childlike happiness for no identifiable reason? If so, and your waking circumstances don't exactly fill you with joy, perhaps you had a wish-fulfillment dream in which your real-life worries had vanished without trace and you felt as carefree as you did when you were little.

Related Dreams

My Hatred Dreams

----

* * * * * * * * * * * * * * * * * * *

Nasty Gestures

Were you shocked in dreamland by an aggressive display of hostility, and did you recognize the person who expressed his loathing of you in this manner? If this is the case, ask yourself whether anything on your conscience may have triggered your dream, or, conversely, whether—and if so, why—you provoke feelings of anger or rivalry in that individual in the waking world.

HATRED

✳✳✳✳✳✳✳✳✳✳✳✳✳✳✳✳✳✳✳✳✳✳✳✳✳✳✳✳✳✳✳✳✳✳✳✳✳✳✳

We are not likely to dream that we hate someone or something unless we harbor some underlying negativity toward this person or thing in the waking world, whether or not we are consciously aware of our feelings. Therefore, it is important to pay attention when we have a dream in which we are filled with hatred, because this may be the unconscious's way of highlighting trouble in real life.

Symbolic and Verbal Associations
- A negative obsession
- Enemies; conflict
- Anger; unhealed emotional wounds
- Self-loathing; internal struggles

Positive Interpretations: Did you have a dream in which you were so overwhelmed by your hatred for someone that you expressed your emotion in a way that you would never think of doing in the real world? For example, if you really hate your job, did your dream self pour gasoline all over your office building and cheerfully set it ablaze? Or if you can't stand your neighbor's cat, who continually overturns your garbage cans and soils your garden, did you have a dream in which you called in the pound to pick up your feline foe? Any dream in which we commit atrocious acts of meanness or violence against someone or something that we abhor may be serving a safety-valve purpose, allowing us to blow off our steam in an extreme way in the dream world, where no one will actually be harmed and where there are no lasting consequences. Our dream selves having done so, we may find that we are able to cope better and more calmly with our adversaries in the waking world.

Negative Interpretations: Sometimes dreams in which we are filled with hatred are simply meant to reinforce, or to alert us to, our waking feelings of negativity. In such cases, your unconscious may depict you as engaging in some sort of conflict in order to enlighten you with regard to the source and nature of your loathing. Dreams of physically fighting with someone are probably pointing to feelings of hostility, or to a personal conflict or struggle with someone in the waking world. If you were engaged in a dream battle, whose side were you fighting on? And against whom were you fighting (or whom might your enemies have represented in the real world)? Whatever the dream scenario, it is important to try to work out who or what the focus of your dream hatred represented, and what each dream player symbolized in your waking life. And if these dreams are recurring, they may signal an unhealthy negative obsession on your part, in which case you should seek ways to abate your anger or to distance yourself from whatever is upsetting you in the real world. But what if you did not recognize the object of your dream self's hatred? Particularly if it was a person of the same sex as you, consider whether he or she represented some aspect of yourself that you loathe.

Related Dreams

pages 106, 129, 190,
255, 256 & 281

HOMESICKNESS

THE EMOTIONAL ROLLERCOASTER

Dreams that transport us back to a happier, more secure time and place may leave us with a cavernous feeling of homesickness. Having this sort of dream may point to our current unhappiness and dissatisfaction with our waking lives. However, by reminding us of the happy times that we once took pleasure in, they may also give us hope that we may eventually experience such joy once again.

Symbolic and Verbal Associations
- Nostalgia; the past
- Loss and yearning
- Happier times
- Childhood memories; feeling carefree
- Security, safety, and comfort
- Family bonds

Positive Interpretations: In your dream, were you transported back to a happy time and place, perhaps to a scene from your childhood, when you felt comforted and secure, and all seemed right in the world? Or did you dream of a long-lost loved one? If so, your unconscious mind may have chosen to remind you of the happier times in your past in order to comfort you and to compensate you for your current unhappiness, and perhaps also to encourage you to believe that such happiness can be possible again and to seek it out with passion and conviction.

Negative Interpretations: If you felt saddened upon waking from a pleasant dream of a past time and place, ask yourself why you awoke feeling this way. Is something missing from your current real-world life—something that you once had but that you somehow lost? If so, do you know what? Is it the intimacy of a romantic relationship? The closeness and companionship of good friends? The security and sense of belonging that being among family brings? Or is it some aspect or quality of your character, such as idealism, trust, or childlike innocence? Whatever your unconscious has identified that you are lacking, the message of your dream may be that you should take positive action to rebuild or replace it in your life. However, if you awoke feeling disturbed or upset because you had dreamed about some unhappy incident in your past, then it is probable that you have never fully come to terms with whatever happened at that time. For instance, did your dream take you back to an all-too-typical scene from your early childhood, when you would hide under your bed with your hands over your ears to block out the sound of your parents fighting? Perhaps you have tried to put these unhappy scenarios out of your conscious mind, in which case, in forcing you to relive the incident in your dream, your unconscious was probably signaling that it is necessary, for your own peace of mind, for you to acknowledge and come to terms with your painful memories.

My Homesickness Dreams

Pining Away

If you dreamed that you had been exiled from home—perhaps you were a soldier fighting overseas—and were gripped with longing for someone special there, do you fear that you are losing touch with your loved one? This dream may have pointed toward emotional, rather than literal, separation, so consider whether coldness or distance is creeping into your real-life relationship.

Related Dreams

pages 89, 158, 178, 266 & 272

THE EMOTIONAL ROLLERCOASTER

My Hostility Dreams

----

* * * * * * * * * * * * * * * * *

Yadda, Yadda

Did you dream that your partner was interrogating you, prompting you to feel uncomfortable, and to resent his intrusive questioning? If so, ask yourself honestly whether your real-life feelings toward him have cooled, perhaps because of his possessiveness, or whether your dreaming hostility could have been a reflection of something that you feel guilty or defensive about.

HOSTILITY

Certain people may incite feelings of hostility in us in our dreams, just as they do during our waking hours. When we have a dream that focuses on someone toward whom we feel hostile, there is usually a good reason. Our unconscious may be giving us a warning, alerting us to our feelings, or simply reinforcing our waking dislike for a certain person.

Symbolic and Verbal Associations
- Anger
- Dislike
- Physical, emotional, or verbal abuse
- Irritating personal qualities
- The shadow

Positive Interpretations: Sometimes people may provoke hostility in us because they exhibit qualities or characteristics that we loathe within ourselves. This is because it is often easier to point out the flaws in others than to objectively evaluate our own shortcomings. If you were perplexed by a dream in which someone whom you are fond of in the waking world behaved out of character, in such a way as to cause you to become irritated and hostile toward him or her, then you should consider whether your unconscious mind was actually attempting to draw your attention to your own irritating behavior. For example, if you dreamed that your normally modest friend drove you into a rage with his incessant bragging, could it be you who is actually the annoying braggart? Similarly, if your dream self met a stranger of the same sex as you, whose personality or behavior elicited feelings of hostility in you, you may have met your archetypical shadow, the part of yourself that embodies those qualities that you particularly despise in others—and in yourself. The conscious mind seeks to suppress your shadow, often leaving your dreams as its only outlet for expression. When you meet your shadow in dreamland, this is likely a cue that it is a good time for you to confront and come to terms with those qualities that your shadow exemplifies—which are, after all, part of what make you a whole personality.

Negative Interpretations: If your loud-mouthed and annoying cousin, whom you detest in the real world, evoked feelings of hostility in your dream self when he strutted across the stage of your dream, then your unconscious was most likely just mirroring your true feelings for him. However, your dream may have been warning you about a possible threat that your cousin poses to you. Is it possible that you have unconsciously detected that your cousin has been slandering your name throughout the family by spreading scandalous and untrue rumors about you? In this case, your dream may have been your unconscious's way of preparing you to defend yourself, and possibly to launch a counterattack.

Related Dreams

pages 106, 129, 107, 253, 262 & 256

JEALOUSY

THE EMOTIONAL ROLLERCOASTER

* *

Though we may feel jealous for a number of different reasons—whether we are envious of someone's looks, talents, or possessions, or whether we fear that our partner has feelings of attraction for someone else—the bottom line of any dream of being jealous is that we perceive ourselves as being somehow inadequate.

Symbolic and Verbal Associations

- Feelings of inadequacy
- Envy; the green-eyed monster
- Hostility
- Relationship insecurities
- Fear of rejection

Positive Interpretations: Were you surprised by a dream in which you jealously vied for the attention of someone who, in the waking world, is merely a casual friend or acquaintance? For example, in your dream, did you find yourself amidst a party of people, and were you competing with others for the attention of your sister's boyfriend's mother's cousin, a person whom you barely know? If so, your dream may be a sign that you have romantic feelings for him or her, whether or not you have realized or acknowledged these feelings in your conscious mind, or else that you are attracted to some special quality or qualities that this person possesses, and that you wish to develop a closer friendship with him or her.

Negative Interpretations: If you had a dream that placed a spotlight on the fact that you were jealous of someone, chances are that something about this person makes you feel deficient in some way. So, can you identify how? If you were envious of his or her charm or grace, for example, might these be the sort of qualities that you would benefit from nurturing within yourself? Alternatively, you may be able to defuse your feelings of jealousy by accepting and telling yourself that—while you admire such and such characteristics within a certain person—you, yourself, have a multitude of other good qualities that more than make up for your self-perceived shortcomings in this regard. However, if you dreamed that someone else was jealous of you, do you know why they were jealous? Your unconscious mind may have detected that this person harbors hostility toward you in the real world. Finally, did you have a dream in which you felt jealous of someone's hold over the attentions of your real-life partner, or in which your partner cheated on you or actually left you for someone else? If so, your unconscious may have been reflecting your feelings of insecurity with regard to the strength of your relationship or the consistency of your partner's love for you, coupled with a fear of rejection. You need not take your dream as an ill omen, however, unless you have been experiencing serious difficulties in your relationship or you have some actual reason to believe that your partner's affections may be waning or directed elsewhere.

Related Dreams

pages 107, 114, 106, 218 & 264

My Jealousy Dreams

----

* * * * * * * * * * * * * * * * * * * *

Out in the Cold

If you are a parent who dreamed that your children were engrossed in a game or project that didn't involve you, to the extent that you felt hurt and excluded, maybe you have been feeling guilty about not spending enough time at home lately. If so, talk over the situation with your family, and maybe try to find ways of improving your work–life balance.

THE EMOTIONAL ROLLERCOASTER

My Loneliness Dreams

----

* * * * * * * * * * * * * * * * *

After the Love Has Gone

Dreams of feeling alone and inconsolable are very common after breaking up with a girlfriend or boyfriend. If you had a dream like this, and you have indeed recently split up with someone, perhaps you are trying to conceal your pain by putting on a brave face in the waking world, but are privately still grieving deeply for your lost love.

LONELINESS

****

As social creatures, most humans need a fair amount of social interaction in order to be happy. And if we become too physically distanced or emotionally withdrawn (if we are overly fixated on our work, for example), a sense of isolation may creep up on us—perhaps without us even realizing it—and our feelings of loneliness may make themselves known in our dreams.

Symbolic and Verbal Associations

- Emotional distance or withdrawal
- Physical isolation
- Becoming disconnected from family, friends, and other loved ones
- Solitude
- Abandonment; rejection

Positive Interpretations: Did you have a dream in which you experienced utter "aloneness" without feeling lonely? What's more, did you luxuriate in the peace and tranquility that you experienced? If so, is your daily life hectic and strained? Do you wake up before sunrise to get the kids off to school before rushing off to your job, which you do not leave until after sundown, when you then face an endless list of errands, duties, and obligations, not least of which are the running and maintenance of your household? If this sounds familiar to you, then your dream of being alone may have been your unconscious's way of giving you some much-needed downtime, if only in dreamland. And, if the stress and chaos of your life is beginning to get to you, heed the message of your dream and try to work some quality time into your relationships, before you become frazzled and isolated.

Negative Interpretations: Loneliness may present itself in a number of different dreamland scenarios, such as in dreams of being widowed, if you are married in the real world. If you had a dream that highlighted your feelings of loneliness, is this how you are feeling in your waking life? Have you been feeling sad ever since you had your dream, which seems to have uncorked and spilled out the loneliness that you had been keeping bottled up inside you (which you may not even have been previously conscious of)? And if so, do you know why you feel lonely? For instance, have you recently switched to a new job or moved to a new city, where you have yet to form significant bonds of friendship? Or have all of your best friends departed or moved away? Or is your partner "too busy" with his or her career to give you the attention and affection that you need, so that an emotional distance has developed between you? If you are lonely in the real world, then your dream may have simply been a literal reflection of your feelings—and, in highlighting your emotional isolation, your unconscious was probably trying to urge you to connect, or reconnect, with those around you, or to build new relationships.

Related Dreams

pages 100, 92, 107, 218, 229 & 252

LOVE

THE EMOTIONAL ROLLERCOASTER

****

There are a number of reasons why your unconscious might cause you to dream of loving someone or of feeling loved: the dream may have been reflecting your waking feelings of love, reminding you how intensely you once felt about someone, alerting you to your feelings of attraction for someone, or reflecting a yearning to be in love.

Symbolic and Verbal Associations
‹ Affection
‹ Emotional closeness
‹ Euphoria
‹ Romance
‹ Physical attraction; sexual desire

Positive Interpretations: If you had a dream in which you experienced the joy and exhilaration of being in love, or in which you basked in the love and affection of someone else, and if this is how you feel in the waking world, then your unconscious was likely just mirroring your waking good feelings. However, if you had such a dream and you are not currently in love with anyone in the real world, then your dream may have been signaling your longing to love and be loved by someone, and perhaps reaffirming your desire to seek out a mate in the real world. Or, if the passion between you and your partner has cooled, and you had a dream in which you were once again filled with the heady, idealistic love that he or she once inspired in you, then your unconscious may have been urging you to rediscover the romantic excitement that you once felt. Alternatively, if you believe that your true feelings of love for someone have been revealed to you through a dream, then your unconscious may have been encouraging you to express your feelings for this person in the waking world.

Negative Interpretations: Did you dream that you were madly in love with someone who did not reciprocate your affections? If this person is your real-life partner, then your dream may have been mirroring your feelings of insecurity with regard to the strength of your relationship. Otherwise, was the object of your dream self's love someone you are attracted to, but who you fear does not have similar feelings for you? Or were you troubled by a dream in which you were in love with someone whom you consider to be an inappropriate object of such affection? For example, you may have felt this way if you, or the person whom your dream self was in love with, are already in a settled relationship with someone else in the waking world. If so, your unconscious may have been trying to force you to acknowledge your real-life feelings of attraction for, or even genuine love for, this person, as disturbing as this may be to your conscious mind. Remember, the dream world is a safe environment in which to explore and help resolve your feelings, because, no matter what happens, no harm is actually done to anyone in the real world.

My Love Dreams

----

* * * * * * * * * * * * * * * * * * *

Two's Company
Was your dream of being intimately entwined with a besotted lover a euphoric expression of passionate love? If so, you may either have had a wish-fulfillment dream about someone to whom you are strongly attracted or, if you are single and have been feeling lonely, simply about being romantically involved. Was your unconscious telling you that it's time to "get out there" again?

Related Dreams

pages 94, 102, 112, 116, 242 & 261

THE EMOTIONAL
ROLLERCOASTER

My Lust Dreams

....

....

....

....

....

....

....

....

....

✱ ✱ ✱ ✱ ✱ ✱ ✱ ✱ ✱ ✱ ✱ ✱ ✱ ✱ ✱ ✱

Feel the Heat

Although lust-filled dreams can have an obvious explanation, particularly if you are trying to suppress your attraction to someone while you are awake, they can highlight nonsexual issues, too. By portraying you enthusiastically "doing what comes naturally" with an appreciative partner, your unconscious may have been encouraging you to shed your inhibitions and have confidence in your ability to win others' approval, for instance.

LUST

✱✱

The sexual urge is so strongly inherent in human nature, it is no wonder that it often makes its way into our dreams. And because sexual desire is such a basic and powerful drive, and yet there are so many social strictures surrounding sex, most people are likely to react to their erotic dreams with extreme emotions, either positive or negative.

Symbolic and Verbal Associations
‹ Sexual desire; ecstasy
‹ Urges or desires perceived as being "obscene" or "dirty"
‹ Repression; guilt

Positive Interpretations: Did you have a dream in which you sexually desired someone whom you also lust after in the real world? If so, then your dream was probably just mirroring your waking attraction to him or her. But if you dreamed that you felt desire for a stranger of the opposite sex, then you may have encountered your anima (the feminine aspects of your character, if you are a man) or your animus (the masculine aspects of your character, if you are a woman), possibly symbolizing your unconscious longing to unite or better integrate your masculine and feminine qualities. Also, since sex can be an act that leads to procreation, your dream self's sexual desire may have been an unconscious reference to the stirring of your creative powers. And if your dream depicted you actually having sex with someone to whom you are strongly attracted in the waking world, then your dream was probably a form of wish-fulfillment—though if you have been feeling unattractive or unlovable during your waking hours, your unconscious may also have been attempting to boost your self-esteem.

Negative Interpretations: Though erotic dreams are quite normal, if you are feeling sexually unfulfilled in the real world, then your sex drive may be compelled to seek its release in dreamland. And if you think sexual frustration may be the reason for your erotic dreams, the implications may not be entirely negative, as these dreams may offer you enlightenment or insight into your sexual desires. The same can be said if you had an erotic dream that disturbed or upset you, as it is important to remember that dreamland is a safe space in which the unconscious may experiment with your sexual urges. So if you are a heterosexual who dreamed that you lusted after someone of the same sex, your unconscious may have been exploring your feelings of, or else your curiosity about, same-sex sexual attraction; however, it is also possible that your dream was simply emphasizing the intensely intimate emotional relationship that you enjoy with this person. Many sexual dreams have a nonsexual meaning. For example, if you are a woman who feels guilty because you dreamed that you lusted after your brother-in-law (whom you like but you would never consider sleeping with), it may be that you would like to have a closer, more intimate (but nonsexual) relationship with him.

Related Dreams

pages 47, 51, 112,
242, 260 & 279

PITY

✶✶✶✶✶✶✶✶✶✶✶✶✶✶✶✶✶✶✶✶✶✶✶✶✶✶✶✶✶✶✶✶✶✶✶✶✶✶✶

In the world of dreams, we may take pity on someone, empathizing with or feeling compassion for them as a means of allowing ourselves to work through and let go of any past pain they may have caused us, thereby freeing ourselves from any further pain and anguish resulting from those old wounds.

Symbolic and Verbal Associations
‹ Compassion; kindness
‹ Sympathy and understanding
‹ Mercy; forgiveness
‹ Feeling sorry for oneself; throwing "a pity party"

Positive Interpretations: Were you surprised by a dream in which you took pity on, or felt compassion for, someone whom you may have deemed as undeserving of such consideration? For example, did your dream self feel pity for the cantankerous old woman who lives a few stories down in your building—a woman who is always bitterly complaining and yelling at everyone for things that you and others perceive as being trivial or irrelevant? Perhaps, in your dream, you helped her to carry her groceries up to her apartment. If so, then your dream may have been an unconscious attempt to make you empathize with your neighbor and to realize that she is troubled and suffering, which is why she treats others the way that she does. A similar meaning may apply if you dreamed that you forgave someone whom you hold a grudge against because of some past hurt that they caused you. For instance, you may have dreamed that your ex-husband—whom you haven't seen since your divorce from him, after he left you and the children with no money so that he could pursue his life with another woman—came to you and begged your forgiveness, saying what a terrible person he had been and how sorry he is, and that you took him in your arms and told him that you forgave him. In a scenario such as this, your unconscious was likely trying to help you to forgive your ex-husband as a way to let go of your own pain and to allow you to move on with your life—regardless of whether he really has repented for his wrongs in the waking world.

Negative Interpretations: In your dream, did you wish that others would recognize that you were suffering and take pity on you? For example, did you dream that you were sick or injured, and did you act in ways (such as whining or complaining) that you hoped would elicit the sympathy of those around you? And have you been moping around and feeling sorry for yourself in the waking world? Do you wish that those around you would pay more attention to you? If so, your dream was probably just mirroring this waking desire, which may be a sign of low self-esteem. And if you think this may be the case, is there a real problem you should address, or would others pay you more attention if you were to stop focusing on your own suffering and seek to interact with them in more positive ways?

Related Dreams
pages 76, 107, 122, 193, 260 & 272

My Pity Dreams

✶✶✶✶✶✶✶✶✶✶✶✶✶✶✶✶✶✶✶✶✶

Road to Nowhere
Sometimes our dreaming emotions change, indicating that our real feelings are also changing. Did you dream that your ex, who humiliated you by two-timing and then dumping you, had run out of gas and found himself stranded? If so, and your vengeful glee turned to pity, perhaps you've let go of your anger and have realized that he is the loser, not you.

THE EMOTIONAL ROLLERCOASTER

My Pride Dreams

----

* * * * * * * * * * * * * * * * * * *

Glittering Prizes

Did you receive the top prize in your dream graduation ceremony, even though you haven't yet submitted your dissertation in the waking world? Such a dream may have been a wish-fulfilling experience, but encouraging you to keep working toward your goal by giving you a taste of how proud you would feel should you achieve it could also have been an unconscious exercise in self-motivation.

PRIDE

reams of feeling proud may be forms of wish-fulfillment, or they may reflect the real-life pride that we take in ourselves, our talents, our accomplishments, and our ideas. Alternatively, these dreams may be meant to encourage us to pursue our interests and ambitions.

Symbolic and Verbal Associations
- Satisfaction; pleasure in one's accomplishments
- Goals and ambitions
- Self-esteem
- Arrogance; conceit

Positive Interpretations: Did you have a dream in which you felt exceedingly proud of something that you had accomplished? For instance, if you are a student and your dreaming mind depicted you graduating with the highest honors, your dream probably reflected your waking feelings of pride in your academic performance. Or if you dreamed that you were filled with pride when you were presented with a prize or trophy, your dream may have been reflecting your desire for your knowledge, skills, actions, and/or hard work to be acknowledged by others. It is also possible that such a dream was an unconscious attempt to encourage you to pursue your talents in whatever field or area your dream self was honored in. So if you dreamed that you received a prize for painting or sculpture, might your unconscious have been encouraging you to explore your artistic talents? These sorts of dreams may also be somewhat literal. For example, if you dreamed of being crowned, have you recently received a big promotion within the company that you work for? Alternatively, if you have no children in the real world, but you dreamed that you were very proud of a son or daughter, your dream child may have represented a cherished project or idea that you wish to protect and nurture in the waking world.

Negative Interpretations: If you feel that you are unacknowledged or underappreciated by others in the real world for your abilities or achievements, then your dream of being filled with pride when you were given an award may have been an unconscious attempt to compensate for the lack of rewards, respect, or acknowledgment that you receive during your waking hours. Likewise, if you dreamed that you gave a magnificent stage performance and that you felt great pride when the audience rewarded you with boisterous applause and a standing ovation, your unconscious may have been compensating you for others' inability to recognize or refusal to celebrate your waking talents. Or, finally, did you have a dream in which you were repulsed or offended by someone else's smugness or self-importance? If so—particularly if this person was a stranger of the same sex as you—might he or she have represented your own waking qualities of arrogance and conceit?

Related Dreams
pages 50, 90, 129, 195, 198 & 245

RELIEF

✳✳✳✳✳✳✳✳✳✳✳✳✳✳✳✳✳✳✳✳✳✳✳✳✳✳✳✳✳✳✳✳✳✳✳✳✳

THE EMOTIONAL ROLLERCOASTER

When we suffer physically or emotionally, the sudden absence of suffering may seem like the sweetest, most pleasurable sensation possible. Sometimes the unconscious may provide us with a temporary relief from our suffering in the form of a compensatory or wish-fulfillment dream in which we are released from whatever pain we have been enduring.

Symbolic and Verbal Associations
- Release; liberation
- Respite or reprieve; relief from pain or mental anguish
- Taking a break or a rest
- Receiving help or assistance

Positive Interpretations: Did a dream cause a feeling of relief to wash over you? If so, what did your dream self feel relieved from? If you are in some legal trouble in the real world, for instance, and you dreamed that it was all just a big mistake, then you most likely experienced a wish-fulfilling, escapist fantasy that your unconscious concocted in order to provide you with some temporary peace of mind. Likewise, if you suffer from chronic pain during your waking hours and you had a dream in which the pain was miraculously taken away, your unconscious was probably attempting both to fulfill your sincere wish for your misery to end and to give you a temporary respite from your suffering. If there is a daunting load of work before you in the waking world, did you have a dream in which someone came and offered to help you? In this case, your unconscious may have been signifying that this person is able to offer you some sort of assistance in the real world (though not necessarily in the way that was depicted in your dream). For example, if you are remodeling your home and you have been saving money by doing much of the labor yourself—a task that has proven much harder than you ever thought it would be—did you dream that your uncle, a retired carpenter, came to help you? If so, your uncle may not be willing or able to help you to actually do the work on your house, but he may be able to give you some good advice that will make your job a lot easier! In all of these examples, the purpose of your unconscious may also have been to hearten and encourage you in your time of trouble.

Negative Interpretations: If you had a dream in which you were relieved from some pain or suffering that you have been experiencing in the real world, you may have felt somewhat disappointed and saddened upon waking and realizing that it was only a dream. If this is the case, you should ask yourself what is causing you to suffer, and if there is anything that you can do to change your situation in the real world. For instance, if you are suffering from drug or alcohol addiction, and you dreamed that you had beaten your addiction and were living "clean," your unconscious may have been encouraging you to seek help in freeing yourself from your addiction in the waking world.

Related Dreams
pages 56, 144, 248, 254, 257 & 258

My Relief Dreams

✳ ✳ ✳ ✳ ✳ ✳ ✳ ✳ ✳ ✳ ✳ ✳ ✳ ✳ ✳ ✳ ✳ ✳

Oasis

If you dreamed that you were lost in the desert, parched and desperate for water, and then saw an oasis, relief must have flooded over your dreaming self. The simplest explanation for a dream like this could be literal thirst. Alternatively, the oasis may have symbolized something of which you feel deprived in waking life, like someone's affection, and thus potential relief.

My Sadness Dreams

✱✱✱✱✱✱✱✱✱✱✱✱✱✱✱✱✱✱

Little Girl Lost

Did you dream that you were a child again, distraught over the loss of your beloved pet? If you have suffered a recent loss, your unconscious may have made an earlier painful experience agonizingly acute once more as a reminder that you eventually came to terms with your grief. Could your dream have been encouraging you to draw hope for the future from the past?

SADNESS

✱✱✱✱✱✱✱✱✱✱✱✱✱✱✱✱✱✱✱✱✱✱✱✱✱✱✱✱✱✱✱✱✱✱✱✱✱✱✱

Though they may leave us weeping, dreams of being sad are not always completely negative. On the contrary, these dreams may serve some very important functions, such as informing us about the nature or cause of our waking unhappiness, bringing repressed feelings out into the open, and providing an outlet for buried emotional pain.

Symbolic and Verbal Associations
- Grief
- Melancholy
- Depression
- Loss
- Emotional release; catharsis

Positive Interpretations: Did you have a dream in which you were so overcome with sadness that when you woke up you were weeping uncontrollably? If so, it is probable that there is some cause for sadness or grief in your waking life, though you may have repressed your feelings rather than allowing yourself to face them head on. Since emotional release is important to mental health, your unconscious may have been providing a cathartic outlet for your sadness via your dreams; this may be especially true if you are a person who rarely, if ever, allows yourself to cry during your waking hours. And, though you may have woken from your dream with a feeling of melancholy, you probably also felt somewhat relieved.

Negative Interpretations: Sometimes our dreams may enlighten as to the underlying reason or reasons for our feelings of sadness or depression, especially when we have pushed these painful feelings out of our waking consciousness. Can you remember what caused your dream self to feel sad? Dreams of grieving for someone who has actually died can usually be taken at face value. However, there may be a number of explanations for a dream in which you grieved for someone who is still alive. For instance, your unconscious may have chosen this person to represent something in your life that you feel you have lost, or else something that you'd like to rid yourself of, or it may be that you fear that your relationship with this person is in jeopardy; however, if the person you dreamed of is actually ill, or if you feel they are in some sort of danger, your dream may have been your unconscious's way of trying to prepare you for the worst. (For more on this, see this chapter's entry on bereavement.) If you dreamed that you were saddened by having failed to achieve a goal or having missed an important opportunity, your dream may also have been fairly literal. Whatever the specifics of your dream sadness, you will probably find it helpful to try to think through its meaning rationally, during your waking hours. Finally, if you often find yourself grief-stricken or crying in your dreams, your unconscious may be highlighting a general depression, in which case you should consider seeking professional help.

Related Dreams

pages 92, 193, 252, 254, 266 & 271

SHAME

★★★★★★★★★★★★★★★★★★★★★★★★★★★★★★★★★★★★★

S hame is a means that society uses to keep individuals from acting "out of line," so to speak. And, likewise, when our dream selves feel ashamed, we may have done something in the waking world that we unconsciously feel guilty about.

Symbolic and Verbal Associations
- Guilt about wrong actions
- Disgrace; dishonor
- Embarrassment; humiliation
- Ridicule and derision
- Insecurity; feeling out of place

Positive Interpretations: If your dreaming mind cast you into a situation in which you acted in a way that, upon waking reflection, caused you to feel ashamed, it is important to remember that the language of dreams is not always literal. For example, did you dream that you had sex with your sister—something that would cause you great shame if you had done it in the real world, and that causes you to feel ashamed even knowing that you merely dreamed about it? If so, you can rest assured that your dream was probably not pointing to a real-life attraction to your sister; instead, there are two likely explanations: your unconscious may have been mirroring the intensely close relationship that you have with your sister, or it may have been highlighting your desire to cultivate a closer, more intimate (nonsexual) relationship with her.

Negative Interpretations: In your dream, were you transported back to the sixth grade, to when your teacher made you sit in the corner wearing a dunce's cap after you failed to turn in your homework assignment? If so, might your dream have been triggered by some public shaming that you have recently been put through during your waking hours? For instance, has your neighborhood association recently sent around a list of members who have failed to pay their annual dues, and was your name at the top of the list? If so, your dream may have been an unconscious reminder for you to pay up what you owe, which will both alleviate your conscience and help to remove some of the stigma that you may feel has been placed upon you. Or, in your dream, had you committed some atrocious crime that you were being publicly punished for? Perhaps you dreamed that you were locked in medieval stocks, in full view of passersby. If so, do you know why your dream self was being shamed in this way? If it was for public drunkenness, are you feeling embarrassed about your recent tendency to drink too much at social events? Or have you committed some transgression that your unconscious is attempting to make you feel more remorse about? Alternatively, if you had a dream in which you found yourself in a shame-inducing predicament, such as being inappropriately clothed or naked in public, this may indicate that you are feeling insecure or out of place, exposed, or vulnerable, or that you are worried that you are an object of ridicule and derision.

My Shame Dreams

★★★★★★★★★★★★★★★★★★★★

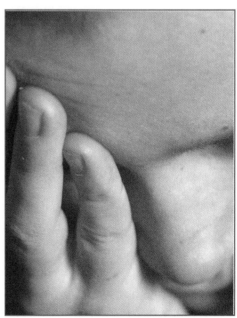

Hiding Your Face
If you felt an overwhelming sense of shame in your dream, but cannot remember what made you cringe, it may be that you have self-esteem issues in the waking world that are not necessarily of your making. Ask yourself whether you really deserve to feel shamefaced, or is someone telling you that you should be ashamed of yourself in order to victimize or control you?

Related Dreams
pages 176, 193, 224, 237, 256 & 260

My Tenderness Dreams

....

....

....

....

....

....

....

....

* * * * * * * * * * * * * * * * * * *

A Maternal Embrace

If you watched a mother embrace her baby in dreamland, could the baby have symbolized you, and your yearning for the love and support that your mother gave you when you were a youngster? Or if you are the mother of a teenager who shrugs off your tender hugs, could your dream have expressed your nostalgia for the days when you could cuddle your "baby"?

TENDERNESS

* *

In the world of dreams, expressions of tenderness, such as touching and kissing, may highlight affectionate feelings that you didn't realize you had for someone, or else a longing for greater emotional intimacy during a time when you are feeling isolated or lonely.

Symbolic and Verbal Associations
- Unconditional affection and love
- Gentleness
- Warmth and comfort
- A sense of wellbeing
- Emotional support
- Relaxation and pampering

Positive Interpretations: Did you have a dream that depicted you expressing your affection for someone by giving them a tender hug? Or, in your dream, did you enjoy having your neck and shoulders massaged by someone—not because it gave you any sexual pleasure, but simply because it made you feel relaxed and comforted and gave you an overall sensation of wellbeing? Either of these dream scenarios may signify your tender feelings for the person whom you dreamed of touching or being touched by, even though you may not be consciously aware of your fondness for him or her (whether this entails feelings of love, friendship, or admiration). Alternatively, by portraying you in a relaxed and tranquil state, your unconscious may have been hinting at your need to slow down and take the time to pamper yourself physically, mentally, and emotionally. And if your dream depicted you touching or massaging someone tenderly, your unconscious may also have been mirroring your feelings of sympathy for this person and your desire to comfort him or her; the specific dream scenario, together with this person's waking-life situation, will help you to decide if this latter interpretation may apply.

Negative Interpretations: Did you dream that you were blissfully engulfed in the warm and gentle embrace of a friend, acquaintance, or loved one? Or, in your dream, did you witness two other people tenderly touching and embracing one another, and did their display of love and affection for each other cause you to feel envious or excluded? These sorts of dreams often signify a basic need and desire for the unconditional love, affection, comfort, and support that we take pleasure in when we are the objects of love (whether this love is platonic or romantic). If physical contact and emotional intimacy are lacking in your current life, your dream of being tenderly touched may have been a form of wish fulfillment, as well as an unconscious attempt to compensate for that which is missing from your waking hours. Your dream may also be a sign that your levels of self-esteem and self-worth are running low and need boosting with the reassuring, unconditional love and affection of those who are close to you.

Related Dreams

pages 34, 89, 113, 116, 266 & 267

CHAPTER 14
HUMAN ACTIVITIES

A dream of indulging in an activity that you enjoy, but haven't
had much time for, in the waking world, may have been a
wish-fulfillment dream. Otherwise, your unconscious may have
been urging you to undertake that activity when you awake and
thus get it off your conscience, be it weeding your neglected garden
or making that difficult phone call. Or could the dream activity
have had symbolic significance? Could a dream of playing a team
sport have been signaling the need to interact as a team with
your colleagues during your working hours in order to beat
"the competition," for instance?

My Acting Dreams

✱ ✱ ✱ ✱ ✱ ✱ ✱ ✱ ✱ ✱ ✱ ✱ ✱ ✱ ✱ ✱ ✱

Silent Movie

If your dream scene was played out in silence by a mime artist, the protagonist's lack of words and exaggerated gestures could have referred to someone whose voice is not being heard and who is trying to attract attention to something important in the real world. Were you the mute actor, or were you watching someone else? Can you remember the message being acted out?

ACTING

✱✱✱✱✱✱✱✱✱✱✱✱✱✱✱✱✱✱✱✱✱✱✱✱✱✱✱✱✱✱✱✱✱✱✱

Because acting is an art of illusion, a dream that cast you in the role of an actor may have been making a comment on how well you are presenting your chosen image or persona to your real-world "audience."

Symbolic and Verbal Associations
- Drama
- Illusion; deception; the world of "make believe"
- Image; persona
- The need to "get your act together"

Positive Interpretations: Each of us does a certain amount of role-playing during the course of our day-to-day lives. That is, from time to time, we all project a persona that isn't completely faithful to our true selves. We may do this for a number of reasons—to make people like us, or to make ourselves appear powerful, or weak, or smart, or to seem to possess any other characteristic that we feel will benefit us in any given situation. So did you dream that you stepped out into the bright, hot spotlights of the stage and that you began to act out the role of the main character in a theatrical drama? If so, how did the audience react to your performance? Your dream may have been an unconscious statement about how well your audience is receiving your waking act. If you had them "eating out of your hand," for instance, then you may be playing a convincing role in the waking world. When interpreting your dream, it is important to note that the part that you were playing, and the scene in which you were acting, are likely to parallel the real-life situation on which your dream was commenting. And if your dream depicted you as being unwilling to walk out onto the stage and perform your part, might this be because you are reluctant to "put on an act," or to attempt to deceive others by pretending that you are something that you are not, in the waking world? (Of course, a dream like this may also refer to your dislike of being the center of attention—especially if you have to deliver a speech or chair a meeting in the near future.)

Negative Interpretations: In your dream of stage-acting, did your audience heckle and boo you—or worse, pelt you with tomatoes? If so, your unconscious may have been telling you that the image or character that you are attempting to present to the world is not very believable. Or, in your dream, did you forget your lines? If so, your dream may signify that you are suffering from a loss of confidence in the waking world, or that you feel unprepared (or unrehearsed) for the role that you are being called upon to play. And if someone helped you out by whispering your lines to you, you may be unconsciously aware that, if you are to succeed in pulling off your role, you will need someone else's assistance. Alternatively, your dream may have been an unconscious reminder that your life is not a dress rehearsal, and it is therefore important to "get your act together," or to organize yourself better in line with your goals in the real world.

Related Dreams

pages 66, 125, 196, 202, 243 & 240

CLIMBING

When we climb something, we are ascending toward a higher level, usually, but not necessarily always, toward a definite goal. In the language of dreams, the meaning of climbing is dependent on what you were climbing, how large the scale was, the ease or difficulty of your journey, the location of your end goal, and whether or not you reached it.

My Climbing Dreams

Symbolic and Verbal Associations
- Working toward a goal
- "Setting your sights high": aspirations
- Ascending the "social" or "corporate" ladders
- Spiritual elevation; the path of enlightenment
- An "uphill struggle"; a near-impossible task

Positive Interpretations: Dreams of climbing are likely to do with a desire to attain a higher professional, social, or spiritual status. In your dream, were you climbing a ladder, a flight of stairs, a hill, or a mountain? Or were you making your ascent in an elevator or on an escalator? If you dreamed of climbing a ladder, this may refer to either the "corporate" or the "social" ladder. Each rung of a dream ladder and each step in a dream flight of stairs is likely to represent a step toward your ultimate aspiration. A dream ladder may also be a phallic symbol, denoting masculine drive and power—qualities that you may feel that you will need to adopt in order to succeed. If you dreamed of climbing a hill, this may signify a longer and more difficult challenge than that presented by a ladder or stairs, while climbing toward the peak of a mountain may represent the ultimate test of your abilities, strength, stamina, and will. A dream of ascending may also refer to spiritual enlightenment—even if you dreamed of making your ascent in an elevator or an escalator! For instance, depending on your religious background and beliefs, you may have dreamed that you were ascending to heaven. If you are familiar with the stories of the Bible, you may have dreamed of climbing "Jacob's ladder," which the angels used to travel from heaven to Earth and back again.

An Uphill Struggle

In your dream, were you feeling exhausted, even doomed, as you slogged up a snowbound slope with a heavy burden and no end in sight? And were you alone in your apparently hopeless predicament? If so, and you are not actually contemplating a risky, extreme-sport vacation, ask yourself whether you have taken on an impossible task in waking life that is wearying you.

Negative Interpretations: As your dream self was climbing, did you get stuck, slip, fall, become weary, or even stop? Did you face your uphill struggle with confidence and endurance, or with trepidation and a defeatist attitude? Was your goal continually within your sights, or was it often shrouded in mist? Did you encounter obstacles, such as gullies, ice, or fallen rocks? If so, how did you tackle them? And were you able to overcome the obstacles and carry on, or did they stop you in your tracks? If you had a climbing companion, did he or she help or hinder your progress? Examining all of these elements of your dream will tell you much about the nature of your approach toward your goal—how well you are doing, how far you may have to go, and, ultimately, your relative chances of success.

Related Dreams

pages 53, 141, 160, 195, 247 & 374

My Communicating Dreams

✶ ✶ ✶ ✶ ✶ ✶ ✶ ✶ ✶ ✶ ✶ ✶ ✶ ✶ ✶ ✶ ✶

Bolt From the Blue

If you dreamed that you got a call from some-one with whom you have long since lost touch, or who is no longer alive, be wary of con-cluding that the caller was trying to commu-nicate something to you. Perhaps your unconscious conjured him or her up to air a sensitive issue that you are finding it difficult to discuss with others in waking life.

COMMUNICATING

✶ ✶

Though all of our dreams can convey messages, sometimes the unconscious sends us its dream message in a form that we can readily recognize, such as a letter, a fax, an e-mail, an instant message, or a telephone call.

Symbolic and Verbal Associations
- The anticipation of receiving news (good news and bad news)
- Speaking or writing "in code"
- Something that is "in writing" or "on the record": a formal promise or agreement
- Getting your "wires crossed"
- Sending "a message in a bottle"

Positive Interpretations: Did you dream that you were poised over a sheet of paper, pen in hand? In the language of dreams, a blank page may symbolize fresh opportuni-ties, and a pen a means by which to express your thoughts. What were you planning to write? If it was a letter to your long-lost friend, your unconscious may have been urg-ing you to make contact with him in the real world. Or was it a poem? If so, might your unconscious be encouraging you to nurture your artistic side? A dream of sitting in front of a blank computer screen may have held a similar message, but if you associate com-puters with your job, then your unconscious may have been making a reference to a work task. If you dreamed of anxiously waiting to receive a letter from someone, your unconscious may have picked up on this person's desire to communicate with you, or else on your desire to receive some news from him or her. Any of these interpretations may also apply to a dream of writing or receiving a fax, e-mail, or instant message, though the urgency of the message may be different. A dream of communicating tele-pathically with someone may denote the intense closeness of your relationship.

Negative Interpretations: Did you dream that your mother wrote you a postcard in shaky script? The handwriting in any dream communication may be an unconscious comment on the sender's mental state—in this case, possibly your mother's vulnerabil-ity. A typewritten message may imply a more impersonal connection between the sender and the recipient. If you have recently applied to a school, did you dream of getting a rejection letter? If so, your unconscious may simply have been mirroring your fears. Or did you dream that you ranted angrily about someone in an e-mail that you accidentally sent to everyone in your address book? If so, your unconscious may have been warning you to restrain your temper and your tendency to act impulsively. If you had a dream phone conversation with your aunt in which you became annoyed with her for not lis-tening to you, your unconscious may have been encouraging you to be more assertive. Finally, if you dreamed of receiving a message in code, your unconscious may have been highlighting the importance of secrecy in your communications with someone, or else to your difficulty in understanding this person in the waking world.

Related Dreams

pages 110, 222, 263, 285 & 292

CREATIVE ACTIVITIES

When the unconscious mind depicts us engaging in creative activities, it may be urging us to pursue the interest in the particular art, hobby, or craft that your dream self enjoyed. However, the unconscious may also use a creative activity as a metaphor for some other type of inspirational action that it is encouraging us to take in waking life.

Symbolic and Verbal Associations
‹ Beauty and pleasure
‹ Productivity; mental fertility
‹ Building or assembling the pieces of one's life
‹ Emotional release; art as therapy
‹ Inspiration; imagination; innovation

Positive Interpretations: Did you dream that you had written a best-selling novel, or that you were creating a beautiful painting or sculpture? If so, and if you have literary or artistic inclinations, your unconscious may have been urging you to explore your creative talents. In your dream, were you engrossed in the work of sewing a quilt? If so, and if this is a project that you have been putting off for lack of time, or if quilting is an activity that you have been meaning to take up, then your unconscious may have been trying to tell you that now is the perfect time to do so. Otherwise, if neither of these interpretations seems to fit, might your unconscious have been calling for you to piece or join together the different, varied aspects of your life into a more harmonious whole? If your dream depicted you as working in a quilting bee, with other people, your unconscious may have been encouraging you to work together with others on a waking project or endeavor. Did you dream of building a tree house? Because dream homes often represent the whole self, might your unconscious have been reflecting your desire to "raise yourself" to a higher, more spiritual (and perhaps ascetic) existence? Or did your dream refer to your desire to have a personal sanctuary or hideaway?

Negative Interpretations: If you dreamed of watching an artist at work—especially if you felt envious as you looked on—your unconscious may have been reflecting your frustration at your inability, for whatever reason, to express your own creativity, and, at the same time, encouraging you to release your own "artist within." But if you had a dream in which you painted or drew a picture or took a photo that was skewed or distorted, what was the image that you were trying to create or capture? The message from your unconscious may have been that you have a skewed or distorted viewpoint or opinion of this subject. Alternatively, if you dreamed that you were a movie director, and that you cursed and hollered at your cast and crew, do you use your creative energy and talents in an effort to control those around you in a tyrannical way, in order to make them do your bidding in the waking world?

My Creative Activities Dreams

----

* * * * * * * * * * * * * * * * * * *

Artist's Block
A dream that focused on brushes laid idle on an artist's palette could signify an interruption to a creative process. Were you in the midst of, or trying to start, a dream painting, but found that you lacked inspiration, or could not replicate the image in your mind's eye? If so, try to identify what is blocking your imagination during your waking hours.

Related Dreams
pages 91, 171, 200, 206, 258 & 283

DANCING

A dream of dancing may be a simple reference to the joy that we feel in our waking life, or be highlighting a romantic attraction to someone with whom we danced in dreamland. A dream in which we danced with others may be a commentary on whether we are "in" or "out" of step with those around us.

My Dancing Dreams

....
....
....
....
....
....
....
....

★ ★ ★ ★ ★ ★ ★ ★ ★ ★ ★ ★ ★ ★ ★ ★ ★ ★

Dancing Queen

Are you relatively shy, or do you feel as though you have "two left feet," and yet, in your dream, were you sashaying confidently on the dance floor, scantily clad and thoroughly enjoying the attention of your fellow partygoers or clubbers—or perhaps of one special onlooker? Depending on your audience and surroundings, this dream may have been a deeply pleasurable, erotic experience.

Symbolic and Verbal Associations
- Joy; celebration
- Sensuousness; eroticism
- Dancing "cheek to cheek" with someone
- Being "in step" with someone; working in unison
- Stepping "out of line": failure to conform

Positive Interpretations: Did you have a dream in which you were dancing all by yourself? Perhaps, in your dream, you were leaping and spinning like a ballerina, delighting in performing such wonderful moves that you never knew you were capable of? In the language of dreams, dancing on your own—with no audience and no one to please but yourself—may symbolize your waking feeling of joyousness. But if you dreamed that you were dancing with your eye on someone to whom you were attracted—and perhaps you hoped to use your sensuous moves to lure him or her into dancing with you, "cheek to cheek"—then your dream may have had an erotic meaning. Did you recognize the person for whom you were dancing? It may be that your unconscious has picked up on your waking attraction to this person, whether or not you are consciously aware of your feelings. And if your dream depicted you and someone else ballroom dancing together, who was your partner? And how well did the two of you dance together? If, in your dream, the two of you were dancing together so fluently that it seemed as though you were one dancer, then your dream may have been highlighting someone who is, or whom you wish to be, your partner in real life—be it a spouse, a business partner, or a good friend. In fact, any time that you dream of dancing "in step" with another person or persons, the implication may be that you are working in pleasurable harmony with this person or these persons in the waking world. Likewise, if your dream depicted you country-line-dancing with members of your family, your unconscious may have been commenting on your tendency to dance in line with your family's values or to conform with "the common line" of family thought.

Negative Interpretations: If you dreamed of dancing "out of step" with someone, your unconscious may have been pointing to the disharmony in your relationship in the waking world. And, similarly, if you dreamed of dancing "out of line" with others, your unconscious may have been making an inference about your inability or refusal to conform with those around you, or else to your habit of "stepping out of line" in your social circle, familial group, or workplace.

Related Dreams

pages 112, 119, 202, 214, 245 & 261

FIGHTING

★ ★

Like real ones, dream fights can vary greatly in nature and level of seriousness—from arguments, to fistfights, to conflicts with weapons and out-and-out warfare. Such clashes are likely to highlight a conflict in the real world, including an internal battle or spiritual crisis.

Symbolic and Verbal Associations
- Conflict; violence
- The attempt to impose one's will on another
- Opposing opinions or ideologies
- An internal battle; indecision

Positive Interpretations: A dream of fighting with someone may simply have been mirroring your waking dislike of this person, his or her dislike of you, or your mutual antipathy toward each other. In this case, your dream may have served a safety-valve purpose, allowing you a safe outlet to express your anger and frustration—especially if it was you who instigated and dominated the fight. If you dreamed of fighting with a stranger, especially if he or she was of the same sex as you, then your adversary may have been yourself, thereby highlighting an internal conflict. And if you think that this interpretation may apply, considering what you were fighting over or what was said during the fight may give you a clue as to your inner battle. Did your dream fight end peacefully? If so, your unconscious may have been indicating that it is possible for you and your opponent (which may be yourself) to come to such a peaceful resolution in the waking world; the specifics of your dream may give you clues about the best or most likely way of doing so, whether it involves surrender, compromise, or arbitration.

Negative Interpretations: If you dreamed of fighting with someone with whom you have a relatively peaceful relationship in the real world, then your unconscious may have been alerting you to your feelings of anger toward this person (which you may have buried because you consider them to be ugly or inappropriate), or else to this person's hostility toward you. In any dream of fighting, the level of severity of the fight will denote both the intensity of the waking battle and the difficulty of your ongoing struggle, and the outcome may indicate how well you are faring in your real-world conflict (as well as your likely chances of winning). But if your dream fight wasn't settled, the implication may be that the conflict represented is likely to be ongoing in the real world. Did you dream of fighting in a battle or full-scale war between "savages" and an ultramodern force? If so, these armies may have been warring aspects of yourself. So whose side were you on? If it was the "savages," your true allegiance is likely to lie with your heart, or your instincts. If, however, you fought on the side of the ultramodern army, it may be that you tend to follow the rule of your head, or your conscious, logical mind. A dream battle may also symbolize a conflict between two groups of people.

Related Dreams

pages 34, 82, 93, 106, 114 & 253

My Fighting Dreams

★ ★ ★ ★ ★ ★ ★ ★ ★ ★ ★ ★ ★ ★ ★ ★ ★ ★

Schoolyard Bully

In your dream, were you transported back to your schooldays, into the presence of the bully who tormented you then? If you fought back in your dream, perhaps you have now overcome your fear of the bully, or have grown in confidence. But if you were the bully, perhaps it's time to acknowledge this aspect of yourself and to mend your ways in real life.

My Games Dreams

✱ ✱

Playing the Odds

If your dream depicted you playing a game of chance, do you feel that you are losing control of some important aspect of your life, or leaving decisions to the hand of fate? And if you dreamed that you were gambling, are you considering risking everything in the waking world, perhaps by investing in a venture (financial or emotional) in which the odds are stacked against you?

GAMES

✱✱✱

In the world of dreams, games can denote intellectual challenges in the waking world, or how well we are playing the hand that fate has dealt us.

Symbolic and Verbal Associations
- A challenge
- How well you are "playing your hand"
- Intellectual performance
- Formulating a "game plan"
- Mastery of a "winning strategy"

Positive Interpretations: Did you dream of playing a game of strategy and intellect, such as chess? Both your opponent and the game pieces may bear significance. For instance, the white and black pieces may denote benevolence and malevolence, respectively. The king may have represented either yourself or your partner—the center of your world, who is in need of defending at this time. If your dream focused on a pawn, might your unconscious have been alluding to the other meaning for the word "pawn," which is someone who is manipulated by another? Or if you dreamed of playing cards, did you "play your cards right"? Whatever game you played, did you devise a "winning strategy"? Did you feel confident because you had a powerful hand or because you knew that you had "an ace up your sleeve" (or a secret weapon)? If your dream focused on a particular card, could it have symbolized a person or a quality that has relevance to your waking situation? For example, hearts can denote love; diamonds, aspirations; and clubs, finances. And if, in your dream, you won a fortune on a bet, your unconscious may have been encouraging you to set caution aside and to take a risk on someone or something (but not necessarily a financial risk) in your waking world.

Negative Interpretations: In your dream game, were you on the defensive? Did your opponent confuse you with unforeseen tactics? If so, your unconscious may have been mirroring your performance in some aspect of your life, although your dream may also have simply reflected your fears and anxieties. Did a dream game turn unpleasant when you accused your opponent of cheating? If so, might this person be deceiving you in the real world? Or are you the one who is doing the deceiving? And if it was time for you to "lay your cards on the table," was your unconscious encouraging you to "come clean" with those around you? Could a dream that demonstrated the "domino effect" have been warning that an action that you are contemplating is likely to have widespread repercussions? If you dreamed of the ace of spades, which some people consider to be an omen of disaster, your unconscious might have been warning you of some sort of danger that it has detected. Aces may also symbolize obstacles. And if you pulled the card of the joker, did this symbolize the archetypal trickster, or a mischievous person who is "playing games" with you during your waking hours?

Related Dreams

pages 114, 131, 190, 250, 276 & 287

GARDENING

✦✦✦

Perhaps for obvious reasons, dream gardens are likely to represent personal growth, while dreams of gardening may also reflect a waking creative endeavor.

Symbolic and Verbal Associations
- Personal growth
- Potential
- Sowing the "seeds" of love, wisdom, change, etc.
- Overgrowth; neglect
- Virulence

Positive Interpretations: In symbolic terms, the earth is associated with bounty and fertility; it is the source of sustenance, stability, and security. Did you dream of tilling or cultivating the soil, sowing a seed, or watering the plants in your garden? If so, can you draw a parallel with your waking situation? For instance, if your dream depicted you planting a seed, might the seed have symbolized the child that you and your partner are hoping to conceive in real life, and the rich, dark soil, the physical and emotional nurturing that you would give to your child, allowing him or her to grow and thrive in a loving and warm family environment? If having a child is not on your agenda, could your dream have been referring to an intellectual or creative seed that you have recently sown in the fertile ground of your imagination? If you dreamed that the plants in your garden were flourishing with an abundance of colors, smells, and textures, your unconscious may have been suggesting that your waking ventures (perhaps your children, if you are a parent) are thriving, or else that your personality has begun to flourish and bloom, giving you a deep sense of satisfaction and happiness.

Negative Interpretations: Were the flowers and plants in your dream garden arranged in a carefully regimented manner? Or did your garden appear meager and sterile, with no blooms at all? If so, are you so controlling and strict in your waking life that you quash any potential for creativity or fun? Or do you have a tendency to "nip yourself in the bud," thereby preventing your personality from flowering or achieving its fullest potential? Alternatively, if your garden was overgrown and full of weeds, might this be a sign that you have been neglecting to take proper care of yourself or to nourish your potential? Or did you dream that you were trying to scratch out a garden in a patch of dusty, barren-looking soil? If so, perhaps the demands of your current waking life are depleting your emotional and physical reserves. Did you dream that the flowers in your garden began to droop and that the earth that should have been sustaining them was arid and parched? Because water symbolizes emotions and the unconscious, and the earth, stability, your dream may have signaled that you have been neglecting your emotional life and that your wilting relationships are in urgent need of nurturing if they are to survive.

My Gardening Dreams

....
....
....
....
....
....
....
....
....

✦ ✦ ✦ ✦ ✦ ✦ ✦ ✦ ✦ ✦ ✦ ✦ ✦ ✦ ✦ ✦ ✦ ✦ ✦

Invasive Growth

In your dream, did you react with horror when you saw that your normally well-tended garden had been overwhelmed by a fast-growing weed that was strangling your vegetables and plants? If so, the real-world reference may have been to your new boss, whose jarring working style is ruining your pet project or performance, or perhaps to a pushy new member of your circle of friends.

Related Dreams
pages 91, 159, 185, 358, 360 & 368

My Jumping Dreams

----

* * * * * * * * * * * * * * * * * * *

A Bold Leap

Leaping across a deep ravine in dreamland may symbolize a conscious decision to take action despite the grave risk that it poses. In your dream, did you soar confidently over the chasm, or were you infused with white-hot fear? And were you making a "leap in the dark," into unknown territory? The answers to these questions should provide clues as to the waking-world parallel.

JUMPING

* *

In the waking world, jumping is a way of moving from one position to another, and also a means by which we may clear a hurdle. In terms of dream symbolism, jumping may signify rapid progression toward an ambition or goal.

Symbolic and Verbal Associations
- "Jumping for joy"
- A need to "get hopping," or working; "jumping to it"
- Jumping hurdles
- Advancing "by leaps and bounds"; making "a quantum leap"
- A "leap in the dark"; "making the leap"

Positive Interpretations: If you dreamed of jumping, your dream probably had little or nothing to do with physical movement in the waking world (unless you are physically unable to jump during your waking hours, in which case your dream may have been a form of compensation or wish fulfillment). In interpreting your dream, it is important to take a careful look at its different aspects. First of all, do you know why you were jumping, or what you were jumping toward? For example, if your dream depicted you "jumping for joy," is there something in your waking life that is a cause for celebration? If not, it is also possible that your unconscious purpose was to comfort and hearten you during a difficult or unhappy time in your waking life. Or, in your dream, did you see yourself "jumping ahead"? If so, what was the goal that you were pursuing? Did your body perform its leap effortlessly, as if you were literally flying through the air? If so, your unconscious was probably commenting that your progress toward a waking goal is proceeding swiftly and smoothly. In your dream, did you feel ecstatic or triumphant when you finally reached your destination? If so, you probably feel fairly confident that your goal is a worthy one, and that its attainment will bring you happiness.

Negative Interpretations: As you were leaping toward your dream goal, did you begin to feel tired and breathless, so that you felt you couldn't go on? Did you stumble as you tried to clear a hurdle? Or did you fall short of your target? If the answer to any of these questions is "yes," then it is likely that your unconscious was using your dream to warn you of difficulties that you may encounter as you advance toward your goal. And if, in your dream, you felt somewhat disappointed or let down when you finally reached your ultimate destination, your unconscious may have been trying to prepare you for the sense of anticlimax that you might feel when you reach your real-world goal. Finally, if you dreamed that you were in despair, so that you were about to jump off a bridge or a building, do you feel as if you can no longer bear your problems in the waking world, and do you often wish that you could just give it all up? If so, your dream may have been expressing your real-world feelings of depression, in which case your unconscious was probably urging you to acknowledge your sadness and perhaps to seek help.

Related Dreams

pages 53, 195, 214, 225, 257 & 261

LISTENING TO MUSIC

* *

Because music is such a powerful tool for expressing emotion, any dream in which you were listening to music is likely to have been a reference to your emotional reaction to a waking situation. When interpreting your dream, it is important to take into account the type of music that you were listening to, as well as how it made you feel.

Symbolic and Verbal Associations
(Relaxation
(Emotional expression
(Inner harmony; being "in tune" with the world around you
(Feelings of being "out of tune" with yourself or others; internal discord

Positive Interpretations: Did the sound of music cause your dream self to feel great joy? If so, is there something that you are happy about in your waking life? You may be able to make a connection between the type of music that you heard and a real-life situation or feeling. For instance, if you were moved by a beautiful melody in dreamland, the melody may have expressed your waking sense of inner harmony, or your feeling of being "in tune" with your environment and those around you. If you dreamed of lying in a lovely meadow in springtime, listening to the sweet sounds of the birds in the trees, might this have reflected the sweetness of your waking hours, perhaps because you have recently received some uplifting news (as in "a little bird told you" something good)? Or if you only listen to rap music in the waking world, did you have a dream in which you took pleasure in listening to a round of Irish jigs and reels—the music that your parents always listened to when you were growing up? If so, your unconscious may have been highlighting your desire to "return to your roots" or to reconnect with your family and its traditions in the waking world. And if you dreamed of listening intently to music that you would never think of tuning into in the waking world, such as a classical symphony, might your unconscious have been urging you to "open your ears" to other people's viewpoints?

Negative Interpretations: If you dreamed that the sound of clashing, disharmonious notes filled your ears, your unconscious may have been reflecting your internal emotional discord, or else your feeling of being "out of tune" with others. Did you dream of wincing with displeasure as you listened to your child practicing the violin, and did you clandestinely cover your ears in order to shut out the cacophonous squalling that her sawing produced? If so, it is likely that your unconscious mind was making a reference to your child's constant whining and the effect that it is having on your nerves during your waking hours. Alternatively, if you are a lapsed Christian, did you dream of being overwhelmed by the deafening sound of a church organ? If so, might your unconscious have been mirroring your waking fear that you have offended God by disobeying fundamental principles of the Church's teachings?

My Listening to Music Dreams

----

* * * * * * * * * * * * * * * * * * *

Private Performance
Did you dream that you were wearing headphones, immersed in a world of your own and enjoying your favorite music? A dream like this may have signified that you crave privacy, especially if your possessive friend or interfering relation is refusing to respect your emotional boundaries in the waking world. Or were you tuning into music in order to avoid hearing something or someone?

Related Dreams
pages 42, 261, 263, 278 & 286

HUMAN ACTIVITIES

My Parties Dreams

✶ ✶ ✶ ✶ ✶ ✶ ✶ ✶ ✶ ✶ ✶ ✶ ✶ ✶ ✶ ✶ ✶ ✶

The Demon Drink

Did you have a nightmare in which you drank too much at a work-related party and behaved inappropriately in front of your boss, colleagues, and clients? Such a dream may have been warning that your real-life heavy drinking is becoming obvious to others and could threaten your job. But if you don't drink excessively, it was probably an anxiety dream reflecting your insecurity at work.

PARTIES

✶✶✶✶✶✶✶✶✶✶✶✶✶✶✶✶✶✶✶✶✶✶✶✶✶✶✶✶✶✶✶✶✶✶✶✶✶✶

Like their real-world equivalents, dream parties bring us together with people for a common purpose, whether it is to celebrate a special occasion, to network, or just to have fun with like-minded individuals. The unconscious may use these dreams to comment on the nature of our interaction with others.

Symbolic and Verbal Associations
- Celebration; a special occasion
- One's social set
- Good company
- Someone who is a "party animal"
- Self-confidence, or, alternatively, insecurities

Positive Interpretations: In your dream, were you creating an e-mail invitation to a party that you were planning? If so, can you remember why you were throwing the party, and whom you invited? If you were planning to host a reunion with old friends with whom you have lost touch, your unconscious may have been mirroring your desire to get in touch with people from your past. Otherwise, your dream of throwing a party may have reflected your desire to make new friends or to relax and enjoy yourself among the friends that you have. But if your social life has withered almost to nothing (perhaps because you have been working long hours at the office) and you dreamed that you were ecstatic to receive an invitation to a party given by one of your friends, then your unconscious may have been urging you to revitalize your social life by reconnecting with the people whose company you enjoy. Did your dream depict you having a good time as you confidently socialized at a party? Perhaps, in your dream, you enjoyed an interesting conversation with someone? If so, the dream may have been a simple reflection of the pleasure that you derive from this person's company. Any dream that placed a spotlight on festive party items—such as champagne, colored streamers, or a piñata—may have been mirroring your real-life elated mood. And if you dreamed that your friends threw you a party and showered you with gifts, you may have experienced a wish-fulfillment dream, particularly if your relationships with your friends are currently strained or if you are feeling underappreciated by those around you.

Negative Interpretations: Did you attend a dream party at which you found yourself nervously hiding in a dark corner, fearing that someone might approach you or talk to you? If so, this may signal that your self-esteem is running low. But if your dream more or less accurately characterized how you behave at real-life parties, perhaps the dream served to underline the fact that your shyness is causing you to miss out on potentially enriching social opportunities. And if you dreamed that an annoying person pestered you as you tried to enjoy yourself at a party, do you feel bothered by this person in the waking world?

Related Dreams
pages 102, 168, 261, 278, 280 & 285

PLAYING

HUMAN ACTIVITIES

Playing is an activity that we associate with the carefree days of childhood, though adults play as well, and often for the same reasons that children do. In the language of dreams, playing may symbolize a childlike state of innocence, fun, and relaxation, but also boredom, immaturity, and "playing" with someone's emotions.

Symbolic and Verbal Associations

- Childhood; a carefree existence
- Fun and relaxation
- "Playing" or "toying" with someone's mind or emotions
- Boredom; diversions
- The need to "get serious" or to "grow up"

Positive Interpretations: Did you dream that you were a child again, with no worries or cares on your mind, thinking only of the colorful building blocks that sat before you on the floor? If so, your unconscious may have been reminding you of this happy, carefree time in order to encourage you to play and have fun more often in your current waking life—especially if your life is particularly lacking in this regard. Similarly, if your dream depicted you as a child again, having fun on the playground surrounded by all of your friends, your unconscious may have been underlining your current lack of fun and excitement, and perhaps your need to socialize more. However, another interpretation for a dream such as this is that it simply reflected your nostalgia for your lost childhood.

Negative Interpretations: A dream of playing with toys may be a sign that you are bored with your waking life. Have you sought, in vain, to alleviate your waking boredom by purchasing all manner of "toys" and gadgets? For instance, has your new sports car failed to fill the empty feeling inside you? If you think that this may have been the point of your dream, then your unconscious may have been telling you that it is time to "put away such childish things," to "get serious," and to spend your time more productively, doing or seeking out whatever it is that will really make you happy. If you dreamed that you were "playing" with a doll, which you were hitting, yelling at, or even sticking pins into, then your dream probably represented a transference of the anger that you feel for someone in your waking world, which you may have repressed. So do you know who your dream doll may have represented? Alternatively, might your dream of playing have been an unconscious reference to someone (perhaps you) who is "playing" or "toying" with someone else's mind or emotions? Finally, if you dreamed that you were cast into the middle of a group of rambunctious, shrieking children, and if you felt aloof from them or shrank from their ear-splitting games, then your dream may have been a signal of your waking disdain for the immature behavior that is being exhibited by a group of people, such as your colleagues, in your current waking life.

My Playing Dreams

----

* * * * * * * * * * * * * * * * * * *

You Cannot Be Serious!

If you made silly faces in your dream while someone was trying to communicate something important to you, was the person trying to alert you to a real-life problem to which you should be paying attention? Who was the individual whom you aren't taking seriously? If it was your husband, could you be ignoring signs that he is unhappy in your relationship?

Related Dreams

pages 66, 89, 131, 258, 282 & 284

HUMAN ACTIVITIES

My Reading Dreams

✱ ✱ ✱ ✱ ✱ ✱ ✱ ✱ ✱ ✱ ✱ ✱ ✱ ✱ ✱ ✱

Shock, Horror!

In your dream, was someone reading a newspaper and reacting to a story about you with shock or amazement? Was the reader your parent or partner, who was horrified by the news that you had committed a crime? Or perhaps the reader was amazed to learn of your recent act of courage. If you were reading the headlines yourself, what shocking news did they tell you?

READING

If you had a dream in which you were reading, the meaning of your dream will be dependent upon what you were reading—a newspaper, a history book, a novel, a book of poetry, or even another person's words or their facial expression—as well as your reaction to what you read.

Symbolic and Verbal Associations
- Knowledge; education
- Stories; adventure
- Poetry; emotions; romance
- "Reading" someone's words, facial expression, or body language
- News; current events

Positive Interpretations: Did you dream that you were deeply absorbed in reading a history book? If this is a subject that you actually study in the waking world, then your unconscious was probably simply underlining your interest in the topic. Or, in your dream, were you avidly reading an epic novel that had you so enthralled that you could barely wait to turn from one page to the next? If so, your dream may have been pointing to a desire to incorporate more excitement and adventure into your life. And if your dream depicted you reading a book of poetry, your unconscious may have been fulfilling your need for emotional stimulation, passion, and romance. Alternatively, in your dream, were you reading a book of a religious or spiritual nature? If you were reading the sacred scriptures of the religion that you follow, then your unconscious may have been either affirming your religious beliefs or else hinting that you might find the solution to a waking problem by consulting your personal religious authority. Otherwise, if you dreamed of reading the scriptures of the religion that you were brought up in, but have since fallen away from, your dream may have been mirroring your desire to reconsider your former religion's teachings. Of course, if you dreamed of reading any book on spiritualism, your unconscious may have been pointing to your general quest for enlightenment.

Negative Interpretations: In your dream, were you reading a newspaper, and did you find yourself becoming more and more disheartened and depressed as you read page after page of bad news? If so, your unconscious may have been pointing to your negative waking feelings about the world. If you think that this is the case, your unconscious may have been urging you to make an effort to focus on the positive things that exist in the world and the positive contributions that you can make. Finally, did you dream that you were "reading" the (perhaps, though not necessarily, negative) message in someone's words, facial expression, or body language? If so, do you feel that this person is trying to hide his or her true feelings from you in the waking world, or else that he or she is attempting to communicate with you in a roundabout manner?

Related Dreams

pages 43, 197, 206, 278 & 330

RUNNING

A dream of running may reflect any of this activity's literal or symbolic meanings, including escape, pleasure, or release, progression toward ambitions or goals, running against rivals or the clock, or an attempt to woo or "catch" someone.

Symbolic and Verbal Associations
- Exhilaration; release; escape
- Advancement; ambitions; goals
- Competition
- Urgency; "running late"
- Chasing after, or trying to "catch," someone; a romantic intrigue

Positive Interpretations: Did you have a dream in which you were running for the pure pleasure, energy, and release that it gave you? If so, and if you often run for exercise or pleasure in the waking world, then it is possible that your dream was simply mirroring your enjoyment of this activity. However, there are a number of other possible symbolic interpretations that are associated with running. Do you remember what you were running toward (or away from)? Your unconscious may have been commenting on your progression toward your goals or ambitions. Were you racing against anyone, such as your coworkers? If so, your dream was likely a reference to the progression of your career. If so, did you run swiftly and smoothly past your fellow runners? If any other runners were on your team, do you perceive these people to be your allies in the pursuit of your real-world goals? And did you reach your final destination with a triumphant feeling? If so, your unconscious may have been trying to give you a glimpse of how you may feel when you finally achieve your ambitions, perhaps in an effort to spur you onward. Alternatively, did you dream that you were running in pursuit of another person? If so, is this someone whom you've been "chasing," or seeking to make a romantic connection with, in the waking world? Do you feel that he or she would be "a real catch"?

Negative Interpretations: If you think that your dream of running symbolized your advancement toward your goals, did you become tired, trip, fall, or come up against an obstacle that blocked your way? If so, your unconscious may have been pointing out some problems that you might encounter in your pursuit of your ambitions, or else it may have been reflecting your fears and worries. If you were running to beat the clock, do you feel that "time is running out" for you to complete some task, or address an important issue, in the real world, or that your days are so packed with activities that you are continually rushing around? Or if you dreamed of chasing after your daughter, has she been emotionally withdrawing or "running away from you" in the waking world? And finally, if you were running to escape from someone or something, ask yourself whether you feel stalked, threatened, or "put upon" by someone or something in the waking world.

Related Dreams

pages 53, 172, 189, 221, 250 & 290

My Running Dreams

----

* * * * * * * * * * * * * * * * * *

Endurance Test

Were you and your spouse running an exhausting marathon in your dream? If so, have you jointly bitten off more than you can chew in real life, perhaps by signing up for an enormous mortgage that is forcing you to work overtime? The message may have been that you should consider dropping out of the "rat race" and adopt a less demanding lifestyle.

My Sports Dreams

·····························
·····························
·····························
·····························
·····························
·····························
·····························
·····························
·····························

★ ★ ★ ★ ★ ★ ★ ★ ★ ★ ★ ★ ★ ★ ★ ★

Extreme Skiing

If you were flying through the air down a dream ski slope, were you exhilarated and pumped full of adrenaline? Were you in control, or were you recklessly courting danger by skiing too fast or exploring back-country terrain? Depending on the answers to these questions, your dream could have been a reference to freedom and excitement, or to risking everything for a short-lived thrill.

SPORTS

★ ★

A dream of playing a sport may reflect a conscious preoccupation with that sport, or may be an unconscious encouragement to engage in pleasurable activities. Dream sports may also be a metaphor for how the dreamer is faring or performing in some aspect of waking life.

Symbolic and Verbal Associations
- A "team mentality"
- Someone who is amiable, or "a good sport"
- Performance; success
- Competition; victory or defeat
- Pleasurable activities

Positive Interpretations: In your dream, were you transformed into a professional basketball player, and did you steal the ball away from a player on the opposing team, turn, charge down the court, and make a spectacular lay-up amidst the cheering of the crowd? If so, and if you play basketball in the real world, then your unconscious may have been mirroring your fixation on your favorite sport. But if this explanation seems unlikely, then could your dream have been a metaphor for some recent success in the waking world? For instance, if your dream teammates were the people on your company sales team, was your unconscious reliving the strategic maneuver that you used to carry your team to the top of the sales charts? Or if you dreamed of playing a fun and leisurely volleyball game with relatives, was your unconscious highlighting the harmonious workings of your family? In your dream, were you "a good sport" when the other team scored against you? Alternatively, if you dreamed that you skipped work and spent the entire day playing golf—an activity that you take great pleasure in, but that you rarely find the time to play—then your unconscious may have been encouraging you to take more time off from your busy schedule to engage in relaxing activities that bring you enjoyment.

Negative Interpretations: Did you dream that your bowling team was trounced by your main rival? If so, and if there is a tournament coming up in which you will have to face this team, your unconscious may have been reflecting your worries about your team's form. However, if it's unlikely that your dream was a literal reference to bowling because you're not on a team, then an examination of the details of the dream may provide you with clues to its meaning. For instance, in the dream, were you frustrated when you bowled a string of gutter balls? If so, is your lack of focus in the real world causing your professional or intellectual performance to suffer? Or if you dreamed of losing a game, did you behave like "a bad sport"? Did you feel as though the game was lost unfairly, perhaps because the other team cheated? Or did you dream that you resorted to cheating in order to win?

Related Dreams

pages 114, 188, 190, 214, 250 & 289

SWIMMING & DIVING

While a dream of frolicking in the water may be an unconscious encouragement for you to relax and have fun in your waking life, dreams of diving, floating, and swimming are most likely to refer to emotions and the unconscious.

Symbolic and Verbal Associations
("Diving into" something "head first"
("Making a splash"; gaining attention
(Something that is going "swimmingly," or very well
(Being "over your head" in difficulties, etc.; being "out of your depth"
(Your emotional state; emotional wellbeing; unconscious feelings and desires

Positive Interpretations: Did you take a dream dive into the sea, where you were met with the loving embrace of the person whom you are dating? If so, your unconscious may have been reflecting your desire to "dive into" a relationship with him or her "head first," without thinking. Or did you dream that you were floating weightlessly and peacefully on the surface of a sunny lake, as the warm water caressed and held your buoyant body? If so, and if you spend most of your waking hours anxiously rushing around, then your unconscious may have been trying to comfort you and to compensate for your lack of peace and tranquility in the waking world. Your dream may also have reflected your desire to be able to float effortlessly through life, letting all of your cares and worries wash over and away from you. And if you dreamed that you were swimming swiftly and smoothly through the water, is your waking life also going "swimmingly"?

Negative Interpretations: Did you dream that you were diving into the ocean? If you have been deliberating over a dilemma in the waking world, then your dream self may have been "diving in" to search for insight in the depths of your unconscious. While you were under water, did you experience a "dream within a dream" in which you and your friends were having fun and interacting as if you were on dry land? If so, then your unconscious may have been suggesting that you have been so busy with other things that you have been neglecting to take the time to connect emotionally with the people who are important to you. Or did you dream that you were filled with a sense of anxiety or unease as you drifted upon the ocean waves? And do you feel as though you lack direction or control in the waking world? Are you merely "treading water," with no clear destination or goal? If so, your unconscious may have been mirroring these feelings. If you dreamed that you were struggling as you swam against a strong current, it may be that your conscious mind is doing battle with an unconscious urge, or else that you feel as though you are "swimming against the tide" or the "current" of opinion in the waking world. And if you found yourself stranded far out in the deep waters of the ocean, do you feel as though you are "out of your depth" with your boyfriend, perhaps whose unpredictable mood swings make you feel as if you have no control over the relationship?

Related Dreams
pages 79, 223, 257, 258, 290 & 383

My Swimming & Diving Dreams

----

* * * * * * * * * * * * * * * * * *

Diving Deep
A dream of exploring the underwater world may have portrayed a metaphorical swim through the "waters" of your unconscious mind. If you enjoyed your swim and admired beautiful, colorful fish, you are probably comfortable with your emotions. But if you were afraid, and felt that you were swimming among sharks and piranhas, are you fearful of facing up to your personal demons?

WATCHING TV

Television is a source of news, entertainment, and diversion—all of which may play into the meaning of a dream of watching TV. However, instead of coming from a media network, the message that we receive via dream television comes straight from our own unconscious.

My Watching TV Dreams

----

* * * * * * * * * * * * * * * * * * *

Soap Opera

If you dreamed that you and your family were happily engrossed in watching a TV show together, could your dream have recalled the congenial evenings that you used to spend at home before you moved away to another city in the real world? Are relations currently strained or awkward, and are you feeling nostalgic for the days when you could relax in one another's company?

Symbolic and Verbal Associations
(Entertainment and diversion
(Intuition; a "news flash" broadcast from the unconscious
(Life drama; memories
(Boredom and restlessness; loneliness: watching TV for company
(Someone who is a "couch potato"; invalids and convalescence

Positive Interpretations: If you watched an exciting or compelling movie on TV before going to bed, and then that night you dreamed about its plot or characters, your unconscious may simply have been recalling the memory of your real-life viewing experience. However, it is also possible that your unconscious was treating you to an interesting diversion from the boredom or anxiety that fills your waking hours. But if your dream self felt particularly caught up in the drama of a movie, then the plot may have had some bearing on your unconscious urges or preoccupations. For instance, if you dreamed that you were watching a romantic movie and that you wept for joy when the leading man and woman finally confessed their love for one another, do you wish that a similar scene would play itself out between you and a certain person in your waking life? Alternatively, if you dreamed that you were engrossed in a documentary on dog breeds, might your unconscious have been mirroring your desire to get a puppy?

Negative Interpretations: Was your dream self upset, angered, or saddened by a program about the issue of child abuse? If so, might your unconscious have been tapping into your own unhappy childhood memories? (And if you dreamed that the program was a video or DVD recording, it is even more likely that it originated from your own memory.) If you think that this may be the case, your dream may have been an unconscious attempt to force you to face your painful memories and to come to terms with your childhood anger or fear. Or if you dreamed of watching a talk show about people who have run themselves deep into credit-card debt, was your unconscious trying to draw your attention to your own tendency to spend beyond your means? In another scenario, did you dream that you were slumped on your sofa, staring blankly at the monotonous flickering of your television screen as you used the remote control to channel-surf aimlessly? If so, do you feel bored and restless in your waking life, and does nothing seem to hold your attention for long? Or if your dream accurately depicted how you spend a large number of your waking hours, might your unconscious have been pointing out what a "couch potato" you have become?

Related Dreams

pages 41, 100, 123, 162 & 202

CHAPTER 15
TRAVEL

Unless a vacation or change of scenery really is on your mind, dreams in which you are traveling will usually tell you more about how smoothly, quickly, and enjoyably you are progressing along life's path at present. You may, for example, be being frustrated by all manner of holdups, be weighed down by your "baggage," or may even have lost your way altogether. On the other hand, life may be "plain sailing" at the moment, and your dream may also have indicated that you are negotiating potentially tricky emotional transitions and pitfalls with effortless ease.

My Accidents Dreams

....
....
....
....
....
....
....
....
....

* * * * * * * * * * * * * * * * * *

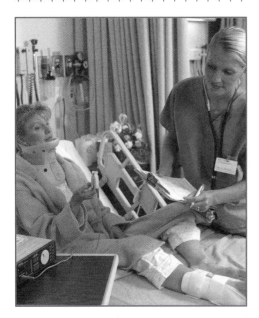

A Clean Break

If you dreamed that you were being treated for fractures and whiplash sustained in a traffic accident, the message may have had more to do with your survival than your injuries. Perhaps you are facing a difficult real-life dilemma in which damage cannot be avoided. If so, your dream may have indicated that you can live with the outcome, no matter what the fallout.

ACCIDENTS

* *

D ream accidents are likely to denote mishaps and calamities in the journey along life's path. They may be a sign that the unconscious has detected danger ahead, or they may simply be an expression of our unconscious fears and anxieties.

Symbolic and Verbal Associations
- Mistakes
- Catastrophe
- Fate; ill luck
- Anxieties, fears, and worries
- A warning of danger
- Strength to overcome misfortune

Positive Interpretations: Did you dream that you were involved in a catastrophic accident, such as a train or plane wreck, but that you emerged from the wreckage virtually unscathed? If so, your unconscious mind may have been trying to hearten and bolster you with the knowledge that, whatever troubles or misfortunes come your way in your life, you have the strength to withstand and overcome them. And if, in your dream, you rescued someone from the scene of the accident, he or she may symbolize something or someone in your life that is either worth saving or that is in need of salvaging. For example, if you pulled a child from the wreckage, he or she may have denoted your innocence or potential. If it was an older person, he or she may have represented your wisdom or maturity, while your partner may have symbolized love or trust.

Negative Interpretations: If you dreamed that you were involved in an accident, your unconscious may have sensed that danger lies ahead, in which case it may have sent you the dream as a warning. The message of your dream may have been either literal or metaphorical. For instance, did you dream that you were driving along a dark road at night, when, at a bend in the road, your automobile suddenly spun out of control and plowed into a tree? If so, there are a few possible explanations. It may be that your unconscious mind has picked up on a mechanical problem with your vehicle, in which case it sent you your dream in order to alert you to the need to have it serviced. Or could your dream have been a literal warning that someone you know drives too dangerously? (Is it you?) Another possibility is that your unconscious was making a comment on the treacherous "course" that your life has been taking. Have you been living your life in the "fast lane"? Have you set yourself on a "collision course"? Are you in danger of "losing control," or of suffering from an emotional or financial "crash"? And if you dreamed that you hit someone with your automobile, who was it? (Perhaps it was your brother-in-law, with whom you can't seem to agree on anything?) And did anyone else witness ,or become involved in, the accident? (Such as your sister, who tries to keep the peace between you and her husband?)

Related Dreams

pages 56, 131, 208, 226, 257 & 370

AIRPLANES

I n the language of dreams, air is a symbol of spiritual or intellectual aspirations. Other possible meanings for a dream of taking to the sky in an airplane may involve "fast-tracking" toward worldly ambitions, or simply a desire to take a vacation.

My Airplanes Dreams

----

* * * * * * * * * * * * * * * * *

Symbolic and Verbal Associations

- Vacations and holidays; "jet-setting"
- "Flying high"
- Traveling "first class"; "fast-tracking"
- Carrying emotional "baggage" or "traveling light"
- Surrender of control
- Spiritual transcendence to a "higher" consciousness

Positive Interpretations: In your dream, were you excitedly boarding an airplane, in the expectation that it would carry you to your dream vacation destination? A dream such as this may have been a simple reflection of your yearning or eagerness to go on a trip—especially if you have one planned, or if your recent day-to-day life has been particularly exhausting. And if you were "traveling light," with just a small tote bag, this may denote your feeling of, or desire for, freedom, independence, or emotional lightness (as in having a lack of emotional "baggage"). Dream departures may also denote a parting from your old circumstances as you embark on a new journey or direction in life, while dream arrivals may indicate that you have either achieved your goal or can envisage yourself doing so. A dream of ascending toward the heavens in an airplane may also indicate a desire to explore your spirituality or to attain a higher level of consciousness. Alternatively, such a dream may have a more material meaning, such as the depiction of the "fast-track" career path that you are (or would like to be) on.

Negative Interpretations: If you dreamed of checking in to board an airplane, were you weighed down by a great amount of luggage? If so, your dream burden may have represented the real-life burden of emotional "baggage" (from past issues or problems) that you are carrying around with you, which may be holding you back or preventing you from moving as freely as you would like. And if you dreamed that your flight was delayed or grounded due to inclement weather or mechanical problems, do you feel as if your real-world ambitions are being hindered (perhaps by unforeseen or uncontrollable forces)? Finally, in your dream, were you piloting a fighter plane? If so, your unconscious may have been advising you of the need to defend yourself or perhaps to go on the intellectual attack during your waking hours. And if you dreamed that you parachuted out of your plane after it was hit by enemy fire, your unconscious may have been warning you of the need to make a hasty retreat in the real world.

Flying High

Dreaming of piloting an airplane and of performing aerial acrobatics in a clear sky is often a sign of confidence and success. If you were enjoying the exhilaration and freedom of swooping through the air in your dream, while surveying panoramic views of the landscape below, you are probably in control of your destiny and comfortable with whatever risks you are undertaking in waking life.

Related Dreams

pages 141, 197, 248, 258, 302 & 304

My Automobiles Dreams

✶ ✶ ✶ ✶ ✶ ✶ ✶ ✶ ✶ ✶ ✶ ✶ ✶ ✶ ✶ ✶ ✶ ✶

Bumper to Bumper

In your dream commute, were you stuck in traffic, frustrated because you couldn't cruise along in your sporty convertible? Does this dream scenario resemble your daily reality? This could point to an incipient mid-life crisis. Maybe your daily routine is becoming stifling, and perhaps you bought the convertible (or dreamed of driving it) to feel more dashing, or to spice up your flagging love life.

AUTOMOBILES

An automobile bestows freedom and independence on us, which are possible meanings for a dream car or truck. But automobiles may also symbolize many other things in the language of dreams, including energy and stamina, personal image, and the amount of control that a person has over his or her life.

Symbolic and Verbal Associations
- ❮ Independence and freedom
- ❮ Living life "in the fast lane"; loss of control
- ❮ Being stuck in a traffic jam, or coming up to a "roadblock"; frustration
- ❮ Running out of "fuel" or "gas"
- ❮ Traveling down a "one-way street"
- ❮ Being "taken for a ride"

Positive Interpretations: Your dream car or truck's performance is likely to symbolize your own performance in life. So if you dreamed that you were cruising smoothly down an open road, you probably have a sense that you are in control of your life, enjoying an "easy ride," with enough strength, energy, and stamina to carry you to your journey's end. Dream automobiles may also take on the symbolism of freedom and independence, or represent the driver's actual or desired image or persona. So if you dreamed of driving down the highway, what did your dream car look like? Was it a large, safe, and sturdy van? Was it a small, sleek, and sporty symbol of status and wealth? Or was it a rugged, all-terrain sport-utility vehicle?

Negative Interpretations: In your dream, were you embarrassed to be seen driving an old, rattling "rust bucket" (which was the only car that your dream self could afford)? If so, do you suffer from waking feelings of inadequacy, perhaps because you are having financial troubles? Or if you dreamed that you were gleefully behind the wheel of your friend's automobile, do you admire his or her image so much that you wish to copy it? If you dreamed that you were a passenger in a car, do you feel that you are not in control of your own life? Who was your driver? Might your unconscious have been hinting that this person is controlling or manipulating you, or that he or she is "taking you for a ride" (or deceiving you) in the real world? Or is this someone who is "driving you crazy" during your waking hours? However, if you were driving someone else around, do you feel responsible for "steering" him or her "in the right direction" in life? If your passenger annoyed you with his or her "backseat driving," is he or she someone who constantly gives you unwanted advice about how to live your life? If you dreamed of running out of gas, your unconscious may have been warning you that your waking physical or mental energies are running low on fuel. Alternatively, if you dreamed of speeding in an out-of-control manner, are you living your life "in the fast lane," so that you are heading for a "crash"? Or are you headed down a "one-way street" toward a dead end?

Related Dreams

pages 125, 157, 179, 226, 289 & 294

BICYCLES & MOTORCYCLES

TRAVEL

Because bicycles allow us to go places by our own power, but faster than on foot, dream bikes are likely to represent the effort that we are making to "power" or advance ourselves through life. Meanwhile, dream motorcycles may denote one's sex drive, especially for male dreamers—and also possibly youth and rebellion, if there are associations for the dreamer.

Symbolic and Verbal Associations
- Self-powered progress; personal effort
- Self-control
- Advancing speedily through life
- Sex drive (in the case of a dream motorcycle)

Positive Interpretations: Did you dream that you jumped onto a bicycle and began to pedal down the street? If so, do you remember where you were heading? When we ride a bicycle in the real world, we have to put much more effort into powering and controlling our movement than we would if we were walking—though cycling allows us to get from one place to another much faster and to cover much greater distances than we could if we were to go on foot. So if you dreamed that you were biking smoothly and rapidly along a flat road that led to your real-world college, your unconscious may have been commenting on the relatively smooth and easy time that you are having in completing your degree. And if, in your dream, you had built up so much momentum that you felt as though you barely had to touch the pedals, the message from your unconscious may have been that your past efforts continue to carry you at an easy pace through the current phase of your waking life. If you dreamed that you were exhilarated to find yourself coasting downhill, are you enjoying a similar "free ride" in the waking world? Cycling is a leisure activity, as well as a competitive one, and a dream of cycling may also carry either of these meanings, depending on the specifics of the dream scenario. Alternatively, if your dreaming mind depicted you mounting and revving up the engine of a motorcycle, your unconscious may have been referring to your sex drive, particularly if you are a man. Motorcycles are also often associated with youth and countercultural rebellion, so these meanings should also be taken into consideration if you dreamed that you were riding one.

Negative Interpretations: In your dream, were you struggling to pedal your bicycle up a steep hill? If so, do you feel as if you are facing an extremely difficult, uphill climb in some aspect of your waking life? Or did the chain fall off your dream bicycle, so that you found yourself pedaling in vain? If so, do you feel as if your waking efforts to get ahead or advance yourself are all for naught? (Or was your unconscious simply reminding you that it's time to take your bike in for a tune-up?) Did your dream bicycle have a flat tire? If so, has someone in the real world "deflated" or "pricked" your ego?

Related Dreams
pages 84, 214, 231, 277 & 289

My Bicycles & Motorcycles Dreams

Spin Cycle
If you were careering down a steep hill at top speed on your dream bicycle, were you exhilarated or did you feel out of control? This dream could have been a warning from your unconscious to pay attention to your current waking-life behavior. Are you doing something reckless, yet feel that you cannot, or don't want to, stop? It may be time to slow down.

My Boats Dreams

....

....

....

....

....

....

....

....

★ ★ ★ ★ ★ ★ ★ ★ ★ ★ ★ ★ ★ ★ ★ ★ ★ ★ ★

We Are Sailing

The dreaming mind sometimes uses sailing as a symbol for how effectively we are negotiating the business of living life in the waking world, and especially for how we are feeling at this stage in our life's "journey." So if you dreamed of sailing smoothly through calm, inviting-looking waters, you are probably finding this phase of your life "plain sailing," or easy and perhaps enjoyable.

BOATS

★ ★

Boats are vessels that carry us over water, which is a symbol of the unconscious. Therefore, in the language of dreams, embarking upon a boat journey may denote a real-life journey of emotional self-exploration.

Symbolic and Verbal Associations
- "Smooth sailing"
- Trying to "stay afloat"
- Feeling "lost at sea"
- Instincts and emotions
- A desire to "drop anchor" somewhere, or to "anchor yourself" to someone

Positive Interpretations: Did you have a dream in which you were sailing the high seas all alone in a little sailboat? If so, your dream may have symbolized a real-world voyage of emotional self-discovery—perhaps a voyage that you have already embarked upon, or else one that your unconscious is urging you to take. So who or what did you encounter in your dream? Did you do battle with, and defeat, great sea monsters? Did you meet up with a beautiful mermaid? Discover a strange new land? And if you dreamed that you dropped anchor at a port, might your unconscious have been highlighting your desire to "anchor yourself" in a loving relationship, or even in a particular location (particularly if you have been moving around from one place to another)? In your dream, did you enjoy lots of sunshine, good weather, and "plain" or "smooth sailing"? If so, do you feel as if your waking life (or else a particular waking venture) has been going equally smoothly? And if you had a crew, who were they? Your unconscious may have been trying to tell you that these persons may be of help to you in some way in the real world—either as emotional support, or as "helping hands" in some project or endeavor.

Negative Interpretations: In your dream sailboat, were you beleaguered by bad weather and rough seas? Did a storm buffet your little ship to and fro, so that you thought that all would be lost for sure? If so, have you recently hit a "rough patch" in the real world? Have you been living through an emotional tempest—perhaps because you have been arguing bitterly with a loved one? Or do you feel "lost at sea," or confused as to which direction to move in during your waking hours? In your dream, did you find yourself sailing through shark-infested waters? Or were you attacked by a band of pirates? If so, your unconscious may have been warning you of some person or persons who may mean to do you harm in the waking world. Was your dream boat beset by problems, such as a torn sail or a leaky hull? Or did your dream self suffer from illness or thirst? If so, you may want to undertake some free association in order to try to determine what possible real-world problems or hindrances your unconscious may have been referring to.

Related Dreams
pages 79, 145, 146, 291, 383 & 387

BRIDGES

Just as a bridge spans the gap between one physical place and another, a metaphorical or dream bridge may span two otherwise disconnected oppositional viewpoints. A bridge may also represent the past, present, and future, or even the transition point between different phases of life or states of consciousness or being.

Symbolic and Verbal Associations
- Past, present, and future
- Moving from one consciousness or state of being to another; a rite of passage
- A meeting place between opposing viewpoints
- "Bridging the gap": coming to an agreement
- "Burning your bridges"

Positive Interpretations: Did you dream that you had reverted to your child self and that you began to cross a bridge, and, as you did so, did you feel yourself gaining in age, maturity, and wisdom? If so, your unconscious was likely to have been reflecting upon how far you have come in life—and possibly also how far you have yet to go. (And, in your dream, could you see past the end of the bridge to your potential future? If so, what did it look like?) A dream such as this may also be the unconscious's way of highlighting a life transition or rite of passage that you are about to go through, such as getting married, having a baby, or retiring from work. If you dreamed of building or crossing a bridge, you should also consider whether your unconscious was making a reference to the act of "bridging the gap" between your own and someone else's (opposing) beliefs or viewpoints. Or if you dreamed that you were wondering whether or not you should cross a bridge, could you see what was waiting for you on the other side? Whether it was a person, a landscape, a city, or whatever else, can you make an association between him, her, or it and someone or something in your waking life? Is it a person, place, or thing that you would like to make a commitment to, or are you ambivalent about your desire to do so?

Negative Interpretations: In your dream, did you find yourself in the middle of a treacherous, swinging rope bridge that was suspended above a chasm so deep that you couldn't see all the way to the bottom? And did the bridge creak and sway unreassuringly with each step that you took? If so, might your unconscious have been alluding to a dangerous crossing or transition that you are making in the real world? Alternatively, as you attempted to cross a dream bridge, were you challenged and tormented by a troll that lived beneath it? If so, has someone in the waking world been hindering either your progress or your attempts at peacemaking? In your dream, did you set fire to a bridge after you'd crossed it? If so, have you recently "burned your bridges" (or destroyed any possibility of reconciliation) with someone in the real world?

My Bridges Dreams

....
....
....
....
....
....
....

* * * * * * * * * * * * * * * * * * *

Bridging the Gap
Dream bridges have the same essential function as real-world bridges, which is to enable us to cross from one place to another. In dreams, their purpose is metaphorical rather than literal, however, so that they may represent a transitional phase or shortcut in life, or else a means of "bridging the gap," or bringing people with different viewpoints together across, perhaps, a cultural "divide."

Related Dreams

TRAVEL

My Buses & Trains Dreams

----

* * * * * * * * * * * * * * * * * *

Doing the Locomotion

Did you dream of watching high-speed trains rush past you in a blur? The key to interpreting such a dream lies in how you were feeling. If you were excited by the prospect of boarding a train, the dream was probably a reflection of your stimulating waking life at the moment. Or do you feel that life is passing you by?

BUSES & TRAINS

****

A dream of riding on a bus or a train may have to do with the surrendering of personal control, frustration at being unable to change the path that we are on, the necessity or desire to abide by "official rules" or to travel "on the straight and narrow," or even (in the case of a dream train) with issues of sexuality.

Symbolic and Verbal Associations
- Surrender of control
- Authority; official rules
- "Missing the bus" or train: missed opportunities
- Being "on the straight and narrow"
- Sex and virility

Positive Interpretations: Freudians associate trains with sexuality (with a train symbolizing the penis, and a tunnel, the vagina). So if you are a man who dreamed of driving or riding on a steam train that was charging toward a tunnel, your dream may have been making an unconscious statement about your "steamy" sex life or your charging virility. Alternatively, did you dream that you were riding a bus or a train to work? If so, your unconscious mind may have been reflecting upon your career path. How did your dream self feel? Was your seat clean and comfortable? Were you riding in first class? Were you sitting at the front of the bus? Was your dream of riding on a train an indication that you are "on the straight and narrow," "on the right track," or traveling along "the right lines"? Or was your dream a reference to the fact that you are moving steadily toward a goal, or toward your destiny?

Negative Interpretations: When we travel on public transportation, we give up a good deal of our ability to control where we go and how soon we get there. Therefore, in the language of dreams, buses and trains may symbolize the surrender of our powers—perhaps to an authority such as a corporate or state entity, or even to a person, as represented by a dream bus driver or train conductor—or, in the case of a train, an inability to deviate from the course of the tracks that we are traveling on. For instance, in your dream, did you notice that your fellow passengers were your real-life coworkers? And was your supervisor cast in the role of the conductor? If so, did you argue with him or her, acting out your waking resentment of the authority that he or she wields over you, or did you sit quietly in your seat and abide by the "company rules"? If your dream self tried to disembark from the train, do you wish to quit your job in the real world? A dream of sitting at the back of a bus may reflect a waking shortage of self-esteem, or else a feeling of being treated like a "second-class" citizen. And finally, if you are a man who dreamed that you were on a train that broke down just as it was about to enter a tunnel, you may want to consider whether your unconscious was mirroring your unsatisfactory sex life or your feelings of impotence in the waking world.

Related Dreams

pages 121, 226, 268, 289, 304 & 385

BUSINESS TRIPS

✦✦

A dream of going on a business trip may have a number of different meanings. Such a dream may denote your waking excitement or boredom during your working hours, your level of responsibility, or even your professional image. However, because a dream business trip is essentially about travel, the root meaning is likely to have to do with your career path.

Symbolic and Verbal Associations
- ❮ Duty and responsibility
- ❮ Your career path
- ❮ Excitement and adventure; boredom
- ❮ A "professional" image or persona

Positive Interpretations: Did you dream that you were on an airplane, sharing cocktails and good conversation with your coworkers as you flew to a conference in a sunny resort city? And did your dream depict you and your coworkers enjoying a fun night on the town after the daytime conference activities were finished? If so, and if you find your job stimulating and enjoyable in the real world, then your unconscious may have been reflecting and reaffirming your waking experience. Your dream may also have been an unconscious commentary on the exciting career path that you are on. Are you really "going places" in your company? Do your bosses and your coworkers consider you to be "a mover and a shaker"? Have you jetted to the top of your profession? Otherwise, if your waking job is dull and repetitive and your work experience is never anything like the one that your dream self experienced, then your unconscious may have been treating you to a wish-fulfillment dream in an attempt to compensate for the drudgery of your real-life nine-to-five existence. And if you have been thinking of seeking out a more exciting job, then your dream may have been your unconscious's way of encouraging you to explore this possibility.

Negative Interpretations: In your dream of being on a business trip, did you find yourself alone in a hotel, thousands of miles away from your family, whom you missed desperately? If so, is the excessive amount of time that you spend at work during your waking hours causing you to become emotionally isolated from your family? Or did you dream that your company sent you on a business trip on which it seemed that everything that could possibly go wrong did go wrong? For example, did you dream that your flight was delayed, that the taxi took you to the wrong hotel, and that your secretary forgot to reserve your room? Did you lose your wallet and drop your cell phone into the gutter? If so, are the hassles, nuisances, and irritations of your work duties causing you to feel immensely frustrated? Is your career path littered with obstacles? Or if you became lost or confused on your dream business trip, is your real-world career path without direction, or are you confused as to which profession is right for you?

My Business Trips Dreams

....

....

....

....

....

....

....

....

....

✶ ✶ ✶ ✶ ✶ ✶ ✶ ✶ ✶ ✶ ✶ ✶ ✶ ✶ ✶ ✶ ✶ ✶ ✶

Corridors of Power
When you checked into your dream hotel, how did you feel? If you were relishing the prospect of an evening of comfort, with room service just a phone call away, you are probably enjoying the challenges and trappings of your career. But if you were weary and unable to locate your room in your dream, is your unsettled lifestyle getting on top of you?

Related Dreams
pages 70, 82, 155, 209, 278 & 302

My Luggage Dreams

_____

_____

_____

_____

_____

_____

_____

_____

* *

Bags and Baggage

When they weigh us down in dreamland, bags and baggage often symbolize the emotional baggage that we—often unwillingly—carry around with us. And because hatboxes, or bandboxes, are designed to enable the safe transportation of hats, which are in turn designed to protect or draw attention to the head, their appearance in a dream may refer to cherished or encumbering thoughts or memories.

LUGGAGE

* *

While the most obvious interpretation for dream luggage is that it is emotional "baggage," a dream of carrying a suitcase may simply denote travel, your anticipation of going on vacation, or a new direction in your life.

Symbolic and Verbal Associations
- Burdens
- Emotional "baggage"
- Feeling "weighted down" with duties and responsibilities
- A change of direction in life
- A desire to "lighten your load"

Positive Interpretations: Did you dream that you were walking out of your house with a suitcase in your hand? If so, do you wish that you could leave your old life behind and embark upon an entirely new journey? Do you long for your life to take a new direction? Or have you already set off on such an adventure? Did you know where your dream self was headed, or did you relish the thrill of heading off into "the great unknown"? In your dream, did you arrive at your destination? If so, the meaning may be that you have already achieved your waking goal, or else that you can see yourself doing so. Alternatively, was your unconscious simply reflecting your excitement over an upcoming trip that you have planned? Did you have a dream in which you left your heavy luggage behind and exhilarated in traveling light, with only a small satchel and the clothes on your back? If so, have you finally found the strength to cast off the emotional "baggage" that you had been carrying around with you—to rid yourself of the burdensome memories of past problems and hurts that had long ruled your life and your relationships?

Negative Interpretations: In your dream, did you labor and struggle with the large and heavy suitcases that you were pulling along with you? Did you feel completely defeated when you came to a long and steep stairwell that you would need to ascend in order to continue your journey? If so, do you feel "weighted down" by your real-world duties and responsibilities? Is someone or something in your life placing such a burden on you that you feel unable to carry on with your own agenda? Do you feel "saddled" and "yoked" like a "beast of burden"? In your dream, were you embarrassed because your luggage was shabby and stained? Did your rolling suitcase squeak and rattle as you pulled it along? Did it have a broken wheel? If so, are you feeling "worn out" or unattractive in your waking life? Do you feel ill-equipped to make your journey through life? And if you dreamed that your suitcase broke open, spilling all of your clothing and personal items onto the sidewalk, do you fear that your private emotions are in danger of "spilling out" for all to see?

Related Dreams

pages 75, 209, 226, 233, 248 & 301

NAVIGATION

* *

In the world of dreams, the direction in which you are moving may denote the sorts of goals that you are pursuing in the waking world. Further meaning may be inferred from how well you navigated your dream course, and what sort of landscape or terrain you traveled over.

Symbolic and Verbal Associations
- Having or lacking "direction" in life
- "Going around in circles"
- "Moving backward"
- Traveling "off the beaten path"
- "Turning a corner"
- "Losing your way"

Positive Interpretations: Did your dream depict you successfully clearing a difficult jump or turn? If so, your unconscious may have been mirroring a recent maneuver that you have used in order to come through a real-world "tricky spot." Otherwise, if your dream self turned a corner, have you recently set off in a completely new direction in your life? Did a dream shortcut denote a shortcut that you have taken in your pursuit of a goal? If you became lost, did you consult a map or a compass? If so, your unconscious may have been attempting to hearten you with the knowledge that you have the means to find your own way in life. So in which direction did you go? If you went north, your unconscious may have been urging you to follow your intellect (although the north may also represent cold, darkness, winter, or old age). If you went south, you may want to consider taking a more relaxed approach to life (and the south may also signify warmth, light, and vitality). If you went toward the east, the place where the sun rises, your unconscious may have been advising you to take a spiritual path—while going west, in the direction of the setting sun, may denote the need to rest because your energies are waning. A right-hand or upward direction may have been pointing toward taking a rational approach to the world, while a left-hand or downward direction may have implied turning inward and exploring your own unconscious.

Negative Interpretations: In your dream of walking along a path, did you become distracted by something and lose the trail that you had been traveling on? If so, are you being sidetracked or diverted from the pursuit of your waking goal? Might your unconscious have been advising you of the need to "get back on track"? If you felt hopelessly lost, was your dream a metaphor for your feeling that you have lost your sense of direction, or your purpose, in life? Are you just "going around in circles"? Or did you dream that you were moving backward? If so, your unconscious may have been commenting on your waking frustration because you seem to be losing ground on some advancement you had previously made, which may be decreasing your quality of life.

Related Dreams
pages 234, 238, 277, 284, 289 & 306

My Navigation Dreams

----

* * * * * * * * * * * * * * * * * *

"X" Marks the Spot

If you dreamed of stopping to consult a map while out hiking, can you remember why? Were you seeking guidance, or trying to "get your bearings," because you were lost? If so, could it be that your unconscious was highlighting your uneasy sense of having lost your way in life? And did your dream map show you the best route to take?

TRAVEL

My Stations & Airports Dreams

✱ ✱ ✱ ✱ ✱ ✱ ✱ ✱ ✱ ✱ ✱ ✱ ✱ ✱ ✱ ✱ ✱

Diverse Destinations

When decoding a dream that featured a station or airport, remember that just as these places are points of departure to diverse destinations in the real world, so they can represent potential new directions in the dream world. But unless your dreaming self knew exactly where you were going, and thus which train or plane to catch, they can also signify confusion and missed opportunities.

STATIONS & AIRPORTS

✱ ✱

As points of transition, dream stations and airports are associated with periods of change or transition in life. Other symbolic associations include departures, waiting periods, uncertainties, feeling stuck or unable to move forward, and missed opportunities.

Symbolic and Verbal Associations
- A transition in life
- A period of waiting
- Uncertainty
- Feeling as if you are "stuck at the station"
- "Missing the bus"

Positive Interpretations: Did you have a dream in which you were walking determinedly toward an airport departure gate or a bus or train terminal? If so, your unconscious may have been trying to tell you that it is time for you to depart from one phase of your life and to embark upon another—and, perhaps, a new opportunity has already presented itself to you. For instance, have you recently received a job offer that would require you to relocate to another city or state? And have you been negating the possibility of taking this new job because it would require such a big life change? If so, your unconscious may have been revealing your true, inner desire to take this job—especially if you are feeling unhappy or unfulfilled in your current life. In your dream, do you remember what gate or terminal number you were departing from? If so, does this number hold any significance for you (for instance, is it your age, or your "lucky" number)? Similarly, if you dreamed that you were excitedly purchasing a ticket for the next bus or train that would take you away to someplace else, your unconscious may have been reflecting your desire to "move on" in life. (And do you remember where you were going? Did you wave goodbye to anyone in particular?)

Negative Interpretations: In your dream, did you find yourself upset and confused as you wandered aimlessly around a train station? Were you unsure as to where you wanted to go, or even how to purchase a ticket? Did other people bump into you and shove you as they rushed off to catch their trains? A dream such as this was likely to be indicating your desire to move on in life, together with your uncertainty about where to go next (or how to get there). Or if you dreamed of standing at a station and watching bus after bus (or train after train) pull away, your unconscious may have been reflecting your frustration and sadness at having "missed the bus" or "the train" (i.e., an important opportunity) in your waking life. Do you feel as if you are continuously "stuck at the station"? Have you been waiting for too long for your life to change? If so, your unconscious may have been urging you to take charge of your life, to take the initiative to make a change, and to follow a new waking direction—in other words, to "get on the bus!"

Related Dreams

pages 209, 231, 240, 248, 295 & 300

TRAVEL DOCUMENTS

✦✦✦✦✦✦✦✦✦✦✦✦✦✦✦✦✦✦✦✦✦✦✦✦✦✦✦✦✦✦✦✦✦✦✦

In the world of dreams, travel documents—including passports and other means of identification; bus, plane, and train tickets; itineraries; and boarding passes—may symbolize personal identity, image, or persona, official business, adherence to the rules, or small (but important) details that you must take care of.

Symbolic and Verbal Associations
- Personal identity
- Image or persona
- Being "official"; adherence to the rules
- Important details
- Something in your life that is "out of date"

Positive Interpretations: Did you dream that you approached an airline check-in desk and presented the clerk with your passport and plane ticket? If so, and if an upcoming real-world business trip or vacation has been on your mind, then your dream may simply have reflected your anticipation of, or excitement about, your planned journey. But what if, in your dream, you were surprised to see that the photo on your passport was not of your face, or that it bore a different name to your own? How did your dream self react? If you were pleased with your new face or name, ask yourself why. Did you feel that the new passport face was prettier or more handsome than yours? Did you appear to be kinder or gentler? Or tougher and stronger? Was your new name more poetic or cosmopolitan than your old one? Your dream may have been an indication that you wish to take on a new identity or to present a new image or persona to the world (and you will not necessarily need to change your name or appearance in order to achieve this).

Negative Interpretations: Did you have a frustrating dream in which you were trying to board a plane but the airline staff turned you away because there was a problem with your ticket or because your passport was out of date? If so, was your unconscious trying to tell you that you need to update your passport or double-check your flight ticket for an upcoming trip? However, if this explanation seems unlikely, you may want to ask yourself whether your waking ambitions are being hindered, either by an authority figure's rigid insistence that you abide by the official rules or else because of your own failure to keep on top of the small, yet crucial, details of your life. And if your dream self argued with the airline staff, have you been battling it out with whoever has authority over you during your waking hours? (Or if you have not been waging such a real-world battle, your unconscious may have been advising you to do so—especially if your dream depicted you as winning the argument.) Finally, did you dream that you lost your ticket or passport? If so, do you feel that you have lost your identity in the real world, perhaps because you have recently had to give up some part of your life that once defined you? Or is your waking disorganization causing you to miss important opportunities?

Related Dreams
pages 125, 121, 233, 248, 301 & 304

My Travel Documents Dreams

✦✦✦✦✦✦✦✦✦✦✦✦✦✦✦✦✦✦✦

Passage to Ride
If you have booked a vacation and dreamed that you presented your passport to a check-in clerk, only to be told that it was out of date and you were going nowhere, you'd be wise to take your dream literally. But if you don't think that this was an unconscious warning that your passport really has expired, what could be holding you back in life?

TRAVEL

My Walking Dreams

....

....

....

....

....

....

....

....

* * * * * * * * * * * * * * * * * * * *

Stepping Out

If you dreamed of being a child, and of clutching your father's hand as you set off on a walk together, could your unconscious have depicted your current sense of vulnerability and lack of direction, and your consequent desire for a father figure's protection and guidance? Or are you simply feeling nostalgia for your childhood and the companionable relationship that you and your father enjoyed?

WALKING

* *

When we walk, we power ourselves along in life with our own two legs and feet, which is why, in the language of dreams, walking is associated with self-reliance and with being in control of one's life. Other dream meanings of walking have to do with how we walk (i.e., alone, softly, quickly, or with a crippled or hobbled gait).

Symbolic and Verbal Associations
- Traveling through life at a slow, leisurely pace
- Independence and self-reliance: standing "on your own two feet"; being in control
- "Treading a lonely path"; "going it alone"
- The need to tread "lightly" or "softly" around someone; walking "on eggshells"
- Feeling as if you are "hobbled" or "crippled"

Positive Interpretations: As in the term "standing on your own two feet," a dream of walking may suggest that you are leading an independent life. Therefore, if you had a dream in which you were walking along quickly, with energy and purpose, the message may be that you are advancing effectively in the waking world by your own efforts, and that you are in control of your own life and destiny. If, in your dream, you found yourself walking along a straight, level road, it is likely that you are following a direct, uncomplicated route toward your real-world goal or objective. If the day was pleasant and sunny, and if there was a gentle wind at your back that helped to push you along, then the message from your unconscious implies optimism about your future. And if you strolled along at a leisurely pace as you enjoyed the warmth of the sunshine and the beauty of the scenery, then your unconscious may have been reflecting your waking enjoyment of life, or else it may have been encouraging you to slow down, to begin to live "in the moment," and to take the time to notice and appreciate the beauty of the world around you.

Negative Interpretations: If you dreamed that you walked along a wooded trail that twisted and turned, or if you felt as if you were wandering around without aim, then the message from your unconscious may be that you are finding your journey toward a waking goal to be extremely slow and muddled, or else that you are having trouble "finding your way" in life. And if you dreamed that you sorely missed the companionship of others as you walked on alone, your unconscious may have been implying that you are "treading a lonely path" through life (in which case, your unconscious was probably encouraging you to seek out a like-minded traveler to share your waking journey). Otherwise, if you found your dream self creeping along as if you were afraid of making any noise, do you feel as if you have to "tread lightly" or "walk on eggshells" around someone in your waking life? And finally, if your dream self struggled forward with a limping gait, is a needy person in your waking life making you feel "hobbled" or "crippled" in your freedom of movement?

Related Dreams
pages 45, 53, 69, 239, 289 & 303

CHAPTER 16
THE ANIMAL KINGDOM

If an animal featured in your dream, the crucial question to ask
yourself is what you associate that animal with. Having identified
the quality or "animal instinct," then ask yourself how that may
have relevance to your waking world. For instance, if you
dreamed of a lion and decide that it represented courage, was
your unconscious telling you that you should try to be as brave
as a lion in a confrontational waking situation?

My Amphibians & Reptiles Dreams

★ ★ ★ ★ ★ ★ ★ ★ ★ ★ ★ ★ ★ ★ ★ ★ ★

Cold-blooded Characters

The symbolic parallels that the dreaming mind draws with amphibians and reptiles are rarely complimentary, whether the association is with a "lounge lizard" (a social climber), a "cold-blooded" person (someone who is unfeeling, dispassionate, or maybe even cruel), or a "toad" (a loathsome individual). A dream chameleon may be a more positive symbol, however, often denoting someone's ability to blend into any social scenario.

AMPHIBIANS & REPTILES

★★★

When reptiles or amphibians feature in a dream, the unconscious message is likely to do with either menace (perhaps indicating a person who is slick or sly) or transcendence (particularly if it was a creature of water, which is a symbol of the unconscious).

Symbolic and Verbal Associations

- Malicious intent; a slick or sly person
- "Crocodile tears": an insincere emotional display
- Someone who is a "lounge lizard" or a social climber
- A chameleon: someone who can blend into any environment
- Transcendence; higher consciousness

Positive Interpretations: If you dreamed of a frog—an amphibian that begins its life as an egg and transforms itself into a tadpole and, finally, into a frog—then the symbolism was likely to do with transformation. Is someone in your life (perhaps you) like the fairytale frog, who is transformed into a prince by the kiss of a princess? Because they produce masses of eggs, frogs are also symbols of fertility. Therefore, might your dream have been a reference to your desire to have children? As a prolific egg-layer, the turtle is also a symbol of fertility—and, because of its longevity and its wizened face, a symbol of wisdom, too. The turtle may also represent the cosmos (as, in some mythologies, the turtle is said to carry the world on its back). So if you dreamed that you saw a turtle that was stuck on its back, waving its legs in a frantic attempt to right itself, do you feel as if your own waking world has been "turned upside down" recently? Because many lizards resemble snakes, a dream lizard may share the symbolic associations of the serpent. So if you had a positive reaction to a dream of a snakelike lizard, you should consider whether it bore some of the more positive associations of the snake, including healing, spiritual or intellectual illumination, or dormant energy and potential.

Negative Interpretations: Was your dream of a toad a reference to someone in your waking life who is ugly or poisonous (i.e., loathsome or malicious)? If you had a negative reaction to a dream of a lizard, it may have bone some of the more sinister associations of the snake: danger, someone who is venomous, evil, treachery, or emotional iciness. But if you dreamed of watching a chameleon change its hue, was the reference to someone in your life who is fickle (is it you?), or to someone who can change or alter their personality to suit any particular situation? (Or was your unconscious pointing to the advisability of camouflaging your true feelings in the waking world?) A dream in which you were frightened by an alligator or a crocodile is likely to indicate that you are being threatened by a dangerous person in the real world. You should also consider whether someone is attempting to deceive you by their shedding of "crocodile tears," an insincere display of sadness, in order to draw you closer and then swallow you up.

Related Dreams

pages 137, 175, 326, 338, 385 & 387

APES & MONKEYS

As some of the most intelligent of creatures in the animal kingdom, monkeys and apes are naturally curious, which makes them both playful and mischievous—two of the chief dream associations of these animals. Also, because of their likeness to humans, there are a number of ape and monkey metaphors for different types of human behavior and personality traits.

Symbolic and Verbal Associations
- "Aping," or copying, someone
- "Monkeying around" or "monkey business"; playfulness
- An irritating person
- Someone who is "a big ape" (i.e., stupid and brutish)
- "The monkey on your back"; addiction, madness, or obsession

Positive Interpretations: Did you have a dream in which a monkey amused you with its antics? If so, your dream may have been an unconscious reflection of your need to incorporate more playfulness into your life. (When was the last time that you spent the day "monkeying around" with your friends?) It is also possible that the dream monkey was a symbol of someone in your life whom you find is fun to be around, in which case your unconscious may have been advising you to spend more time with this person. Alternatively, did you dream of the classic organ grinder and his pet monkey, who, dressed in a little red suit and cap, runs around with a tin cup that he holds out for spectators to drop coins into? If so, might the monkey have represented someone in your life who needs your help or support (either financial or emotional)? Or, was your unconscious simply imploring you to be more generous with others?

Negative Interpretations: In your dream, did a monkey's mischief-making cause you to become extremely irritated? For instance, did you dream that a monkey stole your hat off your head and raced around the room with it, climbing the walls and swinging from the chandeliers, so that you could not catch it? If so, is someone's "monkey business," immature practical jokes, or annoying, attention-seeking behavior getting on your nerves in the real world? Or was your dream monkey the archetypal trickster, whom your unconscious mind summoned in order to tell you not to take yourself quite so seriously? Did your dream of "a big ape" really refer to someone in your waking life whom you consider to be stupid and brutish? Or was your dream ape an unconscious reference to your habit of copying or "aping" everything that your best friend says and does? Finally, did you dream that a screeching monkey had latched itself onto your back and that, try as you might, you could not shake it off? If so, your unconscious may have been referring to an unhealthy obsession or addiction that you are struggling with in the real world (and if you think that this interpretation might be correct, consider seeking professional help for your problem).

My Apes & Monkeys Dreams

Monkey Business
Monkeys, and especially apes, bear such a marked resemblance to humans that the unconscious sometimes summons them into a dream as a reference to someone in the dreamer's social circle. So if one of these creatures was monkeying around in your dream, did its behavior remind you of anyone in particular? Your impish, playful child, for example, or perhaps your hulking, gorillalike brother-in-law?

Related Dreams
pages 122, 131, 138, 235 & 359

My Asses & Mules Dreams

....
....
....
....
....
....
....
....
....

✳ ✳ ✳ ✳ ✳ ✳ ✳ ✳ ✳ ✳ ✳ ✳ ✳ ✳ ✳ ✳ ✳ ✳

Feeling Mulish

A dream ass or mule is likely to have embodied a pun, and the pun may provide the key to interpreting your dream. So when your dreaming mind conjured up an ass, was it referring to someone's foolishness? And if a mule dug in its heels and refused to plod on in dreamland, was the reference to your own "mulish," or obstinate or mutinous, behavior?

ASSES & MULES

✳✳✳✳✳✳✳✳✳✳✳✳✳✳✳✳✳✳✳✳✳✳✳✳✳✳✳✳✳✳✳✳✳✳✳✳

As beasts of burden, asses (or donkeys) and mules are likely to indicate work duties or burdens in the language of dreams. Mules are also particularly noted for their stubbornness—a meaning that should also be considered if you dreamed of one of these animals.

Symbolic and Verbal Associations
‹ Hard work and stamina; a good work ethic
‹ Carrying "a heavy load on your back"
‹ A stubborn person
‹ Someone who is grumpy
‹ Someone who is behaving foolishly, like "an ass"

Positive Interpretations: Because they can be stronger and have greater endurance than horses, mules are desirable both as laborers and for riding. Therefore, if you dreamed of this animal, you may want to consider whether it represented strength, endurance, stamina, or a good work ethic, characteristics that you perhaps already possess, or that your unconscious is perhaps encouraging you to adopt. And just as a dream of riding a horse is likely to represent your vitality, energy, and drive—as well as your sex drive—a dream of sitting astride a donkey or a mule may signify a vitality or drive that is "slow, but sure" (and perhaps also a bit humble, as these creatures are generally not considered to be as noble or as beautiful as horses).

Negative Interpretations: If your dreaming mind cast a spotlight on an ass or a mule who was carrying a heavy load on its back, have you been feeling weighed down by burdens during your waking hours? Are the demands of others placing a large load on your back? If so, how did your dream donkey or mule react to its burden? If it plodded along without complaining, despite the load that it carried, then your unconscious may have been using your dream to set an example for you, so that you might learn to have more patience and stamina in dealing with your own responsibilities. However, if your dream mule came to a halt and refused to go any farther, might your unconscious have been encouraging you to carry out a similar mutiny in the waking world? Or was your unconscious attempting to draw a parallel with someone in your waking life who is "as stubborn as a mule," or else with someone who is grumpy and uncooperative? You may also want to consider whether a dream donkey was a reference to someone in the real world who is behaving "like an ass" (could it be you?) Finally, if you are familiar with the breeding of mules, which are produced by mating a donkey and a horse, and which are almost always sterile, then might your dream of a mule have been a reference to someone in the real world (perhaps you) who is emotionally sterile, or else to someone's impotence or lack of virility?

Related Dreams

pages 35, 259, 306, 317, 328 & 302

BATS

Perhaps the most infamous of bats, vampire bats—like the bloodsucking monster that they are named for—survive by feeding on the blood of other animals, including cows, pigs, horses, birds, and occasionally even humans. Because of this, and because of the nocturnal nature of these animals, bats have strong symbolic associations with black magic, malevolence, and vampirism.

Symbolic and Verbal Associations
- Danger; a sinister attack
- A person who "sucks you dry" or who saps your energy
- Someone who is "batty," "bats," or "as crazy as a bat"
- An "old bat": a derogatory term for an eccentric older woman
- Being as "blind as a bat"

Positive Interpretations: Bats are creatures of the air (which, in symbolic terms, is associated with aspirations and with spirituality). And as mammals that have the rare power of flight, bats naturally have a certain amount of mystique about them. So if you had a positive reaction to a dream of a bat, it is possible that your unconscious was making a reference to spiritual elevation and enlightenment, or to the pursuit of goals and aspirations. Otherwise, because bats are creatures that use sonar to detect their usual prey of flying insects, your unconscious may have been making a reference to your own heightened powers of intuition—i.e., your "sixth sense."

Negative Interpretations: In your dream, were you awakened at midnight by the sound of a large, black bat flapping its wings outside your bedroom window, under the light of the full moon (a sight that filled your heart with sheer terror)? If so, before you went to sleep, did you watch a scary movie in which an evil vampire transformed himself into the form of a bat in order to fly through the night air? However, if this explanation seems unlikely, it may be that your unconscious has detected that you are being threatened in the real world by a sinister person or persons. (The possibility of this meaning being pertinent is redoubled if you are familiar with stories and folklore in which bats are cast in the role of a witch's familiar—a creature who aids the witch in her evil-doing—or if bats in your area may be rabid.) Or was the unconscious reference to someone in your waking life who is "sucking" your energy or sapping your vitality? Is there a person in your life with malicious intent, who has the ability to "transform" his or her personality in order to escape detection or to disguise his or her true, evil nature? On a lighter note, you may want to consider whether your dream bat was a reference to someone in your life who is "batty" or "bats," or who has "bats in the belfry" (i.e., someone who is crazy or eccentric), but perhaps harmless—an association that comes from the erratic flight patterns that these winged creatures display. The details of your dream, together with your reaction to the bat, will help you to decide which interpretation is more correct.

Related Dreams

pages 134, 145, 211, 315, 316 & 363

My Bats Dreams

----

* * * * * * * * * * * * * * * * * * *

Bat Out of Hell

Unless you are fond of bats, you probably regard them as sinister creatures of the night, and perhaps even as blood-sucking vampires. So if you awoke from a nightmare in which you were being mobbed by hundreds of swooping bats, do you feel as though you are being besieged by countless malevolent forces in the waking world, all apparently intent on "bleeding you dry"?

My Bear Dreams

✶ ✶ ✶ ✶ ✶ ✶ ✶ ✶ ✶ ✶ ✶ ✶ ✶ ✶ ✶ ✶ ✶

Beware of the Bear!

Bears are notoriously bad-tempered, and if you dreamed that an enraged bear charged at you before rising up on its hind legs and swiping viciously at you with its massive paws, who has been behaving like a "bear with a sore head" in the waking world? Have you been lashing out at others, just like the infuriated bear that rampaged through your dream?

BEARS

✶✶✶✶✶✶✶✶✶✶✶✶✶✶✶✶✶✶✶✶✶✶✶✶✶✶✶✶✶✶✶✶✶✶✶

Bears are powerful animals that have powerful symbolism. They are known for their ferocity and their strength (unless, of course, they come in the guise of the gentle teddy bear), and for their fierce maternal instincts in protecting their cubs. They are notorious for their bad temper, too.

Symbolic and Verbal Associations

- Someone (especially a man) who is "a teddy bear" (i.e., gentle and loving)
- Fierceness and strength
- A person who is bad-tempered
- Emotional retreat or "hibernation"; physical rest
- Someone whom you cannot "bear"
- Basic instincts and urges

Positive Interpretations: If you dreamed of a mother bear who was fiercely protecting her cubs, the unconscious reference might have been to your own (or to someone else's) powerful maternal instincts, or even to the archetypal mother. But if you dreamed of a bear that was retiring into a cave to hibernate for the winter, your unconscious may have been mirroring your desire to withdraw emotionally from others, or else your need for a period of physical rest and relaxation. Otherwise, if a teddy bear featured in your dream, might the reference have been to a man who is gentle, loving, and comforting (or perhaps just big and hairy)? Or if you dreamed of watching a polar bear catch fish through a hole in the ice, might your unconscious have been urging you to look underneath (or past) someone's veneer of emotional iciness?

Negative Interpretations: In your dream, did you accidentally cross the path of an ill-tempered bear, which roared and snarled as it reared up on its back legs to threaten you? If so, is someone in your waking life behaving in a similar manner by refusing to "pick on someone their own size"? For example, does your husband roar at your children whenever they do something that he doesn't like? Or is it you yourself who is growling like "a bear" at every move that the kids make? Alternatively, is there someone or something in your life that you simply cannot "bear"? Finally, if you dreamed that you were being pursued by a voracious bear, there are a number of possible meanings. It could be that your unconscious was alerting you to a dangerous or predatory person in your waking life, or your dream may have been a metaphor for a memory of a past incident in which someone sought to do (and perhaps succeeded in doing) you harm. It is also possible that your unconscious used the bear to represent a dangerous or wild part of yourself that is threatening to escape from its tethers, or that your dream was a warning that you have been unhealthily suppressing a natural basic instinct or urge—in other words, that the source of your fear lies within yourself!

Related Dreams

pages 89, 113, 221, 257, 364 & 374

BEETLES & BUGS

✦✦✦✦✦✦✦✦✦✦✦✦✦✦✦✦✦✦✦✦✦✦✦✦✦✦✦✦✦✦✦✦✦✦✦✦✦✦✦

Although the term "bug" actually only applies to one order of insects, most people refer to all insects as "bugs." Beetles are of another order that is easily distinguished by the hardened covering over their forewings, which protects their soft bodies. Many people view most bugs as pests, which is why the most obvious symbolism of a dream bug is a person who is "bugging," or bothering, you.

Symbolic and Verbal Associations
- Feeling as "snug as a bug in a rug"
- Smelling a "stink bug"
- A person who is "bugging," or bothering, you
- Someone whom you wish would "bug out" (i.e., leave quickly)
- Putting "a bug in someone's ear" (or discreetly giving them useful information)

Positive Interpretations: If you dreamed that a shiny red beetle scuttled before you, might your unconscious have been referring to that other shiny, red "Bug," or Volkswagen Beetle, that you have been wishing for? Or was your dreaming mind thinking of the new, digitally remastered Beatles album that you are planning to purchase? Did you dream that a beautiful ladybug flew onto your shoulder? The ladybug (which is actually a beetle, and is also sometimes called the lady beetle or ladybird beetle) is widely considered to be lucky (and killing one of these insects is said to be unlucky). So your dream may have signaled your optimistic outlook on life, or your feeling that you are a lucky person, with much to be thankful for. And if you made a wish over the ladybug before it flew away, what did you wish for? (The answer may surprise you as it may be a desire that you have thus far hidden from your conscious mind.) Alternatively, did you dream that you were as "snug as a bug in a rug"? If so, do you feel comforted, loved, and protected in your waking environment?

Negative Interpretations: If you dreamed of being pestered by a bug, is someone in the real world "bugging," or pestering, you? Or has your unconscious detected a "stink bug" (or a noxious or offensive person) in your midst? Alternatively, in your dream, did you drop a bug into your friend's ear? If so, is there some important (but sensitive) information that you feel you need to tell her in the waking world—in other words, do you want to "put a bug in her ear"? Or did someone put a "bug," or listening device, on your dream telephone and hear all the bad things you've been saying behind his back? If you still cannot make out the meaning of a dream bug, it may help to perform some word association. For example, does something have you "bug-eyed" with shock or fear? Do you wish that an annoying person in your life would just "bug out," or are you yourself ready to "bug out" on (or quickly abandon) some person or situation in your waking world?

Related Dreams

pages 42, 256, 316, 329 & 340

My Beetles & Bugs Dreams

✦✦✦✦✦✦✦✦✦✦✦✦✦✦✦✦✦✦✦✦✦

Beetling Around

Unless you really have been preoccupied with beetles and bugs—be they insects or automobiles—during your waking hours, a dream through which a bug and its relatives beetled may have been a reference to something that has been contaminated or infested by "verminous" influences in the real world. Otherwise, could the reference have been to your intrusive neighbors, who are currently "bugging" you?

My Big Cats Dreams

✶ ✶ ✶ ✶ ✶ ✶ ✶ ✶ ✶ ✶ ✶ ✶ ✶ ✶ ✶ ✶ ✶

The Leonine Lead

If you are a woman and one of the highlights of your dream was the sight of a sleek and powerful lioness stalking fearlessly across the savannah, could your unconscious have been setting you an example to follow? Does a difficult situation in your waking world require resolution, and could you achieve this by confronting it head-on, with courage and confidence, for instance?

BIG CATS

✶ ✶

The big, wild cats of nature (including lions, tigers, cheetahs, leopards, and lynxes) are universal symbols of power, stealth, pride and—in the case of the lion, in particular—nobility, the sun, and fire. If your unconscious summoned one of these magnificent creatures into your dream, it is likely that it had an important message to impart.

Symbolic and Verbal Associations

❛ Nobility
❛ Courage
❛ Power and stealth
❛ Pride
❛ The sun; fire
❛ Someone who, like a leopard, can never "change their spots" (i.e., disguise or transform their character)

Positive Interpretations: In your dream, did you watch as a mighty lion strolled across the horizon? The lion is known as "the king of the beasts," and symbolically, the lion represents nobility, courage, and power. So is it possible that your unconscious was encouraging you to cultivate these qualities within yourself? (This may be especially true if you know that you must soon face a real-world challenge or battle.) Alternatively, if you are a man who dreamed of watching a male lion surrounded by a pride of lionesses and cubs, was your unconscious mirroring your "pride" and satisfaction at being the "king cat" or the alpha male in your family? The lion is also the symbol of the zodiacal sign of Leo (which is associated with fire), so you may want to consider this when interpreting your dream. For instance, might your dream lion have represented someone in your life who was born under the sign of Leo? Or if you dreamed of a lynx, was your unconscious telling you that you need to be "lynx-eyed," or have keen vision (i.e., to stay alert or to consider all possibilities) in the waking world?

Negative Interpretations: If you dreamed of watching a powerful lion turn tail and flee, do you feel as if your pride or courage has left you during a difficult time in your life? Are you disappointed because you feel that you, or someone that you admire, has acted with cowardice? It is important to note that all of the big cats share many of the lion's symbolic associations. For instance, lions—as well as all big cats—are also a symbol of danger, so if your dream self had a fearful reaction to one of these felines, your unconscious may have been warning you that it has detected that you may be under great threat from someone or something. The tiger, in particular, has a "man-eating" reputation. So if you are a woman who dreamed of witnessing a tigress prey on a helpless man, might your unconscious have been highlighting your own aggressive, perhaps sexually voracious, tendencies? If your dream focused on a leopard, might your unconscious have been referring to someone (perhaps you) who, like the leopard, can't "change his spots"?

Related Dreams

pages 118, 221, 257, 281, 318 & 384

Birds of Prey

Blackbirds and ravens are birds that feast off carrion, or dead animals, which is why their chief symbolic association is with death. Death is also symbolized by birds of prey (or raptors)—including vultures (whose main diet is also carrion), eagles, hawks, and falcons—rapacious hunters that use their claws to capture and kill their prey. However, depending on the context, there are also a number of other possible interpretations for a dream that featured one of these birds.

My Birds of Prey Dreams

....
....
....
....
....
....
....
....
....

Symbolic and Verbal Associations
- Death; the circling of the "vultures"
- "Crowing," or bragging
- Wanting to "pick over the bones" of something
- Having "a bone to pick" with someone
- "Picking" someone's brain

Positive Interpretations: If you dreamed of watching a buzzard pick over the bones of a carcass, the symbolism need not have to do with death, demise, or ruination. For instance, your unconscious may have been reflecting your desire to "pick over the bones" (or to salvage what is left) of a failed relationship. Or do you "have a bone to pick" (or a grievance to bring up) with your sister? Do you wish to "pick" your friend's brain about a subject that he or she has expert knowledge of (but about which you know very little)? Thinking about the context of your dream and your dreaming reaction to the bird and its actions should help you to determine the message that your unconscious was trying to send to you.

Negative Interpretations: Apart from their macabre diet, ravens, crows, and blackbirds are also associated with death because of the funereal coloring of their plumage. However, it is important to note that a dream having to do with death is likely to be an unconscious reference to a symbolic death—such as the termination of a project or the end of a period in your life—and not necessarily to an actual physiological death. Did you dream that you were being eyed by a hungry raven? If so, do you feel that some aspect of your waking life is nearing its demise? For example, is the company that you own and run about to go bankrupt? Did you dream that the "vultures were circling," impatiently waiting to dine on your company's remains? If you did dream of the latter scenario, might your unconscious have been pointing to a group of persons who would like to see your business go under because it would somehow be to their benefit? In another scenario, if you dreamed that a crow was making a great, raucous din with its incessant cawing, was your unconscious making a reference to someone in the real world who is annoying others with their "crowing" or arrogant bragging? Blackbirds are also known for their highly territorial behavior. So, if you dreamed that you watched as a male blackbird chased off other males, are you feeling territorial over some aspect of your waking life?

* * * * * * * * * * * * * * * * * * *

Rich Pickings

If watching hungry vultures tearing at the flesh of a dead zebra turned your stomach in dreamland, did your dream self's reaction mirror the feeling of disgust that has beset you in real life? It may be, for example, that your brother's business has gone bust and that you have been nauseated by the way that his creditors have been greedily picking over the pieces.

Related Dreams
pages 118, 92, 175, 324, 339 & 363

THE ANIMAL
KINGDOM

My Butterflies & Moths Dreams

....
....
....
....
....
....
....
....

* * * * * * * * * * * * * * * * * * *

Transcendent Beauty

Many dream interpreters believe that butterflies symbolize the soul, or else the essence of our characters, or, alternatively, our inner beauty. So if an exquisitely marked butterfly fluttered through your dream, what could it have represented? Your recently deceased grandmother, perhaps, now free of the suffering that blighted her final years, or the essential goodness at the core of your own being?

BUTTERFLIES & MOTHS

Butterflies are among the most loved of insects. They are beautiful and graceful and they pollinate flowers. In the language of dreams, butterflies may signify the spirit, transcendence, and freedom, while their larval stage, the caterpillar, is a symbol of latent potential. Moths, which tend to be more drab than butterflies, and are also destructive to crops and clothing, may bear a more negative dream meaning.

Symbolic and Verbal Associations
‹ Latent potential
‹ Transformation; metamorphosis
‹ The spirit or soul; spiritual enlightenment or transcendence
‹ Beauty
‹ Freedom
‹ Someone who is a "social butterfly"
‹ Something that has been "moth-eaten"; destruction

Positive Interpretations: In your dream, did you watch as a caterpillar spun itself a cocoon? If so, do you feel as if you are about to undergo a marvelous metamorphosis in your life, just as a caterpillar emerges from its chrysalis only after it has been transformed into a winged butterfly? Such a change can be physical or spiritual. For example, have you scheduled an appointment with your hairdresser, and are you planning to have your hair cut in a way that will present a radical "new you" to the world? Or have you signed up for a meditation class that you hope will help you to transform your spirit? While the caterpillar and the chrysalis are symbols of latent potential, the butterfly itself symbolizes the manifestation of that potential in all of its glorious splendor. And because butterflies and moths are creatures of the air, their appearance in dreams may also signify spiritual transcendence or enlightenment. Traditionally, the souls of those who have died are said to take the form of butterflies. So if you have been recently bereaved and you dreamed that a butterfly landed on your shoulder, your unconscious may have been trying to comfort you with the knowledge that your loved one is still with you "in spirit," and that he or she is now happy and free.

Negative Interpretations: If you dreamed that you admired a butterfly as it floated from flower to flower and that you wished, in frustration, that you yourself could be so free, are you feeling tied down or held back by your real-world commitments and responsibilities? If so, your unconscious may have conjured up the butterfly in order to encourage you to hope that you, too, may attain such a feeling of freedom for yourself. Alternatively, if you dreamed that you were saddened because your favorite sweater was moth-eaten, might the sweater have represented some aspect of your life that is being eaten away by something? Or if you watched as a moth flew into a flame and perished, was your unconscious hinting that you are somehow "playing with fire"?

Related Dreams
pages 36, 92, 143,
313, 350 & 363

CAMELS

Because it is able to withstand long treks through the hot, dry desert without drinking any water, the camel is a symbol of stamina, patience, perseverance, temperance, and self-control. In the ancient East, it was a symbol of royalty and dignity.

Symbolic and Verbal Associations
‹ Stamina
‹ Patience and perseverance
‹ Temperance; self-control
‹ Royalty and dignity
‹ Preparedness
‹ Humility and obedience

Positive Interpretations: Did you dream that a fat-humped camel traveled across your field of vision? If so, was your unconscious signaling that you would do well to begin saving or storing your resources in preparation for "lean times" or a "dry spell," just as the camel stores fat in its hump? For example, if you know that the company that you work for isn't doing well financially, your unconscious may have been warning you that you had better begin saving your money in case you are laid off from your job. Otherwise, could your unconscious have been using the camel in order to encourage you to trust in your stamina and to persevere in a difficult real-world endeavor? Alternatively, if you dreamed of watching a camel kneel down in order to accept its burden, might your unconscious have been mirroring your own humility (or else urging you to nurture this quality within yourself)? Or did your unconscious call up the image of the kneeling camel in order to encourage you to be obedient to your superiors?

Negative Interpretations: If you dreamed of a camel and you are trying to quit smoking, did your unconscious call forth the mascot on the label of your favorite brand of cigarettes? If so, your dream was probably indicative of your battle with your addiction. (And, in your dream, did you mount and ride the camel, or did you shoo it away?) If you dreamed of a camel whose back was loaded up with heavy bundles, are you feeling overloaded, overburdened, or weighed down by your own waking duties and responsibilities? (If so, your unconscious may have been encouraging you to accept your burdens with the calm dignity, patience, and perseverance of the camel.) Or do you feel as if you must pass through a spiritual or emotional desert or wasteland in your waking life, just as the camel must travel across the desert before it may drink again? For example, does the completion of your education mean that you must go to live for a time in an unfamiliar country? If so, your unconscious was likely using the image of the camel to hearten you with the knowledge that you have the ability to overcome the ordeal before you.

My Camels Dreams

....
....
....
....
....
....
....
....
....

* ★ * ★ * ★ * ★ * ★ * ★ * ★ * ★ * ★ *

I Will Survive!

Camels are perhaps best known for their ability to survive for long periods without water in scorching desert environments, thanks to their humps, and it may therefore be that your unconscious summoned a camel into your dream to reassure you that although you are experiencing an arid spell in your life—maybe your creativity has dried up—your inner resources will see you through it.

Related Dreams

My Cats Dreams

✶ ✶ ✶ ✶ ✶ ✶ ✶ ✶ ✶ ✶ ✶ ✶ ✶ ✶ ✶ ✶ ✶ ✶ ✶

A Pussy Cat

How you feel about cats is significant when trying to decode the meaning of a dream that focused on an appealing bundle of fluffy fur. If you like them, the reference may have been to a "pussy cat," or an amiable softy, in your social circle. But if you don't, could the message have been that someone is manipulating you by pretending to be vulnerable?

CATS

Cats were first domesticated by the ancient Egyptians, to whom this animal was a sacred guardian of temples and homes. In Western cultures, cats were once considered to be witch's familiars, with magical powers of their own. In symbolic terms, this animal is strongly associated with feminine mystery, wisdom, and intuition.

Symbolic and Verbal Associations
- Femininity
- Mystery
- Wisdom
- Intuition
- Independence and aloofness

Positive Interpretations: If you dreamed of a cat, was your unconscious highlighting its qualities of independence and aloofness in order to set an example for you? If so, are you too emotionally dependent on others? But if you dreamed of holding a tiny kitten, your dream may have been reflecting your desire to have a baby. A dream of petting a cat may also signify someone in your waking life who is in need of emotional "petting" or "stroking." Cats have amazing instinctive survival skills, which is why they are often said to have "nine lives." So did your unconscious call up a dream cat in order to point out your own survivalist spirit? Or was your unconscious telling you to rely on your instincts in dealing with a waking problem? If you like cats and you dreamed of one, it may have been a manifestation of one of the positive feminine archetypes (the mother, the princess, the amazon, or the high priestess or wise woman). And if you are familiar with Egyptian mythology, you may want to consider whether your dream cat was actually Bast or Bastet, the cat goddess, who is associated with pleasure and joy, music and dance, love and the moon.

Negative Interpretations: In folklore, black cats are considered to be bad luck. So if you had a dream in which you were filled with dread because a black cat crossed your path, are you feeling worried that things are about to go wrong in your waking world? If you generally dislike cats (perhaps because you consider them to be cruel or evil), then it is likely that you had a bad reaction to any feline that you came across in dreamland. If this is the case, your dream cat may have symbolized a negative feminine archetype (the terrible mother, the siren, the huntress, or the evil witch). If you dreamed that an aloof cat sauntered by you and refused to come at your beckoning, did it represent a woman in your waking life who is cool and aloof toward you? Or has your girlfriend been behaving "cattily" or spitefully? Alternatively, did your dream cat symbolize your own smugness, as in "the cat that ate the canary"? Was your unconscious warning you that "curiosity killed the cat"? Or, if you are a man who dreamed of a tomcat, was your unconscious pointing out your own tendency or desire to "tomcat" around with women?

Related Dreams
pages 113, 118, 127, 134, 142 & 314

CATTLE

✦ ✦

Throughout history, cows and bulls have been venerated by many peoples, and cows are still sacred among the Hindus in India. Among other things, a dream cow may represent nurturing, maternal instincts, a "cash cow" or income source, or complacency, while dream bulls may be indicative of masculine virility, power, and anger.

Symbolic and Verbal Associations
- ◖ Nurturing; the archetypal mother
- ◖ A "cash cow"
- ◖ Complacency; a tendency to "go along with the herd"
- ◖ Masculine virility, power, and anger
- ◖ Courage; "taking the bull by the horns"
- ◖ Someone who is clumsy or awkward, "like a bull in a china cabinet"

Positive Interpretations: If you are a woman who has children, or who is thinking of beginning a family, and you dreamed of watching a fat milk cow nursing her young calf, then your unconscious mind may have been mirroring your maternal instincts and desires. But if you have a waking preoccupation with finances and you dreamed of a cow, could it have represented a "cash cow," or a profit source, that you are hoping will pay off for you? In stock-market lingo, a "bull market" refers to a market in which prices are rising, so a similar interpretation may apply if you dreamed of a bull. Or if you are interested in astrology and you dreamed of a bull, you may want to consider whether it represented someone in your waking life who was born under the sun sign of Taurus. If you dreamed that you took a bull by its horns, have you met a waking difficulty with courage?

Negative Interpretations: If you dreamed of watching a herd of cows complacently chew their cud, was your unconscious reflecting your own complacency, placidness, or "bovine" nature? Do you have a tendency to "go along with the herd" rather than think for yourself? In your dream, did an angry cow try to attack you? If so, has a woman in your waking life, or have you, been behaving unkindly toward others, like "a cow"? If you dreamed of watching a team of oxen (castrated bulls) pulling a plow, do you feel as if you have been placed "under a yoke" and are being forced to work for the profit of others during your waking hours? Bulls are temperamental animals that can be extremely dangerous, especially when provoked. Therefore, in the language of dreams, bulls often symbolize masculine virility, power, and anger. In your dream, were you cast in the role of a matador in a bull fight, and were you waving your red rag to gain the attention of a furious, snorting bull? Especially if you are a man, your dream may have denoted your struggle to control "the beast within," which is possibly your sex drive. But if you are a woman who dreamed of being attacked by a bull, could it have represented a sexually aggressive man whom you feel threatened by in the real world?

My Cattle Dreams

✦ ✦ ✦ ✦ ✦ ✦ ✦ ✦ ✦ ✦ ✦ ✦ ✦ ✦ ✦ ✦ ✦

Milking Money

Did you dream of milking a cow, and of feeling enormous satisfaction as you filled bucket after bucket with gallons of rich, warm milk? If so, are you currently making lots of money from a business venture during your waking hours? In this instance, it may be that your dream cow symbolized the "cash cow" that you are "milking" so successfully in the real world.

Related Dreams

pages 113, 181, 310, 328, 331 & 336

My Chickens & Geese Dreams

_____

_____

_____

_____

_____

_____

_____

_____

_____

✶✶✶✶✶✶✶✶✶✶✶✶✶✶✶✶✶✶✶✶✶

A Fox Among Chickens

If you and your friends turned into chickens in dreamland, and huddled anxiously together as you craned your necks in an attempt to identify the danger that you had detected, can you draw a real-life parallel? Is your cozy clique being threatened by a predatory outsider? Has a sly old fox or a foxy lady already got his or her claws into one of you?

CHICKENS & GEESE

✶✶✶

A dream chicken may have varying meanings, depending on whether it was a hen (which is likely to symbolize maternal instincts) or a rooster or cock (which may denote male power, "cockiness," lust, or an early start to the day), while dream eggs or chicks may represent ideas, plans, or ambitions. A dream goose may denote a silly or unwise person.

Symbolic and Verbal Associations
- A "mother hen"
- A fearful person, as in a "chicken"
- Playing "chicken": a battle of nerves
- The cock that "rules the roost"
- Arrogance, or "cockiness"
- "Counting your chickens before they are hatched"
- "The goose that lays the golden egg"
- A "silly goose"

Positive Interpretations: If you dreamed of a chicken, was it a hen or a rooster? Because they lay and hatch their eggs, hens are said to embody the maternal instinct. So if you dreamed of a hen who was sitting on her clutch of eggs, there are a few possible explanations. If you are a woman, did your dream denote your wish to have children? Or if you have children already, was your dream mirroring your own feelings of motherliness? Otherwise, do you wish to be cosseted and fussed over by a "mother hen" figure in the waking world? Alternatively, is there some plan that you are carefully and patiently "hatching"? If you dreamed of a cock crowing, was your unconscious reminding you not to oversleep because you have to get up at "cock crow"?

Negative Interpretations: If you saw a goose in dreamland, could your unconscious have been warning you that you have been acting foolishly or behaving like a "silly goose" in the real world? Or did you dream of "killing the goose that lays the golden egg," an unconscious reference to a bad or hasty real-world business decision? If your dream involved chicken eggs, was your unconscious warning you against "counting your chickens before they are hatched," or becoming carried away by your ambitions, which may never be realized? Alternatively, did your dream chicken represent someone (perhaps you) who is a coward or a fearful "chicken"? Or did you dream that "the chickens" had "come home to roost," a metaphor for something foolish or malicious that you have done in the waking world that is about to bounce back at you? But if you dreamed of watching a rooster or cock strut across the barnyard, might it have represented some male in your waking life (such as your husband, your father, or even you) who "rules the roost," or the home, and who keeps his "hens" in line? Or did the cock represent your own "cockiness" or boasting arrogance, or else someone's virility?

Related Dreams

pages 113, 175, 178, 315, 327 & 339

DEER

In symbolic terms, a dream doe in flight may signal a warning from the unconscious, a skittish or frightened person, or even someone who is "dear" to you. Because antlers are phallic symbols, dream stags are often representative of male virility or lust, though they may also denote rivalry.

Symbolic and Verbal Associations
- A person who is "dear" to you
- Someone who is frozen "like a deer in headlights"
- A skittish person
- A warning
- A bachelor, as in a "stag party"
- The phallus; male virility
- Rivalry

Positive Interpretations: Did you dream of watching a deer grazing peacefully in a sunlit meadow? If so, could it have represented someone in your waking world—perhaps a gentle and timid person—whom you hold very "dear" to your heart? Or did a dream fawn represent someone whom you wish to flatter or "fawn" over (or else someone whom you wish would "fawn" over you)? Did you dream of a stag with a great rack of antlers? If you are a man, the dream stag may have symbolized your pride or your virility—especially if you are a bachelor who is seeking a mate in the real world. But if you are a woman who dreamed of a stag, could it have symbolized the single man whom you are interested in?

Negative Interpretations: In your dream, did you see a white-tailed deer run past you with her tail in the air? When this animal senses danger, it raises its tail, exhibiting a large flash of white as it flees, which both warns other deer of danger and helps the doe's fawn to follow along behind her. So it is possible that your dream was an unconscious attempt to warn you of some danger that it has detected in the waking world. Does are usually shy of humans, and are known for their skittishness. So did the running doe represent a person (particularly a female) in your waking life who is shy or skittish—perhaps someone whom you yourself have frightened by lavishing attention on her? Alternatively, did you dream that you were driving along a dark road, surrounded by woods, when a deer suddenly ran out in front of your car and stopped in the middle of the road? If so, did the dream deer signify a person in the real world who is paralyzed or frozen with fear, "like a deer in headlights"? If you are a man who dreamed of watching two stags lock horns, it is possible that your unconscious was mirroring your rivalry with another man, particularly over the attention of a woman. And if you dreamed of hunting a stag, your dream may have denoted your desire to cull or rein in your libido, your competitive nature, or your aggression.

Related Dreams
pages 114, 221, 239, 257, 274 & 342

My Deer Dreams

---

* * * * * * * * * * * * * * * * *

Doe, a Deer

Unless you dreamed of a mighty stag, a dream deer is likely to have signified someone in your waking world—perhaps even you yourself—whom you consider "a dear." This person may share some of the dream deer's traits, so if you can't make an immediate connection, who in your life is "doe-eyed," or has a melting gaze? Or who is shy and skittish?

THE ANIMAL KINGDOM

My Dinosaurs Dreams

✱ ✱ ✱ ✱ ✱ ✱ ✱ ✱ ✱ ✱ ✱ ✱ ✱ ✱ ✱ ✱ ✱

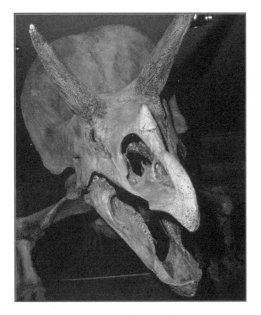

A Prehistoric Relic

There are a number of reasons why a dinosaur may have dominated your dream. It may have represented something that petrifies you, something monstrous, menacing, and dangerous, for instance. But if your dreaming self simply regarded it as a curiosity, it may be that it symbolized the dinosaur in you, such as your outdated beliefs or your liking for styles that were fashionable decades ago.

DINOSAURS

✱✱✱

Although they have been extinct for about 65 million years, dinosaurs do live on in our psyche—and when one of them (or any primitive animal) rears its head in a dream, the message from the unconscious may have to do with something that (or someone who) is outdated or out of style, with primal or "primitive" instincts or desires, or with a sense of pending doom (i.e., the threat of extinction). Different types of dinosaurs and other extinct species may carry specific meanings, such as the dodo bird, which may symbolize a person who is stupid, clumsy, or ineffectual.

Symbolic and Verbal Associations
‹ Being outdated or out of style, as in being "extinct"
‹ Pending doom
‹ Someone who is a "dodo" (i.e., stupid and/or clumsy)
‹ A person who is ineffectual (as represented by the dodo bird, which could not fly)
‹ Primal or "primitive" instincts

Positive Interpretations: In recent years especially, dinosaurs have become a sort of cultural obsession in the Western world—due, in large part, to the continuing discoveries of science, as well as to popular movies that simulate how these beasts may have looked, sounded, and behaved. Did you dream that you were on safari in a primitive landscape, and that you were filled with a sense of awe as you watched as a tyrannosaurus chased and captured its prey or as a triceratops munched on some high-growing grasses as a flying pterodactyl swooped overhead? If so, and if you have just viewed a natural-history show on public television, or if you have recently watched one of the *Jurassic Park* films, then your dreaming mind may have simply been remembering and reflecting upon what you saw. Or if you have a great interest in this topic, could your unconscious have been encouraging you to pursue a degree in archaeology? But if neither of these sorts of explanations seem to apply and you are still perplexed by your dream, then you may want to consider whether your unconscious was making a reference to primal or "primitive" instincts or desires that may be "buried" beneath the surface of your unconscious, but that are yearning for discovery.

Negative Interpretations: In your dream, did you open your closet door to find that a dinosaur was wearing your favorite outfit? If so, do you feel that your wardrobe is outdated or out of style? Is your style a leftover from the "cave days," or is your particular taste in fashion virtually extinct? If so, your unconscious may be craving a new outward physical expression. Otherwise, if you dreamed of a dinosaur or of another extinct creature, is it your ideas that are out of date? If you had a scary dream about dinosaurs, do you feel as if some "monster" (maybe an internal one) is after you in the real world? Or is it that you feel "doomed to extinction"?

Related Dreams

pages 145, 146, 147, 308, 325 & 335

DOGS

THE ANIMAL KINGDOM

W̲hile cats tend to be symbols of femininity, dogs often represent masculinity. In the world of dreams, a dog may denote friendship, companionship, or a protector. More negative interpretations of a dream dog vary widely, including a person from your waking life whom you consider to be a "bitch" or a "dog" (i.e., a lowlife), or something that makes you feel as "sick as a dog."

Symbolic and Verbal Associations
- Masculinity
- Friendship; companionship
- Protection
- Feeling as "sick as a dog"
- A person whom you consider to be a "bitch" (i.e., a person who is nasty)
- Someone whom you consider to be a "dog" (i.e., a lowlife)

Positive Interpretations: In the language of dreams, dogs often represent friends and companions, just as they are our friends and companions in the real world. Therefore, if you like dogs and a friendly one pranced across your dream stage, it may be that you are wishing for more friendship, companionship, and/or fun in your waking life. Since dogs are said to be faithful companions and protectors, it is also possible that your unconscious sent you your dream in order to highlight these qualities within yourself, or else to reflect your desire to have a real-world friend whose faithful companionship would shield or buffer you from the distresses of the waking world. If you dreamed that you were cuddling or playing with a small puppy, it is possible that your unconscious was signaling your desire to have a human baby. And if you dreamed that you were petting a dog, you may want to consider whether it represented someone in your waking life whom you feel is in need of emotional "petting."

Negative Interpretations: In your dream, were you walking a pack of dogs, each of them pulling at the leash in a different direction and becoming entangled with the others, so that you had to strain with all of your strength to hold onto them? If so, your inability to control the dream dogs may represent a waking struggle that you are having with your human "pack" (i.e., your friends or comrades). Do you feel that your friends have gotten out of control, and are you attempting to rein them in before they go completely wild? And if, in your dream, the dogs did indeed break away from you, are you fearful of losing your friends' loyalty? If you dreamed that a large dog was barking fiercely at you, it may be that the dog represented someone in your waking life who has been acting like a "bitch" toward you, or someone whose moral standards are so low that you consider them to be a "dog." Otherwise, it may have been an unconscious warning that the "animal" within you (perhaps your aggression) is trying to break free. Or are you "in the dog house"?

My Dogs Dreams

_____
_____
_____
_____
_____
_____
_____
_____
_____

The Black Dog

Unless the meaning of your dream is instantly obvious, always consider dog-related puns and phrases when mulling it over. If a black dog shadowed your steps in dreamland, could it have signified a shady issue that is "dogging you" in the real world, for example? Or if you suffer from depression, could the dream dog have been a manifestation of your personal "black dog"?

Related Dreams

pages 110, 126, 287, 318, 327 & 342

My Doves Dreams

_____

_____

_____

_____

_____

_____

_____

_____

_____

Messenger of Hope

The dove is a universal symbol of peace, and probably signified your yearning for precisely that if it alighted on a nearby branch in your dream, particularly if you feel as though you are on a war footing during your waking hours. Are you tired of feuding with your siblings? Was the dream dove a message from your unconscious that you'd welcome a truce?

DOVES

Doves are a worldwide symbol of hope and peace, perhaps because of the Old Testament story in which, after the Flood, the dove that Noah had sent out to search for dry land returned to the Ark bearing an olive branch. In Christianity, the dove is also a symbol of the Holy Spirit. Depending on the context, dream doves may also denote gentleness, mourning, or love and marriage.

Symbolic and Verbal Associations
- Peace
- Hope
- Christ; the Holy Spirit
- Gentleness
- Mourning (as in a "mourning dove")
- Love and marriage (as symbolized by turtledoves)
- "Doves and hawks"

Positive Interpretations: In your dream, did a dove alight on your windowsill bearing an olive branch in its beak? If so, the message from your unconscious was likely to have been one of hope and of peace—especially if you have recently gone through a harrowing time in your waking life, just as in the Biblical story of Noah and the Ark, when the dove came bearing the message that "the floodwaters are receding." And if you are a Christian and you dreamed of a dove (which is also a symbol of Christ and the Holy Spirit), you may want to consider whether your dream was reflecting your desire for salvation or spiritual fulfillment. Alternatively, in your dream, did you find yourself on the front line of a bloody war, and were all of your terrors relieved when you saw a white dove fluttering before you? If so, your unconscious was likely trying to give you hope and a sense of peace during a time of conflict, whether this is due to an internal or an external clash. Or did you dream of watching a pair of turtledoves as they billed and cooed happily together in their nest? If so, are you longing to find a gentle, kind partner with whom to settle down and spend your life?

Negative Interpretations: Did you have a dream in which you were being attacked by a bunch of swooping, squawking hawks that bit at you with their beaks and scratched at you with their claws? And, in your dream, did a team of beautiful, soft doves cover your body with their wings and carry you away to safety? If so, do you feel as if you are caught up in a debate between "doves and hawks" (or peacemakers and warmongers) during your waking hours? Finally, if you dreamed that you heard the sorrowful cooing of a "mourning dove," was your dream a reflection of the sadness or grief that you feel within your heart? If you think that this is so, and you have never expressed your sadness in the real world, then your unconscious was probably trying to encourage you to do so as a step toward helping you to release yourself from it.

Related Dreams

pages 112, 175, 267, 274, 315 & 339

ELEPHANTS

Elephants are generally considered to be wise and friendly, which are two of the most obvious meanings that may apply to a dream elephant. And as elephants are considered sacred among certain Eastern peoples, a dream elephant may also denote spirituality and the path toward enlightenment. Also, because of their large size and their strength, a dream elephant may portend potential chaos and destruction.

Symbolic and Verbal Associations
- Wisdom
- Friendship and congeniality
- Spirituality
- A "white elephant" (something that is burdensome or unwanted; a failure)
- Memory: "an elephant never forgets"
- Danger; destruction
- Something big that is of "mammoth" proportions

Positive Interpretations: Among Hindus, elephants are considered to be the sacred incarnation of the god Ganesh, an elephant-headed deity who rides atop a tiny rodent. Buddhists consider light-colored or "white" elephants to carry special significance, and white elephants are revered as powerful spiritual icons across Asia. Therefore, if you are at all familiar with any of these traditions and you had a positive reaction to a dream elephant, you may want to consider whether your dream held a spiritual meaning. For instance, if you are a Hindu or you are interested in Hinduism and you dreamed of watching Ganesh serenely meditate, might your unconscious have been expressing your desire to seek spiritual enlightenment, or at least to meditate on a daily basis? Otherwise, could a dream elephant have represented a wise person whom you consider to be an advisor during your waking hours, or else a person whom you consider to be a good friend? Or if you dreamed of an elephant or of its extinct relative, the mammoth, could it have been a reference to some waking issue or plan that is so big (of "mammoth" proportions) that it looms large even in your unconscious thoughts?

Negative Interpretations: If you dreamed of a white elephant, but you are fairly certain that your dream did not hold any spiritual significance, then could it have been an unconscious reference to a symbolic "white elephant" that is troubling you during your waking hours? For example, is the white elephant actually the financial investment that you have recently made in a new business that, upon reflection, you are worried will be a failure? If you dreamed of an elephant that was wild with fear or rage, so that it was causing havoc, is there something (perhaps a "wild streak" within yourself) that is threatening to cause upset and destruction in your waking life? Or if you had a guilty reaction to a dream elephant that looked you in the eye, was it the elephant that "never forgets," come to remind you of a misdeed that is weighing on your conscience?

Related Dreams

My Elephants Dreams

....
....
....
....
....
....
....
....
....

* * * * * * * * * * * * * * * * * *

Rogue Behavior
If a mean-looking elephant went on the rampage in dreamland, trampling trees under foot as though they were matchsticks while trumpeting its defiance, the reference may have been to someone who is behaving like a "rogue elephant" in your waking world. Is it you who has broken away from "the herd" and is now bent on destroying everything that crosses your path? If so, why?

My Fish Dreams

----

* * * * * * * * * * * * * * * * * *

A Good Haul

If you are an angler or make your living from selling fish, a dream of landing an abundant haul of plump, glistening fish is likely to have been a wish-fulfillment fantasy. Otherwise, could the fish have represented a "catch" beyond your wildest dreams, perhaps an audience that you have "hooked" and then "reeled in" with persuasive talk, or else a wealth of fresh ideas?

FISH

* *

As creatures of water, fish are symbols of emotions, unconscious instincts, intuition, and also creative inspiration. Different breeds of fish may hold specific significance, though there are countless universal meanings having to do with fish, including the idea of "fishing" for something (complements, for example), someone considered to be "a catch," a "fishy" situation, or a "slippery fish" (i.e., someone who is evasive).

Symbolic and Verbal Associations
- Emotions
- Unconscious instincts and intuition
- Creative inspiration
- Restriction; being stuck "in a fishbowl"
- Smelling a "fishy" situation
- A person who is "a catch"; someone you would like to "hook"
- Discomfort; feeling like "a fish out of water"

Positive Interpretations: In your dream, did you watch as a silvery fish leapt above the surface of the water and quickly dove back underneath the waves? If so, the leaping fish may have symbolized a flash of intuition, a basic emotion or instinct, or a creative inspiration—perhaps something that has been swimming deep within your unconscious, but that is now beginning to rise closer to the surface. And if you dreamed of fishing, could it be that you are trying to "fish out" a submerged insight that would help you to solve a waking problem? Or is there someone whom you have a romantic interest in—a person whom you consider to be "a catch," whom you would like to "bait" and "hook"? If you are a Christian, for which the fish is one of the oldest symbols (as Christ was called a "fisher of men"), then you may want to consider whether a dream of seeing a fish, of fishing, or of eating fish was a reflection of your yearning for spiritual sustenance. If you dreamed of a salmon, was it a reference to wisdom (from Celtic lore)? Was a dream carp a sign of good luck, love, or courage (from Japanese tradition)? Or was your dream fish a symbol of someone in your waking life who was born under the sign of Pisces?

Negative Interpretations: Did you dream of gazing into an aquarium full of fish? If so, might your unconscious have been making a reference to aspects of your personality, or instincts or emotions, that are unable to find free expression? Or, similarly, do you feel restricted in your waking life, or do you feel as if you are under constant scrutiny, as if you were living in a "fishbowl"? If you dreamed of watching a fish flopping around on dry land, do you feel like "a fish out of water" in your current waking situation? If, in your dream, you failed to grab the fish, was it representative of someone who is a "slippery fish" (i.e., evasive)? Was a dead fish a reference to someone who is a "cold fish" (i.e., dispassionate or unemotional)? Or, if your dream highlighted a carp, was your unconscious drawing your attention to your tendency to "carp at" or nag others?

Related Dreams

pages 179, 223, 291, 334, 335 & 387

FOXES

✳ ✳

In many folklore traditions around the world, including Native American tradition, the fox is a symbol of intelligence, cunning, and trickery, which are this animal's chief meanings in terms of dream symbolism. The term "foxy" has also come to mean "attractive" or "sexy," which may be another meaning for a dream fox.

Symbolic and Verbal Associations

- ❬ Cunning
- ❬ The archetypal trickster
- ❬ A person whom you need to "outfox" or outwit
- ❬ Someone who is as "sly as a fox"
- ❬ A person who is unreliable or untrustworthy, "like a fox in a henhouse"
- ❬ Someone whom you think is "foxy" (or sexy)

Positive Interpretations: In your dream, were you walking across a field, or through the forest, when you were suddenly stopped in your tracks by the flash of a red fox darting across your vantage point? If so, how did the dream fox make you feel? Did you feel in awe of its speed and its stealth? Were you highly impressed by the fox's furtiveness as it flushed out and captured its prey? If so, your unconscious may have been using the fox to set an example for you to follow in dealing with a waking situation. For instance, is there a need for you to "outfox" or outwit someone who is conniving against you? Is the best way for you to prevail in some waking situation or conflict to use your cunning and your intellect (rather than your brawn) in order to trick someone into doing your bidding? Was the dream fox really an appearance of the shape-shifting trickster archetype, the wild and rebellious maverick who acts on whim and impulse? If so, have you been taking yourself too seriously during your waking hours? Was your unconscious encouraging you to be more like the trickster yourself—to let yourself be a little bit wild, to play more, and to allow yourself to be silly and whimsical? Alternatively, did the dream fox represent someone in the real world whom you think is "foxy" or sexy? Or, especially if you are a woman, did the fox symbolize your own feelings of being attractive, like a "fox"?

Negative Interpretations: Just as the fox is a symbol of the trickster, who may use his cunning for ill, as well as good, a dream fox may also bear a warning of dishonesty or deception. So if you dreamed of watching as a fox slunk into a henhouse, eliciting screams from the residing chickens, and then slipped out with a fat hen in its jaws, could your dream have symbolized someone in the real world who is sly like a fox, and who is using his or her cunning toward the advancement of ill ends? For example, do you suspect a coworker of hacking into your computer files in order to steal your work or ideas for his own?

Related Dreams

pages 131, 143, 221, 320, 323 & 342

My Foxes Dreams

✳ ✳ ✳ ✳ ✳ ✳ ✳ ✳ ✳ ✳ ✳ ✳ ✳ ✳ ✳ ✳ ✳

Feeling Foxed

Foxes have such a reputation for slyness in the real world that this association is often pertinent in the dream world, too. So if you dreamed of glimpsing a furtive-looking fox, and consequently of preparing to protect your henhouse, only to see it sprint away with a chicken in its mouth, your unconscious may have been warning that someone is about to "outfox" you.

My Horses Dreams

★ ★ ★ ★ ★ ★ ★ ★ ★ ★ ★ ★ ★ ★ ★ ★ ★

Harnessing Horsepower

In the language of dreams, horses generally symbolize "animal" energy, urges, and drives, which will typically run amok unless controlled by a rider, who in turn signifies intelligence or conscious willpower. If you dreamed of a horse, the details are therefore important. Was the horse fenced in? Did it roam far afield, wild and free? Or did it happily cooperate with a rider?

HORSES

A dream horse may symbolize nobility (which is an ancient association of this animal), and also energy, drive, and sexual urges—which, like real-life horses, may be either tame or wild-acting. Other symbolic and verbal associations having to do with horses include "unbridled" passion, "riding high," riding "on a high horse," "riding roughshod," and "horsing around."

Symbolic and Verbal Associations

‹ Energy and drive
‹ Sexual urges
‹ "Unbridled" passion or emotions
‹ "Horseplay"; "horsing around"
‹ "Riding high"
‹ Being "on a high horse": arrogance or condescension

Positive Interpretations: A dream of mounting or sitting astride a horse may bear an obvious sexual meaning, and a dream horse itself may symbolize your sex drive. The behavior of the horse and your dream self's ability to control it will be very telling as to how to interpret your dream. Are your unconscious needs and/or your sexual urges harnessed and under control? In your dream, did you find yourself mounted upon a powerful, magnificent, galloping horse that seemed to anticipate your every desire as the two of you charged joyously forward? If so, your dream horse may have symbolized your healthy energy level and vigorous driving force. And because of the symbiotic way in which your dream self and the dream horse worked together, the implication is that your rational mind and emotional needs are also working together in harmony. Are your more wild urges being reined in? Alternatively, if you dreamed that your mount was shod with gleaming new horseshoes (a symbol of luck), do you feel blessed with good fortune in your waking life? In interpreting your dream, you should also consider any verbal associations that may apply. For example, are you "riding high," or feeling confident and assured, in the real world? Are you so happy with your girlfriend that "wild horses couldn't drag you away" from her?

Negative Interpretations: Did you have a dream in which the horse that you were riding bucked and kicked wildly, so that it was all that you could do just to stay on its back? If so, are you trying in vain to restrain an emotion or urge that is raring to break free of its reins? Is it your sex drive? Whatever it is, your unconscious may have been warning you that it will not be held back for much longer. If your dream horse ran away, with you on its back, despite your efforts to stop it, is someone in the real world "taking you for a ride" (i.e., taking advantage of you)? Is a waking "nightmare" running out of control in your psyche? Have you been "riding on a high horse," or behaving arrogantly? Or are you "riding roughshod" over someone else's feelings in the waking world?

Related Dreams

pages 112, 118, 132,
214, 268 & 310

MICE & RATS

✦✦✦✦✦✦✦✦✦✦✦✦✦✦✦✦✦✦✦✦✦✦✦✦✦✦✦✦

In the language of dreams, as in the real world, rats have few positive associations. A dream rat may signify a detestable person in the real world, or a person who has "ratted you out" or tattled on you. Among other things, a dream mouse may symbolize a shy or "mousy" person, or else a person who is a coward.

Symbolic and Verbal Associations
- A human "rat" (a detestable person); smelling "a rat"
- Someone who has "ratted you out" or informed against you
- A person who is meek or "mousy"
- Someone who is playing "a game of cat and mouse" with you (or toying with your feelings)
- A person who is a coward, or "a mouse"
- Magic; witchcraft

Positive Interpretations: In your dream, did a tiny mouse go scurrying across the kitchen floor and into a crack in the wall? If so, could your unconscious have been making a reference to your meek or timid nature? Or was the reference to your shy new employee at work, who is "as quiet as a church mouse"? If you are familiar with Hinduism, you may want to consider whether your dream rodent represented your desire to serve humanity, as it does in association with the elephant-headed god Ganesh (who rides upon a rodent, which is usually depicted at the god's feet). In Western culture, mice and rats have also been associated with magic and witchcraft (in particular, they have sometimes been said to be witches' companions or familiars), so you may want to take this type of interpretation into account when you are trying to decide the meaning of a dream that highlighted a rat or a mouse.

Negative Interpretations: If you had a dream in which the sight of a mouse sent you shrieking and climbing onto the nearest tabletop, was your unconscious simply reflecting your waking phobia of these creatures, which may have been brought to the surface of your consciousness because you recently found evidence that mice have taken up residence in your home? Or was your dream a reference to someone whom you consider to be "a mouse" or a coward? Alternatively, if you dreamed that you were afraid of or disgusted by a scurrying rat, has your unconscious detected or "smelled a rat" (a detestable person) in your waking presence? Or has one of your siblings "ratted" on you to your mother about your severe credit-card debt? Alternatively, in your dream, did you watch in horror as a cat pawed and batted at the tiny, live (but injured) mouse that it had caught? Did the cat allow the mouse to escape just a little bit, only to recapture and play with it some more? If so, has someone in the real world been playing "a game of cat and mouse" (or toying) with your emotions? Or is it you who has been toying so cruelly with someone's feelings?

Related Dreams
pages 140, 143, 211, 218, 311 & 313

My Mice & Rats Dreams

....
....
....
....
....
....
....
....
....

✦✦✦✦✦✦✦✦✦✦✦✦✦✦✦✦✦✦✦

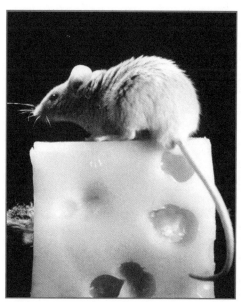

Victim or Vermin?
Did a bright-eyed mouse heroically elude a predatory cat to reach its cheesy reward in your dream, or did a scaly-tailed rodent nibble greedily away at your prized Gruyère? The first scenario suggests that you identify with the mouse—a potential victim who triumphs over the odds—while the second implies that you fear an aspect of your life being overrun by "vermin," or lowlifes.

THE ANIMAL KINGDOM

OWLS

★★★★★★★★★★★★★★★★★★★★★★★★★★★★★★★★★★★★★★★

In times past, the owl was associated with evil, death, and witchcraft—no doubt this was due, in large part, to the fact that the owl is a nocturnal hunter that swoops almost silently through the air to capture its prey. However, in symbolic terms, the owl is now more often considered to be a symbol of wisdom.

My Owls Dreams

★★★★★★★★★★★★★★★★★★★

Symbolic and Verbal Associations
- Wisdom; a mentor
- Vision; illumination (as in "night vision")
- Someone who is a "night owl"
- Evil
- Death
- Magic and witchcraft

Positive Interpretations: In symbolic terms, the owl is a powerful emblem of wisdom, probably because of its large, round eyes and its excellent night vision. Did you have a dream in which you were sitting on a park bench at night when a wise-looking old owl landed on the seat beside you and stared at you with her big, piercing eyes? If so, did your unconscious send you your dream in order to fulfill your wish for a guide or a mentor—a "wise old owl" to lead you through your life's journey? Is it possible that your dream owl represented someone in your waking life whom you consider to be your mentor already, or else a certain person whom you think may be able to fill that role for you? Or could the owl have been a manifestation of the archetypal wise old man (the high priest) or woman (the high priestess), who came to you in your dream in order to shed illumination upon a dark corner of your unconscious mind? In attempting to interpret your dream, it will help to think about how the owl made your dream self feel and what thoughts came into the fore of your dreaming mind. Alternatively, did the owl simply represent someone in your waking life (perhaps you yourself) who is a "night owl"? And if the owl called out "hoo hoo," was this your unconscious's way of asking you "who" you really are, thereby prompting you to engage in some intensive self-exploration?

Look and Learn

Some species of owls appear to be wearing spectacles, giving them a bookish appearance, but it is these nocturnal birds' ability to see in the dark (or, in symbolic terms, to discern things that remain obscure to others) that has made them a symbol of wisdom. So if an owl alighted in your dream, did it bring you an enlightening or illuminating insight?

Negative Interpretations: In your dream, did the sight or the sound of an owl send a chill running through your bones? If so, what associations does the owl bring up for you? If you consider this bird to be a "night hag," or an agent of sinister magic or witchcraft, then your dream may have been mirroring your waking fear of being targeted by evil forces. For example, are you worried that your neighbor, whom you know is interested in the occult, has secretly put a spell or curse on you? Or if you consider the owl to be an omen of death, do you fear that some aspect or phase of your waking life is in danger of meeting with an untimely end?

Related Dreams

pages 43, 133, 134, 143, 199 & 315

PIGS & HOGS

The meaning of a dream pig, hog, swine, or wild boar will depend, in large part, upon the associations and prejudices that you harbor for these animals. For instance, while some people consider pigs to be intelligent and friendly creatures, others think of them as lazy, filthy, and gluttonous.

Symbolic and Verbal Associations
- Intelligence
- Friendliness
- Gluttony and greed
- Filth
- Laziness
- Someone who is a "bore"

Positive Interpretations: In your dream, did you watch as a large sow was raised to the county-fair winner's platform and a blue ribbon was put around her neck? If so, do you consider pigs and hogs to be clean, intelligent, friendly animals, whose character should set an example for all of us? Or did the dream pig represent a person in your waking life, perhaps a good friend whom you look up to for her intelligence and who you feel is deserving of public praise and recognition? Or if you are familiar with the Chinese zodiac, did your dream of a boar represent someone in your waking life who was born in the year of the boar (and "boar people" are said to be sincere, good-natured, kind, generous, friendly, and open-hearted)?

Negative Interpretations: Do you consider pigs, hogs, and all of their relatives to be dirty, lazy, gluttonous animals, and did you dream of watching one of these creatures as it squealed and rolled in the mud? If so, was your unconscious trying to warn you that you have been behaving like a "pig" in the real world? Are your manners bad, your hair uncombed, and your body and clothing unwashed? Do you gorge yourself on food to the point of sickness? Do you treat others in an uncaring manner? Have you been behaving like a "swine" to your family? Is your office, your bedroom, or your entire home a dirty and disorganized "pigsty"? Or if you are a man, have you been acting like a "male chauvinist pig" toward your girlfriend, your wife, or your female friends or coworkers? Are you being stubborn or "pig-headed" over some waking issue or problem that you should give way on? Or if your dreaming mind highlighted a boar, are you being a "bore" and wearying others by your tendency to go on and on in a purely self-indulgent way about whatever it is that is on your mind? Or did your unconscious send you your dream in order to point out someone else whom you consider to be a "pig," a "hog," a "swine," or a "bore"?

Related Dreams

pages 62, 176, 182, 319 & 336

My Pigs & Hogs Dreams

----

* * * * * * * * * * * * * * * * * *

This Little Piggy

If you are a city-dweller, you may be wondering why you dreamed so vividly of a pig. Thinking about the many expressions associated with pigs may give you a persuasive explanation. So could the message from your unconscious have been that you have been "pigging out," or gorging yourself, recently? Or have you been behaving "like a pig," or disgustingly, to your loved ones?

My Rabbits & Hares Dreams

----

* * * * * * * * * * * * * * * *

Honey Bunny

In the harsh real world, defenseless, herbivorous rabbits are the hunted rather than the hunters, and being so eye-catching, white rabbits are particularly vulnerable, as well as especially cute. So if a fluffy bunny hopped into your dream, could it have represented someone whom you feel is currently exposed to danger, and who therefore needs your protection in the waking world?

RABBITS & HARES

B ecause of their high fecundity, rabbits and hares are world-wide symbols of fertility (and therefore of creativity, inspiration, and new beginnings). In the language of dreams, these animals may also be associated with the qualities of gentleness, emotional sensitivity, and nervousness. A dream hare may also represent a person who is "as mad as a March hare," or a "harebrained" or foolish idea.

Symbolic and Verbal Associations

- Fertility; creative inspiration; springtime; new beginnings
- Speed and alertness
- Gentleness
- Emotional sensitivity
- Nervousness
- Someone who is "as mad as a March hare"
- A "harebrained" (crazy or foolish) idea

Positive Interpretations: If a fluffy rabbit went hopping through your dream, might it have symbolized someone in your waking world who is gentle, kind, and sensitive? For example, did the rabbit denote your new family doctor, who exhibits these qualities in her excellent "bedside manner"? Or else did the rabbit symbolize a shy or nervous person whom you should treat with the utmost gentleness (perhaps, if you are a schoolteacher, the new pupil in your class)? If you dreamed that you saw a mother rabbit surrounded by her babies, do you yourself wish to be the parent of many children? Or were the dream babies a metaphor for your inspiration and your creative urges? Do you long to begin working on a new plan or project that you hope will multiply fruitfully? If you dreamed of watching a rabbit race across a field at top speed, might it have represented your desire to streak ahead in your life? Or did the rabbit denote your "quick" wit or intellect?

Negative Interpretations: In calling up the dream image of the gentle and timid rabbit, was your unconscious advising you to be more kind and gentle in your relationships and your dealings with others in the waking world? In another dream scenario, is some waking situation or problem making you feel nervous or fearful, like a rabbit that is caught in the headlights of an approaching automobile? Alternatively, did you dream of watching a pair of hares boxing with each other (standing on their back legs and punching each other with their front paws), as the males and females are often seen to do during their mating season, in the springtime, before they actually mate? If so, have you and/or someone you know been behaving as though you were "as mad as a March hare"? Is it you and your boyfriend, who have been having "lover's spats"? Or did your dream hare come bearing the unconscious message that a waking idea or attitude of yours is "harebrained" or foolish?

Related Dreams

pages 142, 257, 289,
323, 327 & 385

SEA BIRDS & WATER BIRDS

Because sea and water birds are creatures of the air (which represents aspirations, ideals, and spirituality), as well as of the water (which denotes unconscious instincts and emotions), their meaning in dreams may pertain to both of these realms.

Symbolic and Verbal Associations

‹ Enthusiasm; "like a duck to water"
‹ Babies and children (in association with dream storks and pelicans)
‹ The act of "ducking" a problem or a difficulty
‹ Having "an albatross around your neck": a burden that is borne as a penance
‹ A "swan song," or farewell
‹ Someone who is an "ugly duckling"

Positive Interpretations: If a duck waddled through your dream, thinking about the many verbal associations having to do with ducks may help you in interpreting its meaning. For example, have you taken to a new hobby or activity "like a duck to water"? Are you immune to your mother's criticisms of you, so that they are sliding off you "like water off a duck's back"? If you dreamed of watching a swan glide gracefully through the water, do you admire the beauty and grace of someone in your waking life? Or do you wish that you could idly "swan around" during your waking hours? Both storks and pelicans are associated with babies and children—storks because they were once said to "deliver" newborns to their parents, and pelicans because they were once believed to peck open their own breasts in order to feed their children with their blood. So if you dreamed of a stork or a pelican, you may want to consider whether your unconscious was reflecting your desire to have children, or the waking sacrifices that you are making in order to care for the children that you already have.

Negative Interpretations: Did a dream duck bear the message from your unconscious that you are trying to "duck," rather than face, a waking issue or problem? For example, have you been avoiding talking to your husband about his excessive drinking, choosing to ignore it instead? Or if you dreamed of watching a bunch of ducklings swim across a pond, and if your attention was drawn to one duckling who looked very different from the rest, was your unconscious mirroring the fact that you feel like an "ugly duckling" in comparison with your brothers and sisters, perhaps because you are so unlike the rest of them? Other sea and water birds have various symbolic and verbal associations. Did a dream swan's beautiful lament signify a waking "swan song" (i.e., a final farewell)? For example, if you are a musician who is about to retire, are you about to give your final (or "swan-song") performance with the orchestra that you play for? Or if you dreamed of an albatross, could it have represented an "albatross around your neck" (i.e., a burden) that you feel forced to bear, perhaps as a penance for some past misdeed?

Related Dreams

pages 291, 298, 315, 378 & 383

My Sea Birds & Water Birds Dreams

Feed Me!

Storks and pelicans are closely associated with babies in the language of dreams, but whatever the species of chick who squawked so desperately at you in your dream, it probably denoted needy offspring. So if you are a parent, are you feeling harried and hassled by your child's demands, or was the reference otherwise to a developing "brainchild" that currently requires your undivided attention?

THE ANIMAL KINGDOM

My Sea Creatures Dreams

----

* * * * * * * * * * * * * * * * * * *

A Stinging Encounter

If seas and oceans represent the unconscious mind in dreams, the creatures that navigate their depths can symbolize the nebulous thoughts and instincts that inhabit it. If a jellyfish drifted into your dream path as you were swimming, and administered a painful sting when you collided, could it have signified a memory that, although ghostly, or half-forgotten, still has the power to hurt you?

SEA CREATURES

****

In symbolic terms, sea creatures (including things like starfish, squid, octopuses and mollusks, crabs and other crustaceans, and sea nettles or jellyfish) are associated with aspects of the unconscious or instinctive mind—with such things as basic emotions, intuitions, and creative inspirations.

Symbolic and Verbal Associations
- Destiny (as represented by a starfish)
- Emotional armor (as in the armor-plated bodies of mollusks, crabs, and other crustaceans)
- A "crabby" mood or personality
- A formerly shy person who has "come out of their shell"
- Female genitalia (as symbolized by a mollusk shell)
- Having "the world as your oyster"

Positive Interpretations: Did a dream crab represent someone in your waking life who was born under the zodiacal sign of Cancer? If you dreamed of an octopus with its many arms waving, did it represent your knack for multitasking your many duties and responsibilities having to do with your work and your family? Or, in your dream, were you wandering along a beach picking up shells? Because mollusk shells, such as cowries and scallops, tend to look like female genitalia, your unconscious may have been commenting on your sex life. A similar interpretation may apply if you dreamed of collecting or eating oysters, which are said to be an aphrodisiac. If you picked up an oyster and its shell was clamped firmly shut, might it have contained a "pearl" of wisdom that you are longing to possess, or else a female "pearl" (such as your ideal partner)?

Negative Interpretations: If you dreamed of a crab, might it have symbolized your "crabby" mood or way of relating to others? Did it wave its pincerlike claws in the same way that you threaten and ward off those around you? Do you work to prevent others from penetrating your tough, outer shell of emotional armor? Alternatively, if your dream self saw a soft, fleshy mollusk without its shell, did it mirror your own emotional vulnerability? (Or have you simply "come out of your shell"?) If you dreamed that a crab scuttled sideways as you approached it, do you (or someone whom you know) evade the advances of anyone who tries to become too emotionally close to you in the waking world? Did you dream of stooping to pick up a shell on the beach, only to realize with disappointment that it was empty? If so, was your unconscious reflecting your belief that life's opportunities have passed you by and your feeling that the world is no longer your "oyster"? Or, finally, if you dreamed that a squid blew a cloud of blinding black ink into your face, does someone in your life (perhaps your partner) have a habit of confusing or obscuring the difficult issues that you face?

Related Dreams
pages 291, 326, 333, 335, 383 & 387

SHARKS & WHALES

A s creatures of the water, which is a symbol of the unconscious, dream dolphins, sharks, and whales may represent unconscious instincts and emotions. When sharks surface on the waters of dreamland, their meaning is rarely positive; instead, thay are likely to be a warning of danger. Dolphins—known for their intelligence and friendliness—may represent either of these qualities, as well as a source of help or guidance. Dream whales, meanwhile, are likely to symbolize maternal instincts or the womb.

Symbolic and Verbal Associations

‹ Danger; a deadly predator (symbolized by a shark)
‹ A "loan shark"
‹ Intelligence, friendliness, and help or guidance (symbolized by a dolphin)
‹ The dolphin as a symbol of Christ; spiritual salvation
‹ The womb (symbolized by the whale)
‹ Enjoyment; having "a whale of a time"

Positive Interpretations: In the language of dreams, as in the real world, the symbolism of dolphins is almost always overwhelmingly positive. They are intelligent, playful creatures that are friendly toward humans, and they were traditionally believed to lead lost or misguided sailors to safety and to guide the spirits of the dead to the afterlife (which is why the dolphin is also a symbol of Christ). So if you had a dream in which you were swimming or sailing through the ocean accompanied by a group of jovial dolphins, your unconscious may have been reflecting your hope and desire for spiritual salvation, or perhaps your craving for fun and friendship—but whichever interpretation might apply, you probably awoke feeling extremely uplifted! The whale is a symbol of the womb—probably because of its enormous belly, and also because, as a mammal, it gives birth to live young (unlike most fish)—and also of motherhood and maternal instincts. So if you dreamed of watching a whale as it dove and pitched at the surface of the water, or if you dreamed that you watched as a mother whale nursed her baby, are you longing to return to the warmth and protection of the womb? Or was your unconscious mirroring your own maternal instincts toward your children, or else your desire to become pregnant?

Negative Interpretations: In your dream, were you afloat in a small boat, with one or more hungry sharks circling you? In the language of dreams, a shark is usually an unconscious warning that a predatory person has set their sights on you—as in a "loan shark," a person who lends money at an incredibly inflated rate of interest. Or, in your dream, were you terrified by the sight of a great whale? If so, and you are familiar with the biblical story in which Jonah was swallowed by a whale, could your dream whale have represented the archetypal terrible mother? Do you live in fear of being "devoured" by someone who is an abusive mother figure in your life ?

My Sharks & Whales Dreams

----

* * * * * * * * * * * * * * * * * * * *

Jaws of Jeopardy

A dream of an approaching shark is likely to have been an anxious experience at best, and a fully fledged nightmare at worst, for these marine creatures symbolize danger, destruction, and death when they glide into our sleep. So if you had such a dream, can you connect the shark with a vicious, predatory someone who is circling you hungrily in the real world?

Related Dreams

pages 87, 113, 223, 291, 326 & 383

My Sheep & Goats Dreams

✶ ✶ ✶ ✶ ✶ ✶ ✶ ✶ ✶ ✶ ✶ ✶ ✶ ✶ ✶ ✶ ✶

Be a Lamb

The significance of a dream that featured a lamb is likely to be influenced by your religious and cultural background, although an association with sacrifice is almost universal. If you are a Christian, maybe your dream lamb represented Christ, or the "lamb of God." Otherwise, could the lamb have signified you, and the enormous sacrifice that others are demanding of you in the waking world?

SHEEP & GOATS

✶✶✶✶✶✶✶✶✶✶✶✶✶✶✶✶✶✶✶✶✶✶✶✶✶✶✶✶✶✶✶✶✶

Dream sheep may symbolize a number of things, including timidity, gentleness, or having a flock mentality. Dream lambs, in particular, may denote innocence and sacrifice, as in the saying "like a lamb to the slaughter," while dream rams (male sheep) may denote confidence or male sexuality. Dream goats, on the other hand, are likely to represent individualism (or stubbornness), mischief, or lust (if male).

Symbolic and Verbal Associations
‹ Timidity; gentleness
‹ Innocence
‹ Sacrifice; "like a lamb to the slaughter"
‹ Having a flock mentality
‹ Male sexuality (as symbolized by the ram or the billy goat); lust
‹ Mischievousness

Positive Interpretations: If you dreamed of a lamb, you may want to consider whether it represented someone in your waking life who is gentle and innocent like a lamb, or else someone (perhaps you?) who has been willing to sacrifice themselves for the good of others. If you dreamed of a ram, might it have symbolized a confident man in your waking life? Or if you are a man who dreamed of a ram, could it have symbolized your own sexual needs? Alternatively, did your dream ram or goat represent a person whom you know who was born under the zodiacal sun sign of Aries or Capricorn respectively? Did you dream that you were "separating the sheep from the goats"? Goats are well-known for their individualism (which sometimes gives way to stubbornness), their mischievousness, and their lustfulness. So if you dreamed of watching a goat munching his way through your garden, you may want to ask yourself whether this dream beast represented someone in your waking life who delights in being naughty, or else whether it symbolized an aspect of your own personality that is vying for expression during your waking hours.

Negative Interpretations: In your dream, did you find yourself in the midst of a flock of sheep? If so, might your unconscious have been trying to tell you that you are behaving too timidly in the waking world? For example, are you not assertive enough at work? Do you allow your family members to dominate you? Do you go along with their flock mentality? If you dreamed of watching as a tiny, bleating lamb was about to be butchered, do you allow others to take advantage of your gentle and innocent nature, so that you feel like "a lamb to the slaughter"? Or if you dreamed that you were having a battle of wills with an ornery goat, has your father been behaving like a "stubborn old goat" in his refusal to accept your life choices? Or is someone in the waking world "getting your goat" or annoying you?

Related Dreams

pages 149, 180, 319, 323, 331 & 342

SNAILS, SLUGS & LEECHES

Although they are very different animals, snails, slugs, and leeches share certain physical and behavioral characteristics and associations that render them somewhat close together in terms of dream symbolism. When they appear in dreams, they may denote—among other things—slowness, lethargy, a person who is "slimy," or (with regard to leeches) a "bloodsucker."

Symbolic and Verbal Associations
- "Slow as a snail"
- Wanting to retreat "into your shell"
- Spinelessness; cowardice
- A person who is lazy or lethargic; a "slug"
- An unctuous or "slimy" person
- Someone whom you'd like to "slug" (or punch)
- A "bloodsucker" (someone who saps your time, energy, emotions, money, etc.)

Positive Interpretations: In your dream, were you feasting on a delicious dish of cooked snails (or escargots) in a French restaurant? If so, was your dreaming mind anticipating the next time that you will get to enjoy your favorite delicacy (and perhaps the dream was triggered because you went to bed hungry)? Or if escargots are not part of your usual diet, could your unconscious have been encouraging you to take in the snail's slow-paced energy because you have been running yourself ragged by living life at top speed? Blood-sucking leeches have been used for medical purposes for thousands of years. Today, they are similarly employed in various types of surgeries as the natural anticoagulants that they secrete help to restore proper blood circulation to inflamed areas of the body. So if you dreamed that you were calmly lying on a medical table as a doctor applied leeches to your chest, might your unconscious have been encouraging you to focus more on your feelings—i.e., to increase the emotional "blood flow" to your heart?

Negative Interpretations: Did you dream that you were watching as a snail made its slow, painstaking way across the roadway? If so, do you feel as if your own life or some aspect of it (your career, for instance) is moving "at a snail's pace"? Or if the dream snail retreated into its shell, are you feeling so uncomfortable in your waking situation that you wish that you, too, could retreat "into your shell"? If you dreamed of a slug or a leech, might it have represented a person in your waking life whom you consider to be "spineless," or else an unprincipled, "slimy," lazy, or "sluglike" person? Is it you? Is there someone whom you'd like to punch or "slug"? Or did a dream leech denote someone in your waking life whom you consider to be a "bloodsucker," perhaps because he or she is sapping your time, your energy, your emotions, or your financial resources?

Related Dreams
pages 174, 256, 283, 334, 377 & 378

My Snails, Slugs & Leeches Dreams

A Snail's Pace
If you are a horticulturalist who is currently waging a war of attrition on garden pests in real life, a dream that homed in on a voracious snail probably simply reflected your waking preoccupation with "the enemy." But if this isn't the case, with what do you associate snails, and how may this relate to your waking world? To your frustatingly slow progress at work, perhaps?

My Snakes Dreams

----

* * * * * * * * * * * * * * * * * *

A Forked Tongue

Unless you have a liking for these creatures, your dreaming self probably recoiled in horror when confronted by a snake, but why would your unconscious have inflicted this cause and effect on you? Could it have been to warn you that someone in your waking world is a "snake in the grass," or a traitorous friend who speaks with a "forked tongue," or insincerely?

SNAKES

There are a number of possible explanations for a dream through which a snake slithered. The dream snake may have signified dormant energy and potential, powers of healing, transformation, and transcendence, the stirrings of male sexuality, or else death, danger, or deceit.

Symbolic and Verbal Associations

- An atavistic symbol of danger; a phobic symbol
- Renewal and healing energy
- The penis, according to Freudians
- Satan, the tempter of Eve, and the architect of humankind's downfall, according to Judeo–Christian belief
- "A snake in the grass," that is, a betrayer

Positive Interpretations: If you were unafraid of your dream snake, and regarded it with equanimity, or even with affection or longing, it is likely that it symbolized a powerful source of transformational energy. Because snakes shed their old skins and emerge "renewed," they can signify a fresh start, or a new you, for instance, and it may be that you are unconsciously yearning to slough off your old persona or "baggage" and leave your past behind you. Snakes can also represent healing potential (and it is not for nothing that a snake-entwined staff, or the caduceus, is a symbol of medicine), an association that may be especially pertinent if you are suffering from an illness or feel somehow psychologically wounded or damaged. Freudians associate snakes with the penis, primarily on account of their shape, and if this interpretation of your dream snake strikes a chord, your dreaming reaction to it should help you to understand whose sexuality was denoted, and how you unconsciously respond to it.

Negative Interpretations: Most animals, humans included, are instinctively wary of snakes, who, depending on their species, have the power to paralyze or kill their prey, be it by sinking their fangs into its body and injecting it with venom, or by encircling it and crushing it to death within their muscular coils. If you dreamed that you were terrified of a dream snake, it may be that your unconscious was reinforcing a conscious phobia that may recently have been triggered, maybe by a natural-history documentary featuring snakes that you saw on television before going to sleep. The dream snake may alternatively have represented a person whom you have identified—consciously or unconsciously—as posing a danger to your welfare. If you are familiar with the pivotal role that the serpent played in the fall of Adam and Eve, as told in the Old Testament, you may feel that your dream snake represented either someone who is trying to tempt you into behaving disastrously or even a person who is fundamentally evil, despite his or her friendly or helpful manner.

Related Dreams

pages 137, 218, 227, 239, 308 & 340

SONGBIRDS

✶✶✶✶✶✶✶✶✶✶✶✶✶✶✶✶✶✶✶✶✶✶✶✶✶✶✶✶✶✶✶✶✶✶✶✶✶✶✶

If you dreamed of a songbird, the meaning of your dream will depend, in large part, on your dream self's reaction to the sound of the song that it sang, whether positive or negative. Positive associations include happiness, new beginnings, courtship and romance, and good news. Negative associations, particularly with talking birds, include gossip and mindless "parroting," or mimicry.

Symbolic and Verbal Associations
- Happiness and joy
- Spring- and summertime; youth; new beginnings
- Courtship and romance
- The "sweet sound" of good news
- Gossip
- A tendency to mimic or "parrot" the behavior or opinions of others

Positive Interpretations: Did you dream that you were walking on a crisp, sunlit morning, and that you were filled with a sense of joy by the sound of the birds singing sweetly in the trees? If so, your unconscious may have been reflecting your waking happiness (in other words, your feeling that "life is sweet"). Have you recently begun a new romance? Or are you simply happy that it's finally springtime? Another interpretation for this sort of dream is that you are anticipating or hoping to hear some "sweet" good news—something that will be "like the sound of music" to your ears. Did you dream that a little bird whispered something in your ear? If so, do you remember what it said to you? Have you recently been made privy to some secret information in the real world? Alternatively, if you dreamed of a lark, was your unconscious pointing to your desire to "lark around," or to spend some fun time simply frolicking around with your friends, during your waking hours? Or was your unconscious advising you to rise "with the lark," or very early, in the morning?

Negative Interpretations: In your dream, were you alarmed or annoyed by the loud trill of a canary? If so, was your unconscious drawing your attention to your little brother's habit of "singing like a canary," or telling your mother about everything that you get up to in the waking world, even though you have sworn him to secrecy? Or is it you who has trouble keeping secrets? If you dreamed of listening to the chatter of a "talking" bird, such as a parrot, a mynah, or a budgerigar, what did it say? It is possible that it bore an important message from your unconscious—perhaps some advice or a potential solution to a waking problem. Or was your unconscious merely reflecting your own "bird-brained," or unthinking, habit of "parroting" or mimicking others' behavior or ideas without understanding them or thinking them through? For example, do you pay lip service to a particular political party or agenda simply because theirs or it is the opinion that your husband espouses?

Related Dreams
pages 175, 315, 324, 320, 330 & 359

My Songbirds Dreams

✶ ✶ ✶ ✶ ✶ ✶ ✶ ✶ ✶ ✶ ✶ ✶ ✶ ✶ ✶ ✶ ✶ ✶ ✶ ✶

A Sweet Soundtrack
Just as movie-makers use different types of music to evoke a particular mood and thus set the scene, so the unconscious mind may conjure up a songbird to provide the soundtrack for a dream's dramatic action. So if your dreaming self was enraptured by a songbird's sweet trills, did your dream reflect your current waking joy, or was it more concerned with wish-fulfillment?

THE ANIMAL
KINGDOM

My Spiders & Scorpions Dreams

✱ ✱ ✱ ✱ ✱ ✱ ✱ ✱ ✱ ✱ ✱ ✱ ✱ ✱ ✱ ✱ ✱

Lying in Wait

If you suffer from arachnophobia, a nightmare in which you were confronted by a menacing spider may simply have been triggered by a waking encounter with one of its smaller brethren during the day. If you don't mind spiders, however, could the monster in your dream have signified a predatory someone in the real world, and your fear of falling victim to him or her?

SPIDERS & SCORPIONS

✱✱✱✱✱✱✱✱✱✱✱✱✱✱✱✱✱✱✱✱✱✱✱✱✱✱✱✱✱✱✱✱✱✱✱✱

In the language of dreams, spiders and scorpions are strong symbols of danger, either from a predatory or dominating person, or from "poisonous" thoughts or ideas. A dream spider's web may signify a trap, an intricate plan, complexities and entanglements, or the World Wide Web. A dream scorpion, specifically, may point to a metaphorical "sting in the tail."

Symbolic and Verbal Associations

- A warning of danger; a trap
- "Poisonous" thoughts or ideas
- A predatory, dominating person (especially a woman)
- An intricate plan, or complexities and entanglements (as symbolized by a spider's web)
- The World Wide Web
- A "web of deceit"
- A metaphorical "sting in the tail"

Positive Interpretations: If you dreamed of a spider and you are interested in ancient mythology, did your dream have to do with the spider's ancient associations with the cosmos and fate? For example, are you in a period of transition in your life, so that you are constantly wondering and anticipating what fate will next befall you? If you had a positive reaction to a dream that placed a spotlight on a spider's web, could it have been a reference to the intricate plan that you have "spun" for your future, or else to your interest in the Internet, or the World Wide Web? For instance, in your dream, if you knew that the web was the work of a money spider, was your unconscious mirroring your waking belief that an Internet business venture that you recently signed onto will prove to be lucrative? Or if you dreamed of observing a scorpion without having a fearful reaction, might it have symbolized a person in your waking life who was born under the zodiacal sun sign of Scorpio?

Negative Interpretations: If you dreamed of cringing with fear at the sight of a giant, hairy, black spider, was your unconscious merely reflecting your arachnophobia? Or was your dream triggered by your waking sense of fear and helplessness in the presence of a dominating and predatory person in your life (probably a woman, as spiders are symbolically associated with femininity)? If so, was your dream spider a representation of the terrible-mother archetype? If you are a man who dreamed that you were under attack by a female black widow spider (who consumes the male after he has mated with her), was your unconscious drawing a parallel with your increasingly aggressive and dominating wife? If you dreamed of a spider's web, you may want to consider whether it warned of a trap that someone has set for you in the real world, to a "web of deceit," or to the complexities and entanglements of a waking situation.

Related Dreams
pages 113, 118, 145, 227, 257 & 338

SWARMING INSECTS

Stinging, biting, and swarming insects may bear a number of meanings when they come buzzing into a dream. For example, they may signify a swarm of problems that are "plaguing" you, a pesky person, or someone who is "sucking you dry." More positively, dream ants and honey bees may denote hard work, self-sacrifice, discipline, and cooperation.

Symbolic and Verbal Associations

- A swarm of problems; something that is "plaguing" you
- A pesky person, whom you'd like to "swat"
- Someone who is "sucking you dry" (i.e., draining your energy or your resources)
- Behaving in a "lousy" manner, or like a "louse"
- Hard work, self-sacrifice, discipline, and cooperation (as symbolized by ants and honey bees)
- Feeling "antsy," or having "ants in your pants"
- Having "a bee in your bonnet" (an obsessive preoccupation)
- A "stinging" comment, or an emotional "sting"

Positive Interpretations: Whether or not you appreciate encountering them in the real world, both ants and honeybees live in highly organized, cooperative colonies, and both are models of discipline, hard work, and self-sacrifice. So if you had a dream that placed an emphasis on either of these insects busily going about their duties, it may be that your unconscious sent you your dream in order to encourage you to follow industrious their example and to labor in cooperative harmony with your coworkers, your family, or your friends. Or if you dreamed of watching a fly landing on a wall, do you wish that you could be a "fly on the wall" and secretly observe the intimacies of others' lives?

Negative Interpretations: In your dream, were you descended upon by a swarm of insatiable mosquitos? If so, could it have represented the swarm or horde of problems that you are dealing with in the real world? Is there some issue that is "plaguing" you during your waking hours? If you dreamed of being bitten by a blood-sucking insect, such as a gnat, a mosquito, a flea, or a louse, is someone in the waking world "sucking you dry" of your energy or other resources? Or could your dream have been a warning that you have been behaving like a "louse" toward those around you? If you dreamed that you accidentally sat on an anthill and suffered the consequences, are you feeling "antsy," or do you have "ants in your pants" in the real world? If you dreamed that a bee flew under your hat, do you have "a bee in your bonnet" (or an obsessive preoccupation) during your waking hours? Or, finally, if you dreamed that you were stung by a wasp or a hornet, was the unconscious reference to a "stinging" rebuke or an emotional "sting" that you have suffered in the waking world?

My Swarming Insects Dreams

----

* * * * * * * * * * * * * * * * * * * *

Busy Bees

A dream in which you were a beekeeper and were confidently tending to your charges and checking on their honeycombs may have been a metaphor for the project-management job that you are currently performing in the real world. Is your home or office a "hive of activity"? And are you directing everyone's activities toward a common aim in the hope of reaping a sweet reward?

Related Dreams

pages 259, 311, 313, 338, 340 & 377

My Wolves & Coyotes Dreams

----

* * * * * * * * * * * * * * * * *

Trickster Alert!

If you were aware of a coyote lurking suspiciously on the periphery of your dream, and you are familiar with its characterization as a trickster in Native American lore, this association may be pertinent to your waking situation. Could your unconscious have summoned the coyote into your dream to warn you that a devious and unscrupulous opportunist is sniffing around you in real life?

WOLVES & COYOTES

In terms of dream symbolism, a wolf may denote anger and rage, survival, a "lone wolf," a predatory male stalker, "a wolf in sheep's clothing," or a "pack mentality." In Native American tradition, the coyote is considered to be a trickster or a prankster, and so is associated with deception.

Symbolic and Verbal Associations

- Rage
- A "lone wolf"
- Predatory masculine sexuality; a stalker
- Having a "pack mentality"
- "A wolf in sheep's clothing"
- Survival
- Tricks and deception (as symbolized by the coyote)

Positive Interpretations: In your dream, did a thrill shoot through your body when you heard the sound of a wolf howling in the night? Or, in your dream, were you walking through the forest when you caught a glimpse of a wolf's eyes reflected in the moonlight? If so, do you empathize with the wolf's solitary character? Do you wish that you could be happy living as a "lone wolf" during your waking hours? Or if you have recently been feeling as if the drudgery and the woes of the waking world are getting the better of you, is it possible that your unconscious called up the image of the wolf in order to set an example for you of this animal's instinctive proficiency at survival? And if you dreamed that a wolf was observing you, it may have been reminding you not to forget or neglect the qualities within yourself that it represents—be that solitariness, survival skills, or the capacity for anger and rage (see below).

Negative Interpretations: If you dreamed of a vicious, snarling wolf, you may want to consider whether you yourself are harboring a ferocious rage that you are trying to keep caged up during your waking hours. If so, your unconscious may have been trying to bring this rage to your conscious attention so that you can acknowledge it and either express or deal with it in a controlled manner. In dreams, the wolf may also symbolize the predatory and stealthy aspect of male sexuality. So if you are a woman who dreamed that a wolf was chasing or attacking you, might it have denoted a male stalker in your waking life—perhaps someone who is "a wolf in sheep's clothing"? Or if you are a man who dreamed of a wolf, might it have denoted your own "wolfish" behavior? Alternatively, if you dreamed of a pack of wolves, was your unconscious highlighting your own or others' "pack mentality"? And, finally, if you dreamed of a coyote, which in Native American tradition is considered to be a trickster, is someone in the real world attempting to deceive you, perhaps with a prank?

Related Dreams

pages 131, 221, 266, 323, 327 & 336

CHAPTER 17
THE PLANT KINGDOM

In the symbolic language of dreams, seeds and buds can signify
potential; blossoms and flowers can denote an emotional, physical,
or intellectual "blooming" or "flowering"; fruits can symbolize
sweet rewards; while a dream tree may represent the dreamer.
Your dream of a fir tree may have had more to do with Christmas
than your "evergreen" vitality, however, so always bear any personal
associations in mind when trying to work out what your dream
of a plant may have meant.

My Buds Dreams

----

* * * * * * * * * * * * * * * * * * *

Budding Beauty

When the dreaming mind accords buds particular prominence, it often does so to highlight something or someone in the first flush of youth, whose potential looks promising, but has yet to be realized. So if you dreamed of gazing intently at a bud, could it have represented your young daughter, who is on the verge of developing into a beautiful woman?

BUDS

✶✶✶✶✶✶✶✶✶✶✶✶✶✶✶✶✶✶✶✶✶✶✶✶✶✶✶✶✶✶✶✶✶✶✶✶✶

Because they hold the promise of a blossom, dream buds may denote a latent potential, or an idea or plan (i.e., the early growth of a brainchild). The unconscious may also use buds to symbolize babies or children, or a "budding" relationship. Other associations include something that you want to halt, or to "nip in the bud."

Symbolic and Verbal Associations
- A "budding" relationship
- Latent potential
- Children
- An idea or a plan; the early growth of a brainchild
- Something that you want to halt, or to "nip in the bud"
- Someone who is your "buddy"

Positive Interpretations: In your dream, did you step outside on a cold morning in March, and were you surprised and filled with joy to find that the tree outside your house had tiny pink buds on its branches? If so, and if you had your dream in the wintertime, before the first spring buds, your unconscious may have been trying to offer you some relief from your winter blues, while showing you a glimpse of the promise of spring. Or, if you have recently begun dating someone new, could your dream have been a reference to the "budding" of your relationship? Or did the dream buds denote your own latent potential, perhaps your talent as a painter or a sculptor? In the language of dreams, buds may also represent children. So did your unconscious send you your dream in order to highlight your waking desire to have a baby? Or was the reference to the potential of your young son or daughter? But if none of these interpretations seems to apply, you may want to consider whether your dream was an unconscious reference to the budding of an idea or plan (i.e., a brainchild) that you have come up with. Trying some free association may also help you to determine the meaning of your dream. For instance, was your unconscious mind drawing your attention to someone in the waking world whom you consider to be your good "buddy"? Perhaps your old friend Bud?

Negative Interpretations: Did you dream that you walked out to the garden with a pair of shears in your hand, and that you went straight for the rose bush and clipped off one of its new buds? If so, might your unconscious mind have been signaling that there is something in your waking life—perhaps an idea or a plan—that you should "nip in the bud" before it is allowed to develop any further (possibly in order to encourage the lateral growth of other, more "fruitful," branches of your life)? Or if you dreamed that you went on a mad pruning spree, clipping off all of the buds on every plant in sight, could your dream have been reflecting your anger and dismay that your father drinks way too much of his choice beer, "Budweiser" (which you would just as soon expel every drop of from your household)?

Related Dreams

pages 105, 110, 274, 283, 350 & 357

CHRISTMAS GREENERY

My Christmas Greenery Dreams

----

* * * * * * * * * * * * * * * * * * *

Although they come from different traditions, Christmas trees, holly, ivy, and mistletoe are all symbols of Christmas. Therefore, if any of these plants are highlighted in a dream, they may bear some associations having to do with this Christian holiday—associations such as happiness, celebration, the comfort of friends and family, or the promise of everlasting life (as symbolized by the birth of Jesus). The specific message will depend on the context of the dream and the dreamer's personal beliefs and traditions.

Symbolic and Verbal Associations
- Comfort
- Happiness; joyous celebration
- Friends and family
- Romance; love; someone you want to kiss
- Wintertime

Positive Interpretations: If you dreamed of a gaily decorated and brightly lit Christmas tree surrounded by presents, and if you have warm memories of your childhood Christmases, then your dream probably evoked comforting and joyous memories of times spent with your family and friends. And if you are currently feeling lonely or isolated in your waking life, then your unconscious likely sent you your dream in order to comfort and console you. However, if you have never celebrated Christmas and have no particular feelings about Christmas trees, but you dreamed of one, it may be that your unconscious mind was tapping into traditional, mythical, or religious symbolic associations that you have picked up from the culture around you—even though you might not be consciously aware of them. Some of these associations include eternal life (because it is an evergreen, which stays green all year) and spiritual illumination and warmth (symbolized by the lights, which were traditionally candles). Similar interpretations may be applied if you dreamed of holly (which was sacred to the Roman god Saturn, and which is said to represent Christ's crown of thorns), ivy (another evergreen that is an ancient symbol of immortality), or mistletoe (which is a symbol of femininity in the Druidic tradition, and which it is also traditional to embrace or kiss beneath—so is there someone in your waking life whom you want to kiss?)

Negative Interpretations: Did you have a negative reaction to a dream that highlighted a Christmas tree, holly, ivy, or mistletoe? If so, do you have negative past associations with Christmastime, perhaps because a loved one passed away at this time of year, or because your family holidays had a tendency to erupt in arguments? If so, are you dreading this year's approaching holiday season? Or is some difficult situation in your current waking life reawakening to those earlier memories?

All Is Bright
Christmas is such an important family holiday in the West that any Yuletide dream may speak of your relationship with your nearest and dearest rather than of the birth of Jesus. So did the lights of your dream Christmas tree illuminate happy memories of Christmases past spent in the bosom of your family or signal your dread of the inevitable—and looming—family fights?

Related Dreams

pages 89, 178, 263, 286, 349 & 359

CHRYSANTHEMUMS

My Chrysanthemums Dreams

★ ★ ★ ★ ★ ★ ★ ★ ★ ★ ★ ★ ★ ★ ★ ★ ★

Golden Years

If you dreamed of carefully arranging a crop of chrysanthemum stems in a vase, did you do so with a feeling of contentment or sadness? And do you consciously equate these flowers with anything? Depending on your answers, your dream may have signified that you are anticipating enjoying many happy years of retirement or that you fear that death is about intrude in your life.

Because it blooms in the fall, the chrysanthemum is an ancient Chinese symbol of fall and harvest, rest, ease, and scholarly retreat. Japanese tradition associates chrysanthemums with the sun, and the Japanese consider the mum's unfolding petals to be a symbol of perfection. In general, this flower signifies cheerfulness, with individual colors bearing more specific messages (i.e., red for love and white for truth). In Italy, chrysanthemums are associated exclusively with the dead, and therefore they are considered suitable only for funerals.

Symbolic and Verbal Associations
- Fall; harvest
- Rest and ease
- Scholarly retreat
- Cheerfulness
- China or Japan
- The sun
- Perfection
- Death

Positive Interpretations: If your dreaming mind focused on a chrysanthemum, what associations do you have with this flower? Especially if you are of Chinese descent, or if you are familiar with Chinese traditions, then you may want to ask yourself whether this dream flower signified the fall and the rest and ease that, for a farm community, would come after the final harvest. (For example, was your unconscious encouraging you to relax?) And since Chinese tradition also associates this flower with scholarly retreat, might your dream have been reflecting your desire to study a new topic or to write an academic paper? For the Japanese, chrysanthemums are a symbol of the sun, and also of perfection—two avenues of interpretation that you may also want to consider. Since the sun appears on the Japanese flag, could your unconscious mind have been making a reference to Japan or to Japanese culture? Or perhaps the meaning of your dream is something as simple as the fact that you are happy because the weather has been warm and sunny. If you dreamed that someone gave you a gift of a chrysanthemum, what color was it? Red chrysanthemums are associated with love, while white mums are said to symbolize truth.

Negative Interpretations: Did you have a negative reaction to a dream that highlighted a chrysanthemum flower? If so, the meaning will depend on your associations with chrysanthemums. If this flower signifies the fall for you, do you dread going back to school in September? If you associate it with scholarship, are you feeling anxious about an upcoming exam? (If so, your unconscious was probably encouraging you to study!) Or does it speak to you of death, or of your allergy to pollen?

Related Dreams

pages 96, 283, 344, 350, 379 & 384

DAISIES

There are a number of diverse interpretations for a dream in which a daisy was emphasized, ranging from childlike innocence and fun to optimism, solar and summertime symbolism, or a "daisy chain"—which, in addition to flowers, can refer to a series of connected events or a chain of simultaneous sexual activity.

Symbolic and Verbal Associations
- Optimism
- Innocence
- Childlike fun and play
- The sun; summertime
- A series of connected events: a "daisy chain"
- A "daisy chain" of sexual activity: an orgy

Positive Interpretations: Did you have a happy dream in which you were running joyously through a field of daisies? Was your unconscious mind harking back to the blissful summers of your childhood, when the days were long and filled with fun and play in the endless-seeming sunshine? If so, are you finding your current waking life tedious and lacking in fun, perhaps because you are working from morning until night, without any time to socialize or unwind? Do you wish that you could return to a state of blissful innocence? Or have you become overly pessimistic, and was your unconscious mind attempting to infuse you with a healthy dose of optimism? Or do you have the wintertime blues, and are you thirsty for the sunshine of summer? In another scenario, did you dream that you were wandering across a green lawn full of daisies, which you plucked one by one and wove into a necklace that you then placed around your neck? If so, might your unconscious really have been referring to a metaphorical "daisy chain"—a series of connected real-world events or experiences? For example, in the real world, have you recently met someone by chance who knows someone who has a cousin who is in a position to help you with a budding business venture? Or was your unconscious simply reminding you to clean the house because your tidy aunt Daisy is coming to visit?

Negative Interpretations: In your dream, were you saddened to see that a golden-eyed daisy that you had picked in its prime was beginning to slump and wither? If so, do you feel as if the "summer" of your life is past, and that the "flower" of your prime has begun to wither and fade? If so, your unconscious was likely encouraging you to face up to the inevitability of the aging process, which is a part of life, and to enjoy the "bloom" of your latter years. Alternatively, were you troubled by an erotic dream in which you were participating in a "daisy chain"—an orgy. If so, do you know why your dream disturbed you so much? Is it because you consider such activity immoral? Or was your unconscious telling you that you have been overindulging in something, during your waking hours?

Related Dreams
pages 89, 242, 273, 283, 350 & 384

My Daisies Dreams

....
....
....
....
....
....
....
....
....

* * * * * * * * * * * * * * * * * *

Fresh as a Daisy

In the West, daisies often symbolize childlike innocence, a connotation that may have relevance to your waking existence if you perhaps picnicked on a sun-dappled, daisy-strewn lawn in dreamland. Is life in the real world currently so stressful and complicated that your unconscious may have been trying to give you a break by recalling the simple pleasures and lack of responsibility inherent in your childhood summer vacations?

My Deciduous Trees Dreams

✳ ✳ ✳ ✳ ✳ ✳ ✳ ✳ ✳ ✳ ✳ ✳ ✳ ✳ ✳ ✳ ✳

Leaves Equal Life

If you dreamed of a deciduous tree, were its branches covered with tightly furled, green buds or a multitude of fully formed leaves, or were its boughs bare? The answer may help you to decide whether your dream tree represented you, and your time of life (youth, maturity, or old age), or whether it simply mirrored the passing of the seasons in the real world.

DECIDUOUS TREES

Because deciduous trees drop their leaves in fall and grow them anew each spring as part of their eternal life cycle, their seasonal appearance in dreams is likely to mirror the stages of human life. In addition, the state of a dream deciduous tree's foliage is likely to be the key to the meaning of the dream, with new leaves symbolizing new beginnings or fresh interests; withered leaves, waning enthusiasm or affection; and fallen leaves, the past and things that have ended.

Symbolic and Verbal Associations
- The dreamer's age (as symbolized by the seasonal appearance of the dream tree)
- Change; ephemerality
- New beginnings or fresh interests (symbolized by new leaves)
- Waning enthusiasm or affection (symbolized by withered leaves)
- Mortality; the past (symbolized by fallen leaves)
- The eternal life cycle

Positive Interpretations: Did you dream of a deciduous tree that was filled with the tiniest green leaves of early spring? In the language of dreams, new leaves signify fresh beginnings or the development of new interests. So is there something new and exciting in your waking life? Perhaps a new academic interest, a new hobby, or a new love affair? Or was your dream a reference to your young daughter, who is just beginning to explore the world on her own? When attempting to interpret the meaning of a dream such as this, it is important to note that buds, blossoms, or new leaves on a dream tree may also indicate youthful vigor, fertility, and potential. And if you dreamed of a deciduous tree that was covered in mature, lush, dark-green foliage—indicating summertime—then do you feel as if you are in the prime of your years? Or is a waking relationship or endeavor thriving? Alternatively, if you dreamed of watching (as if through a time-lapse camera lens) as a tree rapidly went through its seasonal changes, might your unconscious have been reminding you of the necessity of change and of the ephemeral, yet eternal, nature of life?

Negative Interpretations: Did your dreaming mind highlight a tree whose foliage was withered or shriveled? If so, is the passion or enthusiasm in some area of your life waning? Is it your relationship with your girlfriend? Your interest in playing the guitar? Or simply your lust for life? And if your dreaming mind homed in on a tree that was beginning to drop its fall leaves, might your unconscious have been making a reference to something (perhaps some aspect of your life) that is now over and done with, a thing of the past? Or are you feeling saddened because you have entered middle age, the beginning of the "autumn" of your life? And, finally, if your dream self stood looking at a bare winter tree, your unconscious was likely to be making a reference to old age.

Related Dreams

pages 283, 344, 349, 351, 352 & 359

EVERGREEN TREES

Unlike deciduous trees, evergreen trees retain their leaves (or needles) throughout the year, a characteristic that lends them the dreamland symbolism of enjoying health and youthfulness, a vigorous approach to life, or things that are perennially fresh or interesting. And because many of these trees are found in the more northern, colder climates, a dream evergreen tree may also signify wintertime, old age, and wisdom.

Symbolic and Verbal Associations

‹ Everlasting health
‹ A vigorous approach to life
‹ Youthfulness
‹ Someone who is "needling" you
‹ The north; wintertime
‹ Wisdom and old age

Positive Interpretations: In your dream scenario, were you hiking across a mountain crowded with dark-green evergreen trees, and did you relish the scent of the pine sap and the crisp sound and feeling of the pine needles and pinecones as they crunched beneath your feet? If so, did your unconscious call up the image of the "ever-green" trees in order to mirror your waking sense that you are in the best of physical, mental, and spiritual health? Have you enjoyed a recent rush of youthful feelings and urges? Do you approach life with vigor and zeal? Or, in another scenario, did you dream that a great evergreen tree was the only green thing to be seen in the midst of a vast, ice- and snow-covered tundra? If so, have you been feeling as if your waking world is barren or lifeless? Do you feel lonely or are you saddened because you are growing older? Or do you simply feel down because the winter days are cold and sunless? If so, it is possible that your unconscious sent you the image of the evergreen tree as a symbol of life, to bring cheer and hope for the future spring in the face of death and darkness? (And is it possible that the tree was a metaphor for someone or something in the real world that lifts your spirits?)

Negative Interpretations: Did you have a dream in which you were camping in the woods, but you couldn't get comfortable in your sleeping bag because you were being scratched, itched, and stuck by the bed of pine needles that covered the ground? If so, was your unconscious attempting to draw your attention to the fact that someone has been "needling" you (i.e., goading or teasing you) during your waking hours? Or, finally, did you dream that you saw a pine tree that had dropped nearly all of its leaves, so that it stood dried, brown, and lifeless? If so, do you feel that your vitality and your energy have dried up or been "sapped" in the real world? Or did the dead tree represent someone in your life whose death you are grieving?

Related Dreams

pages 345, 348, 351, 359, 374 & 379

My Evergreen Trees Dreams

---

* * * * * * * * * * * * * * * * * *

An Evergreen Outlook

Should evergreen trees have seemed significant in a dreamscape, ask yourself what they could have represented. If you are looking forward to spending your vacation hiking in the fir-clad hills, they are unlikely to have harbored a deeper meaning, but if you can make no such obvious connection, could the key to your dream's meaning somehow lie in the word "evergreen," as in "eternally young"?

THE PLANT KINGDOM

My Flowers Dreams

★ ★ ★ ★ ★ ★ ★ ★ ★ ★ ★ ★ ★ ★ ★ ★ ★

In Full Flower

The stages of the floral life cycle symbolize the ephemeral nature of human life, with buds signifying youth, blooms in full flower denoting the prime of life, and fading flowers, old age. So if you dreamed of a bloom that had attained the peak of perfection, did it represent someone in your life—maybe you—who is at the height of his or her powers?

FLOWERS

Flowers are universal symbols of beauty, and when given to someone, they are an expression of love and admiration. Because their bloom is so fleeting, flowers are also associated with melancholy, mortality, and the ephemeral nature of existence— yet since flowers do contain the reproductive organs of their respective plants, dream blossoms may signify sex and sexuality, reproduction, and therefore hope for the future.

Symbolic and Verbal Associations
- Springtime
- Beauty and melancholy
- Love and admiration
- Mortality; the ephemeral nature of existence
- Hope for the future
- The "blossoming" of potential; fulfillment
- Sex and sexuality; reproduction

Positive Interpretations: If the stamen (the pollen-producing reproductive organ) of a dream flower was particularly prominent, or if your dream self was struck by the depth and receptivity of the flower's concavity, you may want to consider whether your dream had a bearing on your sexuality or your sex life (or whether you wish to produce a child). If you dreamed of marveling at the beauty of a glorious bloom, could your unconscious have been reflecting your "blossoming" potential, or your feeling of fulfillment because you have the sense that you are in the "full bloom" of your prime? Have all of the incongruent facets of your waking life finally come together in harmony, or do you feel that you have fully realized your potential, having blossomed as an individual? If you dreamed that you gave flowers to someone, who was that person? Was your unconscious simply mirroring the waking love and admiration that you have for him or her? Or if, in your dream, someone presented you with flowers, was your unconscious attempting to lift your spirits by giving you hope for the future?

Negative Interpretations: In your dream, were you saddened by the sight of a vase of drooping, dying flowers? If so, are you experiencing waking melancholy or depression because you are fixated on your own mortality, or else on the ephemeral nature of human existence? Was your dream reflecting your anxiety and sadness about the inevitability of the aging process? Are you afraid that "the flower of your youth has faded"? If you dreamed of watching a flower drop its petals one by one, do you feel regret at having entered the middle years of your life? But if your dream self was upset because you found that a lovely blossom had been knocked or cut off from its stem, do you fear that the blossom of your own talent has been severed from you? For example, if you are a professional dancer, have you recently suffered an injury that may put an end to your stage career?

Related Dreams

pages 36, 47, 91, 245, 267 & 344

FORESTS & WOODS

Dreamland forests and woods can symbolize a real-world community, a peaceful and harmonious environment, or the unconscious state. A dream in which a forest produced negative feelings may signify anxiety or apprehension, the feeling of being "overshadowed" by others, or a sense of being trapped or entangled.

Symbolic and Verbal Associations

(A community; community relations
(A peaceful and harmonious environment
(The state of the unconscious
(Feeling "overshadowed" by others
(A sense of being trapped, stuck, or helplessly entangled (as if in barbs)
(Apprehension

Positive Interpretations: In your dream, were you walking through a fragrant, calm, sun-dappled forest? Just as a single dream tree may represent the dreamer, a dream forest (which is made up of different species of trees and other plants that coexist with each other) may represent some waking community or domain (be it a neighborhood, a city, school, work, etc.) that you are part of—with the different species and individuals represented the various persons in the community. So if your dream forest was pleasant and peaceful, was your unconscious mirroring the pleasant peacefulness of your real-world community? Are people in your waking life living and working together happily and harmoniously? In the language of dreams, a wood or a forest may also signify the current state of your unconscious. So did your peaceful dream forest reflect your waking desire to escape the demands and the mayhem of the real world and to retreat into your own private world for purposes of meditation, self-contemplation, and emotional rejuvenation?

Negative Interpretations: Were you dismayed by a dream in which you were wandering through a forest in which many of the trees had been felled, so that those few that remained were at some distance from one another? If so, did your dream reflect your own depopulated community? For example, have certain of your relatives recently stopped socializing with the rest of the family, perhaps due to a bitter disagreement or a falling out, with the result that there is a good deal of emotional distance between those of you who are still on speaking terms? Or did you have a nightmare in which you were completely lost in a dark forest, or in which you had become helplessly entangled in a patch of brambles and barbs? If so, are your real-life circumstances currently filling you with apprehension? Do you feel overshadowed by others during your waking hours—perhaps by your seniors at work—or do you feel trapped or ensnared in some abrasive waking situation from which you are struggling to regain your freedom?

Related Dreams

pages 234, 306, 348, 349, 359 & 377

My Forests & Woods Dreams

----

* * * * * * * * * * * * * * * * * * *

Friends or Foes?

A dream of walking in a forest is likely to have mirrored how you relate to those in your waking life at the moment. If your dreaming self felt embraced and protected by the surrounding trees, do your friends and family make you feel the same in the real world? But if the trees seemed somehow threatening, is certain people's hostility making you feel fearful?

My Fruit Trees Dreams

✳ ✳ ✳ ✳ ✳ ✳ ✳ ✳ ✳ ✳ ✳ ✳ ✳ ✳ ✳ ✳

Bearing Fruit

Fruit's association with sweet rewards is hard-wired into the human brain, which is why any delectable fruit that you dreamed about probably had this meaning. But if your dream fruit was worm-eaten, could the project (symbolized by the fruit tree) that you have been laboriously nurturing in real life have been infested by destructive outside influences, so that its "fruition" is already tainted?

FRUIT TREES

✦✦✦✦✦✦✦✦✦✦✦✦✦✦✦✦✦✦✦✦✦✦✦✦✦✦✦✦✦✦✦✦✦✦✦✦

Because fruits are the reproductive product of the trees that bear them, a dream fruit tree is likely to signify fertility, children, creativity, or new ideas or plans. Humans have long venerated fruit trees for the food that they provide, and, likewise, a dream fruit tree may symbolize emotional sustenance, or else the harvest of a metaphorical "crop." And in Christianity and Judaism, the Tree of Life that grew in the Garden of Eden is said to have born twelve types of fruit, which, if eaten, gave everlasting life.

Symbolic and Verbal Associations
- Fertility; children
- Creativity; the flourishing of new ideas
- Spiritual or emotional sustenance
- The Judeo-Christian Tree of Life
- "Blooming" talents; a "budding" relationship, etc.

Positive Interpretations: If you dreamed of a tree that was heavy with fruit, could it have denoted your creative drive, a crop of new (or ripe) ideas or endeavors, or your desire to have children (an interpretation that may also apply if you dreamed of a fruit tree that was laden with its first spring blooms)? And if you dreamed of a specific type of fruit tree, ask yourself what associations you hold with regard to this particular species. For instance, since bananas may be phallic symbols, was a dream banana tree a reference to your sex life? If you are a Buddhist, did your unconscious conjure up a fig tree as a reference to the sacred bodhi tree, under whose shelter the Buddha gained enlightenment? In the Jewish and Christian traditions, the dove that Noah sent out from the Ark returned bearing a branch from a tree that grew on the Mount of Olives, which is why olives branches have come to symbolize peace (originally, the peace between God and humans). So if it was an olive tree that you dreamed of, was your unconscious advising you to hold out a metaphorical "olive branch" toward, or to make peace with, someone with whom you have quarreled in the waking world? But because olives are a valuable source of oil, a dream olive tree may also symbolize fertility, prosperity, and wealth. Or did you dream of the Judeo-Christian Tree of Life, whose fruit, if eaten, is said to have imparted everlasting life? If so, was your unconscious referring to your belief in the immortality of the spirit? Or if you are familiar with Chinese tradition and you dreamed of a mulberry tree, which the Chinese consider to be a symbol of industry, was your unconscious making a comment on your current productivity in the real world?

Negative Interpretations: Did you dream of a fruit tree from whose branches hung rotten or mealy fruits, or that was draped in withered, dead blooms? If so, has a formerly sweet aspect of your life (perhaps a relationship) gone sour, foul, or otherwise bad? Do you feel that you are past your prime? Or, if you are a woman, do you yearn to have a baby, but are you worried that you are too old to do so safely?

Related Dreams
pages 177, 184, 348, 351 & 359

IVY & CLIMBING PLANTS

Because it is an evergreen that lives on in its full greenness throughout the turning seasons, ivy is an ancient symbol of immortality. And because ivy and other climbing plants travel upward toward the sunlight, a dream of one of these plants may also denote emotional or spiritual elevation, higher consciousness, or even someone who is a "social climber." Unless, of course, you dreamed of poison ivy, which is likely to denote an irritation or an annoyance.

Symbolic and Verbal Associations
(Immortality (as symbolized by ivy)
(Emotional or spiritual ascension
(Higher consciousness
(Lofty ideals
(Someone who is a "social climber"
(Poison ivy: an irritation or an annoyance
(Something to be avoided

Positive Interpretations: Did you dream that you were using an ivy plant to clamber upward toward the heavens, in much the same way as the fabled Jack who climbed the bean stalk into the sky? If so, is it possible that your unconscious was reflecting your elevated mood, or else the lofty ideals that you hold in the real world? Otherwise, do you desire to make a spiritual ascension, or to tap into a higher consciousness? If you dreamed of a flowering climbing vine, such as a wistaria, sweet pea, clematis, or morning glory, consider the associations that you have with these plants. For example, was your unconscious mirroring your waking notion that life is fragrant, sweet, or glorious? (Also, you may want to refer to this chapter's entry on flowers.)

Negative Interpretations: If you dreamed that you were walking through the woods and that you recoiled at the sight of a patch of poison ivy, your unconscious may have been making a reference to something in your waking life that is an irritation or an annoyance to you, or else to something that is dangerous and to be avoided. Or, in your dream, did you see a sturdy, twisting tree that you wanted to climb, but were disappointed to see that the tree was wrapped in a thick, hairy vine of glistening poison ivy? If so, is something in the waking world preventing you from ascending toward your goals, or from achieving the happiness that you long for? Or is something harmful preventing you from seeking the elevated vantage point that you desire? Otherwise, if you dreamed of an ivy or another climbing plant that was growing up a tree, a trellis, or any other structure, you may want to ask yourself if it represented someone in your waking circle who is a "social climber." And, finally, did you dream that your house (which is a symbol of the self) was covered from ground to roof in wild, thick ivy? If so, have you been neglecting your personal care or emotional needs?

Related Dreams
pages 159, 211, 277, 345, 349 & 350

My Ivy & Climbing Plants Dreams

----

* * * * * * * * * * * * * * * * * * *

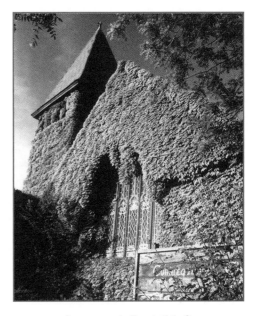

Immortal, Invisible?
If you dreamed of an ivy-covered building, did that building mean anything special to you? A dream church may have symbolized your religious beliefs, for example, while your home may have signified you. As for the dream ivy, it may have signaled the "evergreen," that is, enduring, spiritual attitudes that you present to the world or, alternatively, your neglect of your appearance.

My Lilies Dreams

✱ ✱ ✱ ✱ ✱ ✱ ✱ ✱ ✱ ✱ ✱ ✱ ✱ ✱ ✱ ✱ ✱

Pictures of Lily

If your dreaming vision homed in on a lily, did you have a Christian upbringing in the real world? If so, consider whether your dream lily shares the symbolism of the lily as associated with the Virgin Mary, that is, did it signify purity and innocence, and perhaps even chastity? But if it evoked the words "lily-white," could the reference have been downright racist?

LILIES

✱ ✱

Because lilies are often employed as funereal flowers, many people associate them with death and mourning, but this same association also lends them the added symbolism of the afterlife—a symbolism that corresponds with the Christian association of lilies with Easter (the celebration of Christ's resurrection) and therefore also with everlasting life. In dreams, a white lily may also denote a wedding, virginity, innocence, hope, purity, truth, or compassion.

Symbolic and Verbal Associations

- A wedding; virginity, innocence, and hope (as symbolized by a white lily)
- Purity and truth (also represented by a white lily)
- Everlasting life (in association with Easter)
- Compassion (in connection with the Christian example of Mary)
- A funeral; death, mourning, and the afterlife

Positive Interpretations: If you are a Christian and you had a dream that highlighted a lily, were you reminded of this flower's association with the New Testament story of the Annunciation, in which the Archangel Gabriel appeared before the Virgin Mary to inform her that she would give birth to Christ? If so, are you a woman who is hoping to conceive a child? Or was your unconscious advising you to follow Mary's example of compassion during your waking hours? For Christians, the lily is also associated with Easter, the celebration of Christ's resurrection, which lends it the added symbolism of everlasting life. The details and the context of your dream should help you to determine how to interpret it. For example, if you are soon to be married in the real world, then you should consider whether your dream of a white lily signified virginity (either your own or that of your betrothed), spiritual innocence, or hope. Or if you dreamed that someone gave you a white lily, do you feel that this person is imbued with the qualities of purity and truth?

Negative Interpretations: If you associate lilies primarily with funerals, then your dream self probably had a negative reaction to a dream in which this flower made an appearance. And, if so, was your dream a reference to a metaphorical death—perhaps the end of a friendship or of a phase of your life? Or are you currently mourning the passing of a loved one? It is important to remember that, just as lilies are a symbol of death, they are also a symbol of eternity and the afterlife—and your unconscious may have been reminding you of this in order to bring you some peace and hope in your sorrow. Or, if you are allergic to members of the lily family, as many people are, did you dream that you accidentally sat in a bed of lilies and that, as a result, your skin broke out in an angry, red, and itchy "lily rash"? If so, you may want to ask yourself whether someone in your waking life been irritating you—perhaps a person who is esthetically pleasing, though noxious if you get too close to him or her.

Related Dreams

pages 91, 96, 102, 346, 350 & 357

LOTUSES

****

O f all of the various flowers, the lotus is the one that has the most symbolic associations in the Eastern world. It is, and has been considered, sacred in ancient Egyptian belief, Taoism, and Hinduism, and it is honored as a heavenly bloom in Islamic and Buddhist traditions.

Symbolic and Verbal Associations

- The unity of the underworld, Earth, and the spiritual realm
- The cycle of death, rebirth, and enlightenment
- The Buddha, "the Jewel in the Lotus"
- The yogic chakras or energy centers within the human body
- Summer (in Chinese tradition)

Positive Interpretations: Because of its unusual ability to flower in murky waters, the lotus has long been venerated in the East as a cosmic sign of the unification or oneness of the underworld, the Earth, and the spiritual realm, and also as a symbol of the cycle of death, rebirth, and, finally, enlightenment. So if you dreamed that you were worshiping or praying before the loveliest lotus flower that you had ever seen, you should ask yourself whether your unconscious was reminding you of the connectedness of all things. And if you consider yourself to be on a path toward enlightenment during your waking hours, then it is also possible that your unconscious sent you the image of the lotus as a mandala to help you to focus on your waking desire to transcend desire and suffering and to attain a state of nirvana. If you are a Buddhist, did your dream lotus represent the Buddha himself, who is called "the Jewel in the Lotus"? Alternatively, if you hold the yogic belief that the human body contains energy centers or chakras, and you had a dream in which you saw a lotus that was blooming at the location of one of your chakras (at your third eye, for instance, the point of wisdom and imagination), then it is possible that your unconscious was trying to help you to develop, or open your energy flow to, this chakra. And if you dreamed of a lotus and you are familiar with Chinese tradition, in which this flower is a symbol of summertime, was your unconscious reflecting your excited anticipation of the coming summer?

Negative Interpretations: In your dream, were you distraught to find a lotus that had been uprooted or ripped and torn apart? If so, was your unconscious mirroring your waking feeling of there being a disastrous disconnection between the different aspects of your life (perhaps, even between your physical, mental, and spiritual energies). Or do you feel stuck in your spiritual progression, so that the enlightened state that you desire seems hopelessly unattainable? (If so, your unconscious was likely trying to bring this to your conscious attention so that you may work toward freeing yourself from whatever is holding you back.)

Related Dreams
pages 283, 344, 350, 357, 378 & 387

My Lotuses Dreams

----

* * * * * * * * * * * * * * * * * * * *

The Lotus Position

If you are familiar with the concept of the chakras, or the energy centers that are said to range from the base of the spine to the crown of the head, could your unconscious have prompted you to dream about a lotus to highlight one of yours? If you think that this could be so, the health of the dream lotus may have been significant.

My Poppies Dreams

....

....

....

....

....

....

....

....

....

....

★ ★ ★ ★ ★ ★ ★ ★ ★ ★ ★ ★ ★ ★ ★ ★ ★

Remembrance and Forgetfulness

Poppies can send diametrically opposed messages when they bloom in dreamland, but their meaning usually accords with your conscious association with these flowers. So do red poppies remind you of the sacrifice that a generation of young men made on the fields of Flanders between 1914 and 1918? Or do opium poppies signal oblivion to you, or maybe your longing to forget your real-life woes?

POPPIES

★ ★

The ancient Greeks considered poppies to be a symbol of fertility and love, and eating poppy seeds was thought to imbue one with health and strength. This flower is also associated with oblivion, emotional numbness, and death, probably because poppies are used in the production of opium, morphine, codeine, and heroin. But if the poppy is considered to be a symbol of death, it has also come to symbolize rebirth, remembrance, and commemoration, ever since red poppies sprang up over the bloody battlefields of Flanders in World War I.

Symbolic and Verbal Associations
- Oblivion; emotional numbness
- Death
- Commemoration; remembrance (in association with World War I)
- Rebirth
- Fertility and prosperity
- Love; matters of the heart

Positive Interpretations: Did you dream that you looked out of your window to see that a field of blood-red poppies had sprung up overnight, and do you associate this flower with World War I, during which this flower bloomed over Europe's battlefields? If so, is it possible that your unconscious sent you your dream to reflect your sense of having waged a costly battle in the waking world? Do you wish to undergo a spiritual rebirth? Or do you have other associations with the poppy? If you consider it to be a sign of fertility and prosperity, as the ancient Greeks did, then might your dream have denoted your wish to become pregnant or to gain a fortune? Or was your unconscious reflecting your recent burst of creative energy? Greek mythology also tells how poppies sprang from the tears of Aphrodite as she mourned for Adonis, and this flower's association with Aphrodite made it a popular ingredient in medieval love potions. So if you associate the poppy with love and matters of the heart, did your dream of a poppy signify your waking desire to find a mate? Or did it point toward the romantic feelings that you have for someone in particular in the real world? Alternatively, could your dream have simply been a reference to your memories of Pop, your father, or Poppy, a friend?

Negative Interpretations: If you had a negative reaction to a dream that highlighted a poppy, could your unconscious have been attempting to draw your attention to your own emotional numbness? Or if you associate poppies with death, did your dream denote your sorrow and mourning over the passing of a loved one? But if none of these interpretations seems to apply, trying some free association may help you to understand your dream. For example, was it a reference to how sad you recently felt when you saw that little dog with the "poppy" eyes as you were walking by, and looking into the window of, the corner pet store?

Related Dreams

pages 92, 37, 159, 211, 254 & 350

ROSES

In the Western world, no flower has been more celebrated than the rose. Red roses are the classic floral symbol of love, romance, sexuality, and feminine beauty, and their symbolism has been elaborated on by countless poets and lyricists. White roses, which are often carried by brides, signify virginity, while yellow roses are a sign of friendship and joy. But because this flower's stem is studded with sharp thorns, a dream rose may also be an unconscious warning of danger.

Symbolic and Verbal Associations
- Love, romance, and sexuality (as signified by red roses)
- Beauty and femininity
- Virginity, innocence, and purity (as signified by white roses)
- Friendship and joy (as signified by yellow roses)
- Appreciating the beauty in the world, as in "smelling the roses"
- Optimism: seeing the world through "rose-colored glasses"
- A thorn; danger; something to be avoided

Positive Interpretations: If your dreaming mind conjured up the image of a long-stemmed red rose, are you in love in the real world? If so, your unconscious was likely reflecting the primacy of romance and sexuality in your current life. Or, since a red rose is also a symbol of feminine beauty, you may want to consider whether your dreaming mind was drawing a parallel between the rose and a woman in your waking life whom you consider to be beautiful and graceful. If you dreamed that you were carrying a bouquet of white roses, was your unconscious making a comment on your virginity, your innocence, or your purity of spirit? If you dreamed that someone gave you a gift of yellow roses, was your unconscious reflecting your feelings of friendship for this person? Otherwise, is he or she someone whom you would like to be friends with? Or does he or she simply make you feel happy during your waking hours? Alternatively, did you dream that you were wandering through a rose garden, feeling joyful and relaxed as you breathed in the sweet smell of the flowers? If so, your unconscious may have been advising you to slow down your fast-paced lifestyle and to take some time to appreciate the beauty of the world around you—in other words, to stop a moment and "smell the roses."

Negative Interpretations: In your dream, were you alarmed to find that the entire world had turned into shades of rose-colored reds and pinks? If so, and if you have indeed been viewing the waking world through "rose-colored glasses," could your unconscious mind have been warning you against such blind optimism, because it could cause you to miss crucial warnings of danger? And, finally, danger may have been implied if your dreaming mind focused on the thorn on a rose's stem—perhaps a danger that is hidden or unexpected because it comes as part of a beautiful package.

Related Dreams
pages 36, 102, 112, 245, 267 & 344

My Roses Dreams

---

* * * * * * * * * * * * * * * * * *

A Rosy Outlook

If you dreamed of being surrounded by a sea of beautiful, fragrant roses, did the experience mirror your feeling that your waking life is currently so wonderful that it could be described as being a "bed of roses"? But if your real-world circumstances are anything but "rosy" at the moment, could your unconscious have sent you a heartening contrary, compensatory, or wish-fulfillment dream?

My Seeds & Nuts Dreams

....
....
....
....
....
....
....
....

* * * * * * * * * * * * * * * * * * *

Nature's Bounty

A dream of grabbing a handful of nuts and seeds in order to make granola may have been your unconscious mind's way of urging you to ditch your usual, high-fat breakfast for a more healthy option. Alternatively, could the sight of a wealth of nature's "riches" in dreamland have been encouraging you to "squirrel away" your own real-life riches, or earnings?

SEEDS & NUTS

* *

Seeds and nuts share many associations in terms of dream symbolism. Because they are the means by which the next generation of plants is brought forth into existence, seeds and nuts signify fertility and reproduction, unborn children, and also prosperity and wellbeing. For this same reason, seeds and nuts may denote sexuality, and also because nuts and seeds can be equated with testicles and semen, and because the shape of almonds resembles female genitalia. Other associations include new ideas, hidden wisdom, and challenges (as in "a tough nut to crack").

Symbolic and Verbal Associations

- Fertility and reproduction
- Unborn children
- Prosperity and wellbeing
- Sexuality
- The "germ" of a new idea; "the seeds of" love, change, peace, etc.
- Hidden wisdom; challenges: "a tough nut to crack"

Positive Interpretations: If your dreaming mind focused on a certain type of nut, there may have been a sexual meaning. For example, because almonds resemble female genitalia, and because the almond is also a symbol of the Christian Virgin Mary, you may want to consider whether a dream almond represented a girl's virginity. When trying to interpret a dream that featured seeds or nuts, you should also remember that "nuts" is a slang word for testicles, and that seeds can be equated with semen. So if you are a man whose dream featured nuts or seeds, was your unconscious making a comment on your sex life? Alternatively, if you are a man or a woman who dreamed of seeing a tree, flower, or fruit that was dripping with seeds, could this have represented your desire to start a family, or else your wish for prosperity and wellbeing? Or might your dream have denoted the "germ" of a new idea that you have had, or "the seeds" of something new in your life (such as love, change, or peace).

Negative Interpretations: In your dream, were you trying with all of your strength to break open the hard shell of a nut? If so, was your unconscious referring to someone in the waking world who is "a tough nut" (i.e., someone who presents a hardened persona to the outer world, but in whom you can see sweetness), or else to a difficult waking problem or situation that is proving to be "a tough nut to crack"? In attempting to determine the meaning of your dream, you should also consider the other meaning associated with the word "nuts": for instance, was your dream mirroring the craziness of your current life? In another scenario, if you dreamed of biting into a fruit and getting a mouthful of seeds, could your unconscious have been pointing out the "seediness" (or disrepute) of the new bar that you've been hanging out at in the real world?

Related Dreams

pages 47, 97, 105, 175, 177 & 359

TREES

THE PLANT KINGDOM

From ancient times, the tree has been an archetypal symbol of knowledge, life, family, the cosmos, and more. In dreams, however, a tree is more likely to denote the self: the dreamer's past, present, and future, and his or her physical, emotional, and spiritual growth. Further, the condition of a dream tree's roots, trunk, branches, and leaves may have significant meaning, as may the tree's environment.

Symbolic and Verbal Associations
- Knowledge
- Life
- Family lineage
- The cosmos
- Past, present, and future
- Physical, emotional, and spiritual growth

Positive Interpretations: Did your dreaming vision fix itself on the roots of a dream tree? In dreams, roots can represent both your unconscious mind and your past (i.e., your family, childhood, and geographical "roots"). So if your dream roots appeared strong and sturdy, your unconscious was likely saying that your past influences were stable, supportive, and sustaining, implying that you are "well rooted" in the past. If the dream tree was a young sapling whose roots were just beginning to branch out, are you about to "put down roots," or to establish yourself in a new place, perhaps with a committed partner? A dream tree's trunk, which links the roots and the branches, represents the conscious mind, and also individuality. If you dreamed of a tree with a very straight trunk, do you pride yourself on having a straightforward or rational approach to life? Were your dream tree's branches strong and widespread? If so, could your unconscious have been referring to the various ways that you have "branched out" in your life, whether in terms of your career development or personal interests? Or did the dream tree's proliferating branches represent the branches of your family tree?

Negative Interpretations: In the language of dreams, a tree's bark is likely to denote the façade or persona that you present to the world. And if you had a dream in which a tree's bark was peeling away, could your unconscious have been pointing out the fact that your façade is beginning to erode, so that others can see through it to the "real you"? If you think that this interpretation may be right, was your unconscious encouraging you to strip away that façade, which is failing anyway, and to allow others to see and know you as you truly are? Alternatively, if you dreamed of a tree with a twisted or distorted trunk, might this have denoted your (or someone else's) "twisted" views or ideologies? And if you dreamed that a multitude of insects was feasting on a tree's sap (which can be equated with blood), is your own vitality being "sapped" by a horde of paltry frustrations?

Related Dreams

pages 108, 125, 348, 349, 351 & 352

My Trees Dreams

✳ ✳ ✳ ✳ ✳ ✳ ✳ ✳ ✳ ✳ ✳ ✳ ✳ ✳ ✳ ✳ ✳ ✳

Branching Out

If you found yourself fascinated by a well-branched tree in dreamland, your dreaming interest may simply have reflected a waking preoccupation with trees, perhaps because you are currently studying various woodland species at school. Otherwise—and particularly if your hobby is genealogy, or if you've just welcomed a baby niece into the world—could the tree have symbolized your burgeoning family, or "family tree"?

My Weeds Dreams

★ ★ ★ ★ ★ ★ ★ ★ ★ ★ ★ ★ ★ ★ ★ ★ ★

Out of Place

Dreaming of seeing a huge, green weed growing incongruously among a well-regimented row of unexceptional-looking bedding plants may have reflected how you are feeling during your waking hours. Are you feeling awkward and out of place, for example, perhaps because you have just left school, landed a job, and found yourself in an office where everyone seems to behave an orderly, conventional fashion except you?

WEEDS

★ ★

As unwanted overgrowth in the garden of dreams, weeds may denote neglect of self or of one's personal growth, so that there is confusion or loss of control. Dream weeds may also symbolize an invasion of rogue ideas or foreign, unwanted influences, and a dream of being entangled in weeds may signify a waking feeling of being choked or suffocated. More positively, a fast-growing dream weed may represent a growing and developing child.

Symbolic and Verbal Associations
- Neglect of self or personal growth
- Loss of control
- Confusion
- Negativity; a rogue invasion of ideas, etc.; negative or useless influences
- A child
- Feeling choked or suffocated

Positive Interpretations: In your dream, were you weeding, or chopping and clearing away the weeds that had run amok in your dream garden? If so, your unconscious may have been reflecting your efforts, or your desire, to purge yourself of negative thoughts or actions in order to free your mind and spirit and to allow your positive self to flourish. Such a dream may also signify your desire to correct or make amends for your past self-neglect (whether physical, emotional, mental, or spiritual). And if your dream depicted you plucking out the few scant weeds that were growing in an otherwise beautifully tended garden, then your unconscious may have been reflecting the healthy way in which you tend to your physical, mental, and/or spiritual needs. Otherwise, if you felt pride or joy at watching a weedy-looking plant grow taller and taller, might this have reflected the pride and joy that your real-world self gains by watching a once weakly child grow and develop?

Negative Interpretations: Did you dream that your garden was completely overgrown with a tangled thicket of spiny and vinelike weeds? If so, was your unconscious reflecting the fact that you have been neglecting yourself or your personal growth? Have you let go of your control over your own life, so that you are in a constant state of chaos and confusion? Alternatively, might your dream have been a warning that you have been under the influence of an invasion of negative or useless influences or ideas? Perhaps your weed-choked garden represented the invasive influence of a dominant or charismatic person in your life, who is making you feel as if you are suffocating or choking (an interpretation that may be particularly relevant if your dream self was caught and struggled in the thicket). Whatever they represented, your dream may have been a call to action for you to clear away those weeds that have been inhibiting your personal growth and to begin nurturing your own ideas, desires, needs, and talents.

Related Dreams

pages 159, 211, 283, 368, 377 & 379

CHAPTER 18
THE ELEMENTS & LANDSCAPES

Be particularly alert to possible puns when thinking about a dream
in which fire, air, water, the earth, the weather, or the landscape
seemed particularly significant, for a pun may tell you something
pertinent about your emotional reaction to your current situation
in the waking world. Are you "burning" with anger or close to
"exploding" or "erupting" with fury, for instance? Do you feel that
making progress at work is akin to "climbing a mountain"? Or do
you feel so "swamped" by overwhelming emotions that you are on
the verge of dissolving into "floods" of tears?

My Abysses & Valleys Dreams

----

* * * * * * * * * * * * * * * * * *

The Great Divide

If your waking hours have been marred by a bitter disagreement between you and your partner, and you dreamed that you were walking and talking together when the ground suddenly parted beneath your feet, leaving you standing on one side of an abyss and your partner on the other, could this scenario have represented your dramatically divided viewpoints? And was there any "common ground"?

ABYSSES & VALLEYS

Though they bear some symbolic similarities because they are all depressions in the earth, the explicit meanings of dream abysses, canyons, gorges, ravines, chasms, and valleys will vary. Specifically, a valley may symbolize security and groundedness, or else limited horizons, while a chasm or an abyss may signify instability and danger, a ravine may denote a rift in a relationship, and an abyss may represent a deep emotional depression.

Symbolic and Verbal Associations

- Danger; a hazard or a trap (as in a "pitfall")
- Emotional depression
- A rift in a relationship; a pronounced difference of opinions
- Security and groundedness
- Limited horizons
- The archetypal terrible mother

Positive Interpretations: In your dream, were you frolicking in the tall, green grass of a warm, sunlit valley? Because real-world valleys and dells offer protection from the wind-driven elements, your unconscious may have sent you your dream in order to reflect your waking sense of security and groundedness (perhaps because you are dwelling, or spending your waking hours, amongst a group of warm, loving people), even though your protected environment may mean that your viewpoint or horizons are being limited by the persons or structures that are protecting you.

Negative Interpretations: A chasm, abyss, or gorge is a deep, steep-sided depression in the earth, and their symbolism in dreams is likely to do with insecurity or danger, but may also be related to emotional depression. For instance, if you dreamed that you were trembling or teetering on the edge of a gorge or a chasm, do you feel dangerously close to falling into some sort of trap or hole during your waking hours? Perhaps it is a dangerous plan that someone is trying to draw you into, or else a deep emotional depression that you feel coming on? Or if you dreamed that a hole or an abyss suddenly opened up in the earth before you, might your unconscious have been warning you that you have a false sense of security during your waking hours, and that an unsuspected "pitfall" may be looming before you? Alternatively, if you dreamed that you were scrambling to keep your footing on the edge of a ravine, or that you found yourself straddling a crevice, with one foot on each side and a long, dark drop below you, then was your dream referring to a rift in one of your real-world relationships, perhaps due to a pronounced differing of opinions? And if you found that your dream self had fallen and was lying motionless at the bottom of a profound pit or abyss, was your unconscious drawing a parallel with the emotional pit that you feel unable to pull yourself out of? Finally, a dangerous hole or chasm in the earth may represent the good Earth Mother gone bad.

Related Dreams

pages 113, 159, 204, 225, 238 & 284

Air & Sky

✲✲✲

Air is essential to our survival, which is why it is a symbol of life and wellbeing, and the sky, which comprises air, is associated with inspiration (which can also be defined as the inhalation of air into the lungs), spiritual aspirations, and higher ambitions. To dream of flying or of gliding through the air may symbolize a sense of adventure or liberation, or else a desire to rise above the mundane details of day-to-day existence to get "a bird's-eye view" of life.

Symbolic and Verbal Associations
- Life and wellbeing
- Spiritual aspirations; inspiration
- Intellectual or career ambitions
- Adventure and liberation (as signified by a dream of flying)
- A desire to rise above the mundane
- Seeing the bigger picture; getting "a bird's-eye view"

Positive Interpretations: In your dream, did you feel giddy with excitement and energy after filling your lungs with crisp, clean mountain air? If so, was your unconscious mirroring your sense of being stimulated and inspired in the real world? For example, do you feel intoxicatingly "airy" now that you have quit a dead-end job, called a halt to an unhappy relationship, or begun a new art project that you are enjoying immensely? Alternatively, did you dream that you were flying or gliding high above the earth as you swooped and laughed with pleasure? Different dream analysts believe many different things about flying dreams. For instance, some believe that they are a form of out-of-body experience. However, if you dreamed of flying, you may want to consider whether your dream reflected your waking sense of joyful freedom and liberation (like "walking on air"), your spiritual, intellectual, or career aspirations, or your desire to rise above the mundane or to gain a "bird's-eye view" of life. Similar interpretations may be applied if you dreamed of flying a kite, releasing a helium balloon, or floating in a hot-air balloon. Or you may want to consider whether a dream that focused on air was a reference to someone in your life who is imbued with the traditional associations of air, optimism and confidence—perhaps someone born under one of the zodiacal air signs (Gemini, Libra, or Aquarius).

Negative Interpretations: If you dreamed that you were gasping or fighting for air, your unconscious may have been reflecting upon the psychological or intellectual suffocation that you are suffering during your waking hours. For instance, is the dreariness of your job killing your desire to create or to learn new things? Do you desperately desire "inspiration"? Or if you dreamed that you were unable to breathe properly because the air in the room was foul or smoke-filled, might your unconscious have been advising you of the need for you to "clear the air," or resolve a tense situation, in the real world?

My Air & Sky Dreams

✲✲✲✲✲✲✲✲✲✲✲✲✲✲✲✲✲✲✲✲

Up, Up, and Away

A dream of seeing the familiar features of your daily life—your home, school, or workplace, your family and friends—recede into the distance as, cocooned in the gondola of a hot-air balloon, you floated ever upward into the rarified atmosphere above may have signaled your desire to leave your mundane existence behind in order to focus exclusively on spiritual or cerebral matters.

Related Dreams

pages 213, 219, 225, 295, 315 & 373

My Caves Dreams

✱ ✱ ✱ ✱ ✱ ✱ ✱ ✱ ✱ ✱ ✱ ✱ ✱ ✱ ✱ ✱

Returning to the Womb

In dreams, dark, enclosed spaces like caves can represent the womb, or a warm, safe haven into which we long to retreat in order to escape the perils and problems of the real world, somewhere where we can curl up in the fetal position and sink into a state of blissful oblivion, secure in the knowledge that Mother Earth will protect us.

CAVES

✱✱✱✱✱✱✱✱✱✱✱✱✱✱✱✱✱✱✱✱✱✱✱✱✱✱✱✱✱✱✱✱✱✱✱✱

Because their shape is reminiscent of the vagina, which leads to the womb, and also because they are places within the earth where we might seek protection from the elements, dream caves are often symbolic of the archetypal mother, or Mother Earth. Related associations include escape or retreat, sanctuary and protection. Also, the symbolic association between the subterranean earth and the unconscious mind lends caves the added symbolism of insight, intuition, and memory.

Symbolic and Verbal Associations
- The vagina
- The womb; the archetypal Mother Earth
- Retreat; sanctuary; protection
- Oblivion
- The unconscious mind; insight, intuition, and memory

Positive Interpretations: Did you have a dream in which you were making your way through the cold wind and pounding rain, shivering and soaked to the core, and that you rejoiced to stumble upon the opening to a dry, warm cave? If so, was your unconscious depicting your symbolic return to the womb? Is your waking life so emotionally inhospitable or unbearable that you long to escape to a protected sanctuary—a warm, welcoming, embracing cocoon where you can hide away from all of your problems? If you dreamed of entering a warm cave, you may also want to consider whether your dream cave represented a vagina, thereby reflecting your desire to have a sexual relationship with a woman. However, if none of the above interpretations seems correct, then it is possible that your dream cave denoted the realm of your unconscious mind. This type of interpretation may be especially true if your dream self was searching for something within the cave—perhaps an insight, intuition, or memory that would help you to solve a problem that is weighing on your mind during your waking hours.

Negative Interpretations: Did your dream of being in a dark cave turn into a nightmare when you realized that you had wandered too far and that you couldn't find your way back out to the light of day? If so, your unconscious may have been warning you that you have descended into oblivion, or an absence of rational thought that you are finding it difficult to make your way out of. Your dream may have also signified that you are suffering from depression. You may originally have retreated into this place (possibly via the use of drugs) in order to escape your waking problems, but you now find that you have lost your ability to think critically and clearly. If this interpretation rings true, you may want to heed the message of your dream and to consider seeking professional counseling. Alternatively, did you dream that you became trapped in a cave by falling rocks? If so, are you feeling trapped, overwhelmed, or suffocated by an overbearing or overzealous mother figure in the real world?

Related Dreams

pages 113, 220, 311, 312, 368 & 385

CLIFFS

THE ELEMENTS & LANDSCAPES

✳✳✳✳✳✳✳✳✳✳✳✳✳✳✳✳✳✳✳✳✳✳✳✳✳✳✳✳✳✳✳✳✳✳✳✳✳✳

Dream cliffs may represent many things, including: ambitious goals or expectations that will be difficult to realize, hard-won achievements, or futility. Dreams of losing one's balance or of falling from a cliff may point toward insecurities, or to a fear of losing control or of failing.

Symbolic and Verbal Associations
- Ambitious goals, or high expectations, which will be difficult to realize
- The rewards of hard work; alternatively, a futile upward struggle
- Insecurity; fear of losing control
- Fear of failure
- A "cliff-hanger"; suspense; something unresolved
- An obstacle, or a dead end

Positive Interpretations: Did you dream that you were rock climbing, making a slow, but sure, ascent toward the pinnacle of a tall, steep cliff? If so, the cliff's pinnacle may have represented your professional, spiritual, or social aspirations. In your dream, did you reach the pinnacle, and were you standing confidently as you looked down upon the landscape far below? If so, your unconscious may have been mirroring your pride and security in having fulfilled the high expectations that you have for yourself, or that others have for you. Did you feel a sense of euphoria at having climbed to the rocky high point where you stood? If so, have you overcome the obstacles that were standing in your way in the real world, and are you now at the "pinnacle" of your success?

Negative Interpretations: Did you dream that you were clinging to the sheer, rocky wall that you were attempting to climb as you gazed up, toward the edge of the cliff that you felt that you would never be able to reach? If so, the cliff's pinnacle was likely to have symbolized ambitions or goals that you will find it extremely difficult to achieve in the waking world. Or was your dream a reference to your suspense surrounding an unresolved waking problem—i.e., a "cliff-hanger"? Alternatively, in your dream, did you stand teetering at the edge of a cliff, in terror that you would plummet into oblivion? If so, the dream cliff may represent the high expectations that you have for yourself, or the high expectations that others have for you, and your fear of falling may mean that even though you may have met these expectations in the real world, you fear that you will not be able to "stay on top" of them. Your dream may also have represented your fear of falling from grace, power, your social position, or from anything else that you value. If you dreamed that you were hiking along when you were suddenly stopped in your tracks because you came to the edge of a cliff, was your unconscious referring to an obstacle in your waking life, or perhaps to a dead end? Did you dream that you lost your footing and clung to a shrub as you fought desperately not to slip from the cliff's edge? If so, are you clinging to a relationship that it may be better to let go of?

Related Dreams
pages 225, 238, 277, 369, 374 & 383

My Cliffs Dreams

....
....
....
....
....
....
....
....

✳✳✳✳✳✳✳✳✳✳✳✳✳✳✳✳✳✳✳✳✳

A Career Cliff-hanger
The conscious mind sometimes intervenes in dreams, especially when we find ourselves in scary situations, such as dangling off the edge of a cliff while clinging onto some scrubby vegetation for dear life. If you had a cliff-hanging dream experience like this, are you at a make-or-break point in your real-world career, and are you consciously petrified of "losing your grip" and entering free-fall?

DAMS & CANALS

My Dams & Canals Dreams

----

* * * * * * * * * * * * * * * * * *

Dam-busters

Dams divert and hold back reserves of water, which, in the dream world, can symbolize the emotions. So was your dreamland dam fulfilling its purpose efficiently, or did you spot a weak point in its wall that the accumulated water was threatening to breach? If the latter, do you feel under such emotional pressure in waking life that an outburst or breakdown seems imminent?

In dreams, a dam or a canal may signify successful, restrained control of the unconscious emotions, but may also denote unhealthy emotional restraint or an emotional blockage. A dream dam may also symbolize potential, stored energy, or productivity, while a dream canal may denote a vagina or a birth "canal."

Symbolic and Verbal Associations
‹ Emotional control
‹ A healthy outlet for emotions
‹ Potential; stored energy
‹ Productivity; someone who is "a busy beaver"
‹ An emotional blockage; unhealthy emotional restraint
‹ A vagina or a birth "canal" (as denoted by a dream canal)

Positive Interpretations: Did your dreaming mind alight upon a peaceful dam, perhaps with the sun reflecting off the surface of the water and bright fish leaping here and there? If so, your dream may have been making a positive comment regarding how well your waking, rational mind is controlling your unconscious emotions (which may have been symbolized by both the water and the fish). And if your dream self noticed the water that cascaded gently down the wall at the dam's outlet, the message from your unconscious may have been that, while you are in emotional control in the real world, you are also providing a healthy (controlled) outlet for your emotions. However, if neither of these explanations seems to apply to your dream of a dam, is it possible that your unconscious was referring to your (or someone else's) potential? Remember, too, that a dream dam may point to a source of stored energy that may be available for your use. Alternatively, did you dream that you watched as a beaver worked very hard to cut sticks and branches from trees and to pile them up with stones and mud on the bed of a stream, so that the water flow gradually slowed and widened into a pond where the beaver could fish? If so, might your unconscious have been attempting to draw your attention to someone in the real world (perhaps you) who is as productive as a "busy beaver"—perhaps to set an example for you to follow? If you are pregnant and you dreamed of a canal, consider whether it symbolized your birth canal (was it flowing smoothly?) and thus your anticipation of giving birth to your baby.

Negative Interpretations: Did you have a negative reaction to a dream that focused on a water dam? Just as a dream dam may denote emotional control, it may also point toward unhealthy emotional restraint. In your dream, was a dam bulging with water so that it seemed about to break open? Or did the dream dam actually give way, so that all of the water that it held rushed out in a massive, fast-flowing river? If so, is your own conscious control of your welling emotions about to give way? Your unconscious may have sent you your dream to encourage you to allow yourself a healthy emotional release.

Related Dreams

pages 87, 223, 238, 291, 372 & 378

DESERTS

✱✱

A dream of a relatively desolate, infertile desert landscape may point toward an emotional drought (which is perhaps due to your real-world isolation from others), or to your feeling of having been "deserted" by someone. Other symbolic associations include infertility and "the sands of time." A dream of being overheated in a desert may denote many things, including an overheated emotional reaction, passion, peril, and unpleasantness.

Symbolic and Verbal Associations
- Being emotionally "parched" (i.e., lacking love and affection)
- Loneliness; feeling "deserted"
- Infertility; barrenness
- "The sands of time"
- Passion or lust; someone whom you have "the hots" for
- Peril; being in a "hot seat," or in a "hot spot"
- An overheated emotional reaction
- Someone who is making your life "hot" (or unpleasant)

Positive Interpretations: If you dreamed that you were wandering through a hot, dry desert as you felt precious moisture leaving your body in the form of sweat, might your unconscious have been referring to the overheated passion or lust that you feel for someone whom you have "the hots" for in the waking world? And if, in your dream, you watched as the desert sands gathered themselves to fill an hourglass, was your dreaming mind thinking of the time that you have to wait until you next see your love again? Alternatively, in your dream, did you feel as though you were dying of thirst in the desert sun, and were you thankful when someone came along and gave you a cool drink of water (which is a symbol of emotional revitalization)? If so, who was it? Your unconscious may have been attempting to give you hope that your period of emotional drought is near its end, perhaps because of the kindness or affection of someone whom you know in the real world.

Negative Interpretations: In your dream, were you crawling across the hot, blowing sands of a dry, barren, sun-cracked desert landscape? If so, was your unconscious mirroring your waking feelings of loneliness and emotional isolation? Is your spirit parched for want of love and affection? Otherwise, if you are normally a creative person, have you been going through a period of artistic barrenness? Or, if you desire to have children, are you worried or concerned about your potential infertility—perhaps because you are worried that "the sands of time" are running out for you? But if none of these explanations seems to apply, you may want to consider whether your dream was a warning of peril (are you in a "hot seat" or a "hot spot" in the waking world?), or whether someone in the real world is making your life unpleasantly "hot."

Related Dreams
pages 51, 185, 219, 317, 376 & 384

My Deserts Dreams

✱ ✱ ✱ ✱ ✱ ✱ ✱ ✱ ✱ ✱ ✱ ✱ ✱ ✱ ✱ ✱ ✱ ✱ ✱

An Emotional Desert
A dream of gasping for water while staggering through the hot sands of an apparently endless, sun-baked desert may merely have been your unconscious mind's way of depicting how stifled you were feeling on that baking summer night in the real world. If you dreamed your dream in a cool bedroom, however, could the reference have been to your arid emotional life?

THE ELEMENTS
& LANDSCAPES

My Earth Dreams

✳ ✳ ✳ ✳ ✳ ✳ ✳ ✳ ✳ ✳ ✳ ✳ ✳ ✳ ✳ ✳ ✳

Calling Planet Earth

Were you a reluctant astronaut in your dream, frantically struggling with the controls of your spacecraft in the hope of locking it onto an Earth-bound course? If so, have you been feeling "spaced out" or "out there" during your waking hours—perhaps due to an "alien," or deeply weird, situation—and do you long to "come back down to Earth," or to feel more grounded emotionally?

EARTH

✦✦✦✦✦✦✦✦✦✦✦✦✦✦✦✦✦✦✦✦✦✦✦✦✦✦✦✦✦✦✦✦✦✦✦

In Western zodiacal belief, people born under the earth signs of Taurus, Virgo, and Capricorn are said to be patient and emotionally grounded, or "earthy"— associations that should be taken into account when interpreting a dream that highlighted the earth. And because it is the source of the food that we grow, the earth is also symbolic of bounty and fertility, sustenance, stability, and security (all symbolized by the idea of "Mother Earth"). But because all that lives must also die, a dream of the earth may also denote death and/or rebirth.

Symbolic and Verbal Associations

- Patience and emotional solidity; "groundedness"
- Cultivation or refinement of the self
- Bounty and fertility
- "Mother Earth"; sustenance, stability, and security
- Death and rebirth
- Loss of reputation (having your name "dragged through the mud")

Positive Interpretations: If you had a dream in which the earth was highlighted, was your unconscious referring to someone who was born under one of the earth signs (Taurus, Virgo, or Capricorn), who is imbued with the "earthy" qualities of patience and emotional stability or "groundedness"? If you dreamed of gardening or of harvesting the bounty of "Mother Earth," was your unconscious reflecting your waking feelings of stability and security, perhaps because you have all of the physical, mental, and/or emotional sustenance that you require? Or was your dream of cultivating the earth really a reference to the "cultivation" that you have been undergoing (perhaps through reading literature or attending the opera)? Alternatively, if your dreaming self witnessed the living plants of the earth die in the winter and come to life again in the spring, do you wish to undergo a profound transformation, to undergo a metaphorical death and to be "reborn" as a new person?

Negative Interpretations: In a dream of slipping or losing your footing because the ground gave way beneath your feet, your unconscious may have been mirroring your insecurity or lack of emotional "groundedness" in the real world. It was once thought that the human body was imbued with four "humors," one being earth, which would impart melancholy or gloom if it existed in overly large quantities. So if your dreaming mind conjured up a dark or gloomy landscape, consider whether your unconscious was pointing out your waking sadness, perhaps to encourage you to seek ways to brighten your mood. If you dreamed of trudging through mud, do you feel that you have suffered a loss of reputation in the waking world (with your name "dragged through the mud")?

Related Dreams

pages 113, 159, 207, 220, 283 & 385

EARTHQUAKES

✴✴✴✴✴✴✴✴✴✴✴✴✴✴✴✴✴✴✴✴✴✴✴✴✴✴✴✴✴✴✴✴✴✴✴✴✴✴✴

A dreamland earthquake is likely to be an unconscious warning that your foundations are shaky, and may signify or forebode seismic shifts and changes in your waking circumstances, or else a massive emotional upheaval. A similar interpretation may be applied to a dreamland landslide or avalanche, but a dream of one of these natural disasters may also reflect a feeling of being overwhelmed by a "landslide" or an "avalanche" of duties and responsibilities.

Symbolic and Verbal Associations
- A shift in your waking circumstances
- Tremendous changes
- A shaky foundation
- Emotional upheaval
- Being overwhelmed by a "landslide" or an "avalanche" of work, etc.
- New possibilities; renewal

Positive Interpretations: If your dream depicted you experiencing a natural disaster such as an earthquake or a landslide, your unconscious may have been trying to prepare you for the possibility of mass changes in your waking circumstances. These changes may take place in any realm of your life (for instance, your work, your family, or your relationships); the details of your dream—such as where you were and what you were doing at the time of the disaster—may help you to decode the message from your unconscious. (Of course, a dream such as this is not necessarily a predictor of any upheaval, but it may mean that your unconscious has detected that your foundations have begun to tremble or shift.) If you did have such a dream, it is important to remember that—just as in the real world—this sort of disaster brings not only destruction, but also the opportunity to start creating anew.

Negative Interpretations: Was your dreaming self jolted from whatever dreamland activity you were engaged in by the rumbling and shaking of the earth around you? If your dream self was indoors, did you feel terrified as the walls and ceiling begin to crumble and collapse around you? If you live in an area of the world that is prone to such natural catastrophes, or if you have recently experienced some sort of mass disaster in the waking world, then your dream may simply have been reflecting your anxiety about experiencing such a real-world catastrophe. However, if this explanation seems unsatisfactory, you may want to consider whether your unconscious was foretelling seismic changes that are about to happen in your waking life. Perhaps you have consciously or unconsciously detected that you are dangerously close to losing your job, or that your spouse or partner is on the verge of walking out on you. Alternatively, if you dreamed that you were overcome by an avalanche or a landslide, was your unconscious warning you that you are standing upon a shaky "foundation" in the real world?

My Earthquake Dreams

✴✴✴✴✴✴✴✴✴✴✴✴✴✴✴✴✴✴✴✴✴✴✴

A Crushing Catastrophe
A driving dream that ended disastrously when rock and debris from either side of the highway collapsed onto your automobile may have been a warning. This warning may not have been literal (unless you live in an earthquake zone), but may instead have concerned your smooth progress through life, which may soon be halted by someone dramatically "dumping on," or "offloading onto," you.

Related Dreams
pages 211, 220, 225, 238, 368 & 385

THE ELEMENTS & LANDSCAPES

My Explosions Dreams

----

* * * * * * * * * * * * * * * * * *

Blowing a Gasket

If you dreamed that the traffic was so heavy as you were driving to work that you were reduced to a crawl, whereupon steam started pouring out of your vehicle's innards, followed by a devastating explosion, was your dream a metaphor for how you are currently feeling? Are you now so frustrated by your lack of career progress that you may soon explode with fury?

EXPLOSIONS

* *

While dream fireworks or rockets may denote a celebration of achievements, ecstasy, or sexual climax, any sort of dream explosion may symbolize a thrilling experience, "going out with a bang," a person with "a short fuse," or an explosion of rage.

Symbolic and Verbal Associations
- A celebration (as denoted by fireworks)
- Feelings of ecstasy or sexual climax (symbolized by fireworks or rockets)
- Getting a "bang" or a fleeting thrill out of something
- "Going out with a bang"
- Exploding rage
- Having "a short fuse"

Positive Interpretations: Did you have a dream in which you delighted in the sights and sounds of a fireworks display against the night sky? Unless your unconscious was simply reflecting your excitement with regard to your upcoming Independence Day plans, your dream may have pointed to a remarkable real-world achievement that is a cause for celebration. For example, have you finally kicked your cigarette habit for good? If so, your dream was probably highlighting your intense feelings of ecstasy regarding your waking accomplishment. However, in the language of Hollywood movies, fireworks are also often used to symbolize sexual climax, so you may want to consider whether this interpretation has some relevance to your dream (especially if the fireworks were rockets, which are also phallic symbols). Alternatively, did you dream that you detonated a bomb, and that you "got a bang" or a thrill out of the big explosion that it created? If so, is there something in the real world that you wish to end in a dramatic way, thereby "going out with a bang"? It may help you to understand the meaning of your dream if you can remember what it was that your dream self blew up and if you can make a connection between this object and some aspect of your waking life. For instance, if you dreamed that you blew up your microwave oven, was your unconscious referring to your desire to stop eating microwave dinners and to start eating more freshly prepared foods?

Negative Interpretations: If your dream self was extremely irritated by the sound of a loud, explosive bang, could it simply have been a real-world noise (such as the sound of street construction, or even a gunshot) that your sleeping self incorporated into your dream? Otherwise, might your unconscious have conjured up the dream explosion in order to parallel your own pent-up fury, which periodically finds an outlet in the form of explosive rage? Do you have a "short fuse," or a quick temper, that is easily detonated by the slightest irritation? If so, your negative reaction to the dream explosion may signal your desire to seek ways to assuage your anger and to achieve greater inner peace and harmony.

Related Dreams

pages 204, 226, 253, 259, 371 & 386

FIRE

Because it consumes or changes everything that it touches, fire is a powerful symbol of transformation and purification. Depending on the context, a dream fire may also denote domestic happiness, and a candle (which is a source of illumination) is likely to denote intellectual or spiritual enlightenment. In addition, a dream fire may be a reference to anger and aggression, or to a person with a volatile temper—perhaps someone born under one of the zodiacal fire signs (Aries, Leo, or Sagittarius).

Symbolic and Verbal Associations

‹ Passion
‹ A volatile or bad temper; anger and aggression
‹ Transformation and purification
‹ Domestic happiness; the metaphorical hearth fire
‹ Knowledge; intellectual or spiritual enlightenment

Positive Interpretations: Did you have a dream in which you were busily lighting or stoking a fire? In the language of dreams, kindling a fire may signify that you have summoned a new, vital source of energy into your life. If it was a hearth fire, your dream may have been referring to the happiness and contentment of your familial life. Or if the day-to-day demands of your life have caused you to neglect your real passion, might your dream of stoking a fire have been encouraging you to stoke and revitalize your passion, which has the power to transform you? If you dreamed that you lit a candle in preparation for a romantic dinner for two, this may have denoted the "flame" of your passion for whomever it was that you were dining with. (And when you awoke, did you see this person in "a new light"?)

Negative Interpretations: In your dream, did you pile up all of your belongings in the yard and set fire to the lot? If so, you may have felt relieved upon waking to know that you hadn't actually done such a thing, but you may want to pay close attention to the message of your dream as your unconscious may have been signaling that it's time for you to clear away some of your old mental and/or emotional clutter! If you had a dream in which you had to feed, fan, or stoke a fire in order to keep it lit, or if the dream fire actually went out, might your unconscious have been pointing out that the love, passion, or creativity that your dream fire represented is beginning to flicker and is in danger of dying unless you do something to renew it? For example, do you need to "fan the flames" of your love affair? Or if you blew out a candle that stood between you and another person, was your unconscious indicating that this person is now nothing more than "an old flame" for you? Finally, a dream of a destructive or uncontrolled fire may be a sign of anxiety. Has your unconscious detected an actual fire hazard in your home? Or are you worried about someone in your life whose anger you have recently inflamed—perhaps your bad-tempered sister, who is prone to volatile fits of aggression?

Related Dreams

pages 51, 141, 164, 253, 370 & 386

My Fire Dreams

....
....
....
....
....
....
....
....
....

* * * * * * * * * * * * * * * * * * *

Campfire Camaraderie

When it is controlled, fire is a symbol of warmth, happiness, and contentment, and a dream of talking and laughing around a campfire with your friends is therefore likely to have portrayed the warm emotional bond that you have with these individuals in the waking world. And just as campfires keep wild animals at bay, so your close-knit circle may be inhibiting predatory opportunists.

My Floods Dreams

----

* * * * * * * * * * * * * * * * * * * *

Drowning in Emotion

Did you have to pile up sandbags in dream-land to keep the floodwaters at bay? Water can symbolize the emotions when it assumes center stage in dreams, so did your dream parallel the torrent of feelings that have recently swamped you in the real world? Have you been trying to stem someone's floods of tears (or else your own) during your waking hours?

FLOODS

* *

To dream of a flood may denote a flood of emotions (either your own or someone else's)—perhaps a positive, cathartic release of emotions that you had previously kept pent up inside. A dream flood may also be a sign of feeling overwhelmed by something (perhaps by problems or by work), or—if it was an apocalyptic flood—may reflect your feeling that the world has gone very bad and is thus doomed, or else your worries about the frailty of humankind.

Symbolic and Verbal Associations
- Feeling deluged by emotions
- Catharsis: a deep release of emotions
- Feeling overwhelmed or inundated (by problems, work, etc.)
- The floodwaters of birth; renewal; rebirth
- Apocalypse; annihilation

Positive Interpretations: In your dream, did you feel exhilarated or deeply cleansed and purged when a great flood of water welled up around you? If so, could your dream have represented your waking desire to open the floodgates of your emotions and to allow yourself to have a healthy, cathartic release of all of the feelings that you have been keeping bottled up inside you? If you are a woman who is pregnant, or who wants to become pregnant, did the dream flood represent the floodwaters of birth? Or was it a reference to the flooding of your creative energies? Alternatively, do you wish to undergo a great transformation—a sort of symbolic death or baptism—so that you can begin anew in the floodwaters of your own rebirthing?

Negative Interpretations: Did you dream that you were wading through a swirling flood as you struggled to stay on your feet, or else that you slipped beneath the churning waters as you kicked and thrashed in an effort to raise your head above the water's surface? If so, are you feeling deluged or flooded by someone's emotions in the real world? Is it your girlfriend, who depends on you for emotional support, and who seems to do nothing but cry whenever the two of you are together? Or was the dream flood representative of your own emotions, which are flowing out of control so that they are overwhelming you and those around you? Alternatively, did the dream flood reflect your waking feeling of being overwhelmed by problems, work, family duties, social obligations, or anything else that has been draining away the little time that you have to focus on yourself and your own needs and desires? Or, finally, did you dream of a flood of apocalyptic proportions that swamped the entire world and all within it? If so, there are a few possible explanations. Are you a Christian who feels that the world has become a terrible place that is bound for certain total annihilation, just as God once punished humankind for its sins by causing the seas and oceans to rise? Or are you concerned about the frailty and the ephemeral nature of human existence?

Related Dreams
pages 154, 223, 291, 382, 383 & 387

FOG & MIST

THE ELEMENTS & LANDSCAPES

Dreams into which fog or mist creeps may point toward uncertainty or confusion, a lack of clarity, a feeling of being lost, or an inability to see a person or a situation properly or to proceed in safety (i.e., to make progress). Dream fog and mist may also signify emotions that are clouding your rational view, hidden truths or secrets that are being kept from you, or even weepy sentimentality.

Symbolic and Verbal Associations
- Confusion; uncertainty; a lack of clarity; feeling lost
- The inability to make progress
- Emotions that are clouding your rational view
- Hidden truths
- Sentimentality (as in being "misty-eyed")

Positive Interpretations: In your dream, did the thick fog that had been obscuring your vision and preventing you from moving forward suddenly lift, so that the bright sunshine shone upon you and you were able to see everything plainly and clearly for what it really was? And have you been feeling as though you are in a "fog of confusion" during your waking hours? If so, your unconscious may have sent you your dream in order to assure you that the fog will soon clear from your waking mind, revealing things and people and relationships for what they really are—and perhaps also exposing some hidden truths—so that you will soon have the information that you need in order to decide how best to proceed in your life.

Negative Interpretations: Did you dream that you were in the midst of thick, blinding fog or mist, so that you stumbled along without knowing where you were or which way to go? Did you strain in vain to identify the mist-shrouded faces of the person or persons whom you knew were near you? If so, your unconscious may have been reflecting your current waking state of confusion. Do you feel lost? Are you unable to make progress because you do not know how, or which way, to proceed in safety? Are you lacking clarity, so that you are unable to make sense of a waking relationship or problem? Perhaps you feel as though you are unable to see someone (maybe your new boyfriend or girlfriend) for who they really are. And because fog and mist are made up of suspended, condensed water vapor, and because water is a symbol of the emotions, you may want to consider whether your dream was signaling that it is your own feelings that are clouding your view. Alternatively, do you feel as if others in the real world are plotting to keep important secrets from you, so that you feel as though you are "in a fog" about what is really going on in your life? But if none of these interpretations seems to apply to your dream, you may want to try some free association regarding fog and mist. For instance, was your dream highlighting your mother's "misty-eyed" sentimentality, which inhibits you from acting according to your own needs and desires?

Related Dreams
pages 43, 234, 303, 363, 380 & 387

My Fog & Mist Dreams

---

* * * * * * * * * * * * * * * * * *

Purple Haze

If fog or mist obscured the details of your dream, the implication is that you are not seeing a situation or personality clearly, or for what it really is, during your waking hours. Ask yourself what this might be, and why your perception of it is hazy. Could it be because you are "misty-eyed" with sentiment, or has a "fog" of rage clouded your objectivity?

My Hills & Mountains Dreams

★ ★ ★ ★ ★ ★ ★ ★ ★ ★ ★ ★ ★ ★ ★ ★ ★ ★

Giddy Heights

In the language of dreams, the summit of a hill or mountain can represent a significant challenge, which, if conquered, promises to reward the successful climber with one of life's "pinnacles," "peaks," or "high points." So what happened to you on your dream mountain, and can you equate the experience with a real-life test of your courage and ambition, strength and stamina, or willpower and determination?

HILLS & MOUNTAINS

✶ ✶

In dreamland, a hill or a mountain is likely to symbolize ambitious goals, achievements, status, the "pinnacles" of success, or, more negatively, daunting challenges, immovable problems or obstacles, or even a "mountain" of work.

Symbolic and Verbal Associations

- ◖ Ambitious goals
- ◖ The pinnacles of success
- ◖ Achievement; achieving a high status
- ◖ Daunting challenges
- ◖ Immovable problems; obstacles
- ◖ A "mountain" of work, etc.

Positive Interpretations: In dreamland, were you hiking eagerly toward a range of mountains, with your focus, perhaps, on one particularly high peak? Unless your dreaming mind was looking forward to your next hiking excursion, your dream of advancing toward a mountain range may have denoted your progression toward an ambitious waking goal (be it professional, social, or spiritual). The height of the mountain that your dream self was intent on climbing will be a clue as to how difficult or challenging your unconscious feels that it will be to reach your goal. So was it a massive, rocky, snow-topped mountain? Or was it really just a foothill? In dreams, a crag may also symbolize the course of your life. So if you dreamed of standing at the base of a mountain and looking up at its peak, might your dream have represented you as you are, just embarking upon your career? Have you set your sights on reaching the apex of your profession? If you began to scale the mountain and found the going to be relatively easy, your unconscious may have been hinting that you'll find the path of your career advancement to be equally easygoing. And if you found yourself standing upon the mountaintop, feeling proud and exhilarated as you looked down upon the valley that you had come from, have you conquered the obstacles that you came across, and are you now at the zenith of your success? Alternatively, if you dreamed of descending a mountain with a sense of relief and anticipation, was your unconscious mirroring your pleasure in coming "back down to earth" now that a challenging task has been completed?

Negative Interpretations: A steep, high dream mountain may represent a difficult, daunting real-world challenge or ambition. Did your dream self struggle to clamber up the mountainside, perhaps occasionally slipping and sliding back downward? If so, your unconscious may have been warning you of the difficulties that you will encounter in realizing your goal in the waking world. And if your dream self gave up, turned around, and began to descend the mountain, do you similarly wish that you could abandon your real-life struggle?

Related Dreams
pages 213, 219, 225,
277, 365 & 386

ICE & SNOW

Because ice and snow are made up of water (itself a symbol of the emotions) that has become frozen, a dream that highlights ice or snow is likely to be a reference to someone's icy feelings, or emotional numbness, in the waking world. Such dreams may also denote an emotionally "chilly" atmosphere, together with feelings of emotional isolation, and perhaps even sexual inhibition or frigidity.

Symbolic and Verbal Associations
- Icy feelings; emotional coldness or numbness; a "chilly" atmosphere
- Emotional isolation
- Sexual frigidity
- A significant problem or obstacle (as symbolized by an iceberg)
- Walking on "thin ice"
- Feeling "snowed under," or overwhelmed, by work

Positive Interpretations: If your dream self was encamped in a barren, frozen wilderness, were you filled with hope when you noticed that the sun had broken through the clouds and that the ice and snow were beginning to thaw? If so, and if you have been feeling emotionally cold or numb during your waking hours, your unconscious may have sent you your dream in order to hearten you with the suggestion that your emotions are beginning to come to life again. Or if it is your partner whose emotions have been put "on ice" or icy lately, your unconscious may have noticed that his or her iciness is beginning to thaw and that, as a result, the chilly atmosphere in your home is slowly beginning to warm up.

Negative Interpretations: Did you dream that you were slowly tramping across a silent, white, frozen landscape of ice and snow? If so, do you feel emotionally numb or cold during your waking hours, so that nothing seems to touch or move you at all—not even the love that your family and friends show to you—perhaps because you are still suffering from some sort of real-world shock, such as the death of a loved one or the failure of a relationship? Or did the frozen landscape of your dream denote someone else's emotional iciness? For instance, has your partner "frozen you out" with his or her emotional coldness and/or sexual frigidity? Alternatively, in your dream, were you attempting to steer your boat clear of a looming iceberg? Unless you think that the iceberg may have represented a person in your life who is behaving "icily" toward you, your dream may have denoted a major problem or obstacle that is impeding your real-world progress. Did you dream that you were making your way across the precarious surface of a semi-frozen lake? If so, is someone in your waking life making you feel so nervous or vulnerable that you feel as though you are walking on "thin ice" whenever you are in this person's presence? And if you dreamed that an avalanche of snow and ice landed on you, did your dream denote your feeling of being "snowed under" by your responsibilities?

Related Dreams

pages 40, 80, 238, 239, 380 & 387

My Ice & Snow Dreams

Snowed Under

If you dreamed of trudging wearily through a snow-blanketed landscape, finding the going increasingly difficult as you grew colder and colder, and number and number, so that in the end you could hardly feel your extremities at all, could your unconscious have been mirroring your waking circumstances? Has someone who usually gives you vital emotional support suddenly begun to "freeze you out" with his or her icy demeanor?

My Islands & Beaches Dreams

----

* * * * * * * * * * * * * * * * *

An Island Idyll

If you dreamed of being alone on an unspoiled island, the key to your dream's meaning is likely to lie in how you felt. If you relished your solitude, as well as your natural surroundings, it may be that you need a break from others, and perhaps also a vacation. If you felt lonely, however, are you feeling emotionally isolated in the real world?

ISLANDS & BEACHES

Because they are set in the water, which is primarily associated with the unconscious mind, dream islands are symbolic of emotional retreat, solitude, peace, privacy, and self-contemplation, but they may also denote loneliness and emotional isolation. Dreamland beaches are symbolic of the transition point between the conscious (solid, rational) and the unconscious (fluid, emotional) realms, and may also indicate a shifting in one's foundations.

Symbolic and Verbal Associations

- Solitude, peace, and privacy; emotional retreat
- Self-contemplation; self-sufficiency
- Emotional isolation; loneliness
- A desire to be rescued
- A transitional point between the conscious (rational) and the unconscious (emotional) worlds
- The shifting of seemingly solid foundations

Positive Interpretations: In your dream, did you revel in the peace and solitude inherent in being the only inhabitant of a remote desert island? Were you quite happy and content to spend your days strolling along the beach or collecting berries and coconuts, and your nights sleeping soundly in the cozy, thatched hut that you had built for yourself? Do you wish that you could get away from everyone and everything, to be entirely self-sufficient, even if for just a little while? If you spend your waking life rushing around at a frenzied pace, with little or no time to relax and unwind, then your unconscious may have sent you your dream as a sort of wish-fulfillment, and also to compensate for the chaos of your waking hours. Alternatively, did you dream of diving into the ocean and relishing the shocking sensation of the cold, or of pulling yourself out of the ocean to lie blissfully on the warm sand and feel the sun as it dried your skin? Because they are places where the land (which is symbolic of the rational, conscious mind) meets the sea (which symbolizes the emotional unconscious), a dream of diving into, or of emerging from, the ocean is likely to denote your transition between these two realms (the rational and the emotional), such as at the end of a period of emotional introspection or instability.

Negative Interpretations: Did you have a dream in which you were stranded on a remote island, and that you had built a fire on the beach in desperate hope of attracting a passing ship to come to your rescue? If so, do you feel lonely or emotionally isolated from those around you during your waking hours? Or did your dream of being marooned on an island reflect your waking sense of being stranded in a sea of emotions (either your own or someone else's)? If so, maybe the only way to escape your situation is by diving in and swimming through those very emotions (i.e., "taking the plunge").

Related Dreams

pages 79, 209, 248, 291, 298 & 387

JUNGLES

In the language of dreams, a jungle or rainforest may signify a feeling of being trapped or caught in an urban "concrete jungle," or an extremely competitive environment that includes exposure to the ruthless pursuit of ambitions. And since many dangerous wild animals live in the jungle, such a dream may also point toward dangerous or predatory persons in the waking world.

Symbolic and Verbal Associations
‹ An intensely competitive environment
‹ The "concrete jungle" (the city)
‹ Feeling trapped
‹ Danger; predatory or ruthless persons

Positive Interpretations: In your dream, were you the "king" or "queen" of the jungle? Did you roar with delight and thrill to your own power and freedom as you swung by vine from tree to tree? Did the wild animals of the jungle come to your call and lie prostrate at your feet? If you had a dream such as this, are you at the very top of the "food chain" in the jungle of your corporate workplace? Far from being turned off by the ruthlessly competitive environment in which you spend your days, do you instead relish and savor every bit of it? Have you "tamed" those predatory persons whom you are the boss of, who are now always ready to do your bidding and would never dream of questioning your authority? If so, your dream was most likely mirroring your waking pleasure and happiness in your career success. Otherwise, if this explanation seems unlikely, might your dream have been reflecting your happiness and success in another competitive, junglelike area of your life, such as the amateur hockey league in which you play?

Negative Interpretations: Did you have a dream in which you were hacking and clawing your way through a vine-entangled rainforest or jungle, with mosquitoes biting your flesh and a venomous spider or snake seemingly lurking around every tree? Did your dream self become increasingly fatigued and frustrated as you sought in vain to find your way out of the jungle? If so, did you awake feeling stressed by the knowledge that you had to get up and prepare to spend another day in the "concrete jungle" of the city in which you work? Do you dread the traffic- and people-jammed commute to your office, and is your job a constant source of anxiety and frustration to you? Do you regard your office as a "hothouse" of fierce competition and backstabbing rivalries? And might the dangerous animals that lived in your dream jungle have represented your predatory coworkers, who seem to be doing their best to destroy your chances for career advancement? If your job is making you so miserable that you cannot achieve peace even in your dreams, you may want to consider looking for alternative employment.

Related Dreams

pages 114, 118, 200, 234, 238 & 314

My Jungle Dreams

Jungle Fever

When casting around for a scenario with which to mirror the dreamer's waking circumstances, the unconscious sometimes alights on a jungle environment. So if you found yourself fighting your way through triffidlike vegetation in your dream, while dodging the evil-looking snakes, spiders, and leeches in your path, can you draw a parallel with your real-life office, and with the characters that work, or lurk, there?

THE ELEMENTS & LANDSCAPES

LAKES & PONDS

✳✳

My Lakes & Ponds Dreams

✳✳✳✳✳✳✳✳✳✳✳✳✳✳✳✳✳✳✳✳✳

Still Waters

If a lake exerted a strange fascination upon you in dreamland, were you keen to know what lay beneath the enigmatic-seeming surface? Maybe you were fishing in your dream, and were waiting with bated breath to see what you would hook. If so, could your unconscious have been commenting that you may be surprised by your own hidden depths, should you care to explore them?

As still bodies of water, lakes and ponds are likely to denote a still or calm emotional approach to the world when they appear in your dreams. These bodies of water may also symbolize mystery and the "hidden depths" of your own unconscious, and many dream analysts also associate lakes with the womb. Negative associations include deep-seated emotional turmoil and mental or emotional stagnation.

Symbolic and Verbal Associations
- Calm emotions
- Mystery; "hidden depths"; unconscious instincts
- The womb
- A calm surface obscuring deep emotional turmoil
- Mental or emotional stagnation

Positive Interpretations: Did you have a dream in which you were sitting quietly and contemplatively beside a beautiful, still lake? If so, was your unconscious mind echoing the calm emotional approach that you take toward the world? Or if this seems unlikely, might your dream have denoted your desire to invite more calmness and serenity into your waking life? If, in your dream, you were staring at your own reflection on the surface of the water, was your unconscious referring to your desire for some peaceful self-reflection during your waking hours? And if a dream lake seemed to you to be full of mystery, could your unconscious have been reminding you that "still waters run deep" (i.e., that your own "hidden depths" are available for exploration)? Did you see a fish swim to the water's surface? If so, could it have represented an unconscious urge or instinct that is beginning to take shape in your conscious mind? Alternatively, did your dream of sitting next to, or of diving into or swimming in, a lake represent your waking desire to take refuge from the anxieties of the real world by retreating to a place of safety, or did it denote your desire to be "reborn" as a new, better person? Or, if you are a woman, did your dream of a lake symbolize your desire to become pregnant?

Negative Interpretations: In your dream, did the sight of the still surface of a lake or pond fill your dream self with anxiety or with a feeling of ominous foreboding? If so, was your unconscious reflecting the fact that—although you appear to be calm and collected to those around you—you are actually in a state of deep emotional turmoil? If you think that this interpretation might be accurate, your unconscious may have sent you your dream in order to encourage you consciously to acknowledge your pain so that you can work through it in a positive manner. But if your dream pond was stagnant and lifeless, have you mentally or emotionally stagnated in the real world? If so, your unconscious was likely trying to encourage you to seek out new sources of inspiration.

Related Dreams

pages 159, 223, 291, 298, 326 & 387

PARKS

Like their real-world equivalents, dreamland parks are places of unconscious enjoyment, satisfaction, and relaxation. They may denote an idyllic waking setting or situation, or your sense that your life is "flourishing." And because they are shared public spaces, parks are also symbolic of societal rules and regulations, and of a diversity of people and personalities.

Symbolic and Verbal Associations
- Satisfaction
- A sense that your life is "flourishing"
- An idyllic setting or situation
- Relaxation
- Societal rules
- A diversity of personalities

Positive Interpretations: In your dream, were you walking through a sunny park that was in full greenery and bloom, and did you feel nothing but bliss as you took in the sights, smells, and sounds of the natural beauty that surrounded you? There are a few likely explanations for a dream such as this. Your dream may have been mirroring your current satisfaction with your waking life. (Does your life seem to be flourishing in every way?) Otherwise, your dream may have been mirroring your desire to enjoy an idyllic state of affairs (in which case your unconscious probably sent you your dream in order temporarily to fulfill your wishes). This sort of dream may also reflect your waking sense of peace and relaxation, or else your desire to be peaceful and relaxed. And because parks are public spaces that must be shared with others and that are subject to certain rules and regulations, your dream of enjoying a park experience may have denoted your happy willingness to follow society's rules, and/or your peaceful coexistence with the diversity of people and personalities in your waking life.

Negative Interpretations: Did you have a dream in which you were trying to relax in a park, but were being irritated or disturbed, either by swarming or biting insects or by the activities of others around you? If you were trying to eat your lunch while a troop of ants harassed you, could your dream have represented the minor (yet extremely irritating) annoyances that are preventing you from enjoying an otherwise idyllic waking situation? Or if your dream self was disturbed by the loud music and carrying-on of your park neighbors, is the obnoxious behavior of others in the real world spoiling a place or a situation that you once considered to be like a paradise? Alternatively, in your dream, were you prevented from enjoying the park by a tyrannical set of rules and regulations, such as "no picnicking," "no sleeping," or "no dogs"? If so, is your waking self being inhibited by an overly restrictive rule code? And if your dream self delighted in breaking the park rules, do you long to stage a similar rebellion in the real world?

Related Dreams
pages 159, 261, 283, 288, 350 & 359

My Parks Dreams

Rest and Relaxation

Dreams sometimes set a healthy example to follow, as may have been the case if you dreamed of sitting in a park, dressed in your working clothes, relishing both a wholesome sandwich and the refreshing breeze that ruffled your hair. If you never take a lunch break in the real world, could your unconscious have been urging you to follow your dreaming self's reinvigorating lead?

My Rain, Clouds & Hail Dreams

----

* * * * * * * * * * * * * * * * * * *

It's Raining Again

A rainy backdrop does not always make for a depressing dream: if gardening is your passion and there has been a drought in your region in the waking world, a dream of watching big, fat drops of rain splash on your flowerbeds may have been fulfilling your dearest wish, for instance. But if the sight of raindrops saddened you in dreamland, did they symbolize tears?

RAIN, CLOUDS & HAIL

When it rains in the world of dreams, the unconscious may be drawing a parallel with a real-world outpouring of emotions (as symbolized by the falling water, which can be equated with the emotions and also with tears). And just as rain nourishes vegetation in the real world, dream rain may denote a nourishing of the emotional self, or it may also denote an emotional cleansing (brought about by the washing-away of your problems). A cloudy or overcast dream environment may represent a gloomy atmosphere, while dream storm clouds may foretell danger, and dream hail may represent stinging abuses.

Symbolic and Verbal Associations
- An outpouring of emotions; tears
- Emotional hydration or nourishing
- Wishing that your problems could be washed away; emotional cleansing
- A gloomy atmosphere
- An ominous foreboding
- Stinging abuse (as symbolized by hail)

Positive Interpretations: In your dream, were you elated when the sky opened up and rain began to fall? Did your dream self walk out into the open, stretch your arms wide, and raise your face to the heavens so that the water could drench you completely? If so, has your waking life become so emotionally arid that you would welcome a heavy emotional outpouring such as that represented by your dream rainstorm—perhaps even the emotional release that the shedding of tears would give you? Do you long to experience love and passion—to be emotionally revived and nourished, perhaps by a new romance? Or do you wish that your past problems and difficulties could be washed away, leaving you feeling emotionally cleansed and ready to face life anew? In another scenario, was your dream self sulking on a gloomy, overcast day, when the clouds suddenly parted and a bright shaft of sunshine broke through? If so, and if you have been feeling sad or depressed during your waking hours, your unconscious may have sent you your dream in order to depict the ray of hope that may soon break through your sadness and lighten your days.

Negative Interpretations: Did your dream self feel shocked, cold, and miserable when you were soaked by a sudden rain shower? If so, are you worried that a real-world onslaught of emotions (either your own or someone else's) is about to soak you thoroughly, leaving you feeling overwhelmed and wretched? Or did the downpour represent the sad tears that you have shed during your waking hours? Alternatively, if you dreamed that the day was dark and overcast with clouds, was your unconscious reflecting your own sadness, or else the gloomy atmosphere of your waking hours? Did a dream of gathering storm clouds denote a warning of danger, or else your pessimistic outlook on life?

Related Dreams
pages 80, 373, 375, 381, 387 & 389

RAINBOWS

✳ ✳

To dream of a rainbow may imply happiness, hope for the future, good fortune, or spiritual deliverance. In many cultures, the rainbow is said to link the earth with the heavens (and, in ancient Greece, the rainbow was said to represent Iris, the messenger of the gods), and Hindus and Buddhists consider it to be a sign of transcendence.

Symbolic and Verbal Associations

◖ Hope for the future
◖ Happiness
◖ Good luck; hidden treasure, or a "pot of gold" (in the Celtic tradition)
◖ A link or bridge between heaven and earth (or between the gods and humans)
◖ Transcendence (to Hindus and Buddhists)
◖ Spiritual deliverance; divine reconciliation (according to Judeo–Christian tradition)
◖ Diversity

Positive Interpretations: Did you dream that a storm had finally ended and that you were enchanted and uplifted when you looked up to the sky to see that a shimmering rainbow was arching over the treetops? If so, your unconscious was, almost without a doubt, sending you a message of hope for the future (perhaps because a stormy or troubled period of your life is about to come to an end). In interpreting your dream, you may also want to consider some other associations of the rainbow. For instance, in Norse mythology, and also in Chinese and African belief, the rainbow is said to link the earthly world with the divine heavens—a belief that is akin to the ancient Greek association of the rainbow with Iris, messenger of the gods, and also to the Judeo–Christian association of the rainbow with spiritual deliverance and divine reconciliation. So might your dream rainbow have symbolized your desire to feel more connected to God, or your wish to attain a state of higher consciousness? (And if you think that this interpretation may be correct, you may be interested to note that Hindus and Buddhists consider the rainbow to be a symbol of transcendence). Otherwise, might the appearance of your dream rainbow have represented your feeling that you are a lucky person, or else your desire for good fortune (an association that comes from the Celtic tradition of there being a pot of gold at the foot of a rainbow). Or did your dream rainbow bear the more modern message of the celebration of human diversity?

Negative Interpretations: In your dream, did you follow the rainbow to its fabled pot of gold, only to despair as you watched your treasure disappear in your hands? If so, have you suffered the loss of something that was promised to you or that you feel entitled to? Or did you dream that you saw a rainbow and wished that you could fly off to the better place that you imagined lay beyond it? If so, are you feeling unhappy in waking life, and do you long for your dreams to come true "somewhere over the rainbow"?

My Rainbow Dreams

✳ ✳ ✳ ✳ ✳ ✳ ✳ ✳ ✳ ✳ ✳ ✳ ✳ ✳ ✳ ✳ ✳ ✳ ✳

Colors of the Rainbow

If you admired a shimmering rainbow in your dream, your unconscious may have conjured it up as a heartening sign that a troubled time in your life is ending. Otherwise, consider the rainbow's relevance to your waking world as a beautiful example of the color spectrum. Are you considering redecorating your home? And was any particular color especially pronounced in the dream rainbow?

Related Dreams
pages 144, 271, 299, 363, 380 & 384

My Rivers & Streams Dreams

----

* * * * * * * * * * * * * * * * * *

RIVERS & STREAMS

****

Dreamland rivers and streams may represent your feelings as you navigate your way through life—which, depending upon the shape of the river or stream, can be characterized either by emotional twists and turns or by a straightforward emotional passage. A fast-flowing river may indicate that you are powering your way through life, while a still river may indicate a lack of drive, and ripples on the water's surface may denote a feeling of going around in circles. A flooding river may denote overflowing emotions, and a river that flows beneath a bridge may symbolize a release of the past.

Symbolic and Verbal Associations
‹ Your feelings as you go through life; your current emotions
‹ Emotional twists and turns, or else a straightforward emotional passage
‹ Dynamism
‹ A lack of drive or direction; a sense of going around in circles
‹ Feeling swamped by emotions
‹ Letting go of the past, as if it were "water under a bridge"

Positive Interpretations: If you dreamed of a river or a stream, was it gently twisting and turning, or was its course straight and direct? The answer may indicate the nature of your current emotional life. So if you dreamed of the former scenario, your unconscious may have been reflecting the many emotional twists and turns that you are currently going through in your life. But if you dreamed of the latter scenario, it is likely that you are navigating a straightforward emotional passage through the real world. Did you take note of how fast your dream river or stream was flowing? If it was a rapidly flowing river, your dream may have paralleled your tendency to power your way through life—although such a dream may also have indicated the quick or strong current of your emotions. In another scenario, did you dream of standing on a bridge that spanned a river and of watching the water as it rippled and flowed beneath you? In the language of dreams, bridges are a symbol of transition. Therefore, your dream may have indicated your desire to let go of the past (i.e., your feeling that the events of the past are now "water under the bridge").

Life's Course
A dream river may have symbolized your feelings as you wend your way through this phase of your existence in the real world. If it sluggishly followed a meandering path, it may be that you are currently feeling unmotivated and uncertain about how best to proceed in your waking life, for example. And if the water was polluted, are you feeling unhealthy or somehow tainted?

Negative Interpretations: Did you dream of a quiet and static, moonlit river? If so, might your unconscious have been commenting on your own lack of direction or drive in the waking world? Or have you come to a temporary standstill in your life, perhaps because you are going through a necessary period of self-contemplation? If your dream river had dried up to the point that it had become merely a trickle, are you going through an emotional dry spell during your waking hours? Or were you "swamped" by a rising dream river?

Related Dreams
pages 299, 366, 372, 378, 387 & 388

SEAS & OCEANS

✴✴✴

If water symbolizes the emotions, instincts, and urges of the unconscious mind, seas and oceans are the largest, deepest, and most changeable of its manifestations. Seas and oceans are a symbol of life (which is believed to have had its origins in these salty waters), and therefore also of the mother archetype. Depending on the specific scenario, a dream sea may denote the ebb and flow of feelings, emotional turbulence, or, more dramatically, a tidal wave of emotions. And, finally, to dream of a sea monster may denote unconscious fears.

Symbolic and Verbal Associations
- ◖ Life; origins
- ◖ The mother archetype
- ◖ The unconscious mind (emotions, instincts, and urges)
- ◖ The ebb and flow of feelings
- ◖ Emotional turbulence; a tsunami or tidal wave of emotions
- ◖ Unconscious fears (as symbolized by a sea monster)

Positive Interpretations: Did you dream that you were in a boat that was floating peacefully on the calm sea? If so, is your waking life relatively untroubled by worries or pain, so that you are in a state of peace and harmony? And, in your dream, did you cast a fishing line into the deep waters? If so, and if you are mulling over an important decision or dilemma during your waking hours, then your dream may have represented you "fishing around" in your unconscious for a solution (and, when you awoke, had an answer surfaced in your mind?). Alternatively, did your dream self exhilarate in riding or surfing upon the high, rolling waves of the ocean? If so, is your real-world self "riding high" on the waves of a new love affair? Or, if you dreamed of swimming through the ocean depths, was your unconscious mirroring the deep self-exploration that you are undertaking during your waking hours?

Negative Interpretations: In your dream, did your tiny boat bounce and toss on the rough waves of the sea, so that you feared that you and your vessel would be lost forever? If so, is your waking emotional life equally tumultuous? For example, are you and your spouse considering splitting up, so that you feel as if you are in a constant state of confusion? Or are you afraid that a conflict with your parents will end up getting the better of you and "dragging you under"? If you dreamed that you were deluged by a massive tidal wave or tsunami, do you feel as if you are drowning in a wave of emotions (either your own or someone else's)? Or, finally, did you have a dream in which a horrible, shrieking sea monster sought to drag you to the bottom of the sea? If so, might the monster have symbolized an unconscious fear—perhaps even an aspect of yourself that is so frightening to you that your conscious mind has suppressed and relegated it to the dark depths of your unconscious.

Related Dreams
pages 113, 145, 223, 291, 298 & 387

My Seas & Oceans Dreams

✴ ✴ ✴ ✴ ✴ ✴ ✴ ✴ ✴ ✴ ✴ ✴ ✴ ✴ ✴ ✴ ✴

Hidden Treasure

If your dreamscape was a seascape, and the sea is not part of your everyday life, consider the possibility that the watery dream vista represented your own unconscious mind. Now think about your dream self's actions and try to relate them to your inner being. If you were deep-sea diving in your dream, for instance, are you searching for a personal truth or insight? Did you find "treasure"?

My Sun Dreams

✶ ✶ ✶ ✶ ✶ ✶ ✶ ✶ ✶ ✶ ✶ ✶ ✶ ✶ ✶ ✶

A Ray of Sunshine

Sunshine infuses us with the feel-good factor in both the real and dream worlds, so if your dream self saw the sun peeping through the dark clouds that had previously cast a gloomy shadow over your dream, it must have been a cheering sight. And if you are currently enduring a miserable time in the waking world, did the appearance of the sun in your dream brighten your mood?

SUN

Dreamland sunshine is likely to denote radiant joy, warm feelings, a "sunny" mood, or a positive outlook on life. And because the sun is the Earth's most important source of heat and energy, a dream of bright sunshine may be symbolic of your own high energy. To dream of being sunburned may imply an overexposure to a "hot" or dangerous situation, or a danger of being "burned," or cheated.

Symbolic and Verbal Associations

- Radiant joy; a "sunny" mood
- Warm feelings
- Energy
- A positive outlook on life
- Overexposure to a "hot" situation; a danger of being "burned" (as denoted by dream sunburn)
- Illumination; the intellect

Positive Interpretations: Did you have a happy dream in which you and your partner were basking in the warm sunshine? A dream such as this may have been reflecting your "sunny mood," or the radiant joy in your life—perhaps because of the warm feelings that exist between you and your partner, or because you feel energetic and have a positive outlook on life. Do you feel that you are gazing out upon a bright, blue, cloudless horizon? However, if the reality of your life is that you are far from happy and content, then your unconscious may have sent you your dream as a form of wish-fulfillment, to provide you with a temporary escape from your conscious troubles, and also to encourage you to believe that that brighter times are on the way. However, if none of the above interpretations seems to apply to your dream, consider some of the sun's other associations. For example, did your dream symbolize the illumination of your intellect that is occurring in your current studies? Did your dream of watching the sun rise signal your recent enlightenment with regard to some aspect of your life (as in the expression, "it dawned on me")?

Negative Interpretations: Did your dream of blissful sunbathing take a drastic turn for the worse when you dreamed that you awoke to find that your skin was red and blistering from painful sunburn? If so, are you worried that your current happiness in a waking situation may be spoiled by a looming problem? Your dream of being sunburned may have been an unconscious warning that you are in jeopardy of being overexposed to a "hot" or dangerous person or situation in the waking world. Could it be your new business associate, who you fear is not being completely honest with you? If so, your dream may have been signaling that you are in danger of being "burned" or cheated. Alternatively, might your dream have been a warning that you are in danger of becoming exhausted, or suffering intellectual "burnout"?

Related Dreams

pages 57, 79, 248, 261, 363 & 371

TUNNELS & HOLES

I n the language of dreams, a tunnel or a hole in the ground may symbolize the vagina or the womb, a protective place of retreat, or "underground" (or subversive) tastes or interests. Tunnels may also be symbolic of transition and transformation. More negatively, a dream of being down in a hole may also denote depression, a feeling of being "buried" beneath your problems, or an unconscious warning that someone in the real world would like to see you "dead and buried."

Symbolic and Verbal Associations

- The vagina, or the womb
- A desire to "hole up" or to retreat from the world
- Depression; feeling "buried" beneath your problems
- Hostility; someone who would like to see you "dead and buried"
- "Underground," or subversive, tastes or desires
- Transformation; a transitional phase in life (as symbolized by a tunnel)
- Salvation; seeing "the light at the end of the tunnel"

Positive Interpretations: Did you dream that you were busily tunneling through the earth? If so, do you know what your purpose was? Since dream holes and tunnels can be equated with the vagina, is it possible that your dream had a sexual meaning? Or was your unconscious mind highlighting your "underground," or unusual or subversive, tastes or interests (which, perhaps, you feel unable to express in the light of day)? Also, it is important to note that a dream tunnel may symbolize a point of transition, while the depths of the earth may symbolize your unconscious. Therefore, might your dream of tunneling underground have symbolized your journey into your own unconscious in order to find the key to your potential transformation? What did your dream self see or find underground? If, while making your underground journey, you saw a "light at the end of the tunnel," was your unconscious promising you that the end of a difficult waking situation is near, so that you may soon begin a new, better phase of life?

Negative Interpretations: If you dreamed that you were digging a hole or a tunnel, has your waking life become so unbearable that you wish that you could retreat into the warm, protective sanctuary of the womb? Do you long to "hole up," or to take cover from the outside world, perhaps in order to regain your strength or to recover from your wounds? Alternatively, did you have an anxiety dream in which you were buried in a hole against your will? In your dream, did you scramble, kick, and claw in an effort to climb out of the hole, but did your efforts only cause more soil to fall in upon you? If so, have the demands and worries of your daily life gotten the better of you, so that you have sunk into a depression and feel as if you are at the bottom of a "black hole" from which you cannot escape, and for which you should seek help? Or has your unconscious detected that someone in the real world want to see you "dead and buried"?

My Tunnels & Holes Dreams

Tunnel of Love

The code may seem crude, but the symbolic language used by the unconscious mind is not always subtle, so if you are a man who dreamed of entering a velvety-dark, welcoming tunnel, could your unconscious have been commenting on your sex life? Alternatively, and whatever your gender, could the dream tunnel have been heralding a time of transition in your waking world?

Related Dreams

pages 87, 113, 220, 299, 364 & 368

VOLCANOES

To dream of a volcano may symbolize the building or mounting of "fiery" emotions, such as rage or fury, so that you feel as though you are about to "blow your lid." A dream volcano may also symbolize someone else's volatile temper. More positively, an erupting volcano may denote a positive, cathartic emotional release.

My Volcanoes Dreams

Symbolic and Verbal Associations

- Mounting passions or emotions
- Fury
- The feeling that you will "blow your lid"
- A volatile temper
- An emotional release or catharsis; a purging of suppressed emotions
- An explosive situation; a violent dispute

Positive Interpretations: Did you have a terrifying dream in which you were visiting a famous volcano, such as Mount Saint Helens or Mount Etna, when everyone suddenly started running away because the volcano was beginning to erupt? And did you flee for your life as the volcano began to roar and spew molten lava all around you? However, at this point in your dream, were you surprised to find that you weren't seriously hurt at all by the falling ash and lava, and that you actually felt better and happier than before? If so, your dream may have been referring to your own mounting emotions, which you fear will soon erupt from you during your waking hours. However—especially in light of your dream—it is important to remember that although it is likely to be a difficult and painful experience, such a release of your pent-up and suppressed emotions is likely to be a cathartic experience that will leave you feeling relieved, purged, and ready to move on in your life.

Fire and Brimstone

Did you dream of watching a volcano suddenly erupt, and cheer as it sent stream after stream of red-hot lava shooting up into the air? If so, and if you experienced a strange sense of release when you awoke, could it be that your unconscious channeled your own pent-up feelings of rage into the dream eruption, thereby providing a safe outlet for your mounting frustration?

Negative Interpretations: If you had a nightmare about an erupting volcano, have you been struggling during your waking hours to suppress your mounting emotions, lest you "blow your lid" and do or say something that you might later regret? If so, your unconscious may have been warning you that your suppression of your passions is only serving to build up the pressure within you, making it even more certain that you will erupt some time in the future. Alternatively, could your dream volcano have denoted someone else's fury? Is it your boyfriend, whose volatile temper predisposes him to explosive (possibly violent) outbursts of rage? Or is it your mother, who is calm on the outside, but you know is a virtual volcano of suppressed feelings that is just waiting to explode? Otherwise, if none of the above explanations seems to apply to your dream, could your unconscious have been referring to an explosive situation in the waking world, or to a violent dispute that you are caught up in?

Related Dreams

WATER

✦✦✦

In symbolic terms, water is strongly associated with the unconscious (emotions, instincts, and urges, and because it is so crucial to survival, it is also an ancient symbol of life. In both the real world and the dream world, water has the power to cleanse the body and the spirit (which is why Christians are baptized with water), and it also invites relaxation and reinvigoration.

Symbolic and Verbal Associations
- The unconscious mind
- "The waters of life"
- Cleansing and purification (spiritual, as well as physical)
- Relaxation and reinvigoration; calmness
- A person born under one of the zodiacal water signs (Cancer, Scorpio, or Pisces)
- Femininity; gentleness and changeability (according to zodiacal lore)

Positive Interpretations: Did you have a dream in which you found yourself swimming in blue, warm waters, with shafts of gentle light shining down on you from above? There are a number of possible interpretations for a dream such as this. For instance, your dream may have been reflecting your waking desire to explore the depths of your own unconscious. Or your dream may simply have been highlighting your awareness of, and your joy in, being alive. It is also possible that your unconscious was mirroring your desire for spiritual purification (and, if you are a Christian, might your dream have been a reference to baptism?) Alternatively, if your daily waking life is extremely hectic and stressful, did you dream that you were relaxing in a warm-water-spa retreat? If so, your unconscious probably sent you your dream as a wish fulfillment, and also to provide you with the peace and calm that you desire (if only in the fleeting world of dreams). However, if none of the above explanations seems right, it may be important to remember that a dream of water may symbolize someone born under one of the zodiacal water signs (Cancer, Scorpio, or Pisces), which are said to bestow the "feminine" qualities of gentleness and changeability.

Negative Interpretations: Did you have a dream in which you suffered from a ravaging thirst, or—the opposite—in which you felt that your bladder was so full that it would burst? If, when you awoke, you didn't make a desperate beeline for a glass of water or for the toilet, then your unconscious was likely sending you a message about your current emotional state. Since water is a symbol of the emotions, a dream of being thirsty may imply that your waking life is emotionally arid (perhaps because some emotional trauma has caused you to shut down), whereas a dream of having a full bladder may denote an overabundance of emotions that are pressing for release in the waking world. In another scenario, did you have a nightmare in which you were drowning? If so, are you currently feeling overwhelmed by emotion?

Related Dreams

pages 154, 185, 223, 291, 383 & 388

My Water Dreams

....

....

....

....

....

....

....

....

....

✦✦✦✦✦✦✦✦✦✦✦✦✦✦✦✦✦✦✦✦

Unfathomable Depths

Water can symbolize many things when it is highlighted in dreamland, which is why it is important to take your dreaming self's feelings and behavior into account when trying to decode your dream. So were you petrified and panicking because you were drowning in tumultuous waves, or were you feeling relaxed and happy because you were enjoying a refreshing dip in a sheltered lagoon?

My Waterfalls & Wells Dreams

----

* * * * * * * * * * * * * * * * * *

Cascading Creativity

If you were white-water-rafting in your dream, and found yourself whooping with exhilaration as the fizzing rapids and cascading waterfalls bore you swiftly along, can you draw a parallel between your dreaming self's excitement and sense of being slightly out of control and your real-life reaction to your waking circumstances? Is it your sizzling creativity that is making you feel so deliriously happy?

WATERFALLS & WELLS

* *

In dream symbolism, a gushing waterfall may denote energy and euphoria, creativity, or male sexuality (because of its association with ejaculation). Wells are ancient symbols of wish fulfillment, and both wells and springs are symbolic of the womb, and therefore of birth and life, as well as creative potential. In addition, a dream spring or fountain may represent a "font" of knowledge. And because they are of the element of water, any of these things may denote the unconscious mind or emotions.

Symbolic and Verbal Associations

- Energy and euphoria (as symbolized by a waterfall)
- Birth; the womb (as symbolized by a well, spring, or fountain)
- Creative potential
- A "wishing well"; desires; wish-fulfillment
- Physical or psychological healing
- Sexuality

Positive Interpretations: In your dream, were you laughing with joy at the sight of a cascading, tumbling waterfall? If so, was your unconscious mirroring your waking ebullient mood? And if so, why are you feeling so euphoric? Is it because your creative powers have begun flowing at full speed? Or, if you are a man, did your gushing and spurting dream waterfall symbolize ejaculation, and, therefore, your current happiness with your sex life? If your dreaming mind homed in on a fountain or a spring, could it have represented someone in your waking life who is a "font" of knowledge or wisdom? Or was your unconscious encouraging you to employ your own powers of knowledge and wisdom in order to solve a real-life dilemma? Alternatively, if you dreamed of a spring or a well—which both gain their waters from deep within the earth, itself a symbol of the womb—could your dream have symbolized your desire to become a mother (if you are a woman), or else your untapped creative potential? Did you dream of tossing a coin into a wishing well? If so, what did you wish for? The answer may be symbolic of something that would bring you great happiness in the real world. (In fact, wishing wells have been said to have divine wish-granting powers since Romano–Celtic times, when sacred wells were believed to provide a direct link to a particular god or goddess.) To dream of drawing or drinking water from a well may also symbolize your unconscious mind and emotions (i.e., your inner wisdom).

Negative Interpretations: It has long been said that the water from certain wells and springs is imbued with magical powers of healing. So if you dreamed of drawing, or of drinking, water from a well, might the unconscious implication have been that you are in need of physical or psychological healing? Or if you dreamed that you were thirsty and went to a well or a spring to get a drink of water, has your waking life become so emotionally parched that you are thirsting for a restorative flood of feeling?

Related Dreams

pages 185, 223, 366, 372, 382 & 387

WIND

When the wind blows through dreamland, it may carry a message to do with the inspiration or reinvigoration of the spirit or the intellect (as in "a breath of fresh air"), or it may signal a strong life force and wellbeing. Other verbal associations include a "breezy," or carefree, approach to life (which is also implied by the desire simply to "blow in the wind"), "the winds of change," a "whirlwind" of activity, and a "whirlwind romance."

Symbolic and Verbal Associations
- The life force; spirit, intellect, and wellbeing
- Inspiration or reinvigoration; "a breath of fresh air"
- Messages, carried "on the wind"
- A "breezy," or carefree, approach to life; unpredictability; the desire just to "blow in the wind"
- "The winds of change"
- A "whirlwind" of activity; a "whirlwind romance"

Positive Interpretations: Was your dream self reinvigorated and revitalized when you stepped out of a warm, stuffy building and were greeted by a cool, refreshing breeze? If so, are you feeling mentally stagnant due to the monotony of your daily routine, so that you could desperately use "a breath of fresh air" (i.e., inspiration or reinvigoration) in your life? Your unconscious may have sent you your dream as a means of advising you to adopt a more "breezy," or carefree, approach to life. Or, in your dream, did you relish the sensation of being carried along by strong gusts of wind? If so, do you long for more unpredictability during your waking hours? Do you wish that you could give up your duties and responsibilities and simply "blow in the wind" instead? Or if you dreamed that you were joyously caught up in a whirl-wind, was your unconscious mind making a reference to the "whirlwind romance" that you have recently embarked upon?

Negative Interpretations: In your dream, were you feeling chilled and disheveled as you were buffeted and blown about by a tempest of strong winds? If so, is your exposure to powerful external forces causing you to feel vulnerable in the real world? And if, in your dream, you summoned up all of your strength in order to hold your ground against a severe wind that threatened to blow you off course, consider whether your unconscious was referring to "the winds of change," or to the pressure of others who have been try-ing to force you to switch directions, or objectives, in the real world and to pursue their goals instead. Alternatively, if your dream self was assaulted by a full-out wind storm, might your unconscious have been warning that a tempest of violent emotions (either your own or someone else's) is on the way? Or are you caught up in such a "whirlwind" of activity that you scarcely know whether you are coming or going?

Related Dreams
pages 219, 298, 303, 306, 363 & 380

My Wind Dreams

Whipping up a Storm
Dreaming of cowering in the eye of a storm while observing with horror the havoc that a howling hurricane was wreaking around you may have mirrored your real-life position. Have you been forced to watch your support structures being "blown away" by a dramatic change of circumstances in the waking world? Has a restructuring exercise at work cost you your job, for instance?

You see things; and you say, "Why?"
But I dream things that never were;
and I say, "Why not?"

GEORGE BERNARD SHAW

RECORDING
YOUR DREAMS

Even when you've developed your dream-decoding skills, you'll gain far more from your unconscious mind's nocturnal messages if you record them.

Why? Well, very few people have faultless memories, and it's entirely possible that you will forget a potentially significant dream sooner or later. Having a written record of it will preserve it and will consequently ensure that it does not disappear for good. Another reason for writing up your dreams is that having an archive of dream material—in effect, raw data—to analyze may help you to identify any dream themes, trends, and patterns and maybe, by comparing your dream diary with your everyday diary or appointment book, to link them with real-world triggers.

Pages 30 to 31 of this book contain advice on ways of capturing your dreams on paper or tape before they fade from your memory, as well as on ways of interpreting them. You may also have noticed that there is space in the margin of each dream-theme page where you can jot down a few notes on your own dreams relating to that particular subject. Write whatever you wish here, but it's advisable to note down at least the date, or dates, on which you had the relevant dream, or dreams, before reading the text alongside to try to work out what your dream could have meant.

Keeping a Dream Diary

As is explained on pages 30 to 31, it's crucial that you scribble down, or dictate, the details of a dream as soon as you regain consciousness—leave it any longer, and you run the risk that they'll elude your powers of recollection.

Later on, you may find it helpful to write up your dream from your initial notes according to a set format, such as the example given on the opposite page (and see page 394 for a sample completed dream-diary entry). You could either photocopy these blank pages or create a similar template on your computer to fill in yourself. As your dream diary grows, you could keep its pages or documents in a dedicated ring-binder, card index, or computer folder.

Indexing Your Dreams

Remember to create an index to your dreams, and to update it every time that you add a new dream, to make locating and referring to a particular dream, and perhaps also categorizing your dreams, easier. Your index could consist of the information at left.

Below: A card-index system can be a convenient dream decoder's database.

Index

Dream number: . . . .

Date: . . . .

Title: . . . .

Type(s): . . . .

* *

My Dream Diary

Dream number: . . . .
Dream type(s): . . . .
Day of the week: . . . .
Date: . . . .

Title: . . . .

The prevalent atmosphere/how you were feeling: . . . .
. . . .
The setting: . . . .
The characters: . . . .
. . . .

What happened? . . . .
. . . .
. . . .
. . . .
. . . .
. . . .
. . . .
. . . .

Any puns or punning imagery? . . . .
. . . .

Possible trigger: . . . .

Possible interpretation: . . . .
. . . .
. . . .
. . . .

Possible message: . . . .

Possible link with dream number: . . . .

* *

✴ ✴

Sample Dream-diary Entry

Dream number: *5*

Dream type(s): *literal; nightmare; precognitive. (?)*

Day of the week: *Thursday*

Date: *May 19, 2005*

Title: *Computer Catastrophe!*

The prevalent atmosphere/how you were feeling: *initially relaxed, even complacent; then fraught; eventually panicked and despairing*

The setting: *my office*

The characters: *me; my great-aunt Prudence; my pet mouse Clutterbuck*

What happened? *I was typing the final words of a masterpiece of a novel, which I somehow knew had taken me years to write, on my computer, when I clicked "Save." I was concerned when the computer didn't seem to respond, and then became increasingly panic-stricken when the screen turned black and clicking the mouse and hitting keys didn't have any effect. The computer had died, and I'd lost my bestseller! I was distraught! Then Aunt Prudence appeared by my side, clutching Clutterbuck, my pet mouse, and said, "Better safe than sorry!" Then I woke up.*

Any puns or punning imagery? *Clutterbuck could have represented my computer mouse.*

Possible trigger: *Spending the previous day inputting a lot of important information into my computer.*

Possible interpretation: *I am unconsciously aware that I am risking losing my work on my computer by not copying it and storing it safely. My dream was urging me to mend my lazy ways by exposing me to this worst-case scenario, and reinforced the message by conjuring up Aunt Prudence to impart her words of wisdom.*

Possible message: *Back up everything on my computer that I would be devastated to lose.*

Possible link with dream number: *2*

✴ ✴

Explanatory Notes

1. Number your dreams in the order in which you have them. When it comes to analyzing your dreams, you'll find identifying and referring to dream "5" a lot more convenient than to "the nightmare about my computer."

2. For example: literal, factual, processing; physiological; punning; problem-solving; inspirational; cathartic or safety-valve; contrary, compensatory, wish fulfillment; recurring; nightmare; anxiety; precognitive; telepathic (see pages 17 to 28).

Indexed Summary

Dream number: . . . . . .5. . . . . .

Date: . . . May.19, 2005. . . . . .

Title: . . Computer Catastrophe!

Type(s): . . literal; .nightmare; . . .
. . . . .precognitive (?). . . . .

Left: *As you awake each morning, your dreams may still seem vivid, but the details will soon fade unless you record them straight away.*

Index

Illustrations are shown in *italic* type.
Chapter themes are shown in **bold** type.

✶✶

✶✶

Acknowledgments

The publisher would like to thank Clare Haworth-Maden, Chitra Ramaswamy, Claire Black, Celine Clavel, and Alastair Hall for their assistance in the making of this book. The design of this book is based on a companion title, *The Ultimate Birthday Book*, designed by Ziga Design. Grateful acknowledgment is made to © **2005 JupiterImages Corporation** for permission to reproduce illustrations and photographs.

Sources referred to in the preparation of this book: Gibson, Clare, *The Secret Life of Dreams*, Thunder Bay Books, San Diego, 2003; Keightley, Thomas, *The World Guide to Gnomes, Fairies, Elves and Other Little People*, Avenel Books, New York, 1978; Néret, Gilles, *Devils*, Taschen Books, Cologne, Germany, 2003. Online Sources: Dream Moods; The Dream Dictionary (My Jellybean); Dream Interpreter (Dreamhawk).

Dreams—a microscope through which we look at the hidden occurrences in our soul.

Erich Fromm